The I-Series

Microsoft® Excel 2002

Complete

Stephen Haag
University of Denver

James T. Perry
University of San Diego

McGraw-Hill
Irwin

Boston   Burr Ridge, IL   Dubuque, IA   Madison, WI   New York   San Francisco   St. Louis
Bangkok   Bogotá   Caracas   Kuala Lumpur   Lisbon   London   Madrid   Mexico City
Milan   Montreal   New Delhi   Santiago   Seoul   Singapore   Sydney   Taipei   Toronto

McGraw-Hill Higher Education

A Division of The **McGraw-Hill** Companies

The I-Series: Microsoft Excel 2002, Complete

Published by McGraw-Hill/Irwin, an imprint of The McGraw-Hill Companies, Inc. 1221 Avenue of the Americas, New York, NY 10020. Copyright © 2002 by The McGraw-Hill Companies, Inc. All rights reserved. No part of this publication may be reproduced or distributed in any form or by any means, or stored in a database or retrieval system, without the prior written consent of The McGraw-Hill Companies, Inc., including, but not limited to, in any network or other electronic storage or transmission, or broadcast for distance learning.

Some ancillaries, including electronic and print components, may not be available to customers outside the United States.

This book is printed on acid-free paper.

3 4 5 6 7 8 9 0 WEB/WEB 0 9 8 7 6 5 4 3

ISBN 0-07-245906-9

Publisher: *George Werthman*
Sponsoring editor: *Dan Silverburg*
Developmental editor: *Melissa Forte*
Manager, Marketing and Sales: *Paul Murphy*
Senior project manager: *Jean Hamilton*
Production supervisor: *Rose Hepburn*
Coordinator freelance design: *Mary L. Christianson and Jennifer McQueen*
Lead supplement producer: *Marc Mattson*
Senior producer, Media technology: *David Barrick*
Interior freelance design: *Asylum Studios*
Cover freelance design/illustration: *Asylum Studios*
Compositor: *GAC Indianapolis*
Typeface: *10/12 New Aster*
Printer: *Webcrafters, Inc.*

Library of Congress Control Number: 2002101838

http://www.mhhe.com

INFORMATION TECHNOLOGY AT MCGRAW-HILL/IRWIN

InformationTechnology

At McGraw-Hill Higher Education, we publish instructional materials targeted at the higher education market. In an effort to expand the tools of higher learning, we publish texts, lab manuals, study guides, testing materials, software, and multimedia products.

At McGraw-Hill/Irwin (a division of McGraw-Hill Higher Education), we realize that technology has created and will continue to create new mediums for professors and students to use in managing resources and communicating information to one another. We strive to provide the most flexible and complete teaching and learning tools available as well as offer solutions to the changing world of teaching and learning.

McGraw-Hill/Irwin is dedicated to providing the tools for today's instructors and students to successfully navigate the world of Information Technology.

- **SEMINAR SERIES**—McGraw-Hill/Irwin's Technology Connection seminar series offered across the country every year demonstrates the latest technology products and encourages collaboration among teaching professionals.

- **MCGRAW-HILL/OSBORNE**—This division of The McGraw-Hill Companies is known for its best-selling Internet titles, *Internet & Web Yellow Pages* and the *Internet Complete Reference*. For more information, visit Osborne at www.osborne.com.

- **DIGITAL SOLUTIONS**—McGraw-Hill/Irwin is committed to publishing digital solutions. Taking your course online doesn't have to be a solitary adventure, nor does it have to be a difficult one. We offer several solutions that will allow you to enjoy all the benefits of having your course material online.

- **PACKAGING OPTIONS**—For more information about our discount options, contact your McGraw-Hill/Irwin sales representative at 1-800-338-3987 or visit our Web site at www.mhhe.com/it.

THE I-SERIES PAGE

By using the I-Series, students will be able to learn and master applications skills by being actively engaged—by *doing*. The "I" in I-Series demonstrates <u>I</u>nsightful tasks that will not only <u>I</u>nform students, but also <u>I</u>nvolve them while learning the applications.

How will The I-Series accomplish this for you?

Through relevant, real-world chapter opening cases.

Through tasks throughout each chapter that incorporate steps and tips for easy reference.

Through alternative methods and styles of learning to keep the student involved.

Through rich, end-of-chapter materials that support what the student has learned.

I-Series titles include:

- Microsoft Office XP, Volume I

- Microsoft Office XP, Volume I Expanded

- Microsoft Office XP, Volume II

- Microsoft Word 2002 (Brief, Introductory, Complete Versions) 12 Chapters

- Microsoft Excel 2002 (Brief, Introductory, Complete Versions) 12 Chapters

- Microsoft Access 2002 (Brief, Introductory, Complete Versions) 12 Chapters

- Microsoft PowerPoint 2002 (Brief, Introductory Versions) 8 Chapters

- Microsoft Windows 2000 (Brief, Introductory, Complete Versions) 12 Chapters

- Microsoft Windows XP and Bonus Books to come!

To accompany the series:
The I-Series Computing Concepts text (Introductory, Complete Versions)

For additional resources, visit the I-Series Online Learning Center at www.mhhe.com/i-series/.

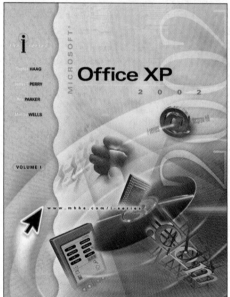

GOALS/PHILOSOPHY

The I-Series applications textbooks strongly emphasize that students learn and master applications skills by being actively engaged—by *doing*. We made the decision that teaching how to accomplish tasks is not enough for complete understanding and mastery. Students must understand the importance of each of the tasks that lead to a finished product at the end of each chapter.

Approach

The I-Series chapters are subdivided into sessions that contain related groups of tasks with active, hands-on components. The session tasks containing numbered steps collectively result in a completed project at the end of each session. Prior to introducing numbered steps that show how to accomplish a particular task, we discuss why the steps are important. We discuss the role that the collective steps play in the overall plan for creating or modifying a document or object, answering students' often-heard questions, "Why are we doing these steps? Why are these steps important?" Without an explanation of why an activity is important and what it accomplishes, students can easily find themselves following the steps but not registering the big picture of what the steps accomplish and why they are executing them.

I-Series Applications for 2002

The I-Series offers three levels of instruction. Each level builds upon knowledge from the previous level. With the exception of the running project that is the last exercise of every chapter, chapter cases and end-of-chapter exercises are independent from one chapter to the next, with the exception of Access. The three levels available are

Brief   Covers the basics of the Microsoft application and contains Chapters 1 through 4. The Brief textbooks are typically 200 pages long.

Introductory   Includes chapters in the Brief textbook plus Chapters 5 through 8. Introductory textbooks typically are 400 pages long and prepare students for the Microsoft Office User Specialist (MOUS) Core Exam.

Complete   Includes the Introductory textbook plus Chapters 9 through 12. The four additional chapters cover advanced level content and are typically 600 pages long. Complete textbooks prepare students for the Microsoft Office User Specialist (MOUS) Expert Exam. The Microsoft Office User Specialist program is recognized around the world as the standard for demonstrating proficiency using Microsoft Office applications.

In addition, there are two compilation volumes available.

Office I   Includes introductory chapters on Windows and Computing Concepts followed by Chapters 1 through 4 (Brief textbook) of Word, Excel, Access, and PowerPoint. In addition, material from the companion Computing Concepts book is integrated into the first few chapters to provide students an understanding of the relationship between Microsoft Office applications and computer information systems.

Office II   Includes introductory chapters on Windows and Computing Concepts followed by Chapters 5 through 8 from each of the Introductory-level textbooks including Word, Excel, Access, and PowerPoint. In addition, material from the companion Computing Concepts book is integrated into the introductory chapters to provide students a deeper understanding of the relationship between Microsoft Office applications and computer information systems. An introduction to Visual Basic for Applications (VBA) completes the Office II textbook.

Approved Microsoft Courseware

Use of the Microsoft Office User Specialist Approved Courseware logo on this product signifies that it has been independently reviewed and approved to comply with the following standards: Acceptable coverage of all content related to the Microsoft Office Exams entitled Microsoft Access 2002, Microsoft Excel 2002, Microsoft PowerPoint 2002, and Microsoft Word 2002, and sufficient performance-based exercises that relate closely to all required content, based on sampling of the textbooks. For further information on Microsoft's MOUS certification program, please visit Microsoft's Web site at www.microsoft.com.

STEPHEN HAAG

Stephen Haag is a professor and Chair of Information Technology and Electronic Commerce and the Director of Technology in the University of Denver's Daniels College of Business. Stephen holds a B.B.A. and an M.B.A. from West Texas State University and a Ph.D. from the University of Texas at Arlington. Stephen has published numerous articles appearing in such journals as *Communications of the ACM, The International Journal of Systems Science, Applied Economics, Managerial and Decision Economics, Socio-Economic Planning Sciences,* and the *Australian Journal of Management.*

Stephen is also the author of 13 other books including *Interactions: Teaching English as a Second Language* (with his mother and father), *Case Studies in Information Technology, Information Technology: Tomorrow's Advantage Today* (with Peter Keen), and *Excelling in Finance.* Stephen is also the lead author of the accompanying *I-Series: Computing Concepts* text, released in both an Introductory and Complete version. Stephen lives with his wife, Pam, and their four sons, Indiana, Darian, Trevor, and Elvis, in Highlands Ranch, Colorado.

JAMES PERRY

James Perry is a professor of Management Information Systems at the University of San Diego's School of Business. Jim is an active instructor who teaches both undergraduate and graduate courses. He holds a B.S. in mathematics from Purdue University and a Ph.D. in computer science from The Pennsylvania State University. He has published several journal and conference papers. He is the co-author of 56 textbooks and trade books such as *Using Access with Accounting Systems, Building Accounting Systems, Understanding Oracle, The Internet,* and *Electronic Commerce.* His books have been translated into Dutch, French, and Chinese. Jim worked as a computer security consultant to various private and governmental organizations including the Jet Propulsion Laboratory. He was a consultant on the Strategic Defense Initiative ("Star Wars") project and served as a member of the computer security oversight committee.

RICK PARKER

Rick Parker received his bachelor's degree from Brigham Young University. He received his Ph.D. in animal physiology at Iowa State University. After completing his Ph.D., he and his wife, Marilyn, and their children moved to Edmonton, Alberta, Canada, where he completed a post-doctorate at the University of Alberta. He accepted a position as a research and teaching associate at the University of Wyoming, Laramie, Wyoming.

Rick developed a love for the power and creativity unleashed by computers and software. After arriving at the College of Southern Idaho, Twin Falls, in 1984, he guided the creation and development of numerous college software courses and software training programs for business and industry. He also led the conversion of an old office occupations technical program into a business computer applications program, which evolved into an information technology program. During the early adoption of computers and software by the college, Rick wrote in-house training manuals and taught computer/software courses.

Rick currently works as a professional-technical division director at the College of Southern Idaho. As director, he supervises faculty in agriculture, information technology and drafting, and electronics programs. He is the author of four other textbooks.

MERRILL WELLS

The caption next to **Merrill Wells'** eighth grade yearbook picture noted that her career goal was to teach college and write books. She completed an MBA at Indiana University and began a career as a programmer. After several years of progressive positions in business and industry, she returned to academia, spending 10 years as a computer technology faculty member at Red Rocks Community College and then becoming an information technology professor at the University of Denver, Daniels College of Business. She completed her first published book in 1993 and began presenting at educational seminars in 1997. Other publications include *An Introduction to Computers, Introduction to Visual Basic,* and *Programming Logic and Design.*

Each textbook features the following:

Did You Know Each chapter has six or seven interesting facts—both about high tech and other topics.

Sessions Each chapter is divided into two or three sessions.

Chapter Outline Provides students with a quick map of the major headings in the chapter.

Chapter and MOUS Objectives At the beginning of each chapter is a list of 5 to 10 action-oriented objectives. Any chapter objectives that are also MOUS objectives indicate the MOUS objective number also.

Chapter Opening Case Each chapter begins with a case. Cases describe a mixture of fictitious and real people and companies and the needs of the people and companies. Throughout the chapter, the student gains the skills and knowledge to solve the problem stated in the case.

Introduction The chapter introduction establishes the overview of the chapter's activities in the context of the case problem.

Another Way and Another Word Another Way is a highlighted feature providing a bulleted list of steps to accomplish a task, or best practices—that is, a better or faster way to accomplish a task such as pasting a format onto an Excel cell. Another Word, another highlighted box, briefly explains more about a topic or highlights a potential pitfall.

Step-by-Step Instructions Numbered step-by-step instructions for all hands-on activities appear in a distinctive color. Keyboard characters and menu selections appear in a **special format** to emphasize what the user should press or type. Steps make clear to the student the exact sequence of keystrokes and mouse clicks needed to complete a task such as formatting a Word paragraph.

Tips Tips appear within a numbered sequence of steps and warn the student of possible missteps or provide alternatives to the step that precedes the tip.

Task Reference and Task Reference Round-Up Task References appear throughout the textbook. Set in a distinctive design, each Task Reference contains a bulleted list of steps showing a generic way to accomplish activities that are especially important or significant. A Task Reference Round-Up at the end of each chapter summarizes a chapter's Task References.

MOUS Objectives Summary A list of MOUS objectives covered in a chapter appears in the chapter objectives and the chapter summary.

Making the Grade Short answer questions appear at the end of each chapter's sessions. They test a student's grasp of each session's contents, and Making the Grade answers appear at the end of each book so students can check their answers.

Rich End-of-Chapter Materials End-of-chapter materials incorporating a three-level approach reinforce learning and help students take ownership of the chapter. Level One, review of terminology, contains a fun crossword puzzle that enforces review of a chapter's key terms. Level Two, review of concepts, contains fill-in-the blank questions, review questions, and a Jeopardy-style create-a-question exercise. Level Three is Hands-on Projects.

Hands-on Projects Extensive hands-on projects engage the student in a problem-solving exercise from start to finish. There are six clearly labeled categories that each contain one or two questions. Categories are Practice, Challenge!, On the Web, E-Business, Around the World, and a Running Project that carries throughout all the chapters.

We understand that, in today's teaching environment, offering a textbook alone is not sufficient to meet the needs of the many instructors who use our books. To teach effectively, instructors must have a full complement of supplemental resources to assist them in every facet of teaching, from preparing for class to conducting a lecture to assessing students' comprehension. The **I-Series** offers a complete supplements package and Web site that is briefly described below.

INSTRUCTOR'S RESOURCE KIT

The Instructor's Resource Kit is a CD-ROM containing the Instructor's Manual in both MS Word and .pdf formats, PowerPoint Slides with Presentation Software, Brownstone test-generating software, and accompanying test item files in both MS Word and .pdf formats for each chapter. The CD also contains figure files from the text, student data files, and solutions files. The features of each of the three main components of the Instructor's Resource Kit are highlighted below.

Instructor's Manual Featuring:

- Chapter learning objectives per chapter
- Chapter outline with teaching tips
- Annotated Solutions Diagram to provide Troubleshooting Tips, Tricks, and Traps
- Lecture Notes, illustrating key concepts and ideas
- Annotated Syllabus, depicting a time table and schedule for covering chapter content
- Additional end-of-chapter projects
- Answers to all Making the Grade and end-of-chapter questions

PowerPoint Presentation

The PowerPoint presentation is designed to provide instructors with comprehensive lecture and teaching resources that will include

- Chapter learning objectives followed by source content that illustrates key terms and key facts per chapter

- FAQ (frequently asked questions) to show key concepts throughout the chapter; also, lecture notes, to illustrate these key concepts and ideas
- End-of-chapter exercises and activities per chapter, as taken from the end-of-chapter materials in the text
- Speaker's Notes, to be incorporated throughout the slides per chapter
- Figures/screen shots, to be incorporated throughout the slides per chapter

PowerPoint includes presentation software for instructors to design their own presentation for their course.

Test Bank

The I-Series Test Bank, using Diploma Network Testing Software by Brownstone, contains over 3,000 questions (both objective and interactive) categorized by topic, page reference to the text, and difficulty level of learning. Each question is assigned a learning category:

- Level 1: Key Terms and Facts
- Level 2: Key Concepts
- Level 3: Application and Problem-Solving

The types of questions consist of 40 percent Identifying/Interactive Lab Questions, 20 percent Multiple Choice, 20 percent True/False, and 20 percent Fill-in/Short Answer Questions.

ONLINE LEARNING CENTER/ WEB SITE

The Online Learning Center that accompanies the I-Series is accessible through our Information Technology Supersite at http://www.mhhe.com/catalogs/irwin/it/. This site provides additional review and learning tools developed using the same three-level approach found in the text and supplements. To locate the I-Series OLC/Web site directly, go to www.mhhe.com/i-series. The site is divided into three key areas:

- **Information Center** Contains core information about the text, the authors, and a guide to our additional features and benefits of the series, including the supplements.

- **Instructor Center**   Offers instructional materials, downloads, additional activities and answers to additional projects, answers to chapter troubleshooting exercises, answers to chapter preparation/post exercises posed to students, relevant links for professors, and more.

- **Student Center**   Contains chapter objectives and outlines, self-quizzes, chapter troubleshooting exercises, chapter preparation/post exercises, additional projects, simulations, student data files and solutions files, Web links, and more.

RESOURCES FOR STUDENTS

Interactive Companion CD   This student CD-ROM can be packaged with this text. It is designed for use in class, in the lab, or at home by students and professors and combines video, interactive exercises, and animation to cover the most difficult and popular topics in Computing Concepts. By combining video, interactive exercises, animation, additional content, and actual "lab" tutorials, we expand the reach and scope of the textbook.

SimNet *XPert*   SimNet *XPert* is a simulated assessment and learning tool. It allows students to study MS Office XP skills and computer concepts, and professors to test and evaluate students' proficiency within MS Office XP applications and concepts. Students can practice and study their skills at home or in the school lab using SimNet *XPert*, which does not require the purchase of Office XP software. SimNet *XPert* will contain new features and enhancements for Office XP, including:

NEW!* Live Assessments! SimNet *XPert now includes live-in-the-application assessments! One for each skill set for Core MOUS objectives in Word 2002, Excel 2002, Access 2002, and PowerPoint 2002 (total of 29 Live-in-the-Application Assessments). Multiple tasks are required to complete each live assessment (about 100 tasks covered).

NEW!* Computer Concepts Coverage! SimNet *XPert now includes coverage of computer concepts in both the Learning and the Assessment sides.

NEW!* Practice or Pretest Questions! SimNet *XPert has a separate pool of 600 questions for practice tests or pretests.

NEW!* Comprehensive Exercises! SimNet *XPert offers comprehensive exercises for each application. These exercises require the student to use multiple skills to solve one exercise in the simulated environment.

ENHANCED!* More Assessment Questions! SimNet *XPert includes over 1,400 assessment questions.

ENHANCED!* Simulated Interface!** The simulated environment in **SimNet *XPert has been substantially deepened to more realistically simulate the real applications. Now students are not graded incorrect just because they chose the wrong submenu or dialog box. The student is not graded until he or she does something that immediately invokes an action.

DIGITAL SOLUTIONS FOR INSTRUCTORS AND STUDENTS

PageOut   PageOut is our Course Web Site Development Center that offers a syllabus page, URL, McGraw-Hill Online Learning Center content, online exercises and quizzes, gradebook, discussion board, and an area for student Web pages. For more information, visit the PageOut Web site at www.pageout.net.

Online Courses Available   OLCs are your perfect solutions for Internet-based content. Simply put, these Centers are "digital cartridges" that contain a book's pedagogy and supplements. As students read the book, they can go online and take self-grading quizzes or work through interactive exercises.

Online Learning Centers can be delivered through any of these platforms:

McGraw-Hill Learning Architecture (TopClass)

Blackboard.com

College.com (formerly Real Education)

WebCT (a product of Universal Learning Technology)

Did You Know?

A unique presentation of text and graphics introduce interesting and little-known facts.

did you
know?

the Penny is the only coin currently minted in the United States with a profile that faces to the right. All other U.S. coins feature profiles that face to the left.

the world's largest wind generator is on the island of Oahu, Hawaii. The windmill has two blades 400 feet long on the top of a tower, twenty stories high.

the only house in England that the Queen may not enter is the House of Commons, because she is not a commoner. She is also the only person in England who does not need a license plate on her vehicle.

former U.S. Vice President Al Gore and Oscar-winning actor Tommy Lee Jones were roommates at Harvard.

Chapter Objectives

- Plan and document a workbook
- Create formulas containing cell references and mathematical operators (MOUS Ex2002-5-1)
- Write functions including Sum, Average, Max, and Min (MOUS Ex2002-5-2)
- Use Excel's AutoSum feature to automatically write Sum functions
- Learn several ways to copy a formula from one cell to many other cells
- Differentiate between absolute, mixed, and relative cell reference (MOUS Ex2002-5-1)
- Adjust column widths (MOUS Ex2002-3-2)
- Set a print area (MOUS Ex2002-3-7)
- Move text, values, and formulas (MOUS Ex2002-1-1)
- Insert and delete rows and columns (MOUS Ex2002-3-2)
- Format cells (MOUS Ex2002-3-1)
- Create cell comments (MOUS Ex2002-7-3)

CHAPTER

2

two

Planning and Creating a Worksheet

Chapter Objectives

Each chapter begins with a list of competencies covered in the chapter.

task reference

Changing Relative References to Absolute or Mixed References

- Double-click the cell containing the formula that you want to edit or click the cell and then press **F2**
- Move the insertion point, a vertical bar, to the left of the cell reference you want to alter
- Press function key **F4** repeatedly until the absolute or mixed reference you want appears
- Press **Enter** to complete the cell edit procedure

Task Reference

Provides steps to accomplish an especially important task.

SESSION 2.1   *making* **the grade**

1. Explain how AutoSum works and what it does.

2. Suppose you select cell A14 and type D5+F5. What is stored in cell A14: text, a value, or a formula?

3. You can drag the _____, which is a small black square in the lower-right corner of the active cell, to copy the cell's contents.

4. Evaluation of a formula such as =D4+D5*D6 is governed by order of precedence. Explain what that means in general and then indicate the order in which Excel calculates the preceding expression.

5. Suppose Excel did not provide an AVERAGE function. Show an alternative way to compute the average of cell range A1:B25 using the other Excel statistical functions.

Making the Grade

Short-answer questions appear at the end of each session and answers appear at the end of the book.

Copying a formula from one cell to many cells:

1. Click cell **G4** to make it the active cell. The cell's formula, =F4/B4, appears in the formula bar

2. Click **Edit** on the menu bar and then click **Copy** to copy the cell's contents to the Clipboard. Notice that a dashed line encloses the cell whose contents are on the Clipboard

tip: *You can press Ctrl+C instead of using the Copy command. Those of you who keep your hands on the keyboard may favor this keyboard shortcut.*

3. Click and drag cells **G5** through **G8** to select them. They are the target range into which you will paste the cell G4's contents

4. Click **Edit** on the menu bar and then click **Paste.** Excel copies the Clipboard's contents into each of the cells in the selected range and then adjusts each cell's formula to correspond to its new location. Notice that the Paste Options Smart Tag appears below and to the right of cell G8 (see Figure 2.16). The Paste Options Smart Tag provides several formatting and copying options in its list. You can access the options by clicking the Smart Tag list arrow

FIGURE 2.16
Copied formulas' results

	A	B	C	D	E	F	G	H
1	Aluminum Can Recycling Contest							
2								
3	City	Population	Jan	Feb	Mar	Total	Per Capita	
4	Arcata	15855	10505	24556	12567	47628	3.003974	
5	Los Gatos	28951	24567	21777	26719	73063	2.523678	
6	Pasadena	142547	10					
7	San Diego	2801561	271					
8	Sunnyvale	1689908	152					
9	Total		437					
10	Minimum		1					
11	Average		875					
12	Maximum		271					
13								
14								

tip: *You can press Ctrl+...*
paste the Clipboard's conte...

5. Press **Escape** to cl...
line from the source...
and view the formul...

' Work Hours

...r Wexler's Tool and
...ge a group of five
...r group has a differ-
...record on a weekly
...ch employee works,
..., and percentage of
...t each employee's
...ing the information
...icient way to record
... Alan Gin, the com-
..., wants you to pre-
...report your group's
...ges. You create a
...nd wages.

Wages.xls and

...n sheet and then
...ove to that work-

...all the employees'
...
...e row 1: Click cell
..., and release the
...e Menu bar and

...he range and type
...
...click cell **C1,** type
...e **Wages,** click cell

hands-on projects

LEVEL THREE

practice

12. Click cell **E3** and type the formula that represents the employee's percentage of the total wages: **=D3/D$8*100**

13. Copy the formula in cell E3 to the cell range **E4:E7**

14. Select cell range **A1:E8,** click **Format,** click **AutoFormat,** select the **Simple** format, and click **OK**

15. Select cell range **E3:E7** and click the **Decrease Decimal** button enough times to reduce the displayed percentages to two decimal places

16. Click cell **A10** and type your first and last names

17. Set the left, right, top, and bottom margins to two inches

18. Either execute **Print** or execute **Save As,** according to your instructor's direction

2. Creating an Invoice

As office manager of Randy's Foreign Cars, one of your duties is to produce and mail invoices to customers who have arranged to pay for their automobile repairs up to 30 days after mechanics perform the work. Randy's invoices include parts, sales tax on parts, and labor charges. State law stipulates that customers do not pay sales tax on the labor charges. Only parts are subject to state sales tax. State sales tax is 6 percent. Create and print an invoice whose details appear below.

anotherword

... about Smart Tags

Microsoft Office Smart Tags are a set of buttons that are shared across the Office applications. The buttons appear when needed, such as when Excel detects you may have made an error in an Excel formula, and gives the user appropriate options to change the given action or error.

task reference roundup

Task	Location	Preferred Method
Writing formulas	EX 2.9	• Select a cell, type **5,** type the formula, press **Enter**
Modifying an AutoSum cell range by pointing	EX 2.11	• Press an arrow key repeatedly to select leftmost or topmost cell in range, press and hold **Shift,** select cell range with arrow keys, release **Shift,** press **Enter**
Writing a function using the Paste Function button	EX 2.17	• Select a cell, click **Paste Function,** click a function category, click a function name, click **OK,** complete the Formula Palette dialog box, click **OK**
Copying and pasting a cell or range of cells	EX 2.21	• Select source cell(s), click **Edit,** click **Copy,** select target cell(s), click **Edit,** click **Paste**
Copying cell contents using a cell's fill handle	EX 2.23	• Select source cell(s), drag the fill handle to the source cell(s) range, release the mouse button

---

Step-by-Step Instruction

Numbered steps guide you through the exact sequence of keystrokes to accomplish the task.

Tips

Tips appear within steps and either indicate possible missteps or provide alternatives to a step.

End-of-Chapter Hands-on Projects

A rich variety of projects introduced by a case lets you put into practice what you have learned. Categories include Practice, Challenge, On the Web, E-Business, Around the World, and a running case project.

Screen Shots

Screen shots show you what to expect at critical points.

Another Way/ Another Word

Another Way highlights an alternative way to accomplish a task; Another Word explains more about a topic.

Task Reference RoundUp

Provides a quick reference and summary of a chapter's task references.

APPROVED COURSEWARE

What does this logo mean?

It means this courseware has been approved by the Microsoft® Office User Specialist Program to be among the finest available for learning *Microsoft Word 2002, Microsoft Excel 2002, Microsoft Access 2002, and Microsoft PowerPoint 2002*. It also means that upon completion of this courseware, you may be prepared to become a Microsoft Office User Specialist. The I-Series Microsoft Office XP books are available in three levels of coverage: Brief level, Intro level, and the Complete level. The I-Series Introductory books are approved courseware to prepare you for the MOUS level 1 exam. The I-Series Complete books will prepare you for the expert level exam.

What is a Microsoft Office User Specialist?

A Microsoft Office User Specialist is an individual who has certified his or her skills in one or more of the Microsoft Office desktop applications of Microsoft Word, Microsoft Excel, Microsoft PowerPoint®, Microsoft Outlook® or Microsoft Access, or in Microsoft Project. The Microsoft Office User Specialist Program typically offers certification exams at the "Core" and "Expert" skill levels. * The Microsoft Office User Specialist Program is the only Microsoft approved program in the world for certifying proficiency in Microsoft Office desktop applications and Microsoft Project. This certification can be a valuable asset in any job search or career advancement.

More Information:

To learn more about becoming a Microsoft Office User Specialist, visit www.mous.net

To purchase a Microsoft Office User Specialist certification exam, visit www.DesktopIQ.co

To learn about other Microsoft Office User Specialist approved courseware from McGraw-Hill/Irwin, visit http://www.mhhe.com/catalogs/irwin/cit/mous/index.mhtml

.

---

* The availability of Microsoft Office User Specialist certification exams varies by application, application version and language. Visit www.mous.net for exam availability.

Microsoft, the Microsoft Office User Specialist Logo, PowerPoint and Outlook are either registered trademarks or trademarks of Microsoft Corporation in the United States and/or other countries.

acknowledgments

The authors want to acknowledge the work and support of the seasoned professionals at McGraw-Hill. Thank you to George Werthman, publisher, for his strong leadership and a management style that fosters innovation and creativity. Thank you to Dan Silverburg, sponsoring editor, who is an experienced editor and recent recruit to the I-Series. Dan quickly absorbed a month's worth of information in days and guided the authors through the sometimes-difficult publishing maze. Our special thanks go to Melissa Forte, developmental editor, who served, unofficially, as a cheerleader for the authors. The hub of our editorial "wheel," Melissa shouldered more than her share of work in the many months from prelaunch boot camp to bound book date. We are grateful to Gina Huck, developmental editor, for her dedication to this project. From the project's inception, Gina has guided us and kept us on track. Sarah Wood, developmental editor, paid attention to all the details that required her special care.

Thank you to Valerie Bolch, a University of San Diego graduate student, who did a wonderful job of creating some of the end-of-chapter exercises and tech editing the Excel manuscript. Ron Tariga, also a graduate student at the University of San Diego, helped categorize and display several Office XP toolbar buttons. Stirling Perry, a University of San Diego undergraduate student, took screen shots of all of the Office XP toolbar buttons and organized them into logical groups. Wendi Whitmore, a University of San Diego undergraduate student, provided screen shots of Office 2000 toolbars, prior to the release of Office XP. Many thanks to Linda Dillon, who provided creative input and feedback for the PowerPoint end-of-chapter materials. Also, the labor of Carolla McCammack in tech editing many of the Access chapters has been invaluable.

Thank you to Marilyn Parker, Rick's partner for 32 years, for her help, support, and tolerance. She helped with some of the manuscript details, supported Rick's need for time, and tolerated his emotional absence. Rick's sons, Cole, Morgan, Spence, and Sam, were patient and helpful during the time required for all the steps in the production of this book. All of them filled in and did "his" chores at times as they tolerated his distractions. Also, thanks to Mali Jones for her excellent technical editing.

We all wish to thank all of our schools for providing support, including time off to dedicate to writing: University of San Diego, University of Denver, and the College of Southern Idaho.

If you would like to contact us about any of the books in the I-Series, we would enjoy hearing from you. We welcome comments and suggestions that we might incorporate into future editions of the books. You can e-mail book-related messages to us at i-series@mcgraw-hill.com. For the latest information about the I-Series textbooks and related resources, please visit our Web site at www.mhhe.com/i-series.

dedication

TO my daughter, Kelly Allison Perry

You say "I will do that," and then you do! What an amazing, bright, and lovely young woman you are. You have taught me more than you realize.

J.T.P.

brief contents

table of contents

8 CHAPTER 8

DEVELOPING MULTIPLE WORKSHEET AND WORKBOOK APPLICATIONS EX 8.1

9 CHAPTER 9

USING DATA TABLES AND SCENARIOS EX 9.1

Common Microsoft Office XP Features

Chapter Objectives

In this chapter you will:

- Be introduced to the Office XP suite

- Find out what new features exist in Office XP

- Become familiar with the different versions of Office XP and which four applications are included in all versions

- Learn about the common screen elements such as the title bar, menu bar, and toolbars

- Learn how to switch between two or more open applications

- Learn how to use Office XP's newest features: the task pane and smart tags

- Become familiar with how to get help in an application

- Learn how to customize your Office Assistant

- Learn about the newest Help features: Answer Wizard and Ask a Question

CHAPTER OUTLINE:

1.1 Introducing
Microsoft Office XP

INTRODUCTION

Office XP is the newest version of the popular Microsoft integrated application suite series that has helped personal computer users around the world to be productive and creative. Specifically, an *application* is a program that is designed to help you accomplish a particular task, such as creating a slide-show presentation using PowerPoint. An *integrated application suite,* like Office XP, is a collection of application programs bundled together and designed to allow the user to effortlessly share information from one application to the next.

SESSION 1.1 INTRODUCING MICROSOFT OFFICE XP

There are several versions of Office XP available to users with a diversity of personal and business needs. They include the Standard edition, the Professional edition, the Professional Special edition, and the Developer edition. Each edition comes with a collection of different programs, but all include the basic applications of Word, Excel, Outlook, and PowerPoint, which is the collection known as the *Standard edition*. The *Professional edition* adds Access to the collection, whereas the *Professional Special edition* includes Access, FrontPage, and Publisher. A summary of some of the more popular applications available in Office XP is listed in Figure 1.1.

FIGURE 1.1

Application programs available in Microsoft Office XP

Office XP Application	Summary of What the Program Does
Word 2002	Word is a general-purpose word-processing tool that allows users to create primarily text-based documents, such as letters, résumés, research papers, and even Web pages.
Excel 2002	Excel is an electronic spreadsheet tool that can be used to input, organize, calculate, analyze, and display business data.
PowerPoint 2002	PowerPoint is a popular presentation tool that allows users to create overhead transparencies and powerful multimedia slide shows.
Access 2002	Access is a relational database tool that can be used to collect, organize, and retrieve large amounts of data. With a database you can manipulate the data into useful information using tables, forms, queries, and reports.
Outlook 2002	Outlook is a desktop information management tool that allows you to send and receive e-mail, maintain a personal calendar of appointments, schedule meetings with co-workers, create to-do lists, and store address information about business/personal contacts.
FrontPage 2002	FrontPage is a powerful Web publishing tool that provides everything needed to create, edit, and manage a personal or corporate Web site, without having to learn HTML.
Publisher 2002	Publisher is a desktop publishing tool that provides individual users the capability to create professional-looking flyers, brochures, and newsletters.

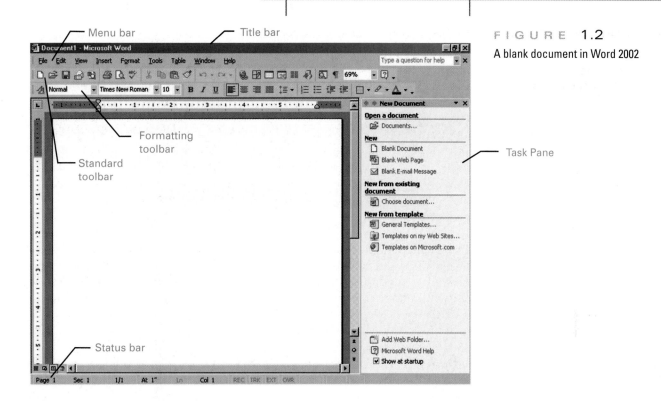

FIGURE 1.2
A blank document in Word 2002

Identifying Common Screen Elements

When you open two or more of the Microsoft applications, you will notice the similarities in the programs. This design is done intentionally so that as you learn to use one application, you will be able to quickly navigate through the remaining Office XP programs. When you first open Word, you will find a blank document as seen in Figure 1.2. In this exercise you will get to preview a blank document in Word and a blank workbook in Excel. Notice the common features of the two programs as you work with them. These features will be explained over the next few pages.

---

*another*word

. . . on the Office XP Suite

Collectively, the programs are officially referred to as ***Microsoft Office XP,*** but individually each application is referred to as version 2002.

Opening multiple applications in Office XP:

1. Click the **Start** button on the taskbar to display the pop-up menu

2. Move your cursor up the menu and stop on **Programs.** Another menu will appear listing all the programs available on your computer

3. Locate **Microsoft Word** in the program list and click it. After a few seconds you should see a blank document as previously seen in Figure 1.2. Now compare the screen layout with that found in Excel

4. Click the **Start** button, then point to **Programs,** once again

5. This time locate and click **Microsoft Excel** in the program list. After a few seconds you will see a blank workbook, similar to the one found in Figure 1.3

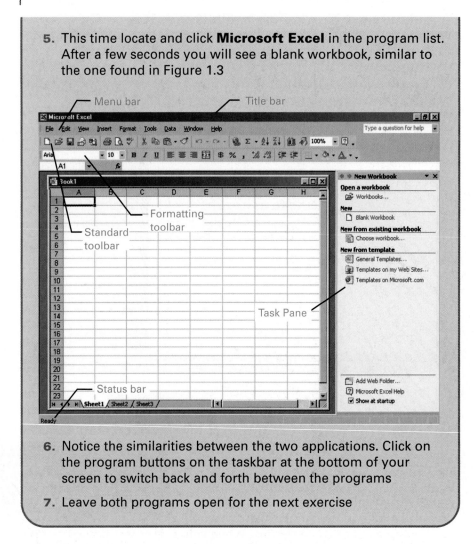

FIGURE 1.3

A blank workbook in Microsoft Excel

6. Notice the similarities between the two applications. Click on the program buttons on the taskbar at the bottom of your screen to switch back and forth between the programs

7. Leave both programs open for the next exercise

Title Bar, Menu Bar, and Toolbars

As you examine the Word and Excel programs, you will notice that each application contains similar elements such as a title bar, a menu bar, a toolbar, and a status bar. The *title bar* at the top of each screen displays the application's icon, the title of the document you are working on, and the name of the application program you are using.

The *menu bar* displays a list of key menu options available to you for that particular program. In addition to a few program-specific menu items, all of the Office XP applications generally will contain the identical menu options of File, Edit, View, Insert, Tools, Window, and Help. To use these menus, you simply click one time on the desired menu, and a sub-menu will then appear with additional options.

On the third row of each application is the *toolbar,* which is a collection of commonly used shortcut buttons. A single click on a toolbar button activates a program feature that also can be found in one of the menu options. Most office applications will display the *Standard toolbar,* which contains the popular icons such as Cut, Copy, and Paste. The table displayed in Figure 1.4 shows a list of these common buttons and their functions.

Another popular toolbar found in Office XP applications is the *Formatting toolbar,* which allows you to change the appearance of text,

*another*way

. . . . to switch between applications

You also can switch between applications by using what is known as the Alt+Tab sequence. Press and hold the **Alt** key, then press **Tab** one time. Let go of both keys when you see the gray box in the middle of your screen displaying program icons. This will allow you to quickly cycle back and forth through any open programs.

FIGURE 1.4

Standard toolbar buttons and their function

New	▯	Opens a new blank document, workbook, presentation, or database.
Open	☞	Opens a previously created document, workbook, presentation, or database.
Save	▣	Allows you to quickly save your work. The first time you save, you will be prompted for a file name and location.
E-mail	▤	New to Office XP, this button lets you quickly send the existing document as an email message.
Print	▤	Prints a document.
Cut	✂	Removes selected information from your document and temporarily places it on the Clipboard.
Copy	▤	Duplicates selected information and places it on the Clipboard.
Paste	▤	Copies information on the Clipboard to the current document.
Undo Typing	↶ ▾	Reverses the last action or keystroke taken. This is a great safety net for those uh-oh type mistakes!

such as bold, italicize, or underline. There are many toolbars available to display and some will appear as you use certain features in Office applications.

Task Panes, Clipboard, and Smart Tags

Most of the Office XP applications include a new feature known as the **Task Pane** as shown in Figure 1.5. This window allows you to access important tasks from a single, convenient location, while still working on your document. With the Task Pane window you can open files, view your clipboard, perform searches, and much more. By default, when you open an Office XP application, the Task Pane window is displayed to allow the user to open a file. As you select various functions of the application, the contents of the task pane will automatically change. You can close the task pane at any time by clicking on the close button, and redisplay the window by selecting it from the View menu.

One of the options available on the task pane is the **Clipboard,** which is a temporary storage location for selected text. In Office XP, you can actually view the contents of up to 24 items that have been cut or copied to the clipboard. This is a very powerful tool that will allow you to collect 24 sets of data and then let you quickly paste those data to a new location or document. When you paste any of the clipboard contents to your document, a Smart Tag button will appear next to the text. This smart tag, known as the **Paste Options button,** will prompt the user (when clicked) with additional features such as allowing you to paste with or without the original text formatting. There are additional **smart tag buttons** that appear as needed to provide options for completing a task quickly. In this next exercise you will get to practice using the Task Pane, Clipboard, and Paste Options smart tag button.

*another*way

. . . to activate a menu option

You also can activate a menu option by using shortcut key strokes. In the menu you will notice that one letter of each option is underlined. These designated letters can be used in conjunction with the Alt key to quickly access a menu task. For example, you can press **Alt+F+S** to save your file.

*another*word

. . . on the Clipboard

It is important to note that the Clipboard contents are available to all applications and not just the original application from where it was extracted.

FIGURE 1.5

Task Pane in Microsoft Word

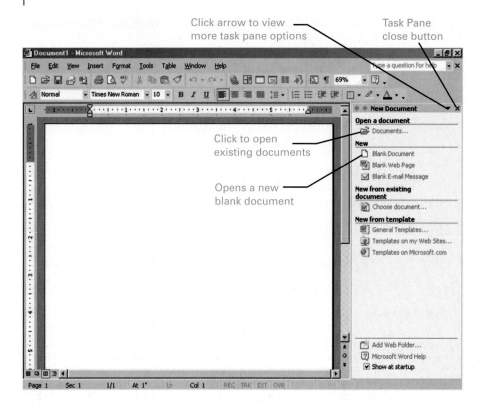

Working with the Task Pane

1. In the Excel application, type **Hello Office XP!** in cell A1 and press **Enter**

2. Click cell A1 and then change the font size of the text to size **22.** Click the **Italic** button on the Formatting toolbar to italicize your text as shown in Figure 1.6

3. Click the **Copy** button on the Standard toolbar. This will copy the contents of cell A1 to the clipboard

4. Press **Alt+Tab** to switch back to the Word program

5. Click the **Paste** button and press **Enter.** The text should appear in the blank document exactly as it was typed and italicized

6. At the top of the Task Pane window, click the **drop-down menu arrow** and select **Clipboard** from the drop-down list. You can now view the Clipboard task pane and the text that was copied to it

7. In the Clipboard Contents task pane, click on the **Hello Office XP!** item as indicated in Figure 1.7. This will paste the text a second time into your document

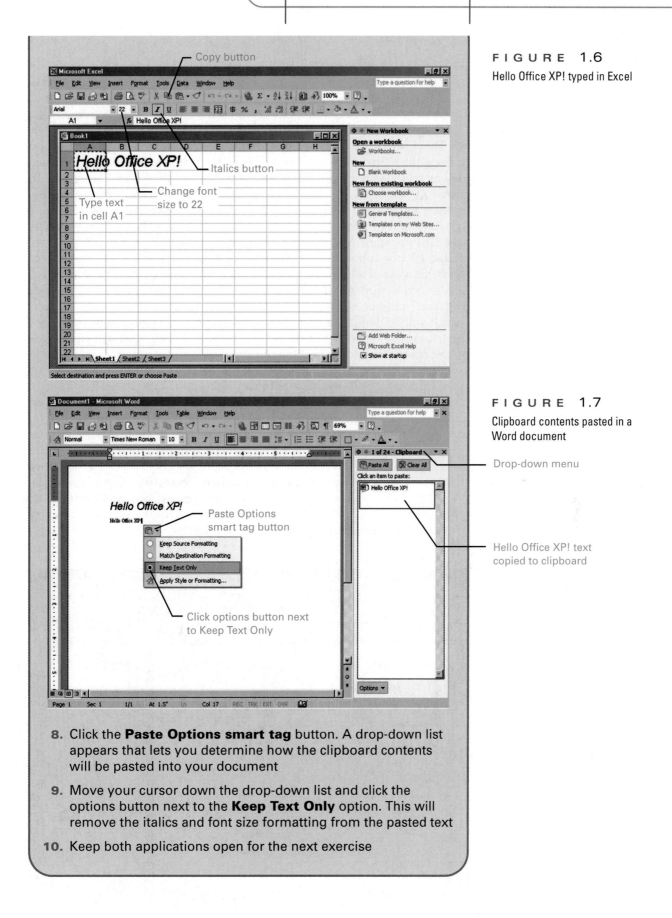

FIGURE 1.6
Hello Office XP! typed in Excel

FIGURE 1.7
Clipboard contents pasted in a Word document

8. Click the **Paste Options smart tag** button. A drop-down list appears that lets you determine how the clipboard contents will be pasted into your document

9. Move your cursor down the drop-down list and click the options button next to the **Keep Text Only** option. This will remove the italics and font size formatting from the pasted text

10. Keep both applications open for the next exercise

Getting Help

When you use any of the Office XP applications, you may find yourself in need of some assistance. There are several ways to obtain help, and fortunately for the user, they are once again consistent across the applications. To get help, the user can use the <u>H</u>elp menu option, press F1, or use the Office Assistant, Answer Wizard, or Ask a Question text box.

The most common way of getting help is to use the Help menu option or press the F1 function key. If you do ask for help, an ***Office Assistant*** will appear ready to help you with your question as shown in Figure 1.8. In Office XP applications, the Office Assistant is hidden by default and only appears when Help is activated. One of the fun aspects about the Office Assistant is that you can select your favorite character to help you. The standard assistant is known as ***Clippit*** (the paper clip), but you also can choose ***F1*** (the robot), ***Links*** (the cat), or ***Rocky*** (the dog), among others.

Regardless of which one you use, once you request help and your assistant appears, you must then type in your help question in the Office Assistant balloon and click on the Search button. The results of your search will be displayed in a Help window for you to review or print. For those users who prefer not to use an Office Assistant, you can right-click on the character and choose the option to hide the assistant.

The ***Answer Wizard,*** located in the Microsoft Help dialog box, is another means of requesting help through your application. In order to use the Answer Wizard, you must first hide the Office Assistant and then click on Help menu. Once the Help dialog box is displayed, simply click on the Answer Wizard tab and type in your question in the text box. Another way to get help without using the Office Assistant is to use the new feature called ***Ask a Question.*** Located in the top-right corner of your window, this is perhaps the most convenient method for getting help because the user simply has to key in a search topic in the text box and press enter, without having to launch the Answer Wizard or Office Assistant. You will get to practice requesting help in the next exercise.

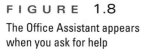

FIGURE 1.8

The Office Assistant appears when you ask for help

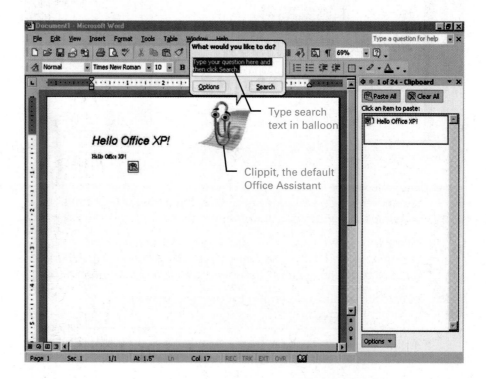

To get help:

1. In your Word document or Excel workbook, press the **F1** function key. This should activate your Office Assistant to the screen

   tip: *If the office assistant does not appear, click on the **Help** menu and select **Show the Office Assistant***

2. In the Office Assistant balloon, type **Speech Recognition,** then click the **Search button**

3. In the next balloon that appears, click the **About Speech Recognition** bullet. This will open up the Microsoft Help window with the speech recognition search results as shown in Figure 1.9. Press the **ESC** key on your keyboard to remove the Office Assistant balloon

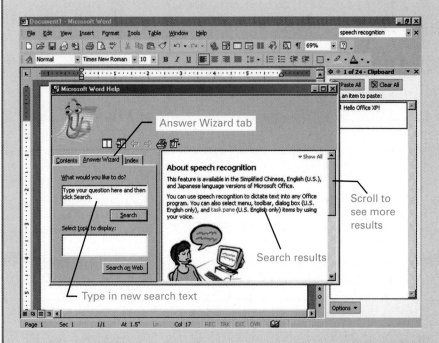

FIGURE 1.9
Results of search displayed in Microsoft help window

4. After looking over your search results, click the **Close** button of the Help window

5. Right-click the **Office Assistant** and, in the menu that pops up, select **Choose Assistant**

6. Click either the **Back** or **Next** button in the Office Assistant dialog box as shown in Figure 1.10 until you find an assistant that you like, and then click **OK**

7. Right-click the **Office Assistant** again, and this time select **Hide.** This will hide the Office Assistant until you request help again

8. **Close** any open documents and programs

FIGURE 1.10
Office Assistant dialog box

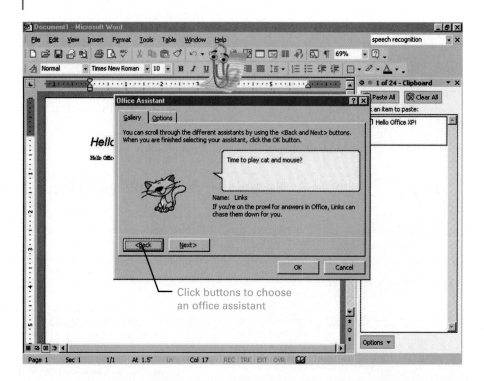

Click buttons to choose
an office assistant

SESSION 1.1   *making the grade*

1. What four application programs are available in all versions of Office XP?

2. What is the default Office Assistant character?

3. How many items can be posted to the clipboard contents?

4. Which two toolbars are the most frequently used in all applications?

5. What is the quickest and most convenient method for getting help in any of the Office XP applications?

SUMMARY

In this chapter you have been introduced to the common elements of Microsoft's newest integrated application suite, known as Office XP. Regardless of which version of the program you are using, you always will have access to the Word, Excel, PowerPoint, and Outlook applications. As you learn to navigate through these applications, you will notice many similarities that allow the user to easily adapt from one application to the next. These common features include the title bar, the menu bar, and toolbars. You learned that the standard and formatting toolbars are the most commonly used toolbars in Office XP, but that there also are many toolbars available for users to select from or that automatically appear when completing a task.

Through the exercises in this chapter, you learned how to use one of Office XP's newest features, the task pane. This window allows the user quick access to various task sequences such as opening a file, viewing the Clipboard contents, performing a search, and inserting clip art. While the

Clipboard is not new to Microsoft products, it is more powerful in this version because it allows the user to post up to 24 different items in its contents. Finally, when in desperate need of answers, the user can always turn to the many help modes of Office XP. You can use one of the customized Office Assistants such as Clippit, use the Answer Wizard in the Help dialog box, or use the Ask a Question text box to find a quick solution to a problem.

task reference roundup

Task	Page #	Preferred Method
Switch between applications	OFF 1.3	• Press **Alt+Tab**
Copy and Paste using Clipboard task pane	OFF 1.5	• Highlight/select text to be copied
		• Click the **Copy** button on the toolbar
		• Place cursor in desired paste location
		• Click on item in Clipboard task pane to paste
Obtaining Help	OFF 1.8	• Press **F1** or click **Office Assistant**

review of terminology

CROSSWORD PUZZLE

Across

2. The dog Office Assistant
6. Office XP version that consists of Word, Excel, PowerPoint, and Outlook
7. Relational database tool that can be used to collect, organize, and retrieve large amounts of data
8. Is located in the Help dialog box and provides another means of requesting help
10. A popular presentation tool that allows users to create multimedia slide shows
11. Temporary storage location for up to 24 items of selected text that has been cut or copied
13. This window allows you to view clipboard contents in addition to other important tasks
14. A collection of commonly used shortcut buttons

Down

1. Toolbar that allows you to change the appearance of your text
3. The cat office assistant
4. Button that appears when you paste into your document
5. Buttons that appear as needed to provide options for completing a task quickly
9. The paper clip Office Assistant
12. Displays a list of key menu options available to you for that particular program

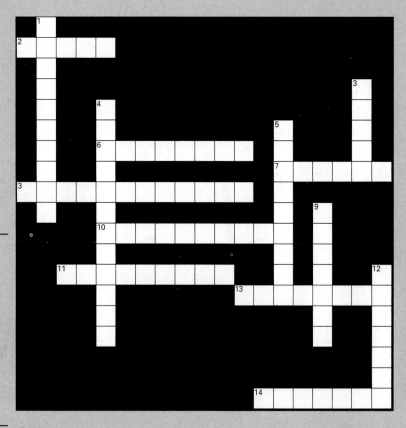

FILL-IN THE BLANKS

1. _____ is the newest version of the popular Microsoft integrated application suite series.

2. An _____ is a program that is designed to help you accomplish a particular task, such as creating a slide-show presentation.

3. By default, when you open an Office XP application, the _____ window is displayed to allow the user to open a file.

4. The standard Office Assistant is known as _____ (the paper clip), but you can also choose _____ (the robot), _____ (the Cat), or _____ (the dog).

5. In Office XP, you can actually view the contents of up to _____ items that have been cut or copied to the clipboard.

6. A single click on a toolbar button activates a program feature that also can be found in one of the _____ options.

7. Most office applications will display the _____ toolbar, which contains the popular icons such as Cut, Copy, and Paste.

REVIEW QUESTIONS

1. What are some of the common features found in all Office XP applications?

2. What tools can you use to get help or search for additional information?

3. What is the Task Pane window used for?

4. What are smart tag buttons and when do you have access to them? Give an example of one.

5. What are the four basic applications that are included as part of all versions of Office XP?

MATCHING

Match the term with the related definition.

1. _____ Access 2002

2. _____ Clipboard

3. _____ Excel 2002

4. _____ Formatting toolbar

5. _____ PowerPoint 2002

6. _____ Standard toolbar

7. _____ Task pane

8. _____ Word 2002

a. A temporary storage location for up to 24 items of selected text that has been cut or copied.

b. Collection of buttons that allows you to change the appearance of text, such as bold, italicize, or underline.

c. Collection of buttons that contains the popular icons such as Cut, Copy, and Paste.

d. Electronic spreadsheet tool that can be used to input, organize, calculate, analyze, and display business data.

e. General-purpose word-processing tool that allows users to create primarily text-based documents.

f. A popular presentation tool that allows users to create overhead transparencies and powerful multimedia slide shows.

g. Relational database tool that can be used to collect, organize, and retrieve large amounts of data.

h. This window allows you to access important tasks from a single, convenient location, while still working on your document.

OFFICE

CHAPTER

1

Chapter Objectives

- Start Excel
- Open a workbook (MOUS) Ex2002-2-1
- Move around a worksheet using the mouse and arrow keys
- Select a block of cells
- Type into worksheet cells text, values, formulas, and functions (MOUS) Ex2002-1-2
- Edit and clear cell entries (MOUS) Ex2002-2-1
- Save a workbook (MOUS) Ex2002-2-3
- Adding a header and a footer (MOUS) Ex2002-3-6
- Previewing output (MOUS) Ex2002-3-7
- Print a worksheet
- Print worksheet formulas
- Exit Excel

one

Creating Worksheets for Decision Makers

Western University Rugby Team

Rugby is a popular sport around the world and is played at many universities in the United States. The sport has a loyal group of people who attend most of the games in the region. Often, U.S. collegiate rugby teams play on open fields that are not fenced. Occasionally, they play in soccer stadiums or on football fields where they can control access of fans and charge a nominal fee—a donation—to view a rugby game.

Western University is a small private school with a rugby team composed of 21 varsity players and 15 freshman and novice players. Stirling Leonard is a senior on the team and one of its co-captains. He is responsible for ensuring that everyone is available for each week's game and for overseeing the athletes' pregame warm-up regimen. He has also taken a lead role in organizing the annual fundraising campaign for the team.

Unlike football or soccer, which are varsity sports at Western University, rugby is a club sport and not eligible to receive financial support from the university. The team's annual costs include transportation to games, replacement of some game uniforms each year, and sundry supplies such as tape and bandages. These costs at Western amount to over $24,000 per year—a small amount compared to the cost of a varsity sport, but a daunting cost for rugby team members to provide. Each team member must pay a fee to offset the projected cost of running the team. Some of Western's rugby team members pay their fees directly, whereas others help with the team's annual fundraising and use the funds they raise to pay their fees.

Past fundraising activities included monthly car washes, club T-shirt sales, and the annual rug-

FIGURE 1.1
Scrip Sales Projection worksheet

		Percent Donation	Unit Value	Projected Unit Sales			Detail Donation	Retail		
Scrip Sales Projection										
Specialty Stores										
	Circuits West	4.50%	$10	300			$135.00	$3,000.00		
	Enterprise Electronics	5.00%	20	400			400.00	8,000.00		
	Radio Hut	6.50%	10	300			195.00	3,000.00		
	University Bookstore	10.00%	5	900			450.00	4,500.00		
						Subtotal	$1,180.00	$18,500.00		
Restaurants										
	Burgers 'R Us	12.00%	$10	600			$720.00	$6,000.00		
	Country Cupboard	5.00%	5	670			167.50	3,350.00		
	McCrackens	6.00%	10	500			300.00	5,000.00		
	Taco King	8.00%	10	400			320.00	4,000.00		
						Subtotal	$1,507.50	$18,350.00		
							Total Donation	Total Retail		
							$2,687.50	$36,850.00		

by alum game. This year, Stirling has devised a new and innovative way to raise money for the team: selling scrip issued by local specialty and fast-food stores near the college. Scrip is special paper issued by various merchants that are evidence of payment for a good or service from that merchant. Similar to a gift certificate, a store's own brand of scrip is the same as cash at the issuing merchant's store. Teams make money on the difference between the wholesale price at which they purchase scrip and the retail price at which they sell the scrip to customers.

Using Microsoft Excel 2002, Stirling has created a worksheet that he and the team can use to calculate the total scrip sold each month as well as the team's profit. He has to complete the worksheet by entering the scrip sales quantities and some formulas to compute the donation value and retail value of the sales this month.

In this chapter, you will learn how to complete the Scrip Report to determine how well the team is doing toward its goal of raising the money it needs to support the team. Figure 1.1 shows the completed Scrip Sales Projection worksheet.

INTRODUCTION

Chapter 1 introduces you to Excel. You start Excel and examine the Standard toolbar, Formatting toolbar, Task Pane, and other features of a new Excel's window. You learn several ways to move around a worksheet, including using arrow keys and the mouse. Select worksheet cells by clicking a cell and then dragging the mouse across a contiguous group of cells.

Excel worksheet cells can contain text, values (constants), formulas, functions, and a combination of these. You enter text into a cell by clicking it and then typing. You enter values, which are numbers, by typing the number preceded by an optional plus or minus sign. Formulas always begin with an equals sign (=). Following the equals sign you can type an arbitrarily complex expression involving values, mathematical operators, and Excel functions. Excel functions are built in or prerecorded formulas that provide a shortcut for complex calculations. Writing Excel functions saves time and trouble. For example, it is far easier to write a SUM function to total several worksheet cell values than it is to write a long formula containing the plus operator and individual cell references to be summed.

Edit a cell that contains an error and then press Enter to complete the work. Alternatively, you can completely replace a cell's contents by typing a new formula. Clear a cell to empty its contents with the Clear command on the Edit menu. Attempting to clear a cell by typing a space usually leads to problems as you develop a worksheet. Specify a worksheet's print area consisting of any rectangular group of cells. When you print the worksheet, Excel remembers each worksheet's print area and prints only cells within the print area.

SESSION 1.1 GETTING STARTED

In this section, you will learn how to start Excel, open a workbook, and observe the anatomy of an Excel worksheet and its window. You will investigate several ways to move around an Excel workbook using the mouse, arrow keys, and combinations of keyboard keys that employ shortcuts to move the worksheet cursor quickly to a particular worksheet cell. Finally, you will learn how to select a block of cells.

INTRODUCTION TO EXCEL

Excel is a computerized spreadsheet—an automated version of an accountant's ledger. A *spreadsheet* is a popular program used to analyze numeric information and help make meaningful business decisions based on the analysis. Spreadsheets are used for a variety of applications ranging from financial analysis of stock portfolios, manufacturing and production quantity assessment, inventory turnover and cost estimation, budgeting, and simple household record keeping.

Dan Bricklin and Bob Frankston invented the electronic spreadsheet in 1979. Bob Frankston joined Dan Bricklin, a Harvard MBA student, to cooperatively write the program for the new electronic spreadsheet. They formed a new company called Software Arts, Inc. and called their spreadsheet product VisiCalc. Bricklin and Frankston later sold VisiCalc to Lotus Development Corporation, where it developed into the PC spreadsheet Lotus 1-2-3. VisiCalc was the first of several spreadsheet programs to develop over the next two decades.

Spreadsheet software has been one of the most popular pieces of software of all time. Why is it so popular? Consider the way people performed a typical spreadsheet task before the advent of the electronic version. A typical application of a hard copy, paper and pencil method of creating and maintaining a spreadsheet is projecting net profit. Prior to the advent of electronic spreadsheets, accountants used paper ledgers and wrote entries in pencil so that they could easily modify various entries in the spreadsheet and then recalculate, using a calculator, the new values. Bricklin once said, "VisiCalc took 20 hours of work per week for some people and turned it out in 15 minutes and let them become much more creative."

Figure 1.2 shows a facsimile of a manual accounting spreadsheet showing projected net profit of a product whose unit price is $200. Expenses for marketing, manufacturing, and overhead are but a few of the

F I G U R E   **1.2**

Hard copy accounting spreadsheet

expenses needed to advertise the product and bring it to market. People who worked with ledger spreadsheets like the one shown in Figure 1.2 often had to modify projected sales numbers, unit sale prices, and other values and then recalculate values such as net profit. Any change to a hard copy worksheet can take a lot of time for even the simplest alteration because many values that are dependent on the change must be recalculated. Making changes to spreadsheets and reviewing their effect on other values is a classic use of spreadsheets and is called **what-if analysis**—one of the popular uses for today's electronic spreadsheets. With electronic spreadsheets, any changes you make to a spreadsheet automatically recalculate to quickly reveal new values. Formulas give Excel its power.

People refer to spreadsheet programs as electronic spreadsheets or simply spreadsheets. Using Excel 2002, you create a document called a **workbook,** which is a collection of one or more individual **worksheets.** Worksheets are so named because they resemble pages in a spiral-bound workbook like the ones you purchase and use to take class notes. You will probably hear the terms *spreadsheets, workbooks,* and *worksheets* used interchangeably.

STARTING EXCEL AND OPENING A WORKSHEET

Stirling's alarm clock wakes him at 6:30 A.M. He's an early riser and wants to get started on the worksheet so that he can show it to his rugby coach, Rod Harrington, for his comments. Stirling has discovered which of the nearby merchants and restaurants offer scrip, and he has learned that he must purchase the scrip through a broker whose warehouse contains scrip from hundreds of stores in the region. After talking to the scrip distribution center manager, Stirling was able to get a special deal: He can request and receive up to $10,000 worth of scrip to be delivered to the university's athletic office and he will have up to 45 days to pay for it.

Start Excel to design the worksheet to calculate the scrip profits and project how many units to order next time.

Starting Microsoft Excel:

1. Make sure Windows is running on your computer and the Windows desktop appears on your computer screen

2. Click the taskbar **Start** ⬛Start button to display the Start menu, then point to **Programs** to display the Programs menu

3. Point to **Microsoft Excel** on the Programs menu and then click **Microsoft Excel.** Within a few seconds, the Microsoft Excel copyright information page appears. Then the Excel window containing an empty worksheet appears. When both Excel and its worksheet are maximized, your screen should look like Figure 1.3

4. Microsoft Excel should fill the screen and show an empty worksheet. If it does not, then click the **Maximize** ⬜ button found in the upper-right corner of the Excel window

5. If the empty worksheet is not maximized, then click the worksheet **Maximize** ⬜ button

EXCEL

FIGURE 1.3

Excel program window containing an empty worksheet

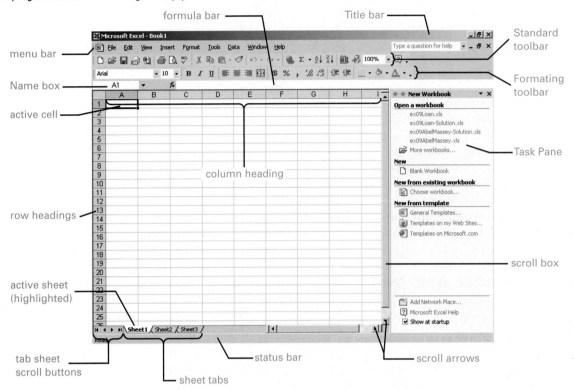

ANATOMY OF THE EXCEL WINDOW

The Excel program window shown in Figure 1.3 is typical of many Microsoft Windows applications. The Excel application is divided into several important areas. These will become very familiar to you as you gain experience with Excel.

Task Pane

A *Task Pane* is a dockable dialog window that provides a convenient way to use commands, gather information, and modify Excel documents. An Excel Task Pane can contain one or more pages, and each page is broken up into sections. The Excel Task Pane in Figure 1.3 contains sections for opening a workbook, creating a new workbook, and creating a workbook from a template. The Task Pane puts relevant features one click away.

Menu Bar

The *menu bar,* which is visible no matter which Excel activity is taking place, contains the Excel menus. Clicking a command on the menu bar reveals the menu's associated commands. Menus are arranged in a familiar way beginning on the left with the File, Edit, and View menus. Clicking the File menu, for example, reveals the New, Open, Close, and Save commands, among others, that are typical of all Windows File menu commands. Normally the menu bar appears just below the Title bar, but you can click the menu handle at the left end of the menu bar and drag the menu bar to any location on the screen, or you can dock it on any of the other three sides of the screen.

Toolbars

Toolbars allow you to execute commands with a single click. Most of the frequently used commands appear in one of the several Excel toolbars. The *Standard toolbar,* which normally appears below the menu bar, contains buttons that execute popular menu bar commands such as Print, Cut, and Insert Table. The *Formatting toolbar* contains buttons that change the appearance of a worksheet. For example, you can set the typeface or underline entries by pressing Formatting toolbar buttons.

Formula Bar

The Formula bar appears below the menu bar and toolbars just above the Workbook window. The *formula bar* displays the active cell's contents, appearing at the top of the screen, in which you can enter cell contents or edit existing contents. *Cell contents* are the text, formulas, or numbers you type into a cell. A cell's contents can look different from the value it calculates and displays in a cell. A discussion of these differences appears later in this chapter. The *name box,* appearing on the left of the formula bar, displays either the active cell's address (A1 in Figure 1.3) or its assigned name. (More information about cell addresses and names appears later in this chapter.)

Workbook Window

The document window is called the *workbook window* or *worksheet window.* It contains the workbook on which you are working. A workbook can contain up to 255 worksheets, and each worksheet contains columns and rows that are labeled with letters and numbers respectively. A worksheet can contain up to 256 columns with labels A through IV to uniquely identify each column. A worksheet contains 65,536 rows with numeric labels from 1 to 65536. A *cell* is located at the intersection of a row and a column and identified by a cell reference, such as A1. The *cell reference,* or cell address, is a cell's identification consisting of its column letter(s) followed by its row number. The cell located at the intersection of column D and row 42 is identified as D42, for example. A worksheet cell contains data that you enter such as text, numbers, or formulas. Each cell is like a small calculator, capable of computing the value of any arbitrarily complex formulas you type. The *active cell* is the cell in which you are currently working. Its name or cell reference appears in the name box, its contents appear in the formula bar, and a dark rectangle surrounds the active cell (see Figure 1.3).

Sheet Tabs

Each of a workbook's sheets has a unique name. That name appears in its *sheet tab.* When you create a new workbook, the number of sheets varies. By default, new sheets are named Sheet1, Sheet2, and so on. You can change the name of any sheet to something more meaningful. Clicking a sheet tab makes the clicked sheet active. The sheet tab of the active sheet— the one into which you are entering data—is bright white whereas inactive sheet tabs are dark gray. If your workbook contains many worksheets, only a few sheet tabs appear just above the status bar. To move to another worksheet whose tab is not shown, click the *sheet tab scroll buttons* to scroll through the sheet tabs until you find the sheet you want. Then click the sheet tab to make the sheet active.

Status Bar

The *status bar* is located at the very bottom of the window—below the sheet tabs and above the Windows task bar. This shows general information about the worksheet and selected keyboard keys. Status indicators on the right side tell you about the current state of selected keys. For instance, one indicator displays NUM whenever the NumLock key is active. Another status indicator displays CAPS when the Caps Lock key is active.

Mouse Pointer

The *mouse pointer* indicates the current position of the mouse as you move it around the screen. It changes shape to indicate what duties you can perform at the location over which the mouse pointer is positioned. When the mouse is over a worksheet, it appears as a white plus sign. Move the mouse to a menu and it changes to an arrow, which indicates that you can select an item by clicking the mouse. When you move the mouse to the formula bar, it changes into an I-beam shape, which indicates that you can click and then type data.

MOVING AROUND A WORKSHEET

In order to enter information into a worksheet, you must first select the cell to make it the active cell. There are a number of ways to select a cell.

Using the Keyboard

Excel provides several ways to move to different cells in your worksheet. Pressing Ctrl+Home always makes cell A1 the active cell. Pressing the right arrow key moves the active cell one cell to the right. Other arrow keys move the active cell corresponding to the arrow's direction (right, left, up, and down). Figure 1.4 shows keys that select different worksheet cells.

F I G U R E   **1.4**

Keys to move around a worksheet

Keystroke	Action
Up arrow	Moves up one cell
Down arrow	Moves down one cell
Left arrow	Moves left one cell
Right arrow	Moves right one cell
PgUp	Moves active cell up one screen
PgDn	Moves active cell down one screen
Home	Moves active cell to column A of current row
Ctrl+Home	Moves the active cell to cell A1
Ctrl+End	Moves to the lower, rightmost active corner of the worksheet
F5 (function key)	Opens the Go To dialog box in which you can enter any cell address

Using the Mouse

The mouse is a quick and convenient way to select a cell. Simply click the cell you want to make the active cell by placing the pointer over the cell and clicking the left mouse button. Moving to cells not yet visible on the screen is simple too. Use the vertical and horizontal worksheet scroll bars or arrow keys to scroll to the area of the worksheet containing the cell to which you want to move. Then click the cell to select it.

Try moving to different parts of the worksheet. Prepare for this short exercise by ensuring that an empty Excel worksheet is open. Then do the following:

Making a cell the active cell:

1. Close the Task Pane by clicking the **Task Pane Close** button in the New Workbook title bar. Position the mouse pointer over cell C4, then click the left mouse button to make cell C4 the active cell

2. Click cell **G7** to make it the active cell

3. Click cell **N53.** (You will have to use the horizontal and vertical scroll bars to bring cell N53 into view on your screen prior to selecting it)

4. Press the **Home** key to move to column A and make cell A53 the active cell

5. Finally, press **Ctrl+Home** to move to cell A1

6. Press the **PgDn** key to scroll the screen down one screen. The active cell is column A and a row below row 20. The exact row that becomes the active cell depends on the size and resolution of your screen. A new, previously hidden set of rows is revealed in any case

7. Press **F5** to open the Go To dialog box

tip: *Ignore any contents in your Go To panel and the Reference text box. If there is already an entry in your Reference text box, simply type over it*

8. Type **CD451** in the Reference text box and click **OK.** Cell CD451 becomes the active cell

9. Press **F5** to open the Go To dialog box again

10. Type **IV65536** and click **OK.** Cell IV65536 becomes the active cell

11. Click the **vertical scroll bar down arrow** three times to move the display up three rows, and then click the **horizontal scroll bar right arrow** two times. Notice that cell IV65536 is located at the highest row and right-most column in the worksheet (see Figure 1.5)

12. Press **Ctrl+Home** to move to cell A1

anotherway

. . . to Move to a Worksheet Cell

Press **Ctrl+G** to display the Go To dialog box

Type in the Reference text box the cell reference to which you want to move

Click the **OK** button

EXCEL

F I G U R E   1.5

Moving to the last cell on an
Excel worksheet

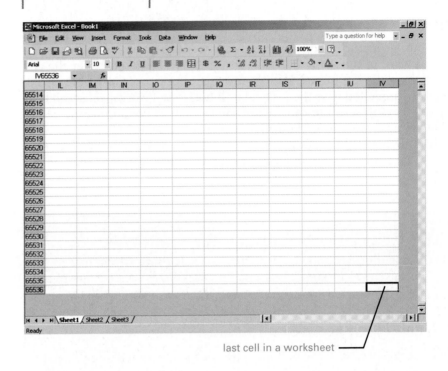

last cell in a worksheet

MOVING FROM SHEET TO SHEET

Workbooks can contain more than one worksheet, because worksheets are
a convenient way to organize collections of related sheets. An inventory
manager might keep each month's raw materials purchases on separate
worksheets by month. Similarly, stockbrokers can keep records about their
clients' purchases in one Excel workbook, assigning one page per client.
You can move from one worksheet to another within one workbook by
clicking its sheet tab. The new sheet becomes active. You can use the sheet
tab scroll buttons to reveal hidden sheet tabs when necessary.

OPENING AN EXISTING WORKBOOK

When you want to examine, modify, or work with a workbook you or
someone else created previously, you must open it first. When you open a
workbook, Excel locates the file on your disk, reads it from the disk, and
transfers the entire file into your computer's main memory, called Random
Access Memory (RAM). The disk-to-memory loading process is complete
when the worksheet appears on your computer's monitor. Loading a worksheet from a removable disk takes more time than loading the same worksheet from a hard disk—a time difference you will notice. Once loaded into
memory, a worksheet resides both in memory and on disk. Any changes
you may make to the worksheet should be saved back to the removable
disk. If you maintain your worksheets on a removable disk, remember to
first save any worksheet changes before you remove the disk. Otherwise,
the worksheet stored on your removable disk may be out of synchroniza-
tion with the one stored in memory.

Stirling has created a workbook called **ex01Scrip.xls** to help you and
the team estimate how much scrip they must sell to raise money for the
team.

task reference

Opening an Excel Workbook

- Click **File** and then click **Open**
- Ensure that the Look In list box displays the name of the folder containing your workbook
- Click the workbook's name
- Click the **Open** button

Opening an existing Excel workbook:

1. Place your data disk in the appropriate drive

2. Click **File** on the menu bar and then click **Open**

3. Click the **Look in** list arrow to display a list of available disk drives. Locate the drive containing your data disk and click the drive containing your data disk. The window displays a list of folders and Excel workbook file names

4. Locate and double-click the folder name **Ch01,** then click the Excel file **ex01Scrip.xls** to select it

5. Click the **Open** button located on the Standard toolbar. The first page of the Scrip workbook opens and displays the documentation worksheet. See Figure 1.6

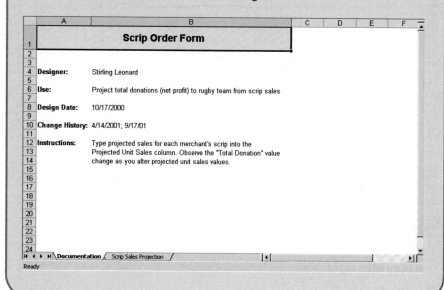

FIGURE 1.6

Scrip workbook documentation worksheet

Scrip Worksheet Design

The Scrip workbook created by Stirling consists of two worksheets, which Stirling name "Documentation" and "Scrip Sales Projection." The first worksheet is labeled Documentation. This sheet name appears on its tab (see Figure 1.6) and contains information about the workbook's designer, its use, when the workbook was created, a list of dates when the workbook was changed, and brief comments. Stirling explains that the Documentation worksheet conveys important information about the Scrip workbook to anyone who works with it. The instructions description is particularly helpful because it provides a reminder of how to use the workbook. That's especially helpful, he explains, when you work with several workbooks and want a quick reminder of how to use this particular workbook. The Documentation worksheet is not typical of most Excel worksheets as it contains no grid lines and no column or row headings. Excel provides options to remove those features. Because the Documentation worksheet is unlike others, removing the gridlines reduces confusion.

After you review the Documentation worksheet with Stirling, he opens the Scrip Sales Projection worksheet by clicking the Scrip Sales Projection worksheet tab. Figure 1.7 shows the Scrip Sales Projection worksheet. Stirling describes the two major parts of the Scrip Sales Projection worksheet. The left half of the sheet contains merchants grouped into the two categories Specialty Stores and Restaurants. Under each category heading are lists of merchants offering scrip—one row for each merchant. The Specialty Stores category contains the three most popular stores near campus: Circuits West, Enterprise Electronics, and Radio Hut. Similarly, beneath the Restaurants category label are four restaurants popular with students and close to campus. Each merchant row contains the percent donation, which is the percentage profit that the club makes on the sale of that merchant's scrip, and the scrip denomination available. The fourth column, Projected Unit Sales, is the column into which you will enter different values, later in this chapter, and the estimate of projected sales, in units, for each merchant. Cells E6 through E16 in that column are a critical part of the worksheet because they contain the assumptions you will be exploring. A change in the projected sales for one or more merchants' scrip causes changes in other worksheet locations.

Under the Donation and Retail columns are the projected values of the revenue that the club keeps—its profit—and the total retail value of the scrip respectively. Cells H6 through H8 display the dollar value that the club receives if they sell the scrip units listed in cells E6 through E8. Similarly, Cells H13 through H16 display projected rugby club profits for restaurant scrip sales for the listed restaurants. To the right, cells I13 through I16 show the total retail value of each merchant's scrip based on

FIGURE **1.7**

Partially complete Scrip Sales Projection worksheet

	A	B	C	D	E	F	G	H	I	J	K
1	Scrip Sales Projection										
2					Projected			Detail			
3			Percent	Unit	Unit						
4			Donation	Value	Sales			Donation	Retail		
5	Specialty Stores										
6		Circuits West	4.50%	$10	300			$135.00	$3,000.00		
7		Enterprise Electronics	5.00%	20	400			400.00	8,000.00		
8		Radio Hut	6.50%	10	300			195.00	3,000.00		
9											
10									$14,000.00		
11											
12	Restaurants										
13		Burgers 'R Us	12.00%	$10	600			$720.00	$6,000.00		
14		Country Cupboard	5.00%	5	670			167.50	3,350.00		
15		McCrackens	6.00%	10	500			300.00	5,000.00		
16		Taco King	8.00%	10	400			320.00	4,000.00		
17									$18,350.00		
18											
19								Total	Total		
20								Donation	Retail		
21									$32,350.00		
22											
23											
24											
25											

Documentation \ Scrip Sales Projection /

Ready

the projected scrip units sold shown in column E. Likewise, Cell I21 displays the scrip's total face value. You can see that the projected total value of all projected scrip retail sales is $32,350.00, but the club's total profit (Total Donation) on those sales for both specialty stores and restaurants is not yet displayed (under the heading Total Donation).

The percent donation column, representing the profit percentage, or discount, that the rugby club receives, is fixed by the merchant and thus unlikely to change. The single variable in the scrip sales worksheet that most determines the success of the scrip sales effort is the column into which Stirling will type in different numbers to see the effect—the projected unit sales. These are called the worksheet's *assumption cells,* which are cells upon which other formulas depend and whose values can be changed to observe their effect on a worksheet's entries. A change in some or all of these values directly affects the total sales and therefore the profit that the rugby team generates. Under the current assumptions, the best single profit-making scrip is Burgers 'R Us, because their scrip yields 12 percent profit—the highest percentage of any scrip in the current set—and the projected sales of 600 units is the current largest. Of course, the value 600 is an assumption and not a record of actual sales. If Burgers 'R Us proves to be popular, the team may want to focus its efforts on selling more Burgers 'R Us scrip.

Overall, the Scrip Sales Projection worksheet provides Stirling with an estimate of how much scrip the team must sell in order to make a real dent in their team expenses. If the total donation value were very small, then the team might consider alternative fundraising activities. The Scrip Sales Projection worksheet is a valuable decision-making tool because it provides a clear picture of the how scrip sales can translate into team profits.

making *the grade*

SESSION 1.1

1. A popular program used to analyze numeric information and help make meaningful business decisions is called a _____ program.

2. _____ analysis is observing changes to spreadsheets and reviewing their effect on other values in the spreadsheet.

3. An Excel spreadsheet is called a(n) _____ and consists of individual pages called _____.

4. Beneath Excel's menu bar is the _____ toolbar, which contains button shortcuts for commands such as Print, and the _____ toolbar containing button shortcuts to alter the appearance of worksheets and their cells.

5. The _____ cell is the cell in which you are currently entering data.

SESSION 1.2 ENTERING DATA, SAVING WORKBOOKS, AND PRINTING WORKSHEETS

In this session, you will learn how to enter data into worksheet cells, enter formulas into worksheet cells, save a workbook, and print a worksheet. Stirling wants you to modify the Scrip Sales Projection worksheet by adding another store and modifying projected scrip sales. In particular,

EXCEL

you will learn how to enter text entries, values, formulas, and functions. You will learn how to remove information from one or more worksheet cells. You will save your workbook and print the worksheet and its formulas. When you have completed your work on the Scrip Sales Projection worksheet, you will close it and exit Excel.

EXCEL DATA TYPES

You can enter three types of data into Excel worksheet cells: text, formulas, and values. You will learn the difference between these three data types in this session. Each type has a slightly different purpose. First you will learn about text entries, because they are straightforward and yet fundamental to good worksheet design.

ENTERING TEXT, VALUES, FORMULAS, AND FUNCTIONS

Worksheet cells can contain text, value, formula, and function entries. Text entries document and identify important elements in a worksheet. Important worksheet input numbers, such as the Scrip Sales Projection worksheet's projected unit sales, are values. More complicated entries are formulas consisting of mathematical operators, cell references, and Excel functions. Formulas compute and display numeric or text entries that usually change when you alter values upon which the formulas depend. Functions are prerecorded formulas that make calculations easier for you. Each of these types of cell entries has an important role to play, and each one is introduced next.

Text

Text entries are any combination of characters that you can type on the keyboard including symbols ($, #, @, and so on), numbers, letters, and spaces. While text can be used as data, it almost always identifies and documents important worksheet columns, rows, and cells. (Sometimes text entries are called labels.) The Scrip workbook contains many text entries. Text appears in the Documentation sheet shown in Figure 1.6. All the entries in column A are text. Column B contains almost all text, with the exception of cell B8. (Cell B10 contains dates separated by a semicolon and is text.) A payroll worksheet, for example, contains employee names in several rows under a particular column. Expense reports contain the days of the week as column labels.

To enter text into a worksheet cell, first select the cell by clicking it and then type the text. As you type the text, it appears both in the formula bar and the selected cell. Excel aligns text entries on the left. Whenever text is longer than the cell containing it, the text visually spills over into the adjacent cell—if the adjacent cell is empty. If the adjacent cell already contains an entry, then the long text appears to be cut off at the boundary between the two cells. In either case, the text is completely contained within the cell you select, whether you can see all of it or not. Figure 1.8 shows the same long text entered into cells B2 and B4. Cell C2, which is adjacent to cell B2, already has an entry, so the long text in B2 appears cut off. Cell C4 is empty, so the long text in Cell B4 is completely visible.

Just today, Stirling has convinced another merchant that selling their scrip will benefit the merchant and the team. Happily, the new merchant is the university bookstore. Stirling wants you to add the newly recruited merchant's name to the Specialty Stores listed in the Scrip Sales Projection worksheet. Enter the new store in the list.

active cell, containing long label, is visually truncated at the cell border

formula bar matches contents of cell B2, proving long label is complete

Long text entries

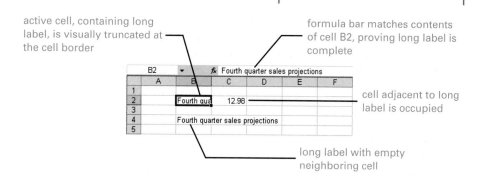

cell adjacent to long label is occupied

long label with empty neighboring cell

Entering text labels:

1. If you closed the Scrip workbook following the end of the previous session, make sure Excel is running and that the Scrip Sales Projection worksheet is showing. (Click the Scrip Sales Projection worksheet tab to open it)

2. Click cell **B9** to make it the active cell

3. Type **University Bookstore** and then press the **Enter** key. The text appears in cell B9, and cell B10 becomes the active cell

tip: *If you press a keyboard arrow key instead of pressing the Enter key, you complete entering text into the current cell and control which cell becomes the active cell*

4. Click cell **G10** to make it the active cell, type **Subtotal,** and then press the **Enter** key

tip: *You may notice the text in G10 is right aligned—contrary to what you read earlier about text entries. This is because the cell has been formatted to align text on the right. You will learn about formatting in Chapter 2*

5. Click cell **G17** to make it the active cell and type **Subtotal.** Excel completes the entry because a similar entry already exists in the column. Figure 1.9 shows the worksheet after you have entered the three text values, also called labels

Next, you need to enter the percent donation, scrip unit value, and the projected unit sales.

Values

Values are numbers that represent a quantity, date, or time. A value can be the number of students in a class, the quantity ordered of some vehicle part, the height in meters of a building, and so on. Examples are 15456, −35.8954, and 17. Values can be times and dates, too. For example, if you were to type 10/17/2001, Excel recognizes that value as a date. Similarly, if you were to type 15:32:30, Excel would interpret your entry as a time value. In other words, Excel can determine automatically whether you are entering text or a value based on what you type. For instance, if you were to type −9435, Excel would recognize the entry as a value and, by default,

EXCEL

F I G U R E   1.9

Worksheet after entering text

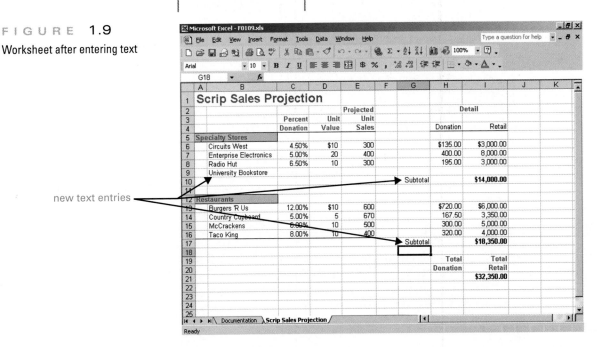

new text entries

would place it right justified in the cell. Similarly, if you typed <u>28 ways to win</u>, Excel would recognize the entry as text. A number enclosed in parentheses such as (9876) is also a value—a negative value.

Common entries that appear to be values sometimes are not. For example, Excel considers a social security number such as 123-45-6789 to be text, not the value of 123 minus 45 minus 6789. Telephone numbers, with or without area codes or country codes, are text also. The key difference between text and values is that cells containing text cannot be used in a meaningful way in mathematical calculations.

Next, you will enter the values for the University Bookstore's percent donation, and scrip unit values. In addition, Stirling talked to you this morning and asked you to enter 900 for the projected unit sales. While this may be an optimistic figure, Stirling thinks that students will like the idea of spending their scrip on campus.

Entering values:

1. Click cell **C9** to make it the active cell. Type **10%** and press the **right arrow** key. The value 10.00% appears in cell C9 and cell D9 becomes the active cell. By pressing the right arrow key, you save a step because you do not have to use the mouse to select the next cell prior to entering data into the cell—in the step that follows

2. Type **5** into cell D9 and then press the **right arrow** key. The value 5 appears in cell D9 and E9 becomes the active cell

3. Type **900** into cell E9 and press the **Enter** key. See Figure 1.10

Next, you will enter formulas that will calculate the total donation value and total retail value for the newly added University Bookstore row. This row will contribute to the subtotal and grand totals, as you will see after you complete the following steps.

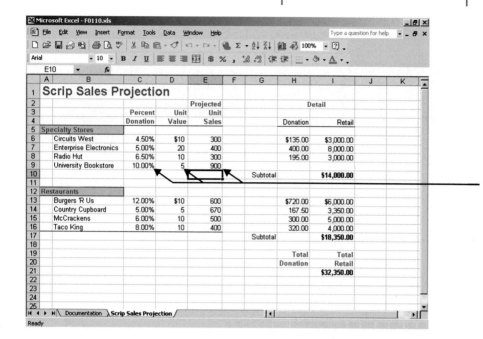

FIGURE 1.10
Worksheet after entering values
in three cells

three new values entered

Formulas

A *formula* is an expression that begins with an equal sign and can contain cell references, arithmetic operators, values, and Excel built-in functions that result in a calculated value that is displayed in a worksheet cell. Without formulas, Excel would be little more than a word processing program, incapable of producing what-if analysis and not even as capable as an inexpensive calculator. Formulas give Excel its power. Formulas that contain a reference to another cell automatically compute new results whenever you change *any* cell in the worksheet. A formula can be as simple as the sum of two numbers or cells, or it can be as complex as the calculation of the present value of a lottery prize that is paid once a year for 22 years. Formulas contain arithmetic operators such as addition, subtraction, multiplication, and division. Figure 1.11 lists the arithmetic operators available in Excel.

Formulas begin with an equal sign. The equal sign informs Excel that you are entering a formula, not a label. A formula can contain values, arithmetic operators, and cell addresses. For example, the formula $=(C5-C7)/(D43+D28)*54.987$ references cells and contains a constant. The formula mathematically combines the values in cells and the constant using parentheses, division, addition, and multiplication.

task reference

Entering a Formula

- Select the cell in which you want to type a formula

- Type = followed by the remainder of the formula

- Type cell references in either uppercase or lower case, or use the mouse or the arrow keys to select cells as you type the formula

- Press the **Enter** key to complete the formula

EXCEL

FIGURE 1.11

Arithmetic operators

Arithmetic Operator	Operator Name	Example Formula	Description
( )	Parentheses	=(1+B4)/B52	Alters the way in which the expression is evaluated: Add 1 to the contents of cell B4 and divide the result by the value in cell B52
^	Exponentiation	=E4^6	Raises the value stored in cell E4 to the 6th power
		=17.4^B2	Raises 17.4 to the value stored in cell B2
*	Multiplication	=B4*D4	Multiplies the value in cell B4 by the value in D4
		=A21*B44*C55	Multiples the values of cells A21, B44, and C55
/	Division	=D1/C42	Divides the value in cell D1 by the value in cell C42
		=A53/365.24	Divides the value in cell A53 by the constant 365.24
+	Addition	=A4 + B29	Adds the contents of cell A4 and the contents of cell B29
		=10/17/46	Divides 10 by 17 and then divides that result by 46
-	Subtraction	=A2-A1	Subtract the value of cell A1 from the value of cell A2
		=100-A2	Subtract the value of cell A2 from the constant, 100

Stirling explains that you must enter a formula to compute the donation and retail values for the University Bookstore row. The subtotal and grand totals automatically include the new calculated values you are about to add because the subtotal and grand total formulas have been written to do so. Stirling asks you to complete the University Bookstore row.

Entering formulas to calculate donation and retail amounts:

1. With the Scrip Sales Projection worksheet displayed, click cell **H9** to select it, type the formula **=C9*D9*E9** (remember to type the equal sign first) and then press **Enter** to complete the formula. The formula multiplies the percent donation (C9), unit value (D9), and unit sales value (E9) for the University Bookstore. In this example, the formula calculates 10 percent of 900 units at 5 dollars per unit sold. The value 450.00, the result, appears in cell H9

tip: *If you make a mistake while typing a formula but <u>before</u> you press Enter or an arrow key, simply press the **Backspace** key to erase the mistake and then type the correction. If you make a mistake <u>after</u> you press Enter or an arrow key, simply select the cell again and retype the formula.*

2. Click cell **H9** again to observe the formula, which appears in the formula bar. See Figure 1.12

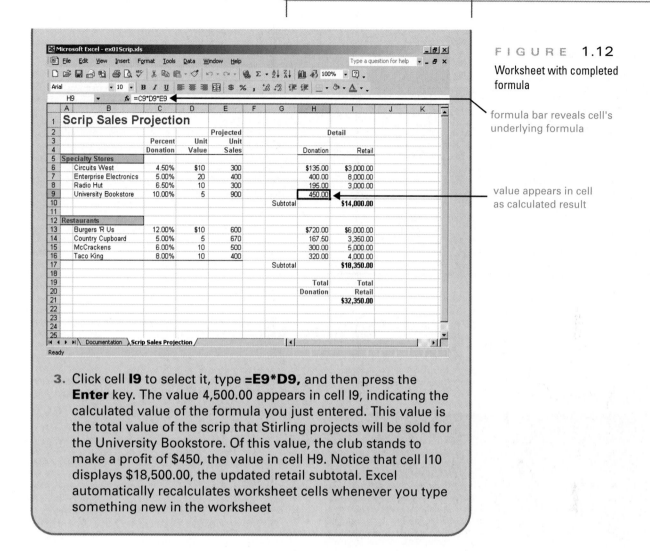

FIGURE 1.12
Worksheet with completed formula

formula bar reveals cell's underlying formula

value appears in cell as calculated result

3. Click cell **I9** to select it, type **=E9*D9,** and then press the **Enter** key. The value 4,500.00 appears in cell I9, indicating the calculated value of the formula you just entered. This value is the total value of the scrip that Stirling projects will be sold for the University Bookstore. Of this value, the club stands to make a profit of $450, the value in cell H9. Notice that cell I10 displays $18,500.00, the updated retail subtotal. Excel automatically recalculates worksheet cells whenever you type something new in the worksheet

Functions

A **function** is a built-in or prerecorded formula that provides a shortcut for complex calculations. Excel has hundreds of functions available for your use. One example is the Excel statistical function SUM. The SUM function is a handy shortcut for summing the contents of any collection of worksheet cells. Instead of writing a long formula such as =A1+A2+A3+A4+A5+A6+A7 to sum the values stored in cells A1 through A7, you can write a shorter equivalent formula =SUM(A1:A7). The SUM function, like all Excel functions, starts with the function's name followed by opening and closing parentheses that optionally contain a list of cells or other expressions upon which the named function operates. In the preceding example, the SUM function adds the values in the cell range designated by A1, which is the upper-left cell in the range, through cell A7, which is the lower rightmost cell in the range. The function calculates and displays the sum in the cell in which the function is written. A *cell range* consists of one or more cells that form a rectangular group. You specify a cell range by typing the name of the upper-left cell, a colon, and the name of the lower-right cell. For example, the cell range B4:C6 consists of the six cells B4, B5, B6, C4, C5, and C6. Because Excel imposes a limit on the size of a formula you can write, the Excel function SUM solves the problem of

FIGURE 1.13

FIGURE 1.13

Cell range examples

cell range C2:J2

cell range B4:B4

cell range B6:B17

cell range D6:G12

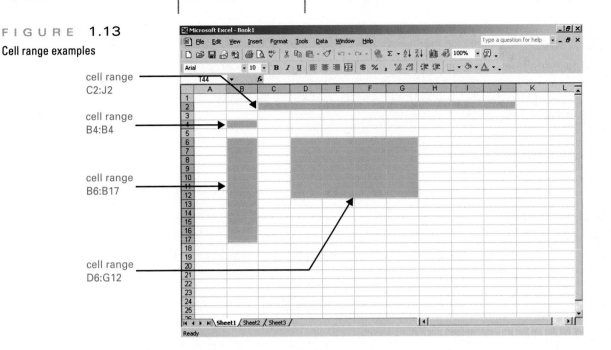

anotherword

. . . on Cell Ranges

A SUM function can contain more than one cell range. For example, the function =SUM(A1:A5,B42:B51) totals two cell ranges. Place commas between distinct cell ranges within the SUM function. The collection of cells, cell ranges, and values in the comma-separated list between a function's parentheses is its **argument list**

writing an extremely long formula that contains a potentially large number of cell addresses. For example, without the SUM function, adding up a column of 600 retail sales values would be impossible, because a formula consisting of 600 cell references separated by addition operators would exceed Excel's limit on formula size. Figure 1.13 shows several examples of cell ranges.

Stirling points out that there are three cells into which you can place the SUM function. Two of those SUM functions will calculate the subtotal of the donations for each of the two categories of merchants. The third SUM function will add the two donation subtotals to calculate and display the grand total donation value—the projected dollar value that the team can use to underwrite some of its costs.

task reference

Entering the SUM Function

- Select the cell in which you want to type a formula
- Type **=**
- Type **SUM** in either uppercase, lowercase, or a mixture of both, followed by a left parenthesis. Do not place a space between "SUM" and the left parenthesis
- Type the cell range to be summed followed by a right parenthesis
- Press **Enter** to complete the SUM function

Entering SUM functions:

1. With the Scrip Sales Projection worksheet displayed, click cell **H10** to select it, type the formula **=SUM(H6:H9)** and press **Enter** to complete the formula. The SUM function adds the four donation amounts and displays it in cell H10

2. Click cell **H17** to select it. This time, you will type part of the formula, use the mouse to indicate the cell range to sum, and finish the formula by typing the final right parenthesis. Using the mouse to select a cell range while writing a formula is called *pointing*. Pointing has the advantage that you are less likely to type an incorrect cell range

3. With cell H17 the active cell, type **=SUM(**

4. Next, click cell **H13,** drag the mouse pointer down to cell **H16,** and release the mouse. Notice that Excel writes the cell range into the function for you as you drag the mouse. A moving dashed line surrounds the selected cell range. See Figure 1.14

	A	B	C	D	E	F	G	H	I	J
1		Scrip Sales Projection								
2					Projected			Detail		
3			Percent	Unit	Unit					
4			Donation	Value	Sales			Donation	Retail	
5		Specialty Stores								
6		Circuits West	4.50%	$10	300			$135.00	$3,000.00	
7		Enterprise Electronics	5.00%	20	400			400.00	8,000.00	
8		Radio Hut	6.50%	10	300			195.00	3,000.00	
9		University Bookstore	10.00%	5	900			450.00	4,500.00	
10							Subtotal	$1,180.00	$18,500.00	
11										
12		Restaurants								
13		Burgers 'R Us	12.00%	$10	600			$720.00	$6,000.00	
14		Country Cupboard	5.00%	5	670			167.50	3,350.00	
15		McCrackens	6.00%	10	500			300.00	5,000.00	
16		Taco King	8.00%	10	400			320.00	4,000.00	
17							Subtotal	=SUM(H13:H16		
18										
19								Total	Total	
20								Donation	Retail	
21									$36,850.00	
22										

FIGURE **1.14**
Pointing to specify a cell range

the dashed line highlights the selected cell range

Excel automatically fills in cell references as you drag the mouse

5. Type **)** (a right parenthesis) and press **Enter** to complete the function

tip: *You can click the Enter button, (a green checkmark button appearing on the left end of the formula bar) whenever you enter data into a cell instead of pressing the Enter keyboard key. The difference between the two methods is that pressing the keyboard Enter key makes another cell active, whereas clicking the Enter button on the formula bar does not make another cell active*

6. Click cell **H21,** type **=SUM(H10,H17)** and press **Enter** to complete the function

tip: *Notice that you place a comma between the two cell references in the SUM function, not a colon. In this formula, SUM is adding two single-cell ranges, not the cell range H10 through H17. Sum can have a large number of cell ranges separated by commas in one function, indicating that all the cells in the several cell ranges are summed.*

EXCEL

You show your nearly complete worksheet to Stirling. He likes the work you have done, but points out that the entry Country Cupboard is incorrect. The merchant's name is Country Kitchen. Stirling asks you to make that correction.

EDITING CELL ENTRIES

Periodically, you may want to make changes to text, values, formulas, or functions. The change may be small and subtle, or you may want to completely replace the contents of a cell. When you modify the contents of a cell, that process is called *editing.*

---

task reference

Editing a Cell

- Select the cell that you want to edit
- Click in the formula bar and make any changes
- Press **Enter** to finalize the changes

or

- Select the cell that you want to edit
- Press **F2** and make changes in the selected cell or in the formula bar
- Press **Enter** to finalize the changes

or

- Double-click the cell and make changes to it
- Press **Enter** to finalize the changes

Editing a text entry by using the F2 edit key:

1. Select cell **B14** and press the **F2** function key
2. Press the **Backspace** key eight times to erase Cupboard
3. Type **Kitchen** and press **Enter** to complete the change and move to cell B15

You notice that McCrackens is misspelled. The correct spelling contains an apostrophe before the letter *s:* McCracken's.

Editing a text entry by typing in the formula bar:

1. Make sure that B15 is the active cell and then click in the formula bar

2. Press the **left arrow** key to move the insertion point between the letters *n* and *s*

3. Type **'** (apostrophe) and press **Enter** to complete the change

Stirling learned that the University Bookstore misquoted their donation percentage. Instead of 10 percent, the correct value is 7.5 percent. Also, he thinks that 900 units is a bit optimistic and asks you to reduce the projection for University Books scrip to 650 units. Stirling asks you to make those changes. When changes to a cell are extensive, you can save time by simply typing a completely new formula, which replaces the original formula when you press Enter or select another cell. Next, you make the changes that Stirling requests.

Replacing worksheet cells with new contents:

1. Click cell **C9** to make it the active cell, type **7.5%,** and press **Enter** to replace the University Bookstore percentage donation value with 7.5%

2. Click cell **E9** and type **650**

3. Press **Enter** to complete the change to cell E9. See Figure 1.15

	A	B	C	D	E	F	G	H	I	J
1		Scrip Sales Projection								
2					Projected			Detail		
3			Percent	Unit	Unit					
4			Donation	Value	Sales			Donation	Retail	
5		Specialty Stores								
6		Circuits West	4.50%	$10	300			$135.00	$3,000.00	
7		Enterprise Electronics	5.00%	20	400			400.00	8,000.00	
8		Radio Hut	6.50%	10	300			195.00	3,000.00	
9		University Bookstore	7.50%	5	650			243.75	3,250.00	
10							Subtotal	$973.75	$17,250.00	
11										
12		Restaurants								
13		Burgers 'R Us	12.00%	$10	600			$720.00	$6,000.00	
14		Country Kitchen	5.00%	5	670			167.50	3,350.00	
15		McCracken's	6.00%	10	500			300.00	5,000.00	
16		Taco King	8.00%	10	400			320.00	4,000.00	
17							Subtotal	$1,507.50	$18,350.00	
18										
19								Total	Total	
20								Donation	Retail	
21								$2,481.25	$35,600.00	
22										

edited cells

FIGURE 1.15
Worksheet with cell edits completed

SAVING A WORKBOOK

Whenever you first create a workbook or make extensive changes to a workbook, you should save your work frequently. By storing a workbook as a file on a disk, you can later recall it, make changes to it, and print it without retyping all the cell entries. When you save a workbook, the computer saves the contents of your computer's internal memory holding the entire workbook to a disk file. You can save a workbook under a new file name by selecting Save As in the File menu or, for existing workbooks, you can click Save to replace the workbook with the newer version. If

EXCEL

anotherword

. . . on Saving Workbooks

You can never save your workbook too frequently. If your computer should fail, your current work in memory is lost. Saving your work frequently avoids having to re-enter large amounts of information that was lost as a result of the computer failure.

you save a file under a new name (Save As), the original workbook file remains on disk unchanged. Always choose the Save As command when you create a workbook and save it for the first time. Also choose the Save As command when you want to preserve the original workbook. Use the Save command when you want to replace the original workbook stored on disk with the new one using the same name. The Standard toolbar has a Save button for your convenience, because Excel users save their workbooks frequently.

task reference

Saving a Workbook with a New Name

- Click the **File** menu and then click **Save As**

- Make sure the Save in list box contains the name of the disk and folder in which you want to save your workbook. If not, use the mouse to navigate to the correct disk and folder

- Change the file name in the File name list box

- Click the **Save** button

You have made a number of changes to the Scrip Sales Projection workbook and it is time to preserve those changes.

Saving an altered workbook under a new file name:

1. Click **File** on the menu bar and then click **Save As.** The Save As dialog box opens and displays the current workbook name in the File name text box

2. If necessary, click the **Save in** list box arrow and then select the disk and folder in which you want to save your workbook

3. Click in the **File name** list box, drag across the file name to select the entire name, and type **Scrip2.xls**

4. Ensure that the Save as type list box specifies "Microsoft Excel Workbook (*.xls)" (see Figure 1.16)

5. Click the **Save** 🖫 button to save your Excel workbook under its new file name. After you save a workbook, you will notice that the new workbook name (Scrip2) appears in the Excel title bar

Stirling tells you that the workbook is designed so that anyone using it can change the values in the Projected Unit Sales column and observe the changes to the worksheet. He wants to save the workbook without any assumptions about the values in the Projected Unit Sales column. That

FIGURE 1.16

Saving a workbook under a new
file name

the workbook will be stored in the folder you select

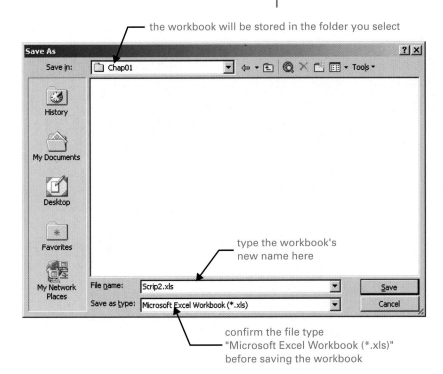

type the workbook's
new name here

confirm the file type
"Microsoft Excel Workbook (*.xls)"
before saving the workbook

way, a new user can load the Scrip Sales Projection workbook and type in
a new set of unit sales assumptions without first deleting the previous
assumptions. You are not sure how to empty or delete a cell's contents, and
you wonder if simply selecting the cell and pressing Spacebar or typing a
zero will clear out the cells. You remember Stirling telling you that whenever you have questions and no one is available for help, you can go to
online help. You decide to investigate Excel's online help to answer your
question.

GETTING HELP

Excel provides online help to answer many of your questions. If you don't
know how a function is written, or if you have a question about how to
complete an Excel task, use Excel's extensive Help feature. Help in Excel is
similar to Help in the other Office products. You can obtain help from the
Office Assistant, from the Excel Help menu, or from Microsoft's Web site.

task reference

Obtaining Help

- Click the **Microsoft Excel Help** command from the **Help** menu (or
  click the Microsoft Excel **Help** 🔲 button on the Standard toolbar)

- Click the **Answer Wizard** tab

- In the *What would you like to do?* text box, type an English-language
  question (replacing the words displayed and highlighted in blue) on the
  topic with which you need help and click the **Search** button

Using Help, you can locate an answer to your question about deleting
cells' contents.

Obtaining help:

1. Click **Help** on the menu bar and then click **Microsoft Excel Help.** The Microsoft Excel Help dialog box appears

2. If necessary, click the **Answer Wizard** tab

3. Type **how do I delete cells** in the *What would you like to do?* text box, and then click **Search** to display help alternatives

tip: *You can also press the Enter key instead of clicking the Search key*

4. Click **Clear cell formats or contents** in the *Select topic to display* list to display information about removing cells' contents. See Figure 1.17

5. Read the information and print it out if you wish (click the printer icon on the Help toolbar). Click the **Close** [Close] button on the Microsoft Excel Help Title bar to close the Help dialog box

---

Now you know how to empty cells' contents. Deleting cells is not quite what Stirling wants. He wants the cells to remain but their contents to be emptied. Now that you have obtained help, you know just what to do.

CLEARING CELLS

Periodically you may want to delete the contents of a cell containing text, a value, a formula, or a function. You have a couple of choices. You can empty a cell by selecting it with the mouse and then pressing the Delete key or by clicking Edit on the menu bar, then clicking Clear, and finally

FIGURE 1.17

Obtaining help

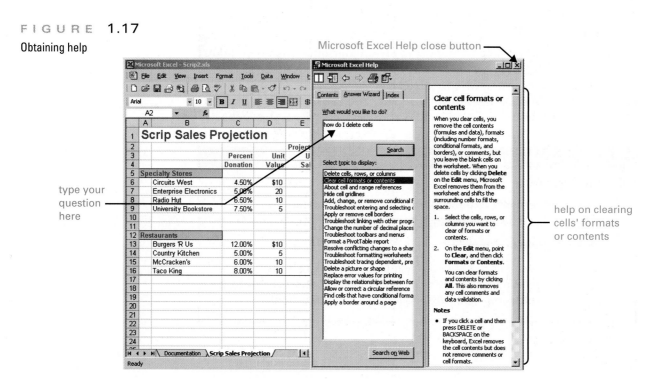

type your question here

Microsoft Excel Help close button

help on clearing cells' formats or contents

clicking Contents from the command list. Either way, Excel erases the cell's contents. You might be tempted to simply select the cell and press the Spacebar key in order to clear the cell. While the cell *appears* to be empty, it is not—it contains a space. This is the "colorless, odorless, tasteless gas" that later can harm your worksheet. Cells containing one or more spaces (blanks) are treated differently from those that are empty and they are very difficult to locate.

---

task reference

Clearing Cells' Contents

- Click the cell or cells you want to empty
- Press the **Delete** keyboard key

or

- Click **Edit** on the menu bar, click **Clear,** and then click **Contents** to empty the contents of the cell or cells you selected

---

All the assumptions for the Scrip Sales Projection worksheet are in column E. Cells E6 through E9 contain the assumed unit sales for the group of specialty stores, and cells E13 through E16 contain the assumed unit sales for restaurants. You are ready to clear those cells' contents.

Clearing several cells' contents:

1. Click cell **E6,** drag the mouse down through cell **E9,** and release the mouse. This selects the cell range E6:E9

   tip: *If you select the wrong cells, simply repeat the click-and-drag sequence in step 1.*

2. Press the **Delete** keyboard key to clear the contents of the selected cells

   tip: *If you delete the wrong cells, click **Edit** in the menu bar and then click **Undo Clear.** Alternatively, you can press the **Undo** ⟲ ▾ button on the Standard toolbar*

3. Click cell **E13,** drag the mouse down through cell **E16,** and release the mouse

4. **Right-click** anywhere within the selected range of cells. A pop-up command list appears (see Figure 1.18)

5. Click **Clear Contents** from the pop-up command list to clear the contents of the selected cell range

6. Click on any cell to deselect the range

7. To save the workbook under a new name, click **File** and then click **Save As**

EXCEL

FIGURE 1.18

Selecting Clear Contents from a
pop-up command list

Clear Contents

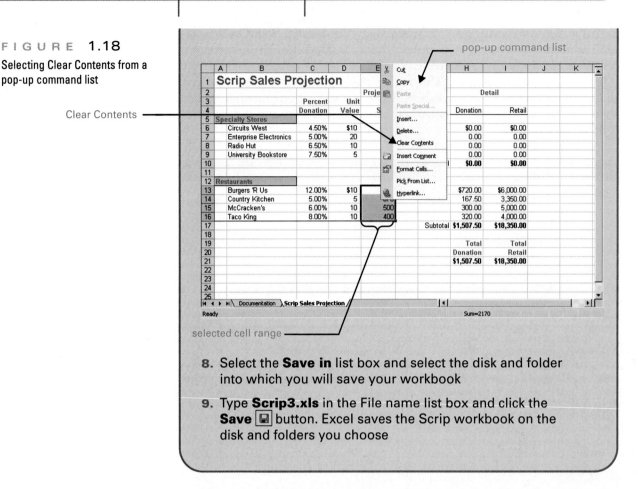

8. Select the **Save in** list box and select the disk and folder into which you will save your workbook

9. Type **Scrip3.xls** in the File name list box and click the **Save** button. Excel saves the Scrip workbook on the disk and folders you choose

You may be alarmed that the subtotal values and the total values are all zero. Do not be concerned. Cells that reference empty cell ranges often display zero because empty cells are treated mathematically as if they contained zero. The moment anyone types a value into any cell in the Projected Unit Sales column adjacent to one of the merchant rows, all the subtotals and totals will recalculate nonzero values. Looking at the calculated values for different sets of input information is performing what-if analysis. Doing so can reveal how many units a factory needs to produce in order to be profitable, or how many scrip units a rugby team must sell to produce $3,000 in profits. You will do that next.

CONDUCTING WHAT-IF ANALYSIS

The power of a workbook lies in its ability to recalculate the entire workbook quickly whenever you enter new values to see the overall affect of the changes you propose. Using your knowledge of students' preferences and how many students are likely to purchase scrip, you can change the values for some or all of the Projected Unit Sales values for each merchant and observe how much profit each combination of values generates. Cell H21 displays the total donations, or club profit. That value is recalculated whenever you enter new data.

You can examine the effect on Total Donations of selling larger numbers of Burgers 'R Us scrip, which pays the highest percentage of total sales. Similarly, you can determine what would happen if you sold 400 units of every merchant's scrip. Trying different combinations of scrip sales units in the worksheet produces results that help the team decide where it wants to focus its scrip sales efforts. What-if analysis like this may reveal whether or not selling scrip generates enough profit to be worthwhile. For example, if everyone agrees that students won't purchase enough scrip to make a significant dent in the club's expenses, they may choose to pursue other fundraising opportunities.

Stirling wants you to try another set of Projected Unit Sales values to see if you can raise at least $2,500. He e-mails you a note with the scrip sales values he wants you to try along with a request that you print out the resulting worksheet. Stirling wants to see the profit generated if the team could sell 400 units of each merchant's scrip, except for Burgers 'R Us. "Let's plug in 850 units for Burgers 'R Us and see what happens," Stirling's e-mail concludes.

Conducting what-if analysis by changing all unit sales values:

1. With the Scrip Sales Projection worksheet open, click cell **E6** and drag the mouse down through cell **E9** to select the cell range E6:E9. After selecting a range of cells, you can enter data into the range by typing each cell's contents and pressing Enter to move to the next cell. Excel proceeds through the entire list of selected cells, eventually returning to the first cell after you have pressed Enter a sufficient number of times. Using this technique can save time

2. With the cell range E6:E9 highlighted, type **400** and press **Enter.** Cell E7 becomes the active cell and Excel recalculates formulas

3. Type **400** and press **Enter.** Repeat this step two more times to fill each of the four selected cells with the value 400

4. Click cell **E13** and drag the mouse down through cell **E16** to select the cell range E13:E16

5. Type **850** and press **Enter.** The value 850 appears in cell E13

6. Type **400** and press **Enter**

7. Repeat step 6 two more times to enter the remaining two values

8. Click any cell to deselect the block of cells. Your worksheet should resemble the worksheet in Figure 1.19

FIGURE **1.19**

What-If analysis example

new unit sales assumptions

rugby team's profit

	A	B	C	D	E	F	G	H	I	J
1	**Scrip Sales Projection**									
2					Projected			Detail		
3			Percent	Unit	Unit					
4			Donation	Value	Sales			Donation	Retail	
5	Specialty Stores									
6		Circuits West	4.50%	$10	400			$180.00	$4,000.00	
7		Enterprise Electronics	5.00%	20	400			400.00	8,000.00	
8		Radio Hut	6.50%	10	400			260.00	4,000.00	
9		University Bookstore	7.50%	5	400			150.00	2,000.00	
10							Subtotal	$990.00	$18,000.00	
11										
12	Restaurants									
13		Burgers 'R Us	12.00%	$10	850			$1,020.00	$8,500.00	
14		Country Kitchen	5.00%	5	400			100.00	2,000.00	
15		McCracken's	6.00%	10	400			240.00	4,000.00	
16		Taco King	8.00%	10	400			320.00	4,000.00	
17							Subtotal	$1,680.00	$18,500.00	
18										
19								Total	Total	
20								Donation	Retail	
21								$2,670.00	$36,500.00	
22										

EXCEL

With the new projected sales units, or sales assumptions, the team will produce a profit of $2,670. That will help a lot to reduce their projected team expenses this season. Naturally, their profit will be more or less if they sell more or fewer units of scrip than shown in the worksheet.

You are ready to show Stirling your work, but you must first print the worksheet so that you can give it to Stirling for review.

PRINTING A WORKSHEET

Printing a worksheet provides you and others with a portable copy that you can peruse, review, and modify with a pen or pencil. When you are ready to try more what-if analysis, take the hand-modified hard copy of the worksheet, enter the changes, save the modified worksheet, and print a copy. You can print an Excel workbook or worksheet using the Print command in the File menu or by clicking the Print button on the Standard toolbar. The toolbar Print button is handy because it is a one-click way to produce output. However, the Print button doesn't offer any printing options. On the other hand, the File menu Print command displays the Print Dialog box allowing you to select a number of values and settings to customize your output. You can adjust a number of important settings such as the number of output copies, which pages to print, whether to print all worksheets in the workbook or just the active sheet or a selected range of cells, and which printer to select. Most importantly, you can click the Print dialog box Preview button to preview your output before you print it—an important way to ensure you don't waste paper when you print the workbook.

First, there are a few preliminary tasks to perform before producing a printed worksheet. One of these important tasks is creating a worksheet header and footer. A *header* contains text that appears automatically at the top of each printed page in the header margin, which is located directly above the worksheet print area on a page. A *footer* contains text that appears automatically at the bottom of each printed page in the footer margin, which is located below the worksheet print area on a page. Though worksheet headers and footers are optional, you will find a well-labeled worksheet is a good way to document and identify your printed worksheets.

Labeling an Output with a Header or Footer

If you are printing your worksheet on a shared printer located in a computer laboratory, several people may be producing the same or similar outputs. To avoid the confusion of determining whose output is whose, you will want to uniquely identify your output so that it is not mistaken for someone else's. The best way to label your output is to either place on the header or footer your first and last names or other identifying information such as your company or student identification number.

There is more than one way to identify your output. You can type your name into one of the worksheet cells, perhaps adding it to a documentation worksheet similar to the Scrip workbook's Documentation worksheet, or you can type your name into the worksheet's header or footer. The advantage of a header or footer is that your identification will appear automatically on *each* output page, not just on the first output page. Having your identification appear on every page, with each page numbered, unequivocally identifies the work as yours. Of course, you want to follow the guidelines your instructor provides for output. Here, you will learn how to create a header and footer prior to printing your worksheet.

---

task reference

Creating a header or footer

- Click **View** on the menu bar and then click the **Header and Footer** tab

- Click **Custom Header** or **Custom Footer**

- Select the Left section, Center section, or Right section

- Type the header text into any or all of the sections

- Optionally, select text in any section and then click the **Font** button to set font characteristics

- Click **OK** to confirm your header or footer choices

- Click **OK** to close the Page Setup dialog box

Many people use the printer in your laboratory where you are building the Scrip Sales Projection worksheet, so you decide to add a header to identify the worksheet and a footer to display a page number in case the worksheet grows to multiple pages.

An Excel header can appear in three sections: left, center, or right. If you type text in the header's Left section, the text will appear on the top left portion of each page. Text typed into the Center section of the Header dialog box appears in the top center of each page. Text typed into the Right section of the Header dialog box appears in the top right of each page. You decide to place your name on the right side of each page top.

Creating a worksheet header:

1. Ensure that the Scrip Sales Projection worksheet is displayed. Click **View** and then click **Header and Footer.** The Header/Footer tab of the Page Setup dialog box appears

2. Click the **Custom Header** [Custom Header...] button, click in the **Right section** text box, type **Modified by,** and then type your first and last names following "Modified by"

3. Drag the mouse over the text in the Right section to select it, click the **Font** [A] button, click **Bold** under the Font style list, and then click **OK.** The Page Setup dialog box reappears

4. Click the Header dialog box **OK** button to complete the header

---

Next, you will ensure that your printed worksheet pages contain numbers by placing a page number in the page footer.

Placing a page number in the worksheet footer:

1. With the Page Setup dialog box open, click the **Custom Footer** [Custom Footer...] button, click in the **Center section** text box, and click the **Page Number** [⊞] button. The

---

characters &[Page] appear in the Center section. The symbol represents a page number variable that automatically numbers pages in sequence beginning with 1

2. Click the Footer dialog box **OK** button. The Page Setup dialog box reappears. Figure 1.20 shows the Page Setup dialog box. Of course, your page header will be slightly different because you have typed your own name where Stirling Leonard appears in the header preview text box

FIGURE **1.20**

Page Setup dialog box with completed header and footer

header appears at the top of each page

page number appears in the footer of each page

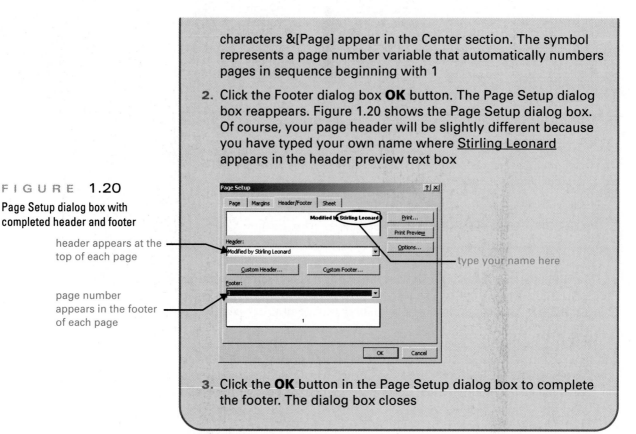

type your name here

3. Click the **OK** button in the Page Setup dialog box to complete the footer. The dialog box closes

Previewing Output

Before you print any worksheet, you should preview the output. Previewing output lets you catch any small errors that might cause more pages to print than you expected. Page margins, font size, and header and footer margins all can affect how many pages you print. Previewing your output gives you a chance to make adjustments so that the worksheet prints correctly and on as few pages as possible.

Previewing output:

1. Click **File** on the menu bar

2. Click **Print Preview** command in the File menu. The first page of output appears on the screen. Although the header and footer are unreadable at the standard magnification, you can zoom in to inspect them

tip: *Preview output quickly by clicking the **Print Preview** button found on the Standard toolbar*

3. Click the **Margins** button, and then move the mouse to the top right portion of the preview page—near the header. The mouse pointer becomes a magnifying glass. Click the mouse to increase the magnification. The enlarged worksheet makes the header easy to read. The dashed lines indicate the page margins. See Figure 1.21

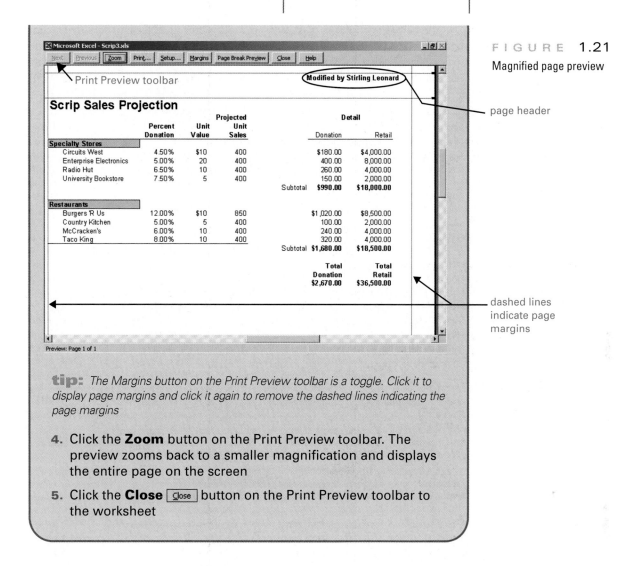

FIGURE 1.21
Magnified page preview

tip: *The Margins button on the Print Preview toolbar is a toggle. Click it to display page margins and click it again to remove the dashed lines indicating the page margins*

4. Click the **Zoom** button on the Print Preview toolbar. The preview zooms back to a smaller magnification and displays the entire page on the screen

5. Click the **Close** [Close] button on the Print Preview toolbar to the worksheet

Printing

The output appears to be fine, and the header and footer are where you expected them to be. You are ready to print the worksheet.

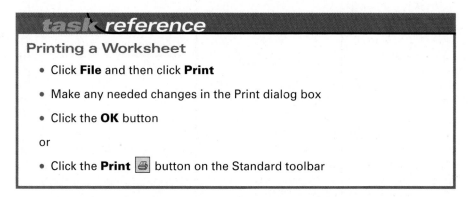

task reference

Printing a Worksheet

- Click **File** and then click **Print**
- Make any needed changes in the Print dialog box
- Click the **OK** button

or

- Click the **Print** 🖨 button on the Standard toolbar

You are ready to print your worksheet. The print preview revealed that the entire worksheet would fit on one page. You decide that you want to check the print settings before printing, so you select the Print command from the File menu rather than risk using the Print button—at least until you become more comfortable with printing.

One of the important settings you will want to check in the Print dialog box is in the *Print what* section of the Print dialog box. Which of the three option buttons you choose determines how much and which portions of the workbook or worksheet print. You can choose one of *Selection, Active sheet(s)*, or *Entire workbook*. Click Selection if you have highlighted a block of cells and want to print only that section of a worksheet. Click Active sheet(s) if you want to print the active worksheet or if you have selected more than one worksheet and want to print the selected worksheets from one workbook. Select Entire workbook if you want to print all of a workbook's worksheets. You will see where these choices appear in the steps that follow.

Checking the print settings and printing the worksheet:

1. If you are using your own printer, make sure it is turned on and contains paper. If you are using a network printer, assume it is turned on and full of paper.

2. Click **File** on the menu bar and then click **Print.** The Print dialog box opens (see Figure 1.22).

FIGURE 1.22
Print dialog box

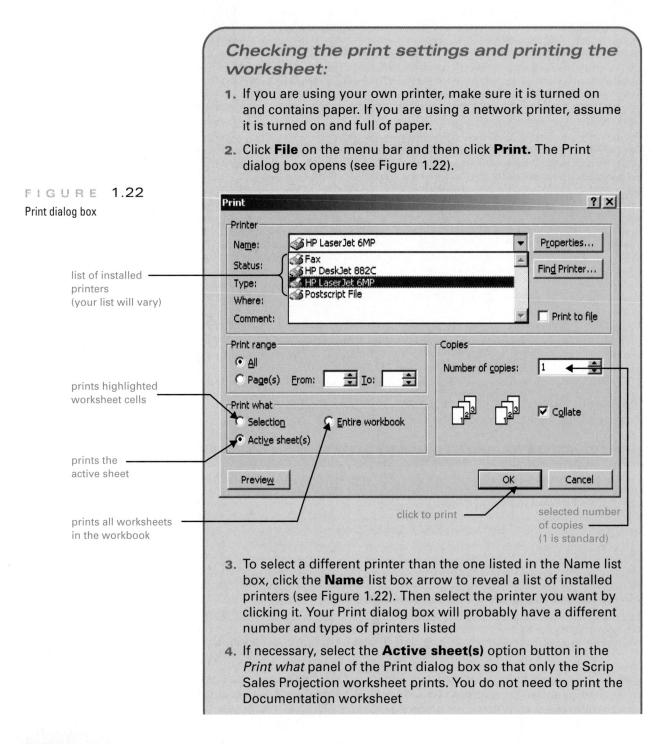

list of installed printers
(your list will vary)

prints highlighted worksheet cells

prints the active sheet

prints all worksheets in the workbook

click to print

selected number of copies
(1 is standard)

3. To select a different printer than the one listed in the Name list box, click the **Name** list box arrow to reveal a list of installed printers (see Figure 1.22). Then select the printer you want by clicking it. Your Print dialog box will probably have a different number and types of printers listed

4. If necessary, select the **Active sheet(s)** option button in the *Print what* panel of the Print dialog box so that only the Scrip Sales Projection worksheet prints. You do not need to print the Documentation worksheet

5. Click **All** in the Print range section, if necessary
6. Ensure that the Number of copies box displays 1. You need only one copy of the worksheet
7. Click the **OK** button to print the worksheet. Figure 1.23 shows the printed worksheet. Of course, your worksheet will contain your name in the header instead of Stirling Leonard

Modified by Stirling Leonard

Scrip Sales Projection

	Percent Donation		Projected		Detail Donation	Retail
Specialty Stores						
Circuits West	4.50%	$10	400		$180.00	$4,000.00
Enterprise Electronics	5.00%	20	400		400.00	8,000.00
Radio Hut	6.50%	10	400		260.00	4,000.00
University Bookstore	7.50%	5	400		150.00	2,000.00
				Subtotal	**$990.00**	
Restaurants						
Burgers 'R Us	12.00%	$10	850		$1,020.00	$8,500.00
Country Kitchen	5.00%	5	400		100.00	2,000.00
McCracken's	6.00%	10	400		240.00	4,000.00
Taco King	8.00%	10	400		320.00	4,000.00
				Subtotal	**$1,680.00**	
					Total Donation $2,670.00	

1

FIGURE 1.23
Printed Scrip Sales Projection worksheet

Printing Worksheet Formulas

Part of documenting a worksheet and learning how Excel works is printing the worksheet's formulas. Typically, businesses do not require that reports showing Excel worksheet results also show the formulas. However, you may want to refer to both the worksheet output and the formulas that produced that output. Additionally, your instructor may want to view the worksheet formulas so that she or he can see exactly what formulas and functions you used to produce the results. Your instructor may request that you print and turn in worksheet formulas along with the regular worksheet printout. In any case, it is helpful to know exactly how to print worksheet formulas in case Stirling wants to study them and give you suggestions.

---

task reference

Printing Worksheet Formulas

- Click **Tools** and then click **Options**
- Click the **View** tab
- Click the **Formulas** check box in the Window options panel to place a checkmark in it
- Click **OK**
- Click **File** and then click **Print**
- Click **OK** to print the worksheet formulas

You ask Stirling if he wants worksheet formulas for documentation. Stirling thinks that is a great idea and thanks you for thinking of it.

Printing worksheet formulas:

1. Click **Tools** on the menu bar and then click **Options.** The Options dialog box opens

2. Click the **View** tab on the Options dialog box

3. Click the **Formulas** check box to check it. The Formulas check box is located in the Window options section of the dialog box. See Figure 1.24

FIGURE 1.24

Selecting the Formulas check box

Formulas check box checked ——

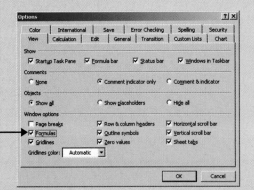

4. Click **OK** to close the Options dialog box

5. Click the Formula Auditing toolbar **close** button, if necessary, to close the toolbar. The Excel worksheet displays its formulas on screen

6. Drag the **horizontal scroll arrow** until columns H and I come into view. See Figure 1.25. With the Formulas option selected, you can print formulas for the entire worksheet or for a selection of cells

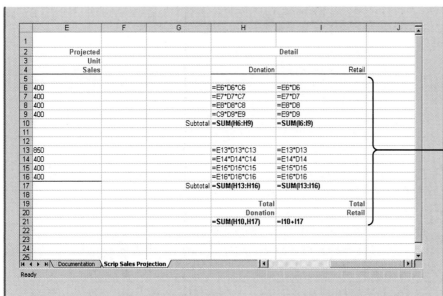

FIGURE 1.25
Excel formulas on screen

formulas that underlie
calculated values

7. Click **File** and then click **Print**

8. Click **OK** in the Print dialog box to print the worksheet formulas. Excel prints your worksheet's formulas

tip: *Excel remembers the settings you choose in the Options dialog box. It is best to return those settings to their original values. Once the worksheet starts printing its formulas, revisit the Options dialog box and clear the Formulas check box before continuing work*

9. Click **Tools**, click **Options,** and then click the **View** tab

10. Click **Formulas** check box to clear it and then click **OK.** Excel redisplays values in place of formulas

CLOSING A WORKBOOK

When you finish a worksheet and the workbook containing it and want to move on to another activity, you close the workbook. If you have made changes to the worksheet that you have not saved, Excel will display a dialog box asking if you want to save the altered workbook before closing it. Normally you should affirm saving a changed workbook, even if you cannot remember making any changes to it. That way, the most current version is saved on disk.

---

task reference

Closing a Workbook

- Click **File**

- Click **Close**

- Click **Yes** to save changes

Your work is finished for now and you are ready to close the Scrip workbook.

Closing an Excel workbook:

1. Click **File** on the menu bar and then click **Close.** A dialog box opens and displays the message "Do you want to save the changes you made to 'Scrip3.xls'?"

tip: *You can close the active workbook by clicking the workbook's **Close Window** button. If the workbook window is maximized, the workbook's Close Window button appears on right side of the Excel menu bar. Always be careful to not click the Close Application button, which is located on the Excel Title bar. That will cause Excel to close all loaded workbooks, not just the active workbook*

2. Click **Yes** to save the changes you made since you last saved the workbook before closing it. (If you click No, Excel does not save the changes before closing the workbook. If you click Cancel, Excel cancels the close operation and redisplays the active worksheet.)

Excel remains available, allowing you to create new workbooks or open existing ones. You can exit Excel because you have finished your work.

EXITING EXCEL

Exiting Excel unloads it from memory and closes any open workbooks. When you are finished using Excel, it is wise to close it so that the internal memory it occupies becomes available to other programs. Follow these steps to close Excel.

Exiting Excel:

1. Click **File** on the menu bar and then click **Exit**

tip: *You can close Excel by clicking the **Close** button on Excel's Title bar.*

Stirling has reviewed your work on the Scrip Sales Projection sheet and is pleased with your work. He's also enthusiastic about the projected sales and is holding a team meeting next Saturday to discuss the details about obtaining and selling scrip to Western University students.

*another*word

. . . on Exiting Excel

Wait to remove your floppy disk containing your Excel worksheets until after you have exited Excel. Sometimes Excel does a final bit of housekeeping on the workbook you stored on your floppy disk, such as writing the last little piece of the workbook to the file just before exiting Excel.

SESSION 1.3 SUMMARY

Excel is a spreadsheet program in which you can type text, values, formulas, and functions and conduct what-if analysis by changing worksheet assumptions and viewing the changes. You can edit worksheet entries by selecting a cell, pressing

making the grade

1. An Excel worksheet cell can contain text, values, formula, and _____ entries.

2. Indicate which of the following cell entries are text, values, or formulas.
   a. =A1+B2
   b. 11/12/02
   c. 42,350
   d. Sum(A1:B2)
   e. 1st Quarter Sales
   f. 401-555-1212
   g. =11/12/19

3. You could write the formula **=B4+B5+B6+C4+C5+C6** to sum values in the six cells, but the SUM function is a better solution. The SUM function to sum the preceding six cells is _____.

4. You can store an Excel workbook on disk by executing the **File** menu _____ or _____ _____.

5. To empty the contents of a worksheet cell, right-click the cell and then click _____ _____ on the pop-up menu.

6. The ability to type into worksheet cells different values and see their effect on a worksheet is called _____ analysis.

7. A worksheet _____ appears on the top of each printed worksheet page.

8. Modify the Scrip Sales Projection worksheet, saved as **scrip v3.xls,** in the following ways: Type **400, 500, 600,** and **700** in cells E6 through E9. In cell E10, type a function to sum the projected sales units for cells E6 through E9. Similarly, type into cell E17 a function to sum the projected sales units for cells E13 through E16. Print the worksheet and then print the worksheet formulas.

F2, and typing the changes. Completely replace cell contents by selecting a cell and typing the new contents. Save a workbook periodically to preserve its contents on disk. Click File and then click Save to save an existing workbook or Save As to save a workbook under a new file name or for the first time.

Clear cell contents by selecting the cell or cells and then pressing the Delete key. Clearing cells empties their contents; pressing the spacebar does not clear a cell—it places a blank in a cell. Click F1 or click Help on the menu bar to search for help on any Excel topic. Preview a worksheet before printing it to ensure that the correct cells and pages will print. Print a worksheet for review or documentation purposes by clicking File, Print, and selecting print parameters.

When you have completed your Excel work, close the workbook and then close Excel. Excel will prompt you to save any workbooks whose contents have changed since they were last saved. You can choose to save the workbook, not save it, or cancel the Excel exit operation. Be sure to visit the series Web site at www.mhhe.com/i-series for more information.

MOUS OBJECTIVES SUMMARY

- Open a workbook (MOUS) Ex2002-2-1
- Type into worksheet cells text, values, formulas, and functions (MOUS) Ex2002-1-2
- Edit and clear cell entries (MOUS) Ex2002-1-2
- Save a wookbook (MOUS) Ex2002-2-3
- Adding a header and a footer (MOUS) Ex2002-3-6
- Previewing output (MOUS) Ex2002-3-7

task reference round-up

Task	Location	Preferred Method
Workbook, open	EX 1.11	• Click **File**, click **Open**, click workbook's name, click the **Open** button
Formula, entering	EX 1.17	• Select cell, type **=**, type formula, press **Enter**
Sum function, entering	EX 1.20	• Select cell, type **=SUM(**, type cell range, type **)**, and press **Enter**
Editing cell	EX 1.22	• Select cell, click formula bar, make changes, press **Enter**
Workbook, saving	EX 1.24	• Click **File**, click **Save As**, type file name, click **Save** button
Help, obtaining	EX 1.25	• Click the **Microsoft Excel Help** command from the **Help** menu (or click the Microsoft Excel **Help** button on the Standard toolbar)
		• Click the **Answer Wizard** tab
		• In the What would you like to do text box, type an English-language question (replacing the words displayed and highlighted in blue) on the topic with which you need help and click the **Search** button
Contents, clearing	EX 1.27	• Click cell, press **Delete** keyboard key
Header/Footer, creating	EX 1.31	• Click **View**, click **Header and Footer**, click **Custom Header** or **Custom Footer**, select section, type header/footer text, click the **OK** button
Worksheet, printing	EX 1.33	• Click **File**, click **Print**, click the **OK** button
Worksheet formulas, printing	EX 1.36	• Click **Tools**, click **Options**, Click the **View** tab, click **Formulas** check box, click **OK**, click **File**, click **Print**, click the **OK** button
Workbook, closing	EX 1.37	• Click **File**, click **Close**, click **Yes** to save

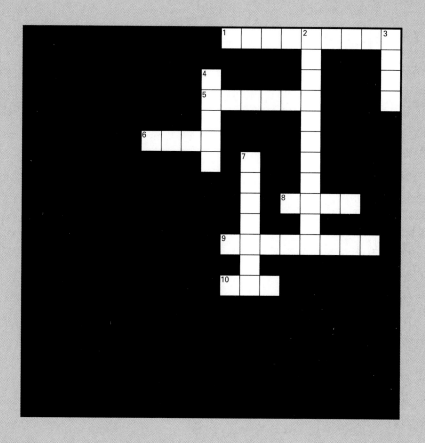

CROSSWORD PUZZLE

ACROSS

1. A single electronic page of a workbook
5. Currently working on this cell, it is the _____ cell
6. A _____ bar contains menus
8. Create a heading with this type of data
9. Prerecorded formulas built into Excel
10. Click to move to another worksheet

DOWN

2. A program used to analyze numeric information
3. The _____ Pane is a dockable dialog window
4. Data representing a quantity, date, or time
7. An expression beginning with an equal sign

FILL-IN

1. A _____ is the name of the entity that holds a text entry, value, or formula.

2. The first spreadsheet program, called_____, was introduced in 1979.

3. To the left of the formula bar is the _____, which contains the name of the active worksheet cell.

4. Click the _____ to make another worksheet of a workbook active.

5. Suppose you type 333-56-8866 in a cell. Excel interprets the entry as a _____ entry.

6. The address of a cell at the intersection of row 43 and column F is _____.

REVIEW QUESTIONS

1. Suppose cells A3 through A5 contained the values 5, 10, and 15, respectively. Discuss what would happen if you typed **SUM(A3:A5)** in cell B15. Hint: You type only the 10 characters shown. Do not assume anything.

2. What is the most important feature of electronic spreadsheet software that makes them especially attractive when compared to the way people created spreadsheets with pencil and paper? In other words, electronic spreadsheets save time. However, which general feature of electronic spreadsheets do you think saves time?

3. Discuss what happens if a text label is wider than the cell in which you enter it and the adjacent cell contains information.

4. Why should you save a workbook to disk?

CREATE THE QUESTION

For each of the following answers, create an appropriate short question.

ANSWER	QUESTION
1. A built-in formula that is a shortcut for complex calculations	_____
2. It is shorter than writing =A1+A2+A3+A4+A5	_____
3. The F2 function key	_____
4. The Office Assistant appears	_____
5. Although the cell appears empty, it is not. It contains the blank text character, and doing this activity can cause problems later	_____
6. You should do this before printing a worksheet to ensure that you don't print more pages than you expected	_____

practice

1. Creating an Income Statement

Carroll's Fabricating, a machine shop providing custom metal fabricating, is preparing an income statement for its shareholders. Betty Carroll, the company's president, wants to know exactly how much net income the company has earned this year. Although Betty has prepared a preliminary worksheet with labels in place, she wants you to enter the values and a few formulas to compute cost of goods sold, gross profit, selling and advertising expenses, and net income.

1. Open the workbook **ex01Income.xls** in your student disk in the folder Ch01
2. Click **File** and then click **Save As** to save the workbook as **Income2.xls** in the folder Ch01
3. Scan the Income Statement worksheet and type the following values in the listed cells: Cell C5, **987453**; cell B8, **64677**; cell B9, **564778**; cell B10, **-43500**; cell B15, **53223**; cell B16, **23500**; cell B17, **12560**; cell B18, **123466**; cell B19, **87672**
4. In cell C10, write the formula **=SUM(B8:B10)** to sum cost of goods sold
5. In cell C12, type the formula for Gross Profit: **=C5-C10**
6. In cell C19, type the formula to sum selling and advertising expenses: **=SUM(B15:B19)**
7. In cell C21, type the formula **=C122C19** to compute net income (gross profit minus total selling and advertising expenses)
8. In cell A4, type **Prepared by** <your name>
9. Click the Save button on the Standard toolbar to save your modified worksheet
10. Print the worksheet

2. Creating a Timecard Worksheet

You have a part-time job at Harry's Chocolate Shop, an ice cream parlor near the university. You work Tuesdays, Thursdays, and Saturdays. Every Saturday, you fill out a time card indicating the hours you worked the previous week and leave it on your manager's desk. Last week, you worked Tuesday, October 15, from 9:30 A.M. to 12:00 P.M., took a one-hour lunch break, and then worked until 3:00 P.M. Thursday, you worked 8:00 A.M. to 11:00 A.M., and on Saturday, you worked from 8:00 A.M. until 5:00 P.M. with an hour break from noon until 1:00 P.M. Fill out your timecard and write a formula to compute your total work hours for the week.

1. Open the workbook **ex01Timecard.xls** in your student disk in the folder Ch01. Notice that there are no worksheet gridlines. This is an option you will learn about later. Several cells, especially those containing formulas, are protected so that valuable prewritten formulas cannot be disturbed inadvertently
2. Click cell **B11** and try to type **10**. An error message dialog box opens, demonstrating that some cells are protected from change
3. Click **OK** to close the dialog box, click cell **A2**, type your first and last names, and then press **Enter**
4. Click cell **A4** and type **334**; click cell D4 and type **25**; click cell F4 and type **12**; click cell G4 and type **123-45-6789**
5. Click cell **B6**, type **10/14/02**, and press the **right arrow** key to move to cell C6
6. Repeat step 5 a total of six times, typing the remaining dates, in sequence, into cells **C6** through **H6**
7. Click cell **C7** and type **9:30 am** (type a space before "am") and press **Enter.** You notice that cell C11 displays #NUM! Don't be concerned with that error message. It will go away once you enter all your times in and out that day
8. Click cell **C8**, type **12:00 pm** (remember to type a space before "pm"), click cell **C9**, type **1:00 pm**, click cell **C10**, and type **3:00 pm**. Cell C11 should display the value 4.5.

tip: If you see the error message #VALUE! in cell C11, check to make sure you did not type a semicolon instead of a colon in the time entries

9. Type in your hours (see the introductory paragraph before these steps for the hours) for Thursday and Saturday, using step 8 as a guide
10. Click cell **I11** ("eye-eleven") and type a Sum formula to total hours for the cell range C11:H11
11. Print your timecard worksheet
12. Sign and date your timecard on the line above the Employee signature and Date found near the bottom of the timecard

challenge!

1. Creating a Purchase Order

Sheridan's Fresh Flowers is a retail flower store that produces flower arrangements from flowers that the store orders from wholesalers. Allison Sheridan, the owner, did a quick inventory check last night and found that she needed more supplies. Today is the last Friday of the month, and Allison must place her order with her wholesaler for supplies for the next month. By carefully reading her wholesaler's catalog, Allison knows the wholesale price for each of the flower supplies she needs. In addition to the charges for items Allison orders, her wholesaler charges $75 to ship any size order to Sheridan's Fresh Flowers.

Because Sheridan's purchases supplies for resale, it does not pay state sales tax to the wholesaler for its purchases. Allison needs to know how much each item will cost and the total charges, including shipping.

Open a new workbook and create a new worksheet containing the text and values shown in Figure 1.26. In addition, place the title "Sheridan's Fresh Flowers" in the first row of the worksheet. Write formulas to compute each item's total cost and place them in the Item Total Cost column. Write a formula to sum the item costs and place that formula next to the Subtotal label. In the cell to the right of Shipping, place the shipping cost. Finally, write a formula to sum the Subtotal and Shipping values and place it in the cell to the right of the Total label. Place your name in the worksheet header. Print the worksheet and be prepared to turn it in to your instructor.

2. Tracking Inventory with a Worksheet

Thurgood Johnson's Hardware has been offering some new products and wants to see how they are selling. Thurgood Johnson, the store owner, has been keeping track of the number of each item sold. Figure 1.27 shows the number of items Johnson's has sold by month and item.

Open the worksheet **ex01Johnsons.xls**. Modify the worksheet in the following ways. Title the worksheet "Thurgood Johnson's Hardware" by placing that text

in cell A1. Place the label **Products** in the cell above the product names. Write formulas to sum the number of items sold each month, placing each of the six sums in their column in row 10. Type formulas to sum the number of items sold for each item for six months in column H—the column immediately to the right of June. Label the row-totals column **Totals** and place that text next to the "June" text. Finally, in cell H10, write a formula that is the grand total of all the items sold for all six months.

Locate the product that sold the fewest items overall for six months and type the fewest number of items sold to the right of its row sum. Locate the product that sold the largest number of items overall for six months and type largest number of items sold to the right of its row sum. Place your first and last names in one of the unoccupied worksheet cells in row one. Print the worksheet.

FIGURE 1.26
Sheridan's flower supplies order worksheet

Supplies	Quantity Needed	Unit Cost ($)	Item Total Cost ($)
Baskets	10	15.55	
Bows	20	15.95	
Candles	20	4.25	
Cutter	30	7.75	
Knife	40	7.75	
Leafshine	20	5.25	
Ribbons	10	30.45	
Snapper	20	11.25	
Styrofoam	20	13.56	
		Subtotal:	
		Shipping:	
		Total:	

FIGURE 1.27
Johnson's hardware supplies worksheet

	A	B	C	D	E	F	G
1							
2		January	February	March	April	May	June
3							
4	Drills	57	58	54	11	25	10
5	Hacksaws	46	21	36	10	42	19
6	Hammers	45	57	29	59	59	22
7	Levels	34	16	61	10	53	60
8	Pliers	66	13	10	45	45	65
9	Saws	33	12	19	32	50	37

1. Tracking Product Sales by Store Location

The Coffee and Tea Merchant has been selling coffee in the same store in the mall for almost 10 years. They have hired a consultant to build a Web site where they can advertise their store and some of their coffees. The Coffee and Tea Merchant is not ready to build an electronic commerce store, but they do want to be competitive with similar online coffee stores. They want to prepare a worksheet comparing the prices of coffee beans from several coffee regions. Go to the Web and look for three online coffee stores. Record in a worksheet the coffee prices per pound from the three online stores to serve as a comparison. The coffees are shown in Figure 1.28.

Create a new workbook whose worksheet is similar to Figure 1.28. Fill in real store names in place of *Store 1, Store 2,* and *Store 3.* Fill in coffee prices in the columns below the store names. Use the Web and search engines to locate prices per pound for the listed coffee types. Search for online coffee stores by going to www.hotbot.com. Hotbot has an excellent search engine. In the search box, type **coffee beans** and click the **Search** button. Then click several links that Hotbot returns in search of three representative online coffee stores.

Write formulas to compute the average price of each type of coffee by summing the prices for each and dividing by three. Place your name and other required identification information in a worksheet header. Either print the worksheet or execute Save As, according to the direction of your instructor.

2. Building a Product Feature and Price Comparison Worksheet

You want to purchase a new personal computer, but you aren't sure which manufacturer offers the best deal for the machine you want. You've drawn up a list of features that your computer should have and you want to compare machines from three manufacturers: Dell, Gateway, and IBM. First, load and print the worksheet **ex01Computer.xls.** The worksheet lists features in column A and each of the three computer makers' names at the top of a column.

With the preliminary worksheet as your guide, go to the Web and shop for a Dell, Gateway, and IBM desktop computer, noting any additional price for component upgrades listed in the worksheet. Select a PC category called **Home and Home Office** for each manufacturer, and locate and click the **CUSTOMIZE** button when available. The customization process will reveal individual prices for upgraded hardware. When you have jotted down base prices and any additional component costs, load **ex01Computer.xls** and immediately save the worksheet as **Computer2.xls.** Then, enter the values under the manufacturer's column and in the row associated with the machine or component. Write a formula, in the Total row, to compute the total price of each machine. Type your name in cell C1. Print the worksheet.

FIGURE 1.28

Coffee price comparison

The Coffee Merchant					
Coffee Price per Pound Comparison					
					Average
			Store 1	Store 2	Store 3	Price
Ethiopia Sidamo						
Kenya AA						
Kona						
Zimbabwe						

e-business

1. Web Host Price Comparison Worksheet

All About Batteries sells batteries for hundreds of electronic devices ranging from CD players to mobile phones. The business generates most of its revenue through catalog sales. Some customers still prefer to order from the store where they can talk to a salesperson about their needs. Producing and mailing catalogs every three months to thousands of customers and potential customers is costly, and Paul DeMaine, the owner of All About Batteries, wants to open an online store and place the entire catalog online. He knows he must find an online commerce service provider to host his online business. Figure 1.29 shows a list of Web hosting services, their monthly fees for a basic Web hosting package, and the amount of disk storage they provide for their monthly service fees.

Create a workbook that contains this information. Write a formula for each Web host that calculates the cost of the first year of hosting—the setup fee plus 12 times the monthly fee—and place those formulas in the Cost for First Year column. Compute the average monthly cost per megabyte of storage for each listed host, placing that formula in the row corresponding to the Web host name. Place a label next to the Web host that provides the least costly storage per megabyte. Label your output with your name. Execute either Print or Save As, according to your instructor's direction. If you are interested in learning more about Web hosting costs and options, point your Web browser to www.hostcertify.com and read through their pages. Web hosting costs change quickly.

FIGURE 1.29

Web hosts and their fees

Web Hosts					
Company Name	Monthly Service Fee	Disk Storage (MB)	One-time Setup Fee ($)	Cost for First Year	Cost Per Megabyte
HalfPrice Hosting	16.63	100	50		
HostPro	14.95	40	40		
Interland	19.95	150	40		
Webhosting.com	29.95	125	50		
Verio.com	49.95	60	50		

around the world

1. Comparing Gross National Products of Several Countries

Your economics professor has asked you to look up statistics about the population, surface area, and gross national product (GNP) of eight countries. Furthermore, the economics professor would like you to create a worksheet showing the data and displaying the population density and GNP per capita (a measure of productivity) for each country. Start by loading the worksheet called **ex01GNP.xls**, which contains the selected eight countries along with population data and GNP data, and save the worksheet as **GNP2.xls.**

To complete the worksheet, type formulas for population density and GNP per capita for each of the eight countries listed. Population density is the number of people per square kilometer. You calculate that number by dividing the population by the surface area. Remember that the population value is in millions, so you will have to multiply the population in the formula by one million; the surface area of each country is in thousands of square kilometers, so remember to multiply that number in the formula by 1000.

Alternatively, simply divide the population number by the surface area and multiply the entire value by 1000. For example, the per capita GNP is $290.3*1,000,000,000/36*1,000,000. You can divide both the numerator and denominator by 1 million to reduce the value to $290.3*1000/36, or approximately $8,000 per capita. Of course, you will use cell references in place of values in all your formulas. Place your name in the worksheet header and print the worksheet.

running project

Pampered Paws

Pampered Paws is a pet store and provides a sitting service for clients who do not want to board their animals in a kennel. Pampered Paws' pet sitting clients prefer to leave their pets at home—in surroundings that are familiar and comforting to their pets. For a small daily fee, a Pampered Paws' employee will visit a client's pet two or three times per day. During each of the 15-minute visits, the employee plays with the owner's pet and checks the pet's food and water. The employee will walk dogs and, on occasion, cats as part of the service. (They draw the line at turtles, however.) Pampered Pets employs several people on a part-time basis when the service becomes especially busy during the holiday season and summertime. These well-trained part-time employees, known as *walkers,* have varying work schedules that accommodate their other jobs' work requirements. Several of the part-timers have asked for a raise from their current rate of $7.75 per hour to $8.50 per hour. Grace Jackson, the service's owner, wants to compute the total cost of the raise given the typical work schedule of her part-time walkers.

Figure 1.30 shows a worksheet Grace has started. Create a workbook containing a worksheet that looks like Figure 1.30. Fill in the Weekly Current Wage column with formulas that multiply each employee's hours per week times the current hourly rate. Be sure to write the formula to reference the cell containing 7.75 rather than use 7.75 in the formula directly.

Write a similar formula to fill in the Weekly Proposed Wage column, but this time multiply Hours per Week values times the proposed hourly rate cell for each employee. Finally, write formulas in the Wage Difference column to compute the difference between the proposed wage and the current wage for each employee. Sum the Wage Difference column at its foot to see the total effect of the proposed wage increase for the company. Identify your worksheet with your name and print it.

FIGURE 1.30

Employee wage analysis

Pampered Paws Part-time Employees Wage Analysis					
7.75	current hourly rate				
8.50	proposed hourly rate				
			Weekly	Weekly	
First Name	Last Name	Hours per Week	Current Wage	Proposed Wage	Wage Difference
Ellen	Fittswater	12			
Kim	Fong	8			
Ted	Garcia	4			
Randy	Hutto	14			
Luca	Pacioli	9			
Sharon	Stonely	18			

did you

know?

the penny is the only coin currently minted in the United States with a profile that faces to the right. All other U.S. coins feature profiles that face to the left.

the world's largest wind generator is on the island of Oahu, Hawaii. The windmill has two blades 400 feet long on the top of a tower, 20 stories high.

the only house in England that the Queen may not enter is the House of Commons, because she is not a commoner. She is also the only person in England who does not need a license plate on her vehicle.

former U.S. Vice President Al Gore and Oscar-winning actor Tommy Lee Jones were roommates at Harvard.

Chapter Objectives

- Plan and document a workbook
- Create formulas containing cell references and mathematical operators (MOUS Ex2002-5-1)
- Write functions including Sum, Average, Max, and Min (MOUS Ex2002-5-2)
- Use Excel's AutoSum feature to automatically write Sum functions
- Learn several ways to copy a formula from one cell to many other cells
- Differentiate between absolute, mixed, and relative cell reference (MOUS Ex2002-5-1)
- Adjust column widths (MOUS Ex2002-3-2)
- Set a print area (MOUS Ex2002-3-7)
- Move text, values, and formulas (MOUS Ex2002-1-1)
- Insert and delete rows and columns (MOUS Ex2002-3-2)
- Format cells (MOUS Ex2002-3-1)
- Create cell comments (MOUS Ex2002-7-3)

chapter case
Intercity Recycling Contest

Each year for 12 years, a group of five California cities has held a recycling contest to see which city does the best job of recycling plastic, glass, and aluminum. Cities participating in this year's contest are Arcata, Los Gatos, Pasadena, San Diego, and Sunnyvale. Mayors of each of the competing cities elect a contest organizer from a slate of candidates. Although the Recycling Contest Chairperson position is unpaid, it is a great honor to be chairperson. Many candidates vie for the chairperson's position. To avoid any conflict of interest, contest rules require that the chairperson not be a resident of any of the competing cities.

This year's contest chairperson is Kelly Allison. She is a member of the Los Angeles Chamber of Commerce and well known in the Los Angeles area for her work with businesses and the Los Angeles city council. Because chairing the recycling contest is more than a part-time job, Kelly has requested a leave of absence for the contest's three-month duration. She will need help from several volunteers to carry out various tasks associated with the contest, to meet with officials from contesting cities, and to periodically monitor recycling.

This year, the contestants want to recycle aluminum cans. To help keep track of each city's recycling, Kelly has designated several recycling collection points in each of the five cities. The number of recycling centers is proportional to each city's population so that no city has to cope with a recycling congestion problem. Because the populations of the participating cities are wide ranging, a large city such as San Diego will probably recycle the largest number of aluminum cans as its population is over 2.8 million people. To make the contest fair for both large and small cities, the winning city will be the one that recycles the largest number of cans per capita—the number of cans recycled by a city divided by the number of residents of that city.

Each city has a recycling supervisor who monitors and records that city's recycling for every month for the contest's duration. The first of each month, the contest supervisors e-mail the recycling numbers to Kelly Allison. Kelly needs your help to compile the numbers in an Excel worksheet and create the formulas to compute the total recycling by city each month, total recycling for all cities each month, and the all-important per capita recycling value that determines the contest winner. In addition, Kelly wants to know a few statistics about the monthly recycling efforts including the minimum, average, and maximum number of cans recycled.

Figure 2.1 shows the completed Aluminum Can Recycling Contest worksheet. You will be developing the worksheet in this chapter.

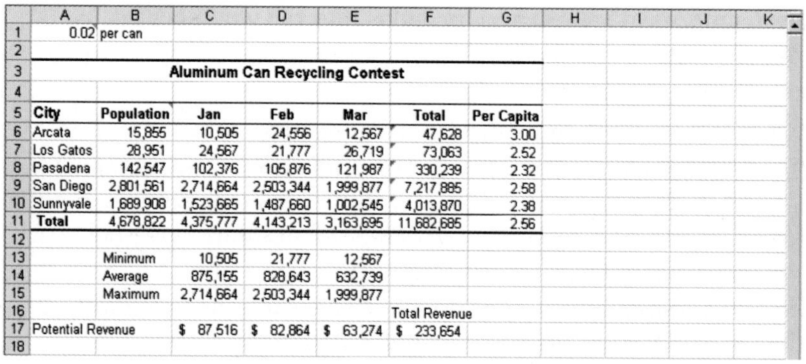

FIGURE 2.1

Completed Can Recycling Contest worksheet

	A	B	C	D	E	F	G
1	0.02	per can					
2							
3			Aluminum Can Recycling Contest				
4							
5	City	Population	Jan	Feb	Mar	Total	Per Capita
6	Arcata	15,855	10,505	24,556	12,567	47,628	3.00
7	Los Gatos	28,951	24,567	21,777	26,719	73,063	2.52
8	Pasadena	142,547	102,376	105,876	121,987	330,239	2.32
9	San Diego	2,801,561	2,714,664	2,503,344	1,999,877	7,217,885	2.58
10	Sunnyvale	1,689,908	1,523,665	1,487,660	1,002,545	4,013,870	2.38
11	Total	4,678,822	4,375,777	4,143,213	3,163,695	11,682,685	2.56
12							
13		Minimum	10,505	21,777	12,567		
14		Average	875,155	828,643	632,739		
15		Maximum	2,714,664	2,503,344	1,999,877		
16						Total Revenue	
17	Potential Revenue		$ 87,516	$ 82,864	$ 63,274	$ 233,654	
18							

INTRODUCTION

Chapter 2 covers writing formulas in worksheet cells, using Excel functions, copying and moving cell contents, and formatting. In this chapter you will create a new workbook from scratch. First, you will type text to identify the worksheet's columns of numbers. You will write expressions using the Excel functions SUM, MIN, AVERAGE, and MAX. Using Excel's AutoSum feature, you will build expressions to total columns by selecting cell groups and then clicking the AutoSum to automatically build the SUM function. You will learn to write formulas and then save time by copying them to other cells in the worksheet to create a family of related formulas. Chapter 2 describes the differences between using relative, mixed, and absolute cell references in expressions and the advantages of each form. You will learn how to use spell-checking to reduce the chances of your worksheets containing misspellings and how to save your workbook. Finally, Chapter 2 describes how to adjust a worksheet page's print settings such as print margins and the print area.

SESSION 2.1 WRITING FORMULAS, USING FUNCTIONS, AND COPYING AND MOVING CELL CONTENTS

In this section, you will learn how to build a worksheet; enter text, formulas, and use Excel functions; and copy and paste formulas to create a family of related formulas.

CREATING WORKBOOKS

Workbooks that endure are well planned and organized. Workbooks designed in a haphazard way grow into finished products that are hard to understand and use. The process from designing a workbook to producing the final printed result follows a series of steps that increase the likelihood of a successful finished workbook.

- First, determine the purpose of the workbook and the worksheets it contains and decide on its overall organization.

CHAPTER OUTLINE

2.1 Writing Formulas, Using Functions, and Copying and Moving Cell Contents

2.2 Formatting Cells, Print Setup, and Printing

2.3 Summary

- Next, enter text, values, and formulas into the worksheet.
- Then, test the worksheet's robustness by entering various values into it and viewing the results.
- Modify formulas that display incorrect results.
- Create documentation such as a description of the worksheet's purpose, the worksheet author's name, names and dates of any modifications, and which cells contain data—the assumptions—and which are formulas.
- Review and implement appearance changes to render the worksheet's displayed values and text more attractive.
- Save the workbook.
- Print the worksheet and its formulas.

PLANNING A WORKBOOK AND ITS WORKSHEETS

Kelly brainstorms with you about the recycling contest and the structure of the worksheet that will record the recycling values reported by contest supervisors. The worksheet should show in the clearest possible way the following:

- What is the overall purpose of the worksheet?
- What are the important results to display in the worksheet?
- What types of data must the supervisors collect and report back to Kelly in order to compute the results?
- What formulas and functions create the answers? The answer to this question specifies the formulas the worksheet designer must write.

With the preceding questions in mind, Kelly creates a list answering the questions. Purposefully general, the answers will guide her in designing the worksheet or directing someone else to do so. The following is a list of specific answers to the preceding worksheet design questions. See Figure 2.2.

FIGURE 2.2

Recycling contest worksheet planning guide

Objective:
Produce a worksheet comparing per-capita recycling among cities

Input Data:
1. City names
2. City populations
3. Recycling amounts by city for each of the three months

Calculated Results (formulas):
- Per capita recycling for each city
- Total recycling per month for all cities
- Smallest recycling amount for each month
- Average recycling amount for each month
- Maximum recycling amount for each month
- Three-month recycling total for each city
- Grand total recycling for all cities for the entire contest period
- Total revenue generated for all recycled cans

With the list of input data values and formulas that Kelly wants to appear in the worksheet, she draws a rough sketch. This helps her decide where totals, labels, and input values look best and allows her to visualize the worksheet's design. Figure 2.3 shows her sketch of the finished worksheet with x representing values or calculated results.

BUILDING A WORKSHEET

Using Kelly's worksheet planning guide (Figure 2.2) and her hand-drawn sketch of the layout (Figure 2.3), you proceed to create the worksheet.

Starting Microsoft Excel:

1. Start Excel by clicking **Start,** pointing to **Programs,** and clicking **Microsoft Excel**

2. Place your floppy disk in the floppy disk drive so that you can save the worksheet later

3. Ensure that both Excel and the empty worksheet are maximized

---

Entering Text

Frequently, people begin building a worksheet by entering most or all of the text (labels). With labels in place, the worksheet has a guide indicating where to place values and formulas. It is a good idea to enter row and column labels first. Leave room for spreadsheet titles above the data and text labels. If you forget to leave space, you can always insert rows and columns where needed. You recall from Chapter 1 that when you enter a label that is wider than its cell, the label spills over into one or more cells to its right. Whenever the adjacent cell is not empty, Excel displays only as much of the label as fits in the cell. Though the entire label may not be visible, it is all stored in a single cell. Begin by entering the worksheet title and column labels.

revenue per recycled can: 0.02

Aluminum Can Recycling Contest

City	Population	Jan	Feb	Mar	Total	Per Capita
Arcata	xxxxxx	xxxxxx	xxxxxx	xxxxxx	xxxxxx	x.xxxx
Los Gatos	xxxxxx	xxxxxx	xxxxxx	xxxxxx	xxxxxx	x.xxxx
Pasadena	xxxxxx	xxxxxx	xxxxxx	xxxxxx	xxxxxx	x.xxxx
San Diego	xxxxxx	xxxxxx	xxxxxx	xxxxxx	xxxxxx	x.xxxx
Sunnyvale	xxxxxx	xxxxxx	xxxxxx	xxxxxx	xxxxxx	x.xxxx
Total # Cans	xxxxxxxx	xxxxxxxx	xxxxxxxx	xxxxxxxx		
Minimum		xxxxxx	xxxxxx	xxxxxx		
Average		xxxxxx	xxxxxx	xxxxxx		
Maximum		xxxxxx	xxxxxx	xxxxxx		
Revenue		xxxxx.xx	xxxxx.xx	xxxxx.xx	xxxxx.xx	

FIGURE 2.3

Worksheet sketch

Typing a worksheet title and column labels:

1. Click cell **A1,** type **Aluminum Can Recycling Contest,** and press **Enter**

   Notice that the title spills over into adjacent cells B1 through C1

2. Click cell **A3** and type **City**

3. Click cell **B3** and type **Population**

4. Enter the remaining column heads as indicated below

tip: *When you are entering data in a row, press the **right arrow** key after typing a cell's entry to finalize the contents and move right one cell in the row. That saves time.*

   Cell C3: **Jan**

   Cell D3: **Feb**

   Cell E3: **Mar**

   Cell F3: **Total**

   Cell G3: **Per Capita**

   See Figure 2.4.

FIGURE 2.4

Worksheet with title and column headings in place

worksheet title

column labels

tip: *If you make a mistake typing any cell's text, select that cell and simply retype it. For short labels, it is usually faster to retype the text than to edit and correct mistakes.*

This year, five cities are entered in the recycling contest. Kelly wants you to enter the city names in alphabetical order in a single column. Enter the city names next.

Entering the names of participating cities:

1. Click cell **A4,** type **Arcata,** and press the **down arrow** keyboard key to move to cell A5

2. Type **Los Gatos** and press the **down arrow** keyboard key to move to cell A6

3. Enter the remaining city names as follows:

   Cell A6: **Pasadena**

   Cell A7: **San Diego**

   Cell A8: **Sunnyvale**

Next, enter summary statistics labels. They identify the values that will appear to their right to indicate the sum, smallest, average, and largest recycling value for each month from the five cities.

Entering summary labels:

1. Click cell **A9,** and type **Total**

2. Click cell **A10** and type **Minimum**

3. Click cell **A11** and type **Average**

4. Click cell **A12,** type **Maximum**, and press **Enter**

Figure 2.5 shows the worksheet containing the labels you just typed.

	A	B	C	D	E	F	G	H	I	J	K	L
1	Aluminum Can Recycling Contest											
2												
3	City	Population	Jan	Feb	Mar	Total	Per Capita					
4	Arcata											
5	Los Gatos											
6	Pasadena											
7	San Diego											
8	Sunnyvale											
9	Total											
10	Minimum											
11	Average											
12	Maximum											
13												
14												

FIGURE 2.5

Worksheet with all labels entered

Entering Values

With a little Web research, Kelly has gotten accurate population data for each of the cities entered in the recycling contest. In addition, the recycling data arrived in Kelly's office and she wants you to enter both the population data and three month's recycling values into the worksheet. Throughout the data entry process, be sure to type the number zero and the number 1 and *not* the letter o ("oh") or the letter l ("ell").

Entering population and recycling values:

1. Click cell **B4** and type **15855**

2. Click cell **B5,** type **28951,** and press **Enter**

3. Enter the remaining population values as follows, pressing Enter after each entry:

   Cell B6: **142547**

   Cell B7: **2801561**

   Cell B8: **1689908**

4. Click cell **C4,** type **10505,** which is the number of cans that Arcata recycled in January, and press the **down arrow** keyboard key

5. Continue entering the recycling values as follows. (Press Enter or the down arrow key to move down the column to the next cell after typing each entry)

   Cell C5: **24567**

   Cell C6: **102376**

   Cell C7: **2714664**

   Cell C8: **1523665**

6. Click cell **D4,** type **24556,** and press **Enter**

7. Continue entering the recycling values for February as follows (press **Enter** after typing each value):

   Cell D5: **21777**

   Cell D6: **105876**

   Cell D7: **2503344**

   Cell D8: **1487660**

8. Click cell **E4,** type **12567,** press **Enter,** and then continue entering the recycling values for March as follows (press Enter after typing each value):

   Cell E5: **26719**

   Cell E6: **121987**

   Cell E7: **1999877**

   Cell E8: **1002545**

Figure 2.6 shows the worksheet with the Population and three months' recycling values entered.

FIGURE 2.6

Worksheet with completed population and recycling values

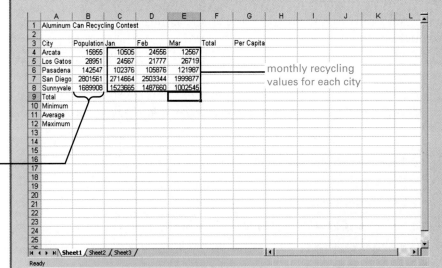

	A	B	C	D	E	F	G
1	Aluminum Can Recycling Contest						
2							
3	City	Population	Jan	Feb	Mar	Total	Per Capita
4	Arcata	15855	10505	24556	12567		
5	Los Gatos	28951	24567	21777	26719		
6	Pasadena	142547	102376	105876	121987		
7	San Diego	2801561	2714664	2503344	1999877		
8	Sunnyvale	1689908	1523665	1487660	1002545		
9	Total						
10	Minimum						
11	Average						
12	Maximum						

monthly recycling values for each city

city population values

Saving Your Worksheet

Once you have invested more than 30 minutes or so developing a worksheet, especially a new one, you should save it—even if you haven't completed it. More times than you can believe, nearly completed worksheets are lost due to power failures, computer glitches, or other mistakes. Because you created the worksheet from scratch, you do not have a back-up copy stored safely on disk. Now is a good time to save it.

Saving your worksheet:

1. Click **File,** and then click **Save As.** The Save As dialog box appears

2. Using the Save in list box at the top of the Save As dialog box, navigate to the disk drive and folder where you want to store your workbook

3. Type **Recycle** in the File name text box to change the workbook's name

4. Click the Save As dialog box **Save** button to save the file. The new name appears in the Excel Title bar

---

Now you have a backup copy safely stored on your floppy disk. If something would happen to reset the computer on which you are working, then you can use the **Recycle.xls** worksheet you stored on disk as the starting point to rebuild any lost work.

WRITING FORMULAS

Now you have the fundamental recycling data on which you can base formulas that compute the results. Among the first results that Kelly wants you to create are the formulas that display each month's minimum, average, and maximum recycling values. The first formula Kelly would like you to write is one to total each month's recycling values.

Creating Excel Sums Automatically

The most frequently used Excel function is SUM. It totals one or more cells. Because the SUM function is so popular, Excel provides the AutoSum button on the Standard toolbar. When you click the AutoSum button, Excel creates a SUM function, complete with a proposed range of cells to be totaled. Excel makes assumptions about which group of contiguous cells you want to total and creates a SUM function based on cells adjacent to the current active cell. You accept Excel's proposed cell range by pressing Enter, or you can select a different range of cells by using arrow keys or the mouse.

---

task reference

Writing Formulas

- Select the cell to contain a formula

- Type **=**

- Type the remainder of the formula

- Press **Enter** or press an arrow key to complete the entry and move to another cell

---

Next, you will use the AutoSum button to create a SUM function to total the recycling values for January.

FIGURE 2.7

Using AutoSum to build a SUM formula

Calculating the number of cans recycled in January:

1. Click cell **C9,** the cell to contain the total cans recycled in January

2. Click the **AutoSum** Σ ▾ button on the Standard toolbar. Excel creates a SUM function in cell C9 and suggests a cell range to sum by placing a dashed line around the cell range C4:C8 (see Figure 2.7). That is the correct cell range. Figures 2.6 and 2.7 show the worksheet with the Population and three months' recycling values entered.

AutoSum button

suggested cell range to sum is enclosed in a dashed rectangle

SUM function that AutoSum builds

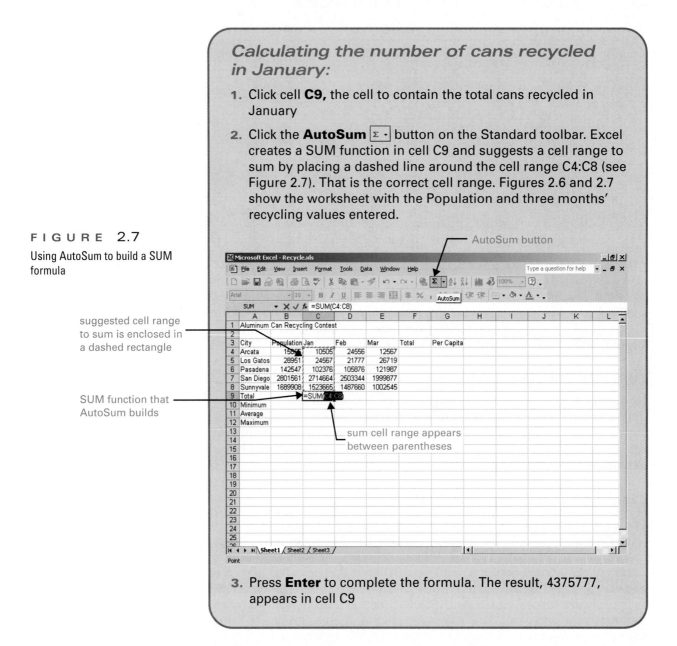

sum cell range appears between parentheses

3. Press **Enter** to complete the formula. The result, 4375777, appears in cell C9

Using the same approach, create the remaining two sums. Notice that Kelly did not ask you to total population for the five cities because the total population is not a meaningful value in this application.

Entering formulas to calculate the number of cans recycled in February and March:

1. Click cell **D9,** the cell to contain the total cans recycled in February

2. Click the **AutoSum** $\boxed{\Sigma \cdot}$ button on the Standard toolbar. Excel creates the appropriate SUM function in cell D9

3. Press **Enter** to complete the formula. The result, 4143213, appears in cell D9

tip: *If the sum your worksheet displays for column D does not match the preceding value, be sure to check the values in cells D4 through D8 to make sure they match the values shown in Figure 2.7*

4. Click cell **E9,** the cell to contain the total cans recycled in March

5. Click the **AutoSum** button. Excel creates the appropriate SUM function in cell E9

6. Press **Enter** to complete the formula. The result, 3163695, appears in cell E9

---

*another*word

. . . on quickly viewing the sum of a selected cell range

If you select a range of cells, their sum appears in the status bar located at the bottom of the worksheet. Selecting a range provides you a quick view of the sum without writing a SUM function in the worksheet.

Modifying AutoSum-Suggested Cell Ranges

Each city's total three-month recycling number is crucial to calculating which city wins the contest. Kelly asks you to enter formulas to total each city's recycling and to create a grand total that is the number of total cans recycled by all cities for three months. Each city's total and the grand total recycling numbers will appear in column F, headed by the column label Total.

---

task reference

Modifying an AutoSum Cell Range by Pointing

- With the AutoSum cell range outlined, press an arrow key repeatedly to outline the leftmost or topmost cell in the range through to the desired starting cell of the range

- Press and hold the **Shift** key

- Press the **right** or **down arrow** key repeatedly to move right or down until reaching the last cell in the cell range

- Release the **Shift** key

- Press **Enter** to complete the AutoSum formula

Create the row totals for each city next.

EXCEL

FIGURE 2.8

Changing the beginning cell in an AutoSum cell range

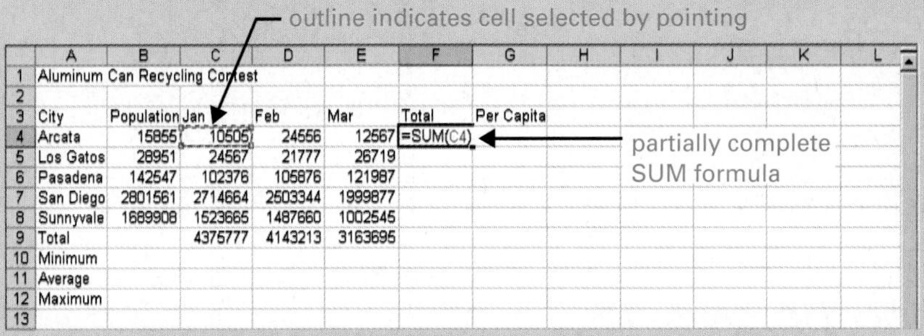

Creating a row total for each city with AutoSum and changing the summed cell range:

1. Click cell **F4,** the cell to contain the total cans recycled by Arcata

2. Click the **AutoSum** button. Excel suggests summing the cell range B4:E4. Because cell B4 is Arcata's population, you will exclude it from the sum in the next steps

3. Press the **right arrow** key to move the outline to cell C4 (see Figure 2.8)

outline indicates cell selected by pointing

	A	B	C	D	E	F	G	H	I	J	K	L
1	Aluminum Can Recycling Contest											
2												
3	City	Population	Jan	Feb	Mar	Total	Per Capita					
4	Arcata	15855	10505	24556	12567	=SUM(C4)						
5	Los Gatos	28951	24567	21777	26719							
6	Pasadena	142547	102376	105876	121987							
7	San Diego	2801561	2714664	2503344	1999877							
8	Sunnyvale	1689908	1523665	1487660	1002545							
9	Total		4375777	4143213	3163695							
10	Minimum											
11	Average											
12	Maximum											
13												

partially complete SUM formula

4. Press and hold the **Shift** key

5. Press the **right arrow** key twice to outline the cell range C4:E4

6. Release the **Shift** key

7. Press **Enter** to finalize the formula. The value 47628 appears in cell F4, along with a cell error Smart Tag symbol that appears in the upper-left corner of the cell. The Smart Tag warns that the sum range has omitted a value adjacent to it. That's okay

You can ask Excel to create more than one SUM function at a time by selecting rows or columns of values with an empty adjacent column or row (respectively) in the range of cells. Then you click the AutoSum button to have Excel build multiple sum functions in one operation.

Creating multiple sum functions at once:

1. Click cell **C5** and drag the mouse through cell **F8** to select the cell range C5:F8

2. Click the **AutoSum** button. Excel automatically creates sum functions in the cell range F5:F8. Additional cell error Smart Tags appear in the cell range F5:F8

3. View a Smart Tag by clicking cell **F5** and then hovering the mouse over the Smart Tag icon. A warning message appears stating "The formula in this cell refers to a range that has additional numbers adjacent to it." (see Figure 2.9)

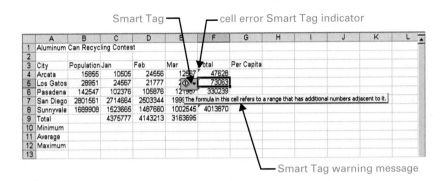

FIGURE 2.9
Smart Tag and warning message

anotherword

. . . about Smart Tags

Microsoft Office Smart Tags are a set of buttons that are shared across the Office applications. The buttons appear when needed, such as when Excel detects you may have made an error in an Excel formula, and gives the user appropriate options to change the given action or error.

Finally, Kelly asks you to write a formula for the grand total—the total number of cans the five cities recycled during the three-month contest. You do that next.

Creating a grand total formula:

1. Select cell **F9,** and then click the **AutoSum** button. Excel suggests the sum range F4:F8

2. Press **Enter** to accept the suggested cell range and complete the SUM formula. The grand total value 11682685 appears in cell F9. This means that the cities involved have recycled nearly 12 million cans (see Figure 2.10)

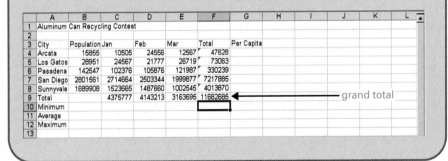

FIGURE 2.10
Worksheet with row totals and grand total

The cell error indicators in cells F4 through F8 are distracting to Kelly and she asks you to remove them.

Removing cell error indicators from cells:

1. Select the cell range **F4:F8**

2. Hover the mouse over the Smart Tag, then click the **Smart Tag list arrow** to open the list of choices

3. Click **Ignore Error** in the list of choices displayed in the Smart Tag list. Excel removes the cell error indicators from all selected cells

4. Click any cell to deselect the cell range

Using Mathematical Operators

Excel formulas begin with an equal sign (=) and are followed by a mixture of cell references, Excel functions, and values mathematically combined into a meaningful expression. When you type an equal sign, you are signaling to Excel that you are writing a formula, not a label or a value. For example, you recall that Excel recognizes 11/22/02 as a value—the date November 22, 2002. However, if you type =11/22/02, Excel knows you are entering a formula that instructs Excel to divide 11 by 22 and divide that result by 02. Excel computes and displays the result, 0.25.

The divide sign (/) is one of several mathematical operators. A *mathematical operator* is a symbol that represents an arithmetic operation. When several mathematical operators occur in a formula, Excel employs the widely recognized *precedence order* to determine the order in which to calculate each part of the formula—which mathematical operators to evaluate first, which to evaluate second, and so on. If a formula contains more than one operator, the order of precedence determines which operations to perform first. For example, Excel evaluates the formula =A1/(B1+B2)*C1^D1 following the precedence order rules. First, Excel computes the value of B1+B2, because that expression is inside parentheses and saves the result temporarily. Then, Excel computes C1^D1, which is the value in cell C1 raised to the power in cell D1 power, and temporarily saves that partial result. When the remaining operators are all of equal precedence, Excel evaluates an expression left to right. Therefore, Excel divides A1 by the value derived earlier for B1+B2. Finally, Excel multiplies the previous partial result, A1/(B1+B2), by the temporarily saved value of C1^D1. For example, the result of the formula =20+2*5−15/3 is 25. Because multiplication and division have precedence over either subtraction or addition, Excel computes 2*5 first, which is 10. Then, Excel computes the value of 15/3—the value is 5. The final expression, with the preceding partial results plugged in, is =20+10−5—the value is 25.

Whenever Excel encounters an expression in which all operators are of equal precedence, it evaluates the expression left to right. For instance, Excel proceeds left to right forming the value of the expression =10*5/2*4, whose evaluation yields 100. Similarly, Excel evaluates the formula =89+A4−B6+B4 left to right, because the addition and subtraction operators are of the same precedence, or importance. How would Excel evaluate the expression =9+12/3? Because division is higher precedence than addition, Excel first divides 12 by 3 and then adds that result to 9. The expression's value is 13, not 7.

On the other hand, if you wanted Excel to first add 9 and 12 before dividing the result by 3, you must rewrite the formula as =(9+12)/3. Excel evaluates expressions enclosed in parentheses first. Thus, Excel divides the sum of 9 and 12 by 3 to yield the answer 7 in the reformulated expression. Figure 2.11 shows the Excel mathematical operators in precedence order, first to last.

Although you may not consider parentheses a mathematical operator, they alter the normal order of precedence wherever they appear in a formula. Therefore, parentheses have highest precedence—they precede all other mathematical operators when Excel evaluates a formula. Figure 2.12 shows other examples of formulas, precedence rules, and computed results. You will write formulas using mathematical operators throughout the book.

Whichever city recycles the largest number of cans during a given period is certainly important, but using that measure to determine the recycling winner would always favor larger cities over smaller ones. You recall that the winner of the recycling contest is the city that has the highest per capita recycling. Per capita (per citizen) recycling is simply the total recycling

Precedence	Operator	Description
1	( )	Parentheses. Alters the order of evaluation. Expressions inside parentheses are evaluated first
2	^	Exponentiation. Raises to a power
3	/ or *	Division or multiplication
4	- or +	Subtraction or addition

FIGURE 2.11

Precedence order of mathematical operators

Formula	Result	Precedence Rule
A1 = **30**	A2 = **20**	A3 = **10**
=A3+A2*A1	610.00	Multiplication first followed by addition
=(A3+A2)*A1	900.00	Parentheses force addition to occur first followed by multiplication
=A3*A2/A1	6.67	Equal precedence among the two operators; proceed left to right
=A1/A2+A3	11.50	Division higher precedence than addition
=A1/(A2+A3)	1.00	Parentheses force addition to occur before division
=A3/A2*A1	15.00	Equal precedence among the two operators; proceed left to right
=A1+A2-A3	40.00	Equal precedence among the two operators; proceed left to right

FIGURE 2.12

Examples of expressions and precedence rules

EXCEL

divided by the city's population. In this contest, the judges compute that number for each city by dividing the city's number of cans recycled in three months by their population. You build that formula next.

Writing Arcata's per capita recycling formula:

1. Select cell **G4** to make it the active cell

2. Type **=F4/B4** and then press **Enter** to complete the formula. The value 3.003974 appears in cell G4. In other words, Arcata's recycling amounted to slightly over three cans per person for every person living in the city

---

While it seems natural to write the remaining Per Capita formulas for the remaining cities, you have a feeling that there may be a better way. You've heard Kelly mention that you can copy formulas that belong to a family of similar formulas, so you wait until you have a chance to talk to her before writing the rest of the per capita recycling formulas in column G.

USING EXCEL FUNCTIONS

Based on Kelly's Recycling Contest Worksheet Planning Guide (Figure 2.2), you need to write formulas to produce statistics for each month. To enter these statistics, you will use three of the Excel functions that are in the same group of functions as the SUM function. The group, called statistical functions, contains several functions including AVERAGE, MAX, and MIN.

An Excel function, you recall from Chapter 1, is a built-in or prerecorded formula that provides a shortcut for complex calculations. Excel functions compute answers, such as the average or maximum, using software instructions that are hidden from view and, frankly, of little interest. Excel has hundreds of functions ranging from a function to generate a random number to a function to compute the monthly payment for a particular loan amount. Excel functions are organized in categories containing related functions. The categories include Database, Date & Time, Engineering, Financial, Information, Logical, Lookup & Reference, Math & Trig, Statistical, and Text.

Functions are written in a particular way. Rules governing the way you write Excel functions are called the function's *syntax.* Syntax rules include properly spelling the function's name, whether or not the function has arguments, and the order in which you list the function's arguments. A function's *argument list* is data that a function requires to compute an answer, and individual list entries are separated by commas. The entire argument list is enclosed in parentheses and follows the function name with no intervening space.

For example, the function SUM(A1, C8:C20, 43.8) contains three arguments in the argument list: a cell reference (A1), a cell range (C8:C20), and a value (43.8). You can write the function name in uppercase, lowercase, or a mixture. Excel converts the function name to uppercase after you enter the complete formula and move to another cell. The general form of an Excel function is this:

Function name($argument_1$, $argument_2$, . . . , $argument_n$)

A function's name describes what action the function takes. AVERAGE, for example, computes the mean of all arguments in its argument list. The function's *arguments,* which specify the values that the function uses to compute an answer, can be values, cell references, expressions, functions, or an arbitrarily complex combination of the preceding that results in a value.

You can enter functions into a cell alone or enter functions as part of a larger expression either by typing the function or by using the Paste Function button located on the Standard toolbar. The Paste Function button opens a dialog box in which you can simply point to the arguments to include in the function, click OK, and let Excel build the complete, syntactically correct function complete with argument list.

MIN Function

MIN is a statistical function that determines the minimum, or smallest value, of all the cells and values in its argument list. It is useful for determining, for example, the lowest temperature from a long list of temperatures or finding the lowest golf score from 800 players' scores. The function is written this way:

$MIN(argument_1, argument_2, . . . ,argument_n)$

Often workbook creators write MIN functions with only one argument—a cell range that Excel examines to determine the smallest value. You must specify multiple arguments when you cannot specify the cells in one cell range. For example, to find the smallest value of those in cells A1, A2, A3, B4, B5, C4, and C5, you must write two arguments, one for each cell range:

MIN(A1:A3, B4:C6)

Like other statistical functions, MIN ignores empty cells and cells containing text when computing its answer.

---

task reference

Writing a Function Using the Insert Function Command

- Click the cell to contain the function

- Click **Insert** on the menu bar, and then click **Function**

- Click the *Or select a category* list and then click the Function category of the function type you want

- Scroll the *Select a function* list, if necessary, to locate the function you want

- Click the function you want in the *Select a function* list box

- Click **OK** to open another dialog box

- Enter information in the edit boxes for each argument

- Click **OK** to close the dialog box and complete building the function in the selected cell

---

Kelly wants you to write the MIN function to produce the smallest recycling value for January.

EXCEL

Building a MIN function using the Insert Function command:

1. Ensure that Excel is running and that the Recycle workbook is loaded

2. Select cell **C10,** the cell in which you want the MIN function built

3. Click **Insert** on the menu bar, click **Function,** and then click the **Or select a category list arrow.** A list of available function categories appears

4. Click **Statistical** in the *Or select a category* list to choose the category containing the MIN function

5. Drag the **Select a function scroll box** until you locate MIN in the alphabetically sorted list of statistical functions

6. Click **MIN** in the Select a function list. Figure 2.13 shows the MIN function syntax in the Insert Function dialog box. A brief description appears there also

FIGURE 2.13

Insert Function dialog box

list of function categories available in the list box

MIN function syntax

MIN function description

some of the statistical functions

Select a function list scroll box

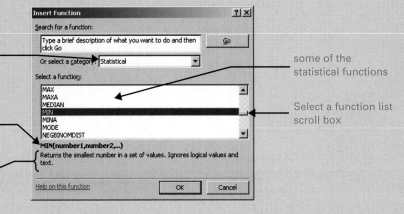

7. Click the **OK** button to open the Function Arguments dialog box. Two text boxes appear, one for each of two arguments. The dialog box also displays a description of the function, a description of the argument list, the current values of the arguments, the current results of the function, and a model of the entire formula. Notice that Excel suggests the cell range C4:C9 for Argument1. That is not the correct cell range, so you will correct it next (see Figure 2.14)

FIGURE 2.14

The Function Arguments dialog box

description of the function and its arguments

current value of the formula containing the function

collapse/expand dialog box button

partial list of function arguments

function's current value

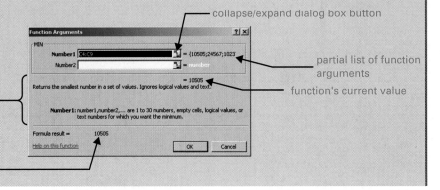

8. Click the **Collapse Dialog Box** button appearing to the right of the Number1 text box. The Function Arguments dialog box collapses to its title bar, making it easier for you to locate and point to the correct cell range

9. Click the **Function Arguments dialog box title bar** and drag it to the right so that you can see cells C3 through C9

10. Click and drag the cell range C4:C8. Notice that as you are dragging the cell range, the ScreenTip 5R x 1C appears, indicating you have selected five rows and one column

11. Click the **Expand Dialog Box** button to restore the collapsed dialog box. Notice that the correct range, C4:C8, appears in the Number1 text box, and the minimum value 10505 appears near the bottom of the dialog box next to the text "Formula result ="

12. Click the **OK** button to accept the MIN formula that Excel built for you and return to the worksheet. The minimum value of the selected range, 10505, appears in cell C10

Based on Kelly's plan, you need to enter two more functions to complete January's statistical information. Those functions yet to be added to the worksheet are AVERAGE and MAX.

AVERAGE Function

AVERAGE is a statistical function that determines the average (arithmetic mean) of all the cells and values in its argument list. It is useful for determining, for example, the average grade of all students taking a test (empty cells or cells with labels are ignored), determining the average price of a stock from a list of weekly closing prices, or computing the average rainfall for the year. The function is written this way:

AVERAGE($argument_1$, $argument_2$, . . . ,$argument_n$)

It is common to see an AVERAGE function with one argument—a cell range—that Excel examines to calculate the average value of the range of values. Similar to other statistical functions, AVERAGE can have up to 30 arguments separated by commas in its argument list.

Kelly wants you to use the AVERAGE function to compute and display the average number of cans recycled each month. You begin by writing an AVERAGE function to determine the average number of cans recycled in January.

Writing an AVERAGE function:

1. Click cell **C11**, if necessary, to make it the active cell

2. Type **=AVERAGE(C4:C8)** and then press **Enter.** Cell C10 displays 875155.4, the average number of cans recycled in January by all five cities

---

The last statistical value you need is the maximum number of cans recycled in January. For that formula, you will use the MAX function.

MAX Function

MAX is a statistical function that determines the largest number. MAX can seek out, for example, the highest-priced real estate from a list of sale prices, the highest examination score, or the largest stock price gain over a time period. The function is written this way:

$MAX(argument_1, argument_2, \ldots ,argument_n)$

MAX, like the other statistical functions, can have up to 30 arguments separated by commas. Arguments can be values, cell references, cell ranges, or arbitrarily complex formulas that calculate a numeric value.

Kelly wants you to write a MAX function to compute and display the value for the largest number of cans recycled in January.

Writing a MAX function by pointing to designate cell ranges:

1. Click cell **C12,** if necessary, to make it the active cell, because that cell will contain the formula displaying the maximum number of cans recycled in January

2. Type **=MAX(** to start the formula

3. Move the mouse pointer to cell **C4,** and then click and drag the mouse to select cells **C4** through **C8.** A dashed line indicates the cells you have selected as you drag the mouse

4. Release the left mouse button and press **Enter.** Excel completes the formula and displays the value 2714664, the largest value in the specified cell range. Notice that Excel automatically adds the terminating right parenthesis when you press Enter. Figure 2.15 shows the worksheet with the three statistical functions displaying January's recycling results

tip: *Excel supplies the right parenthesis automatically when you press Enter.*

FIGURE 2.15

January's statistical functions

	A	B	C	D	E	F	G	H	I	J	K	L
1	Aluminum Can Recycling Contest											
2												
3	City	Population	Jan	Feb	Mar	Total	Per Capita					
4	Arcata	15855	10505	24556	12567	47628	3.003974					
5	Los Gatos	28951	24567	21777	26719	73063						
6	Pasadena	142547	102376	105876	121987	330239						
7	San Diego	2801561	2714664	2503344	1999877	7217885						
8	Sunnyvale	1689908	1523665	1487660	1002545	4013870						
9	Total		4375777	4143213	3163695	11682685						
10	Minimum		10505									
11	Average		875155.4									
12	Maximum		2714664									
13												
14												

statistical functions for January recycling

fill handle

COPYING FORMULAS TO SAVE TIME

Worksheets often contain expressions that are repeated across a row, down a column, or both. Although such expressions may consist of the same mathematical operators and functions, any cell references within formulas are slightly different. Whenever you identify families of expressions—formulas that are identical with the exception of their cell references—avoid creating each expression individually. That approach is time consuming and unnecessary. Instead, take advantage of Excel's ability to create copies of formulas. Examples of functions that you can clone to save time are the MIN, AVERAGE, and MAX. While you could recreate these three formulas manually for the February and March, Excel can do the same job much more quickly.

The key to when you can copy existing formulas is to create a series of formulas. Similarly, you can create four more per capita formulas, or you can copy the existing per capita recycling formula you created for Arcata to the other cities. Unlike a copy operation that Word carries out, Excel copies formulas and then *adjusts* all cell references in the copied formulas. You can choose to copy one cell's contents (a formula, value, or text) to another cell, you can copy one cell's contents to many cells, or you can copy many cells' contents to an equal-sized many-cell group. The copied cell(s) are called the ***source cell(s),*** and the cell or cells to which the contents are copied are known as ***target cell(s).***

There are several equally convenient ways to copy a cell's contents to other cells. You can copy a cell's contents using Excel menu commands, a cell's fill handle, or toolbar buttons. A cell's fill handle is the small black square in the lower-right corner of the active cell (see Figure 2.15).

Copying Formulas Using Copy/Paste

You can copy the contents of one or more cells by copying the cell or cell range to the Clipboard and then pasting the copy into one or more cells in the same worksheet or in a different worksheet. When you copy one or more cells, Excel surrounds the copied cell or cells with a dashed line, or marquee, to indicate the Clipboard's contents. Pressing the Escape key empties the clipboard and removes the dashed line surrounding the copied cells.

The worksheet's plan calls for the cell formula =F5/B5 in cell G5 representing Los Gatos' recycling, =F6/B6 for Pasadena, =F7/B7 for San Diego, and =F8/B8 for Sunnyvale. Rather than create each of those per capita recycling formulas, you can copy the formula in cell G4 to cells G5 through G8. Excel will create a copy of the source cell's contents in each of the target cells and make slight changes to the cell references in the new copied formulas.

---

task reference

Copying and Pasting a Cell or Range of Cells

- Select the cell or cells to copy
- Click the **Edit** menu **Copy** command
- Select the target cell range into which you want to copy the source cell's contents
- Click the **Edit** menu **Paste** command

Copying a formula from one cell to many cells:

1. Click cell **G4** to make it the active cell. The cell's formula, =F4/B4, appears in the formula bar

2. Click **Edit** on the menu bar and then click **Copy** to copy the cell's contents to the Clipboard. Notice that a dashed line encloses the cell whose contents are on the Clipboard

   tip: *You can press **Ctrl+C** instead of using the Copy command. Those of you who keep your hands on the keyboard may favor this keyboard shortcut.*

3. Click and drag cells **G5** through **G8** to select them. They are the target range into which you will paste the cell G4's contents

4. Click **Edit** on the menu bar and then click **Paste.** Excel copies the Clipboard's contents into each of the cells in the selected range and then adjusts each cell's formula to correspond to its new location. Notice that the Paste Options Smart Tag appears below and to the right of cell G8 (see Figure 2.16). The Paste Options Smart Tag provides several formatting and copying options in its list. You can access the options by clicking the Smart Tag list arrow

FIGURE 2.16

Copied formulas' results

	A	B	C	D	E	F	G	H
1	Aluminum Can Recycling Contest							
2								
3	City	Population	Jan	Feb	Mar	Total	Per Capita	
4	Arcata	15855	10505	24556	12567	47628	3.003974	
5	Los Gatos	28951	24567	21777	26719	73063	2.523678	
6	Pasadena	142547	102376	105876	121987	330239	2.316703	copied
7	San Diego	2801561	2714664	2503344	1999877	7217885	2.57638	cells
8	Sunnyvale	1689908	1523665	1487660	1002545	4013870	2.3752	
9	Total		4375777	4143213	3163695	11682685		
10	Minimum		10505					
11	Average		875155.4					
12	Maximum		2714664					
13								
14								

Paste Options Smart Tag

tip: *You can press **Ctrl+V** instead of using the Edit menu Paste command to paste the Clipboard's contents. This may be a faster alternative.*

5. Press **Escape** to clear the Clipboard and remove the dashed line from the source cell. Click any cell to deselect the range and view the formulas' results

If you click any cell in the range of cells you just copied, you will see that Excel has made changes to the copied formula. Cell G6 contains the formula =F6/B6. Similarly, Cell G8 contains =F8/B8. The changed cell reference reflects each copied formula's new location compared to the original source cell. For example, cell G8's formula is exactly four rows higher than the source in cell G4. Excel adds four to the row portion of each cell reference to account for its new location four rows higher than the original.

Cell reference such as the preceding ones are called relative cell references. **Relative cell references** in formulas always change when Excel copies them to another location. When you copy a function or formula horizontally, Excel changes the column letters automatically while leaving the row number unchanged. When you copy a formula or function vertically, the column letters will stay the same, but Excel changes the row numbers automatically. If this did not happen, then copying worksheet cells would merely clone the same values throughout the target range, an activity that would not save you any time.

Copying Formulas Using the Fill Handle

Sometimes you may find it more convenient and quicker to copy a cell's contents by dragging its fill handle. When target cells are adjacent to the source cell, using the fill handle saves time because you do not have to click menus and commands to accomplish the copy and paste operations.

---

task reference

Copying Cell Contents Using a Cell's Fill Handle

- Select the cell whose contents—value, formula, or text—you want to copy. If you want to copy a group of cells, select the cell range you want to copy

- Create an outline of the target cells by clicking and dragging the fill handle of the source cells to the target cells where you want the copied contents to appear

- Release the mouse button

You want to make a copy of the three statistical formulas summarizing January recycling to the other two months, creating six new formulas.

Copying several formulas at once:

1. Click cell **C10** and drag through cell **C12** and release the mouse to select the three cells containing statistical formulas for January

2. Move the mouse pointer over the fill handle in the lower-right corner of cell C12 until the pointer changes to a thin plus sign

3. Click and drag the mouse to the right to outline cells **D10** through **E12.** See Figure 2.17

4. Release the mouse button to complete the copy operation. Excel copies the three formulas from cells C10 through C12 (noted as C10:C12) to cells D10 through E12 and displays the AutoFill Options Smart Tag

5. Click any cell to deselect the range. Figure 2.18 shows the results after copying the statistical functions

EXCEL

FIGURE 2.17

Dragging the fill handle to copy
cells

FIGURE 2.17

Dragging the fill handle to copy
cells

	A	B	C	D	E	F	G	H
1	Aluminum Can Recycling Contest							
2								
3	City	Population	Jan	Feb	Mar	Total	Per Capita	
4	Arcata	15855	10505	24556	12567	47628	3.003974	
5	Los Gatos	28951	24567	21777	26719	73063	2.523678	
6	Pasadena	142547	102376	105876	121987	330239	2.316703	
7	San Diego	2801561	2714664	2503344	1999877	7217885	2.57638	
8	Sunnyvale	1689908	1523665	1487660	1002545	4013870	2.3752	
9	Total		4375777	4143213	3163695	11682685		
10	Minimum		10505					
11	Average		875155.4					
12	Maximum		2714664					
13								
14								

cell contents being copied

target cells receiving copy

FIGURE 2.18

Worksheet after copy operation

	A	B	C	D	E	F	G	H
1	Aluminum Can Recycling Contest							
2								
3	City	Population	Jan	Feb	Mar	Total	Per Capita	
4	Arcata	15855	10505	24556	12567	47628	3.003974	
5	Los Gatos	28951	24567	21777	26719	73063	2.523678	
6	Pasadena	142547	102376	105876	121987	330239	2.316703	
7	San Diego	2801561	2714664	2503344	1999877	7217885	2.57638	
8	Sunnyvale	1689908	1523665	1487660	1002545	4013870	2.3752	
9	Total		4375777	4143213	3163695	11682685		
10	Minimum		10505	21777	12567			
11	Average		875155.4	828642.6	632739			
12	Maximum		2714664	2503344	1999877			
13								
14								

Copy Options
Smart Tag

Creating and Copying a Revenue Formula

Kelly wants an estimate of the total value of the aluminum cans recycled during the contest. Although prices paid at recycling centers vary by city, the average is two cents per can. So, Kelly would like you to add a formula to calculate the total value of the recycled cans for each month, placing those formulas below the maximum statistic for each month. Next, you will create a label to identify the row displaying the approximate value of the recycled cans and a label to identify the value per can.

Adding text and a value for the approximate value of each recycled can:

1. Click cell **A14,** type **Potential Revenue,** and press **Enter**

2. Click cell **H1,** type **0.02,** and press the **right arrow** key to make cell I1 the active cell. The value 0.02 (two cents) is the assumed average value per recycled can

3. In cell I1, type **per can** and then press **Enter.** The text you enter identifies the value to its left. The two cells form the phrase "0.02 per can," which is self-explanatory

Kelly wants you to write a formula for the potential revenue for January for all cans recycled by the five cities.

Writing the recycling revenue formula:

1. Click cell **C14** to make it the active cell

2. Type **=C9*H1** and press **Enter.** The expression is the product of the total number of cans recycled in January and the assumed amount per can, 2 cents. Cell C14 displays the result 87515.54. That is, January's recycling efforts by the five cities have yielded an approximate value of almost $88,000

You ask Kelly why she wants the value .02 in cell H1. Instead, why not write the formula =C9*0.02 for January's potential revenue? She responds that the value per can is an *assumption* that she may want to change later to see the effect on the potential value of the recycled cans. If that assumption were written directly into each formula, what-if analysis would require editing the revenue formulas, an unnecessary activity if the assumption is stored in a separate cell.

Next, you will copy the January revenue formula to the right to fill in formulas for February and March. Then, you will copy a formula to two other cells and cause errors to occur. By performing this operation, you will learn how to avoid the problem in other worksheets.

Copying January's revenue formula using copy and paste:

1. Click cell **C14** to make it the active cell

2. Press **Ctrl+C** to copy the selected cell's contents to the Clipboard

3. Click and drag the cell range **D14:E14** and then release the mouse

4. Press **Ctrl+V** to paste the formula into the target cell range, cells D14 through E14. Figure 2.19 shows the results of the copy operation

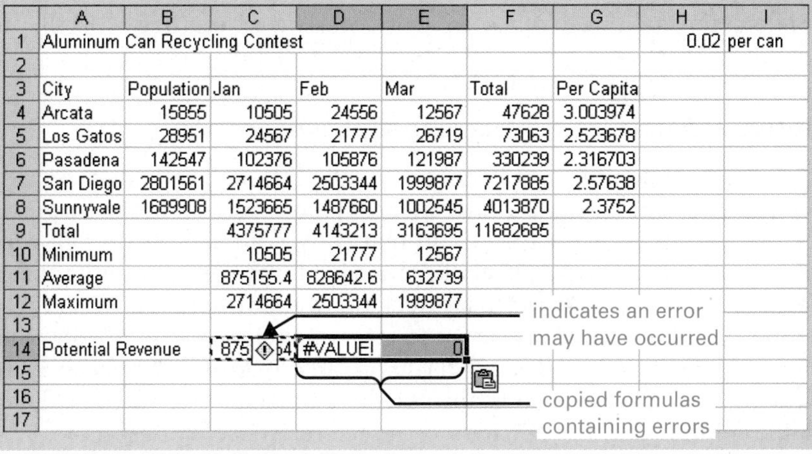

	A	B	C	D	E	F	G	H	I
1	Aluminum Can Recycling Contest							0.02	per can
2									
3	City	Population	Jan	Feb	Mar	Total	Per Capita		
4	Arcata	15855	10505	24556	12567	47628	3.003974		
5	Los Gatos	28951	24567	21777	26719	73063	2.523678		
6	Pasadena	142547	102376	105876	121987	330239	2.316703		
7	San Diego	2801561	2714664	2503344	1999877	7217885	2.57638		
8	Sunnyvale	1689908	1523665	1487660	1002545	4013870	2.3752		
9	Total		4375777	4143213	3163695	11682685			
10	Minimum		10505	21777	12567				
11	Average		875155.4	828642.6	632739				
12	Maximum		2714664	2503344	1999877				
13									
14	Potential Revenue		875◊54	#VALUE!	0				
15									
16									
17									

indicates an error may have occurred

copied formulas containing errors

FIGURE 2.19

Worksheet containing errors in copied formulas

EXCEL

5. Press **Escape** to empty the Clipboard and remove the outline from cell C14

6. Click any cell to deselect the cell range

That did not go as expected. Excel displays an error Smart Tag indicating it has detected an error. Cell D14 displays "#VALUE!" This is a special Excel constant called an ***error value.*** The constant indicates that something is wrong with the formula or one of its components. Cell E14 displays "0," which is not correct either. Whenever you encounter unexpected results from a formula, the best action is to examine the cell's formula carefully to determine the error. You do that next.

Viewing a cell's contents:

1. Click cell **D14** to make it the active cell

2. Press the **F2** function key to display the cell's contents within the worksheet grid. F2 is called the Edit function key because you can edit a cell's contents by first pressing that key and then changing the cell's contents. Excel color-keys both the formula and the cells to which the formula refers so that you can easily see which cells depend on which other cells. Notice that cell D14 contains the formula =D9/I1. The first cell reference, D9, is correct because that is February's recycling total. The second cell reference, I1, is incorrect. It should be H1 instead

3. Click cell **E14** to examine its contents in the formula bar

4. Press the **F2** function key to observe how Excel adjusted the cell references in that formula

5. Press the **Escape** key to end the Edit operation on cell E14

The formula errors occur because Excel adjusts all cell references in copied formulas based on their new position relative to the original cell formula. Occasionally, you alter cell references to avoid the kinds of problems that have occurred here. The answer to avoiding these problems lies in understanding three types of cell references: relative, mixed, and absolute.

Relative, Mixed, and Absolute Cell References

Sometimes, you do not want Excel to adjust all the cell references in a formula that you copy. (Any cell reference you have used so far in this text is a relative cell reference.) Excel automatically adjusts relative cell references to reflect the new location of the copied formulas containing the relative cell references. That is what Excel did to the revenue formula.

When you want a cell reference to remain unchanged no matter where the formula containing it is copied, you use an ***absolute cell reference.*** You indicate that a cell reference is absolute by placing a dollar sign ($) before both the column and row portions of the cell reference. For example, in the formula =C14/H1, you can make the cell reference to cell H1 absolute by rewriting the formula as =C14/$H$1. No matter where you copy that formula, Excel will not adjust the $H$1 reference—it remains anchored to cell H1.

A third type of cell reference allows you to specify that one portion of a cell reference remains fixed while the other can be adjusted. A *mixed cell reference* is a cell reference in which either the column or the row is never adjusted if the formula containing it is copied to another location. For example, if you did not want the row to change in the preceding reference to cell H1, then rewrite the formula to =C14/H$1. An easy way to remember this notation is to substitute the word "freeze" for $. Then a cell reference such as H$1 reads "H freeze 1" and helps remind you that the row is unchanging when copying the formula containing the cell reference. The other form of mixed cell reference is to hold the column portion unchanged, for example, $H1.

To include a dollar sign in a cell reference as you create a formula, type a dollar sign as you type the cell reference. Alternatively, you can press the F4 function key when you edit a cell's contents to cycle through the four combinations of references for a cell. Figure 2.20 shows examples of relative, mixed, and absolute cell references.

FIGURE 2.20

Relative, mixed, and absolute cell references

Formula	Cell reference type
=A43	Relative
=$A43	Mixed
=A$43	Mixed
=$A$43	Absolute

---

task reference

Changing Relative References to Absolute or Mixed References

- Double-click the cell containing the formula that you want to edit or click the cell and then press **F2**

- Move the insertion point, a vertical bar, to the left of the cell reference you want to alter

- Press function key **F4** repeatedly until the absolute or mixed reference you want appears

- Press **Enter** to complete the cell edit procedure

To correct the problem that showed up in the revenue formulas, the best course of action is to correct the original source cell and then re-execute the copy operation. Then both the source cell and the target cells will have a corrected copy of the formula. You want to change the original relative-reference revenue formula in cell C14 from =C9/H1 to the formula =C9/$H1 so that Excel does not adjust the column portion of the reference to the per can recycling cell, H1, when you copy the formula to cells to the right of the existing cell.

Altering a relative cell reference to a mixed reference:

1. Click cell **C14** to make it the active cell

2. Press the **F2** function key to edit the formula in place. Notice that each cell reference in the formula is color coded to an outline surrounding the referenced cell in the worksheet. Called

FIGURE 2.21

Insertion point while editing a cell reference

the **_Range Finder_** feature, it helps you locate cells that the formula references. A cell upon which a formula depends is called a **_precedent cell_**

3. Ensure that the cell insertion point is to the right of the multiplication operator and next to or within the cell reference H1 by clicking the mouse or using the keyboard arrow keys (see Figure 2.21)

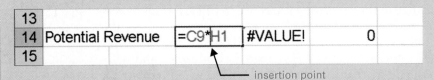

13					
14	Potential Revenue	=C9*H1	#VALUE!		0
15					

insertion point

4. Press the **F4** function key three times to change the cell reference to $H1

tip: _If you press F4 too few or too many times, continue pressing it slowly until the desired reference, $H1, appears_

5. Press **Enter** to complete the formula alteration

Now you can recopy the corrected January recycling revenue cell to cells D14 and E14, corresponding to February and March.

Copying January's corrected revenue formula using copy and paste:

1. Click cell **C14** to make it the active cell

2. Press **Ctrl+C** to copy the selected cell's contents to the Clipboard

3. Click and drag the cell range **D14:E14** and then release the mouse

4. Press **Ctrl+V** to paste the formula into the target cell range, cells D14 through E14

5. Press **Escape** to empty the Clipboard and remove the outline from cell C14

6. Click any cell to deselect the cell range. Figure 2.22 displays the corrected revenue results

MOVING TEXT, VALUES, AND FORMULAS

When you modify a worksheet, you may want to rearrange some blocks of cells containing text, values, or formulas so that they appear in other locations. For example, you might decide that key values should be grouped together so that they appear in the top of the worksheet. Whatever the reason, you can move information from place to place with little effort. When

	A	B	C	D	E	F	G	H	I
1	Aluminum Can Recycling Contest							0.02	per can
2									
3	City	Population	Jan	Feb	Mar	Total	Per Capita		
4	Arcata	15855	10505	24556	12567	47628	3.003974		
5	Los Gatos	28951	24567	21777	26719	73063	2.523678		
6	Pasadena	142547	102376	105876	121987	330239	2.316703		
7	San Diego	2801561	2714664	2503344	1999877	7217885	2.57638		
8	Sunnyvale	1689908	1523665	1487660	1002545	4013870	2.3752		
9	Total		4375777	4143213	3163695	11682685			
10	Minimum		10505	21777	12567				
11	Average		875155.4	828642.6	632739				
12	Maximum		2714664	2503344	1999877				
13									
14	Potential Revenue		87515.54	82864.26	63273.9				
15									

corrected revenue cells

FIGURE 2.22

Worksheet with corrected revenue formulas

you move one or more cells, both the contents and the formatting move to the new location. Unlike copying cells, moving cells involves taking a cell's contents and formatting away from its current location and placing them in a new location.

Formulas are not changed when they are moved. Of course, moving text or labels does not change their value either. For example, suppose you moved the formula stored in cell C14 to compute potential revenue for January, =C9*$H1, to cell C2. After the move operation, cell C14 would be empty and the formula =C9*$H1 would occupy cell C2. In other words, Excel does not adjust cell references in the formula that moves. However, all cells that referenced a moved formula are adjusted. For example, if you were to move cell H1 containing the value of a single can to H5, any formulas that referenced cell H1 are adjusted to reference cell H5 automatically. That is, moving a cell's contents causes all dependent cells to adjust their references to the new location of the moved formula.

There are several ways to move cell contents from one cell to another. You can use the mouse to drag and drop the contents of a cell or block of cells, you can cut and paste one or more cells, or you can insert or delete rows or columns in a worksheet and thus change a cell's position. (How to insert and delete rows or columns is described in the next session.)

---

task reference

Moving Cells' Contents

- Select the cell or cell range that you want to move

- Move the mouse pointer to an edge of the selected range

- When the mouse pointer changes to an arrow, click the edge of the selected cell or cell range and drag the outline to the destination location

- Release the mouse

Kelly would like you to move the four labels in cells A9 through A12 to the right so that they are closer to the values they identify.

Moving four labels:

1. Click and drag the mouse through the cell range **A9:A12**

2. Release the mouse

3. Move the mouse pointer toward an edge of the selected cell range until the mouse pointer changes from a large plus sign to a four-headed arrow.

4. Click any edge of the selected cells and drag the outline to the right so that it surrounds cells B9 through B12 (see Figure 2.23)

FIGURE 2.23

Moving cells' contents

	A	B	C	D	E	F	G	H	I
1	Aluminum Can Recycling Contest							0.02	per can
2									
3	City	Population	Jan	Feb	Mar	Total	Per Capita		
4	Arcata	15855	10505	24556	12567	47628	3.003974		
5	Los Gatos	28951	24567	21777	26719	73063	2.523678		
6	Pasadena	142547	102376	105876	121987	330239	2.316703		
7	San Diego	2801561	2714664	2503344	1999877	7217885	2.57638		
8	Sunnyvale	1689908	1523665	1487660	1002545	4013870	2.3752		
9	Total		4375777	4143213	3163695	11682685			
10	Minimum		10505	21777	12567				
11	Average		875195.4	828642.6	632739				
12	Maximum		2714664	2503344	1999877				
13									
14	Potential Revenue		87515.54	82864.26	63273.9				
15									

selected cells being moved

outline indicates cell block destination

B9:B12

indicates current destination cell range

5. Release the mouse. Excel moves the cells to their new target location

6. Click any cell to deselect the cell range

---

anotherway

. . . to move cells' contents

Drag the mouse across the source cell or cell range you want to move

Click the **Cut** command in the Edit menu

Drag the mouse across the target cell or cell range to which the contents will move

Click the **Paste** command in the Edit menu

Moving a cell's contents to another location is a cut action followed by a paste action. Cutting removes the cell's contents from its current location and places it on the Clipboard temporarily. Pasting moves the Clipboard contents to the new location. Of course, you can move any block of cells in one operation, regardless of its size. If the destination cell or cell range already contains information, Excel issues a warning and asks you if it is okay to overwrite existing contents. Clicking OK approves overwriting cell contents, while clicking the Cancel button calls off the attempted move operation.

RENAMING A WORKSHEET

A handy way to add documentation to a worksheet is to name the sheet in a meaningful way to reflect its contents. Examine the leftmost sheet tab in the recycling workbook you created. Notice the sheet tab is labeled Sheet1, which is the name Excel automatically assigns to the first sheet in a workbook. If your workbook has other worksheets, they are named Sheet2, Sheet3, and so on. (The number of worksheets Excel creates when creating a new workbook depends on how Excel is set up on your computer.) Because your worksheet is nearly complete, you will give it a name that reflects its contents.

> **Renaming a worksheet:**
>
> 1. Double-click the **Sheet1** sheet tab to select it
> 2. Type **Recycling Contest** to replace the current name, Sheet1
> 3. Press Enter to complete the worksheet renaming operation. The sheet tab displays the name "Recycling Contest"

SPELL-CHECKING A WORKSHEET

Excel contains a spell-check feature that helps you locate spelling mistakes and suggests corrections. Comparing words in Excel's dictionary to the words in your worksheet, Excel finds words that appear to be misspelled and suggests one or more corrections. You can choose to leave unchanged each word Excel locates, or you can select an alternative spelling. You should always spell-check your worksheet before presenting it to others. It is easy to overlook misspelled words in any document, and this is especially true for worksheets.

> **task reference**
>
> **Spell-Checking a Worksheet**
>
> - Click cell **A1** to begin spell-checking from the top of a worksheet
> - Click the **Spelling** command in the Tools menu or click the **Spelling** button on the Standard toolbar
> - Choose to correct misspelled words that the spell-checker identifies
> - Click **OK** to close the dialog box

Kelly knows that a lot of people will see the recycling contest worksheet. She wants to make sure that any misspellings in the worksheet are corrected. She asks you to check the worksheet for spelling mistakes.

> **Checking a worksheet's spelling:**
>
> 1. Click cell **A1** to begin-spell checking at the top of the worksheet
> 2. Click **Tools** on the menu bar and then click **Spelling** to start the spell-check operation
>
> **tip:** *you can click the **Spelling** button on the Standard toolbar to check spelling*
>
> 3. Correct any misspellings. A message box opens when all spelling is correct
> 4. Click **OK** to close the message box

EXCEL

SAVING YOUR MODIFIED WORKBOOK

You have made many changes to your worksheet. It is time to save your work permanently on your disk so that you have a portable copy and to preserve it for future use.

> *Saving your worksheet under its current name:*
>
> 1. Click **File**
> 2. Click **Save.** Excel saves the worksheet to your disk

SESSION 2.1

making the grade

1. Explain how AutoSum works and what it does.

2. Suppose you select cell A14 and type D5+F5. What is stored in cell A14: text, a value, or a formula?

3. You can drag the _____, which is a small black square in the lower-right corner of the active cell, to copy the cell's contents.

4. Evaluation of a formula such as =D4+D5*D6 is governed by order of precedence. Explain what that means in general and then indicate the order in which Excel calculates the preceding expression.

5. Suppose Excel did not provide an AVERAGE function. Show an alternative way to compute the average of cell range A1:B25 using the other Excel statistical functions.

SESSION 2.2 FORMATTING CELLS, PRINT SETUP, AND PRINTING

In this session, you will complete the worksheet by formatting it to apply a more professional look, increase the width of a column to accommodate longer text entries, insert rows and columns to provide visual boundaries between worksheet sections, undo worksheet changes, and format groups of cells with Excel's AutoFormat command. You will explore how to establish worksheet headers and footers, set page margins, establish a worksheet's print area, and add cell-level documentation and worksheet-wide documentation.

STRESS TESTING A WORKSHEET

Using an electronic worksheet to produce results sometimes gives the worksheet designer a sense that the formulas and results are correct because the product is, after all, an electronic worksheet. Therefore, the results must be correct. This is not always the case, and mistakes can creep in and linger, undetected, for days or months if you don't examine the results carefully and test the worksheet to prove its validity. Testing need not be a long or complicated procedure. You can choose from several test methods to validate the worksheet's formulas and results.

One way to test a worksheet is to enter valid, small numbers in the input cells and observe the formulas' computed results. For example, you can enter 10 into each city's recycling cells for all three months and then change each city's population to 10. If your worksheets' formulas are correct the recycling per capita will be 3 across all cities—a result you know is correct—and the three-month totals display 30 for all cities. Similarly, the recycling statistical values will all be the same—the minimum, average, and maximum should display 10.

Entering extreme or limit values into a worksheet's non-formula cells is another way to test your worksheet's formulas. For example, if you enter zero into the recycling cells for all cities and all months, then all formulas—totals, per capita recycling, and statistics by month—should all display zero.

Finally, you can try out a few test calculations with your calculator and compare the results with the same values in your worksheet. If the results jibe, your worksheet formulas are correct.

MODIFYING A WORKSHEET'S APPEARANCE

After testing the worksheet, you and Kelly are satisfied that the worksheet is correct. However, Kelly wants to modify the worksheet so that it looks more professional. Cosmetic changes to a worksheet—changes that make the text and numbers *appear* different—occur when you **format** a worksheet. While formatting changes the appearance of the results displayed by text, values, and formulas, formatting never changes a cell's contents.

Kelly has identified a few formatting changes that will render the worksheet more professional and easy to read. She wants you to widen the column containing city names so that they have a bit more space between them and the population column to the right. Additionally, she wants you to insert two rows above the Aluminum Can Recycling Contest title and to insert a blank row between the recycling total row and the row containing the Minimum recycling values for each month. She also asks you to insert a blank row between the Maximum values row and the Potential Revenue row, to make the recycling statistics values display their values with commas and no decimal places, and to display the potential revenue values with currency symbols and commas. Finally, Kelly wants you to move the revenue per can value and its label to cells A1 and B1 so that what-if assumption value is near the top of the worksheet.

Inserting and Deleting Rows

You cannot always anticipate where you will need more columns or rows in order to make room for omitted cells or to add a blank row for aesthetic reasons. Fortunately, Excel allows you to add rows or columns at any point and accommodates existing work by moving existing rows to accommodate inserted or deleted rows. Likewise, if you insert or delete columns, Excel automatically moves columns to accommodate them. Inserting rows or columns follows the same procedure: You select the number of rows or columns you want to insert and then click the Insert command. After Excel repositions existing rows or columns to accommodate the insertion operation, it adjusts all cell references in formulas to reflect the new locations of cells referenced by the formulas.

Kelly wants you to insert two rows above the worksheet title currently in row 1.

task reference

Inserting Rows

- Click any cell above which you want to insert a row or select a range of cells in several rows above which you want to insert several rows

- Click **Insert** and then click **Rows.** Excel inserts one row for each row you selected

Inserting Columns

- Click one or more cells in columns to the left of which you want to insert one or more new columns

- Click **Insert** and then click **Columns.** Excel inserts as many new columns as there are in the range you selected

Inserting rows into a worksheet:

1. Click cell **A1** and drag the mouse through cell **A2** to indicate the row above which you want Excel to insert two additional rows

2. Click **Insert** on the menu bar and then click **Rows.** Excel inserts two rows at the top of the worksheet and moves existing rows down

3. Click cell **A11** to prepare to insert a blank row between the Total row, containing monthly recycling totals, and the Minimum row

4. Click **Insert** and then click **Rows.** Excel inserts the new row 11 (see Figure 2.24)

FIGURE 2.24

Inserting three new rows into a worksheet

click the Undo button to cancel last operation

row inserted in the wrong location

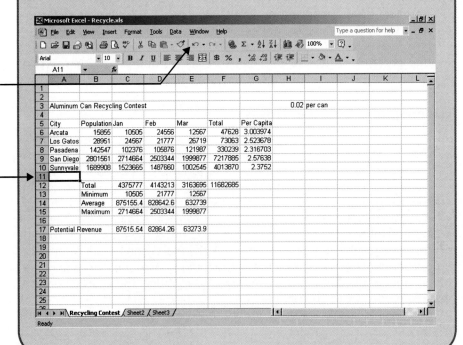

Correcting Mistakes with Edit Undo

The last row you inserted is not where you want it to be. To correct that error, you can delete the newly inserted row or you can click the Undo button to cancel the last operation. You can click the row label to the left of column A to select the entire row. Then, click Delete in the Edit menu to delete the row. You will find the Undo method helpful in so many other situations that you decide to use it to cancel the insert row action. Whenever possible, use the Undo method immediately after you realize that you want to reverse one or more actions.

Canceling the previous row insertion action:

1. Click the **Undo** 🔄 button on the Standard toolbar (see Figure 2.24). Excel deletes the row you previously inserted

Now you are ready to insert a new row in the correct position—between the Total and Minimum rows.

Inserting a row into a worksheet:

1. Click cell **A12** to prepare to insert a blank row between the Total row, containing monthly recycling totals, and the Minimum row

2. Click **Insert** and then click **Rows**. Excel inserts the new row—row 12—and moves all other rows below it down one row

Because it is convenient to place cells in a convenient location when they are used in what-if analysis, you move the recycling value per can assumption and its label to cells A1 and A2. That way, anyone who wants to see the effect of changing the value per can to three cents can locate the cell quickly and change it easily.

Moving cells to another location in a worksheet:

1. With the mouse, select the cell range **H3:I3,** which contains the value and label you want to move

2. Hover the mouse over cell **H3** and slowly move the mouse toward one of the selected cell range's edges until the mouse pointer changes to a four-headed arrow

3. Click the mouse button and hold it down as you drag the outline to cells **A1** through **B1** (see Figure 2.25)

4. Release the mouse button to complete the move operation. The value *0.02* and label *per can* now occupy cells A1 and B1, respectively

EXCEL

FIGURE 2.25

Moving cells' contents

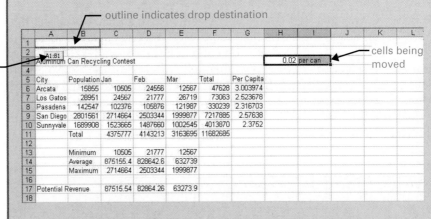

drop cell range
address displayed

outline indicates drop destination

cells being
moved

5. Click any cell to deselect the cell range

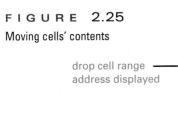

anotherway

**. . . to Move Cells'
Contents**

Select the cell range you
want to move

Press **Ctrl+X** to cut the
selected cells

Select the cell range to
which you want to move
the cells

Click **Ctrl+V** to paste the
cells to their new
location

Using AutoFormat

Excel's AutoFormat feature provides you with a wide selection of predefined formats from which you can select to alter the appearance of your
worksheet. Each of the AutoFormat selections in the portfolio of formats
includes a variety of formatting selections including color, fonts, shading,
and lines. AutoFormat automatically adjusts column widths and heights
and selects cell alignment characteristics that yield the most attractive
presentation. Formatting changes to your worksheet such as those
AutoFormat supplies should be one of the last operations you apply to
your worksheet. If you format cells or cell ranges with AutoFormat or do
so manually before you have built a complete worksheet, you frequently
have to reapply formatting to accommodate larger than expected numeric
values requiring cell width or font size adjustments.

task reference

Applying AutoFormat to Cells

- Click the cell range you want to format

- Click **Format** and then click **AutoFormat**

- Select the format style from the portfolio of styles in the Table Format
  list

- Click **OK** to select and apply the format you choose

Experiment with AutoFormat by formatting rows 3 through 11 of the
recycling worksheet.

Formatting cells with AutoFormat:

1. Select the cell range **A3** through **G11**

2. Click **Format** on the menu bar and then click **AutoFormat**.
The AutoFormat dialog box opens and displays the first of

several AutoFormat styles (see Figure 2.26). A dark outline appears around the Simple format, because it is the currently selected format

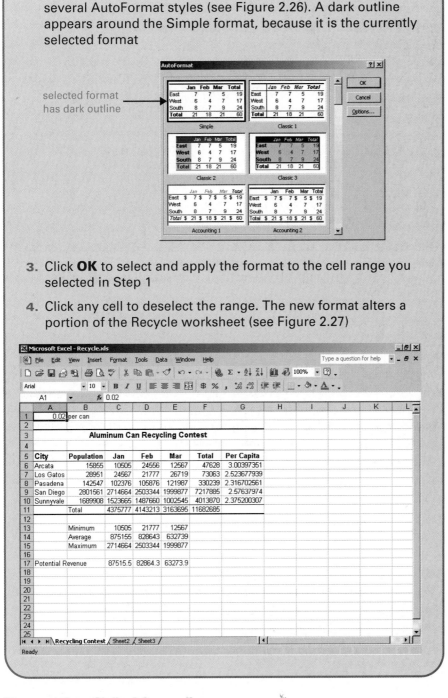

selected format has dark outline

FIGURE 2.26

AutoFormat dialog box

3. Click **OK** to select and apply the format to the cell range you selected in Step 1

4. Click any cell to deselect the range. The new format alters a portion of the Recycle worksheet (see Figure 2.27)

FIGURE 2.27

Worksheet after applying AutoFormat

Formatting Cells Manually

Kelly reviewed your work so far and is pleased. She would like the numeric values to contain commas to make their values easier to read. Kelly would also like you to format the Per Capita column so that the values all contain two decimal places. The Per Capita values are also difficult to read because the decimal points aren't aligned. Finally, Kelly wants the Potential Revenue row values to include currency symbols so that worksheet viewers clearly understand the row contains revenue and not recycling units. You begin by formatting a portion of the worksheet so that numeric values include commas and no decimal places—whole numbers.

Formatting numeric entries to display commas and no decimal places:

1. Select the cell range **B6** through **F15**
2. Click the **Comma Style** ⬚ button on the Formatting toolbar. Several cell entries display ######, which indicates the formatted value is too wide to display the entire value
3. Click the **Decrease Decimal** ⬚ button *twice* (located on the Formatting toolbar) to reduce the number of displayed decimal places to zero. Several cells display values with commas, but some still display the pound sign (#). You will fix that problem soon. Ignore it for now
4. Click any cell to deselect the range

Next, reduce the number of decimal places displayed in the Per Capita column to two.

Formatting numeric entries to display commas and two decimal places:

1. Select the cell range **G6** through **G11**
2. Click the **Comma Style** button on the Formatting toolbar. All values in the Per Capita column display numbers rounded to two decimal places
3. Click any cell to deselect the range

Finally, format the Potential Revenue column so that the currency symbol, $, displays and reduce the number of decimal places to zero.

Formatting numeric entries to display the currency symbol and no decimal places:

1. Select the cell range **C17** through **E17,** which displays the potential revenue for January through March
2. Click the **Currency Style** ⬚ button on the Formatting toolbar
3. Click the **Decrease Decimal** ⬚ button *twice* (see Figure 2.28). The revenue values display a series of # symbols, indicating the column is too narrow to display the value

Though it is not yet apparent, the revenue values you just formatted will display dollar signs and no decimal places. To see the several values in cells that are currently displaying pound signs, you will have to widen the columns to accommodate their increased width. You do that next.

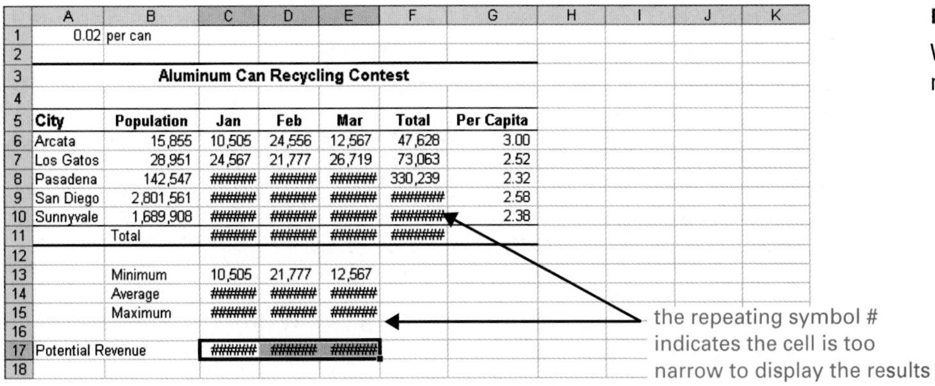

FIGURE 2.28
Worksheet after applying numeric formats

the repeating symbol # indicates the cell is too narrow to display the results

Adjusting Column Width

One way to enhance the appearance of a worksheet is to widen columns. Widening a column to leave some vertical white space between it and its neighbor adds to the worksheet's readability. Several columns in the Recycling worksheet must be widened in order to view the values. The column containing city names is a little narrow also.

There are several ways to alter a column's width. You begin by clicking the column heading—the letter at the top of a column—or drag the pointer to select a series of contiguous columns and then use the Width command in the Format menu to select a width. Alternatively, you can move the mouse to the dividing line on the right side of any selected column header. When the pointer changes to a resize arrow (a double-headed arrow), you can drag the dividing line to the right to increase the column's width or drag it to the left to decrease the column's width. Moving the mouse pointer to the column heading dividing line, you can double-click the right-side dividing line to make the entire column as wide as the widest entry plus one character.

---

task reference

Modifying a Column's Width

- Select the column heading(s) of all columns whose width you want to change

- Click **Format,** point to **Column,** and click **Width**

- Enter the new column width in the **Column Width** text box and click **OK,** or click **AutoFit Selection** to make the column(s), optimal width as wide as the widest entry in the column

  or

- Double-click the right edge of the column heading line to make the column(s) optimal width(s) as wide as the longest entry in the column(s)

  or

- Drag the column heading dividing line of any one of the selected columns to the left to decrease the column width or to the right to increase the column width

EXCEL

Kelly wants you to increase the column widths of columns A through F to display the city names and values completely.

Increasing the width of column A:

1. Move the mouse pointer to the A column header and move it slowly to the right edge of the column heading dividing line. The pointer changes to a resize arrow ⬌

2. Click and drag the **column heading A dividing line** to the right until the pop-up ScreenTip indicates the width is 11 characters or more

3. Release the mouse button

Next, you will increase the width of columns B through F in one operation. You want the columns to be wide enough to accommodate the widest numeric value so that the repeated pound signs disappear and the computed recycling and statistical values appear in their place.

Optimizing the width of several columns at once:

1. Click **column heading B** and drag the mouse through **column heading F** and release the mouse. This selects the five columns whose width you want to alter

2. Move the mouse pointer to the heading dividing line between any two selected columns. The pointer changes to a resize arrow

3. Double-click the column heading dividing line to make the selected columns optimal width (see Figure 2.29)

FIGURE 2.29

Optimizing columns' widths

	A	B	C	D	E	F	G	H	I	J
1	0.02	per can								
2										
3		Aluminum Can Recycling Contest								
4										
5	City	Population	Jan	Feb	Mar	Total	Per Capita			
6	Arcata	15,855	10,505	24,556	12,567	47,628	3.00			
7	Los Gatos	28,951	24,567	21,777	26,719	73,063	2.52			
8	Pasadena	142,547	102,376	105,876	121,987	330,239	2.32			
9	San Diego	2,801,561	2,714,664	2,503,344	1,999,877	7,217,885	2.58			
10	Sunnyvale	1,689,908	1,523,665	1,487,660	1,002,545	4,013,870	2.38			
11		Total	4,375,777	4,143,213	3,163,695	11,682,685				
12										
13		Minimum	10,505	21,777	12,567					
14		Average	875,155	828,643	632,739					
15		Maximum	2,714,664	2,503,344	1,999,877					
16										
17	Potential Revenue		$ 87,516	$ 82,864	$ 63,274					
18										

selected columns whose width is changed

4. Click any cell to deselect the columns. Notice that all the computed results display in the worksheet. The Potential Revenue row values contain commas and currency symbols, just as Kelly wanted

You learned in Chapter 1 how important page headers and footers are in identifying printed output. Kelly wants you to add a header with the title "Aluminum Can Recycling Contest Results" centered on the page. In addition, she wants the worksheet footer to contain your first and last names to identify the worksheet's author.

Creating a worksheet header and footer:

1. Click **View** on the menu bar and then click **Header and Footer**

2. Click **Custom Header,** click in the **Center section,** type **Aluminum Can Recycling Contest Results**, and click **OK**

3. Click **Custom Footer,** click in the **Center section,** type your first and last names, and click **OK**

4. Click the **Print Preview** button on the Standard toolbar to preview the worksheet complete with the new header and footer

5. After you have examined the output to ensure that it looks as you expected, click the **Close** button to close the Preview window and return to the worksheet window

The output looks great. Save the worksheet and then print it so that Kelly can scan the worksheet before you make it available to the public.

Printing a worksheet:

1. Click **File** on the menu bar

2. Click **Print**

3. Click **OK** to print the worksheet

ADJUSTING PAGE SETTINGS

You give the worksheet printout to Kelly so that she can comment on it. She is pleased with your work and suggests that you change the left margin to 1.5 inches and set the top, bottom, and right margins to one inch. She wants another printout that contains only rows 3 through 11 of the worksheet.

Setting the Print Area

Unless you specify otherwise, Excel prints the entire worksheet, including any incidental or scratch areas of the worksheet you may have used. Many times, you want to print just a selected part of a worksheet. To restrict the print output to part of a worksheet, you select the area to be printed and then execute the Excel Set Print Area command to tell Excel the print range.

> ### Setting a worksheet's print area:
>
> 1. Drag the mouse pointer through the cell range **A3:G11** to select it
>
> 2. Click **File,** point to **Print Area**, and then click **Set Print Area**
>
> 3. Click **File,** and then click **Print Preview** to examine the output prior to printing it. Notice that the statistics do not appear in the output. Neither does the value per can assumption cell in row 1 of the worksheet
>
> 4. Click **Close** to return to the worksheet, and click any cell to deselect the area

To print the entire worksheet after you have set the print area, you must remove the print area before printing the worksheet. A worksheet's print area is stored with the worksheet, so Excel remembers if a print area is set or not. Remove the print area by clicking **File**, point to **Print Area,** and click **Clear Print Area**. Once you remove the print area, the entire worksheet will print.

Setting Print Margins

Print margins define the area of a printed page in which a worksheet appears. The left, right, top, and bottom margins define the area. The *left margin* defines the size of the white space between a page's left edge and the leftmost edge of the print area. Similarly, the *right margin* defines the white space between the print area's rightmost position and the right edge of a printed page. Header information appears within the *top margin,* which is the area between the top of the page and topmost edge of the print area. The *bottom margin* is the area at the bottom of the page between the bottommost portion of the print area and the bottom edge of the page. A worksheet's page footer, if any, appears in the bottom margin.

You can set each worksheet's page margins independently using several techniques. Set the margins by executing the Page Setup command in the File menu and clicking the Margins tab. Alternatively, you can click the Margins button in the Print Preview window and move any margin by dragging the dashed line representing each margin.

> ### Setting a worksheet's print margins:
>
> 1. Click **File** on the menu bar
>
> 2. Click the **Page Setup** command. The Page Setup dialog box opens
>
> 3. Click the **Margins** tab
>
> 4. Type **1.5** in the Left spin control box. This sets the left margin to 1½ inches
>
> 5. Type **1** in the Top, Right, and Bottom spin control boxes (see Figure 2.30). This sets the margins to 1 inch

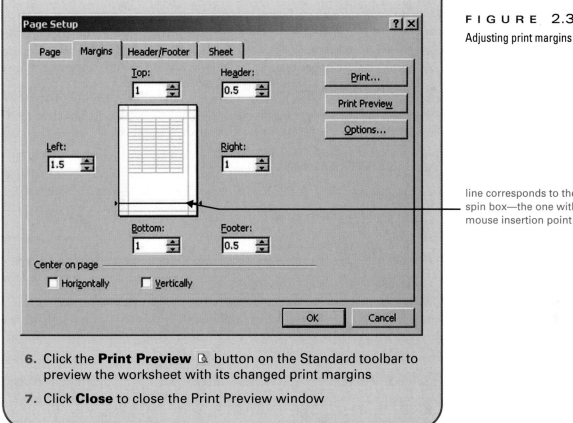

FIGURE 2.30
Adjusting print margins

line corresponds to the active spin box—the one with the mouse insertion point

6. Click the **Print Preview** button on the Standard toolbar to preview the worksheet with its changed print margins

7. Click **Close** to close the Print Preview window

You have made a large number of changes to the Aluminum Can Recycling Contest worksheet since you last saved it. It is time to save your work so that you preserve all the changes.

Saving your worksheet:

1. Click **File** on the menu bar

2. Click **Save**

DOCUMENTING THE WORKBOOK

It is always smart to document your work so that the next person assigned to modify or extend your work can easily and quickly understand the purpose and use of your worksheet. Besides external documentation such as printouts of worksheet formulas and your own notes, you can create internal documentation. As you recall, the first page of a workbook can contain extensive documentation including the author's name, the dates of major changes to the worksheet, and instructions on how to input data and use the worksheet. Small simple worksheets such as the Recycling worksheet require simple instructions. Larger more complex worksheets require more extensive instructions including which cells comprise the input area, which cells contain formulas whose results depend on the input area(s), and which workbook worksheets contain additional information or instructions.

One valuable but often overlooked source of documentation is the Properties dialog box found on the File menu. The ***Properties dialog box*** contains several text boxes that you can fill in with helpful information including the fields Title, Subject, Author, Manager, Company, Category, Keywords, and Comments. A workbook's creator can enter his or her name in the Author field. Another way to document a workbook is to include internal notes on individual worksheet cells. Called ***comments,*** these worksheet cell notes are particularly helpful to indicate special instructions about the contents or formatting of individual cells.

Setting File Properties

Kelly wants you to fill in the Title, Author, and Manager fields of the Property dialog box to record within the worksheet these important pieces of documentation.

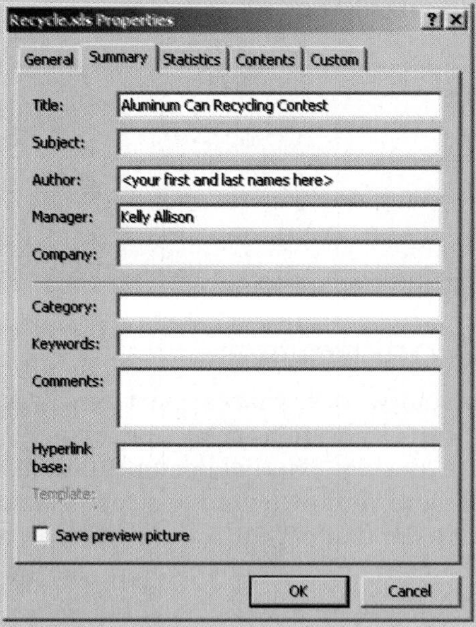

FIGURE 2.31

Completed Properties dialog box

Documenting a worksheet using the Properties dialog box:

1. Click **File** on the menu bar, click **Properties,** and click the **Summary** tab, if necessary

2. In the Title text box, type **Aluminum Can Recycling Contest** and then press the **Tab** key twice to move to the Author text box

3. Type your first and last names in the Author text box and then press the **Tab** key

4. In the Manager text box, type **Kelly Allison** (see Figure 2.31)

5. Click **OK** to close the Properties dialog box

Adding Cell Comments

Kelly also wants you to place a note in cell A1 indicating that the two-cent per can recycling value is approximate. This will help others who use the worksheet in the future to understand that the value is a variable that anyone can change to observe changes in potential revenue from recycling. In cell B5, Kelly wants you to place a comment indicating the source of the population numbers—the World Wide Web.

Cell comments are analogous to sticky notes on which you can write reminders and attach to paper. Like sticky notes, cell comments can remind a worksheet developer or user about special conditions attached to a worksheet or cell, explain any restrictions on user input values, or provide an outline of the steps required to complete an unfinished worksheet.

---

task reference

Inserting a comment

- Click the cell to which you want to add a comment
- Click **Insert** and then click **Comment** to display the comment text box
- Type the comment
- Click any other cell to close and store the comment

Create the cell comment that Kelly asked you to insert in cells A1 and B5.

Insert comment in cells:

1. Click cell **A1** to make it the active cell

2. Click **Insert** and then click the **Comment** command. The comment text box opens

3. If the comment text box contains text, such as a user or computer name, delete the text.

4. Type **Kelly Allison:** (type a space after the colon)

5. Continue by typing the text **Per can value is an approximation. Change it for revenue what-if analysis.** (Be sure to include a period to end the comment's second sentence)

6. Click cell **B5,** click **Insert,** and click **Comment**

7. Repeat steps 3 and 4

8. Type **Population figures obtained from the World Wide Web.** and click any cell besides cell B5 to complete the comment and close the text box

9. View the hidden comment by hovering the mouse pointer over cell **A1.** The Comment text box pops up (see Figure 2.32)

10. Hover the mouse pointer over cell **B5** to view that cell's comment

---

EXCEL

FIGURE 2.32

Viewing a cell comment

red triangle indicates cell
contains a comment

comment text box

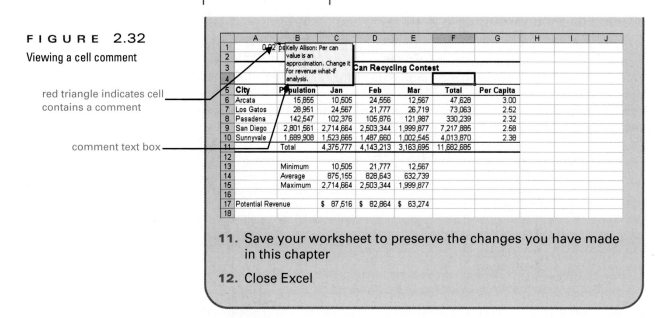

	A	B	C	D	E	F	G	H	I	J
1	0.02 pe	Kelly Allison: Per can								
2		value is an								
3		approximation. Change it		Can Recycling Contest						
4		for revenue what-if								
		analysis.								
5	City	Population	Jan	Feb	Mar	Total	Per Capita			
6	Arcata	15,855	10,505	24,556	12,567	47,628	3.00			
7	Los Gatos	28,951	24,567	21,777	26,719	73,063	2.52			
8	Pasadena	142,547	102,376	105,876	121,987	330,239	2.32			
9	San Diego	2,801,561	2,714,664	2,503,344	1,999,877	7,217,885	2.58			
10	Sunnyvale	1,689,908	1,523,665	1,487,660	1,002,545	4,013,870	2.38			
11		Total	4,375,777	4,143,213	3,163,695	11,682,685				
12										
13		Minimum	10,505	21,777	12,567					
14		Average	875,155	828,643	632,739					
15		Maximum	2,714,664	2,503,344	1,999,877					
16										
17	Potential Revenue		$ 87,516	$ 82,864	$ 63,274					
18										

11. Save your worksheet to preserve the changes you have made in this chapter

12. Close Excel

anotherway

. . . to Insert a
Comment

Right-click the cell to
which you want to insert
a comment

Click **Insert Comment**
on the shortcut menu

Type the comment, and
then click outside the
comment text box

To delete a comment, select the cell containing the comment you wish to delete. Then click Edit on the menu bar, point to Clear, and click Comments to delete the selected cell's comment.

SESSION 2.3 SUMMARY

Enter a value or text into an Excel cell by selecting the cell and typing the value or text. Excel formulas such as $=D3-B4$ begin with an equal sign to indicate the entry is not text. Excel provides AutoSum to automatically build a SUM function whose argument is an adjacent, contiguous row or column of values or expressions resulting in values. When necessary, you can adjust the AutoSum cell range suggested by Excel.

Excel provides standard mathematical operators of exponentiation, multiply, divide, add, and subtract. The mathematical operators conform to a precedence order that dictates which parts of an expression are evaluated before other parts. When you want to alter the order in which Excel evaluates expressions in a formula, you can use parentheses to group parts of the formula. For example, you use parentheses to cause Excel to evaluate the expression $A1+B2$ first in the formula $=B17*(A1+B2)$ even though addition has lower precedence than multiplication.

Three other important statistical functions Excel provides are MIN, AVERAGE, and MAX. MIN determines the smallest value of its arguments. AVERAGE calculates the average value of its argument list. MAX displays the largest value in its list of arguments. Similar to other functions, these three statistical functions ignore empty cells or text cells in argument cell ranges. You can write arguments in the argument list in any order.

Most spreadsheet projects include formulas that are similar to one another. Take advantage of Excel's ability to quickly create formulas by copying a formula to other cells. When you copy a formula such as $=SUM(A1:A4)$ to another cell, Excel creates a copy of that formula and *adjusts* all cell references to reflect the copied formula's new position. Cell adjustment is automatic when you use *relative* cell references. When you do not want Excel to adjust selected cell references in a copied formula, then you must use either *mixed* or *absolute* cell references. Moving a cell's contents to another location has no effect on the formula—all cell references remain unaltered.

making the grade

1. Briefly describe how you might test a worksheet to determine whether its formulas are correct.

2. If you make a mistake in entering a formula, you can reverse the operation by executing the _____ command on the _____ menu.

3. Which of the following is the correct formula to add cells B4 and A5 and multiply the sum by cell C2?
   a. =C2*B4+A5
   b. =B4+A5*C2
   c. =(B4+A5)*C2
   d. =B4+(A5*C2)
   e. none of the above is correct

4. Suppose cell A5 contains the formula =C1+D12 and you *move* that cell's contents to cell C6. After the move, what is the formula in cell C6?
   a. =E2+F3
   b. =C1+D2
   c. =B1+D12
   d. =none of the preceding

5. Modify the recycle worksheet, **Recycle.xls,** in the following ways. In cell **G11** write a formula that will compute the overall average per capita values stored in cells G6 through G10. Move the Total label in cell **B11** to cell **A11.** (You notice that moving a cell's contents removes the source cell's formatting. You will restore that in a moment.) Type a formula in B11 that will compute the total population of the five cities in the contest. Write a formula in cell **F17** to sum the potential revenue row. In **F16,** type **Total Revenue** to identify the summation of revenue. Clear the Print Area so that the entire worksheet prints. Select the cell range **A3:G11** and reformat it with the AutoFormat Simple style. Click cell **A1** to deselect the cell range. Save the worksheet under the name **Recycle2.xls.** Print the worksheet and then print the worksheet formulas.

Insert additional rows or columns into a worksheet wherever needed. Select a cell above which you wish to insert additional rows or to the left of which you wish to insert additional columns and then execute the Insert Rows or Insert Columns command. Excel automatically adjusts all formulas affected by the Insert procedure to reflect the new location of referenced cells, regardless of whether the cell references are relative, mixed, or absolute. Deleting one or more rows or columns is equally simple. Select the row(s) or column(s) to delete and then execute the Edit menu Delete command. When you delete cells, Microsoft Excel removes them from the worksheet and shifts the surrounding cells to fill the space.

Formatting modifies the appearance of cells, but not their contents. AutoFormat provides a predefined set of formats you can apply to a cell range, or you can format cells individually with the Format menu. Correct any mistakes, including unwanted formatting, by executing the Undo command in the Edit menu. If pound signs (#) appear in a cell indicating a column is too narrow to display the formatted numeric value, widen the column or columns by dragging the column heading dividing line located on the right side of the column's label.

Before printing a worksheet, preview your output. If necessary, adjust a worksheet's print margins by executing Page Setup in the File menu and clicking the Margins tab. Set a worksheet's Print Area to specify printing less than all the non-empty worksheet cells. Document a workbook by filling in the text boxes found in the Properties dialog box that you access from the File menu. In addition, you can use comments to attach internal notes to worksheet cells to explain any unusual circumstances or remind the worksheet user or developer about the content of selected cells.

MOUS OBJECTIVES SUMMARY

- Create formulas containing cell references and mathematical operators (MOUS Ex2002-5-1)
- Write functions including Sum, Average, Max, and Min (MOUS Ex2002-5-2)
- Differentiate between absolute, mixed, and relative cell reference (MOUS Ex2002-5-1)
- Adjust column widths (MOUS Ex2002-3-2)
- Set a print area (MOUS Ex2002-3-7)
- Move text, values, and formulas (MOUS Ex2002-1-1)
- Insert and delete rows and columns (MOUS Ex2002-3-2)
- Format cells (MOUS Ex2002-3-1)
- Create cell comments (MOUS Ex2002-7-3)

task reference roundup

Task	Location	Preferred Method
Writing formulas	EX 2.9	• Select a cell, type **5**, type the formula, press **Enter**
Modifying an AutoSum cell range by pointing	EX 2.11	• Press an arrow key repeatedly to select leftmost or topmost cell in range, press and hold **Shift**, select cell range with arrow keys, release **Shift**, press **Enter**
Writing a function using the Insert Function command	EX 2.17	• Click a cell, click **Insert**, click **Function**, click the *Or select a category* list, click the Function category, scroll the list to locate the function you want, click the function, click **OK**, complete the Function Arguments dialog box, and click **OK**
Copying and pasting a cell or range of cells	EX 2.21	• Select source cell(s), click **Edit**, click **Copy**, select target cell(s), click **Edit**, click **Paste**
Copying cell contents using a cell's fill handle	EX 2.23	• Select source cell(s), drag the fill handle to the source cell(s) range, release the mouse button
Changing relative references to absolute or mixed references	EX 2.27	• Double-click the cell, move insertion point to the cell reference, press **F4** repeatedly as needed, press **Enter**
Moving cells' contents	EX 2.29	• Select the cell(s), move the mouse pointer to an edge of the selected range, click the edge of the selected cell or cell range, drag the outline to the destination location, release the mouse
Spell-checking a worksheet	EX 2.31	• Click cell **A1**, click the **Spelling** [icon] button, correct any mistakes, click **OK**
Inserting rows	EX 2.34	• Click a cell, click **Insert**, click **Rows**
Inserting columns	EX 2.34	• Click a cell, click **Insert**, click **Columns**
Applying AutoFormat to cells	EX 2.36	• Select a cell range, click **Format**, click **AutoFormat**, select a format style, click **OK**
Modifying a column's width	EX 2.39	• Select the column heading(s), click **Format**, point to **Column**, click **Width**, type column width, and click **OK**
Inserting a comment	EX 2.45	• Click a cell, click **Insert**, click **Comment**, type a comment, and click another cell

EXCEL

CROSSWORD PUZZLE

Across

5. This list is enclosed in parentheses
7. A mathematical _____ that represents an arithmetic operation
9. General name for cells to which other cells are copied
11. This dialog box contains fields such as Title and Subject that you fill in to provide additional documentation

Down

1. Type of internal documentation, or note, attached to a cell
2. Rules governing the way you write Excel functions
3. A _____ cell is a cell upon which a formula depends
4. When you do this to cells, it changes their appearance but not their contents
6. General name for cells that are being copied
8. The _____ finder color codes cells referenced by the formula you are editing
10. This value occurs when you make a mistake writing a formula

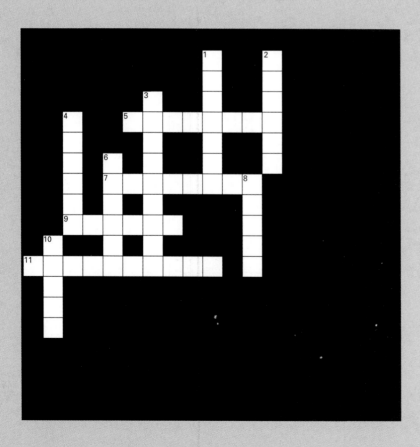

FILL-IN

1. The _____ function totals one or more cells.

2. While writing a formula, you can use a technique called _____ to select a cell range rather than using the keyboard to type the cell range.

3. _____ order determines the sequence in which Excel evaluates expressions containing addition, subtraction, multiplication, division, or exponentiation.

4. If you copy a formula such as =B4−C9, Excel does what to the copied formula's cell references?

5. There are three types of cell references: relative, _____, and _____.

6. The menu bar _____ command helps you write a function and fill in the arguments.

REVIEW QUESTIONS

1. Suppose cell D1 contains 0.14, the proposed salary percentage increase for next year, and cells B5 through B8 contain current salaries. Next year's increased salaries—computed from formulas—are in cells C5 through C8. All other cells are empty. You write the formula **=B5*(1+D1)** in cell C5 and then copy that formula to cells C6 through C8. Explain, briefly, what is wrong with the original formula in cell C5 and how you would correct it before recopying the formula.

2. If Excel did not have an AVERAGE function, how would you write an expression to compute the average of cells A5 through A10 using other Excel functions?

3. Describe in two or three sentences what Excel does to modify *copied* formulas.

4. Briefly describe what Excel does, if anything, to the contents of a formula that you *move* to another location. What happens, if anything, to formulas that refer to a moved cell?

5. Does formatting a cell alter its contents? Explain.

6. Experiment with Excel to answer this question. Describe what happens when you enlarge or narrow a column having an unformatted cell whose formula is =1/7?

CREATE THE QUESTION

For each of the following answers, create an appropriate, short question.

ANSWER	QUESTION
1. Builds a SUM function automatically	_____
2. Provides a variety of predefined formats	_____
3. Do this to view worksheet output before printing	_____
4. Set this to restrict the cells that Excel prints	_____
5. This command can reverse a mistake you made in the previous operation	_____
6. Dragging this object copies formulas to other cells	_____

1. Managing Employees' Work Hours

You are a project manager for Wexler's Tool and Die Manufacturing and manage a group of five people. Each employee in your group has a different hourly rate, and you must record on a weekly basis the number of hours each employee works, the total wages per employee, and percentage of the whole group's wages that each employee's weekly wage represents. Keeping the information on a worksheet is the most efficient way to record and report employee activity. Alan Gin, the company's Chief Operating Officer, wants you to prepare an Excel worksheet to report your group's weekly hours and gross wages. You create a worksheet to track the hours and wages.

1. Open the workbook **ex02Wages.xls** and save it as **Wages2.xls**
2. Review the Documentation sheet and then click the **Sheet2** tab to move to that worksheet
3. Widen column A so that all the employees' names are entirely visible
4. Insert two new rows above row 1: Click cell **C1**, drag through cell **C2**, and release the mouse. Click **Insert** on the Menu bar and then click **Rows**
5. Click cell **A1** to deselect the range and type **Employee**
6. Click cell **B1**, type **Rate**, click cell **C1**, type **Hours**, click cell **D1**, type **Wages**, click cell **E1**, and type **Percentage**
7. Type the following employee hours in the corresponding cells:
   Cell B3: **25**
   Cell B4: **40**
   Cell B5: **30**
   Cell B6: **20**
   Cell B7: **35**
8. Click cell **D3**, type **=B3*C3**, the formula to compute Bushyeager's wage, and press **Enter**
9. Copy Bushyeager's wage formula to the cell range **D4:D7**
10. Click cell **B8** and type **Totals**
11. Select cell range **C8:D8** and click the **AutoSum** Σ button

12. Click cell **E3** and type the formula that represents the employee's percentage of the total wages: **=D3/D$8*100**
13. Copy the formula in cell **E3** to the cell range **E4:E7**
14. Select cell range **A1:E8**, click **Format**, click **AutoFormat**, select the **Simple** format, and click **OK**
15. Select cell range **E3:E7** and click the **Decrease Decimal** button enough times to reduce the displayed percentages to two decimal places
16. Click cell **A10** and type your first and last names
17. Set the left, right, top, and bottom margins to two inches
18. Either execute **Print** or execute **Save As**, according to your instructor's direction

2. Creating an Invoice

As office manager of Randy's Foreign Cars, one of your duties is to produce and mail invoices to customers who have arranged to pay for their automobile repairs up to 30 days after mechanics perform the work. Randy's invoices include parts, sales tax on parts, and labor charges. State law stipulates that customers do not pay sales tax on the labor charges. Only parts are subject to state sales tax. State sales tax is 6 percent. Create and print an invoice whose details appear below.

1. Open the workbook **ex02Randys.xls** on your student disk in folder **Ch02**
2. Insert rows in which you can enter the customer's name and address: Click cell **A5**, drag the mouse down through cell **A8**, and release the mouse
3. Click **Insert** and then click **Rows**
4. Type the following in the indicated cells:
   cell A5: **Customer**:
   cell B5: **Craig Shaffer**
   cell B6: **21121 Bluff Place**
   cell B7: **Lincoln, NE**
5. Click cell **E11** and type the extended price (unit price times quantity) formula: **=A11*D11**

6. Select **E11** and drag its fill handle to copy the formula in E11 to cells **E12** through **E15**

7. Click cell **E17,** drag the mouse down to cell **E18,** release the mouse, click **Insert,** and then click **Rows**

8. Click cell **D17** and type **Subtotal.** Click cell **D18** and type **Tax.** Click Cell **D24** and type **Subtotal,** and click cell **D26** and type **Total**

9. Widen column C by moving the mouse to the dividing line between columns C and D. When the mouse pointer changes to a resize arrow, double-click the mouse

10. Click cell **E17** and type **=SUM(E11:E15)**

11. Click cell **E18** and type **=E17*B1**

12. Click cell **E24** and type **=D21+D22**

13. Click Cell **D26** and type **=SUM(E17,E18,E24)**

> **tip:** *Typing commas between the single-cell references allows you to sum cells that are not adjacent to one another*

14. Click cell **E11** and drag through cell **E26** to select the cell range

15. Click once the **Increase Decimal** button on the Formatting toolbar

16. Select cell range **A2:E26** and then click **File, Print Area, Set Print Area**

17. Click cell **D5**, type your first and last names, and save the worksheet as **Randys2.xls**

18. Either **Print** the worksheet or execute **Save As,** according to your instructor's direction

1. Building a Product Comparison Worksheet

Jacob's Fine Stationers carries different lines of fine pens. You have been asked to help them figure out the profits the store generates from pen sales. The information is as follows: The store has 20 Stylo pens in stock, which sell for $27 each and cost the store $8 each. There are 15 Royal pens in stock, which sell for $45 and cost the store $12. There are 50 Hans pens in the store, which sell for $78 and cost the store $50. There are 6 Tower pens in stock, which sell for $120 and cost the store $60.

Create a spreadsheet with the following column labels: **Pen, Quantity, Cost,** and **Price**. Enter the pen names Stylo, Royal, Hans, and Tower in the column headed by the label "Pen." Write formulas below the Quantity, Cost, and Price columns that indicate the minimum, average, and maximum values for Quantity, Cost, and Price. Create a column labeled **Profit per Pen.** Create a formula and copy it to fill in these cells with the difference between price and cost. Create a column labeled **Total Profits per Pen.** Fill the cells in this column with formulas that multiply profit per pen by quantity in stock for each pen. Add a formula below the last entry in the Total Profits per Pen to compute total profits for all pens, assuming all pens in stock sell.

Widen any columns as needed to view column-top labels. Insert two rows at the top of the worksheet and type your first and last names. Select all numeric cells and then click the Increase Decimal button enough times to display two decimal places for numbers. Print the worksheet.

Change a cell in the worksheet to answer this question: If the store decides not to sell any of their Royal pens, how will total profits be affected? (Type 0 in the Quantity cell for the Royal pen.) Add text to the worksheet indicating that this shows what happens to the total profits if Royal pens are not sold. Print the worksheet.

2. Writing a Payroll Worksheet

Bateman Leisure Properties wants you to create a payroll worksheet that provides management with an overview of the hourly workers' pay and taxes. Alicia Hernandez, the human resources manager, provides you with a preliminary worksheet containing employee names—there are quite a few—column labels, and some tax rate information. She asks you to complete the worksheet and save it under a new name when you are done. She would like you to document the tax rate cell and the overtime rate cell with short comments. In preparation for this exercise, open the workbook **ex02Payroll.xls** stored on your disk (see Figure 2.33).

Start by writing a formula for Patti Stonesifer's gross pay. Compute gross pay as regular pay plus overtime pay. Regular pay is the employee's pay for up to 40 hours and is computed as hourly rate times hours worked. Overtime pay is paid for overtime hours—any hours over 40. Compute overtime pay at an hourly rate that is 1.5 times the regular rate times the overtime hours. Be sure to reference cell C2 in the gross pay formula using a mixed cell reference form, C$2 instead of using the constant 1.5. When her gross pay formula is correct, copy it down through the remaining employees' gross pay cells.

In the Federal Tax column, write one formula and copy it to the other employees' rows. Federal tax is gross pay times the federal tax rate found in

FIGURE 2.33

Payroll worksheet

	A	B	C	D	E	F	G	H	I
1		Fed. Tax R	0.25						
2		Overtime r	1.5						
3				Hourly	Regular	Overtime	Gross	Federal	Net
4	ID	First Name	Last Name	Rate	Hours	Hours	Pay	Tax	Pay
5	1301	Patti	Stonesifer	23.10	40	13			
6	1364	Kevin	Pruski	17.00	22				
7	1528	Luca	Pacioli	19.70	40	8			
8	1695	Ted	Nagasaki	21.80	40				
9	2240	Sharon	Stonely	20.30	13				
10	2318	Helen	Hunter	19.50	40	18			
11	2754	Phillipe	Kahn	16.20	40	19			
12	3370	David	Kole	18.70	19				
13	3432	Melinda	English	24.70	40	16			
14	3436	William	Gates	22.50	14				
15	3458	Alanis	Morrison	25.00	26				
16	3609	Annie	Chang	16.40	17				
17	3692	Steve	Ballmer	18.20	40	11			
18	3700	Larry	Ellison	18.80	24				
19	3892	Brad	Shoensteir	18.60	30				
20	3943	Barbara	Watterson	24.30	40	12			
21	4012	Barbara	Minsky	23.10	40	15			
22	4029	Sharad	Manispour	16.60	32				
23	4057	Giles	Bateman	17.60	40	4			
24	4058	Whitney	Halstead	24.20	24				
25	4082	Hillary	Flintsteel	22.00	40	19			
26	4112	Ted	Goldman	23.90	13				

cell C1. Be sure to reference cell C1 using the mixed reference, C$1. Otherwise, you will not get the correct answer. Write a formula for net pay, remembering that net pay is gross pay minus federal tax (in this example). Copy the net pay formula to other employees' cells.

Next, widen columns B and C so that all names and tax rates are completely visible. Add a blank row between the column labels and the first employee row. Select the Federal Tax Rate value stored in cell C1 and type this comment: **This is a flat tax rate for experimentation.** Click the overtime rate cell and type the comment **Normal overtime rate is 1.5 times regular rate. Change this value to review overall changes to gross pay.** (If the comments remain visible after you press Enter, you can make them disappear by clicking **Tools** on the menu bar, clicking **Options,**

clicking the **View** tab, and clicking the **Comment indicator only** option button in the Comments section.) Select all cells in the Gross Pay, Federal Tax, and Net Pay columns displaying values, click the Decrease Decimals button once, and then click the Increase Decimal button once to display two decimal places for all selected cells.

Create a header in page setup, placing your name in the worksheet header (in the Center section), and then print the worksheet. Print the Gross Pay, Federal Tax, and Net Pay formulas for all employee rows. (Hint: Check the Formulas option on the View tab of the Options dialog box. Set the print area to include only the three columns containing formulas.). Save the worksheet under the name **Payroll2.xls.**

1. Selecting an Online Broker

Erik Engvall is trying to decide which online brokerage firm he should use for trading stocks. After some research, he came up with the following list of five online brokerages that are highly rated. The brokerages are Ameritrade, Charles Schwab & Co., Datek Online Brokerage Services, DLJ Direct, and Fidelity. Figure 2.34 shows the Web addresses of each of these online brokers. To help Eric, you will use the Web to look up how much each service charges for stock transactions. The annual fees vary and are sometimes difficult to find. Assume that the annual charges are as follows: Ameritrade—$49, Charles Schwab—$35, Datek—$20, DLJ Direct—$40, and Fidelity—$50. (The preceding fees are contrived costs—the listed online brokers have different annual fees or none at all.) Arrange this information in columns, with each brokerage firm in a separate row.

Label the columns the following way: **Company, Price per Trade,** and **Annual Fee.** In a cell, enter **4**, which is the number of brokerage transactions per month that Erik estimates he executes with a broker. (That number will be the what-if analysis value you can change to determine the overall cost differences between the brokers you have selected.) Write formulas to compute the minimum, average, and maximum charge per transaction and formulas to compute the minimum, average, and maximum annual fee. Create a column labeled **Total Cost per Month** and label another column to the right of the monthly cost column called **Total Yearly Cost.** Beneath the Total Cost per Month column, write a formula for each brokerage indicating the cost for four transactions (refer to a cell containing 4 that you created earlier). Write formulas for each brokerage row indicating the total annual cost, assuming Erik continues to execute four transactions per month for the year. Remember to add the annual fee.

You forgot to include another important brokerage, E*Trade. Insert a new row between DLJ Direct and Fidelity and enter **E*Trade** under the Company column. Complete the information in the E*Trade row including Price per Trade. Assume they do not charge an annual fee. Copy formulas from DLJ Direct to complete E*Trade's missing formulas.

Use the **Increase Decimal** button on the Formatting menu to cause all numeric entries to display two decimal places. Widen columns as necessary so all entries including brokerage names and column labels display completely. Place your name in your worksheet to identify it and then print the worksheet. Save your worksheet in the Ch02 folder as **Brokerage2.xls.** Based on this information, which online broker is the least expensive?

FIGURE 2.34

Brokerage Web addresses

Brokerage	Web Address
Ameritrade	www.ameritrade.com/
Charles Schwab	www.schwab.com/
Datek	www.datek.com/
DLJ Direct	www.dljdirect.com/
E*Trade	www.etrade.com/
Fidelity	www.fidelity.com/

e-business

1. Investigating E-Commerce Service Providers

Green Gardens is a one-stop gardening store located in Lincoln, Nebraska. They have been a successful brick-and-mortar store for over 22 years, but their owner, Orlando Madrigal, wants to create an online store that will complement their existing store. Because they do not have room nor the expertise to buy computing equipment and software to create an online store, Orlando wants to locate a commerce service provider (CSP) to host the store and provide a complete menu of online services. The CSP provides computer hardware, commerce software, and merchant account processing (to process credit cards). There are several hosting plans available, and each one offers the same basic service. Orlando wants you to find a least-cost provider.

Your investigation reveals that most CSPs charge a one-time setup fee when you sign up for their service, monthly store rental fee to pay for disk space, and transaction fees charged when a customer submits his or her credit card to pay for a purchase. You have found four representative CSPs and want to create a worksheet to compare your costs. Orlando estimates that the online store can sell approximately 10,000 items each month for the first year. Each sale, he estimates, will average $50. Armed with those sales assumptions, you build a worksheet to compare CSP costs.

Figure 2.35 shows the partially complete worksheet. You are to complete the sheet by filling in formulas for the estimated annual cost, the minimum annual cost, and the six statistics showing the minimum, average, and maximum setup fees and monthly rental fee.

Begin by opening the E-Commerce worksheet **ex02E-Merchant.xls** in the folder Ch02 on your student disk. Save the file under the name **E-Merchant2.xls**. Annual costs consist of the sum of the one-time setup fee (for the first year), 12 times the monthly rental fee, and the transaction costs. The transaction costs consist of a fixed per-transaction charge, shown in Column D of Figure 2.35, and a percentage charge for each transaction. For example, Yoddle charges 15 cents for each transaction plus 2.1 percent of the transaction value. In other words, Yoddle charges a transaction cost for selling one $10 garden implement of $0.15 + 0.021 * 10, or a total of $0.36. The four formulas for estimated annual cost should reference the monthly transactions value in cell B1 and the average transaction value, $50, in cell B2.

Print the worksheet and print the worksheet formulas. Based on Orlando's transaction volume and per-transaction value assumptions, which CSP is the least expensive? Which one is the most expensive?

FIGURE 2.35

E-Commerce hosting cost comparison

	A	B	C	D	E	F
1	Monthly Transactions:	10000				
2	Average Trans. Value: ($)	50				
3						Estimated
4		One-time	Monthly	Per-Transaction Costs		Annual
5	Host	Setup Fee	Rental Fee	Fixed ($)	Variable (%)	Cost
6	ClickEnsure	500	200	0	0.016	
7	HostWay	200	400	0.25	0.015	
8	ShopSmart	0	250	0.12	0.017	
9	Yoddle	125	100	0.15	0.021	
10						
11	Minimum				Minimum	
12	Average					
13	Maximum					

write formulas for estimated annual cost

write a formula for minimum annual cost

write statistical formulas for setup and monthly rental

around the world

1. Comparing Living Expenses Around the World

What does it cost to live for a month in a foreign country? You've been considering living in Europe or South America for a month next summer and want to know the total cost of living abroad. Costs include an apartment locator agency fee, one month's rental charges, the cost of food, utilities, transportation to the foreign country, and transportation costs within the country for the month. Using the Web, research the cost of renting a one-bedroom apartment in Florence (Italy), Paris, Buenos Aires, and Santiago. Include cell comments for each city indicating the source—Web URL or other reference—for your rental cost information. Document the workbook by entering information in the Properties dialog box. Print the worksheet.

running project

Pampered Paws

Besides providing pet sitting services, Pampered Paws has a complete line of pet products. Grace Jackson, the company founder and owner, wants to compare the profitability of five different dog food products she's interested in selling. There are several costs associated with purchasing dog food in bulk. A wholesaler, from which Grace purchases the dog food, charges a fixed order fee of $100, a one-time fee charged for each order any customer places with the wholesaler. Bags of dog food costs vary, depending on brand. Shipping costs $0.10 per pound, and the shipper charges $25 to deliver the product to the store. Figure 2.36 shows Pampered Paws' cost and the retail price Pampered Paws can charge for each of the five dog food products in 10-pound bags.

Create a worksheet showing the total cost of each of the products if Grace orders 50 bags of each of the five products. Compute the total profit Grace's store can realize if she sells 50 bags of each of the products. Remember to include the shipping and delivery charges in your calculations. Figure 2.37 displays one way you might organize your worksheet. Wherever the notation *xxxxx* appears in the worksheet, you should create a formula.

FIGURE 2.36

Dog food cost comparison

Brand	Wholesale cost per bag	Retail price per bag
Eukanuba	16.09	22.99
Iams	12.71	16.95
Nutro	12.67	19.49
Pro Plan	11.01	18.99
Vita Rx	13.93	16.99

FIGURE 2.37

Example dog food comparison

	A	B	C	D	E	F
1	Dog Food Cost Comparison					
2						
3	Assumptions:					
4	Order fee ($):		100			
5	Shipping/lb. ($)		0.1			
6	Delivery ($)		25			
7						
8	Purchase				Extended	Extended
9	Quantity (bags)	Brand	Cost	Price	Cost	Price
10	50	Eukanuba	16.09	22.99	xxx.x	xxx.x
11	50	Iams	12.71	16.95	xxx.x	xxx.x
12	50	Nutro	12.67	19.49	xxx.x	xxx.x
13	50	Pro Plan	11.01	18.99	xxx.x	xxx.x
14	50	Vita Rx	13.93	16.99	xxx.x	xxx.x
15				Subtotal	xxxx.x	xxxx.x
16						
17			Order fee	xxx		
18			Shipping	xx		
19			Delivery	xx		
20				Subtotal	xxx	
21						
22				Total	xxxx.x	xxxx.x
23						
24				Net Profit		xxxx

CHAPTER

3

three

Formatting a
Worksheet

did you

know?

the *city in the United States that purchases the most ice cream on a per capita basis is Portland, Oregon.*

the *Great Lakes have a combined area of 94,230 square miles — larger than the states of New York, New Jersey, Connecticut, Rhode Island, Massachusetts, and Vermont combined.*

"However *fascinating it may be as scholarly achievement, there is virtually nothing that has come from molecular biology that can be of any value to human living."—Nobel Prize-winning immunologist Frank MacFarlane Burnett (1899–1985) whose work made organ transplantation possible.*

paul Saffo, *a director of the Institute for the Future, in February 1996 predicted the Web would mutate into "something else very quickly and be unrecognizable within 12 months."*

bricks *are the oldest manufactured building material still in use. Egyptians used them 7,000 years ago.*

you *can attach graphic objects to your worksheet. Read this chapter to find out how.*

Chapter Objectives

- Left-, center-, and right-align text (MOUS Ex2002-3)

- Apply currency and accounting formats to numbers
  (MOUS Ex2002-3-1)

- Modify the typeface and point size of text and numbers
  (MOUS Ex2002-3-1)

- Apply boldface, italic, and underline to cells
  (MOUS Ex2002-3-1)

- Clear all formatting from selected cells (MOUS Ex2002-3;
  Ex2002-1-2)

- Modify column widths and row heights (MOUS Ex2002-3-3)

- Hide and reveal rows and columns (MOUS Ex2002-3-2)

- Remove worksheet gridlines

- Modify a worksheet's print characteristics
  (MOUS Ex2002-3-7)

chapter case

The Exotic Fruit Company

The Exotic Fruit Company is a wholesale exotic fruits, nuts, and roots distributor headquartered in La Mesa, California. Exotic Fruit's customers include most of the large grocery store chains in the western United States. Corporate buyers for the grocery stores contract with Specialty Fruits to supply and ship exotic fruits to stores' warehouses scattered throughout the West. Exotic Fruit's chief procurement officer, Nancy Carroll, oversees the purchase and distribution operations for all divisions from her La Mesa office.

Exotic Fruit also maintains a small Web site from which it sells exotic fruit to consumers. While the online store is not a large part of their revenue stream, it is an essential and growing part of Exotic Fruit's business. Nancy has asked her financial analyst to quickly develop a sales forecast for the coming year of selected exotic fruits, using the previous year's figures as the basis of the projection. Nancy wants to investigate sales predictions based on the assumption that next year's wholesale sales will increase by approximately 10 percent for each product included in the projection.

Due to time constraints, her financial analyst, Angel Hernandez, did not have time to format the worksheet. Consequently, the worksheet looks unprofessional and, frankly, it is a little difficult to read and understand. While Nancy understands that Angel is stretched to the limit and has little time to format the projection, Nancy wants to improve the worksheet's appearance. She asks you to spend a little time formatting it so that the labels and numbers are easier to read and the entire worksheet is ready for presentation at the annual board meeting next month.

Figure 3.1 shows the completed Exotic Fruit Sales Forecast worksheet. You will be developing the worksheet in this chapter beginning with a fundamental worksheet that Nancy and Angel provide for you.

FIGURE 3.1

Exotic Fruit Sales Forecast worksheet

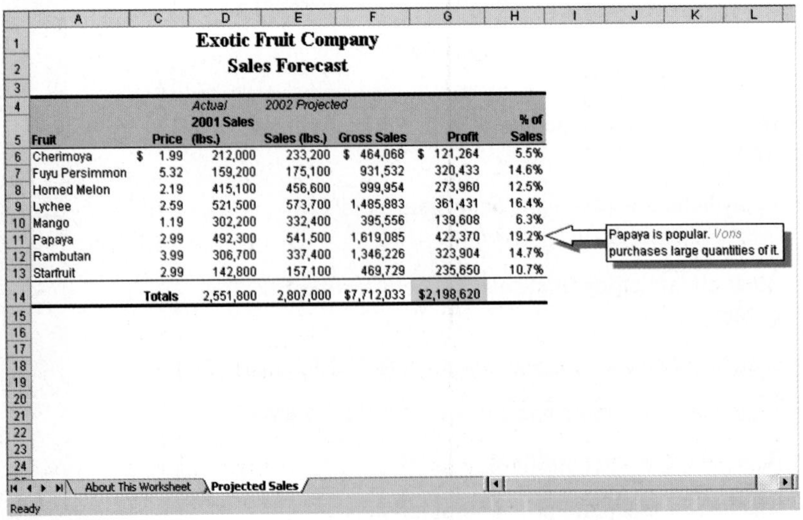

Exotic Fruit Company

Sales Forecast

Fruit	Price	Actual 2001 Sales (lbs.)	2002 Projected Sales (lbs.)	Gross Sales	Profit	% of Sales
Cherimoya	$ 1.99	212,000	233,200	$ 464,068	$ 121,264	5.5%
Fuyu Persimmon	5.32	159,200	175,100	931,532	320,433	14.6%
Horned Melon	2.19	415,100	456,600	999,954	273,960	12.5%
Lychee	2.59	521,500	573,700	1,485,883	361,431	16.4%
Mango	1.19	302,200	332,400	395,556	139,608	6.3%
Papaya	2.99	492,300	541,500	1,619,085	422,370	19.2%
Rambutan	3.99	306,700	337,400	1,346,226	323,904	14.7%
Starfruit	2.99	142,800	157,100	469,729	235,650	10.7%
	Totals	2,551,800	2,807,000	$7,712,033	$2,198,620	

INTRODUCTION

Chapter 3 covers formatting. In this chapter you will open and use an existing worksheet—complete with formulas, text, and values—and apply various formats to its cells. Formats that you will apply include aligning numeric results in columns by their decimal places, controlling the number of decimal places that display, and displaying currency symbols for column-heading monetary values. Other formatting you will apply includes indenting a label and formatting the worksheet title and subtitle by merging several cells and centering the title in the merged cells. Drawing objects can add interest to a worksheet, and Excel has several drawing objects from which you can choose. You will add two of the available objects—an arrow and a text box—to the highlighted example used in this chapter. The chapter concludes by describing ways to customize printing a worksheet including selecting either landscape or portrait orientation, centering output on the page, and printing multiple worksheets at once.

SESSION 3.1 ALIGNING DATA AND APPLYING CHARACTER FORMATS

In this section, you will learn how to render your worksheets more professional looking by using various formatting methods. You will format text so that it wraps to a new line within a cell, indent text, format numeric cells with currency and accounting numbers, paint existing formats over other cells, and explore other numeric formatting details. You will align data on the right and left edges of cells and across several cells. This section introduces how to modify typefaces, apply boldface, apply underline, and modify a typeface point size.

LOCATING AND OPENING THE WORKBOOK

After Nancy outlines what she wants you to do to the Exotic Fruit worksheet to improve it, you outline what your goal and plans are to complete the worksheet as follows:

- Goal: Format the Exotic Fruit worksheet, without changing any formulas or values, so that it is easier to read and looks professional.

- Information needed to complete the work: Exotic Fruit worksheet and Nancy's outline of the changes she wants.

- New formulas or values needed: None. The worksheet's contents are complete and correct.

Angel has entered all the formulas, values, and text. Consequently, Nancy wants you to focus on formatting the cells to maximize their visual impact. You can accomplish this by formatting individual cells and columns so that numbers and text are formatted and by providing visual cues about data and labels that are related. Nancy wants selected areas of the worksheet to draw the reader's attention—to be formatted to attract attention without overwhelming the worksheet and without making the overall design look garish.

You begin by formatting individual cells and columns to maximize their impact. Then you plan to move on to providing larger, worksheet-wide improvements to help readers discern the different sections of the worksheet and how they are related. Begin by opening the worksheet.

Starting Microsoft Excel:

1. Start Excel

2. Ensure that the Excel application window is maximized

You can open the worksheet. Angel cautioned you that she wants to preserve the original worksheet, **ex03Fruit.xls,** just in case she needs to adjust some of the formulas. She asked you to save the worksheet under a different name before beginning work on it. You will save the worksheet under the name **ExoticFruit.xls,** as a safety measure, before you get deeply involved with worksheet formatting changes.

Opening the ex03Fruit.xls worksheet and saving it under a new name:

1. Click **File** and then click **Open** to display the Excel Open dialog box

2. Locate and then double-click the worksheet **ex03Fruit.xls** to open it. The first sheet, Documentation, opens (see Figure 3.2)

FIGURE 3.2

Exotic Fruit documentation worksheet

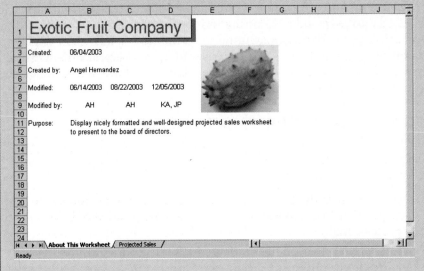

4. Click the **Projected Sales** worksheet tab to move to that worksheet

5. Click **File** on the menu bar, then click **Save As**

6. Click the **File name** text box and type **ExoticFruit.xls** to change the name

7. Click the **Save** button to save the workbook under its new name. Figure 3.3 shows the Exotic Fruit worksheet, Projected Sales. Notice that some labels are partially obscured and that the values are difficult to understand

tip: *If Excel displays a dialog box asking if you want to replace the existing file, click the Yes button to allow Excel to replace an existing version with a new one*

	A	B	C	D	E	F	G	H
1	Exotic Fruit Company							
2	Sales Forecast							
3								
4				Actual	2002 Projected			
5	Fruit	Cost	Price	2001 Sales	Sales (lbs)	Gross Sale	Profit	% of Sales
6	Cherimoya	1.47	1.99	212000	233200	464068	121264	0.055155
7	Fuyu Pers	3.49	5.32	159200	175100	931532	320433	0.145743
8	Horned Me	1.59	2.19	415100	456600	999954	273960	0.124605
9	Lychee	1.96	2.59	521500	573700	1485883	361431	0.16439
10	Mango	0.77	1.19	302200	332400	395556	139608	0.063498
11	Papaya	2.21	2.99	492300	541500	1619085	422370	0.192107
12	Rambutan	3.03	3.99	306700	337400	1346226	323904	0.147322
13	Starfruit	1.49	2.99	142800	157100	469729	235650	0.107181
14			Totals	2551800	2807000	7712033	2198620	

About This Worksheet / **Projected Sales** /

Ready

FIGURE 3.3

The unformatted worksheet, Projected Sales

FORMATTING DATA

Formatting a worksheet is the process of altering the appearance of data in one or more worksheet cells. Formatting is purely cosmetic—changing only the *appearance,* not the contents—of the formulas, values, or text stored in cells. Using the appropriate formatting renders a worksheet easier to read and understand and enhances a worksheet's overall appearance, making it more professional looking. Choosing inappropriate formatting has the opposite effect. It distracts the reader and creates a bad impression that extends beyond the worksheet to the company or activity illustrated by the worksheet.

You have already formatted some cells in the previous chapter. Recall that you used AutoFormat to format both numeric and text cells in one operation. Additionally, you used the increase decimal and decrease decimal buttons to increase or decrease the number of decimal places displayed by cell calculations and values alike. Although AutoFormat is simple to apply, it lacks versatility.

Often, you can provide the exact appearance you desire only by executing particular formatting commands that each make small changes to the appearance of cells. For example, you can apply a currency format with zero decimal places to the value 1234.5678 so that the cell displays $1,234, but the underlying value—the value you typed into the cell—remains unchanged. Only the cell's *appearance* changes. Suppose a cell contains the formula =A1*25.89 and it displays the result 0.6789945. You can format the cell using the Percentage format with two decimal places so that the cell's appearance changes—it displays 67.90% in the cell. When you apply formatting changes to a worksheet carefully, the changes enhance the worksheet tremendously.

By default, Excel formats all worksheet cells with a standard format called General. The *General* format aligns numbers on the right side of a cell, aligns text on the left side, indicates negative numbers with a minus sign on the left side of a number, and displays as many digits in a number as a cell's width allows. When you clear a cell's format, it takes on the General format. General format and no format are synonymous.

You have many ways to format one or more cells. The process begins by selecting the cell range you want to format. Then you can click one or more of the Formatting toolbar buttons to apply various formats to the selected cells or click Format on the menu bar to select formatting alternatives from the menu. Alternatively, you can right-click within the selected range of cells and click Format Cells from the shortcut menu that opens. Applying several formats is a cumulative process of applying one format followed by other formats. For example, you apply bold, italic, and underscore if you want a cell or cell range to display all three formatting characteristics.

Many of the more popular formatting operations appear as buttons on the Formatting toolbar. While many Formatting toolbar icons' graphics adequately describe the formats they apply, others may not. If you have trouble remembering what a particular Formatting toolbar button does, hover the mouse pointer over it and observe the ToolTip that appears within a few seconds. The ToolTip text tersely describes the format that a button applies. Figure 3.4 shows the Formatting toolbar.

FORMATTING NUMERIC ENTRIES

Excel's default numeric format General is not always the best format choice. Numeric entries and formulas that display values should have commas, or thousand separators, every three digits to make the numbers easier to read. The topmost number in a column of numbers representing money should display the currency symbol. Optionally, all values representing money could display the currency symbol. Some values in the Exotic Fruit worksheet represent percents and would look better if they were formatted as percentages with one or two decimal places. Excel provides these formatting choices for cells containing values and many format choices for a wide variety of situations.

Common format choices for numeric entries include General (the default format), Accounting, Currency, Date, Number, Percentage, Scientific, and formats you build yourself called Custom.

- General format displays numbers without commas or currency symbols (the dollar sign in the United States).
- Accounting provides left-aligned dollar signs, comma separators, a specified number of digits after the decimal place, and displays negative numbers inside a pair of parentheses.
- Currency is similar to Accounting, except the currency symbol is just to the left of the most significant digit and negative values are enclosed in parentheses.

F I G U R E   3.4

The Formatting toolbar

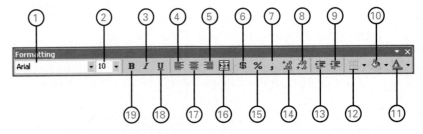

1	Font Style box	6	Currency Style	11	Font Color	16	Merge and Center
2	Font Size box	7	Comma Style	12	Borders	17	Center
3	Italic	8	Decrease Decimal	13	Decrease Indent	18	Underline
4	Align Left	9	Increase Indent	14	Increase Decimal	19	Bold
5	Align Right	10	Fill Color	15	Percent Style		

- Date provides special formats to display month, day, and year.

- Number format lets you designate the number of digits following the decimal place and the option to use comma separators. Negative values display a leading minus sign.

- Percentage inserts a percent sign to the right of the least significant digit and allows you to set the number of decimal places.

- Scientific displays a number between 1 and 10 followed by the letter E representing 10 raised to the exponent that follows E. For example, the number 123.45 formatted with Scientific displays 1.2345E+02, which reads "1.2345 times 10 to the 2nd power." This format is not used much in nonscientific applications.

- Customer allows you to create your own format when none of Excel's built-in number formats is suitable. Consisting of four sections separated by semicolons, you can specify how positive, negative, zero, and text appears with a custom format.

---

task reference

Formatting Numbers

- Select the cell or cell range to which you will apply a format

- Click **Format,** click **Cells,** and click the **Number** tab

- Click the format category you want and then select options for the format choice

- Click **OK** to finalize your format choices and format the selected cell(s)

If you change your mind and decide another format is better, simply select the cell or cell range whose format you want to change, click Format, click Cells, select the new format choices, and click OK.

Applying Accounting and Currency Formats

Reviewing Nancy's Exotic Fruit worksheet, you can see several distinct groups of numeric formats that will improve the worksheet.

another word

. . . on removing all formatting from a cell or cell range

If you decide to remove all formatting from a cell or cell range, select the cell(s) whose formatting you want to remove, click **Edit** on the menu bar, point to **Clear,** and click **Formats.**

Columns B, C, D, F, and G all contain money values and should be formatted with commas. The first entries in those columns and the totals row entries should display currency symbols—a generally accepted format that accountants frequently prefer. Because the values in columns D through G represent relatively large numbers, you will format them so that they do not display any decimal places. Columns B and C, however, represent small numbers and should display two decimal places to represent dollars and cents. Column H represents percentages and should be formatted to look like percentage values. You begin by formatting the whole dollar columns with the Accounting format, no decimal places, and no currency symbol. Then you will come back and add the currency symbol to the top and bottom cells in the range.

Formatting columns D through G with the Accounting format:

1. Select cell range **D6:G14**

2. Click **Format** on the menu bar and click **Cells.** The Format Cells dialog box opens

3. Click the **Number** tab if necessary

4. Click **Accounting** in the Category list box. The Number tab display changes to display options appropriate for the Accounting selection including a list box for decimal places and the currency symbol. Notice that the default number of decimal places (displayed in the Decimal places list box) is 2

4. Type **0** in the Decimal places list box. The default currency symbol is the dollar sign if you installed the U.S. version of Excel

5. Click the **Symbol list box arrow** and then click **None** in the drop-down list (see Figure 3.5)

F I G U R E 3.5

Format Cells dialog box

click the Number tab to display numeric format choices

choose Accounting format category from this list

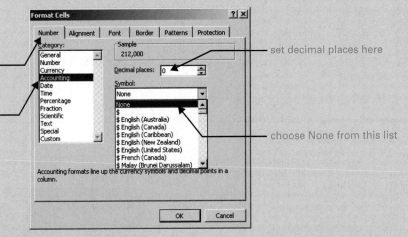

set decimal places here

choose None from this list

6. Click the **OK** button to affirm your formatting choices. The values in the formatted cell range display comma separators and are offset from the right cell wall by one character (see Figure 3.6)

F I G U R E 3.6

Cells with Accounting format and no decimal places

formatted cells

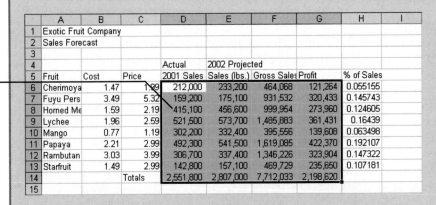

	A	B	C	D	E	F	G	H	I
1	Exotic Fruit Company								
2	Sales Forecast								
3									
4				Actual	2002 Projected				
5	Fruit	Cost	Price	2001 Sales	Sales (lbs.)	Gross Sales	Profit	% of Sales	
6	Cherimoya	1.47	1.99	212,000	233,200	464,068	121,264	0.055155	
7	Fuyu Pers	3.49	5.32	159,200	175,100	931,532	320,433	0.145743	
8	Horned Me	1.59	2.19	415,100	456,600	999,954	273,960	0.124605	
9	Lychee	1.96	2.59	521,500	573,700	1,485,883	361,431	0.16439	
10	Mango	0.77	1.19	302,200	332,400	395,556	139,608	0.063498	
11	Papaya	2.21	2.99	492,300	541,500	1,619,085	422,370	0.192107	
12	Rambutan	3.03	3.99	306,700	337,400	1,346,226	323,904	0.147322	
13	Starfruit	1.49	2.99	142,800	157,100	469,729	235,650	0.107181	
14			Totals	2,551,800	2,807,000	7,712,033	2,198,620		
15									

7. Click any cell to deselect the cell range

Recall from Chapter 2 that a cell displaying a series of pound signs ("######") indicates that the column is too narrow to display the values in the cells as *formatted*. If your display shows a series of pound signs, you must widen the column to see the full formatted number. It is best to wait to widen the columns until you have formatted the remaining numeric values in a column that requires widening. Subtotals and totals, for example, usually are wider than other values because they are the sum of a possible large list of numbers.

Accountants, financial analysts, and others often format the top cell in a column of currency values with the currency symbol. The same is true for cells containing subtotals or totals. Displaying currency symbols on every value in a column creates visual clutter and is distracting.

Next, you will format cells F6 and G6 so that they display leading dollar signs. You want the dollar signs not to appear right next to the most significant (leftmost) digit of the numbers. You choose the Accounting number format with the currency symbol because the currency symbol appears near the left edge of the cell,

Formatting selected cells with the Accounting format and currency symbol:

1. Select cell range **F6:G6**

3. Click **Format** on the menu bar and then click **Cells**

4. Click the **Number** tab if necessary. Notice that the Category list highlights the Accounting category because that is the format assigned to all the selected cells. Notice also that the number of decimal places (displayed in the Decimal places list box) is 0—the formatted number of decimal places of the current cell selection

6. Click the **Symbol list box arrow** and click **$** appearing just below None in the Symbol drop-down list

7. Click **OK** to finalize your formatting selections

8. Click any cell to deselect the range. Figure 3.7 shows the worksheet with currency symbols displayed in cells F6 and G6

	A	B	C	D	E	F	G	H	I
1	Exotic Fruit Company								
2	Sales Forecast								
3									
4				Actual	2002 Projected				
5	Fruit	Cost	Price	2001 Sales	Sales (lbs.)	Gross Sales	Profit	% of Sales	
6	Cherimoya	1.47	1.99	212,000	233,200	$ 464,068	$ 121,264	0.055155	
7	Fuyu Pers	3.49	5.32	159,200	175,100	931,532	320,433	0.145743	
8	Horned Me	1.59	2.19	415,100	456,600	999,954	273,360	0.124605	
9	Lychee	1.96	2.59	521,500	573,700	1,485,883	361,431	0.16439	
10	Mango	0.77	1.19	302,200	332,400	395,556	139,608	0.063498	
11	Papaya	2.21	2.99	492,300	541,500	1,619,085	422,370	0.192107	
12	Rambutan	3.03	3.99	306,700	337,400	1,346,226	323,904	0.147322	
13	Starfruit	1.49	2.99	142,800	157,100	469,729	235,650	0.107181	
14			Totals	2,551,800	2,807,000	7,712,033	2,198,620		
15									

FIGURE 3.7

Worksheet with some currency symbols in place

cells display the currency symbol

Painting Formats onto Other Cells

You recall Nancy's advice that values (or formulas that display values) representing subtotals and totals usually display a currency symbol. Cells F14 and G14 display totals for their respective partial columns. Instead of repeating the command sequence you used above for cells F6 and G6, to save time and effort you will copy the cell format (but not the contents) from cell F6 to the two cells containing sales and profit totals. The Format Painter ✍ button, located on the Standard toolbar, is a quick and convenient way to copy one cell's format to another cell or cell range. The advantage of painting a format instead of using formatting commands is that the painter duplicates *all* of a cell's formats at once.

---

task reference

Copying a Cell Format to a Cell or Cell Range

- Select the cell whose format you want to copy
- Click the **Format Painter** ✍ button
- Click the cell where you want to paint the format, or click and drag the cell range where you want to paint the format

---

Rather than repeat the formatting sequence to apply the currency symbol to cells F14 and G14, you will copy the format with the Format Painter.

Formatting cells with the Accounting format and currency symbol and widening columns:

1. Click cell **F6,** the cell whose format you want to copy to another cell or cells
2. Click the **Format Painter** ✍ button on the Standard toolbar
3. Click and drag the cell range **F14:G14** (see Figure 3.8) to copy the format to those cells. The newly formatted cells probably display ########. Recall that this indicates a formatted numeric value wider than the column can display. You need to widen the columns to accommodate the sums
4. With F14 and G14 still selected, click **Format** on the menu bar, point to **Column,** and click **AutoFit Selection.** Excel widens columns F and G to accommodate formatted cells F14 and G14
5. Click any cell to deselect the cell range

---

*another***way**

. . . to Copy a Cell's Format to Noncontiguous Cells

Click the cell whose format you want to copy

Double-click the **Format Painter** button to permanently engage it

Select a cell or cell range to which you want Excel to copy the format

Select other cells or cell ranges to receive a copied format

When done, click the **Format Painter** button to disengage it

---

OTHER NUMBER FORMATS

You can apply other number formats by using buttons on the Formatting toolbar, shown in Figure 3.4, such as Currency Style, Percent Style, Increase Decimal, or Decrease Decimal. Many other formatting options are available in the Format Cells dialog box, shown in Figure 3.5. Number format options allow you to select whether or not to display a comma to

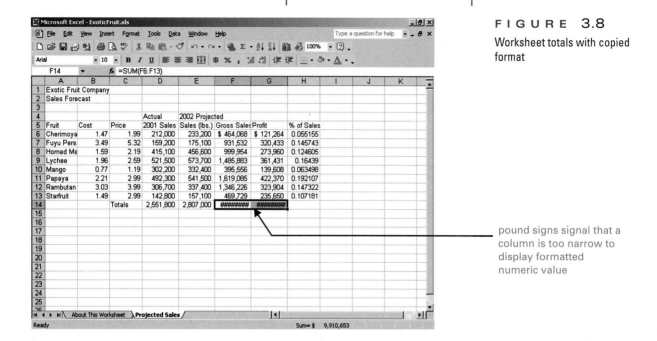

FIGURE 3.8
Worksheet totals with copied format

pound signs signal that a column is too narrow to display formatted numeric value

delimit numbers every three digits, to select the number of decimal places that display, and the exact format of negative numbers.

Percent Style

Column H displays values beneath the column label "% of Sales." These values are percentages, although they are somewhat difficult to interpret because they display five or six decimal places. Nancy wants you to format these column values (such as 0.107181, the Starfruit percentage) to display 10.7% instead—a percentage displaying one decimal place.

Formatting column H with percent and one decimal place:

1. Click and drag the cell range **H6:H13**

2. Click the **Percent Style** % button to apply the Percent Style format to the selected cell range. The default for the Percent Style is to display zero decimal places

3. With the cell range H6:H13 still selected, click the **Increase Decimal** button on the Formatting toolbar to increase, by one, the number of decimal places the selected cells display

tip: If the Increase Decimal button is not visible on the Formatting toolbar, it is farther right on the Formatting toolbar and out of sight—probably sharing space with the Standard toolbar. If so, drag the Formatting toolbar below the Standard toolbar and to the left edge to view the entire toolbar. Then click the Increase Decimal button

4. Click any cell to deselect the range (see Figure 3.9)

EXCEL

FIGURE 3.9

Worksheet cells formatted with the Percent Style

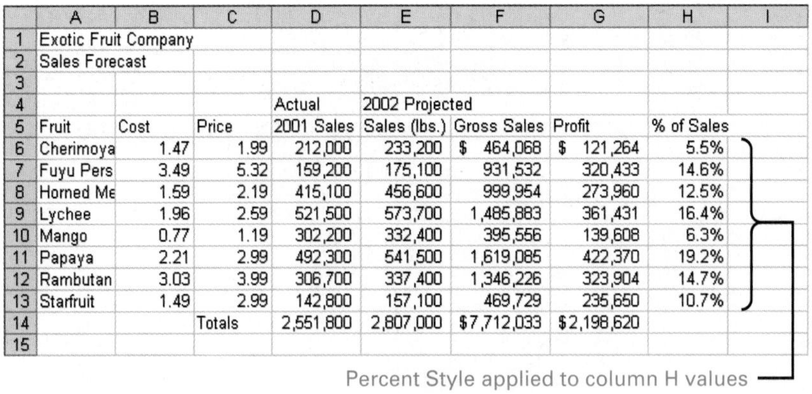

	A	B	C	D	E	F	G	H	I
1	Exotic Fruit Company								
2	Sales Forecast								
3									
4				Actual	2002 Projected				
5	Fruit	Cost	Price	2001 Sales	Sales (lbs.)	Gross Sales	Profit	% of Sales	
6	Cherimoya	1.47	1.99	212,000	233,200	$ 464,068	$ 121,264	5.5%	
7	Fuyu Pers	3.49	5.32	159,200	175,100	931,532	320,433	14.6%	
8	Horned Me	1.59	2.19	415,100	456,600	999,954	273,960	12.5%	
9	Lychee	1.96	2.59	521,500	573,700	1,485,883	361,431	16.4%	
10	Mango	0.77	1.19	302,200	332,400	395,556	139,608	6.3%	
11	Papaya	2.21	2.99	492,300	541,500	1,619,085	422,370	19.2%	
12	Rambutan	3.03	3.99	306,700	337,400	1,346,226	323,904	14.7%	
13	Starfruit	1.49	2.99	142,800	157,100	469,729	235,650	10.7%	
14			Totals	2,551,800	2,807,000	$7,712,033	$2,198,620		
15									

Percent Style applied to column H values ———

Nancy has reviewed your formatting work and suggests that you format the values at the top of the Cost and Price columns to display a currency symbol and two decimal places.

Formatting selected cells with the Accounting format and currency symbol:

1. Click cell **B6** and drag the mouse through cell **C6**
2. Click the **Currency Style** button on the Formatting toolbar
3. Click any cell to deselect the range

Look carefully on your screen at the cell range B6 through C13. Do you notice that cell B6 is not aligned on the right side with cell B7 or the remainder of the cells in the Cost column? Similarly, Cell C6 is no longer aligned on the right side with the other cells in the Price column. This is because the Currency Style also adds one character, a space, to the right side of all values so that there is room for a right parenthesis. Under the Accounting format, negative numbers are surrounded with parentheses.

It is sloppy to leave the values beneath the formatted cell out of alignment with the top value in the column. You can correct this by applying a comma format to the remaining cells in the Cost and Price columns.

Comma Style

Even though commas are not needed for values less than 1000, comma formatting also aligns values the same way the Currency format does—by adding a character to the right side of each value. You will format cells B7 through C13 with the Comma format to align those values the same as the first two entries in each column.

Formatting cells with the Comma Style:

1. Click cell **B7** and drag the mouse through cell **C13**
2. Click the **Comma Style** ⎸,⎹ button on the Formatting toolbar

3. Click any cell to deselect the range. Notice that all values in the Cost and Price columns are aligned (see Figure 3.10)

	A	B	C	D	E	F	G	H	I
1	Exotic Fruit Company								
2	Sales Forecast								
3			Currency format						
4				Actual	2002 Projected				
5	Fruit	Cost	Price	2001 Sales	Sales (lbs.)	Gross Sales	Profit	% of Sales	
6	Cherimoya	$ 1.47	$ 1.99	212,000	233,200	$ 464,068	$ 121,264	5.5%	
7	Fuyu Pers	3.49	5.32	159,200	175,100	931,532	320,433	14.6%	
8	Horned Me	1.59	2.19	415,100	456,600	999,954	273,960	12.5%	
9	Lychee	1.96	2.59	521,500	573,700	1,485,883	361,431	16.4%	
10	Mango	0.77	1.19	302,200	332,400	395,556	139,608	6.3%	
11	Papaya	2.21	2.99	492,300	541,500	1,619,085	422,370	19.2%	
12	Rambutan	3.03	3.99	306,700	337,400	1,346,226	323,904	14.7%	
13	Starfruit	1.49	2.99	142,800	157,100	469,729	235,650	10.7%	
14			Totals	2,551,800	2,807,000	$7,712,033	$2,198,620		
15									

Comma Style format

values aligned and one character to the right of the cells, edges

FIGURE 3.10

Applying the Comma Style to numeric values

ALIGNING DATA

Excel allows you to align data within a cell. Data *alignment* refers to the position of the data relative to the sides of a cell. You alter a cell's alignment with formatting commands. You can align data on the left or right sides of a cell, or you can center it between the two cell walls. A special center alignment command called Merge and Center allows you to center data across several cells in a single row—to create a heading over several columns of numbers, for example. Figure 3.11 shows examples of these four alignment options.

General rules about aligning data have evolved over time. As you know, Excel automatically aligns text on the left side and aligns values or formulas that result in values on the right side. While you certainly can choose data alignment that suits your style and taste, here are some suggestions about cell alignment. Align a column of text on the left side, the default alignment provided by Excel. If you align text on the right, the result can be a disorienting ragged left edge down the column. You can center numeric values if all values have the same number of digits. Examples are employee identification numbers that are all the same

FIGURE 3.11

Cell alignment examples

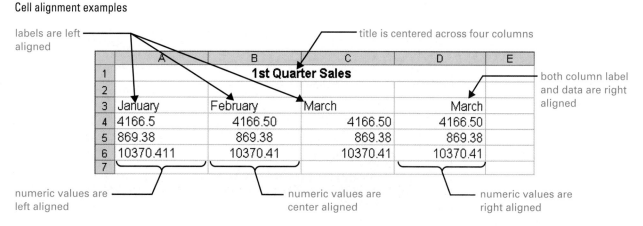

labels are left aligned

title is centered across four columns

both column label and data are right aligned

numeric values are left aligned

numeric values are center aligned

numeric values are right aligned

EXCEL

number of digits long. In a column of numeric values that are not all the same size, align the values so that their decimal places are lined up vertically (column D, Figure 3.11). To do so, you may have to format values to display the same number of decimal places. Text that labels a column of values below it should be right aligned, the same way the values are. This makes the number column easy to identify. For example, column D is easier to interpret than column C, which contains the same values but whose column top label is left aligned. It is often best to center a worksheet title or a text label describing several columns over those columns. In this case, you use the Merge and Center to accomplish the task. Row 1 in Figure 3.11 is an example. The title "1st Quarter Sales" is centered over four columns.

Before altering the alignment of any text or values, you widen column A to accommodate the widest entry in the list of fruit. Notice that two labels identifying the worksheet, "Exotic Fruit Company" and "Sales Forecast," are also in column A (Figure 3.10). This is important because you want to enlarge the column enough to display the fruit names in cells C6 through C13, but the column need not be as wide as the text in cell A1. Widening the column to completely contain the text in cell A1 would make the column far too wide.

> ### Widening column A to accommodate the longer fruit names:
>
> 1. Select cells **A6** through **A13**
>
> 2. Click **Format** on the menu bar, point to **Column,** and then click **AutoFit Selection.** The column widens to one character wider than the widest entry in the selected cells, Fuyu Persimmon
>
> 3. Click any cell to deselect the range. Now each fruit name is visible

Centering Data Across Columns

You will want to center text across multiple columns periodically. A worksheet title or a label that identifies a group of columns is an example. A worksheet title aligned across the columns of the worksheet it identifies can look especially nice. Nancy wants you to center the worksheet title and subtitle found in cells A1 and A2, respectively, across columns A through H.

> ### Centering a worksheet title and subtitle across several columns:
>
> 1. Select the cell range **A1:H2**
>
> 2. Click **Format** and then click **Cells**
>
> 3. Click the **Alignment** tab in the Format Cells dialog box
>
> 4. Click the **Horizontal list box arrow** to display a list of alignment choices (see Figure 3.12)

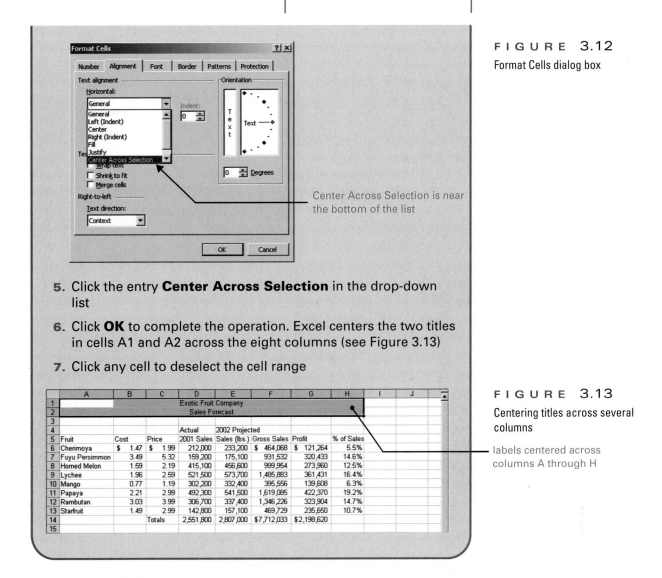

FIGURE 3.12

Format Cells dialog box

5. Click the entry **Center Across Selection** in the drop-down list

6. Click **OK** to complete the operation. Excel centers the two titles in cells A1 and A2 across the eight columns (see Figure 3.13)

7. Click any cell to deselect the cell range

FIGURE 3.13

Centering titles across several columns

labels centered across columns A through H

Right Aligning Data

Text labels that appear above columns containing values often look best if the text labels align the same way as the data beneath them. There are three labels in the Exotic Fruit worksheet, shown in Figure 3.13, which should be right aligned to match the data columns beneath the labels. They are the text in cells B5, C5, G5, and H5. (It is difficult to tell that the text in cell H5 is left aligned, but it is.)

Right aligning text:

1. Click and drag the cell range **B5:C5**

2. Press and hold the **Ctrl** key, click cell **G5,** click cell **H5,** and then release the Ctrl key

3. Click the **Align Right** button on the Formatting toolbar. Excel right-aligns the selected text labels

4. Click any cell to deselect the range

Upon close examination, you notice that the labels Excel right-aligned actually appear one character to the right of the values beneath each text label in columns B, C, and G. You ask Nancy how to correct this, and she tells you that you can use the Accounting format to align text as well as numbers. The advantage of using Accounting format is that it matches the format you applied earlier to the numbers. She explains that the Accounting format adds a space on the right side of the label just as it does for numbers. You change the formatting to improve the worksheet's appearance.

Applying the Accounting format to text:

1. Click and drag the cell range **B5:C5**

2. Press and hold the **Ctrl** key, click cell **G5,** click cell **H5,** and then release the Ctrl key

3. Click **Format**, click **Cells**, click the **Number** tab, click **Accounting** in the Category list, and click **OK** to complete the reformatting process (see Figure 3.14)

FIGURE 3.14

Applying the Accounting format to text cells

Accounting format aligns text to match formatting of numbers beneath

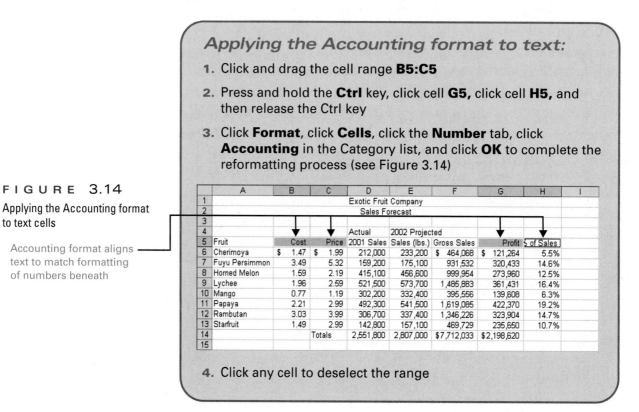

4. Click any cell to deselect the range

That looks better. Now you are ready to modify the format of the remaining column labels.

Wrapping Data in a Cell

Recall that text that is too long to display in a cell extends beyond the cell into the adjacent cell as long as the adjacent cell is empty. If it is not, the long label is visually truncated at the cell boundary. Labels in cells D5, E5, F5, and H5 are all longer than their respective columns are wide. One solution would be to increase the width of the three columns until the labels completely fit within the cells. However, this is not always the best solution because especially long labels force their columns to become exceptionally wide, wider than is attractive. An alternative solution is to format long labels so they appear in multiple rows *within* a cell, much the same way that a text line in a word-processed document wraps around to the next line when it approaches the right margin. Excel uses the same term as Word—*wrap text*—to describe what happens to long text that continues onto the next line of the same cell.

task reference

Wrapping Long Text Within a Cell

- Select the cell or cell range to which you will apply a format
- Click **Format,** click **Cells,** and click the **Alignment** tab
- Click the **Wrap text** check box
- Click **OK** to finalize your format choice

Wrapping the text within cells D5, E5, F5, and H5 will make each label visible and eliminate the need to increase the column widths. It will be a good improvement toward making the worksheet more professional looking.

Wrapping text within a cell:

1. Click and drag the cell range **D5:F5**

2. Press the **Ctrl** key, click cell **H5,** and release the Ctrl key. This adds H5 to the list of selected cells

3. Click **Format,** click **Cells,** and then click the **Alignment** tab

4. Click the **Wrap text** check box, in the Text control panel, to place a checkmark in it

5. Click **OK** to complete the format operation and close the Format Cells dialog box

6. Click any cell to deselect the range (see Figure 3.15)

	A	B	C	D	E	F	G	H	I
1				Exotic Fruit Company					
2				Sales Forecast					
3									
4				Actual	2002 Projected			% of	
5	Fruit	Cost	Price	2001 Sales (lbs.)	Sales (lbs.)	Gross Sales	Profit	Sales	
6	Cherimoya	$ 1.47	$ 1.99	212,000	233,200	$ 464,068	$ 121,264	5.5%	
7	Fuyu Persimmon	3.49	5.32	159,200	175,100	931,532	320,433	14.6%	
8	Horned Melon	1.59	2.19	415,100	456,600	999,954	273,960	12.5%	
9	Lychee	1.96	2.59	521,500	573,700	1,485,883	361,431	16.4%	
10	Mango	0.77	1.19	302,200	332,400	395,556	139,608	6.3%	
11	Papaya	2.21	2.99	492,300	541,500	1,619,085	422,370	19.2%	
12	Rambutan	3.03	3.99	306,700	337,400	1,346,226	323,904	14.7%	
13	Starfruit	1.49	2.99	142,800	157,100	469,729	235,650	10.7%	
14			Totals	2,551,800	2,807,000	$7,712,033	$2,198,620		
15									

FIGURE 3.15

Wrap text format

Wrap text format

Indenting Text

You can indent text within a cell by clicking the Increase Indent or Decrease Indent buttons on the Formatting toolbar. Indenting text allows finer control over text placement within a cell, somewhere between the extremes of left-aligning and right-aligning data. Each time you press the Increase Indent button, Excel moves the text or a value within a cell to the right a few character spaces. Pressing the Decrease Indent button does the opposite: It moves a value or text in a cell to the left a few spaces. You decide to move the label "Totals" in cell C14 right a few spaces.

EXCEL

> ### Indenting text within a cell:
>
> 1. Click cell **C14**
> 2. Click the **Increase Indent** ⊞ button on the Formatting toolbar to indent "Totals" within cell C14
> 3. Since it has been a while since you saved your worksheet, click the **Save** 🖫 button to save your workbook

The basic formatting looks good. All the numbers are visible and contain commas, and selected cells contain the currency symbol. Percentages are formatted to display one decimal place and the percent symbol. Next, you want to alter the typeface and font style of the column headings as well as the worksheet title and subtitle.

CHANGING FONT AND FONT CHARACTERISTICS

Excel allows you to select from a wide variety of typefaces, character formatting characteristics, and point sizes. A *font* is the combination of typeface and qualities including character size, character pitch, and spacing. Typefaces have names such as Garamond, Times Roman, and Helvetica. The height of characters in a typeface is measured in *points,* where a point is equal to 1/72 of an inch. Characters' widths are measured by *pitch,* which refers to the number of characters horizontally per inch. A font is *fixed pitch* (or monospace) if every character has the same width, whereas a font is called a *proportional* font if characters' pitches vary by character. Most people agree that proportional fonts are easier to read than fixed pitch fonts. (The typeface in this book is a proportional font.) Excel provides a large number of fonts from which you can format text and numbers.

Excel also provides the font styles regular, bold, and bold italic. Most fonts are available in a variety of sizes, and you can apply special effects to fonts such as strikethrough, superscript, subscript, a variety of colors, and various types of underlines. You access all of the preceding—fonts, font styles, and font special effects—through the Format Cells dialog box, which opens when you click Format and then Cells. Applying font characteristics is straightforward.

---

task reference

Applying Fonts and Font Characteristics

- Select the cell or cell range that you want to format
- Click **Format,** click **Cells,** and click the **Font** tab
- Select a typeface from the Font list box
- Select a font style and a font size
- Click **OK** to finalize your choices

Applying Boldface

Applying font size and characteristic changes to the worksheet title, subtitle, column headings, and selected cells in the Exotic Fruit worksheet will yield a more professional worksheet. Column labels in row 5 will look better if they stand out, and the label in cell C14 will improve too. Applying boldface to them is just the touch needed to distinguish the labels from the data and enhance the worksheet's appearance.

Applying boldface style to labels:

1. Select the cell range **A5:H5**

2. Click and hold the **Ctrl** key and then click cell **C14**

3. Release the **Ctrl** key

4. Click the **Bold** 🅱 button on the Formatting toolbar. Excel applies the boldface style to the selected labels (see Figure 3.16). Excel also increased the row height of row 5. Notice that the Bold formatting toolbar button is outlined and light blue, indicating that the style is active for <u>all</u> cells in the selected range. The style buttons and the alignment and numeric formatting buttons indicate the formats applied to selected cells in the same way

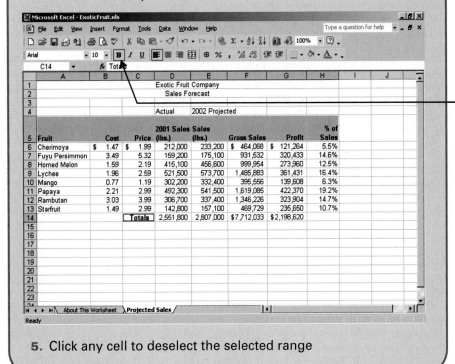

FIGURE 3.16
Bolding column labels

indicates selected range is bold

5. Click any cell to deselect the selected range

Applying Italic

Next, you will italicize the column labels in cells D4 and E4 and the numeric cells D14 through G14 for emphasis.

Applying italic to column labels and values:

1. Select the cell range **D4:E4**

2. Press and hold the **Ctrl** key and click the cell range **D14:G14**

3. Release the Ctrl key

4. Click the **Italic** button $\boxed{I}$ on the Formatting toolbar. Excel applies the Italic style to the two labels and four numeric cells

5. Click any cell to deselect the two cell ranges

Applying Boldface and Changing Point Size and Typeface

The worksheet title and subtitle would look better bolded and with a larger point size. You also want to change the typeface from Arial to Times New Roman. You make those changes in the following steps.

Applying boldface style and modifying the point size and typeface:

1. Select the cell range **A1:A2.** Though the worksheet title and subtitle are centered across several columns, they are actually stored in cells A1 and A2, respectively. To alter their formats, you must click the cells in which they are stored

2. Click **Format** on the menu bar, and then click **Cells**. The Format Cells dialog box opens

4. Click the **Font** tab

5. Drag the mouse across the typeface name displayed in the Font list box to select it and type **Times New Roman.** Notice that the list scrolls automatically to the Times New Roman entry after you type the word *Roman*

6. Click **Bold** in the Font style list box

7. In the Size list box, click the **down-pointing scroll arrow** to locate and then click **16** (see Figure 3.17)

F I G U R E 3.17

Setting typeface and font characteristics

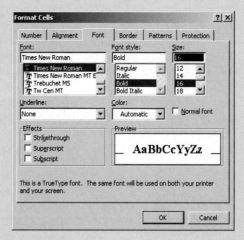

8. Click **OK** to confirm your choices and close the Format Cells dialog box

9. Click any cell to deselect the cell range

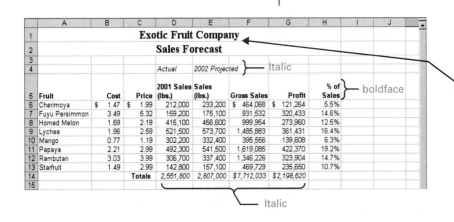

FIGURE 3.18
Worksheet with font and typeface changes

The title and subtitle look better with the larger point size, Times New Roman typeface, and boldface applied (see Figure 3.18).

Removing Selected Formats

Nancy reviewed your worksheet and is pleased with it. However, she believes that the italic style applied to the values appearing in cells D14 through G14 is distracting. She asks you to remove that formatting entirely but to maintain the Accounting format.

> **Removing one style while retaining others:**
>
> 1. Select the cell range **D14:G14.** Notice that the Italic button is outlined and light blue, indicating the entire range has the Italic format
>
> 2. Click the **Italic** button to remove the Italic format from the selected cells. The Italic button is no longer highlighted. (Bold, Italic, and Underline buttons are toggle buttons: You click a button once to activate it and click it again to deactivate it.) The Italic style is removed from the selected cells
>
> 3. Click any cell to deselect the cell range

Clearing Formats

When you want to remove all formatting from a cell or cell range, you use the Clear Formats command. Doing so clears all formats, returning the selected cells to their default, General format.

> **task reference**
>
> **Clearing Formats From a Cell, a Cell Selection, Rows, or Columns**
>
> - Select the cell, cell range, rows, or columns whose format you want to clear
>
> - Click **Edit,** point to **Clear,** and then click **Formats** to remove all formatting

Although you do not need to clear any formats, experiment with the procedure in the following steps. Then you can click Edit, Undo to restore or cancel the Format Clear operation and restore the original formatting.

Clearing one or more cells' formatting:

1. Select the cell range **A5:H5**

2. Click **Edit** on the menu bar, point to **Clear,** and click **Formats.** The cell range formats all return to the General format. Notice that the cells' contents are unaffected. Only the cells' appearances change

3. After observing the cleared formats, reverse the effects of step 2 by clicking **Edit** and then clicking **Undo Clear.** The cell range displays its bold and wrapped text formats

4. Click any cell to deselect the cell range

You have made several changes to your worksheet since you last saved it. Save your worksheet before continuing.

Saving your workbook under a new name:

1. Click **File** on the menu bar

2. Click **Save As**

3. Type **ExoticFruit2.xls** in the File name list box and then click the Save button. Excel saves your workbook under its new name

---

Nancy reviews your progress on the Exotic Fruit worksheet. She's pleased with the worksheet's appearance and makes some suggestions that you note. You will implement her suggested enhancements in the next section of this chapter.

SESSION 3.2 ADVANCED FORMATTING

In this session, you will continue formatting a worksheet. You will alter the row height of a row, enlarging it to add emphasis. Borders delineate particular areas of a worksheet, and you will learn how to apply borders for maximum effect. In order to provide information protection, you will hide information in a column. You will use the Drawing toolbar to add text boxes and arrows to the worksheet to draw attention to especially important elements on it. Finally, you will learn how to add and remove gridlines on the screen and on the printed output and how to specify important print settings such as repeating rows and columns.

CONTROLLING ROW HEIGHTS

Earlier in this chapter, you adjusted several columns' widths. You can adjust the height of rows to provide more room for labels or values or to

making *the grade*

1. What does formatting do to the contents of a cell?

2. By default, Excel worksheet cells are formatted with what format?

3. Excel aligns numbers on the _____ and aligns text on the _____ by default.

4. The Accounting format allows you to specify an optional _____ symbol, specify the number of _____ _____ , and adds a space on the right side of all entries.

5. Modify the Exotic Fruit Company Sales Forecast worksheet, **ExoticFruit2.xls,** in the following ways. First, save the workbook under the name **ExoticFruitModified.xls** to preserve the original **ExoticFruit2.xls** for the next Session. Make these changes. Change the point size of all labels in row 4 to 12 points. Italicize all labels in row 5, and insert your name in the worksheet's header. Save the workbook and then print the worksheet.

simply add emphasis. When you enlarged the worksheet title and subtitle, Excel compensated for the taller characters by increasing the rows' heights automatically. You can increase or decrease the height of one or more rows manually in several ways.

task *reference*

Modifying a Row's Height

- Click the row heading to select the row whose height you want to modify

- Click **Format,** point to **Row,** and click **Height**

- Type the row height in the Row height text box

- Click **OK** to finalize your choices

You decide that row 14 containing totals would look better if it were taller. Increase the row's height by following these steps.

Increasing a row's height:

1. If you took a break at the end of the last session, make sure Excel is running and then open the **ExoticFruit2.xls** workbook that you saved at the end of Session 3.1

2. Click row 14's **row heading**, which is located to the left of column A in row 14. Excel selects the entire row

3. Click **Format,** point to **Row,** and click **Height.** The Row Height dialog box appears

FIGURE 3.19

Row Height dialog box

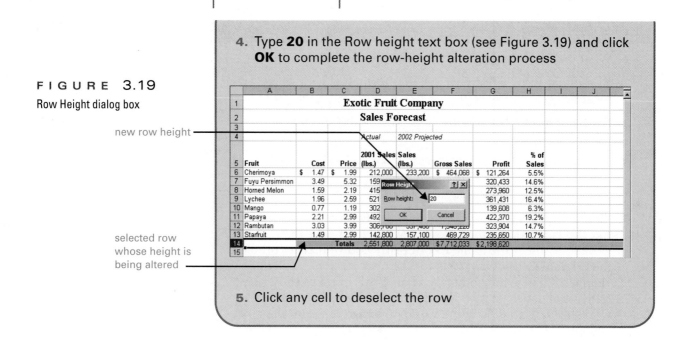

4. Type **20** in the Row height text box (see Figure 3.19) and click **OK** to complete the row-height alteration process

new row height

selected row
whose height is
being altered

5. Click any cell to deselect the row

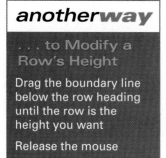

anotherway

. . . to Modify a
Row's Height

Drag the boundary line
below the row heading
until the row is the
height you want

Release the mouse

EMPLOYING BORDERS, A TEXT BOX, AN ARROW, AND SHADING

Like many worksheets, the Exotic Fruit Sales Forecast worksheet has distinct regions or zones that contain groups of related information. Using lines to delineate these groups adds impact to your worksheet and makes the groups easier to identify.

Adding Borders

A ***cell border*** is a format that applies lines of various types to one or more edges (left, right, top, bottom) of the selected cell(s). You create borders among or around selected cells by selecting the Borders button on the Formatting toolbar or by selecting options on the Border tab of the Format Cells dialog box. Using the Outline option, you can place a border around one cell or the rectangle created by a selection of several cells. You can create a horizontal line by selecting cells in the same row and then formatting either the top or bottom edge with a border. Similarly, you create a vertical line by formatting a border on the left or right side of a selection of cells in a single column.

Using the Formatting dialog box, you have several border styles available, including solid lines of various thicknesses, dashed lines, and double lines. The Border button provides a few of the more popular border options. Removing borders from a cell is straightforward with the Format Cells dialog box. You select the cell(s) whose borders you want to remove, click the Border tab of the Format Cells dialog box, and click None.

You want to place a thick line above the column headings in row 4 and a thinner line below the column headings in row 5 to set off the column headings.

Adding a thick line above column labels will help establish the column labels and data beneath them as a separate area. When you want to add a border whose style is not available in the Borders list, you customize border choices by using the Format menu. Next, you will add a border above row 4.

task reference

Adding a Border to a Cell

- Click the cell to which you want to add a border
- Click **Format,** click **Cells,** and click the **Border** tab
- Click the line style in the Style list that you want to apply to the selected cell or cells
- Click one or more of the buttons indicating which cell walls you want to format with a border
- Click **OK** to apply your border formatting choices

  or

- Click the cell to which you want to add a border
- Click the Formatting toolbar **Borders list box arrow** and click the type of border you want

Formatting a border below the column headings:

1. Select the cell range **A5:H5**
2. Click the **Borders button list arrow** ⊞▾ on the Formatting toolbar. A series of borders appears (see Figure 3.20)

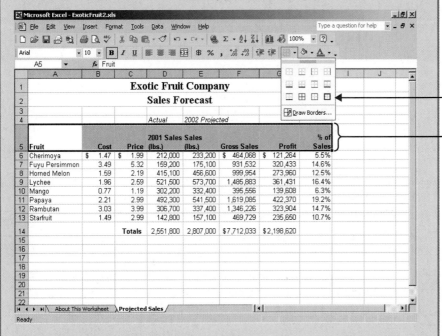

FIGURE 3.20
Border choices

border formatting choices

cells being formatted

3. Click the thin **Bottom Border** button (top row, second from the left). This is the default border that Excel applies if you click the Borders button on the Formatting toolbar. It is helpful for you to view the predefined border sets available from the Borders button list
4. Select any cell to deselect the range

Formatting a border above column headings:

1. Select the cell range **A4:H4**

2. Click **Format,** click **Cells,** and click the **Border** tab on the Format Cells dialog box

3. Click the **thick line** in the Line Style box (the second line from the bottom on the right side of the Line Style box)

4. Click the **top border** button. Excel places a thick line at the top of the Border preview window indicating the relative position of the line in the selected cell range (see Figure 3.21)

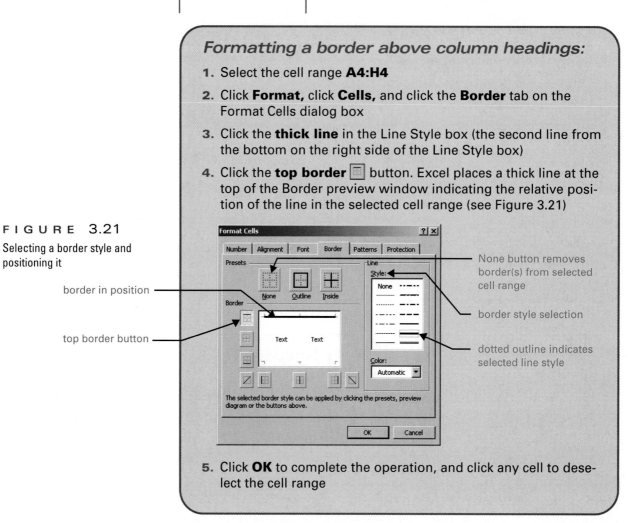

None button removes border(s) from selected cell range

border style selection

dotted outline indicates selected line style

5. Click **OK** to complete the operation, and click any cell to deselect the cell range

The last pair of borders will be similar to the first two you created. A thin line will separate product information from totals in row 14. Finally, you will format the bottom edge of row 14 with a thick border to enclose the product sales information in a pair of thick lines.

Adding a thin and thick border to row 14:

1. Select the cell range **A14:H14**

2. Click **Format,** click **Cells,** and then click the **Border** tab on the Format Cells dialog box

3. Click the **thin line** in the Line Style box (the bottom line on the left side of the Line Style box)

4. Click the **top border** button. Excel places a thin line at the top of the Border preview window indicating the relative position of the line in the selected cell range

5. Click the **thick line** in the Line Style box and then click the **bottom border** button. Excel places a thick button at the bottom of the Border preview window indicating the position of the line in the selected cell range

6. Click **OK** to complete the border formatting procedure and then click any cell to deselect the cell range

Adding and Removing Toolbars

Excel provides several useful drawing tools that allow you to create graphic elements on a special drawing layer of a worksheet. Drawing elements float over the top of a worksheet. They include arrows, text boxes, various lines and connector lines, over 30 basic shapes such as rectangles and trapezoids, WordArt, and clip art. You access these features on the Drawing toolbar.

You are already familiar with Excel's Standard toolbar and Formatting toolbar. In addition, Excel has other toolbars, including the Chart toolbar, Database toolbar, Forms toolbar, and Visual Basic toolbar. Usually only the Standard and Formatting toolbars are visible. To use any toolbar's menus, you must make it appear. If many toolbars are visible simultaneously, there is little room for a worksheet. Normally you make a toolbar visible, use its features, and then remove the toolbar when you are done with it. That way, toolbar clutter is not a problem. ***Activating a toolbar*** is the process of making it appear on the desktop.

FIGURE 3.22

Excel toolbar shortcut menu

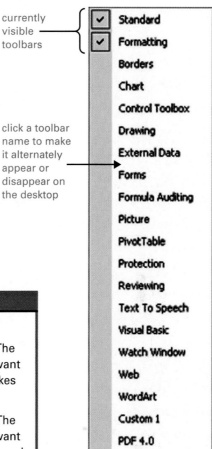

currently
visible
toolbars

click a toolbar
name to make
it alternately
appear or
disappear on
the desktop

task reference

Activating or Removing a Toolbar

- Activate a toolbar by **right-clicking** any toolbar or the menu bar. The toolbar shortcut menu appears. Click the name of the toolbar you want to use, which places a checkmark next to the toolbar name and makes the toolbar appear

- Remove a toolbar by **right-clicking** any toolbar or the menu bar. The toolbar shortcut menu appears. Click the name of the toolbar you want to remove, which removes the checkmark next to the toolbar name and makes the toolbar disappear

If your worksheet is obscured by too many toolbars, you can selectively remove the toolbars you do not want. You can remove all toolbars, leaving only the menu bar visible if you choose. However, in order to use the Drawing toolbar features, you must ask Excel to display the Drawing toolbar. If the Drawing toolbar is not visible, do the following

Displaying the Drawing toolbar:

1. **Right-click** the menu bar. The toolbar shortcut menu appears (see Figure 3.22)

2. Click **Drawing** in the shortcut menu. The Drawing toolbar appears. Usually Excel docks the Drawing toolbar at the bottom of the screen

tip: *If a toolbar is **floating** on the worksheet, it can appear anywhere in the worksheet window. If so, you can dock it on any of the four edges of your display. (When you **dock** a toolbar, it clings to the edge of the window.) Simply click the toolbar's title bar and drag it toward an edge of the worksheet window. It will dock on the edge when the mouse nears it.*

*another*way

. . . to Display or Remove the Drawing Toolbar

Click the **Drawing** button on the Standard toolbar

EXCEL

Adding a Text Box

Excel's *text box* is a rectangular-shaped drawing object that contains text. It floats above a worksheet's cells and is useful to annotate an especially important point. It draws the worksheet reader's attention to the text box and its comments. Excel has other drawing objects including lines, ovals, circles, rectangles, and arrows. All of these graphic elements provide ways to enhance your worksheet. You can move or delete an object easily. First, move the pointer over the object and click it to select it. An object displays small square *selection handles* around its perimeter or on its ends to indicate it is selected. Once you select an object, you can press the Delete key to delete it or click within the object and drag it to a new location. You can adjust the size of an object by clicking one of its selection handles and dragging until the object obtains the desired size.

---

task reference

Adding a Text Box to a Worksheet

- Activate the Drawing toolbar and then click the **Text Box** button
- Click the worksheet in the location where you want the text box
- Drag an outline away from the initial point until the text box outline is the right size and shape
- Type the text you want to appear in the text box
- Click anywhere outside the text box to deselect it

Exotic Fruit's best-selling product this year and projected bestseller next year is Papaya. You want to draw attention to the projected profit and overall percentage of sales for Papaya. A text box is a good way to emphasize the projected sales of Papaya.

Adding a text box to a worksheet:

1. With the Drawing toolbar visible, click the **Text Box** button, and then move the mouse over any cell in the worksheet. Notice that as you move the mouse pointer on the worksheet, the mouse shape changes to

2. Move the mouse pointer to the upper-left corner of cell **J11** and then click the mouse to establish the upper-left corner of the text box. (You may have to scroll the worksheet to the left so that columns J, K, and L are in view.) A narrow box appears with four circular selection handles—one at each corner of the box

3. Move the mouse to the lower-right text box selection handle. The mouse pointer changes to a two-headed arrow

4. Click and drag the mouse to the right until you reach the lower-right corner of cell **L11,** and then release the mouse

5. Type **Papaya is popular. Vons purchases large quantities of it**

6. Carefully move the mouse pointer to any border of the text box until the pointer changes to a four-headed pointer and then **right-click** the border. A shortcut menu appears

7. Click **Format Text box** in the shortcut menu, click the **Colors and Lines** tab, click the **Color** list box found in the Fill section, and click **Automatic,** which appears above the color palette

8. Click the **Color** list box in the Line section of the Format Text Box dialog box, click **Automatic,** which appears above the color palette, and then click **OK** to apply the text box formatting and close the dialog box. Excel places a border around the text box

You can see that the message is longer than the text box can display and it appears that only part of the message is available. Therefore, you need to enlarge the text box just enough so that the entire message is visible.

Modifying the Size of a Text Box:

1. Click the **text box** to select it. Six circular selection handles appear around the text box indicating it is selected

2. Move the cursor until it is directly above the center handle on the bottom edge of the text box. The pointer changes to a double-headed arrow

3. Click and drag the selection handle so that the bottom edge of the text box is aligned with the bottom edge of row 12 so that the text box covers approximately two rows

4. Release the mouse. The text box is large enough to display the entire message (see Figure 3.23)

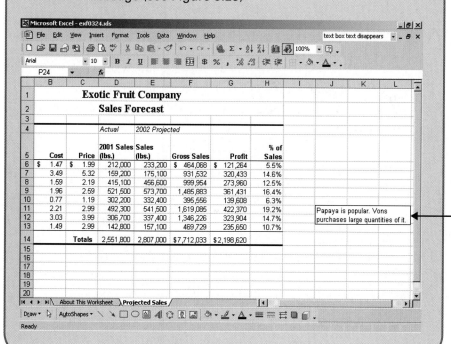

FIGURE 3.23

Adding a text box for emphasis

text box spans approximately two rows

You want to emphasize the word *Vons*, the name of a grocery store chain, with italic and a splash of color.

Italicizing a text box word and changing its font color:

1. Double-click the mouse inside the text box and then use the arrow keys to move the insertion point just ahead of the word "Vons"

2. Hold down the Shift key and press the right arrow key four times to highlight the entire word "Vons"

3. Click the Formatting toolbar **Italic** I button

4. Click the Formatting toolbar **Font Color list arrow** $\underline{A}$ ·. The color palette opens (see Figure 3.24)

5. Click the **Red** button in the color palette (see Figure 3.24)

6. Click any cell to deselect the text box. The font color of the word "Vons" changes to red and is italicized

---

Adding an Arrow

The text box adds just the right emphasis without overpowering the worksheet. You decide to add an arrow leading from the text box to the right end of the Papaya row—to cell H11—so that it is clear to which row the text box refers. There are several arrows available in the Drawing toolbar from which you can choose.

Adding an arrow graphic and placing it in a layer behind the text box:

1. Click the **AutoShapes** menu on the Drawing toolbar

2. Point to **Block Arrows** and then click the **Left Arrow** (see Figure 3.25), which is in the top row, second arrow from the left. The mouse pointer changes to a small plus sign

3. Move the mouse pointer just to the right of the word *Papaya* in the text box

4. Click and drag the mouse to the left and down so that the outline of the arrow completely fills cell **I11** and covers the word Papaya and the tip of the arrow just touches the right edge of cell **H11**. Release the mouse

tip: *If you are dissatisfied with the arrow for any reason (its right end does not cover Papaya, it is too skinny, for example), then select the arrow, press the* **Delete** *key, and repeat the preceding steps until you are pleased with the arrow.*

5. With the arrow selected, move the mouse pointer *inside* the arrow and **right-click** the mouse. A shortcut menu appears

---

6. Point to **Order** on the shortcut menu and click **Send to Back**. Excel places the arrow in a layer beneath the text box and the word *Papaya* becomes visible again (see Figure 3.26)

7. Click in any cell to deselect the arrow

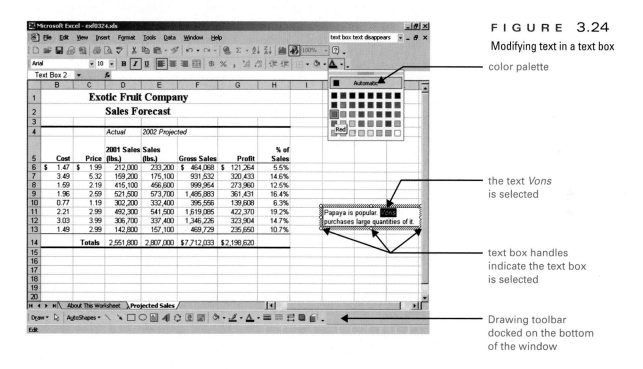

FIGURE 3.24
Modifying text in a text box

color palette

the text *Vons* is selected

text box handles indicate the text box is selected

Drawing toolbar docked on the bottom of the window

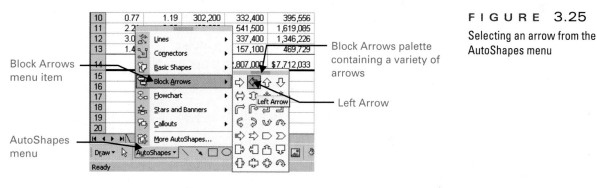

FIGURE 3.25
Selecting an arrow from the AutoShapes menu

Block Arrows menu item

AutoShapes menu

Block Arrows palette containing a variety of arrows

Left Arrow

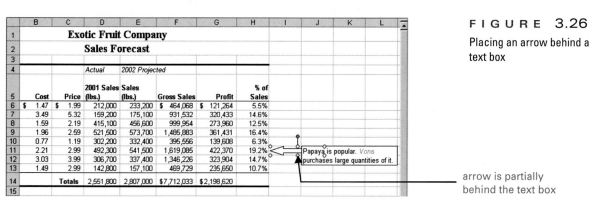

FIGURE 3.26
Placing an arrow behind a text box

arrow is partially behind the text box

Grouping Drawing Objects

You can move the arrow and text box graphics independently of each other. If you selected the text box and moved it to another location, the arrow would remain where it is. It is better if the two objects are combined into one object. That way, if you choose to move the graphics around, you can select the combined arrow and text box graphic and move it as one unit. Joining two graphics into one object is called *grouping.* Once grouped, multiple objects act as one and one set of selection handles surround the larger grouped object. You can ungroup objects later if you want to adjust their position and then regroup them.

Grouping two graphic objects:

1. Click the **text box** to select it. Selection handles appear around the text box

2. Press and hold the **Shift** key

3. Move the mouse over the arrow graphic and **click** the mouse to select the arrow graphic. Both objects should be selected. If not, repeat steps 1 through 3

4. With the mouse within the arrow graphic (the mouse pointer displays the four-headed arrow pointer ⊕) **right-click** the mouse. A shortcut menu appears

5. Point to **Grouping** in the shortcut menu and then click **Group.** The two objects are grouped, and one set of selection handles surrounds the grouped graphic (see Figure 3.27)

F I G U R E 3.27

Grouped objects

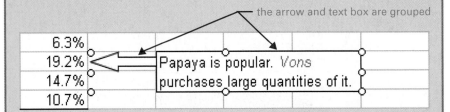

the arrow and text box are grouped

| 6.3% |
| 19.2% | Papaya is popular. *Vons* |
| 14.7% | purchases large quantities of it. |
| 10.7% |

6. Click any cell to deselect the grouped objects

Adding a Drop Shadow

You can make some drawing objects look three-dimensional by adding a drop shadow. A *drop shadow* is the shadow that is cast by the object. Adding a drop shadow to the grouped object—the arrow and text box—enhances the object and adds a little flair.

Adding a drop shadow to a drawing object:

1. Ensure that the Drawing toolbar is visible and then click the arrow and text box grouped object to select it. Selection handles appear around the object

2. Click the **Shadow Style** ◨ button on the Drawing toolbar. A palette of drop shadow choices appears (see Figure 3.28)

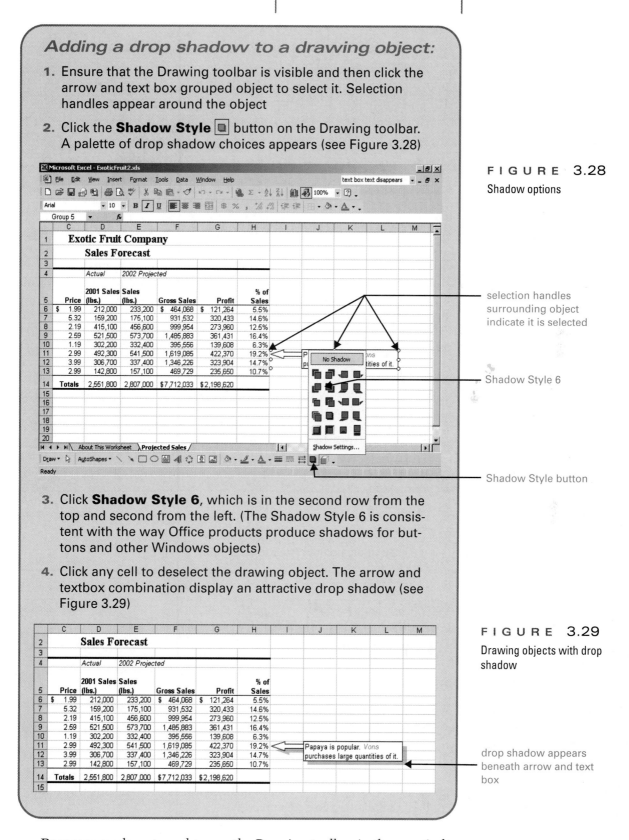

FIGURE 3.28
Shadow options

selection handles surrounding object indicate it is selected

Shadow Style 6

Shadow Style button

3. Click **Shadow Style 6**, which is in the second row from the top and second from the left. (The Shadow Style 6 is consistent with the way Office products produce shadows for buttons and other Windows objects)

4. Click any cell to deselect the drawing object. The arrow and textbox combination display an attractive drop shadow (see Figure 3.29)

FIGURE 3.29
Drawing objects with drop shadow

drop shadow appears beneath arrow and text box

Because you do not need to use the Drawing toolbar in the remainder of this chapter, you can hide it. Doing so provides a little more room for your worksheet.

EXCEL

> **Remove the Drawing toolbar from the work surface:**
>
> 1. Click the **Drawing** 🖉 button on the Standard toolbar. The Drawing toolbar disappears from the work surface and the Drawing button no longer appears highlighted (selected)
>
> 2. Just to be safe, save your worksheet by clicking the **Save** button on the Standard toolbar

HIDING AND UNHIDING ROWS AND COLUMNS

Nancy reviewed the worksheet and is pleased with the way you have formatted it. It is really taking shape. The Cost column contains prices that Exotic Fruit Company pays to its suppliers and is company confidential. Nancy wants you to somehow make that column not appear in any printouts you or any of the managers produce. Naturally, you cannot delete the column from the worksheet because the Profit column depends on the Cost column. The Percent of Sales column depends indirectly on the Cost column. If you deleted the Cost column, Excel would display the error message #REF! in the Profit column and the Percent of Sales column.

Hiding a column is the best solution. Any columns or rows that you hide remain in the worksheet but they are not displayed. When you hide a column, Excel sets its column width to zero. Similarly, when you hide a row, its row height is set to zero.

> **task reference**
>
> **Hiding Rows or Columns**
>
> - Select the rows or columns you want to hide
> - Click **Format,** point to **Row** (or **Column**), and click **Hide**

anotherway

. . . to Hide Rows or Columns

Select the rows or columns you want to hide

Right-click the selected rows or columns to display a shortcut menu

Click **Column Width** in the shortcut menu

Type **0** in the Column width text box and click **OK**

> **Hiding the Cost column:**
>
> 1. Click the **column B header.** Excel selects the entire column
>
> 2. Click **Format,** point to **Column,** and then click **Hide.** Excel hides column B (see Figure 3.30)
>
> 3. Click any cell to deselect the hidden column

Column B disappears, although it is still part of the worksheet because the formulas that depend on column B entries, such as formulas in column G and H, still display correct values.

USING COLOR FOR EMPHASIS

Using colors and patterns carefully can emphasize areas of the worksheet, highlight input areas where users type assumption values, or provide an attractive design element to your worksheet. An important key to effective

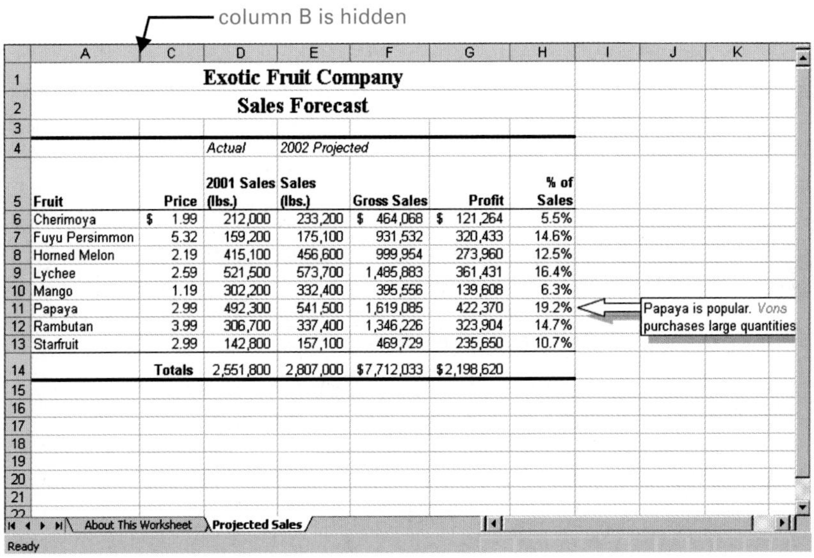

column B is hidden

FIGURE 3.30

Hiding a worksheet column

	A	C	D	E	F	G	H	I	J	K
1			**Exotic Fruit Company**							
2			**Sales Forecast**							
3										
4			*Actual*	*2002 Projected*						
5	Fruit	Price	**2001 Sales (lbs.)**	**Sales (lbs.)**	Gross Sales	Profit	**% of Sales**			
6	Cherimoya	$ 1.99	212,000	233,200	$ 464,068	$ 121,264	5.5%			
7	Fuyu Persimmon	5.32	159,200	175,100	931,532	320,433	14.6%			
8	Horned Melon	2.19	415,100	456,600	999,954	273,960	12.5%			
9	Lychee	2.59	521,500	573,700	1,485,883	361,431	16.4%			
10	Mango	1.19	302,200	332,400	395,556	139,608	6.3%			
11	Papaya	2.99	492,300	541,500	1,619,085	422,370	19.2%			
12	Rambutan	3.99	306,700	337,400	1,346,226	323,904	14.7%			
13	Starfruit	2.99	142,800	157,100	469,729	235,650	10.7%			
14		Totals	2,551,800	2,807,000	$7,712,033	$2,198,620				

Papaya is popular. *Vons* purchases large quantities

About This Worksheet   Projected Sales

Ready

use of color is restraint. Use color sparingly. Too much color or too many colors in a worksheet can yield a garish, unattractive, or confusing overall appearance. On the other hand, the subtle use of color results in an attractive worksheet that others can easily understand and use. If you plan to make color transparencies from your worksheet output, you will need a color printer. However, you can print color-enhanced worksheets on a noncolor printer. Be aware that black text in cells containing a colored background may not be legible. Experiment with different text and cell background colors if you cannot print your worksheet on a color printer. Generally, lighter colors work better on noncolor printers. As an alternative, you can use patterns to emphasize areas when the output device is a noncolor printer.

Nancy's office has both color printers and noncolor printers (sometimes called monochrome printers or black-and-white printers). She wants you to add a splash of color to the worksheet that looks good on both types of printers. After consulting other people in the office, you decide to use light colors such as pale yellow and light gray for emphasis. Those colors don't obscure black text and look good on both types of printers.

task reference

Applying Color or Patterns to Worksheet Cells

- Select the cells to which you want to apply a color or pattern

- Click **Format,** click **Cells,** and click the **Patterns** tab in the Format Cells dialog box

- If you want to apply a pattern, click a pattern from the Pattern list box

- If you want the pattern to appear in color, click the Pattern list box again and click a color from the Pattern palette

- If you want to apply a colored background, click a color in the Cell shading color palette in the Format Cells dialog box

You decide to apply two separate colored backgrounds, but not patterns, to two worksheet areas. A light gray background color would enhance the column labels in rows 4 and 5. To draw the worksheet reader's eye to the important projected profit value in cell G14, you decide to apply a yellow background to that cell.

FIGURE 3.31

Patterns tab of the Format Cells dialog box

Applying a background color to column labels:

1. Click and drag the cell range **A4:H5**

2. Click **Format** on the menu bar, click **Cells,** and then click the **Patterns** tab on the Format Cells dialog box (see Figure 3.31)

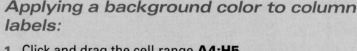
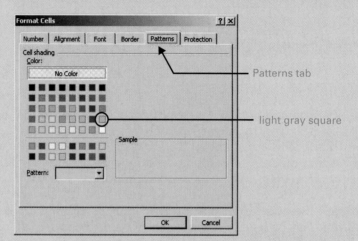

3. Click the **light gray square** (in the fourth row from the top and in the rightmost column) of the Cell shading Color palette

4. Click **OK** to complete the color formatting operation

Next, you will apply another background color to the total profit cell, G14, to highlight that value. Instead of using the Format menu to apply a color, you will use the Fill Color button on the Formatting toolbar, a faster alternative for this type of formatting.

Applying a background color to the total profit cell:

1. Click cell **G14**

2. Click the **Fill Color** button list arrow to display the cell shading color palette

3. Click the **Yellow** color square found in the fourth row from the top and the third square from the left. The background of cell G14 changes to yellow. Figure 3.32 shows the two color formatting changes you have made

4. Press **Ctrl+Home** to make cell A1 active

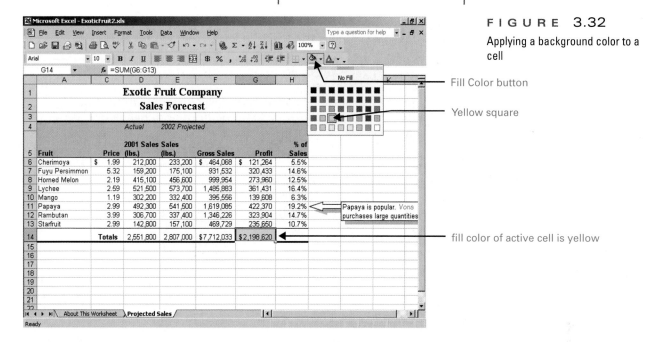

FIGURE 3.32

Applying a background color to a cell

Fill Color button

Yellow square

fill color of active cell is yellow

You have finished applying the formatting changes to the Exotic Fruit worksheet. Nancy has reviewed the worksheet and is very pleased with its overall look. She wants you to make one more change to it, however. Nancy thinks that the gridlines that Excel displays onscreen by default are distracting and lessen the visual impact of the worksheet. She asks you to remove the gridlines displayed onscreen.

CONTROLLING GRIDLINES

Excel normally outlines worksheet cells in black. The black gridlines are very handy because they help you locate cells as you are building your worksheet models. When your worksheet is complete, you may wish to eliminate the onscreen gridlines. Consider the example Exotic Fruit documentation worksheet shown in Figure 3.2. That worksheet page would be much less attractive and a bit confusing if the page displayed gridlines.

You can also control whether Excel displays gridlines on output or not. Normally Excel does not display gridlines on output. However, you may want to display them for documentation or demonstration purposes. Whether or not gridlines display onscreen or in output is completely under your control. Next, you will remove the gridlines from the onscreen display of the Projected Sales worksheet.

Removing and Displaying Gridlines Onscreen

Gridline display is an option that you can set for each worksheet or for all worksheets at once. If you remove the gridlines from one worksheet, they need not be removed from other worksheets in the same workbook.

Removing gridlines from the Projected Sales worksheet:

1. Click **Tools** on the menu bar and then click **Options.** The Options dialog box opens

2. If necessary, click the **View** tab

3. Click the **Gridlines** check box in the Window options section to remove the checkmark and remove the onscreen gridlines

4. Click **OK** to complete your changes, close the Options dialog box, and display the worksheet without gridlines (see Figure 3.33)

FIGURE 3.33

Worksheet without gridline display

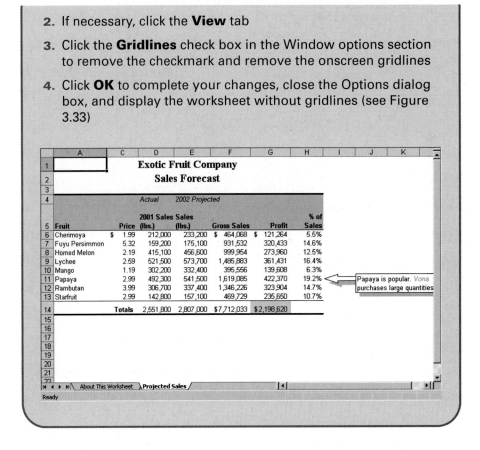

anotherword

. . . on Adding or Removing Onscreen Gridlines

If you want to remove gridlines from more than one worksheet, Shift-click a range of worksheet page tabs or Ctrl-click noncontiguous worksheet tabs

Click **Tools** and then click **Options**

Click the **View** tab

Click the **Gridlines** check box to check it, and click **OK**

Restoring worksheet gridlines is the reverse of the preceding steps. That is, you click Tools, click View, click the Gridlines check box to check it, and click OK.

Removing and Displaying Gridlines on Output

When you want to display worksheet gridlines in *output pages*, set that option prior to printing a page. While output worksheets containing gridlines are not as professional looking as those without gridlines, you may want to print out the worksheet with gridlines as well as the row and column headers as documentation.

Nancy wants you to document the worksheet in hard copy by printing gridlines and row and column headers. First, you will set the option that prints gridlines. Then, you can set another option to print row and column headers. In the steps that follow, you will preview the output but not actually print it. Then you will reset the options so that no gridlines or row and column headings appear.

Adding gridlines and row and column headings to a worksheet to be printed:

1. Click **File** on the menu bar and then click **Page Setup.** The Page Setup dialog box opens

2. Click the **Sheet** tab in the Page Setup dialog box and then click the **Gridlines** check box (in the Print section) to place a check-mark in it. The Gridlines option controls whether or not grid-lines print

3. Click **Row and column headings** check box to place a check-mark in it. The Row and columns headings check box controls whether or not worksheet row and column headings appear in printed worksheet pages (see Figure 3.34)

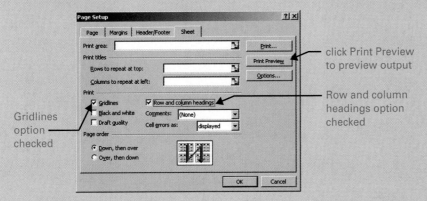

Gridlines option checked

click Print Preview to preview output

Row and column headings option checked

4. Click the **Print Preview** button (see Figure 3.34) to preview the output. Examine the preview for a few moments. Notice the gridlines and row and column headings

5. Click the **Setup** Setup... button in the Print Preview toolbar to redisplay the Page Setup dialog box

6. Click the **Gridlines** check box to clear it and then click the **Row and column headings** check box to clear it. You don't want to print the worksheet gridlines or the row and column headings at this time

7. Click **OK** in the Page Setup dialog box

8. Click the **Close** Close button on the Print Preview toolbar to return to your worksheet

FIGURE 3.34

Setting print options

PRINTING

When you are ready to print a worksheet, you should preview the output using the Print Preview command first. That way, you can check to ensure that the worksheet looks right or check to make sure the output is not several pages long. Keep in mind the rule: Preview before printing. That can save both time and effort. Print Preview shows margins, page breaks, headers and footers, and other elements that you do not see in the worksheet window.

FIGURE 3.35

Print Preview window

an available
Next button
means there is
another page

indicates
number of
pages to print

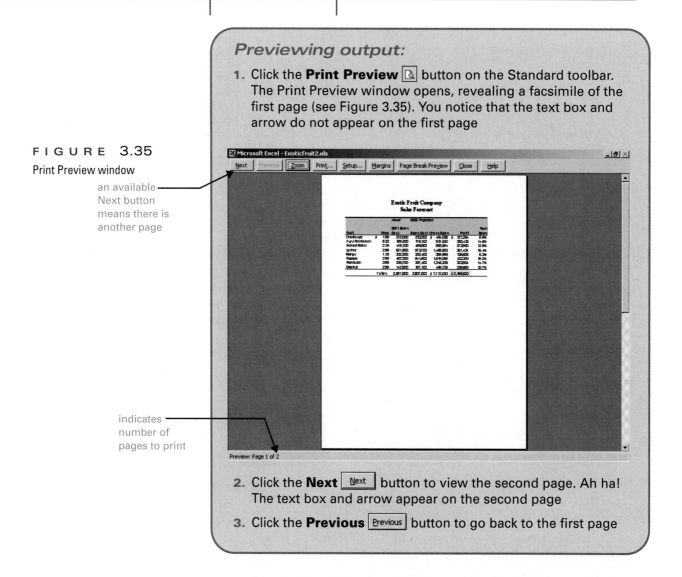

Previewing output:

1. Click the **Print Preview** button on the Standard toolbar. The Print Preview window opens, revealing a facsimile of the first page (see Figure 3.35). You notice that the text box and arrow do not appear on the first page

2. Click the **Next** button to view the second page. Ah ha! The text box and arrow appear on the second page

3. Click the **Previous** button to go back to the first page

Previewing the output reveals that the worksheet is slightly larger than can currently fit on one page. There are several ways to remedy this. One possibility is to reduce the left and right margins until there is enough room to fit all the output on one page. As in this case, this may not be the solution. Another possibility is to reduce the font size of the entire worksheet until it is small enough to squeeze the entire worksheet on one page. This is not often a good choice. An alternative is to reorient the worksheet printout.

Controlling Print Orientation

Excel provides two print orientations called portrait and landscape. ***Portrait*** orientation prints a worksheet so that the paper is taller than it is wide—the standard way books and notebook paper is written. It borrows its name from the way artists paint portraits. ***Landscape*** orientation prints a worksheet that is wider than it is tall. The term landscape reminds you of an artist's painting depicting a landscape, which is often wider than it is tall. The Exotic Fruit is a worksheet that should be printed in landscape orientation to fit nicely on a printed page.

Changing an output orientation to landscape:

1. With the Print Preview window still open, click the **Setup** Setup... button, which opens the Page Setup dialog box

2. Click the **Page** tab and then click the **Landscape** option button in the Orientation section to select Landscape orientation

3. Click **OK** to return to Print Preview (see Figure 3.36). Notice that the entire worksheet fits on the page and the Next button is dimmed, which indicates there is only one output page

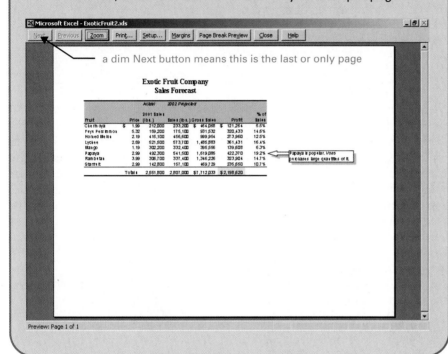

FIGURE 3.36

Landscape orientation

Centering Output on a Page

Before printing the worksheet, you can center the worksheet on a page and add a header and footer. First, center the worksheet.

Vertically centering worksheet output:

1. With the Print Preview window still open, click the **Setup** Setup... button

2. Click the **Margins** tab in the Page Setup dialog box. On this page, you can set left, right, top, bottom, header, and footer margins. In addition, you can check options to center a page horizontally or vertically on a page

3. Click the **Vertically** check box to place a checkmark in the check box (see Figure 3.37)

FIGURE 3.37

Centering output

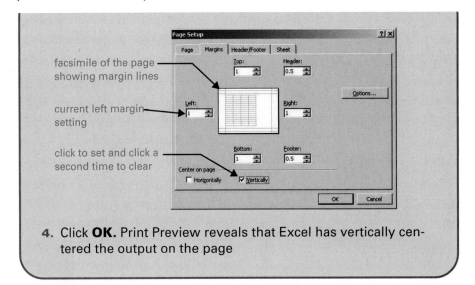

facsimile of the page showing margin lines

current left margin setting

click to set and click a second time to clear

4. Click **OK.** Print Preview reveals that Excel has vertically centered the output on the page

You should place some documentation on the worksheet. In an e-mail message she sent a week ago, Nancy requested that you print the worksheet with the header "Company Confidential" in the center and a footer containing your name and the current date. Nancy did not specify the exact placement of the footer information, so you decide to place your name on the left side of the page and the current date on the right side. You are familiar with worksheet headers and footers, because you have used them in previous chapters.

Placing information in a worksheet header and footer:

1. With the Print Preview window still open, click the **Setup** button

2. Click the **Header/Footer** tab in the Page Setup dialog box

3. Click the **Custom Header** `Custom Header...` button and click in the **Center section**

4. In the Center section, type **Company Confidential** and then click **OK**

5. Click the **Custom Footer** `Custom Footer...` button, click in the **Left section,** and type your first and last names

6. Click in the **Right section** and click the **Date** 📅 button to insert the current date

7. Click **OK** to close the Footer dialog box

8. Click **OK** again to close the Page Setup dialog box. The Print Preview window redisplays and shows the header and footer information you entered

9. Click the **Close** `Close` button in the Print Preview toolbar to close the window. The worksheet window opens

Unhiding a Column

Your work on the Exotic Fruit Sales Forecast worksheet is almost done, and you are ready to give Nancy the printed copy for her to check before her presentation next week. Before you print the worksheet, unhide column B, check the output once more in the Print Preview window, and make any necessary output adjustments. Then you can save the worksheet and exit Excel.

Unhiding column B:

1. Position the mouse pointer over the column A header

2. Click and drag the mouse through the **column C header** to select the three columns (column A, hidden column B, and column C). Notice that the two visible columns are highlighted

3. Right-click anywhere inside the selected columns. A shortcut menu appears

4. Click **Unhide** in the shortcut menu. Column B reappears

5. Click any cell to deselect the three selected columns

6. Click the **Print Preview** button to check the output (see Figure 3.38)

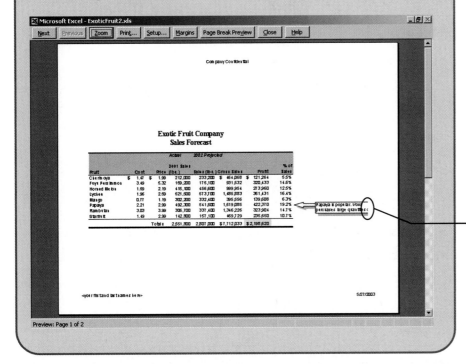

FIGURE 3.38

Preview of expanded worksheet

part of the drawing object may be on the second page (yours may vary)

Depending on where you positioned the drawing objects in the steps presented earlier in this chapter, your output may (still) not fit on one page. The example shown in Figure 3.38 shows a tiny part of the graphic missing from the right end of the text box. One way to handle this kind of problem is to enlarge your worksheet page by adjusting the left and right margins. Any space released by left and right margins is allocated to the worksheet printing area, just enough to print the entire worksheet and drawing object on one page.

Modifying the left and right margins:

1. With the Print Preview window still open, click the **Setup** button. The Page Setup dialog box opens

2. Click the **Margins** tab and double-click the **Left spin control box** to highlight the current left margin number

3. Type **0.5** to set the left margin to one-half inch

4. Double-click the **Right spin control box** to highlight the current right margin number

5. Type **0.5** to set the right margin to one-half inch

6. Click **OK** to close the Page Setup dialog box. The Print Preview window is visible. Unless your arrow and text box drawing boxes are unusually large, the entire grouped drawing object should be visible

tip: *If you still cannot see the entire worksheet on one page, you can force the worksheet to fit by clicking the **Page** tab in the Page Setup dialog box and then click the **Fit to** option button in the Scaling section of the Page tab settings. This shrinks the overall worksheet so that it fits on a single page*

7. Click the **Close** button on the Print Preview toolbar to close the window and return to the worksheet

Printing Several Worksheets

Your work on the Exotic Fruit worksheet is complete. Always save your work when you have completed a significant number of changes. That way, your work is safely stored in case you need to open the latest version of the workbook.

Saving your worksheet:

1. Click the **File** on the menu bar

2. Click **Save**

Nancy asks you to print not only the main worksheet, which you have been working to perfect, but also the documentation sheet. You have printed single worksheets before, but not multiple worksheets in one print statement.

Printing multiple worksheets is almost the same process as printing a single worksheet. There is only one small difference in the procedure: You press and hold the Ctrl key and then click the worksheet tabs corresponding to all the worksheets you want to print. Then release the Ctrl key. Then you print as usual.

When you click multiple worksheet tabs, they turn white to indicate they are selected. You probably noticed that there are three option buttons available in the *Print what* section of the Print dialog box. The default option selected is *Active sheets,* which instructs Excel to print all selected sheets. Selected sheets are called ***active sheets.***

task reference

Printing multiple worksheets

- Press and hold the **Ctrl** key
- Click the sheet tabs of each sheet you want to print
- Release the **Ctrl** key
- Click the **Print** button on the Standard toolbar

Printing multiple Exotic Fruit worksheets:

1. Press and hold the **Ctrl** key
2. With the Projected Sales worksheet displayed (active), click the worksheet tab **About This Worksheet**. Both worksheet tabs turn white, indicating both worksheets are active (see Figure 3.39)

white sheet tabs indicate active worksheets

3. Release the **Ctrl** key
4. Click the **Print** button on the Standard toolbar. Both worksheets print
5. Click the **About This Worksheet** tab to deselect the multiple active worksheets. Only the About This Worksheet tab is active

FIGURE 3.39
Selecting multiple worksheets

anotherword

. . . on Selecting and Deselecting Multiple Worksheets

Select multiple worksheets in a contiguous group by clicking the leftmost worksheet tab in the group

Then press and hold the **Shift** key and click the rightmost worksheet tab in the group (using the tab scroll buttons if necessary)

Ctrl-clicking worksheet tabs allows you to select noncontiguous worksheets

Deselect multiple worksheet tabs by clicking any worksheet tab that is *not* selected

If all worksheet tabs are selected, click any one of the worksheet tabs to deselect all the other tabs

EXCEL

SESSION 3.2   *making* **the grade**

1. Describe how to modify a row's height.

2. Click the _____ tab in the Format Cells dialog box to add borders to selected cells.

3. Activate the Drawing toolbar by right-clicking any _____ or the_____ bar and then clicking Drawing in the list.

4. When you click a drawing object such as a text box, _____ _____ appear around the object.

5. Modify the **ExoticFruit2.xls** worksheet in the following ways. Hide the Cost and Price columns (columns B and C). Change the typeface of the worksheet title and subtitle (cells A1 and A2) to Arial and change the point size of the worksheet title to 18 point and the subtitle to 14 point. Change the worksheet header to **Copyright Exotic Fruit Company, Inc**. Change the formatting of the Gross Sales and Profit numbers to Currency Style with zero decimal places. Modify the % of Sales column to display percentages with two decimal places instead of one. Format the background of each total in row 14 with the color Yellow. Modify the page footer to display the page number in the Center section. Remove the arrow and text box objects from the worksheet. Change the left and right margins to 1.5 inches and center the output horizontally and vertically. Place your name in the Left section of the footer of the *About This Worksheet* page. Save the worksheet as **ExoticFruit3.xls**. Print both worksheet pages.

SESSION 3.3 SUMMARY

Formatting worksheet entries alters the appearance of labels and values but does not alter the cells' contents. By default, Excel formats all cells with the General format. The General format displays values right aligned in a cell and displays text left aligned in a cell. Clicking Clear and then Formats from the Edit menu restores selected cells to an unformatted state. Selected popular format commands appear as buttons on the Formatting toolbar to make them easier to use. Nearly all worksheets contain some formatting. Formatting yields professional-looking worksheets that are suitable for publication in sales brochures and accounting statements that always accompany company annual reports.

Common formatting choices display values with leading currency symbols, allow you to select the number of decimal places to display, and provide comma separators for larger numbers. Formatting can display negative numbers enclosed in parentheses or with a leading minus sign. Other formats present numbers as percentages or dates in a variety of forms. Scientific formats are convenient for engineering and scientific applications in which large numbers display with a number and an exponent. Scientific notation represents the value 123.436 as 1.23E+02, where E+02 means multiply the number preceding E by 100. Applying an Accounting format to numbers displays a left-aligned dollar sign, commas when necessary, and any number of decimal places, including zero.

Excel repeats the symbol # in formatted numeric cells in which the values are larger than the column can display. In that case, widen the column until the # symbols disappear. When possible, delay altering column widths until you complete all formatting. Use the Format Painter button to apply one cell's format characteristics to other cells. Doing so relieves you from executing several multistep formatting commands to apply a series of formats. Other time-saving formatting buttons on the Formatting toolbar include Currency Style, Percent Style, Increase Decimal, and Decrease Decimal. Select a cell or cell range and click the Increase Decimal button to increase the number of displayed decimal places, for example.

Several data alignment formats allow you to align numbers or text on the left, center, or right side of a cell. The Merge and Center Formatting toolbar button centers text across multiple columns by merging the cells in a row and then centering text within the merged cells. You can format especially long labels to fit in narrower columns with the Wrap text option, which is found on the Alignment tab of the Format Cells dialog box. This option creates multiple lines within a cell and automatically increases the row height to accommodate multiline text. Excel includes a wide variety of typeface, point size, and character formatting choices. Typeface choices range from Arial to ZaphDingbats, and you can format text or numbers in point sizes ranging from 4 points to over 96, depending on the typeface you choose. Boldface, Italic, and Underline are popular character formatting choices that you can apply to any cells.

Change the height of a row by typing the new height in the Row Height dialog box, or drag the line between the row headings to adjust a row's height. Sparing use of cell border formatting visually enhances worksheets with vertical and horizontal lines following cell wall boundaries. Excel provides several line styles and widths from which you can choose.

Excel provides several toolbars whose name you can see by right-clicking in the menu or in any toolbar. You can activate a toolbar from the shortcut menu by clicking the toolbar's name. The Drawing toolbar contains graphic objects that you can place on a layer above the worksheet. Objects include arrows, connecting lines, callouts, various geometric shapes including squares and ovals, WordArt, fill colors, drop shadows, and other 3-D effects. A text box is one of the Drawing toolbar's objects. Text boxes contain text enclosed in a sizeable rectangle that you can place anywhere on the worksheet. Text boxes are handy for pointing out special worksheet features or simply noting important facts about the worksheet. Clicking an object selects it and selection handles appear around the object's perimeter. Move objects by selecting and then dragging them to their new locations. Group multiple objects into one object by shift-clicking each object and then grouping them.

Cell background colors, when used tastefully and sparingly, add emphasis and draw the eye to selected features. Colors can also visually group related areas of a worksheet. Foreground color does not affect the contents of cells, and a variety of colors is available. When color is not appropriate—especially for noncolor laser printers—you can pattern cell backgrounds for dramatic and eye-catching effects.

Clicking the Print Preview button allows you to preview output before you print it. If the worksheet is too wide to fit on a page, try landscape orientation rather than portrait. Landscape orientation is wider than it is tall. Print multiple pages of a worksheet by shift-clicking multiple tabs before printing. Modify page margins when needed to provide more space for worksheet output. Hide selected columns when necessary to prevent printing confidential or proprietary information. Select the column and select Column Hide from the Format menu. Hiding a column is synonymous with making its width equal to zero.

EXCEL

MOUS OBJECTIVES SUMMARY

- Left-, center-, and right-align text (MOUS Ex2002-3)
- Apply currency and accounting formats to numbers (MOUS Ex2002-3-1)
- Modify the typeface and point size of text and numbers (MOUS Ex2002-3-1)
- Apply boldface, italic, and underline to cells (MOUS Ex2002-3-1)
- Clear all formatting from selected cells (MOUS Ex2002-3; Ex2002-1-2)
- Modify column widths and row heights (MOUS Ex2002-3-3)
- Hide and reveal rows and columns (MOUS Ex2002-3-2)
- Modify the worksheet's print characteristics (MOUS Ex2002-3-7)

task reference round-up

Task	Location	Preferred Method
Formatting numbers	EX 3.7	• Select cell(s)
		• Click **Format**, click **Cells**, click **Number**
		• Click format category and select options
		• Click **OK**
Copying a cell format to a cell or cell range	EX 3.10	• Select the cell whose format you want to copy
		• Click the **Format Painter** ✐ button
		• Click (click/drag) the target cell(s)
Wrapping long text within a cell	EX 3.17	• Select the cell or cell range to which you will apply a format
		• Click **Format**, click **Cells**, and click the **Alignment** tab
		• Click the **Wrap text** check box
		• Click **OK**
Applying fonts and font characteristics	EX 3.18	• Select the cell or cell range that you want to format
		• Click **Format**, click **Cells**, and click the **Font** tab
		• Select a typeface from the Font list box
		• Select a font style and a font size
		• Click **OK**
Clearing formats from a cell, cell selection, rows, or columns	EX 3.21	• Select the cell, cell range, rows, or columns
		• Click **Edit**, point to **Clear**, and click **Formats**

task reference round-up

Task	Location	Preferred Method
Modifying a row's height	EX 3.23	• Click the row heading
		• Click **Format**, point to **Row**, and click **Height**
		• Type the row height in the Row height text box
		• Click **OK**
Add a border to a cell	EX 3.25	• Click the cell to which you want to add a border
		• Click the Formatting toolbar **Borders list box arrow**, and click the border you want
Activating/removing a toolbar	EX 3.27	• **Right-click** the menu bar
		• Click the name of the toolbar you want to activate or remove
Adding a text box to a worksheet	EX 3.28	• Activate the Drawing toolbar
		• Click the **Text Box** 📰 button
		• Click the worksheet in the location where you want the text box
		• Drag an outline away from the initial point until the text box outline is the right size and shape
		• Type the text you want to appear in the text box
Hiding rows or columns	EX 3.34	• Select the rows or columns
		• Click **Format**, point to **Row** (or **Column**), and click **Hide**
Applying color or patterns to worksheet cells	EX 3.35	• Select the cells to which you want to apply a color or pattern
		• Click **Format**, click **Cells**, and click the **Patterns** tab in the Format Cells dialog box
		• If you want to apply a pattern, click a pattern from the Pattern list box
		• If you want the pattern to appear in color, click the Pattern list box again and click a color from the Pattern palette
		• If you want to apply a colored background, click a color in the Cell shading color palette in the Format Cells dialog box
Printing multiple worksheets	EX 3.45	• Ctrl-click the sheet tabs of each sheet you want to print
		• Click the **Print** 🖨 button

EXCEL

CROSSWORD PUZZLE

Across

2. Name for the combination of typeface, character size, and spacing
4. Print orientation for a narrow but long output
7. Type into the Excel _____ box drawing object
9. Name of the default format for cells
10. The process of making a toolbar appear on the desktop
13. General name for font if characters' pitches vary

Down

1. The cell _____ format applies lines to worksheet cell edges
3. Sheet is _____ when it is selected
4. Metric used to indicate the height of a character
5. The position of data relative the sides of a cell
6. The property of a toolbar that is not attached to one of the four window walls
8. Altering the appearance of data in one or more cells
11. Format drawing objects with 3-D effects with a _____ shadow
12. Name given to the width of a character

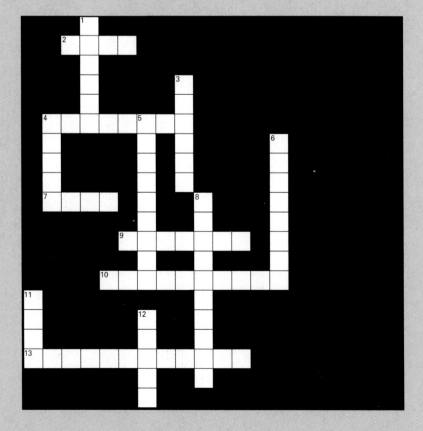

FILL-IN

1. Use the numeric format _____ when you want to format a value such as 0.3478 to display 34.78%.

2. Use the Format _____ to copy the format of one cell to another.

3. The _____ format displays a left-justified currency symbol for numeric entries.

4. Apply a cell _____ format to produce lines and to outline an area of related cells.

5. Click the _____ menu on the Drawing toolbar to display a palette of shapes such as Block Arrows and lines.

6. Select _____ orientation for wide worksheets. The default orientation, _____, is best for narrow worksheets.

REVIEW QUESTIONS

1. Suppose you have a column of numbers representing the wholesale cost of various quantities of produce, and suppose the label "Whole produce cost" heads the column. Discuss how you would format the numeric entries in the column and discuss which formats you might apply to the column's identifying label.

2. Discuss the impact of a worksheet in which five columns each are formatted with a different background color. Is such formatting suitable for professional presentations? What improvements, if any, would you suggest?

3. What are Excel drawing objects and how are they useful? Are drawing objects attached to particular cells, stored as part of the cells' contents, or in some other position in a worksheet? Explain.

4. Explain why you might want to hide one or more columns in a worksheet.

CREATE THE QUESTION

For each of the following answers, create an appropriate, short question.

ANSWER	QUESTION
1. So that the label and numeric values alignments match	_____
2. Selection handles appear when you do this	_____
3. Changes a cell's background color	_____
4. Proportional typeface	_____
5. Excel merges cells and centers text within the merged cells	_____
6. Excel sets the column width to zero	_____

1. Formatting a College Bookstore Book Order

Mr. Waldron Madden is an instructor in the Philosophy department at South-Western College. Each semester for more years than he can remember, Mr. Madden has ordered his books for each semester through the college bookstore using one of their multipart book order forms. A separate book order form is required for each course, although instructors can group courses together on one order form whenever multiple sections of the same course use the same books. While filling out a book order form is not difficult, Mr. Madden has often thought how much simpler it would be if he could simply fill out an electronic form and e-mail it to the bookstore.

This year the bookstore sent a notice to all instructors that the bookstore would accept book orders by fax or e-mail. However, all fax orders must use a copy of the old paper book order form. Instructors wanting to use e-mail could produce a reasonable facsimile of the paper book order form using Word or Excel. Mr. Madden decides to use Excel. He asks you to help him format the worksheet so that it resembles the paper form. Execute each of the steps that follow to create a book order form containing Mr. Madden's book request. First, ensure Excel is running and the application window is maximized.

1. Open the workbook **ex03Bookstore.xls** and then click **File**, click **Save As**, type **Bookstore2** in the File name text box, and click the **Save** button to save the file under a new name. Ensure that the Formatting toolbar is visible.

2. Type the following in the indicated cells:
   Cell B10: **Mr. W. Madden**
   Cell B11: **1, 2, 5**
   Cell F10: **Philosophy 101**
   Cell F11: **Spring, 2003**
   Cell H10: **10/17/2002**

3. Click cell **A1**, click the **Font Size list box arrow** on the Formatting toolbar, and click **36** in the Font Size list box (scroll it if necessary).

4. Click cell **A2**, click the **Font Size list box arrow** on the Formatting toolbar, and click **24** in the Font Size list box (scroll it if necessary).

5. Select cell range **A1:I1** ("eye-one") and then click the **Merge and Center** button on the Formatting toolbar.

6. Select cell range **A2:I2** and then click the **Merge and Center** button on the Formatting toolbar.

7. Alter the column widths of columns A through I by right-clicking each column heading in turn, clicking **Column Width**, and then typing a width—listed below for each column—and then clicking **OK**. Column A: **16**, column B: **21**, column C: **12**, columns D and E: **4**, column F: **21**, columns G and H: **10**, and column I: **12**.

8. Click and drag the cell range **A14:I20**, click the **Borders list box arrow**, and click the **All Borders** square to place borders around all cell walls of the selected cell range.

9. Click and drag the cell range **I21:I24** and click the **Borders** button (the All Borders button appears on the Borders button now).

10. Click and drag the cell range **A14:I14**, click the **Fill Color list box arrow**, and click the **Gray-25%** square to place a light gray background in the selected cells. Click the **Bold** button on the Formatting toolbar.

11. Click **B10**, press and hold the **Ctrl** key, click **B11, F10, F11,** and **H10,** and then release the Ctrl key.

12. Click the **Borders list box arrow** and click the **Bottom Border** square to place a line on the lower edge of each selected cell.

13. Click the cell range **B14:C14** and click the **Center** formatting toolbar button.

14. Click **D14**, press and hold the **Ctrl** key, and click cells **E14, G14, H14,** and **I14,** release the Ctrl key, and click the **Align Right** Formatting toolbar button.

15. Click and drag the cell range **I15:I24**, click **Format**, click **Cells**, click the **Number** tab, click **Accounting** in the Category list, click the **Symbol list box arrow,** and click **None.** Click the **Decimal places spinner** so that it displays 2 and click **OK**.

16. Click the **Format Painter** button and then select the cell range **H15:H20.**
17. Click **I15,** press and hold the **Ctrl** key, click **I21,** click **I24,** release the Ctrl key, click the **Currency Style** button on the Formatting toolbar, and press **Ctrl+Home** to deselect the cell range.
18. Click **View,** click **Header and Footer,** click the **Custom Header** button, replace the text in the Right section with your name, click **OK,** and click **OK** again.
19. Click the **Print Preview** button on the Standard toolbar. Then click the **Setup** button on the Print Preview toolbar, click the **Page** tab, click the **Landscape** option under the Orientation section, click the **Margins** tab, and change the Left and Right margins to **0.75.** Finally, click the Page Setup dialog box **OK** button and then click the Print Preview toolbar **Close** button.
20. Click the Save button on the Standard toolbar, print the worksheet, and close Excel.

2. Creating a Business Card

Carmen Cervantes is the president of the Professional Students Association, which is a club that meets once a month to hear a professional speaker from the community speak about various topics in both business and society. The association has almost 40 members, and Carmen thought it would be nice if the members had cards, similar in format to business cards, that identify each of them as members of the Professional Students Association (PSA). Unfortunately, PSA's budget is very limited. Therefore there is not enough money to supply each member with a set of business cards. As an interim measure, Carmen wants to make business cards using Excel. She can print the cards on heavier stock paper to give the printed output the feel of real business cards. Follow these steps to print a business card similar to Carmen's organization.

1. Start Excel and open a blank workbook.
2. Click **A1** and type **Professional Students Association.**
3. Click **B3** and type your first and last names.
4. Click **B4** and type your school's name.
5. Click **B5** and type the street address of your school.
6. Click **B6** and type the city and state, separated by a comma, where your city is located.
7. Click **B7** and type your telephone number, beginning with the area code. Enclose the area code in parentheses, type a space, and type the rest of your phone number.
8. Click **A1** and click the **Bold** button on the Formatting toolbar. Change the point size of the typeface to **14.**
9. Click **B3** and click the **Bold** button on the Formatting toolbar. Change the point size of the typeface to **12.**
10. Select the cell range **B4:B7** and click the **Increase Indent** button twice.
11. Click **B4** and click the Formatting toolbar **Italic** button.
12. Select cell range **A1:E11.**
13. Click the **Borders** button on the Formatting toolbar and then click the **Thick Box Border** square.
14. Click **File,** click **Save As,** type **BusinessCard** in the File name text box, and click **Save.**
15. Click **File,** click **Print,** and click **OK** to print your business card.

challenge!

1. Formatting a Class Schedule

You just received your Spring 2003 class schedule and you want to create a copy of it using Excel. Once you create the schedule, you can post it to the Web for others to view. Begin by loading the workbook **ex03Schedule.xls.** It contains an example class schedule containing a total of 17 credit hours.

Format and then print the schedule by doing the following. Set the title in A1 to **18** point **Times New Roman** typeface and merge and center it over columns A through E. Set row 1's Row Height to **24. Bold** cell range **A2:E2.** Change the column widths of column A to **5,** columns B and C to **8,** column D to **22,** and column E to **8.** Format cell range A2:E2 with wrap text alignment. Format cells A1 through E7 with the **All Borders** selection so that borders appear around each cell in the range. Remove the gridlines from the onscreen display. Center all entries in column E, and right-align labels in cells B2 and C2. Format the times in columns B and C to display AM or PM. Adjust column widths so that they are no wider than necessary to accommodate the existing data. Finally, color the background of cells A2 through E2 with **Yellow** and the background of cells A3 through E7 with **Light Yellow.** Place your name somewhere in the worksheet header or footer and then execute File, Save As, or print the worksheet according to your instructor's direction.

2. Formatting a Payment Ledger

John Kirry purchased a new automobile last year. He received a bank loan for $10,000 for the car and paid the dealer a down payment of just over $5,000. His bank sent a statement at the end of the year detailing all of his loan payments during 2001. The worksheet shows the amount of John's payment that is applied toward interest and the amount that reduces the outstanding loan balance. John, a commercial airline pilot, understands enough about spreadsheet programs to enter data and save workbooks, but he is reluctant to format the data. He calls you up and asks you to format it for him. (To return the favor,

John promises to take you up in a private plane for an hour to tour the city.) You agree to help John and ask him to send you the worksheet as an e-mail attachment. He does. The file is called **ex03Payment.xls.** You detach it from the e-mail message and load it into Excel. Figure 3.40 shows you the formatted version of the payment ledger.

Reproduce the formatting shown in that figure as accurately as you can. The font is Arial 10 point. Column labels are bold, some column labels are centered, but the labels above numeric values are right aligned. Column-top numeric values contain the Accounting format. Notice the Interest Payment label. It has a superscript—a footnote. Type the word **Payment1** and then highlight the digit 1. Click **Superscript** from the Font tab of the Format Cells dialog box. Follow the same procedure for the text box at the bottom of the figure. It contains the same superscript. The text box and the callout Drawing objects both have drop shadows. Remember to place your name in the header or footer. Set all margins to 1 inch. Use borders and shading as shown in the figure.

FIGURE 3.40

Formatting a payment ledger

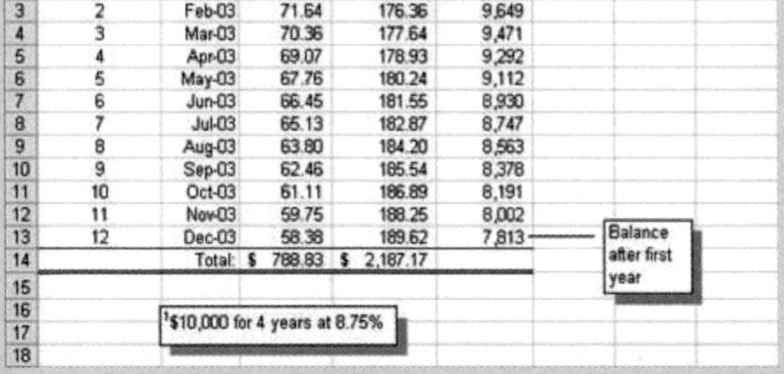

	A	B	C	D	E	F	G	H
1	Payment Number	Date	Interest Payment[1]	Principal Payment	Unpaid Balance			
2	1	Jan-03	$ 72.92	$ 175.08	$ 9,825			
3	2	Feb-03	71.64	176.36	9,649			
4	3	Mar-03	70.36	177.64	9,471			
5	4	Apr-03	69.07	178.93	9,292			
6	5	May-03	67.76	180.24	9,112			
7	6	Jun-03	66.45	181.55	8,930			
8	7	Jul-03	65.13	182.87	8,747			
9	8	Aug-03	63.80	184.20	8,563			
10	9	Sep-03	62.46	185.54	8,378			
11	10	Oct-03	61.11	186.89	8,191			
12	11	Nov-03	59.75	188.25	8,002			
13	12	Dec-03	58.38	189.62	7,813		Balance after first year	
14		Total:	$ 788.83	$ 2,187.17				
15								
16								
17			[1]$10,000 for 4 years at 8.75%					
18								

on the web

1. Building and Formatting a Product Comparison Worksheet

Ernie Kildahl wants to open an online store to carry audio equipment. The real physical store he owns sells a variety of electronic equipment but has only a limited selection of audio equipment. Ernie is particularly interested in offering a variety of brand-name stereo headphones in his online store. He wants you to research a few brands on the Web, collect a bit of information about the headphones, and report back to him. He is interested in the following brands and models: AKG, Beyerdynamic, Etymotic Research, Grado, and Sennheiser. Using Web search engines, locate three prices for each headphone and model and compare their prices on these five brands. The particular models you are to price-shop—one per brand—are in the worksheet **ex03Headphones.xls.** Load and print the worksheet for reference as you conduct your Web research.

After you have collected three prices for each brand and model, format the worksheet with currency symbols, borders, bold, and at least two typefaces—one for the title (Headphone Price Survey) and a different font for the remainder of the worksheet. Bold column titles, and use a larger point size for the column titles than the five product rows. One Web location to get you started is www.headphone.com (what else!). Use one or more search engines such as www.hotbot.com and www.google.com to search for "headphone" to locate prices. If those search results are not satisfying, search for particular brand and model combinations. For example, search for "Grado SR224" and look for any vendor's prices. Identify your worksheet, save it when you are done as **Headphones2.xls**, and print the results.

2. Formatting an "Audio Rippers and Encoders" Comparison Worksheet

You have an extensive collection of MP3 files that you have purchased from various reputable online MP3 distribution sites. Now you want to convert several of your MP3 sound tracks into a CD-compatible format. First, do a little feature, cost, and popularity comparisons before choosing a conversion program by creating a worksheet with features across a row and different encoding and ripping program names down a particular column. Format the results into an attractive worksheet with commas where needed. Start your research by using any Web browser and going to www.download.com. Click the *Rippers and Encoders* link under the heading *MP3 and Audio*. After the browser displays the Rippers and Encoders page, click the Downloads link at the top of the column displaying the number of downloads. This sorts the resulting rows into descending order by popularity. Place the following information into a worksheet, format it, save it, and print it.

In column A (beginning in cell A4, for example), list at least five of the most popular entries in the sorted list of encoders. In row 3, beginning in cell B3, place the following labels left to right: **Software Cost, Date Added to List, Number of Downloads,** and **File Size (KB).** Format these long labels by clicking Format, Cells, and then clicking the Alignment tab. Format the column labels wrap text so that they completely display. Next, fill in the rows and columns with information for each of the five products and their features (software cost, date added to list, etc.). Place a zero in a cell whenever the software cost indicates "free." For "shareware" or "check latest prices" software, determine the software's price by clicking the appropriate links and then insert the price into your worksheet. (Leave it blank if the price is not readily available.) Be sure the file sizes are in thousands of kilobytes so that the units are comparable in the File Size column. List the file size for a 2.9MB file as 2,900 or a 950K file as 950. Remember that 1MB is equal to 1000K. Use cell borders in any way you choose to enhance the worksheet.

Place a worksheet title (such as "Encoder Price Comparison") in row 1 and increase the title's font size. Bold the title to make it stand out. Center the title across all information-containing columns (product name, software cost, and so on). Insert a comment in the cell containing the File Size label. The comment should contain the statement "All information obtained from Download.com." Remember to label your output with your name in the header, footer, or in the worksheet itself. Execute either Print or Save As, according to your instructor's direction.

e-business

1. Developing a Rowing Product Worksheet

Marcia Sandoval was on the lightweight women's crew in college. She rowed for Radcliffe seven years ago and has maintained her passion for rowing ever since. Since she graduated from college, she has been rowing at an all-women's rowing club in Santa Monica. Marcia majored in journalism and she minored in business in college. She has always had an entrepreneurial spirit. Three years ago, she started a mail-order store from her garage selling rowing accessories and athletic equipment. She wants to open a rowing store on the Internet selling her rowing items that appeal to both recreational and competitive rowers. She has created a fundamental worksheet that she will present to her loan officer next Monday, but she has to format it to make it more professional looking.

Open the worksheet **ex03Rowing.xls** and format it to make it more attractive and professional looking. Make at least six formatting changes to the worksheet and print it. Marcia has introduced some indenting that is incorrect. All values should be formatted to two decimal places.

around the world

1. Investigating the Value of the U.S. Dollar

Format a table showing the exchange rate for $100 U.S. Start your research by loading your favorite Web browser. There are several exchange rate calculators on the Web, but you might find one particularly handy because it maintains a history of currency exchange rates. Go to www.exonofinance.com/xrates.html and use their Web pages to locate currency exchange rates. Specifically, you are to find the exchange rate of

$100 U.S. in the following currencies: Australian Dollar, French Franc, British Pound, Italian Lira, and Japanese Yen. Format the worksheet to resemble Figure 3.41. Select any three consecutive months and compute each currency's average value against the U.S. Dollar. Color the $100 red (second row of the figure), shade the column headers, use a background color, and format values in the four columns with commas and zero decimal places. Print your worksheet.

FIGURE 3.41

Formatting a foreign currency table

Value of U.S. Dollar

The value of $100 U.S. is:

Currency	Currency	9/1/2003	10/1/2003	11/1/2003	Average
Australia	Australian Dollar				
France	French Franc				
Great Britain	Pound				
Italy	Lira				
Japan	Yen				

fill in values in these three columns

write formulas for this column

running project

Pampered Paws

Grace Jackson wants to assemble a worksheet showing the first-quarter sales and remaining inventory of dog and cat baked and bottled treats. The worksheet will help her order supplies next month based on sales for the previous period and the amount of inventory on hand. She has created a rudimentary worksheet called **ex03Paws.xls** that she wants you to format so that it is easier to understand and use.

Format the worksheet using borders, at least one text box and arrow combination that points out the inventory item on hand with the largest value, and use some foreground and background color to highlight the product that has the highest total sales. Format the Beginning Inventory, Ending Inventory, and the Units Sold columns using Accounting with zero decimal places. Format the Inventory Value and Total Sales columns with Accounting with two decimal places. Remember to place a dollar sign on each column-top numeric value per product category. Use at least two different typefaces but no more than four in the worksheet. Use foreground and background color for the three product category names and separate the categories with one blank row. Center the worksheet both horizontally and vertically on the worksheet. Save the workbook as **Paws33.xls.** Print the worksheet in landscape orientation.

CHAPTER

4

four

Creating
Charts

Chapter Objectives

- Define a data series and data categories

- Create an embedded chart and a chart sheet
  (MOUS Ex2002-6-1)

- Modify an existing chart by revising data, altering chart
  text, and labeling data (MOUS Ex2002-6-1)

- Use color and patterns to embellish a chart
  (MOUS Ex2002-6-1)

- Add a new data series to a chart (MOUS Ex2002-6-2)

- Alter a chart type and create a three-dimensional chart
  (MOUS Ex2002-6-1)

- Create a pie chart with a title, exploding slice, labels, and
  floating text (MOUS Ex2002-6-1)

- Add texture to a chart (MOUS Ex2002-6-1)

- Delete embedded charts and chart sheets
  (MOUS Ex2002-4-1)

Big Wave Surfboards

Keoki Lahani founded Big Wave Surfboards in 1971 in his garage in Napili, Maui, Hawaii, where he designed and built his first surfboards. Keoki ships surfboards all around the world today. Since 1971, Keoki has enlarged his shop in Napili and created two more surfboard design and manufacturing facilities and accompanying outlet stores in Malibu, California, and Melbourne, Florida. A master board builder at each of his three stores oversees the design and manufacture of Keoki's surfboards, which bear his Big Wave logo.

Each facility builds surfboards from scratch using Keoki's time-honored hand craftsmanship and quality control methods. Starting with a foam blank, a shaper uses foam planers to create the rough shape for each custom-designed board to exacting customer specifications. If a board is going to contain a color or logo, it is applied after the blank is sanded. In the second major step of the four-step manufacturing process, a skilled technician applies fiberglass (called "glassing") followed by a coating of resin to hold the fiberglass in place to supply waterproofing and to give the board strength and integrity. The third step, called sanding, follows the glassing. An experienced sander carefully sands the board to remove any irregularities and ensures that the surface is

smooth and even. The final step is called finishing. A finisher typically applies a gloss finish. The gloss finish supplies the final seal and gives the board a smooth, uniform, glossy look.

Big Wave offers a wide variety of surfboards ranging from smaller boards, called shortboards, that are as short as 5 feet long up to the largest surfboards, called longboards, that can be over 11 feet long. Each of the three manufacturing centers can build any surfboard from shortboards to longboards. Big Wave classifies the surfboards they sell into these groups: Shortboard, Fish, Funboard, Retro, and Longboard. Surfboard length, shape, and features classify them into the different groups.

Keoki and his chief financial officer, Stephen French, have created a worksheet summarizing sales for last year and broken out sales by sales outlet and board type. In this chapter, you will help Stephen create various charts from the raw worksheet data and enhance charts to convey sales information graphically. Charts provide the reader with a quickly understandable and simple picture of the sales patterns. Figure 4.1 shows the completed Big Wave Sales worksheet and accompanying embedded graph.

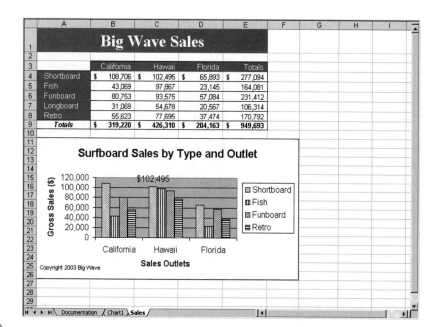

FIGURE 4.1

Completed Big Wave surfboard sales worksheet

INTRODUCTION

Chapter 4 covers creating Excel charts. In this chapter, you will use a worksheet from Big Wave, a surfboard manufacturer and seller. Using the sales values for three separate sales locations and several different surfboard categories, you will create graphs that pictorially display sales in a chart. Using the chart wizard and various chart formatting features, you will create and modify both an embedded chart and a chart stored on a separate worksheet. Formatting and graph features you will explore include altering a chart's title, legend, data markers, X- and Y-axis titles, background colors, and Y-axis scaling. Color and patterns add excitement to a chart. You will learn how to apply both. Three-dimensional charts simplify understanding the values in a worksheet, and you will create a 3-D pie chart with special features such as an exploded pie slice. The chapter concludes by describing how to add various text elements to charts, adding and modifying textures, printing chart sheets, and saving and deleting charts.

SESSION 4.1 CREATING AN EXCEL CHART

In this section, you will learn how to create your first Excel chart from existing sales data supplied in the Big Wave sales worksheet. First you will learn about data series and data categories. Then you will learn about the different chart types available in Excel and which situations favor one chart type over others. Using the Excel chart wizard, you will create an embedded chart displaying sales of different types of surfboards for each sales outlet. After creating a graph, you will update and modify it by changing the underlying data, changing text in the chart, and adding labels

CHAPTER OUTLINE

4.1 Creating an Excel Chart

4.2 Modifying and Improving a Chart

4.3 Summary

EX 4.3

EXCEL

to the charted data. Next you will add color and modify color to enhance the chart's appearance. Finally you will preview the worksheet and chart and then print it.

DATA SERIES AND CATEGORIES

Two important terms you should understand before you work with charts are data series and categories. A *data series* is a set of values that you want to chart. For example, if you want to chart sales of Big Wave surfboards in California, the data series is the set of sales values under the column heading California. Similarly, if you want to chart temperatures in Nebraska for the month of January, the data series is the set of temperature readings for each day of January found in contiguous cells in a row or column. Each data series in a chart can have up to 32,000 values, or *data points,* for two-dimensional charts or 4,000 values for three-dimensional charts. You can chart as many as 255 data series in a chart, although a two-dimensional chart is limited to a total of 32,000 total data points.

You use *categories* to organize the values in a data series. For example, a data series of sales for surfboards sold in Florida contain the categories Shortboard, Fish, Funboard, Retro, and so on (see Figure 4.1). Similarly, the categories for a series of sales values for the past year are January, February, March, and so on—the month names under which sales are recorded. In a chart that plots value changes over time, such as fluctuating prices of a particular stock for the last month, the categories are always the time intervals (days, months, or years). To keep this clear in your mind, simply remember that the data series is the series of values you are charting and categories are the labels or headings under (or next to) which the values are stored.

LOCATING AND OPENING THE WORKBOOK

Stephen French, an avid surfer and Big Wave's chief financial officer, sits down with you and outlines what he wants you to do to the Big Wave sales worksheet. He sets milestones for you to complete in time for the important presentation coming up this month. The result of that meeting with Stephen are these points:

- Goal: Create charts from the Big Wave sales data in an attractive form ready for printing and presentation to the Board of Directors this month
- Information needed to complete the work: Sales data for California, Hawaii, and Florida by surfboard model for previous year
- New formulas or values needed: None. The worksheet data is complete as is. Only charts are missing from the workbook

With Keoki's guidance, Stephen has entered all the formulas, values, and text for the Big Wave workbook. It consists of one worksheet displaying sales for five categories of surfboards broken out by sales location. For example, the worksheet sales figures indicate that shortboard-style surfboards sold far more units in California last year than in either Hawaii or Florida. Similarly, longboards are more popular in Hawaii than they are in either Florida or California based on last year's sales. However, it takes careful study of the sales values to determine the preceding facts. A graph would make that fact obvious more quickly.

You begin by opening the Big Wave workbook.

Opening the Big Wave worksheet and saving it under a new name:

1. Start Excel

2. Open the workbook **ex04BigWave.xls.** The documentation sheet displays (see Figure 4.2)

3. Type your name in the cell to the right of the label Designer and type the current date in the cell to the right of the label Design Date. Notice that the Documentation worksheet does not display column and row headers

4. Save the worksheet as **BigWave2.xls** to preserve the original workbook in case you want to revert to that version

5. Click the **Sales** tab to display that worksheet (see Figure 4.3)

	California	Hawaii	Florida	Totals
Shortboard	$ 198,706	$ 102,495	$ 65,893	$ 367,094
Fish	43,069	97,867	23,145	164,081
Funboard	80,753	123,575	57,084	261,412
Longboard	31,069	154,678	20,567	206,314
Totals	$ 353,597	$ 478,615	$ 166,689	$ 998,901

The Sales worksheet shows sales of four types of surfboards in the three states where Big Wave has outlets—California, Hawaii, and Florida. At the bottom of each state's column is the total value of sales for the year in that state's store. Details of individual models of each type of surfboard are not displayed in the worksheet because the Sales worksheet summarized sales for Keoki. Other worksheets maintained by store managers in each of the three states list each surfboard built and sold. Detailed information on each surfboard includes the exact dimensions, weight, construction, number and size of fins, sale price, and so on. Worksheet data arranged in row categories and column locations are ideal to graph.

CHOOSING A CHART TYPE AND FORMAT

Using Excel, you can create sophisticated charts from worksheet data. Excel provides 14 chart types, each of which has at least two subtypes providing alternative representations. While you may be used to calling the graphical representations of data "graphs," Excel refers to them as ***charts.*** Each of the 14 chart types has a unique use and purpose. For example, a pie chart is a better way to show the relationships of parts to the whole such as the distribution of tax dollars to education, defense, health and human resources, and so on. A bar chart is an excellent graphical representation to compare values of independent data such as sales by different salespersons or charitable contributions raised by different organizations. Figure 4.4 lists the Excel chart types and provides a brief description of their uses.

Chart Elements

Different chart types have different elements. A column chart is typical of an Excel chart. Figure 4.5 shows the elements of a column chart. All of a chart's elements reside in the ***chart area.*** Within the chart area is the ***plot***

F I G U R E 4.4

Excel chart types and their uses

Chart Type	Purpose	Identifying Icon
Area	Shows size of change over time	Area
Bar	Displays comparisons between independent data values	Bar
Bubble	A scatter chart showing relationships between sets of data	Bubble
Column	Displays comparisons between independent data values	Column
Cone	Displays and compares of data represented by each cone	Cone
Cylinder	Displays and compares of data represented by each cylinder	Cylinder
Doughnut	Shows the contribution of each part to a whole at the outer edge	Doughnut
Line	Shows a trend over time of a series of data values	Line
Pie	Shows the relative size of the parts to a whole	Pie
Pyramid	Displays and compares of data represented by each pyramid	Pyramid
Radar	Illustrates data change relative to a central point	Radar
Stock	Displays low, high, open, and close values for stock prices	Stock
Surface	Depicts relationships among large volumes of data	Surface
XY (scatter)	Shows the relationship between two sets of data points	XY (Scatter)

area, which is the rectangular area bounded by the X-axis on the left and the Y-axis on the bottom. By default the plot area is gray, but you can change the color. An *axis* is a line that contains a measurement by which you compare plotted values. The *X-axis* contains markers denoting category values, and the *Y-axis* contains the value of data being plotted. Normally the Y-axis is vertical. The *Y-axis title* identifies the values being plotted on the Y-axis. Above a chart is a *chart title,* which labels the entire chart. Below the X-axis are *category names,* which correspond to worksheet text you use to label data. Below the category names is the *X-axis title,* which briefly describes the X-axis categories. *Tick marks* are small lines, similar to marks on a ruler, that are uniformly spaced along each axis and identify the position of category names or values. *Gridlines* are extensions of tick marks that help identify the value of the data markers. A *data marker* is a graphic representation of the value of a data point in a chart; a data marker can be a pie slice, a bar, a column, or other graphic depending on the graph type. The data marker in the Big Wave sales chart is a column (see Figures 4.1 and 4.5). A chart's *legend* indicates which data marker represents each series when you chart multiple series. The legend in Figure 4.5 contains the series names (Shortboard, Fish, and so on) and the color-coded bar associated with that name. It is always a good idea to include a legend so that the reader can associate a particular data series with its assigned color or fill pattern.

Chart Placement Choices

You can place charts in one of two places: on a worksheet along with the data being charted or on a separate sheet. When you place a chart on a worksheet near the data you are charting, it is called an *embedded chart.* Embedded charts have the advantage that you can see the data and the accompanying chart on the same page. Often you can print both the data and chart on a single page. When you place a chart on a separate sheet, called a *chart sheet,* it is much larger and there are no other data on the chart sheet. In addition, a chart sheet contains no gridlines, which can distract from the chart's usefulness. Chart sheets are particularly handy when

FIGURE 4.5

Anatomy of an Excel column chart

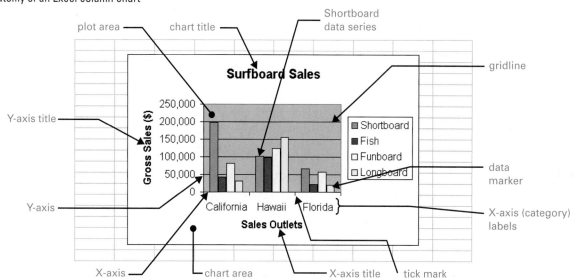

you want to print color transparencies for a presentation. In this first session, you will create an embedded chart. In the second section, you will create a chart sheet.

Developing and Planning a Chart

Prior to creating a chart, take time to plan what it is you want the chart to depict. Consider the following in developing and planning your chart(s):

- What data are to be represented by the chart?
- Which chart type is the best one to represent the data you want to plot?
- Where should the chart be placed—in a worksheet along with the data or on a separate sheet?
- What features should the selected chart type contain—what data markers, whether to include a legend, and what axis labels to include, for example?

Keoki wants you to create a chart summarizing the sales of surfboards. He wants a chart to show the sales by sales outlet and surfboard type. Another chart he'd like to have is total sales of each of the surfboard types, regardless of sales outlet. He has sketched the basic form of the two graphs on an output worksheet page containing sales data. Figure 4.6 shows

FIGURE 4.6

Sketch of two surfboard sales charts

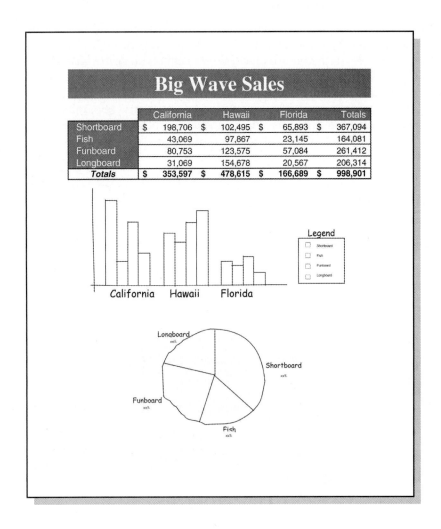

Keoki's sketch. A column graph shows sales by surfboard type for each sales outlet. The pie chart is a good way to show overall sales by surfboard type.

CREATING AN EMBEDDED COLUMN CHART

After calling Keoki and discussing the drawing he faxed, you decide you have all the information you need to create a chart. Creating an Excel chart is a simple two-step process. First, select the worksheet cells you want to chart including any text cells containing row or column headings. Second, launch the Chart Wizard by clicking the Chart Wizard button and follow the multistep Chart Wizard's prompts. The Chart Wizard consists of four steps corresponding to four dialog boxes in which you make choices and proceed to the next step. Figure 4.7 outlines the choices you can make in each step.

Because Keoki wants a printout—on one page—of both the worksheet data and a chart, you choose to create an embedded chart so that both reside on the same page. Create a column chart using the Charting Wizard by selecting the data to be charted in the Big Wave surfboard sales worksheet and then invoking the Chart Wizard.

FIGURE 4.7

Chart Wizard steps and dialog boxes

Dialog box	Tasks and Choices
Chart Type	Select a chart type from a palette of choices
Chart Source Data	Specify or modify the worksheet cell range containing data to be charted
Chart Options	Alter the look of a chart by selecting from a tabbed set affecting gridlines, titles, axes, and data labels
Chart Location	Choose either an embedded chart or a chart sheet style chart

task reference

Creating a Chart

- Select the cell range containing the data you want to chart

- Click the Standard toolbar **Chart Wizard** 📊 button

- Respond to the series of Chart Wizard dialog box choices, clicking the **Finish** button on the last step

Invoking the Chart Wizard to create a column chart:

1. With the Sales worksheet displayed, drag the mouse to select the cell range **A3:D7,** which includes labels at the top of the sales columns and labels on the left of the surfboard data rows. The chart omits the totals column, because it cannot be compared easily to individual sales

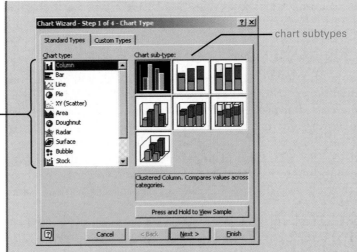

chart subtypes

chart types

tip: *Do not include row 8 in the selected cell range. It contains totals for each numeric column and would be an inappropriate row to include or compare to individual sales.*

2. Click the **Chart Wizard**  button located on the Standard toolbar. The first of several Chart Wizard dialog boxes opens (see Figure 4.8). The dialog box presents the chart types in a list along with a list of chart subtypes

tip: *If the Office Assistant appears, close it by clicking the button next to the message "No, don't provide help now."*

3. Click the **Column** chart choice in the Chart type list, if needed, to select it. In the Chart subtype panel are the seven column chart subtypes including clustered column, stacked column, and several 3-D subtypes of column charts

4. To view a sample of a subtype, click and hold the **Press and Hold to View Sample** button. A sample displays in the Chart subtype panel as long as you hold down the left mouse button. The default subtype, clustered column, is a good choice

5. Click the **Next** button, located at the bottom of the dialog box, to move to the next Chart Wizard dialog box

6. Ensure that the Data range text box displays "=Sales!$A$3:$D$7." The dialog box displays a preliminary chart of your data (see Figure 4.9)

Chart Wizard Step 2 allows you to modify the data series in case you selected an incorrect range accidentally. Notice that the preview of the chart looks different from the chart Keoki wants. Looking closely, you see that the series shown by each bar represent sales outlets, and the four groups represent the four surfboard types. You want just the reverse—series representing each surfboard type and three groups representing the three sales outlets. You modify the way the data series is represented—by rows or columns—with the *Series in* option. You will change this in the steps that follow.

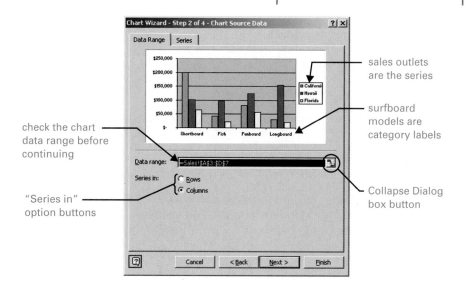

F I G U R E   4.9
Chart Wizard Step 2 dialog box

check the chart
data range before
continuing

sales outlets
are the series

surfboard
models are
category labels

Collapse Dialog
box button

"Series in"
option buttons

Altering the data series and completing the Chart Wizard steps:

1. Click the **Rows** option in the "Series in" section of the Chart Wizard dialog box. Charting will produce a series for each surfboard type and form three groups, one for each sales outlet

2. Click the **Next** button to move to the next Chart Wizard step

3. If necessary, click the **Titles** tab to display chart title text boxes, click the **Chart title** text box, and then type **Surfboard Sales**. After a short pause, the title appears above the chart in the chart preview area of the dialog box

4. Click the **Category (X) axis** text box and then type **Sales Outlets**. After a brief pause, the category title appears below the X-axis in the chart preview area (see Figure 4.10)

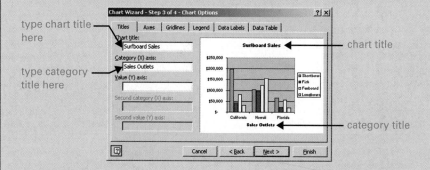

type chart title
here

type category
title here

chart title

category title

F I G U R E   4.10
Chart Wizard Step 3 dialog box

5. Click the **Next** button to proceed to the final Chart Wizard step (see Figure 4.11). In this step, you choose whether to create an embedded chart or a chart sheet. Because you want an embedded chart, you leave unchanged the default option, <u>As object in</u>

EXCEL

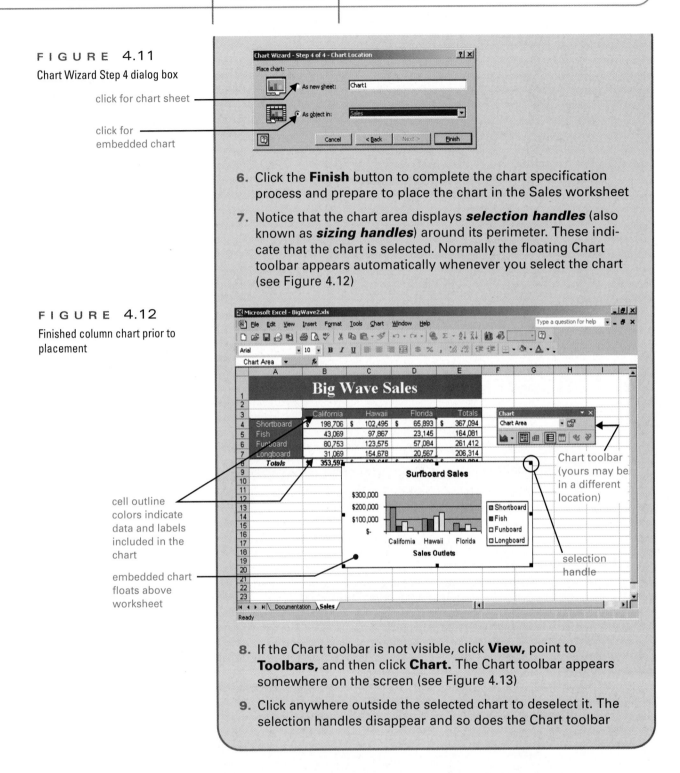

Chart Wizard Step 4 dialog box

click for chart sheet

click for
embedded chart

6. Click the **Finish** button to complete the chart specification process and prepare to place the chart in the Sales worksheet

7. Notice that the chart area displays *selection handles* (also known as *sizing handles*) around its perimeter. These indicate that the chart is selected. Normally the floating Chart toolbar appears automatically whenever you select the chart (see Figure 4.12)

Finished column chart prior to placement

cell outline colors indicate data and labels included in the chart

embedded chart floats above worksheet

Chart toolbar (yours may be in a different location)

selection handle

8. If the Chart toolbar is not visible, click **View,** point to **Toolbars,** and then click **Chart.** The Chart toolbar appears somewhere on the screen (see Figure 4.13)

9. Click anywhere outside the selected chart to deselect it. The selection handles disappear and so does the Chart toolbar

MOVING AND RESIZING AN EMBEDDED CHART

The embedded chart you produced for Keoki is too small to distinguish sales details, and the labels are small as well. It would be nice to somehow enlarge the chart slightly. Because an embedded chart is an object, you can resize it or move it to another location. Like other Windows objects, you modify an object's size by selecting the object and then moving the mouse over one of the object's selection/resizing handles. When the mouse pointer changes to a double-headed arrow, you can drag any selection handle

FIGURE 4.13

Chart toolbar

Icon	Name	Meaning
Chart Area ▾	Chart Objects	List box contains names of all objects on the current chart
	Format	Displays Format dialog box for the selected object (plot area, chart area, and so on)
▴ ▾	Chart Type	List box contains list of chart types (radar, bar, etc.)
	Legend	On/off toggle that adds or removes the legend
	Data Table	On/off toggle that adds or removes a chart data table
	By Row	Displays data series using rows
	By Column	Displays data series using columns
	Angle Text Downward	On/off toggle to angle text down at a 45 degree angle
	Angle Text Upward	On/off toggle to angle text up at a 45 degree angle

away from the object's center to enlarge the object or toward the object's center to shrink it.

Sometimes you want to move an embedded chart to a specific position on a worksheet. For example, you may want to fit a chart exactly within a particular range of cells. Or you might want to modify several embedded charts so that they are the same height and width. In all these cases, you can use a handy Excel snap-to feature to place embedded charts precisely on a worksheet. Otherwise, you can move a chart by clicking the Chart Area and dragging the chart to a new location. (Be careful to click the Chart Area and not the Plot Area or other chart element.)

task reference

Snapping an Embedded Chart into Place

- Select the chart that you want to move or resize

- Press and hold down the **Alt** key

- Drag a chart left, right, up, or down until the chart edge snaps to a cell boundary

- Still holding down the **Alt** key, move the cursor to a chart selection handle

- Click and drag a chart selection handle until the chart's selected boundary snaps to a cell border

- Release the mouse and **Alt** key

Because the chart is too small and obscures part of the data area whose values it charts, you will move and resize the chart. You begin by moving the chart so that its upper-left corner is positioned below the worksheet data.

EXCEL

Moving an embedded chart to a cell boundary:

1. Click in any white area within the chart border, being careful not to click another chart object such as the chart title or the legend

    tip: *Alternatively, you can click the* **Chart objects** *list box on the Chart toolbar and then select* **Chart Area.** *Selection handles appear around the border of the embedded chart.*

    tip: *If the Chart toolbar is in your way, move it to another location by dragging it. You can dock the toolbar on the bottom of the window by dragging it close to the bottom of the screen until it automatically snaps into place.*

2. Press and hold the **Alt** key

3. Drag the chart down and to the left until the upper-left corner is positioned over cell A10 and the top edge of the chart aligns with the bottom edge of worksheet row 9. (The mouse pointer changes to ✛ as you drag the chart)

4. Release the mouse and then release the **Alt** key

Once you move the chart, it no longer obscures the data. However, the chart is still too small. The next task you want to accomplish is to enlarge the chart.

Resizing a chart:

1. Scroll the worksheet up on the screen so that the top of the embedded chart is near the top of the screen and row 25 is also visible

2. Click in any white area within the chart border, being careful not to click another chart object such as the chart title. Selection handles appear around the border of the chart

3. Position the mouse pointer on the bottom-right selection handle

4. When the mouse pointer changes to ◥, drag the selection handle down and to the right until it reaches the bottom of row 25 and the right edge of column F until the lower-right corner of the chart covers cell F25 (see Figure 4.14)

5. Click anywhere outside the chart area to deselect it

You show the Sales worksheet containing the embedded chart to Keoki. He's pleased with the chart but notices that there are three values in the worksheet that are incorrect. Luckily, Keoki catches the errors before you distribute a printed copy. The California Shortboard sales value should

FIGURE 4.14

Resized and relocated chart

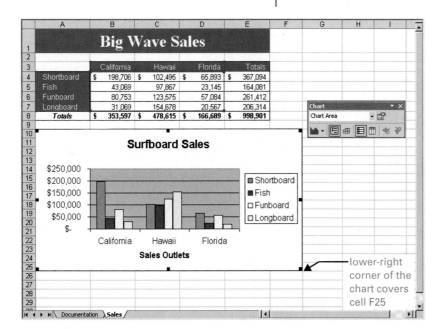

be $108,706. The other two incorrect values are in the Hawaii sales column. Hawaiian Funboard sales should be $93,576, not $123,575. Hawaiian Longboard sales should be $54,678, not $154,678.

UPDATING A CHART

Charts are automatically linked to the data from which they have been created. Consequently, when you change a worksheet value, the portion of the chart representing that data point is automatically updated to reflect the new value. The same is true of worksheet labels that are in the range of cells you selected to create a chart. Any text values in a worksheet that are also part of a chart will change automatically when you change them in the worksheet. An example of this is the text "California" found in cell B3 of the Big Wave Sales worksheet. Changing that cell's contents would also cause the chart category label "California" to change to the new value.

You are ready to make changes to the erroneous data in cells B4, C6, and C7. Any changes you make to the data will change the chart also. Before continuing, notice the leftmost bar in the California category and the rightmost two columns in the Hawaii category. Those bars will decrease in size when you make the changes in the steps below. Notice, in particular, that the first California column almost touches the gridline marked $200,000 and that the third and fourth bars in the Hawaii category are both taller than the first two bars in the Hawaii category.

Changing worksheet data linked to a chart:

1. Scroll the worksheet so that you can see row 1 again, click cell **B4** to select it, type **108706,** and then press **Enter.** Notice that the entire chart plot area resizes as the California Shortboard chart column decreases in height

2. Click cell **C6,** type **93576,** and then press **Enter.** Notice that the third bar from the left in the Hawaii group becomes shorter

EXCEL

FIGURE 4.15

Revised sales data and chart

3. Click cell **C7**, type **54678**, and press **Enter.** Notice that the fourth bar from the left in the Hawaii group becomes shorter (see Figure 4.15)

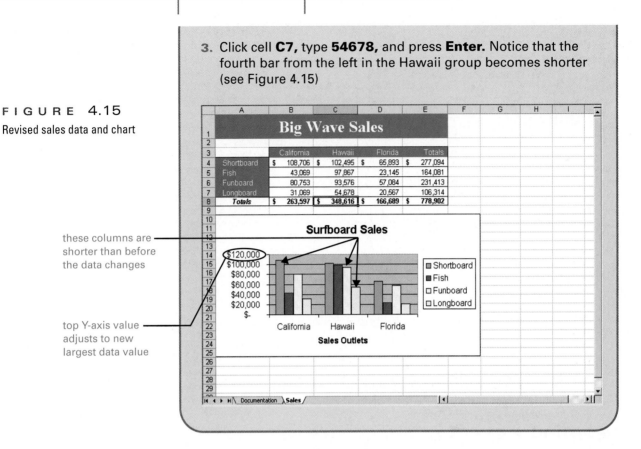

these columns are shorter than before the data changes

top Y-axis value adjusts to new largest data value

After you make changes to the data, the chart automatically changes. One of the most dramatic changes occurs when you reduce the value of the currently largest data point on the chart—the sales value for California Shortboards. The entire chart resizes automatically and the Y-axis values display new values. The embedded chart looks fine. You will make other changes to it after Keoki reviews what you have produced.

MODIFYING A CHART

You can modify every aspect of an Excel chart. For example, you can add a new data series to a chart, modify the foreground and background colors of text objects, alter the colors of data markers in a series, change the typeface of text, and reposition objects on a chart. One of the most dramatic changes you can make to a chart is to add, delete, or hide a series in the chart. You do that by adding, deleting, or hiding rows in the data range of the associated worksheet data. Keoki wants you to add a new line of surfboards to the sales totals so that he can compare their sales to the other types of surfboards.

Adding and Deleting Chart Data Series

Adding a new data series to an existing embedded chart is straightforward. There are several ways to add a series to a chart, but perhaps the simplest way is to add a row to the worksheet and then drag the new data and label cell range to the embedded chart.

You will add the new data to the worksheet. After you add the data, you can add the data series to the embedded chart.

task reference

Adding a New Data Series to an Embedded Chart

- Add the new data, both labels and values or formulas that display values, to the worksheet adjacent to existing chart data

- Select the cell range, including category labels and data, of the data series you want to add to the embedded chart

- Move the mouse to any edge of the selected worksheet cell range

- When the mouse pointer changes to an arrow, click and drag the range into the chart area and release the mouse

---

Inserting a new surfboard category and sales information into the worksheet:

1. Click cell **A8,** click **Insert** on the menu bar, and then click **Rows.** A new row 8 is inserted

2. Type **Retro** in cell A8 and press the **Tab** key

3. Type **55623;** press the **Tab** key, type **77695,** press the **Tab** key, and type **37474**

4. Click cell **E8.** Notice that Excel automatically fills in the SUM function in cell E8. Cell A8 contains a line on its top border because its format is copied from the previous cell A8, which contained "Total." Remove that line in the steps that follow

5. Click Cell **A8,** click **Format** on the menu bar, click **Cells,** and click the **Border** tab

6. Click the top line in the preview panel of the Border section. The top line in the preview panel disappears

7. Click **OK** to close the Format Cells dialog box

tip: *If a dashed line appears along the right edge of column F, Excel is indicating where a page break will occur if you print the worksheet. You can remove the line, if you wish.*

8. To remove the page break indicator, click **Tools** on the menu bar, click **Options,** click the **View** tab, click the **Page breaks** check box in the Window options panel to remove the check mark, and click **OK** to close the Options dialog box

---

Excel automatically adjusts the column sales totals located in row 9 to account for the new surfboard data you added in row 8. However, the new series is not added automatically to the chart. Now that you have added the new surfboard category and sales information for the three sales outlets to the worksheet, you can proceed to add a new series to the existing embedded column chart.

Adding a new series to a chart by dragging the worksheet data:

1. Drag the mouse through the cell range **A8:D8**
2. Move the mouse to the edge of the cell range until it turns into a four-headed arrow
3. Click any line surrounding the cell range, drag the cell range to anywhere in the embedded chart area, and release the mouse to create a new data series (see Figure 4.16)

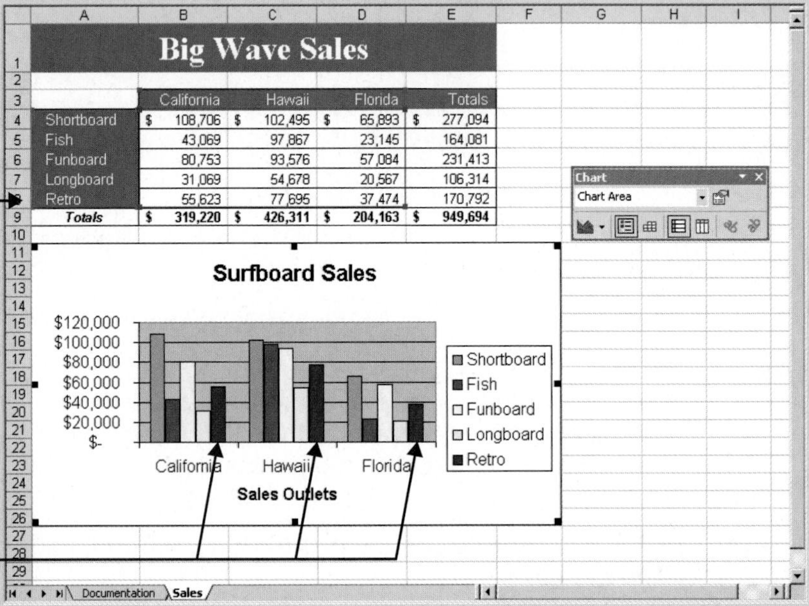

new worksheet data

new data series

FIGURE 4.16
Adding a new data series to an embedded chart

> ***anotherway***
>
> **. . . to Add a New Data Series to a Chart**
>
> Click near the chart border to select the entire chart
>
> Click **Chart** on the menu bar and then click **Add Data**
>
> Select the data you want to plot by dragging the mouse across the worksheet cell range, including the category text, or by typing the cell range in the Range text box
>
> Click **OK**

After examining a chart, you may discover that you have a data series that should not be included in the chart. Similarly, you may decide that the chart should display a different data series. In either case, you can delete a series from a chart without affecting the data series in the worksheet. You can temporarily remove a data series by hiding the data in the worksheet. A more permanent solution is to delete a data series by deleting it from the chart.

task reference

Deleting a Data Series from a Chart

- Select the chart area by clicking anywhere within the chart
- Click the data marker for the series you want to delete
- Press the **Delete** key

Keoki wants to remove the Longboard from the chart but leave it in the worksheet. He asks you to show him the modified chart after you remove the series.

Deleting a data series from a chart:

1. Click the **Chart Objects list box arrow** in the Chart toolbar and then click **Chart Area** in the list to select the Chart

tip: *If the Chart floating toolbar is not visible, click inside the chart to display the Chart toolbar.*

2. Click any of the Longboard data markers (the fourth column in each group). Notice that Excel outlines the corresponding data range in the worksheet—cell range B7:D7—and that a ScreenTip appears identifying the data marker whenever you hover the mouse over it (see Figure 4.17)

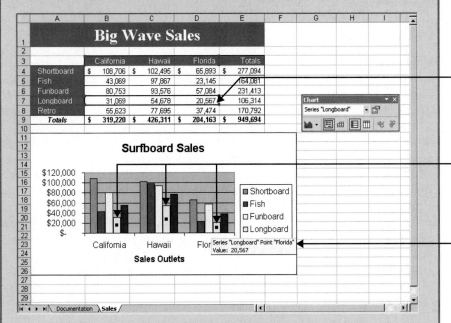

FIGURE 4.17

Selecting a data series prior to deleting it

outline indicates data associated with data markers you select

selected data markers

ScreenTip confirms which data marker is beneath the mouse pointer

3. Press the **Delete** key. The data series disappears from the chart

tip: *If you accidentally delete the wrong series, simply click the **Undo** button on the Standard toolbar, if necessary, and then select and delete the correct data series.*

Hiding Chart Data Series

An alternative to deleting a data series from a chart is hiding it. When you *hide* data (by reducing its row height to zero) in a worksheet that corresponds to a chart's data series, it is removed from the chart temporarily. Removing the data series from the chart is temporary because the data series reappears when you unhide the corresponding worksheet data row or column. Hiding data is handy when you want to print one version of a chart without a particular data series represented in the chart, for instance. Keoki wants you to show him the chart without the Fish data series included.

> ### Hiding a data series by hiding the worksheet data:
>
> 1. Right-click the **row 5 heading label** to select row 5
>
> 2. Click **Hide** from the shortcut menu that opens. Excel hides row 5 and removes the data series corresponding to that row from the chart. You show the resulting chart to Keoki
>
> 3. Because you don't want to hide the data after Keoki examines the new chart, click the Standard toolbar **Undo** ⤺▾ button to reverse the row-hiding operation and then click any cell to deselect row 5. Row 5 reappears

Altering Chart Text

Excel charts can contain several categories of text: attached text, unattached text, and label text. *Attached text* includes tick mark labels, the X-axis title, and the Y-axis title. Excel initially assigns attached text to default positions in the chart area, but you can click and drag attached text to new locations. *Unattached text* includes objects such as comments or text boxes that you add to the chart after creating it. Add unattached text by selecting objects from the Drawing toolbar—objects such as text boxes or callouts. *Label text* includes text such as tick mark labels, category axis labels, data series names (the legend), and data labels. Label text is linked to cells on the worksheet used to create the chart. If you change the text of any of these items on the chart, they are no longer linked to the worksheet cells. The best way to change label text and maintain their links to worksheet cells is to edit the text on the worksheet, not on the chart.

Keoki wants you to change the chart title and add a Y-axis title. Since neither title gets its value from worksheet cells, you can alter and add them directly to the chart.

> ### Altering the chart title:
>
> 1. Click the **Chart Title** object to select it. Selection handles and an outline appear around the chart title. The Name box displays the name "Chart Title" when you select the chart title
>
> 2. Move the I-beam-shaped mouse pointer to the end of the word "Sales" and then click the mouse to remove the selection handles. The blinking vertical bar insertion point appears to the right of the word *Sales*
>
> 3. Press the **Spacebar** and type **by Type and Outlet**
>
> 5. Click anywhere within the chart area but outside the Chart Title object to deselect it

Next, you will add a Y-axis title to identify the values on that axis.

It seems redundant to indicate in the Y-axis title that the values are in dollars and display sales with leading dollar signs in the Y-axis. You will modify the format of the Y-axis values next.

Adding a Y-axis title:

1. If necessary, select the **Chart Area.** Selection handles appear around the border of the entire chart area

2. Click **Chart** on the menu bar and then click **Chart Options** to open the Chart Options dialog box

3. Click the **Titles** tab if necessary, click the **Value (Y) axis** text box, and type **Gross Sales ($)**

4. Click **OK** to complete the process and close the Chart Options dialog box (see Figure 4.18)

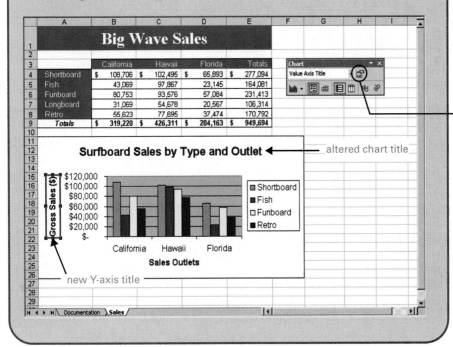

FIGURE 4.18
Chart with altered title and new Y-axis title

Format button (Format Axis, Format Chart, and so on)

Modifying the Y-axis Number Format

Excel determines the values to display on the Y-axis based on the largest and smallest values in the data series you plot. The interval between consecutive Y-axis values is uniform. Excel picks the format for Y-axis values from the formatting of the cell range represented by the data series. You can modify the Y-axis formatting using the same formats Excel provides for formatting numeric entries in a worksheet. You format the Y-axis next to remove the currency symbol, which is indicated in the Y-axis title.

Formatting the Y-axis values:

1. Click the **Y-axis** to select it. Notice that the Chart Objects list box in the Chart toolbar displays "Value Axis" when you select the Y-axis

tip: If the Chart toolbar is not visible, click **View** on the menu bar, point to **Toolbars,** and click **Chart.**

EXCEL

2. Click **Format** on the menu bar, click **Selected Axis,** and click the **Number** tab

tip: *You can also click the **Format Axis** [icon] button on the Chart toolbar instead of Format/Selected Axis (see the Chart toolbar in Figure 4.18)*

3. Click **Number** in the Category list, type **0** in the Decimal places spin control, and check the **Use 1000 Separator** check box

4. Click **OK** to complete the formatting process. The Format Axis dialog box closes and the Y-axis values no longer display the currency symbol to the left of each value along the Y-axis. The value 0 now appears where the Y-axis intersects the X-axis

Labeling Data

While charts provide a handy way to represent numeric data that are easily understood, the exact values of significant data projected by charts is not always clear—especially when you use three-dimensional charts. It is helpful to anyone who reads your charts if you label some or all of the data markers with text that indicates their values. Look at the chart in figure 4.18, for example. If that chart were made into a transparency and presented to an audience and someone in the audience asked you, "What is the value of the gross sales of Shortboards in California?" would you be able to answer them with a precise answer? The best answer you could give is that the value is between $100,000 and $120,000. To precisely answer that question using only a chart, you need to add one or more data labels to your chart. A ***data label*** is the value or name assigned to an individual data point. Data labels are optional.

You can choose to display a data label to all data series in the chart, to one of the data series, or to a single data marker in a data series.

Keoki wants you to add a data label to the data marker corresponding to Hawaiian Shortboard sales. The data marker will indicate the exact value for gross sales represented by the marker.

---

task reference

Adding a Data Label to All Data Series in a Chart

- Select the chart
- Select any data series in the chart
- Click **Chart,** click **Chart Options,** click the **Data Labels** tab
- Click the **Show value** option button and then click **OK**

Adding a Data Label to a Data Series

- Select the chart
- Select the data series
- Click **Format,** click **Selected Data Series,** click the **Data Labels** tab
- Click the **Show value** option button and then click **OK**

task reference

Adding a Data Label to a Data Marker

- Select the chart
- Select the data series containing the data marker to label
- Click the data marker in the series
- Click **Format,** click **Selected Data Point,** and then click the **Data Labels** tab
- Click the **Show value** option button, and then click **OK**

Adding a data label to the Shortboard data marker for Hawaii:

1. Click the chart to select it

2. Click any **Shortboard data marker.** A single square selection handle appears in each of the three Shortboard data markers (columns)

3. Click the **Hawaii Shortboard** data marker. Eight selection handles outline the data marker

4. Click **Format** on the menu bar, click **Selected Data Point,** and click the **Data Labels** tab on the Format Data Point dialog box

5. Click the **Value** check box to place a checkmark in it (see Figure 4.19)

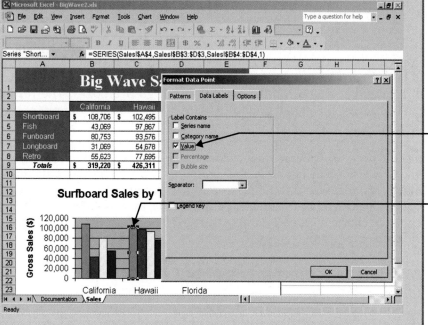

FIGURE 4.19

Adding a data label to a data marker

Value check box

selected data marker
displays selection handles

6. Click **OK** to compete the data label procedure, and click anywhere outside the chart to deselect the data marker (see Figure 4.20)

FIGURE 4.20

Displaying a data marker's value

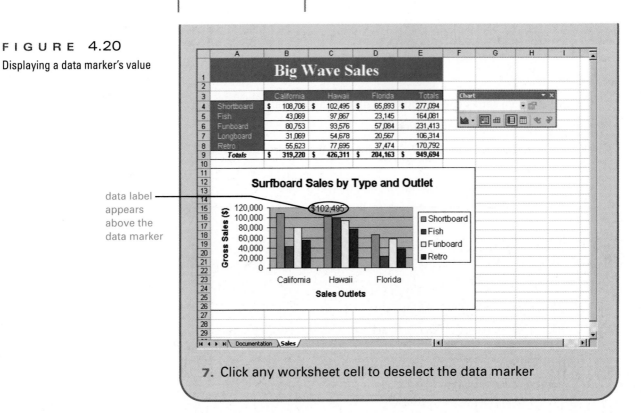

data label appears above the data marker

7. Click any worksheet cell to deselect the data marker

Keoki makes some other suggestions to you about enhancing the chart. You will apply those suggestions next.

EMBELLISHING A CHART

There are a large number of alterations or embellishments you can make to a chart. You can apply foreground and background color to any object on a chart or to the chart background itself. There is a wide selection of patterns and textures you can add to a background also. Gradients, which are color fades that change from dark to light across an object, are available. In fact, the number of enhancements you can apply to a chart is almost endless. However, be careful to not go overboard. The resulting chart can become garish and difficult to view if you use too many colors, textures, and color blends in a single chart.

Remember that not everyone has access to a color printer. Some charts printed on laser printers may yield unreadable text due to the foreground and background color and texture combinations you choose. Data markers may blend together if you choose colors that register as very similar grayscale values on a laser printer. In other words, exercise restraint when you enhance charts with color and textures. The final result will enhance the worksheet rather than detract from it.

Adding a Text Box for Emphasis

Keoki wants you to add text to indicate that the chart belongs to the Big Wave company. The text box should contain the phrase "Copyright 2003 Big Wave" and be placed near the lower-left corner of the chart in 8-point (Arial) typeface.

Adding a text box to the embedded chart:

1. Click the **Chart Area**

2. If the Drawing toolbar is not visible, click **View** on the menu bar, point to **Toolbars,** and click **Drawing.** The Drawing toolbar appears on the screen

3. Click the **Text Box** 🖻 button on the Drawing toolbar

4. Move the mouse to the left side of the chart area near row 25 (scroll the worksheet if necessary), click the mouse to drop the text box onto the chart, and type **Copyright 2003 Big Wave**

5. With the mouse pointer in an I-beam shape, select the text inside the text box by dragging the mouse from right to left across the text within the text box until all the text is selected

tip: *Selecting text in a text box takes a little practice. If the mouse pointer becomes a four-headed arrow* ✥*, you are near the edge of the text box itself. In that case, move back slightly until the mouse changes to an I-beam. Then drag the I-beam mouse pointer across the text until all of it is selected.*

6. Click in the **Font Size list box** on the Formatting toolbar, type **8,** and then click outside the Chart Area (see Figure 4.21)

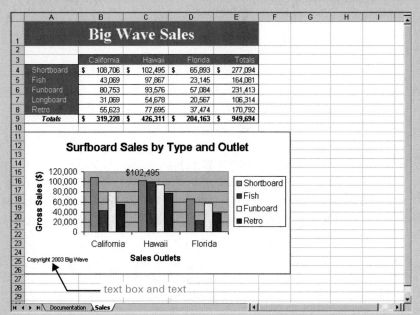

FIGURE 4.21
Adding a text box to a chart

7. If you need to adjust the position of the text box, move the mouse near the text box edge. When the mouse pointer changes to a four-headed arrow ✥, click the text box edge and drag it to the correct position within the Chart Area

8. Click **View** on the menu bar, point to **Toolbars,** and click **Drawing.** The Drawing toolbar closes

Keoki likes the text box you added, and he's satisfied that anyone viewing the chart will know it belongs to Big Wave. Next, you will add a splash of color to your chart.

EXCEL

Emphasizing and Enhancing with Color

There are hundreds of combinations of ways to spruce up a chart including varying the typeface, using color in the background of objects, using color in the text or foreground of objects, and adding graphics. After examining the worksheet for a few minutes, Keoki asks you to experiment with using a dark blue color for the chart title text. Keoki thinks a border or background color might be distracting, though. "Let's try using the dark blue color you will use on the chart title for the value axis title and the category axis title too," Keoki suggests. You open the worksheet and make the requested changes.

FIGURE 4.22

Changing the chart title foreground color

> ### Changing the color of the chart, value axis, and category axis titles:
>
> 1. Click the **Chart Title** object. Selection handles surround the chart title
> 2. Click the **Format** button on the Chart toolbar to open the Chart Title dialog box
> 3. Click the **Font** tab, then click the **Color list box arrow** to reveal the palette of text colors, click the **Dark Blue** square in the palette of color squares (see Figure 4.22), and click **OK** to close the Format Chart Title dialog box
>
>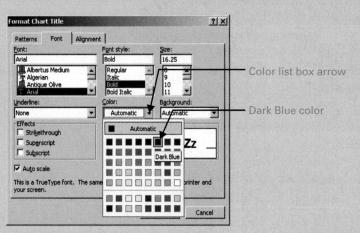
>
> 4. Select the **Value Axis Title** object and repeat steps 2 and 3 above. (The dialog box that opens is called the Format Axis Title dialog box)
> 5. Select the **Category Axis Title** object and repeat steps 2 and 3 above. Press the **Esc** key to deselect the category axis title. All three titles are now dark blue

Changing Patterns and Colors

Colors look great on the screen, but they may not have the same visual impact when you print a worksheet on a noncolor printer. Noncolor laser printers display colors as shades of gray, which can diminish the effectiveness of color. In the absence of color, you can use stripes or textures to differentiate elements of a chart and add impact in a noncolor printer environment. Data markers are particularly difficult to distinguish when they contain the wrong combination of colors. For example, a red data marker is almost indistinguishable from a dark blue data marker. In those cases, it is better to choose stripes and other patterns to uniquely pattern each data series.

Keoki wants you to use different patterns for each of the data markers to avoid confusion about which gross sales are due to each surfboard category.

Applying a data pattern to a data series and changing a data series color:

1. Click any **Shortboard data marker** in the series. Excel selects all data markers in the series

2. Click the **Format** 🖼 button on the Chart toolbar. The Format Data Series dialog box opens

3. Click the **Patterns** tab, if necessary, and click the **Fill Effects** button to open the like-named dialog box

4. Click the **Pattern** tab and then click the **Dark upward diagonal** pattern in the fourth row from the top, third column (see Figure 4.23). The sample pattern you select also appears in the Sample box—a larger version that is easier to view

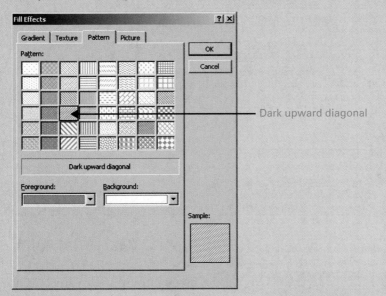

Dark upward diagonal

FIGURE 4.23

Fill Effects dialog box

5. Click **OK** to close the Fill Effects dialog box. Click **OK** to close the Format Data Series dialog box. The new fill pattern appears in the Shortboard data series columns

6. Click any **Fish data marker** in the series and repeat steps 2 through 5, clicking **Dark vertical** pattern (fifth row from the top, fourth column) in step 4

7. Click any **Funboard data marker** in the series, click the **Format Data Series** button on the Chart toolbar, click the **Patterns** tab, click the **Fill Effects** button, and click the **Pattern** tab

EXCEL

8. Click the **Foreground list box arrow** and then click the **Sea Green** square (third row from the top, fourth column) to change the series color

9. Click the **Dark downward diagonal** square (third row from the top, third column)

10. Click **OK** to close the Fill Effects dialog box and click **OK** to close the Format Data Series dialog box

11. Click any **Retro data marker** in the series and repeat steps 2 through 5, choosing **Dark horizontal** pattern (sixth row from the top, fourth column) in step 4

12. Click any worksheet cell to deselect the data marker. Each of the data series has a distinguishable pattern that will be visible even when printed on a noncolor printer (see Figure 4.24)

F I G U R E   4.24

Data markers with patterns applied

another word

. . . on Data Series and Fill Effects

If you decide to *remove* all fill effects from a data series, click any marker of the data series in the chart, click **Edit** on the menu bar, point to **Clear,** and click **Formats**

PREVIEWING AND PRINTING A CHART

You know by now to preview your output before you actually print it, because you can catch small mistakes before printing too many pages. Often a multipage output can be trimmed to one or two pages simply by minimizing the margins or reorienting the output to landscape. Keoki wants you to produce two printouts. The first one is the worksheet and the embedded chart on one page. On the second printout, he wants only the chart, not the worksheet.

Previewing and Printing a Worksheet and Chart

Preview the worksheet and chart prior to printing it. Check to ensure that both the chart and worksheet fit on one page. You will do that next.

task reference

Printing a Worksheet and Embedded Chart

- Ensure that the embedded chart is not selected by clicking any worksheet cell
- Click **File** and click **Print Preview**
- Click **Print** and click **OK**

Saving, previewing, and printing the worksheet and embedded chart:

1. Click **File** and then click **Save** to save the completed worksheet and chart

2. Click cell **A2** to be doubly sure that the chart is not selected

3. Click the **Print Preview** button on the Standard toolbar to open the Print Preview window. Check to ensure that both the worksheet and chart appear on the same page.

tip: *If the entire worksheet does not appear on the first page or if both the worksheet and chart do not appear on the same page, adjust the page margins. Click the Margins button on the Print Preview toolbar. The margin lines appear on the preview. Drag the left and right margin lines toward the edge of the paper to decrease the margins (see Figure 4.25)*

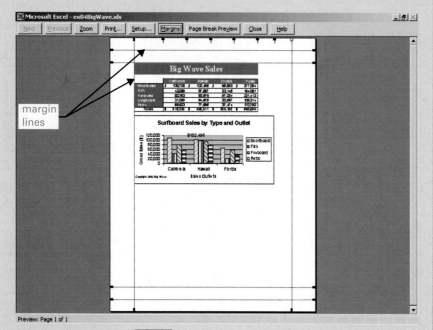

FIGURE 4.25

Preview of worksheet and chart displaying margin lines

4. Click the **Setup** button on the Print Preview toolbar to open the Page Setup dialog box and type your name in the Right section of the header (recall that you click the **Header/Footer** tab, click the **Custom Header** button, click in the **Left section,** and then click **OK** *twice* to close two dialog boxes)

EXCEL

5. Click the **Print** | Print... | button on the Print Preview toolbar to open the Print dialog box, and then click the **OK** button to print the output

Previewing and Printing an Embedded Chart

Printing an embedded chart without the accompanying worksheet is only slightly different from printing the worksheet and chart together. The main difference between the two procedures is that you select the chart before previewing or printing it.

---

task reference

Printing an Embedded Chart

- Click the embedded chart
- Click the **Print** button on the Standard toolbar

Because Keoki wants the embedded chart printed separately, you print it next.

FIGURE 4.26

Embedded chart output

Printing an embedded chart only:

1. Click the **Chart Area.** Selection handles appear around it

2. Click the **Print** 🖨 button on the Standard toolbar to print the chart (see Figure 4.26)

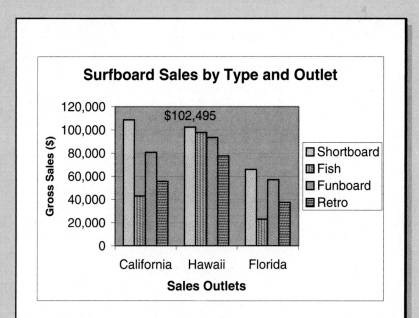

Your work on the embedded chart is done. Keoki is very happy with the results. You can go on to learn about adding another type of graph to the output. This type will be a chart sheet containing a pie chart showing another aspect of Big Wave's surfboard sales.

---

making *the grade*   SESSION 4.1

1. A _____ _____ is a set of values that you want to chart.

2. In a column chart, the labels appearing along the X-axis are called _____ titles.

3. A chart on the same worksheet as the data it represents is called a(n) _____ chart. The other type of chart is called a _____ _____ and resides on its own sheet that is different from normal worksheets.

4. The _____ _____ helps you create a chart by displaying a series of dialog boxes that you fill in to complete the chart.

5. Modify the Big Wave worksheet you saved as **BigWave2.xls** in the following ways. Delete the Funboard data series from the chart. Modify the Y-axis title to **Sales (U.S. Dollars)** and change its point size to 14. Remove the X-axis title completely. Remove all patterns from the data markers so that they all display solid colors. Add data labels to the other two Shortboard data markers (California and Florida). Save the worksheet as **BigWaveModified.xls.** Print the worksheet and chart on one page.

SESSION 4.2 MODIFYING AND IMPROVING A CHART

In this session, you will create a pie chart and learn how to select nonadjacent data ranges for charting. You will learn about three-dimensional chart types including pie charts, exploding a pie slice to emphasize it, and the use of text and titles in three-dimensional charts. You will explore how textures can add interest to charts and learn how to create a chart sheet containing a freestanding chart. Finally, you will create a stacked column chart and learn how to format its components to highlight significant data.

CREATING A CHART IN A CHART SHEET

Keoki wants to look at a broader picture of his surfboard sales in a chart—a chart you will create in a chart sheet. He wants you to create a chart showing total sales of each surfboard type in a pie chart, based on his sketch shown in Figure 4.6. A pie chart is a good chart choice when you want to show the contribution of parts to the whole. In the case of Big Wave, the pie chart will demonstrate visually the contribution of each surfboard type to the overall sales. In a similar way, you could create a pie chart by sales outlet and examine the sales attributable to each sales outlet compared to the sum of all sales.

The pie Keoki sketched contains four slices, one for each type of surfboard. Since then, he added another surfboard to the sales summary—Retro. Therefore, the pie chart will consist of five slices. Each slice should identify the surfboard type represented by the slice and indicate the percentage of sales, compared to the sum of all sales, that it represents.

Defining a Series

Creating a chart begins by first selecting the worksheet cells in the data range to be plotted. Recall that when you specified the data range for the column chart in the previous section, you simply dragged the mouse through a rectangular cell range consisting of all the rows and columns of sales, including the labels above the columns and to the left of each row. This time, the data selection process is different because you want to select two columns from a group of five columns, leaving out three columns in the middle of a range of contiguous cells. Using the sketch in Figure 4.6 as a general guideline, notice that the labels around the perimeter of the pie chart match text in worksheet cells A4 through A8 (A7, originally). Additionally, you speculate that the data represented by pie slices corresponds to the total sales of each surfboard type stored in cells E4 through E8. How do you indicate that you want to chart two noncontiguous cell ranges? The next section describes how to select cells from two noncontiguous ranges prior to calling upon the Chart Wizard.

Selecting Nonadjacent Data Ranges

Prior to launching the Chart Wizard to create a chart, select the cell range(s) that are to be charted. Because the cell ranges are in columns that are not adjacent to each other, you cannot simply drag the mouse through both ranges. Doing so would result in a chart containing two distinct types of data—sales detail information and sales sum information—that should not appear in the same chart. Selecting nonadjacent cell ranges is a common practice when creating charts. When you select nonadjacent cell ranges, each one is highlighted.

---

task reference

Selecting Nonadjacent Cell Ranges

- Click and drag the mouse through the first cell range you want to select
- Press and hold the **Ctrl** key
- Click additional cells or click and drag additional cell ranges
- When finished selecting all cells or cell ranges, release the **Ctrl** key

---

In preparation to create a pie chart, select the two cell ranges consisting of the surfboard labels in column A (cells A4 through A8) and the total sales across all three sales outlets, computed by SUM functions, in column E (cells E4 through E8).

Selecting nonadjacent data ranges in the sales worksheet:

1. If you took a break after the last session, make sure that Excel is running and open to **BigWave2.xls**

2. Click **File**, click **Save As**, type **BigWave3** in the File name list box, and click the **Save** button to preserve the work you completed in the first session

3. Click the **Sales** tab to open that worksheet, select cell range **A4:A8,** which contains names of different types of surfboards, and release the mouse

4. Press and hold the **Ctrl** key, click and drag the cell range **E4** through **E8,** and release the **Ctrl** key. The cell range E4:E8 contains the data points you want to plot on a chart and the two nonadjacent cell ranges, A4:A8 and E4:E8, are selected (see Figure 4.27)

selected, nonadjacent
cell ranges

Creating a Three-Dimensional Pie Chart

Once you have selected the data ranges to chart, you can proceed to create the chart. Keoki wants a pie chart on a separate workbook page—a chart sheet. Charts on separate sheets are convenient to print and you can easily move chart sheets around in the workbook to reorganize their order. You can rename chart sheet tabs with meaningful names to make the charts easy to locate. If you are making a slide presentation, chart sheets are particularly convenient because you can organize the chart sheets in the same order as the slide presentation. Then you can print the chart sheets directly to a color transparency-capable printer.

Selecting nonadjacent data ranges in the sales worksheet:

1. Click the **Chart Wizard** button on the Standard toolbar to start the chart construction process

2. Click **Pie** in the Chart type list box. Several pie chart subtypes appear in the Chart subtypes panel

3. Click the **Pie with a 3-D visual effect** chart subtype (top row, second column) and then click the **Press and Hold to View Sample** button to see an example of the chart. That sample is the chart that Keoki wants. Release the **Press and Hold to View Sample** button

4. Click the **Next** button to proceed to Chart Wizard Step 2. Make sure that the Data range text box displays the data range value =Sales!$A$4:$A$8,Sales!$E$4:$E$8, which is a special form of the cell range notation for the two nonadjacent cell ranges you selected previously

tip: *If the Data range text box does not show the correct cell range, click the Collapse Dialog button and select the two nonadjacent data ranges A4:A8 and E4:E8 before continuing with the Chart Wizard.*

5. Click the **Next** button, click the **Titles** tab, click the **Chart Title** text box, and type **Surfboard Sales by Type**

6. Click the **Legend** tab, and click the **Show Legend** check box to clear it (see Figure 4.28)

FIGURE 4.28

Removing the chart's legend

clear to remove the chart's legend

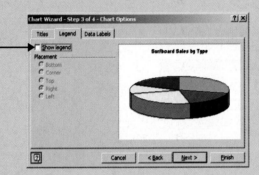

7. Click the **Data Labels** tab, click the **Category name** check box to display category names for each pie slice, and click the **Percentage** check box button to display percentages for each pie slice

8. Click the **Next** button and then click the **As new sheet** option button to create the chart as a chart sheet rather than as an embedded chart

9. Click the **Finish** button to complete the preliminary version of the three-dimensional pie chart on its own chart sheet (see Figure 4.29)

FIGURE 4.29

Preliminary 3-D pie chart

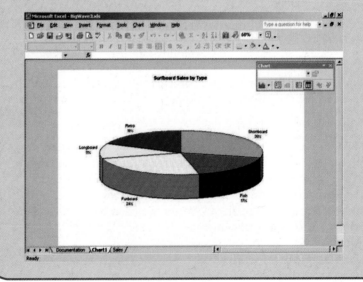

Exploding a Pie Chart Slice

Keoki gives his approval and requests that you find a way to highlight the Shortboard sales to make the data stand out to a viewer. You review several options including special colors and other methods and suggest that the best choice is to pull the Shortboard pie slice away from the rest of the chart.

Exploding a Pie Slice:

1. If necessary, click the chart sheet tab **Chart1** (your chart sheet tab may have a different name) to select the chart sheet Excel just created

2. Click the pie chart. Selection handles appear around the pie, one on each slice, and the Chart Objects list box displays "Series 1"

3. Once you have selected the entire pie, you can select one slice of it. Hover the mouse over the Shortboard pie slice. The ScreenTip "Series 1 Point "Shortboard" Value: $277,094 (30%)" appears

4. Click the **Shortboard pie slice** to select it. Selection handles disappear from all other pie slices

5. Click and drag the **Shortboard pie slice** a short distance away from the center of the pie. An outline appears and shows your progress

6. Release the mouse (see Figure 4.30)

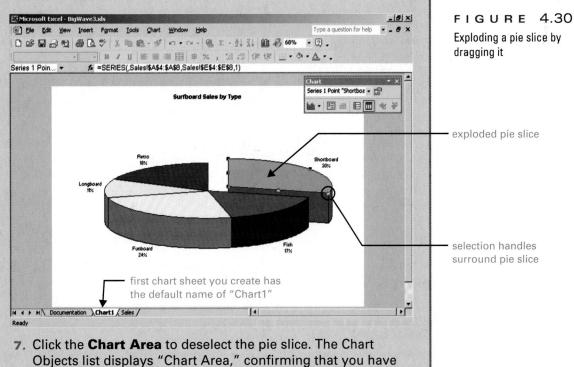

F I G U R E 4.30

Exploding a pie slice by dragging it

exploded pie slice

selection handles surround pie slice

first chart sheet you create has the default name of "Chart1"

7. Click the **Chart Area** to deselect the pie slice. The Chart Objects list displays "Chart Area," confirming that you have clicked the Chart Area

---

EXCEL

Rotating and Elevating a Three-Dimensional Chart

While the 3-D pie chart certainly is impressive and self-explanatory, Keoki thinks the exact proportions of the pie slices are not obvious to a casual reader. He thinks that the pie chart should be tilted up, by raising the back edge, to provide a better perspective. Additionally, Keoki wants the Shortboard pie slice to appear on the right side of the chart at the 3 o'clock position, considering the pie to be a clock face.

FIGURE 4.31

3-D View dialog box

Elevating and Rotating a Pie Chart:

1. With the Chart Area of the 3-D chart sheet selected, click **Chart** in the menu bar and click **3-D View.** The 3-D View dialog box opens. Notice that the Elevation text box displays 15, indicating that the entire pie chart is tilted up 15 degrees (see Figure 4.31)

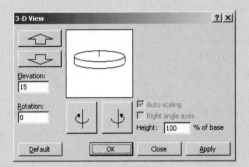

2. Double-click the **Elevation** text box, if necessary, to select its current value and then type **35**

3. Click and drag the **3-D View dialog box title bar** to move the dialog box to a corner of the screen so that you can see the Shortboard portion of pie chart

4. Double-click the **Rotation** text box to highlight its current value, type **20,** and click the 3-D View dialog box **Apply** button. Excel rotates the pie chart clockwise 20 degrees, but that is not quite enough

5. Double-click the **Rotation** text box, type **30** to rotate the pie chart clockwise 30 degrees, and click the **Apply** button. That looks just right (see Figure 4.32)

6. Click the **OK** button to complete the operation and close the 3-D View dialog box

You can see why Keoki wanted you to elevate the 3-D pie chart. It is much easier to see the pie chart and judge the size differences between the five pie slices representing total sales of the five types of surfboards.

CHANGING THE CHART TYPE

Excel has several chart types from which you can choose. You can choose a type as you create a chart. You can choose to change chart types after you have created a chart sheet or an embedded chart. With the current chart selected, you can change to a different chart type by clicking the

Saving the workbook and printing a chart sheet:

1. Click the **Save** 🖫 button on the Standard toolbar to save your workbook

2. If necessary, click the **Chart1** sheet tab to select the chart sheet

tip: *If you have created other chart sheets and deleted them before creating the final chart sheet, your chart sheet tab may not be called Chart1. It may have another name such as Chart2 or Chart3*

3. Click **File,** click **Page Setup,** click the **Header/Footer** tab, click the **Custom Header** button, type your name in the Right section, click **OK** to close the Header dialog box, and click **OK** to close the Page Setup dialog box

4. Click the **Print** 🖨 button to print the chart sheet. After a short pause, the chart sheet prints

DELETING CHARTS

Although you will not delete any charts you have created, you should learn how to delete both embedded charts and chart sheets in case you later need to do so. Delete an embedded chart by selecting it and then pressing the Delete key.

---

task reference

Deleting an Embedded Chart

- Click the embedded chart

- Press the **Delete** key

Deleting a chart sheet is equally simple. Be careful. Unlike deleting an embedded chart, there is no way to reverse the deletion process. You cannot undo a chart sheet deletion. If you mistakenly delete a chart sheet, your only recourse is to reconstruct the chart sheet from scratch or to open a previous version of the worksheet containing the chart sheet.

---

task reference

Deleting a Chart Sheet

- Click the tab corresponding to the chart sheet

- Click **Edit,** then click **Delete Sheet**

- Click **OK**

EXCEL

SAVING A CHART AS A WEB PAGE

Because Keoki wants to share the worksheet with his Big Wave employees in all three locations—Hawaii, California, and Florida—he asks you to create a Web page from the Excel worksheet. For now, Keoki will post the worksheet in a protected area of the Web server that only employees can access.

You can create Web pages from Excel charts about as simply as you can save a worksheet. Once you create the Web pages, make them available to anyone by posting them on a server connected to the Internet that displays Web pages. However, you do not need access to a Web server to create Web pages. You can view your Web pages on any PC that has a Web browser regardless of whether it is connected to the Internet.

---

task reference

Creating Web Pages from an Excel Chart

- Click the chart sheet tab
- Click **File** and click **Save as Web Page**
- Select a drive and folder in the Save in text box
- Click the **Selection: Chart** option
- Click the **Change Title** button, type a Web page title in the title text box, and click **OK**
- Type the Web page file name in the File name text box
- Click the **Save** button

You are ready to create a Web page from the pie chart on the chart sheet you created in this session.

Saving a Chart Sheet as a Web Page:

1. Click the **Chart1** chart sheet tab, if necessary

2. Click **File** and then click **Save as Web Page.** The Save as dialog box opens

3. Select the disk drive and folder in the Save in text box in which you want to save your Web pages

4. Click the **Selection: Chart** option

5. Click the **Change Title** button, type **Big Wave Surfboard Sales by Type** in the Title text box of the Set Title dialog box. The title you type appears in the browser's title bar whenever you open the Web page

6. Click **OK** to close the Set Title dialog box

7. Drag the mouse across the text in the File name text box and type **BigWave** to replace the Excel-suggested file name (see Figure 4.37)

8. Click the **Save** button to save the Web page

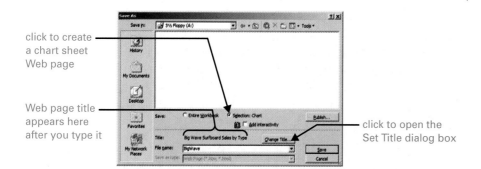

FIGURE 4.37
Saving a chart as a Web page

click to create
a chart sheet
Web page

Web page title
appears here
after you type it

click to open the
Set Title dialog box

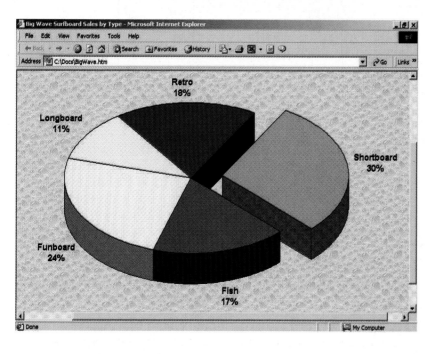

FIGURE 4.38
Big Wave Web page

If you want, you can view the Web page you just created by opening the Web page in your favorite Web browser. Figure 4.38 shows the Web page displayed with Internet Explorer.

CREATING A BAR CHART

Keoki has encouraged competition between his three Big Wave sales outlets by offering incentives if the sales outlet reaches or exceeds selected gross sales goals. He expects gross sales at each outlet to exceed $200,000 per year—the amount he calculates he must make just to keep the sales outlet open. Keoki is pleased when annual sales exceed $200,000 in any sales outlet. He pays a bonus to sales associates in those regions. For sales outlets selling more than $300,000 in one year, Keoki promises a double bonus for the sales associates in those regions.

Keoki thinks that a bar graph is the best way to show the progress of each sales outlet and to display the annual totals to every Big Wave salesperson. Keoki asks you to figure out a way to color-code each segment of a bar so that it colorfully indicates when the sales region reaches the next sales goal.

A bar chart is similar to a column chart and can be used interchangeably. Bar charts can illustrate competitions slightly better than column charts because bar charts are drawn from left to right and resemble progress toward a goal or a race proceeding from left to right. Bar charts

Bar chart with color-coded value alerts

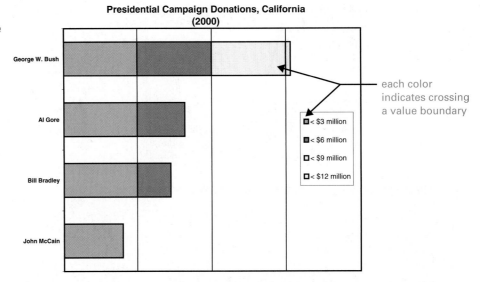

are often used to highlight values that exceed a critical level—blood pressure is too high, temperatures are reaching a critical value, or fuel reserves are below a safety point. One way to highlight critical goals or value points with a bar chart is to color-code a data marker to indicate when the data marker has surpassed one or more critical points. Figure 4.39 illustrates this concept. Each segment of a bar is color coded to indicate when campaign funds for each candidate exceed successive $3 million boundaries. Color codes help a reader quickly grasp the big picture—only George W. Bush raised more than $9 million in California. The paragraphs that follow explain how to create color-coded value alerts using a special type of bar chart.

The **stacked bar chart**, a subtype of the bar chart, combines the data markers in a data series together to form one bar, placing each marker at the end of the preceding one in the same data series. A stacked bar chart is particularly well suited in situations that Figure 4.39 illustrates—when data series comprise a category and you are interested in viewing the sum of the data values in the series. You will use a stacked bar chart to vividly illustrate sales from each sales region that exceed particular milestones. The key is not in the chart but in the data. To create a stacked bar chart similar to the one in Figure 4.39 for Big Wave surfboards, you will create new data and then chart the data.

Creating data series for a stacked bar chart:

1. Click the **Sales** sheet tab to select the worksheet containing the sales data

2. Click cell **G5** and type **California,** click cell **G6** and type **Hawaii,** and click cell **G7** and type **Florida**

3. Click cell **H5**, type **=MIN(B9,200000)**, click cell **H6**, type **=MIN(C9,200000)**, click cell **H7**, type **=MIN(D9,200000)**, and then press **Enter.** These formulas calculate values that

represent the first segment—up to $200,000—of the sales for each sales outlet. Next, you will add another data marker that represents the value between $200,000 and $300,000

tip: *You may want to widen columns H, I, and J, as necessary, to view the results of the formulas.*

4. Click cell **I5,** type **=MIN(B9-H5,100000),** click cell **I6,** type **=MIN(C9-H6,100000),** click cell **I7,** type **=MIN(D9-H7,100000),** and then press **Enter.** These formulas calculate values that represent the second segment—from $200,000 to $300,000— of the sales for each sales outlet

5. Click cell **J5,** type **=B9-H5-I5,** click cell **J6,** type **=C9-H6-I6,** click cell **J7,** type **=D9-H7-I7,** and then press **Enter.** These formulas calculate values that represent the final segment— above $300,000—for each sales outlet (see Figure 4.40)

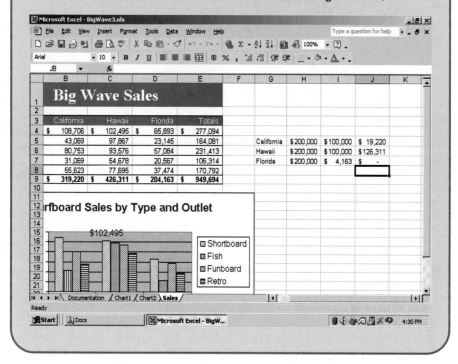

FIGURE 4.40

Creating new data for a stacked bar chart

The new data show the sales for each sales outlet broken down into three segments: 0 to $200,000, $200,001 to $300,000, and greater than $300,000. Using this new data, you can create a stacked bar graph that shows how each series' segment contributes to the total sales represented by a bar in the bar chart. You create the chart next.

Creating a stacked bar chart:

1. Click and drag the cell range **G5:J7**

2. Click the **Chart Wizard** button, click **Bar** in the Chart type list box, click the **Stacked Bar** square in the Chart subtype panel (top row, second column), and click the **Next** button to go to the next Chart Wizard step

3. Click the **Columns** option button and click the **Next** button

4. Click the **Titles** tab, if necessary, and then click the **Chart title** text box and type **Critical Sales Boundaries**

5. Click the **Legend** tab, click the **Show Legend** check box to remove the checkmark, and click **Next**

6. Click the **As new sheet** option button and then click the **Finish** button. The stacked bar chart appears in its own chart sheet, Chart2, following the Chart1 chart sheet (see Figure 4.41)

F I G U R E 4.41

Stacked bar sales chart

Critical Sales Boundaries

bar color change indicates bonus range

color change indicates upper bonus range

Keoki couldn't be happier. He's pleased with all three charts and sends you a nice e-mail expressing how much he appreciates your hard work.

Saving the workbook:

1. Click the **Documentation** sheet tab to make it the active sheet

2. Click **File** on the menu bar, click **Save as,** type **BigWave4.xls** in the File name text box of the Save As dialog box, and click the **Save** button to save the final version of your worksheet to disk under a new name

3. Click **File** and then click **Exit** to exit Excel

You have completed your work in this chapter and have created an embedded chart and two chart sheets.

making the grade

1. You select nonadjacent cell ranges by selecting the first cell range, pressing the _____ key, and selecting the second cell range.

2. A(n) _____ chart resides on a worksheet page, whereas a(n) _____ _____ is on a separate sheet.

3. A _____ chart is a good choice when you want to depict contribution of parts to a whole.

4. You can _____ a three-dimensional pie chart to get a better perspective of it.

5. Open up the original worksheet, **ex04BigWave.xls,** and save it as **BigWave5.xls.** Next, create data similar to that you created in the exercise entitled "Creating data series for a stacked bar chart" above. Click the **Sales** worksheet tab to open that worksheet. Type **Shortboard, Fish, Funboard,** and **Longboard** into cells A11 through A14, respectively. Type the following in the indicated cells:

    Cell B11: **=MIN(E4,100000)**

    Cell C11: **=MIN(E4-B11,100000)**

    Cell D11: **= E4-B11-C11**

    Select cell range **B11:D11** and copy it to cell range **B12:D14** to complete the data area you will chart. Create a three-dimensional stacked bar chart in a chart sheet based on the data in cell range B11:D14 using the Chart Wizard. If necessary, click the Columns option in the Data range panel. Eliminate the legend in Chart Wizard step 3 of 4 and title the chart appropriately. Add your name in the chart sheet header. The chart shows bar color changes when the bars cross $100,000 and $200,000. Click the Documentation tab to make that sheet active and save the worksheet. Print the stacked bar chart sheet and the Sales worksheet. Close Excel.

SESSION 4.3 SUMMARY

Excel charts pictorially display values and provide a graphic way for viewers to easily understand the magnitude or change in data values. You can create either two-dimensional or three-dimensional charts including column, bar, line, pie, scatter, area, and doughnut. For each chart type, you can choose from several chart subtypes. Column subtype charts include simple column, stacked column, and stacked column with a 3-D visual effect. Chart data is called data series—the set of values you chart. Categories organize values in the data series. The X-axis in a column chart displays category names.

Choosing the correct type of chart to display your data is important. Each chart has a different purpose. A pie chart best displays the contribution of parts to the whole—how much of your tax dollar goes to education, for example. Line charts are a good choice to show trends. The plot area contains the chart and other elements surrounding the chart include the chart title, category names, and the X- and Y-axes. Excel supports both embedded charts and chart sheets. Embedded charts appear on a worksheet along with data and float on a layer above the worksheet. A chart sheet is a separate sheet that contains a chart but does not contain worksheet data. Embedded charts and chart sheets are otherwise exactly the same—both types can display any of the Excel chart types.

Chart data—the values represented by the data series—are linked to the data markers. This dynamic relationship means that you can change the value of worksheet data and the chart will automatically adjust to reflect the changes. Category names are linked to worksheet cells too, though they typically display text.

You can modify every aspect of a chart including the overall chart type, the format (color, typeface, and size) of any text or numeric value on a chart, the background color of the plot area or chart area, the color or existence of gridlines and data labels, the format and scaling of Y-axis values, and whether a legend appears on the chart.

Delete data series from a chart by hiding the data in the worksheet (hide the row or column) or by selecting the data series and pressing the Delete key. Print an embedded chart by printing the worksheet on which it resides. Alternatively, click an embedded chart to print just the embedded chart.

Tilt or rotate three-dimensional pie charts until the perspective is just right. Explode a pie slice for emphasis by clicking the pie and then clicking the pie slice. Then drag the pie slice away from the center. Data labels for pie slices can be category names, category names and values, or percentages. You can apply a texture to several chart elements including pie slices, bars, columns, the plot area, or the chart area to add interest and vitality to a chart. You can save an Excel chart as a Web page with the Save As Web Page command in the File menu. After saving the Web pages on your computer disk, you can upload them to an Internet-connected computer so that the world can view your creation.

With a few simple formulas, you can create stacked bar or stacked column charts that display different data segments in a different color to emphasize crossing significant numeric boundaries or goals. Using the MIN function, you can dissect a value into parts that you can chart as a bar with a different color or pattern for each segment that is part of the bar or column.

MOUS OBJECTIVES SUMMARY

- Create an embedded chart and a chart sheet (MOUS Ex2002-6-1)
- Modify an existing chart by revising data, altering chart text, and labeling data (MOUS Ex2002-6-1)
- Use color and patterns to embellish a chart (MOUS Ex2002-6-1)
- Add a new data series to a chart (MOUS Ex2002-6-2)
- Alter a chart type and create a three-dimensional chart (MOUS Ex2002-6-1)
- Create a pie chart with a title, exploding slice, labels, and floating text (MOUS Ex2002-6-1)
- Add texture to a chart (MOUS Ex2002-6-1)
- Delete embedded charts and chart sheets (MOUS Ex2002-4-1)

task reference summary

Task	Page #	Recommended Method
Creating a Chart	EX 4.9	• Select data cell range Click the **Chart Wizard** button
		• Respond to the series of Chart Wizard dialog box choices
Snapping an embedded chart into place	EX 4.13	• Select the chart
		• Press and hold the **Alt** key
		• Drag a chart left, right, up, or down until the chart edge snaps to a cell boundary
		• Release the mouse and Alt key
Adding a new data series to an embedded chart	EX 4.17	• Select the cell range of the data series you want to add
		• Move the mouse to any edge of the selected worksheet cell range
		• When the mouse pointer changes to an arrow, click and drag the range into the chart area and release the mouse
Deleting a data series from a chart	EX 4.18	• Select the data marker
		• Press **Delete**
Adding a data label to all data series in a chart	EX 4.22	• Select a data series
		• Click **Chart**, click **Chart Options**, click the **Data Labels** tab
		• Click the **Show value** option, click **OK**
Adding a data label to a data series	EX 4.22	• Select the data series
		• Click **Format**, click **Selected Data Series**, click the **Data Labels** tab
		• Click the **Show value** option, click **OK**
Add a data label to a data marker	EX 4.23	• Select the data series, click the data marker in the series
		• Click **Format**, click **Selected Data Point**, click the **Data Labels** tab
		• Click the **Show value** option, click **OK**
Printing a worksheet and embedded chart	EX 4.29	• Click any worksheet cell
		• Click the **Print** button
Printing an embedded chart	EX 4.30	• Click the chart
		• Click the **Print** button

EXCEL

task reference summary

Task	Page #	Recommended Method
Selecting nonadjacent cell ranges	EX 4.32	• Select the first cell range
		• Press and hold the **Ctrl** key
		• Select additional cells or cell ranges
		• When finished selecting cells, release the **Ctrl** key
Deleting an embedded chart	EX 4.41	• Click the embedded chart
		• Press the **Delete** key
Deleting a chart sheet	EX 4.41	• Click the chart sheet tab
		• Click **Edit**, click **Delete** Sheet, click **OK**
Creating Web pages from an Excel chart	EX 4.42	• Click the chart or chart sheet tab
		• Click **File**, click **Save as Web Page**
		• Select a drive and folder
		• Click the **Selection: Chart** option
		• Optionally type a page title and click **OK**
		• Click **Save**

CROSSWORD PUZZLE

Across

1. A chart _____ resides on its own workbook page
7. _____ text includes tick mark labels and the X-axis title
8. The _____ area contains all the chart elements
9. A chart's _____ appears above the chart and labels it
10. A(n) _____ chart resides on a worksheet
12. Each data series in a chart can have up to 32,000 values or data _____
13. A data _____ is a graphic representation of the value of a data point
14. A data _____ is the value or name assigned to an individual data point

Down

2. _____ the data in a worksheet, but not delete it, to remove it from a chart
3. _____ marks are small lines uniformly spaced along the axis
4. Organizes the values in one data series under a name
5. Click and drag a _____ handle to resize a chart or other object
6. A _____ is an extension of a tick mark and helps identify the value of data markers
11. A data _____ is a set of values that you want to chart
12. The _____ area is bounded by the X-axis and the Y-axis
15. A line that contains a measurement by which you compare plotted values

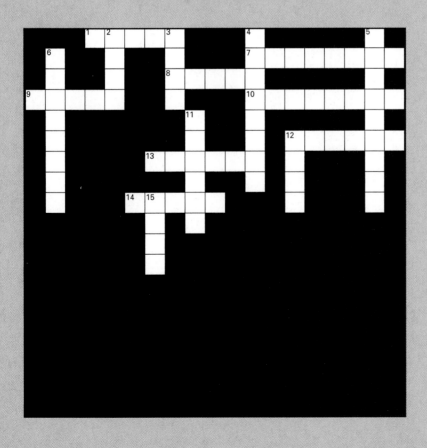

FILL-IN

1. A _____ _____ is a set of values that you chart.

2. The values in a data series are named by a _____.

3. The _____ area of a chart is bounded by the X-axis and the Y-axis.

4. What object in a chart identifies which data marker represents each series when you chart multiple series?

5. A _____ chart is a better choice than a pie chart to represent the daily average temperature in a city for a month.

6. The _____ box is a drawing object into which you can type text and place on a chart to highlight a feature.

REVIEW QUESTIONS

1. Suppose you create a column chart using data from the Big Wave surfboard data in which each row is a data series and row totals are in the rightmost column. You select the cells to plot, but you accidentally include the totals column. The totals are plotted as a separate series in the chart. Explain how to remove the totals column from the chart and still display the totals column in the worksheet.

2. Explain briefly how to remove dollar signs from the Y-axis values in a column chart.

3. The legend Excel created is too small. Legend names are difficult to read. How do you increase the size of the legend? What do you do to make the labels inside the legend larger?

4. You click a chart sheet tab and then click Edit, Delete Sheet, and click OK. You realize you deleted the wrong chart sheet. How do you recover the accidentally deleted chart sheet?

CREATE THE QUESTION

For each of the following answers, create an appropriate, short question.

ANSWER	QUESTION
1. Click Edit and then click Delete Sheet	_____
2. One of the set of values being charted	_____
3. Extensions of tick marks that help identify the value of data markers	_____
4. Click and drag one of these to resize an embedded chart	_____
5. They display the numeric value of a data marker	_____
6. Click this button on the Chart toolbar to change a pie chart into a bar chart	_____

practice

1. Charting Olympic Gold, Silver, and Bronze Medals

Olsen, Kramer, and Shubert (OKS) is a public relations firm that has been hired to do post-Olympic analysis of the games. They have hired Alison Najir and you to produce statistics about the competition and graph the results. In particular, OKS wants you to produce a chart of the medals that competing countries have won. They think a three-dimensional stacked bar chart showing bronze, silver, and gold medals in a single bar for each country would be a good way to chart the results. There are too many countries winning medals to conveniently represent each one, so the company asks you to produce a chart sheet showing the number of medals won by teams winning at least 10 medals total. You have done your Web research and prepared a list of medal winnings—bronze, silver, and gold—in descending order by total medals won. You proceed to produce the chart.

1. Open the workbook **ex04Olympics.xls** and use the Save As command in the File menu to save the workbook under the name **Olympics2.xls**
2. Click the **Medal Data** tab and then drag the mouse to select the cell range **A3:D14** (to include in the chart all countries winning at least 10 medals and the column title row)
3. Click the **Chart Wizard** button, click **Bar** in the Chart type, click the **Stacked bar with 3-D visual effect** in the Chart subtype panel, click **Next** to go to Step 2, and click **Next** again to go to Step 3
4. Click the **Chart title** text box and type **Top Medal Winners, 2000 Olympics**
5. Click the **Value (Z) axis** text box and type **Medals**
6. Click the **Data Labels tab,** click the **Value** check box, and then click **Next**
7. Click the **As new sheet** option button and then click the **Finish** button
8. In the Chart toolbar, click the Chart Objects list arrow, scroll the list, click any **Series "Bronze"** to select all Bronze data markers, click the **Format Data Series** button in the

Chart toolbar, click the **Patterns** tab, and click the **Brown** square (top row, second column) in the Area frame, and click **OK**

tip: *Be careful when selecting a data marker not to select the data label inside a data marker. You select a data marker when the Chart toolbar Chart Object list box contains "Series. . . ."*

9. Repeat Step 8 for the **Silver data marker** (second from the left in any bar), but this time select the **Gray-40%** color square on the Patterns tab (third row from the top, column eight), and then click **OK**
10. Repeat Step 8 for the **Gold data marker** (third from the left in any bar), but this time select the **Light Yellow** square (fifth row from the top, column three) and then click **OK**
11. Place your name in the chart sheet header, click the **Cover Sheet** tab and type your name next to the label "Workbook designer," and enter today's date next to the "Design date" label
12. Print the Cover Sheet and the Chart1 chart sheet, save the workbook, and exit Excel

2. Mapping Rainfall in Hawaii

The field office of the Hawaii visitor's bureau in Kauai, Hawaii, wants you to produce a line chart of the average rainfall for the previous year—January through December. A line chart is the best way to represent this data because it shows trends for each of the five regions. Follow these steps to produce and print the chart.

1. Open **ex04Rainfall.xls**, type your name in the Designer line, type the current date in the Design Date line, and save the file as **Rainfall2.xls** (click **File**, click **Save As,** type the new name, and click the **Save** button)
2. Click the **Rainfall Averages** tab, click cell **A2,** and type your first and last names
3. Click and drag the mouse to select the cell range **A3:M8** and click the **Chart Wizard** button
4. Click **Line** in the Chart type list box and click **Next**

5. Click **Next** again, click the **Chart title** text box, and type **Average Rainfall, Kauai, Hawaii,** click the **Value (Y) axis** and type **Inches,** click **Next**, and click **Finish**

6. Drag the embedded chart until its upper left-corner covers cell A10

7. Click the **chart selection handle** in the lower-right corner of the chart area and drag it down and to the right until the lower-right corner of the chart area just covers cell M30. (Remember, you can press the Alt key as you drag the corner to snap it to exact cell boundaries)

8. Click cell **A1** to deselect the embedded chart

9. Save the workbook again, print the Rainfall Averages worksheet, and then click the **Documentation** tab, print the Documentation worksheet, and exit Excel

challenge!

1. Charting California's Expenditures

The Director of Finance for the State of California, G. Timothy Gage, has collected data about the 2001–2002 Expenditures by fund source for the State of California. The data are in a workbook called **ex04California.xls.** He wants you to help him get the data into shape. Specifically, he wants you to do two things for him. First, he wants you to format the worksheet data so that it looks better—currently it is in raw form and difficult to read. Second, he wants you to produce a two-dimensional pie chart showing the percentage contribution to the total 2001–2002 expenditures. He wants the chart to display a legend and the chart title to be "California Expenditures (2001–2002)." While he leaves other chart formatting details to you, he insists that you emphasize the Education pie slice by exploding it out from the rest of the chart, and he wants the chart on its own chart sheet.

Figure 4.42 shows one way you can format the worksheet. Hint: It is formatted using Merge and Center for the title and subtitle, colors, bold-face, background color, and a shadow around the table. Column A is wide enough to display the widest text in its column.

FIGURE 4.42

Example of formatted Expenditures worksheet

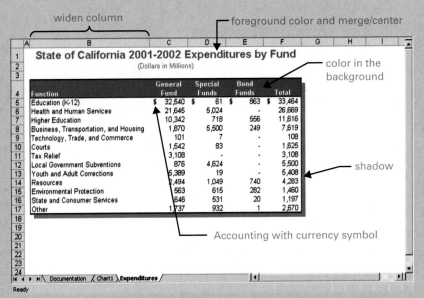

Start by loading **ex04California.xls** and save the worksheet as **California2.xls.** Then type your name on the Documentation worksheet to the right of the "Designer:" text. Type the current date in cell C8. On the Expenditures worksheet, place your name in the worksheet header. Do the same for the Chart1 chart sheet page. Print all three pages.

2. Charting the Rental Car Market

Herb Klein is researching the U.S. rental car market. He conducted part of his research on the Web and through professional magazines. One Web site, Auto Rental News, is chock full of car rental statistics (www.autorentalnews.com) that have helped Herb understand the magnitude of the rental car market. While Herb is a marketing wizard and understands Excel enough to enter data, he has difficulty understanding how to chart the data. He wants you to help him by producing two charts of the data he has collected in a worksheet called **ex04RentalCar.xls.**

Two charts interest Herb. The first one will be a chart sheet column chart showing the estimated U.S. rental revenue by each of nine top car rental companies. The second chart will be an embedded two-dimensional pie chart showing the number of cars in service of each company in comparison to the total cars in service. Start by opening **ex04RentalCar.xls** and immediately save it under the new name, **RentalCar2.xls.** Here are the details of what he wants.

The chart sheet column chart, when completed, will show car rental companies in the X-axis as categories. The Y-axis values should not show currency symbols and should be expressed in whole dollars. The chart title is "U.S. Rental Revenue Est. (Millions)" and is 16-point bold text. The Y-axis title is "Revenue (Millions)" with default formatting. Add data labels to two columns—the highest revenue and the lowest revenue—so those two columns display the amount at their column tops. Place in your name in the chart sheet page header's left section.

Embed the second chart, a two-dimensional pie chart, on the same page as the worksheet data. The chart area should occupy cells A14 through G36. Display values only on the pie segments, display the legend on the left side of the chart area, and create a chart title "Cars in Service" formatted bold and 16-point typeface. Place your name in the page header's left section.

On the Documentation page, type your name and the current date in the underlined areas to the right of Designer and Design Date, respectively. Modify the worksheet data page, called Car Rental Statistics, any way you want or not at all. Print all three worksheets.

1. Graphing Agricultural Production Values

Terry Branson is the county agent for Lancaster County, Nebraska, and is responsible for aiding citizens of the county and state of Nebraska with agricultural questions. Most of the inquiries he receives are from the farming community, and questions range from what type of feed is best for farmers' livestock to which fertilizer is best for tulips. Lately, Terry has been getting a number of inquiries about crop production in Nebraska and neighboring states. Several farmers in the region have been growing sugar beets and alfalfa with some success, but the prices in both those products have been poor in recent years. Many of the questions have been about alternative crops and their viability in Nebraska. Some farming individuals and corporations have asked Terry to research crops such as corn, sorghum, and soybeans and to report to them the average yield of these products per acre in Nebraska. In order to give the farmers the big picture, Terry wants to include productivity rates, measured in bushels per acre, for Kansas, Oklahoma, and Texas as well as for Nebraska. Because Terry does not have these statistics at his fingertips, he asks you to use the Internet to look up statistics about corn, sorghum, and soybean production and produce a graph.

The graph will use a column chart listing the three crops along the X-axis as categories and the bushels per acre plotted along the Y-axis. The four data series will correspond to states. Include a legend listing the four states of Kansas, Nebraska, Oklahoma, and Texas. The chart title should be "Crop Production per Acre," the Y-axis title should be "Bushels/Acre," and the X-axis title should be "Crops." Change the color of all three titles to a dark green, and resize and reposition the chart so that the embedded chart covers the cell range A10 through F30.

Begin by opening **ex04Crop.xls.** Fill in cells B5:E7 with the values for bushels per acre for the crops in the corresponding states. Graph the cell range A4:E7. Here's how you find the bushels per acre values required to complete this assignment: Launch your Web browser and to go www.fedstats.gov and locate the MapStats section of the home page. Start with Kansas. Click the list box arrow beneath MapStats, click **Kansas** in the list (see Figure 4.43), and then click the **Submit** button to the right of the list box. Ensure that the list box for Kansas says "State level only" and click the **Get Profile** button. When the next page appears, click the **Field Crops** link under the Agriculture heading near the top of the page. A *Field Crops in Kansas* page opens. On this page is a table containing crops and their bushels per acre values (in a column labeled "Yield per harvested acre (bushels)"). Write down the values from that column for corn, sorghum, and soybeans. Click the **Fedstats home page** link to return to the FedStats home page. Repeat this Web search procedure for Nebraska, Oklahoma, and Texas. After you gather the twelve values, close your browser, fill in the values in the worksheet, create an embedded column graph, insert your name in the worksheet header, and print the worksheet.

FIGURE 4.43

FedStats home page

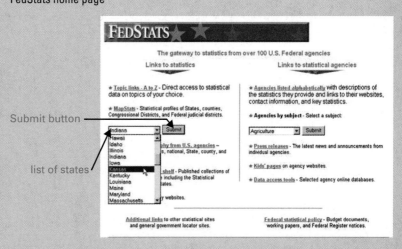

e-business

1. Researching the Largest Coffee Exporting Countries

Jehad Nasser wants to open a Web store to sell coffee beans and coffee supplies. He wants to know which countries export the most coffee and then determine from which countries he will purchase raw coffee beans. To start his research, he has asked you to search the Web for information on coffee bean production and export. One of his acquaintances from Java, Indonesia, suggests Jehad investigate Web sites such as the International Coffee Organization (www.ico.org) to locate statistics on coffee production and export. Jehad has done some work and collected data from the Web including production and export values for 45 coffee-producing nations. He wants you to produce a pie chart showing the percentage of production by the top six coffee exporters. The top six exporters are those who export the largest number of bags of coffee per year. Fortunately, Jehad has gone to the trouble of sorting the list he produced in descending order by the number of bags each country exports.

To accomplish this task, Jehad wants you to complete the Documentation worksheet by doing the following. Start by opening Jehad's preliminary worksheet called **ex04ExportCoffee.xls**. Then add a label such as **Designed by:** and fill in your name. Add a label "Design date:" and fill in the current date next to it. Add a title at the top of the Documentation worksheet that describes, in three or four words, the title of the worksheet. Finally, add a **Purpose:** label and a sentence describing what the workbook contains. Print the documentation in landscape orientation.

Create a two-dimensional pie chart on a chart sheet showing the export percentages of the top six countries and that of all other coffee-producing countries. The "all others" category is the *sum* of export bags for all other countries. (Hint: You will want to add a row after the sixth country that sums the 7th through 45th countries' exports.) In other words, the pie chart will have seven slices. The pie chart data labels should show the percent and the country names. Delete the legend. Title the chart, in 14-point bold typeface, "Top Six Coffee Exporters." Explode the pie slice of the largest exporter, Brazil. Include your name in the header of the chart worksheet.

The Coffee Production and Export worksheet contains the data you will chart. Place your name in the worksheet header. Next, open up a row below the entry for Mexico, place all others in cell B12, and sum up production and export values for Uganda through Benin, placing the sum of production in cell C12 and the sum of export in cell D12. Chart the export values of Brazil through "all others," including the country names as category along with the export values. Set the Coffee Production and Export print range to the first 12 rows (the title through the "all others" row). Save the completed workbook as **ExportCoffee2.xls.** Print the entire workbook.

1. Charting Hourly Compensation Rates around the World

The Bureau of Labor Statistics (www.bls.gov) maintains tables comparing hourly compensation rates, in U.S. dollars, for the employees in the manufacturing sector for several countries. Melissa Franklin, your supervisor at Applied Economics, Inc., wants you to produce a chart of the data that she can present at a talk she is giving to a group of businesspersons next week in Atlanta. The raw data, shown in Figure 4.44, shows the hourly compensation values for seven countries for selected years between 1975 and 1999. Hourly compensation includes wages, bonuses, vacation, holidays, premiums, insurance, and benefit plans.

Begin by loading the worksheet, called **ex04HourlyLabor.xls.** Format the worksheet so that the column labels and the numbers are attractive and easy to read. Then create a chart in a chart sheet that is well labeled and displays, in the best form possible, the information in a chart. Which chart type is best to display the changes in the hourly compensation for a country? Use that chart type choice for all countries. Add a text box displaying your name in the lower-right corner of the chart. Save the workbook and then print the worksheet and the chart.

2. Charting Unemployment Rates around the World

The U.S. Bureau of Labor Statistics (BLS) collects all sorts of information about the U.S. labor force and provides statistical summaries. In addition to tracking the U.S. labor force, the BLS provides comparisons of U.S. labor segments with foreign countries and provides the information in various types of tables. The BLS maintains a large Web site at www.bls.gov and you can use your browser to go to that location and view some of their

reports. (Most reports are in PDF, or portable document format, that are rendered using the free software product called Acrobat Reader.)

Janet Morrison, the Sonoma County chief of labor statistics, is interested in charting unemployment rate trends between the United States and France during the 1960s as an embedded chart. She would like to compare the United States and France to see if there is a trend both for each country and between the two countries. She wants you to produce a line chart of the unemployment rates with the 1960s along the X-axis and unemployment rates along the Y-axis. Change the color of the chart title, Y-axis label, X-axis label, and X-axis category names to dark blue. Place the chart after the last data row so that it will fit along with the worksheet data on one printed page. Add the appropriate chart title and axes titles.

Start by loading the unemployment worksheet called **ex04Unemployment.xls.** Before you make any changes to the worksheet, save it under the new name **Unemployment2.xls** to preserve the original worksheet. To identify the chart as yours, place a text box containing your first and last names somewhere on the chart. Print the chart and be sure to save the altered worksheet before leaving Excel.

FIGURE 4.44

Hourly compensation comparison

	A	B	C	D	E	F	G	H
1	Hourly compensation costs in U.S. dollars for production workers in manufacturing							
2								
3		1975	1980	1985	1990	1995	1999	
4	Canada	5.96	8.67	10.95	15.95	16.1	15.6	
5	France	4.52	8.94	7.52	15.49	20.01	17.98	
6	Italy	4.67	8.15	7.63	17.45	16.22	16.6	
7	Japan	3	5.52	6.34	12.8	23.82	20.89	
8	Spain	2.53	5.89	4.66	11.38	12.88	12.11	
9	Sweden	7.18	12.51	9.66	20.93	21.44	21.58	
10	United States	6.36	9.87	13.01	14.91	17.19	19.2	
11								

running project

Pampered Paws

Grace Jackson, Pampered Paws' owner, wants you to chart the sales of dog food and cat food for the first six months of her business. She has gathered sales information about four of her most popular dog foods and four of the most popular cat foods in a workbook called **ex04Paws.xls.** Grace wants you to create two chart sheets.

The first chart sheet is a stacked column chart sheet showing sales of each of the four dog foods. Each column represents a month, and the four data markers in each column are the sales of each type of dog food. When completed, the stacked column chart sheet will display six columns, one for each sales month. Type the chart title **Dog Food Sales** for the column chart. The legend displays a different color for each dog food brand. The Y-axis displays sales, and values display the currency symbol.

The second chart sheet is a three-dimensional pie chart showing the percent of the total cat food sales each brand contributes. Tilt the 3-D chart 45

degrees and explode the Iams Lamb/Rice pie slice. Title the chart **Cat Food Sales.** Display a legend and label each slice with the percent (only) of each product's sales.

Begin by loading the worksheet called **ex04Paws.xls.** Then write expressions to sum each row's sales beneath the Total column for both dog and cat products. Subtotal dog food sales in the cell next to the label "Subtotal" and do the same for cat food sales. Sum the two subtotals in the cell H16.

Reorient the worksheet containing sales data so that it prints in landscape orientation. Place a page header on all three sheets containing your name in the center section. Print the two chart sheets and the worksheet.

did you know?

Microsoft reports that there are over 250 million users of Office worldwide.

Japan is one of the most competitive soft drink markets in the world; approximately 1,000 new soft drinks are launched in Japan every year, of which only a small number survive.

Thomas Jefferson drafted the Constitution of the United States on a portable desk that carried all of his favorite tools.

team members at Microsoft consumed approximately 115,000 slices of pizza while developing the Microsoft XP suite.

the word "stewardess" is the longest word in the English language that you type with one hand.

a pivot table is also known as a _____. (Find the answer in this chapter.)

Chapter Objectives

- Create and maintain a list

- Freeze rows and columns (MOUS Ex2002e-3-2)

- Sort a list on multiple sort keys

- Enter, search for, modify, and delete records in a list with a data form

- Group and outline structured data (MOUS Ex2002e-7-3)

- Create subtotals (MOUS Ex2002e-7-1)

- Create and apply conditional formatting (MOUS Ex2002e-3-2)

- Create filters with AutoFilter (MOUS Ex2002e-7-2)

- Use worksheet labels and names in formulas (MOUS Ex2002e-4-1)

- Create a pivot table and pivot chart (MOUS Ex2002e-8-1)

Computer Security, Inc.

Computer Security, Inc. (Comsec) is a small computer security contractor that provides computer security analysis, design, and software implementation for the U.S. government and commercial clients. Comsec competes for both private and U.S. government computer security contract work by submitting detailed bids outlining the work they will perform if awarded the contracts. Because all of their work involves computer security—a highly sensitive area—almost all of Comsec's work requires access to classified material or company confidential documents. Consequently, all of the security engineers (simply known as "engineers" within the company) have U.S. government clearances of either Secret or Top Secret. Some have even higher clearances for the 2 percent of Comsec's work that involves so-called "black box" security work. Most of the employees also hold clearances because they must handle classified documents.

Alice Rovik is Comsec's Human Resources (HR) manager. She maintains all employee records and is responsible for semi-annual review reports, payroll processing, personnel records, recruiting data, employee training, and pension option information. At the heart of an HR system are personnel records. Personnel record maintenance includes activities such as maintaining employee records, tracking cost center data, recording and maintaining pension information, and absence and sick leave record keeping—to name a few. While most of this information resides in sophisticated database systems, Alice maintains a basic employee worksheet for quick calculations and ad hoc report generation. Because Comsec is a small company, Alice can take advantage of Excel's excellent list management facilities to satisfy many of her personnel information management needs. One of the worksheets Alice keeps close at hand lists employees' names, departments, titles, and other fundamental information. Figure 5.1 shows the worksheet, which she calls simply the "employee" worksheet. During the course of reading this chapter, you will be asked to manipulate the worksheet in various ways to produce summaries, filter the list, add and delete employee records, and produce pivot tables summarizing department data.

FIGURE 5.1

Employee worksheet

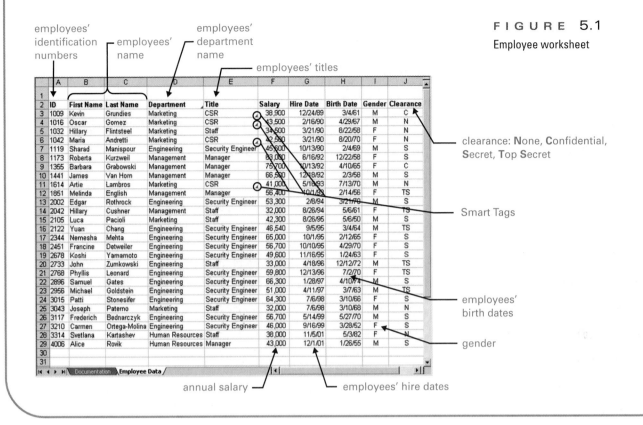

employees'
identification
numbers

employees'
name

employees'
department
name

employees' titles

clearance: None, Confidential,
Secret, Top Secret

Smart Tags

employees'
birth dates

gender

annual salary

employees' hire dates

Chapter 5 covers building and maintaining Excel lists, which are also called databases. In this chapter you will use a personnel worksheet from Comsec, a computer security consulting and contracting company. Using the personnel information already entered in the worksheet, you will sort the data various ways so that the list is in a more useful order. Using Excel's form feature, you will add, modify, and delete values in the list through a simple and intuitive form-based interface, which also facilitates searching for particular values. Creating a data filter allows you to hide selected rows of the list to easily locate groups of records—worksheet rows—that contain the same value. You will learn how to sort a list into related groups and then create salary subtotals and other statistics for each identified group. Creating pivot tables, the capstone feature described in this chapter, illustrates how to create summaries by pairs of variables, or values. For example, you will learn how to use the PivotTable Wizard to quickly create a table displaying the average salary by department—all with a few simple keystrokes. Pivot tables, sometimes known as crosstabs, reveal information hidden in Excel lists, and you will learn how to extract that hidden information.

SESSION 5.1 CREATING AND USING LISTS

In this section, you will learn how to use Excel to manage a list, or database. One of the most common uses of worksheets is to maintain lists of information: names and addresses of business contacts and students, and symbols and purchase prices of stocks, for example. You will learn how to sort the list into a meaningful order, modify the amount of the worksheet that displays on the page, find and replace information in a list, and use a data form to add, modify, and delete data.

BUILDING A LIST

A *list* is a collection of data arranged in columns and rows in which each column displays one particular type of data. A list has the following characteristics:

- Each column contains the same category of information. In the personnel list highlighted in this chapter, for example, the ID column contains employee identification numbers and no other data
- The first row in the list contains labels identifying each column and its contents
- A list does not contain any blank rows
- A list is bordered on all four sides by empty rows and columns, or a list begins in row 1 or column A, each of which serves to delimit the list on the top or the left side, respectively

Figure 5.1 shows the employee worksheet containing a small amount of employee data. It contains fewer rows and columns than a typical employee worksheet to keep the example understandable without sacrificing elegance. Each column of a list is a *field* of related information describing some characteristic of the object, person, or place. Each row is called a *record,* which contains the fields that collectively describe a single object, person, or place. The employee record in this chapter, for example, contains an employee's identification number, first and last names, the department in which he or she works, his or her title, annual salary, hire and birth dates, gender, and U.S. Department of Defense clearance level. A collection of these records constitutes a list. Observe the Hire Date column. It contains only date values, and the dates recorded in the column—field—are the dates when each employee was hired—his or her first day to report to work. Observe one other important attribute about the list shown in Figure 5.1: The labels at the top of the list, or names that identify each column, are unique and formatted differently (boldface) from the information in rows below the label row. This is important, because it helps Excel determine that the first row is a label row identifying each column.

Developing and Planning a List

Before you jump in and begin typing data into your list, you should plan the contents of the list and the way you want to arrange the data in it. It is important to think about and write down the types of reports and printouts you will be creating from a list. Consider whether it is important to organize the columns in a particular order to facilitate creating those reports. Another question to consider is whether a list should be sorted in a particular order. With Excel, you can change the order of rows or columns easily if you change your mind later.

FIGURE 5.2

Employee list definition table

Field Name	Field Description
ID	Unique employee identification number
First Name	Employee's first name
Last Name	Employee's last name
Department	Employee's department
Title	Employee's job title
Salary	Employee's annual salary
Hire Date	Date employee was hired
Birth Date	Employee's birthday
Gender	Female (F) or male (M)
Clearance	U.S. Department of Defense clearance: N (none), C (confidential), S (secret), or TS (top secret)

Each column or field you include is important. Decide which columns to include and define their contents. You can do this with a table that database experts call a *schema,* but you refer to the same definition by its ordinary name, a ***list definition table.*** Figure 5.2 shows the list definition table for the Comsec employee table.

With the list definition table finalized and approved, you can proceed to create the list, beginning with an empty worksheet or one already containing data. Be sure to follow the list guidelines presented above as you create a list: The first row should contain column headings formatted distinctly from the rest of the list, and don't include any blank rows.

Begin your work on the employee workbook by opening it and saving it under its new name.

Opening the Employee worksheet and saving it under a new name:

1. Start Excel

2. Open the workbook **ex05Employee.xls** and immediately save it as **Employee1.xls** to preserve the original workbook in case you want to revert to that version. Excel displays the first worksheet, Documentation, of the Employee1 workbook (see Figure 5.3)

3. Switch to the **Employee Data** worksheet (click the yellow **Employee Data** tab) to display the employee list. The list currently contains 27 employees and displays information about employees whose records appear in rows 3 through 29. Row 2 contains labels that name each column. The labels in row 2 are boldfaced to help Excel distinguish between labels and the columns containing data they identify. Scroll down the

EXCEL

FIGURE 5.3
Documentation worksheet

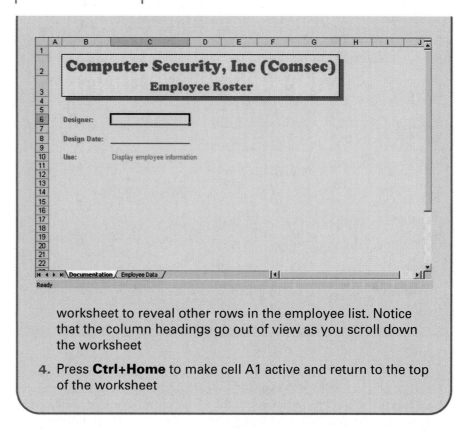

worksheet to reveal other rows in the employee list. Notice that the column headings go out of view as you scroll down the worksheet

4. Press **Ctrl+Home** to make cell A1 active and return to the top of the worksheet

A common problem occurring when you use a long list of data is that the labels identifying the columns soon scroll out of view as you go to the bottom of the list to enter new data. Without the labels at the top of the column, it is difficult to remember what to enter in each column—particularly when two columns contain similar data such as the Hire Date and Birth Date. There is more than one way to handle this problem.

FREEZING ROWS AND COLUMNS

Freezing rows and columns prevents certain columns, rows, or both from scrolling off the screen when you scroll an Excel window down or to the right. When you freeze one or more rows or columns, they form a two-sided frame that remains in place—almost like a two-sided picture frame in which the picture can move up or down while the frame remains in place.

task reference

Freezing Rows and Columns

- Select the cell below and to the right of the row(s) and column(s) you want to freeze

- Click **Window** on the menu bar and then click **Freeze Panes**

You decide to freeze rows 1 and 2 containing the column headings and freeze columns A through C containing the employees' names. Once frozen, you can scroll down the worksheet and the column labels will remain in view. Similarly, you can scroll to the right and the employee IDs and names remain visible in the left three columns.

Freezing label rows and employee name columns:

1. With **Employee1.xls** still open, click cell **D3** to make it the active cell

2. Click **Window** on the menu bar and then click **Freeze Panes.** Notice dark lines appear at the boundaries of the frozen rows and columns

3. Click the **vertical scroll bar down arrow** to scroll down the worksheet. Notice that the labels remain fixed at the top of the worksheet

4. Click the **horizontal scroll bar right arrow** to scroll a few columns to the right. Notice that the first three columns (ID, First Name, and Last Name) remain fixed. Columns appear to scroll beneath the frozen columns (see Figure 5.4)

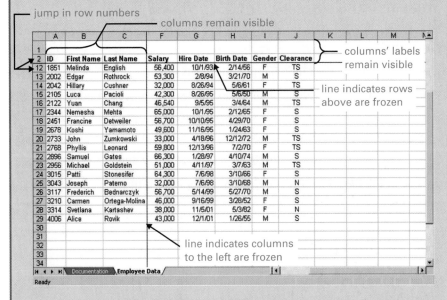

FIGURE 5.4

Freezing rows and columns in place

5. Press **Ctrl+Home.** Notice that D3 becomes the active cell, not cell A1—which is the cell you would expect to become the active cell. When columns or rows are frozen, pressing Ctrl+Home makes active the cell directly below and to the right of frozen rows or columns

You can unfreeze rows or columns by clicking Unfreeze Panes in the Window menu. For now, leave the panes frozen.

USING A DATA FORM TO MAINTAIN A LIST

Alice Rovik has several changes she wants to make to the Employee worksheet. The first change to the list that Alice wants you to make is to add information for a newly hired employee, Steven Ballmer. Second, Alice wants you to modify Sharad Manispour's record. He has worked for Comsec for more than a decade and has been promoted to manager in the Engineering department. Consequently, his new salary as the Engineering department's manager is $54,500. Finally, Alice wants you to delete the record for Joseph Paterno. This week, Joseph accepted a job, after giving Alice his two-week notice, with a dot-com company in San José.

You can perform all of these operations using existing Excel commands to insert a row to add an employee record or delete a row to remove a record. However, you will find it easier to use Excel's Form command. A *data form* is a dialog box displaying one row of a list in text boxes in which you can add, locate, modify, or delete records. One advantage of using a simple Excel data form for record maintenance operations—updates, insertions, or deletions—is that doing so greatly reduces the chances of making data entry mistakes. Because a data form displays a single row at a time, your chance of transposing values from one row to another are smaller.

Adding a Record

> ### task reference
>
> ### Adding a Record to a List Using a Data Form
>
> - Click any cell within the list—even a cell in the label row at the top of the list
> - Click **Data** on the menu bar and then click **Form**
> - Click the **New** button to clear all text boxes and present a blank form
> - Type the values for each field in the corresponding form text boxes, pressing the **Tab** key to move from one text box to another
> - Press the **Enter** key to add the new record (to the end of the list)
> - Click the **Close** button after adding all records to the list

The first modification is to add a new employee to the list of employees on the Employee Data worksheet.

> ### Adding a new record by using the data form:
>
> 1. With **Employee1.xls** still open, click any cell within the list (cell F4, for example)
>
> **tip:** *Be sure to select only one cell in the list. Otherwise, Excel might not display the correct column headings in the form.*
>
> 2. Click **Data** on the menu bar and then click **Form** to display the Employee Data form. You probably notice that the form's title is the same as the sheet tab's name, Employee Data (see Figure 5.5). Labels at the top of each column in the list appear to the left of the form's text boxes
>
> 3. Click the data form's **New** button to clear the text boxes in preparation for entering a new employee record. Notice that "New Record" appears where the record number and total record count were previously

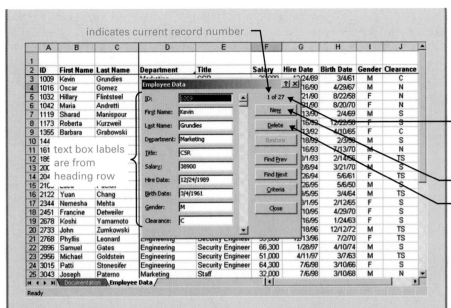

FIGURE 5.5

Employee Data form displaying the first record

indicates current total number of records in list

click to add a record

click to delete current record

tip: *A form displays the current record number and the total number of records in the list. Notice that the* **headings row**—*the list row containing the column headings—is not included in the record count.*

4. Type **4123** in the ID text box and then press **Tab** to move to the next text box

tip: *If you pressed the* **Enter** *key instead of the* **Tab** *key, Excel displays a blank data form and stores the previous information. Click the* **Find Prev** *button to return to the record you were working on and then continue entering information.*

5. Type **Steve** in the First Name text box and then press **Tab** to move to the next text box

6. Type **Ballmer** in the Last Name text box and then press **Tab** to move to the next text box

7. Type **Engineering** in the Department text box and then press **Tab** to move to the next text box

8. Type **Security Engineer** in the Title text box and then press **Tab** to move to the next text box

9. Type **42900** in the Salary text box and then press **Tab** to move to the next text box

10. Type **5/1/2002** in the Hire Date text box and then press **Tab** to move to the next text box

11. Type **4/14/1970** in the Birth Date text box and then press **Tab** to move to the next text box

12. Type **M** (uppercase, please) in the Gender text box and then press **Tab** to move to the next text box

13. Type **N** (uppercase, please) in the Clearance text box

14. Press the **Enter** key to add the record to the list. Excel automatically adds the record to the end of the current data list and displays an empty data form

15. Click the **Close** button to close the data form and return to the worksheet

16. Press and hold the **End** key, then press the **down arrow** key, and release the **End** key to move to the last record in the list. Ensure that the last record in the list is Ballmer's record

17. Press **Ctrl+Home** to make cell D3 the active cell

After adding the new record to the list, you can proceed to make other alterations that Alice requested to the list. Recall that she wants one record deleted and another record edited.

Searching for a Record

The employee list is short and it is easy to locate any particular record by examining the list. In larger lists containing perhaps 500 rows or more, looking for a particular employee's record or a particular customer's invoice could be much more difficult. Fortunately, Excel's data form provides search capabilities. You will use the data form search method to locate a record just as you would for a very large list.

You can search for one or more records by specifying *search criteria,* which are values that the data form should match in specified data form fields. Beginning with the first record in the list, Excel inspects each record in turn until it either finds a record matching the search criteria or it reaches the end of the list without finding a match. If more than one record matches the search criteria, Excel displays the first record it encounters in the data form. When you click the Find Next button, Excel continues the search by searching for the next matching record.

To modify or delete a record from a list, you have to locate it first. The fastest way to locate a record is to use the data form search facility. Once Excel finds the requested record, you can choose to change it, delete it, or do nothing at all to the record.

Searching for a record using a data form:

1. Click any cell within the employee list

2. Click **Data** on the menu bar and then click **Form** to display the first employee record in the data form

3. Click the **Criteria** button. Excel blanks all the form's text boxes

4. Click the **Last Name** text box and type **manispour** to specify the employee's last name for the search criteria

tip: *When typing character search criteria—names, street names, or other text labels—you need not worry about capitalization. Excel ignores the case of the search criteria and matches fields based on spelling, alone*

tip: *You can type information in more than one text box to specify multiple search criteria. All specified criteria must be satisfied to match a record. In other words, you narrow the search for matching records with each additional search criteria*

5. Click the **Find Next** button to display the record that matches the search criteria. Sharad Manispour's record appears in the data form (see Figure 5.6)

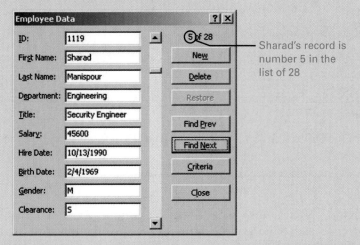

Sharad's record is number 5 in the list of 28

FIGURE 5.6

Employee Data form displaying Sharad Manispour's record

     You have located the correct record. Had there been more than one employee with that last name, you could press the Find Next button to continue the search. If no record could be found matching the criteria, the first record appears in the data form

6. Drag the mouse across the **Title** text box to select its contents, "Security Engineer," and then type **Manager** to correct Sharad's title

7. Double-click the **Salary** text box to select its entire contents and then type **54500** (without a currency symbol or a comma)

8. Click the **Close** button to close the data form. Excel replaces the record with its new contents

9. Examine row 7 to verify that Excel altered the Title and Salary fields for Sharad Manispour

10. Press **Ctrl+Home** to make cell D3 the active cell

The third change to the list Alice wants you to make is to delete Joseph Paterno's record.

Deleting a Record

The procedure you follow to delete a record from a list is similar to updating a record. The only difference is the action you take once you locate the record. In other words, you display the data form for the employee list, click the Criteria button, and type in suitable search criteria. When you locate the record, then you click the data form Delete button.

     Sometimes knowing exactly how to spell a name in a criteria text box or how it is spelled in a list can cause search problems. Unless you specify the exact spelling of text values, the search will fail to locate a matching record. One way to reduce the chance of this happening is to specify fewer characters in the search criteria field and use a wild card character on the end of the search criteria. A **_wild card character_** is a character that stands

task reference

Deleting a Record from a List with a Data Form

- Click any cell within the list—even a cell in the label row at the top of the list

- Click **Data** and then click **Form**

- Click the **Criteria** button and enter the search criteria in one or more text boxes

- Click the **Find Next** button repeatedly until you locate the record to be deleted

- Press the **Delete** button and then click the **OK** button to confirm the deletion

for one or more characters—a "don't care" symbol. Excel has two such characters: asterisk (*) and question mark (?). Use the question mark to substitute for a single character in a search criteria character string. Use the asterisk to match any number of characters. For example, the search text "pat?rno" matches paterno, patorno, or patirno. The more powerful wild character asterisk matches any characters that appear where it does in the search criteria. For example, the search criteria "G*" in the employee Last Name field matches Grundies, Gomez, Grabowski, Gates, and Goldstein. The more characters you specify preceding the asterisk, the more specific the search criteria are because all the characters preceding an asterisk wild card must match the corresponding field in those positions exactly.

To try out a wild card search and maximize your success searching, use the asterisk wild card to search for the last name "Paterno" in preparation to delete the record.

Searching for a record using the asterisk wild card:

1. Click any cell within the employee list, click **Data** on the menu bar and then click **Form** to display the first employee record in the data form

2. Click the **Criteria** button to prepare to enter the search criteria

3. Click the **Last Name** text box and type **pa*** (see Figure 5.7)

4. Click the **Find Next** button to launch the search and display the first record satisfying the criteria. The criteria "pa*" requires that the last name field of a candidate record begin with "pa" followed by any number of additional characters. The data form displays Luca Pacioli's record. That is not the one you want to remove from the list

5. Click the **Find Next** button to continue searching down the list for a record whose last name field begins with "pa." Excel locates and displays Joseph Paterno's record—the record you want to delete

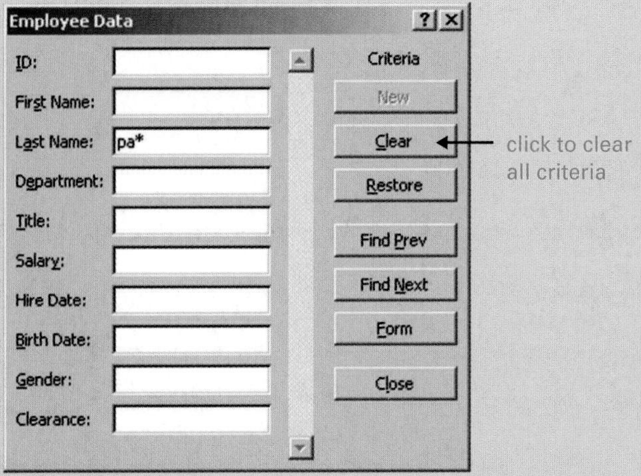

FIGURE 5.7
Using search criteria containing a wildcard

click to clear all criteria

6. Click the **Delete** button. A warning dialog box appears indicating you are about to permanently delete a record

7. Click **OK** to confirm that you want to permanently delete the selected record

8. Click the **Close** button to close the data form and redisplay the worksheet

Scroll down so you can see rows 23 through 26. Prior to the deletion operation, Paterno's record occupied row 25. Notice that Frederich Bednarczyk's record now occupies that row. In other words, when you delete a record with a data form, Excel removes the entire row and moves up rows below it to fill the void.

LOCATING AND MODIFYING DATA WITH FIND AND REPLACE

When you must make a few modifications to various fields in an Excel list, the data form method illustrated above is the best way. However, when you have to make a change to one particular field in the list involving many records, then the Excel Find and Replace command is your best choice. For example, suppose you had to change the entries in the Gender column by replacing "M" with "Male" and "F" with "Female." Modifying each entry by hand would be tedious at best because each of the 27 employee rows would have to be modified individually. Using the find and replace command reduces the effort.

Alice observes the computer security industry trend that engineers working in security engineering and engineering departments typically hold the title "engineer" rather than "security engineer." She wants you to change that name wherever it occurs in the Title column.

Replacing a character string in many cells:

1. Select the cell range **E3:E29,** which are all the record entries in the Title column

tip: *The fastest way to select the range of cells in a single column that contains no "holes"—each cell in the column has a value—is to click the topmost cell in the range, press and hold the* **Shift** *key, tap the* **End** *key, tap the* **down arrow** *key, and then release the* **Shift** *key. Excel highlights the entire range of filled cells between the first cell you select and the bottom-most cell in the range.*

2. Click **Edit** on the menu bar and then click **Replace** to display the Find and Replace dialog box

3. Click the **Find what** text box and type **security engineer** (lowercase is okay)

4. Click the **Replace with** text box and type **Engineer** (be sure to capitalize the title). Figure 5.8 shows the dialog box with both the search text and the replacement text in place

FIGURE 5.8

Replacing text in many cells

search text
(case insensitive)

replacement text
(case sensitive)

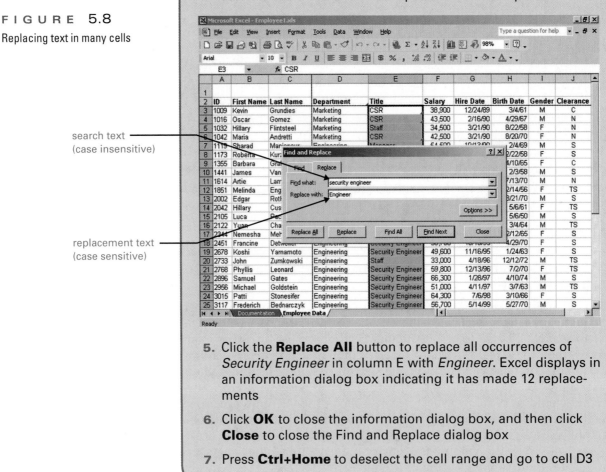

5. Click the **Replace All** button to replace all occurrences of *Security Engineer* in column E with *Engineer*. Excel displays in an information dialog box indicating it has made 12 replacements

6. Click **OK** to close the information dialog box, and then click **Close** to close the Find and Replace dialog box

7. Press **Ctrl+Home** to deselect the cell range and go to cell D3

SORTING DATA

The employee list is kept in Hire Date order. When a new employee joins the company, his or her record is placed at the end of the list. Alice Rovik has a meeting next week with several top management people to discuss retirement benefits, and she wants to have the list in order by the Birth Date field for easy reference.

To sort rows of a list, you use one or more fields to determine the final position in the list that each row occupies. The field or fields you use to sort a list are called *sort fields* (or *sort keys*). For instance, if you wanted to rearrange the rows of the Employee list so that they are in alphabetical order by last name, Last Name is the sort field. If more than one sort field is required to reorder a list, the first sort field is called the *primary sort field.* Other sort fields used to reorder rows break any ties that occur in the primary sort field. This is common in telephone books, for example. Telephone book lists are sorted by last name, then first name, and then by middle initial. The primary sort field is last name, the secondary sort field is first name, and the third sort field (needed to break a tie between two or more with the name Joe Smith, for example) is middle initial.

Once you decide which fields are your list's sort fields, you decide whether to order the list in ascending or descending order for each sort field. *Ascending order* arranges text values alphabetically from A to Z, arranges numbers from smallest to largest, and arranges dates from earliest to most recent. *Descending order* does the opposite—it arranges text values alphabetically from Z to A, arranges numbers from largest to smallest, and arranges dates from most recent to earliest. Whether sorting in ascending order or descending order, blank fields are always placed at the bottom of the list.

While a list in employee ID order may be handy when adding employees, it is not a useful way to organize records when you want to know how many people work in the Engineering department, for example. When you want to look up a particular employee's record, it is easier to do so if the list is in order by last name.

Sorting a List by One Column

You can sort Excel list data on one column by using the Sort Ascending and Sort Descending buttons on the Excel Standard toolbar. Alternatively, you can use the Sort command of the Data menu. If you need to sort a list on only one field, the toolbar method is the fastest and simplest way. For more complex sort operations involving more than one column, use the Sort command.

---

task reference

Sorting a List on One Column

- Click any cell in the column in which you want to sort a list
- Click the **Sort Ascending** or the **Sort Descending** buttons to sort the list

---

Sort the employee list in ascending order by Birth Date so that Alice can locate employees by age in the employee list.

Sorting the employee list in ascending order by Birth Date:

1. Click cell **H3,** a birth date cell for the first employee row

tip: *You do not need to select the entire list nor the entire column on which the list is sorted. Excel determines the list's boundaries by finding blank rows to the left and right of the list and blank columns above and below the list.*

FIGURE 5.9

Employee list sorted by Birth Date

2. Click the **Sort Ascending** ⬇ button on the Standard toolbar. Excel sorts the rows in order by the Birth Date column (see Figure 5.9)

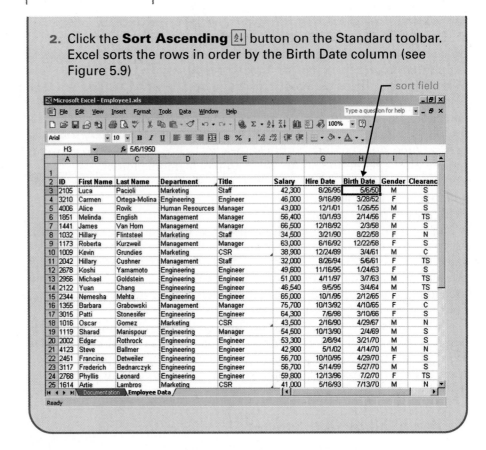

Never select the entire column you want to designate as the sort field because Excel misinterprets your intentions and sorts the entries in the selected column only, rather than sorting the entire record along with the sort field. If you make this mistake, click Undo in the Edit menu to reverse the effects of the incorrect sort operation.

Sorting a List on Multiple Fields

Often, sorting a list on only one field is not adequate to sort the list because larger lists frequently have groups of entries that are identical in a particular field. A *tie* exists when one or more records have the same value for a field. When ties occur, you must sort the groups of records that tie on a particular field by another field—the *secondary sort field*—to break the tie. For large lists, groups of records can match on both the primary sort field and the secondary sort field. In that case, sorting a list on three sort fields is necessary. It is rare that a list has records that match in three fields. Three sort fields are almost always sufficient to sort a list into order and eliminate all ties.

Alice Rovik wants the employee list sorted in order by department and then by employee last name and first name within each department. This type of sort operation goes beyond the capabilities of a single-key sort provided by the Sort Ascending or the Sort Descending buttons on the Standard toolbar. The Sort command of the Data menu provides the multiple-field sorting capability Alice requires.

Alice wants the employee list sorted by department and then by last and first names within each department.

task reference

Sorting a List on More Than One Field

- Click any cell within the list to be sorted

- Click **Data** on the menu bar and click **Sort** to open the Sort dialog box

- Click the **Sort by** list arrow to display the list's column headings. Click the column heading corresponding to the primary sort field, and click the **Ascending** or **Descending** option button

- Click the first **Then by** list arrow to display the list's column headings. Click the column heading of the secondary sort field, and then click the **Ascending** or **Descending** option button for the second sort field

- If necessary, click the second **Then by** list arrow to display the list's column headings. Click the column heading of the third sort field, and then click the **Ascending** or **Descending** option button for the third sort field

- Click the **OK** button to sort the list

Sorting the employee list in order by department and name within department:

1. Click any cell in the list

2. Click **Data** on the menu bar and then click **Sort**

3. Click the **Sort by list box arrow** to display a list of column headings, click **Department,** and, if necessary, click the **Ascending** option button

4. Click the first **Then by list box arrow** to display a list of column headings, click **Last Name,** and, if necessary, click the **Ascending** option button

5. Click the second **Then by list box** arrow to display a list of column headings, click **First Name,** and, if necessary, click the **Ascending** option button. Figure 5.10 shows the Sort dialog box after specifying three sort fields

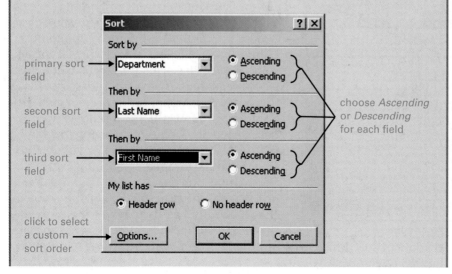

FIGURE   5.10

Sort dialog box

EXCEL

6. Click **OK** to sort the list into order on three sort fields. Excel sorts the list in order by department (first) and then last and first name within each department (see Figure 5.11)

FIGURE 5.11

Sorted employee list

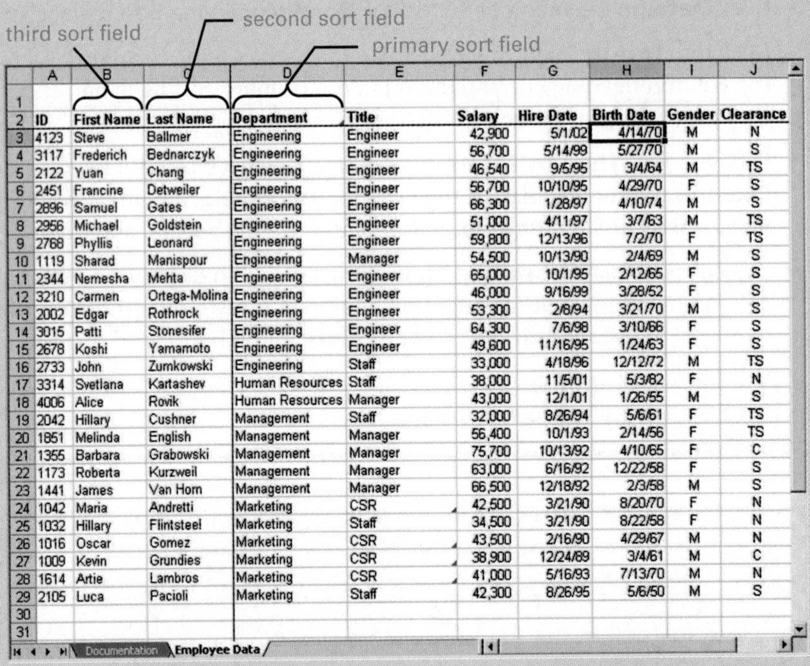

	ID	First Name	Last Name	Department	Title	Salary	Hire Date	Birth Date	Gender	Clearance
3	4123	Steve	Ballmer	Engineering	Engineer	42,900	5/1/02	4/14/70	M	N
4	3117	Frederich	Bednarczyk	Engineering	Engineer	56,700	5/14/99	5/27/70	M	S
5	2122	Yuan	Chang	Engineering	Engineer	46,540	9/5/95	3/4/64	M	TS
6	2451	Francine	Detweiler	Engineering	Engineer	56,700	10/10/95	4/29/70	F	S
7	2896	Samuel	Gates	Engineering	Engineer	66,300	1/28/97	4/10/74	M	S
8	2956	Michael	Goldstein	Engineering	Engineer	51,000	4/11/97	3/7/63	M	TS
9	2768	Phyllis	Leonard	Engineering	Engineer	59,800	12/13/96	7/2/70	F	TS
10	1119	Sharad	Manispour	Engineering	Manager	54,500	10/13/90	2/4/69	M	S
11	2344	Nemesha	Mehta	Engineering	Engineer	65,000	10/1/95	2/12/65	F	S
12	3210	Carmen	Ortega-Molina	Engineering	Engineer	46,000	9/16/99	3/28/52	F	S
13	2002	Edgar	Rothrock	Engineering	Engineer	53,300	2/8/94	3/21/70	M	S
14	3015	Patti	Stonesifer	Engineering	Engineer	64,300	7/6/98	3/10/66	F	S
15	2678	Koshi	Yamamoto	Engineering	Engineer	49,600	11/16/95	1/24/63	F	S
16	2733	John	Zurnkowski	Engineering	Staff	33,000	4/18/96	12/12/72	M	TS
17	3314	Svetlana	Kartashev	Human Resources	Staff	38,000	11/5/01	5/3/82	F	N
18	4006	Alice	Rovik	Human Resources	Manager	43,000	12/1/01	1/26/55	M	S
19	2042	Hillary	Cushner	Management	Staff	32,000	8/26/94	5/6/61	F	TS
20	1851	Melinda	English	Management	Manager	56,400	10/1/93	2/14/56	F	TS
21	1355	Barbara	Grabowski	Management	Manager	75,700	10/13/92	4/10/65	F	C
22	1173	Roberta	Kurzweil	Management	Manager	63,000	6/16/92	12/22/58	F	S
23	1441	James	Van Horn	Management	Manager	66,500	12/18/92	2/3/58	M	S
24	1042	Maria	Andretti	Marketing	CSR	42,500	3/21/90	8/20/70	F	N
25	1032	Hillary	Flintsteel	Marketing	Staff	34,500	3/21/90	8/22/58	F	N
26	1016	Oscar	Gomez	Marketing	CSR	43,500	2/16/90	4/29/67	M	N
27	1009	Kevin	Grundies	Marketing	CSR	38,900	12/24/89	3/4/61	M	C
28	1614	Artie	Lambros	Marketing	CSR	41,000	5/16/93	7/13/70	M	N
29	2105	Luca	Pacioli	Marketing	Staff	42,300	8/26/95	5/6/50	M	S

anotherword

. . . on Sorting Lists on Multiple Fields

The Sort dialog box limits you to three sort fields at a time. To sort on more than three fields, you must sort the list on the three least important fields first, and then continue to sort by three fields at a time until you have sorted the list by the most important field—a type of master primary key. Specify the most important sort field in the Sort by list box on the final sort operation.

anotherword

. . . on Sorting Lists and Removing Sort Fields

Excel remembers the sort fields you used the last time you executed the Sort command. If you do not want to sort by the third or second Then by field, remove them by clicking the **Then by sort list arrow,** scrolling to the top of the list, and clicking the **(none)** choice.

Creating and Using Custom Sort Orders

Excel does not limit you to the standard sorting sequence. If you want to sort a series of labels in a particular order, you can define a custom sorting series. A *custom sorting series* or list is an ordered list you create to instruct Excel in what order to sort rows containing the list items. For example, imagine a list of student records containing a field called Year in School. The Year in School would contain "Freshman," "Sophomore," "Junior," and "Senior." Under normal circumstances, records sorted on the Year in School would rearrange rows so that they appear in this order: Freshman, Junior, Senior, and then Sophomore. However, most schools want the list sorted by year in school beginning with Freshman and ending with Senior. Creating a custom list containing Freshman, Sophomore, Junior, and then Senior—in that order—solves that particular sorting problem. (Excel already has the days of the week and the months of the year as custom sort orders, so you can sort time cards in Monday through Friday order or January through December.)

task reference

Creating a Custom Sort Order

- Click **Tools** on the menu bar, click **Options,** and then click the **Custom Lists** tab

- Click **NEW LIST** in the Custom lists list box

- In the List Entries section of the dialog box, type each item of your list in order and press **Enter** to place each item on its own line

- When the list is complete, click the **Add** button to move the proposed list to the Custom lists panel

- Click the **OK** button to close the Options dialog box after completing the custom sort list

Alice would like you to sort the list in a third way so that the departments appear in this order: Marketing, Human Resources, Management, and Engineering. You begin by defining a custom sort order. Once you have defined the list, you can sort the worksheet rows in order by the custom list.

Creating a custom sort order:

1. Click **Tools** on the menu bar and then click **Options**

2. Click the **Custom Lists** tab, and then click **NEW LIST** in the Custom lists box

3. In the List entries box, type **Marketing** and press **Enter**

4. Type **Human Resources** and press **Enter**

5. Type **Management** and press **Enter**

6. Type **Engineering** and click the **Add** button to add the list you typed to the Custom lists (see Figure 5.12)

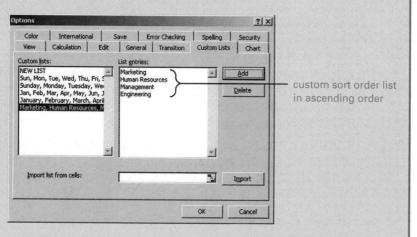

FIGURE 5.12

Defining a custom sort order

7. Click **OK** to complete the custom sort list definition process and close the Options dialog box

*another*word

...on Creating a Custom Sort Order

If the items in your custom list already appear in the correct order as text in your worksheet, you do not have to type them on the Custom Lists tab of the Tools, Options dialog box. Instead, select the list before choosing the Options command of the Tools menu. Your highlighted text list will appear automatically in the dialog box. Simply click the Import button to add the new custom sort order sequence to Excel's custom lists. The lists are remembered for all workbooks you load from Excel on that particular computer.

Now you can test your new custom sort order. You can sort the employee list by department names and then by employee names within the department using a procedure similar to the sort you performed above. This time, you will specify a data sort option and tell Excel to use the custom sort order to sort department names in a special way. The resulting list will be organized in a slightly different order because you redefined how to sort the department names.

To delete a custom sort order list, select the list on the Custom Lists tab and click the Delete button. The list is eliminated. For now, leave the custom list in place to use in the next steps to sort your employee list by department names.

FIGURE 5.13

Selecting a custom sort order

Sorting the employee list using a custom sort order for department names:

1. Click any cell in the employee list

2. Click **Data** on the menu bar and then click **Sort**

3. Click the **Options** button to display the Sort options dialog box

4. Click the **First key sort order list box arrow,** click the **Marketing, Human Resources** entry to notify Excel to use that custom sort order (see Figure 5.13), and then click **OK**

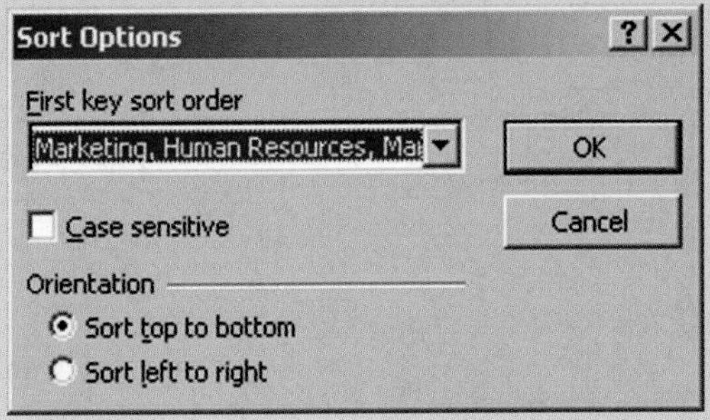

Because Excel remembers the field names and sort order for the Sort by and the two *Then by* sort fields, you do not need to reinstate them. Ensure that they say Department, Last Name, and First Name, respectively.

5. Click **OK** to sort the list into order on three sort fields using the custom sort order for the Department field—the primary sort field. Figure 5.14 shows the list sorted with the custom department sort order.

With the employee list sorted by department and employee names within each department, it will be easier for Alice to look up an employee in a particular department.

a custom sort order based on department

	A	B	C	D	E	F	G	H	I	J
1										
2	ID	First Name	Last Name	Department	Title	Salary	Hire Date	Birth Date	Gender	Clearanc
3	1042	Maria	Andretti	Marketing	CSR	42,500	3/21/90	8/20/70	F	N
4	1032	Hillary	Flintsteel	Marketing	Staff	34,500	3/21/90	8/22/58	F	N
5	1016	Oscar	Gomez	Marketing	CSR	43,500	2/16/90	4/29/67	M	N
6	1009	Kevin	Grundies	Marketing	CSR	38,900	12/24/89	3/4/61	M	C
7	1614	Artie	Lambros	Marketing	CSR	41,000	5/16/93	7/13/70	M	N
8	2105	Luca	Pacioli	Marketing	Staff	42,300	8/26/95	5/6/50	M	S
9	3314	Svetlana	Kartashev	Human Resources	Staff	38,000	11/5/01	5/3/82	F	N
10	4006	Alice	Rovik	Human Resources	Manager	43,000	12/1/01	1/26/55	M	S
11	2042	Hillary	Cushner	Management	Staff	32,000	8/26/94	5/6/61	F	TS
12	1851	Melinda	English	Management	Manager	56,400	10/1/93	2/14/56	F	TS
13	1355	Barbara	Grabowski	Management	Manager	75,700	10/13/92	4/10/65	F	C
14	1173	Roberta	Kurzweil	Management	Manager	63,000	6/16/92	12/22/58	F	S
15	1441	James	Van Horn	Management	Manager	66,500	12/18/92	2/3/58	M	S
16	4123	Steve	Ballmer	Engineering	Engineer	42,900	5/1/02	4/14/70	M	N
17	3117	Frederich	Bednarczyk	Engineering	Engineer	56,700	5/14/99	5/27/70	M	S
18	2122	Yuan	Chang	Engineering	Engineer	46,540	9/5/95	3/4/64	M	TS
19	2451	Francine	Detweiler	Engineering	Engineer	56,700	10/10/95	4/29/70	F	S
20	2896	Samuel	Gates	Engineering	Engineer	66,300	1/28/97	4/10/74	M	S
21	2956	Michael	Goldstein	Engineering	Engineer	51,000	4/11/97	3/7/63	M	TS
22	2768	Phyllis	Leonard	Engineering	Engineer	59,800	12/13/96	7/2/70	F	TS
23	1119	Sharad	Manispour	Engineering	Manager	54,500	10/13/90	2/4/69	M	S
24	2344	Nemesha	Mehta	Engineering	Engineer	65,000	10/1/95	2/12/65	F	S
25	3210	Carmen	Ortega-Molina	Engineering	Engineer	46,000	9/16/99	3/28/52	F	S

Documentation \ Employee Data

Ready

FIGURE 5.14

Sorting with a custom sort order

CHANGING THE ZOOM SETTING OF A WORKSHEET

Sometimes it is handy to get a bird's eye view of a worksheet—to back up and view a larger portion of it on screen. Normally, Excel displays a worksheet at 100 percent magnification. The Zoom command of the View command (or the Zoom list box on the Standard toolbar) provides several preset viewing percentages, or you can specify an exact percentage of magnification. To view more of a worksheet—more columns and rows—you reduce the Zoom percentage. Similarly, you can zoom in and carefully examine a portion of a worksheet by increasing the Zoom percentage. Experiment with the Zoom percentage.

Decreasing the Zoom percentage to view a larger part of the employee list:

1. Click **View** on the menu bar and then click **Zoom** to open the Zoom dialog box

2. Click the **50%** option button to reduce the worksheet display to 50% of its normal size (see Figure 5.15)

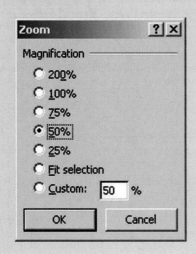

FIGURE 5.15

Zoom dialog box

Reducing a worksheet's Zoom percentage

3. Click **OK** to reduce the worksheet to 50% magnification (see Figure 5.16)

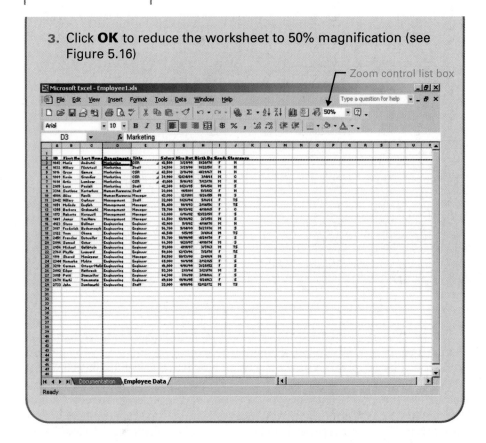

When you want to zoom in for a close inspection of a few cells on the worksheet, you can do so by increasing the Zoom percentage to a value greater than 100 percent.

Increasing the Zoom percentage to view details of the worksheet:

1. Click the **Zoom control list arrow** on the Standard toolbar

2. Click **200%**. Examine the worksheet

3. Return the worksheet to its normal display by clicking the **Zoom control list arrow** on the Standard toolbar and then clicking **100%**

SESSION 5.2 CREATING FILTERS AND SUBTOTALS

In this section, you will learn how to create data filters to hide selected list rows, how to apply conditional formats to draw attention to selected cells in the employee list, and how to insert subtotals beneath groups of employee records.

making the grade

1. A column of a data list is also called a _____.

2. A data list's row is also called what?

3. Execute the _____ _____ command of the Window menu to freeze rows and columns.

4. A _____ _____ is a dialog box displaying one row of a list in text boxes.

5. Modify the employee worksheet you saved as **Employee1.xls** in the following ways. Sort the employee list into ascending order by gender and by descending order by salary within each gender—a two-field sort where Gender is the primary sort field and Salary is the secondary sort field. Place your name on the worksheet or in the header and print the worksheet. Save the workbook as **EmployeeS1.xls.** Sort the employee list into ascending order by the Clearance field where the custom sort order is: N, C, S, and TS. Set the two *Then by* sort fields to (none). Save the workbook as **EmployeeS2.xls** and print the worksheet. Sort the worksheet in ascending order by the Birth Date field, save the workbook as **EmployeeS3.xls,** and print the sorted worksheet.

   Finally, eliminate the Clearance custom sort order so that it does not affect your results in Sessions 5.2 and 5.3. (Excel remembers custom sort orders you have created regardless of which workbook is open.). To eliminate the Clearance custom sort order, click **Tools** on the menu bar, click **Options,** click the **Custom Lists** tab, click the **N, C, S, TS** list in the Custom lists panel, click the **Delete** button, click **OK** to confirm the deletion, and click **OK** to close the Options dialog box.

USING FILTERS TO ANALYZE A LIST

When viewing a long data list such as the employee list or lists with hundreds or thousands of rows, you may want to view just a portion of the list. For example, if you want to view records of customers who live in Michigan from your list of 3,000 customers, then you could sort the list on the State field and then scroll down to the section containing Michigan customers. But sorting and then scrolling down the list is not the best way to locate particular records in a list. Locating a group of records by sorting and scrolling is tedious and time-consuming.

Filtering a List with AutoFilter

Alice frequently needs to have a list of the engineers who work for Comsec. She is putting together a brochure that outlines the background and capabilities of the company and its engineers. She wants to list the names and clearance levels of the engineers. Alice thought about using a data form and specifying the search criteria "engineer" in the Title text box to locate the engineers, but that method displays only one record at a time. The best way to display the list of engineers is to ask Excel to list only records that match particular criteria, hiding the rows that do not. This method is called *filtering*. Other Office products use filtering too. Microsoft Access uses filtering to retrieve rows that satisfy criteria through its query facility.

---

task reference

Filtering a List with AutoFilter

- Click any cell in the list

- Click **Data,** point to **Filter,** and click **AutoFilter** to turn each column into a list box with a list arrow beside each label

- Click the **list arrow** next to the label you want to use as a filter

- Click the criteria in the drop-down list by which you want to filter the list

---

AutoFilter is the filtering command that allows you to hide all rows in a list except those that match the criteria you specify. You will create a filter on the Title column to list the employees with the title "Engineer."

Filtering a list with the AutoFilter command:

1. Save the employee workbook as **Employee2.xls** to preserve the work you completed in Session 5.1

2. Click any cell within the employee list

3. Click **Data** on the menu bar, point to **Filter,** and click **AutoFilter.** Excel places list box arrows next to each label in the list's heading row. You view the filtering criteria by clicking a list arrow

4. Click the **Title column list arrow** to display the filtering criteria available for that column. Excel analyzes each column, sorts it, and removes the duplicate values to form the filtering list for each column (see Figure 5.17)

FIGURE 5.17

AutoFilter filtering values for the Title column

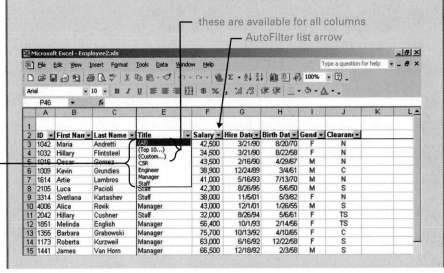

list of filters available for this column

these are available for all columns
AutoFilter list arrow

5. Click **Engineer** to hide all employees except those containing "Engineer" in the Title column. Excel counts the total number of records it filters and the total number of records and displays those numbers in the status bar ("12 of 27 records"). Missing rows are hidden, not deleted (see Figure 5.18)

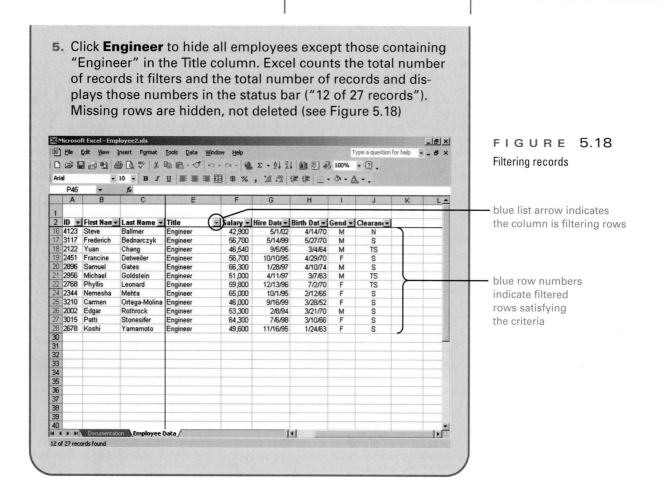

FIGURE 5.18
Filtering records

blue list arrow indicates the column is filtering rows

blue row numbers indicate filtered rows satisfying the criteria

Three filter choices appear in all list columns. They are *All*, *Top 10*, and *Custom*. *All* displays all items in the list and removes filtering from the column. *Top 10* displays the top or bottom *n* items, when sorted, in the list. You can click *Custom* to specify more complex filtering criteria.

The AutoFilter list also displays the choices *(Blanks)* and *(NonBlanks)* at the bottom of the AutoFilter list for any column that contains at least one blank entry. If the column does not contain any blank entries, the preceding choices do not appear in the AutoFilter list. The (Blanks) and (NonBlanks) choices are handy because they allow you to display rows whose selected field contains blanks. Blank entries are often errors, and locating them can be difficult in long lists.

With any criteria in effect, you can refine your query by using several AutoFilter drop-down filters in tandem. Doing so further restricts the rows that appear in the filtered list. For example, if you want a list of engineers who have top secret clearances, you select Engineer from the Title drop-down filter list and then select TS from the Clearance drop-down list to combine filtering criteria.

anotherword

. . . on Filtering a List

Because AutoFilter hides entire rows in the active sheet that do not match the AutoFilter criteria, avoid placing other worksheet information in the same rows as the list. Though outside the list, information in the same list as a hidden row is hidden also.

anotherword

. . . on Blanks

When a column contains blanks, you can eliminate displaying rows in which a particular column contains a blank. Click the AutoFilter drop-down list for the field and select **NonBlanks.** Only rows with nonblank entries in the selected column appear. Select Blanks to reveal rows containing no value in the selected column.

EXCEL

FIGURE 5.19

Using multiple criteria to filter a list

Filtering a list with multiple criteria:

1. With the Title filter criteria ("Engineer") still in effect, click the **Clearance column list arrow**

2. Click **TS** in the Clearance filter list to limit rows to engineers with a top secret clearance (see Figure 5.19)

filter criteria: "Engineer"   filter criteria: "TS"

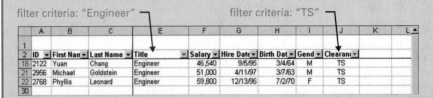

	A	B	C	E	F	G	H	I	J	K	L
1											
2	ID	First Nan	Last Name	Title	Salary	Hire Date	Birth Dat	Gend	Clearani		
18	2122	Yuan	Chang	Engineer	46,540	9/5/95	3/4/64	M	TS		
21	2956	Michael	Goldstein	Engineer	51,000	4/11/97	3/7/63	M	TS		
22	2768	Phyllis	Leonard	Engineer	59,800	12/13/96	7/2/70	F	TS		
30											

3. Remove the Clearance column filter by clicking the **Clearance column list arrow** and then by clicking **(All)** at the top of the list. Excel removes the Clearance filter

task reference

Clearing All AutoFilter Filtering Criteria

- Click **Data,** point to **Filter**

- Click **Show All** to remove all existing filters

Removing all AutoFilter list filters:

1. Click **Data** on the menu bar

2. Point to **Filter** and then click **Show All.** All the records reappear, but the AutoFilter list arrows remain next to each column heading

Using Custom AutoFilters

The AutoFilters you applied in the preceding examples work for *exact match criteria*—criteria in which a row's field exactly matches a particular filter value. Alice needs the capability to specify a *range* of acceptable values. The AutoFilter custom criteria do just that. With custom criteria, you can specify the low and high values range that a field must satisfy instead of a single value.

Custom AutoFilters allow you to specify other relationships besides "is equal to." You specify criteria using any of the six relational operators: Less than, less than or equal to, greater than, greater than or equal to, or not equal to, or equal to. A *relational operator* compares two values, and the expression containing the values and the conditional operator result in either true or false. Relational operators in Excel expressions are written as the symbols <, <=, =, >, >=, <>. In Custom AutoFilters, relational operators appear in a list box as English phrases such as "is greater than or equal to" rather than their symbolic equivalent such as ">=".

Alice wants to send out mailers to all male employees who were born in the 1960s because a company policy change affects their health benefits. While she could sort the list and try to write down the affected employees' names born between 1960 and 1969 (inclusive), she knows that using a custom AutoFilter is a better solution. That way, she can hide all rows except those whose hire date is in a specified range.

Creating a more complex AutoFilter:

1. With all criteria cleared but the AutoFilter list arrows still visible, click the **Birth Date column list arrow.** The criteria filter list appears below the Birth Date column heading

2. Click **(Custom...)** to display the Custom AutoFilter dialog box (see Figure 5.20)

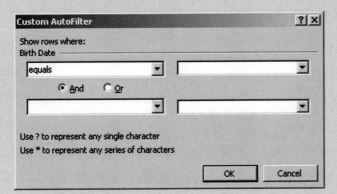

FIGURE 5.20

Custom AutoFilter dialog box

The operator list box contains the six relational operators plus four additional operators. It lets you select a relational operator or special operator by clicking the item in the list. The criteria list box to the right of the operator list box contains unique values from the selected column in ascending order. You can select an item from the list by clicking the arrow and then clicking a list item.

Select the "And" or "Or" option buttons when you want to specify multiple custom criteria on a row. Select "And" when both criteria apply simultaneously. Select "Or" when either criteria apply but not necessarily both criteria.

3. Click the top left list box and then click **is greater than or equal to**

4. Click the top right list box and then type **1/1/1960**

5. Click the **And** option button, if necessary

6. Click the bottom left list box and then click **is less than or equal to**

7. Click the bottom right list box and then type **12/31/1969** in the list box (see Figure 5.21)

8. Click **OK** to apply the custom filter and display the filtered employee list—employees born between January 1, 1960 and December 31, 1969

EXCEL

FIGURE 5.21

Custom AutoFilter dialog box
with filters filled in

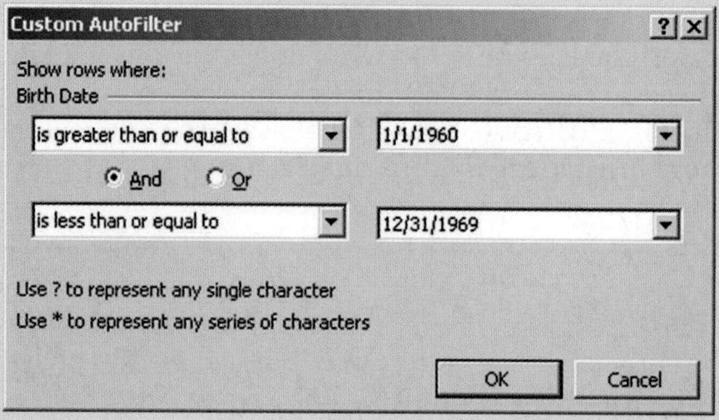

To further restrict selected rows to males, you need to apply a filter to the Gender column. Together, the two filters combine to hide all rows except male employees born in the 1960s

9. Click the **Gender column list arrow.** The criteria filter list appears below the Gender column heading

10. Click **M** in the Gender filter list to further restrict the list to males. Excel filters the list producing the required list of males born in the 1960s (see Figure 5.22)

FIGURE 5.22

Filtered list of males born in the 1960s

criteria 1: born in the 1960s ——   —— criteria 2: Male

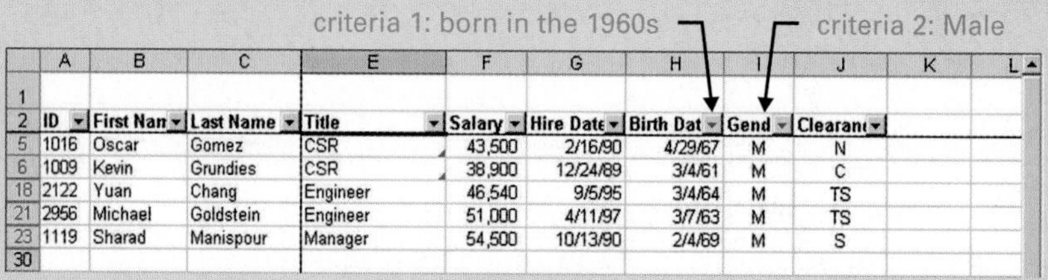

	A	B	C	E	F	G	H	I	J	K	L
1											
2	ID	First Nam	Last Name	Title	Salary	Hire Date	Birth Dat	Gend	Clearan		
5	1016	Oscar	Gomez	CSR	43,500	2/16/90	4/29/67	M	N		
6	1009	Kevin	Grundies	CSR	38,900	12/24/89	3/4/61	M	C		
18	2122	Yuan	Chang	Engineer	46,540	9/5/95	3/4/64	M	TS		
21	2956	Michael	Goldstein	Engineer	51,000	4/11/97	3/7/63	M	TS		
23	1119	Sharad	Manispour	Manager	54,500	10/13/90	2/4/69	M	S		
30											

Alice wants to interview the employees whose records are shown in Figure 5.22 in order of their birth data—oldest to youngest. She asks you to sort the list on the Birth Date field and then show her the resulting list (still filtered). After Alice reviews the list, she wants you to remove the AutoFilter so that all the employee rows reappear.

Sorting a filtered list and then restoring hidden rows:

1. Click any cell in the **Birth Date** column—inside the list, the column label, or outside the list

2. Click the **Sort Ascending** button on the Standard toolbar to sort the list in ascending birth date order. The filtered list appears in ascending birth date order

3. Click **Data** on the menu bar, point to **Filter,** and click **AutoFilter** to remove all filters. (You cannot undo the result of removing an AutoFilter.) Excel removes all filters and restores the list to reveal all previously hidden employee rows

USING SUBTOTALS TO ANALYZE A LIST

Whenever you have an Excel list with data whose columns each contain one type of data—a database or list such as the employee worksheet, for example—you can produce summary information about the numeric columns. The Employee worksheet is a typical example. With data arranged in order by department, it is convenient to insert SUM functions to compute the total salary of each department. Although you could write four SUM functions to total the salaries of all employees in each department, Excel provides a more convenient solution—the Subtotals command.

Subtotals offers several list summary features including count, sum, average, minimum, and maximum—the same features provided by the stand-alone statistical functions of COUNTA, SUM, AVERAGE, MIN, and MAX. Unlike those functions, the Subtotals command automatically creates the appropriate formula when it senses a change in the value of a specified field. For the employee list, that field could be Department. Subtotals also provides the added convenience of outlining whereby you can display the rows that comprise a group or you can collapse the list, hiding all rows except the subtotal rows. Excel handles the details of hiding and revealing list rows as needed. The only requirement for the Subtotals command to do its work properly is that the list be sorted so that it is in order by the field you specify as the grouping field before you use the subtotals command.

How Subtotals Are Built

---

task reference

Subtotaling a List's Entries

- Sort the list by the column whose groups you want to subtotal

- Click any cell inside the list

- Click **Data** and then click **Subtotals**

- In the *At each change in* list box, click the name of the group on which you want a subtotal

- From the *Use function* list box, select the aggregate function you want to use

- In the *Add subtotal to* list box, select the column(s) containing the values you want to aggregate; in the *Add subtotal to* list box, clear the clear the column(s) containing check marks for any values you *do not* want to aggregate

- Click **OK**

Alice wants to view the total salaries by department and the total of all departments' salaries. To prepare to create that report, first sort the list into order by Department, which is the field upon which subtotals are created. Remember, the last time you sorted the list, you used a custom sort list. You have to remove that list to sort the Department field in a "normal" way. First, you will remove the custom sort order.

Canceling a custom sort order:

1. Click **Data** on the menu bar, click **Sort,** and click the **Options** button to open the Sort Options dialog box (see Figure 5.13)

2. Click the **First key sort order** list box, and then click **Normal** at the top of the list

3. Click **OK** to close the Sort Options dialog box, and then click **OK** to close the Sort dialog box

Now you can sort the list in alphabetical order by department, because you cancelled the custom Department sort order.

Sorting a list prior to creating subtotals:

1. Click cell **D3,** the first data cell under the Department column label

2. Click the **Sort Ascending** button on the Standard toolbar to sort the list in order by department name

Now that the list is sorted into department order, you can create summary information about departments. Because Alice wants a sum of salaries by department and the grand total salary value, you use the Subtotals command.

Summing salaries by departments:

1. Click **Data** on the menu bar and then click **Subtotals.** The Subtotal dialog box opens

2. Click the **At each change in** list box and then click **Department** in the drop-down list to tell Excel to create subtotals by department

3. Click the **Use function** list box and then click **Sum.** You want to sum the salary field, not count or average it

4. Scroll to the top of the *Add subtotal to* list box, then slowly scroll down the Add subtotal to list and remove any check marks in the column name check boxes

5. Scroll the list, if necessary, to locate and then click the **Salary** check box to place a check mark in it. Salary is the column you want to sum (see Figure 5.23)

6. Ensure that the *Replace current subtotals* and the *Summary below data* check boxes are checked and that the *Page break between groups* check box is clear (see Figure 5.23)

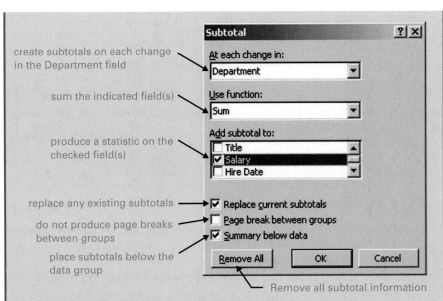

create subtotals on each change in the Department field

sum the indicated field(s)

produce a statistic on the checked field(s)

replace any existing subtotals

do not produce page breaks between groups

place subtotals below the data group

Remove all subtotal information

F I G U R E   5.23
Completed Subtotal dialog box

tip: *By default, the* Replace current subtotals *check box is checked, meaning the subtotal you specify will replace the selected list's current subtotal. However, if you want to use more than one function, sum and average for example, you can execute the Data Subtotals a second time and specify the second subtotal function. The second time, however, deselect the Replace current subtotals check box to display both subtotal functions at once. You can repeat this for as many subtotal functions as you want for a group.*

7. Click **OK** to insert the subtotals below each department group and the grand total below the last group's subtotal (see Figure 5.24)

level 1, 2, and 3 Outline buttons

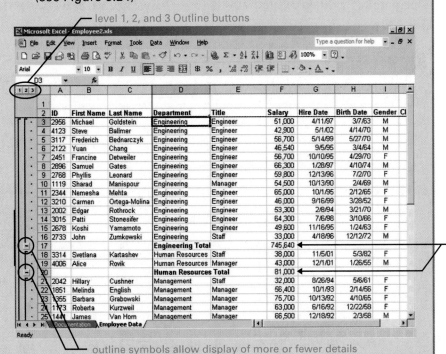

departmental salary subtotal lines

outline symbols allow display of more or fewer details

F I G U R E   5.24
Departments with subtotaled salaries

8. Scroll through the list to view each department's subtotal and the total salary value for all departments (the value is 1,362,940, which is in cell F34)

EXCEL

> **tip:** *If cell F34 displays ###### symbols, the value is larger than the column can display. In that case, widen column F.*

9. If necessary, widen column F so that the total salary displays. Click cell **F34** containing the total salary for all departments, click **Format** on the menu bar, point to **Column,** and click **AutoFit Selection.** The column enlarges enough to display the total in cell F34

Using the Subtotals Outline View

The subtotals by department are very handy and easy to create. Alice also wants to see just the subtotals and not all the details about the rows that are in each department. Upper management people commonly want the "big picture" instead of all the details. Often, the higher up the corporate ladder one is, the fewer details one needs to make sweeping decisions. Fortunately, Excel makes creating summaries a snap with another feature that is part of the Subtotals command—Outlines.

The Subtotals command produces two results when you use it. Not only does it produce subtotal statistics for identified groups, it also outlines the worksheet's list. You can choose how much detail to view in the outline by clicking one of three outline buttons located at the top left side of the worksheet (see Figure 5.24). Commonly, the highest level, 3, is active. It displays all active list members, subtotals, and the grand total. Level 2 hides the individual list-member rows but displays subtotal information. The lowest level of detail, level 1, displays only the grand total information. Try the outline buttons to see how they work by doing the next exercise.

Using the outline feature of the subtotals:

1. Make D3—the upper leftmost cell in the frozen panels—the active cell by pressing **Ctrl+Home**

2. Click the **Level 2 Outline** [2] button (see Figure 5.24). Notice that the departmental salary subtotals and grand total appear, but Excel hides the detail rows (see Figure 5.25)

FIGURE 5.25

Level 2 outline

outline expand buttons

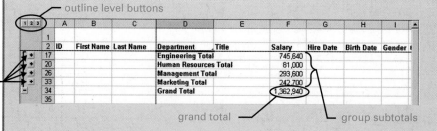

outline level buttons

grand total   group subtotals

3. Click the **Expand** [+] button to the left of row 34 to expand the Management department details

4. Click the **Level 1 Outline** [1] button to hide all information in the list except the grand total

5. Place your name in the worksheet header and print the worksheet.

6. Click the **Level 3 Outline** 3 button to expose all departments' detail rows

Although the employee list is relatively short, you can see how outlining a really long list can be useful. It allows anyone to see an overview of crucial statistics without having to see the details at the same time. Removing details helps a viewer focus on the "bottom line," much the same way a chart does.

Inserting Page Breaks into a List with Subtotals

Alice wants to distribute the employee information to four department heads for their use. Because she wants to keep each department's information confidential among the departments, she wants to print each department's employee information on a separate page so that she can distribute the four one-page reports to each department head. Though the worksheet prints on one page, you can create your own page breaks easily.

You can insert page breaks into any Subtotals list by selecting an option available on the Subtotal dialog box, or you can manually insert page breaks anywhere using the Insert command on the menu bar.

Inserting page breaks into a list containing subtotals:

1. Click **Data** on the menu bar and then click **Subtotals** to display the Subtotal dialog box

2. Click the **At each change in** list box and then click **Department** in the list of fields

3. Click the **Use function** list box and then click **Sum**

4. Click the **Clearance** check box in the *Add subtotal to* list to clear it, and then click the **Salary** check box to place a check mark in it

5. Click the **Page break between groups** check box (see Figure 5.23) to place a check mark in it

6. Click **OK** to close the Subtotal dialog box. Dashed lines appear on the worksheet where Excel inserts page breaks (see Figure 5.26)

7. Click the **Print Preview** button on the Standard toolbar

8. Click the **Next** button on the Print Preview toolbar. Look at the top of the page (zoom in if necessary). Notice that the column labels do not appear at the top of the second page, but they do appear on the top of the first page

9. Click the **Close** button on the Print Preview toolbar to close the Print Preview window

EXCEL

FIGURE 5.26

Page breaks inserted between groups

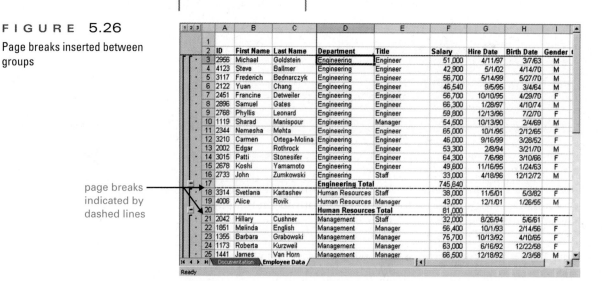

page breaks indicated by dashed lines

Printing Row and Column Titles on Each Page

You noticed as you reviewed the worksheet in the previous exercise that the column headings appear only on the first page printed. Typically, you should display column headings on every page printed so that a reader does not have to leaf back to the first page to see the headings. Similarly, if you have a wide output in which every other page displays columns in the right half of a worksheet, you can tell Excel to print row headings in the first column of every page.

task reference

Displaying Row or Column Headings on Each Page

- Click **File** and then click **Page Setup**
- Click the **Sheet** tab
- Click the **Collapse dialog box** button on the **Rows to repeat at top** or **Columns to repeat at left** text boxes in the Print titles section
- Select the row(s) or column(s) you want to print on each page
- Click the **Expand dialog box** button again to reveal the Page Setup dialog box
- Click **OK**

Alice wants the row containing the column headings, row 2, to print at the top of each page so that the columns are identified on each page.

Printing selected rows on each page:

1. With the employee list subtotals with group page breaks still open, click **File** on the menu bar, click **Page Setup** to open the Page Setup dialog box, and then click the **Sheet** tab

2. Click the **Collapse dialog box** ![collapse] button to the right of the **Rows to repeat at top**

3. Click the **row 2 header** button to select the entire row, and then click the **Expand dialog box** 🔲 button to restore the Page Setup dialog box (see Figure 5.27)

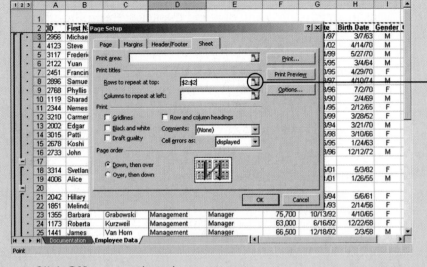

FIGURE 5.27
Seleting a row to repeat on every page

Collapse dialog box button

4. Click **OK** to complete the process

5. Click the **Print Preview** button on the Standard toolbar and then click the **Next** button repeatedly to preview each output page and confirm that the first output line—the column labels—appears on every page

6. Click the **Close** button on the Print Preview toolbar

Clearing All Subtotal Information

You can remove subtotal information by executing the Data Subtotals command and then clicking a button that removes all totals.

Removing subtotals from a list:

1. Click any cell within the list, including a subtotal row, and then click **Data** on the menu bar

2. Click **Subtotals.** The Subtotal dialog box opens

3. Click the **Remove All** button. Excel removes all subtotal rows and closes the Subtotal dialog box

4. Click **Ctrl+Home** to make cell D3 the active cell

Manually Inserting and Removing Page Breaks

Excel removes all subtotal information from the employee worksheet and displays all employee rows. Excel allows you to insert manually your own page breaks without using the Subtotals command. Similar to the way you insert page breaks in Microsoft Word documents, Excel provides a Page Break command on the Insert menu.

Manually inserting page breaks into a worksheet:

1. Click the **row 17 header** button

2. Click **Insert** on the menu bar, and then click **Page Break.** Excel inserts a page break above the selected row and displays a dashed line to indicate the position of the page break

3. Repeat steps 1 and 2 two more times but substitute row headers **19** and then **24** in step 1. When you are done, Excel displays page breaks following rows 16, 18, and 23

4. Click any cell to deselect row 24

5. Click the **Print Preview** button on the Standard toolbar

6. Click repeatedly the **Next** button on the Print Preview toolbar to view each of the remaining three pages. Notice that the column heading row prints on each page because you set that option in an earlier series of steps

7. Click the **Close** button when you are finished previewing the page breaks

You can easily remove all manually inserted page breaks. Do that next.

Removing all page breaks from a worksheet:

1. Click the **Select All** button located at the intersection of the row heading and the column heading of the worksheet

tip: *You can press **Ctrl+A** to select all worksheet cells if you prefer*

2. Click **Insert** on the menu bar and then click **Reset All Page Breaks.** Excel removes all page breaks

3. Press **Ctrl+Home** to make D3 the active cell

APPLYING CONDITIONAL FORMATTING

Managers often want to highlight unusual values in a worksheet to draw attention to them. Perhaps you want to highlight exceptional sales volume, superior quality measures, or cars with unusually high repair costs. One way to highlight exceptional values is to locate a value you want to highlight, click Format on the menu bar, and then specify a series of format changes such as a background color or a change in the font color. While this is one solution, it is both laborious and error-prone.

Excel provides a better solution: *conditional formatting*. Conditional formatting automatically takes effect in a cell when the data in the cell satisfy criteria that you specify when you create the conditional format. Conditional formatting is an easy way to highlight significant values, because you can format a group of cells at once. Only the cells that meet the specified criteria display under the control of the conditional format.

Cells containing the conditional format but not meeting the criteria display normally. For example, suppose you are tracking accounts receivable and want to display groups of values in different font colors. To display accounts with a balance of more than $10,000 in blue, you can use conditional formatting. Balances less than or equal to $10,000 display in their usual black color.

---

task reference

Applying a Conditional Format to Cells

- Click the cell range to which you want to apply a conditional format

- Click **Format** on the menu bar and then click **Conditional Formatting**

- Enter the criteria for which Excel is to apply the special formatting

- Click the **Format** button on the Conditional Formatting dialog box, select the font color, style, underlining, borders, or other formatting to apply conditionally

- Click **OK** to close the Conditional Formatting dialog box

- Click **OK** to apply the conditional formatting to the selected cell(s)

Alice would like to highlight employee salaries that are at least $55,000. This will help her quickly identify the highest-paid employees. She asks you to apply a conditional format to the Salary column so that any value equal to or greater than $55,000 displays a background color of red and a font color of white.

Applying a conditional format to the Salary column:

1. Select cell range **F3:F29**

   tip: You can select a filled partial column of cells by clicking the first cell (F3 in this case), holding the **Shift** key, tapping the **End** key, and then tapping the **Down Arrow** key

2. Click **Format** on the menu bar and click **Conditional Formatting** to open the Conditional Formatting dialog box

3. Ensure that **Cell Value Is** appears in the first text box for Condition 1, because the Salary column contains values, not formulas that compute and display values

4. Click in the **second list box** for Condition 1 to display a list of choices and then click the **greater than or equal to** choice

5. Click in the **third list box** for Condition 1 and then type **55000.** That completes defining the first and only condition on the cell range

6. Click the **Format** button in the Conditional Formatting dialog box. The Format Cells dialog box opens

7. Click the **Font** tab, if necessary, click the **Color list box arrow,** and then click the **white square** (fifth row from the top, eighth column) in the Font Color palette

8. Click the **Patterns** tab and then click the **red square** (third row from the top, first column)

9. Click **OK** to close the Format Cells dialog box (see Figure 5.28)

F I G U R E   5.28

Setting conditional formatting criteria and format options

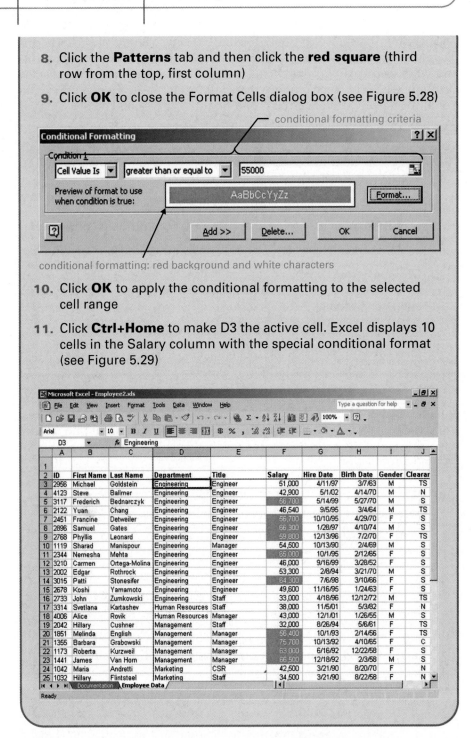

10. Click **OK** to apply the conditional formatting to the selected cell range

11. Click **Ctrl+Home** to make D3 the active cell. Excel displays 10 cells in the Salary column with the special conditional format (see Figure 5.29)

F I G U R E   5.29

Selected cells displaying the conditional format

If the value of any of the Salary cells changes and no longer meets the criteria for the conditional format, then Excel displays the cell in the usual way without the conditional format. The conditional format remains with the cells until you either reformat the cells or clear their formats.

Deleting a conditional format:

1. Select cell range **F3:F29,** the range of cells containing the conditional format

2. Click **Format** on the menu bar and click **Conditional Formatting** to open the Conditional Formatting dialog box

3. Click the **Delete** button on the Conditional Formatting dialog box. The Delete Conditional Format dialog box opens

4. Click the **Condition 1** check box to place a check mark in it (see Figure 5.30), click **OK** to confirm your choice, and close the Delete Conditional Format dialog box

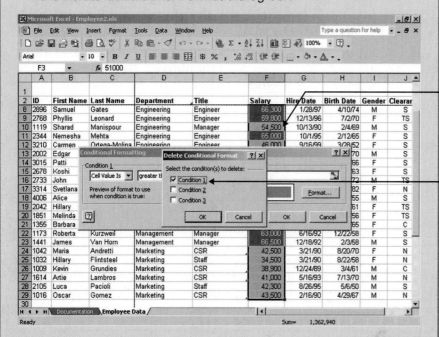

F I G U R E 5.30

Deleting a conditional format

cells with conditional format are highlighted

check Condition 1 to delete that conditional format

5. Click **OK** to close the Conditional Formatting dialog box and remove the conditional formatting from the selected cell range

6. Press **Ctrl+Home** to make cell D3 active

7. Click the Save button on the Standard toolbar to save this version of the Employee worksheet **(Employee2.xls),** close the worksheet, but leave Excel running. If you decide to take a break, close Excel. Remember to open Excel again before beginning Session 5.3

making the grade

1. You have a list of 635 employees who work at the university and you want to print the list of employees who work in Warren Hall. You would use the _____ commands from the menu bar to list the subset of employees who work in Warren Hall.

2. In order to print a list of banks in South Florida in order by City and then by bank name within each city, you would do what?

3. Suppose you want to display employees who earn $40,000 or less per year. How would you produce a list of those employees? Assume that the salary information is in a column called "Salary."

4. A list called Monthly Customer Sales contains sale dates, customer names, customer addresses, and total value of sales in three columns labeled "Sale Date," "Customer," "Address," and "Sales." Any customer may have several sales recorded in the list when he or she makes more than one purchase in the month. Describe in a sentence or two how you would produce a list, grouped by customer name, displaying each customer's list of sales followed by a total of all sales for each customer and a grand total for the month.

5. Modify the employee worksheet you saved as **Employee2.xls** in the following ways. First, load **Employee2.xls** and save it immediately as **Employee52.xls.** Sort the list in ascending order by Clearance. Use conditional formatting to make three conditions to correspond to the three clearance levels as follows: Select the Clearance column and then format the TS clearance so that the background (click the **Patterns** tab on the Format dialog box) is blue (any blue). Create a second condition (click the **Add >>** button) to color the background red in any cell with S (secret) clearance. Add a third condition to color the background green for any Clearance column cell with the value C. Cells containing the clearance N are unchanged. Click cell **J12** and type **TS.** Click cell **J5** and type **N.** Click cell **J25** and type **S.** Click **Ctrl+Home** to make cell D3 active. Place your name in the header and print the Employee Data worksheet. Place your name in cell C6 on the Documentation page. Save the worksheet (File, Save). Print both pages of the worksheet.

SESSION 5.3 CREATING AND USING PIVOT TABLES

In this section, you will learn how to summarize data in an Excel list to provide insights that are otherwise masked by the size and volume of data in a list.

PIVOT TABLE BASICS

Pivot tables provide a three-dimensional view of data that is often too complicated to understand in its raw list form. A *pivot table* is an interactive table enabling you quickly to group and summarize large amounts of data. The employee list is an example of a list that you could create a pivot table from in order to locate hidden information from the list. Pivot tables summarizing longer data lists are particularly valuable tools for revealing the information hidden in the details.

In order to create a pivot table from data, the data must meet certain criteria. First, the data must be in tabular form. Each column must have a unique column label to identify each field. Each row must represent a unique fact or piece of data. Third, date values in the list should be formatted with a date format. Fourth, remove blank rows or columns from the list so Excel can easily identify the complete unbroken list.

Pivot tables can contain these elements: *row fields, column fields,* and *page fields.* Frequently, data such as year, gender, ID number, sales date, birth date, or hire date appear in pivot tables as row, column or page fields.

Numeric data appear in pivot tables' central position—*data fields.* The data fields contain the summary information such as average sales, average age, total sales, number of sales per month, or number of students in the sophomore class, for example. The ability to move row fields to column fields and vice versa—to pivot the data—is the origin of the name for this analytical tool.

Pivot tables can help you simplify and understand the data in an Excel table or list. Consider the example of all the sales transactions for a large corporation, such as the worksheet shown in Figure 5.31 containing over 900 rows of transaction data. The Accounting department creates financial statements from a series of internal financial reports that are based on the thousands of sales transactions, vendor payments, and other transactions. The highest levels of management rarely see transaction details. As you move down through levels of a company's organization, managers at successively lower rungs of the corporate ladder look at progressively more detail. In order to manage effectively, all managers depend on summary information. Pivot tables serve a function of creating summary information from a myriad of details contained in an Excel list of individual transactions. Figure 5.32 shows a pivot table that summarizes the data

SaleID	Date	State	Sales Rep	Gender	Amount
12101	7/3/2003	CA	Watterson, Barbara	F	5470
12102	7/3/2003	NM	Goldman, Ted	M	9687
12103	7/3/2003	TX	Kole, David	M	7495
12104	7/3/2003	WI	Morrison, Alanis	F	5239
12105	7/3/2003	TX	Kole, David	M	5920
12106	7/3/2003	IL	Stonesifer, Patti	F	3349
12107	7/3/2003	CA	Pacioli, Luca	M	4061
12108	7/3/2003	IN	Kahn, Phillipe	M	7658
12109	7/3/2003	GA	Halstead, Whitney	F	6172
12110	7/3/2003	NH	English, Melinda	F	9253
12111	7/3/2003	CA	Minsky, Barbara	F	8586
12112	7/3/2003	TX	Bateman, Giles	M	6666
12113	7/3/2003	IL	Halstead, Whitney	F	6714
12114	7/3/2003	OH	Stonely, Sharon	F	4574
12115	7/3/2003	CA	English, Melinda	F	11150
12116	7/3/2003	ME	Watterson, Barbara	F	7299
12117	7/3/2003	CA	Pacioli, Luca	M	4740
12118	7/3/2003	OK	English, Melinda	F	6614
12119	7/3/2003	IL	Halstead, Whitney	F	3444
12120	7/3/2003	CA	Minsky, Barbara	F	5593
12121	7/3/2003	WI	Gates, William	M	4482
12122	7/3/2003	IA	Flintsteel, Hillary	F	6464
12123	7/4/2003	NV	Kole, David	M	10064
12124	7/4/2003	MI	Pacioli, Luca	M	5480
12125	7/4/2003	IN	Goldman, Ted	M	2458
12126	7/4/2003	CA	Stonely, Sharon	F	5210
12127	7/4/2003	FL	Kahn, Phillipe	M	6390
12128	7/4/2003	TX	Manispour, Sharad	M	10225
12129	7/4/2003	NY	Chang, Annie	F	3085
12130	7/4/2003	OH	Gates, William	M	9821

FIGURE 5.31

Sales list example

EXCEL

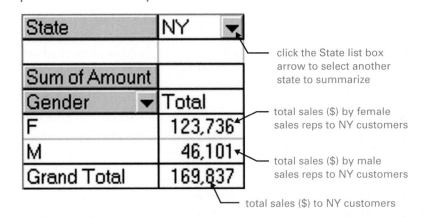

click the State list box
arrow to select another
state to summarize

total sales ($) by female
sales reps to NY customers

total sales ($) by male
sales reps to NY customers

total sales ($) to NY customers

partially displayed in Figure 5.31 and provides a fact that the dollar volume of sales to New York customers by female sales representatives is greater than sales by male sales representatives. By clicking the list box displaying "NY," managers can compare performance of male versus female sales persons in other states.

While managers' financial and database reports are often static objects, pivot tables are dynamic and flexible, providing up-to-the-minute results and in a way that allows managers to alter their view of the summary. Instead of passively reading a report, anyone with an Excel pivot table can slice, dice, twist, and turn it until they change the summary into the information they are looking for. By altering a variable here and moving another variable there, you can make the sales per month by region suddenly jump out of the details of a list, much like viewing a hologram from a different angle.

When should you use a pivot table and when should you not? Pivot tables are useful to summarize data from a relatively long list of individual observations or transactions—hundreds or thousands of invoice lines for the year, a list of dates, times, and measurements of an experiment over time, or a long list of financial transactions. Extensive listings of observations logged into columns of characteristics provide the best material for creating revealing pivot tables. On the other hand, a pivot table is not useful to analyze data that are already in summary form. You can find many examples of already summarized data, data for which a pivot table makes little sense, maintained and available at the U.S. Census bureau. They have collected thousands of statistical facts that summarize level of education by ethnicity, average income level by age, and so on.

CREATING A PIVOT TABLE WITH A PIVOT TABLE WIZARD

Alice wants you to create some pivot tables based on the raw data in the employee worksheet. Even though the list is short, there are several pieces of important information buried in the data list. For example, Alice would like a listing of the average salary by department. Then, she wants you to produce a breakdown of the employees by birth date so that she can get a better picture of the number of employees likely to retire in the next few years.

The best way to create a pivot table, especially if this is your first experience, is to use Excel's PivotTable Wizard. Like other Excel Wizards, the PivotTable Wizard guides you through a few steps to create a pivot table. You begin by opening the Employee workbook and then launching the PivotTable Wizard.

task reference

Creating a PivotTable with the PivotTable Wizard

- Click **Data** on the Standard toolbar and then click **PivotTable and PivotChart Report**

- Specify the data's location (Excel worksheet, external data source, and so on)

- Select the **PivotTable** option

- Click the **Layout** button and then specify the cell range containing the data list to be analyzed by the PivotTable Wizard

- Design the layout by selecting the column fields, row fields, page fields, and data fields

- Designate a location for the pivot table: on its own, separate page, or embedded on an existing worksheet page

Creating a pivot table:

1. If you took a break since the last session, be sure to launch Excel, if necessary, open **Employee2.xls,** and immediately save the workbook under the name **Employee3.xls** to preserve your work from Session 5.2

2. Click **Window** on the menu bar and then click **Unfreeze Panes** to remove the panes you established earlier

3. Click any cell within the list, click **Data** on the menu bar, and then click **PivotTable and PivotChart Report** to launch the Pivot Table and PivotChart Wizard (Step 1) as shown in Figure 5.33

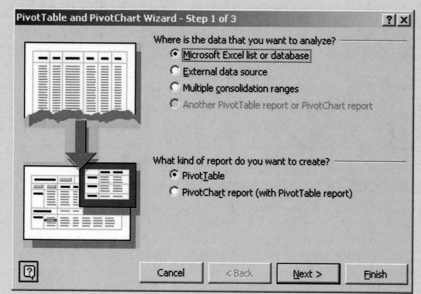

FIGURE 5.33

First dialog box displayed by the PivotTable Wizard

Specify the source of the data that you want to summarize, including all rows and header column

4. Click the **Microsoft Excel list or database** option button, if necessary, click the **PivotTable** option button in the lower panel of the first pivot table dialog box, and then click the **Next** button (see Figure 5.34)

F I G U R E   5.34

PivotTable Wizard, Step 2

cell range of list to analyze

In the second PivotTable Wizard dialog box you specify the exact cell range containing the list (and column headers) to summarize. Because you clicked a member of the list *before* launching the Wizard, Excel correctly identifies the boundaries of your list

5. Click the **Next** button to open the third step dialog box (see Figure 5.35)

F I G U R E   5.35

PivotTable Wizard, Step 3

click to go to the last step

click to design the layout of a pivot table

click to back up one step and make adjustments

In the third PivotTable Wizard, you decide where to place the resulting pivot table—on a separate page or on the worksheet containing the data—and complete the layout of the pivot table

6. Ensure that the **New worksheet** option is selected to place the pivot table on its own page and then click **Finish.** Excel creates an empty PivotTable on a new worksheet (see Figure 5.36)

DESIGNING THE PIVOT TABLE LAYOUT

You can define the initial layout of a pivot table within the framework of the pivot table report. You select the fields you want to place in the row field, column field, page field, and data field whose design is outlined in the empty pivot table report framework. Into the data field of the pivot table frame, you drop the field name(s) from the data list that you want to summarize—to count, sum, average, and so forth. The PivotTable toolbar (see Figure 5.36 and Figure 5.37) contains field buttons that correspond to the list's field names. You can drag a field name button to any of the four areas of the pivot table framework—Drop Row Fields Here, Drop Column Fields Here, Drop Page Fields Here, or Drop Data Items Here—to design the layout of the pivot table.

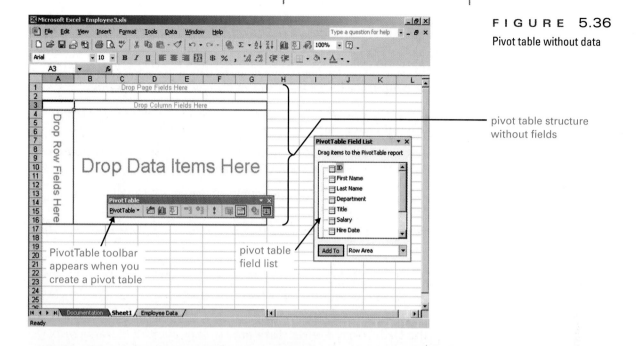

FIGURE 5.36
Pivot table without data

pivot table structure
without fields

PivotTable toolbar
appears when you
create a pivot table

pivot table
field list

FIGURE 5.37
PivotTable toolbar tools

Button Name	Purpose
PivotTable	Drop-down that displays shortcut menu of pivot table commands
Format Report	Displays a list of pivot table report styles
Chart Wizard	Creates a chart sheet from a pivot table
MapPoint	Creates map from PivotTable data (you may not have this icon if you did not install MapPoint)
Hide Detail	Hides detail lines of a pivot table field
Show Detail	Reveals detail lines of a pivot table field
Refresh Data	Updates a pivot table after you have made changes to the underlying data
Include Hidden Items in Totals	Items you have hidden are still counted in the PivotTable totals
Always Display Items	Controls when Excel goes to an external data source to determine a pivot table value
Field Settings	Opens the PivotTable Field dialog box containing options you can apply to the selected pivot table field
Hide/Show Field List	Toggles between hiding and displaying field list

The first pivot table you will create is average salary by department
and gender. The values of the department will appear as row labels and the
gender values will be column headings. In the Data Items area will be the
expression that averages the Salary column in each of the several groups
defined by department/gender value pairs. Create the pivot table layout
next.

EXCEL

task reference

Selecting Pivot Table Fields

- Click and drag each field containing the data you want to summarize to the **Drop Data Items Here** area of the pivot table framework
- Click and drag each field you want to appear in columns to the **Drop Column Fields Here** area of the pivot table framework
- Click and drag each field you want to appear in rows to the **Drop Row Fields Here** area of the pivot table framework
- Click and drag each field you want to appear in pages to the **Drop Page Fields Here** area of the pivot table framework

Creating the pivot table layout:

1. Click and drag **Department** from the PivotTable Field List to the **Drop Row Fields Here** area of the pivot table framework. After you release the mouse, the Department field appears with a list arrow at the top of the Drop Row Fields Here area

   tip: *If you click and drag the wrong field to the pivot table frame, remove the field by clicking the field button and dragging it anywhere off of the pivot table frame*

2. Scroll the PivotTable Field List to reveal the Gender field, and then click and drag **Gender** from the PivotTable Field List to the **Drop Column Fields Here** area of the pivot table framework. After you release the mouse, the Gender field, with a list arrow, appears at the top of the Drop Row Fields Here area

3. Click and drag **Salary** from the PivotTable Field List to the **Drop Data Items Here** area of the pivot table framework. After you release the mouse, values immediately appear in rows and columns corresponding to the salary of each department by gender (see Figure 5.38)

   tip: *The Sum of Salary button at the intersection of the row and column headings indicates the type of statistic displayed in the data area of the pivot table—salary sums.*

The default Excel uses for numeric fields placed in the Drop Data Items Here area of a pivot table is the SUM function. You can change the function to any of several other available statistical functions including COUNT, AVERAGE, MAX, MIN, PRODUCT, and others. The default for nonnumeric data is COUNT. To change the summary value function displayed in the pivot table data field, simply click the Field Settings button on the PivotTable toolbar and select the summary function from the list Excel displays. Next, you will modify the numeric function summarizing the data from SUM to AVERAGE so that you can display average salaries by department and gender.

4. Click **Accounting** in the Category list, double-click the **Decimal Places** spin box, type **0,** click the **Symbol** list box, and click **$** (see Figure 5.41)

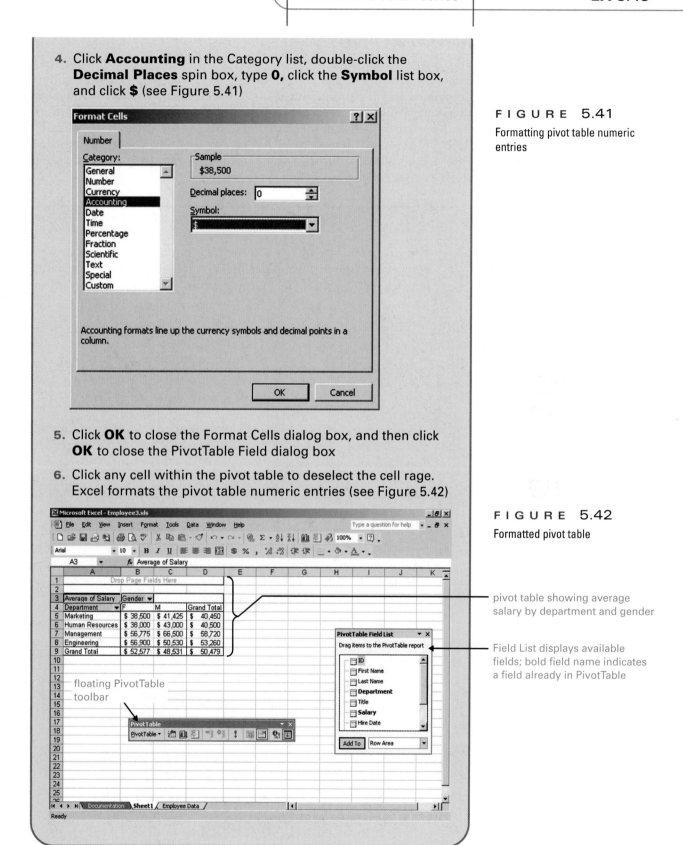

FIGURE 5.41
Formatting pivot table numeric entries

5. Click **OK** to close the Format Cells dialog box, and then click **OK** to close the PivotTable Field dialog box

6. Click any cell within the pivot table to deselect the cell rage. Excel formats the pivot table numeric entries (see Figure 5.42)

FIGURE 5.42
Formatted pivot table

pivot table showing average salary by department and gender

Field List displays available fields; bold field name indicates a field already in PivotTable

The numbers in the pivot table look much better formatted, especially the Grand Total row (row 9), which contains averages rather than grand totals.

ROTATING PIVOT TABLE FIELDS

Perhaps the single most impressive feature of pivot tables is that you can rotate or pivot the values in pivot table column and row fields. By simply dragging a row or column button in a pivot table to a column or row position, you pivot the data to view it from a different perspective. For example, Alice wants to look at the departmental average salaries from a slightly different angle—with two rows for gender and the departments listed across four columns. She asks you to rotate the data so that she can see if she likes that perspective better.

> ### Rotating pivot table fields:
>
> 1. Move the mouse over the Gender field button appearing above cell B3 until the mouse changes to a four-headed arrow
>
> 2. Click the **Gender** field button and drag it below the Department field button—on top of the Marketing label in the PivotTable
>
> 3. Release the mouse button. The pivot table is reorganized so that the Gender is listed in the leftmost column and Department labels are listed in the column to the right
>
> **tip:** Click **Edit** and then click **Undo** and repeat steps 2 and 3 if you do not get the described result.
>
> 4. Hover the mouse over the Department field button in the PivotTable until the mouse changes to a four-headed arrow, click the **Department** field button, and then drag the field button up and just to the right of the Average of Salary label— over cell B3
>
> 5. Release the mouse button. Excel displays Gender in two rows and Departments in four columns. You may have to drag the PivotTable toolbar or the PivotTable Field list out of the way to see the entire PivotTable (see Figure 5.43)

F I G U R E   5.43

Rearranged pivot table fields

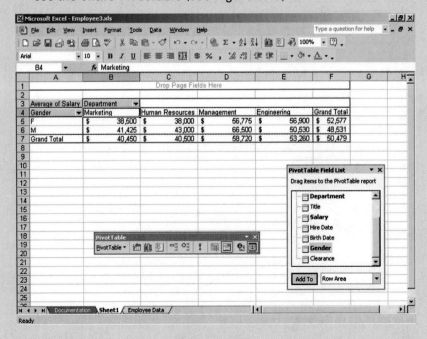

REMOVING AND ADDING PIVOT TABLE FIELDS

You can change the composition of a pivot table anytime you want. If you decide that you want to see average salaries of males versus females regardless of the departments in which they work, you can remove the Department field from the pivot table. If you want to see finer details about salaries, you might want to examine average salaries by gender and clearance level among departments by adding the Clearance field to the pivot table. And, you can even examine salaries by age groups.

Removing a Pivot Table Field

Alice realizes that comparing salaries by considering only gender is complicated by the fact that there are a number of other factors that affect average salary of Comsec employees, such as seniority and clearance level. Nonetheless, she is interested in comparing the companywide difference between the average salaries of females versus males. Creating the pivot table to compute that value involves removing the Department data field and leaving Gender as the only pivot table field.

Removing a field from a pivot table:

1. Click the **Department** field button and drag it to any cell *outside* the pivot table range. When the field button is no longer inside the pivot table, the mouse pointer changes to a small button displaying a red X below it—a symbol used through Microsoft Office to indicate *delete*

2. Release the mouse button. The pivot table is rearranged to display average salaries for males and females. When you remove a field, the original data remains unchanged—only the pivot table changes (see Figure 5.44)

	A	B	C
1	Drop Page Fields Here		
2			
3	Average of Salary		
4	Gender ▼	Total	
5	F	$52,577	
6	M	$48,531	
7	Grand Total	$50,479	
8			

FIGURE 5.44
Pivot table with field removed

Adding a Pivot Table Field

You can add any field to a pivot table that is identified as a column name and displays in the PivotTable toolbar. Simply click and drag one of the field buttons from the PivotTable toolbar to a row field, a column field, or a page field. Add the Clearance column to the column field in the pivot table and add the Department field to the row field to the left of the Gender button in the Pivot table.

Adding a field to a pivot table:

1. Click the **Clearance** field button found in the PivotTable Field List

EXCEL

tip: *If you do not have a PivotTable Field List visible, simply click the Show Field List button on the PivotTable toolbar (see Figure 5.38)*

2. Drag the **Clearance** field button to the column field in the pivot table (cell B3) and release the mouse button. Excel reorganizes the table to display average salaries with Gender in rows and Clearance across four columns

3. Click the **Department** field button, found in the PivotTable Field List, and drag it just to the right of the Gender button so that the mouse pointer hovers over the Gender list arrow and the large gray insertion I-beam appears to the right of the Gender field button (see Figure 5.45)

FIGURE 5.45

Adding a field to a pivot table

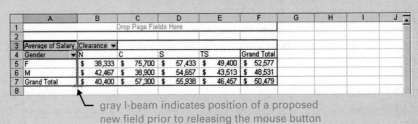

gray I-beam indicates position of a proposed new field prior to releasing the mouse button

4. Release the mouse. Excel displays the newly rearranged format table, containing two row fields and one column field, to display average salaries broken out by Department, Gender, and Clearance level (see Figure 5.46). (You may want to drag the PivotTable Field list out of the way to see the pivot table)

FIGURE 5.46

A three-field pivot table

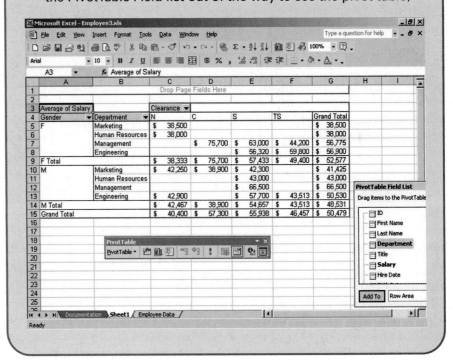

You can sort a pivot table's row or column fields. Your pivot table Clearance fields may be listed in the same order as the custom sort order you created in Session 5.1: N, C, S, and TS. In any case, Alice wants the Clearance fields automatically sorted in ascending alphabetic order (C, N, S, and TS) each time the PivotTable report is updated. You do that next.

Sorting a pivot table by its column field:

1. Click any of the Clearance field column headers (N, C, S, or TS), and then click the **PivotTable** button located on the left end of the PivotTable toolbar. A menu of choices appears

2. Click **Sort and Top 10.** Excel displays the PivotTable Sort and Top 10 dialog box

3. Click the **Ascending** option button found in the AutoSort options panel, click the **Using field** list box, and click **Clearance** (if necessary). This designates the field that Excel will always keep in ascending order within a pivot table

4. Click **OK** to finalize your choices. Excel sorts the Clearance column labels and associated values into ascending order, left to right

HIDING FIELD ITEMS

Perhaps the detail in a pivot table is too much, and you want to focus on one particular value. You can hide field items by clicking the list box arrow next to a field button and then select which items values you want to hide in a pivot table. Alice wants to produce two pivot table reports. The first one shows average salary by department and clearance level for males, hiding the information about females. The other report shows the same information for females, hiding the information about males. You produce the second report, female average salary information, next.

Hiding items in a pivot table:

1. Click the **Gender list box arrow** in the leftmost column of the pivot table to display a list of unique values comprising the Gender rank (see Figure 5.47)

2. Click the **M** check box to clear the check mark and therefore hide the value of that item in the pivot table

3. Click **OK** to redisplay the pivot table with the male row information hidden

4. Print the report

5. Repeat steps 1 through 4, but in step 2 click the **M** check box to place a check mark in it and click the **F** check box to clear that check box

After completing the last step of the preceding series of steps, the pivot table displays average salaries for males only in each department at each of the four clearance levels.

USING PAGE FIELDS

You can use a pivot table's Page field to hide and unhide one or more data items. Page fields provide a slice, or cross section, of your data. You can look at the effect of one particular variable by placing the column in which

EXCEL

FIGURE 5.47

List of unique values in a field item

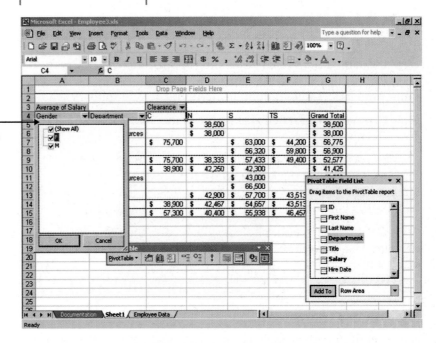

"Show all" and a list of unique field values for the selected pivot table field, Gender

it resides into a page field. While row or column fields allow you to select some or all items from a list of unique values by using check boxes, a page field allows you to select all values or one particular value, similar to option buttons. Page fields are a great choice when you want to view each unique field by itself. In the steps that follow, you will create a new pivot table for Alice that displays average salary by employee title and use the page field to select individual departments, or all departments when Alice wants to aggregate all department salary information.

Creating a new pivot table containing a page field:

1. Click the **Employee Data** sheet tab to make that sheet active and click cell **D3** to make that cell active

2. Click **Data** on the menu bar and then click **PivotTable and PivotChart Report.** The first PivotTable Wizard dialog box opens

3. Click the **Microsoft Excel list or database** option, click the **PivotTable** option, and click the **Next** button

4. Click **Next** to accept the suggested cell range displayed in Step 2. An information dialog box opens explaining that a new report will use less memory if you base it on an existing report. Since this is unimportant for these two small pivot tables, click **No** to proceed

5. If necessary, click the **New worksheet** option to create the pivot table in a new worksheet, and then click the **Layout** button to specify the row, column, and page fields. The PivotTable and PivotChart Wizard Layout dialog box opens

6. Click the **Title** button and drag it to the **ROW** area of the layout in the dialog box, click the **Department** button and drag it to the **PAGE** area of the layout, and then click the **Salary** button and drag it to the **DATA** area of the layout. Excel labels it Sum of Salary (see Figure 5.48)

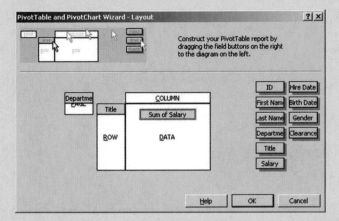

FIGURE 5.48

Selecting pivot table fields in the PivotTable Wizard

7. Double-click the **Sum of Salary** button in the DATA area of the pivot table layout to open the PivotTable Field dialog box, and click the **Average** function in the *Summarize by* list of functions

8. Format the entry by clicking the **Number** button, select **Accounting** in the Category list box, double-click the Decimal places text box, type **0,** select **$** in the Symbol list box, and click **OK** to close the Format Cells dialog box

9. Click **OK** to close the PivotTable Field dialog box, and then click **OK** to close the PivotTable and PivotChart Wizard - Layout dialog box. The Pivot Table Wizard - Step 3 of 3 dialog box reappears

10. Click the **Finish** button to complete the pivot table. Excel creates a new worksheet containing the newly completed pivot table (see Figure 5.49)

11. Click the **arrow** to the right of the Department button, click **Engineering,** and click the **OK** button located near the bottom of the list. The pivot table displays average salaries by job title for members of the Engineering department

12. Click the **arrow** to the right of the Department button, click **(All),** and click the **OK** button located near the bottom of the list to redisplay the average salary by job title for all departments

Experiment with the page field by clicking the arrow and selecting other department names. Notice that you have two choices with a page field: All or a particular value. Unlike Row or Column fields, you cannot select two or three departments to display a salary summary.

FIGURE 5.49

Pivot table with a page field

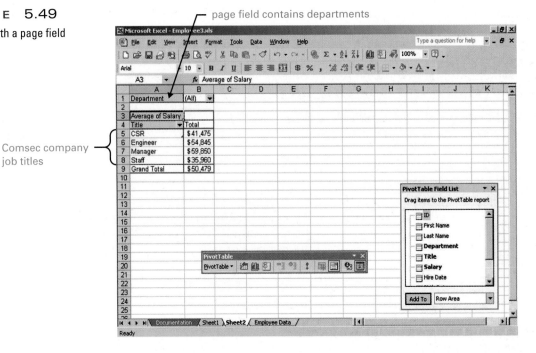

page field contains departments

Comsec company job titles

REFRESHING A PIVOT TABLE

Pivot tables represent summary information computed from a data list. Because pivot table values are calculated from underlying data, the pivot table values cannot be altered. And it makes little sense to do so. However, any data list that underlies a pivot table is likely to change over time. Employees come and go, they get salary raises, and they are promoted. Perhaps you find it odd, but changing data in a pivot table's data list does not alter the values in the pivot table summarizing the list. Whenever you make a change to a data list that is summarized by a pivot table, you must *refresh* the pivot table, that is, make Excel recalculate the values in the pivot table based on the data list's current values.

First, look at Figure 5.49, cell B7, and observe that the average salary of all managers is $59,850. Melinda English has received a 10 percent salary increase following her very favorable semi-annual performance review. Her new salary is $62,040. Update her salary and then observe the effect on the pivot table.

Modifying a data list entry through a data form:

1. Click the **Employee Data** sheet tab to activate it, and then click cell **A3** to ensure that the cell within the data is active

2. Click **Data** on the menu bar and click **Form** to open the Employee Data form

3. Click the **Criteria** button, click in the **Last Name** text box, type **English,** and press the **Find Next** button. Excel displays the record for Melinda English

4. Double-click the **Salary** field, type **62040** to replace the old salary with the new one, and click the **Close** button to close the Employee Data form

5. Click the **Sheet2** sheet tab containing the pivot table displaying the average salary by job title. Notice that the average salary for managers—Melinda English has that job title—is unchanged at $59,850

It is clear that Excel does not automatically refresh a pivot table when the data in its underlying data list changes. You will have to do that manually.

Refreshing a pivot table after modifying its underlying data:

1. Click any cell within the pivot table. (The pivot table *does not* include row 2 separating the Page field from the rest of the pivot table)

2. Click the **Refresh Data** button on the PivotTable toolbar. Excel recalculates the pivot table values. Cell B7 displays $60,790, which is the updated average salary for all managers (see Figure 5.50). Cell B9 also changes because it is an overall average (though it is labeled "Grand Total")

	A	B	C
1	Department	(All) ▼	
2			
3	Average of Salary		
4	Title ▼	Total	
5	CSR	$41,475	
6	Engineer	$54,845	
7	Manager	$60,790	← updated average salary value
8	Staff	$35,960	
9	Grand Total	$50,688	
10			

FIGURE 5.50
Refreshed pivot table

CREATING A CHART FROM A PIVOT TABLE

Recall that one of the benefits of using pivot tables is that they display summaries such as averages, sums, and subtotals based on the current grouping you have defined. You can add a pivot chart to the report. Like the pivot table, a pivot chart changes as you change the pivot table to which it is linked. You can examine the impact of one data grouping of a data list by using a page field and plotting the results in a pivot chart.

anotherway

. . . to Refresh a Pivot Table

Click any cell within the pivot table

Click **Data** on the menu bar and then click **Refresh Data**

EXCEL

You can create a chart from a pivot table just as you would with any other type of worksheet data by using the Chart Wizard or selecting the Chart command from the Insert menu. For convenience, the PivotTable toolbar contains a copy of the Chart Wizard button.

Alice wants to create a chart, which will graphically illustrate the differences in average salary among the four job titles currently held by Comsec employees. She also wants to examine average salaries between males and females with the same job title. Alice asks you to create a Clustered bar chart, based on the pivot table, displaying average salaries among those with the same job title.

Refreshing a pivot table after modifying its underlying data:

1. Click any cell within the pivot table (probably on worksheet Sheet2) that you just created

2. Click the **Hide Field List** button on the PivotTable toolbar to hide the PivotTable Field List

3. Click the **Chart Wizard** [icon] button on the PivotTable toolbar. A Stacked column chart and Chart toolbar appear on a new chart sheet, Chart1

4. To see the chart without all the toolbars, click **View** on the menu bar and then click **Full Screen** (see Figure 5.51).

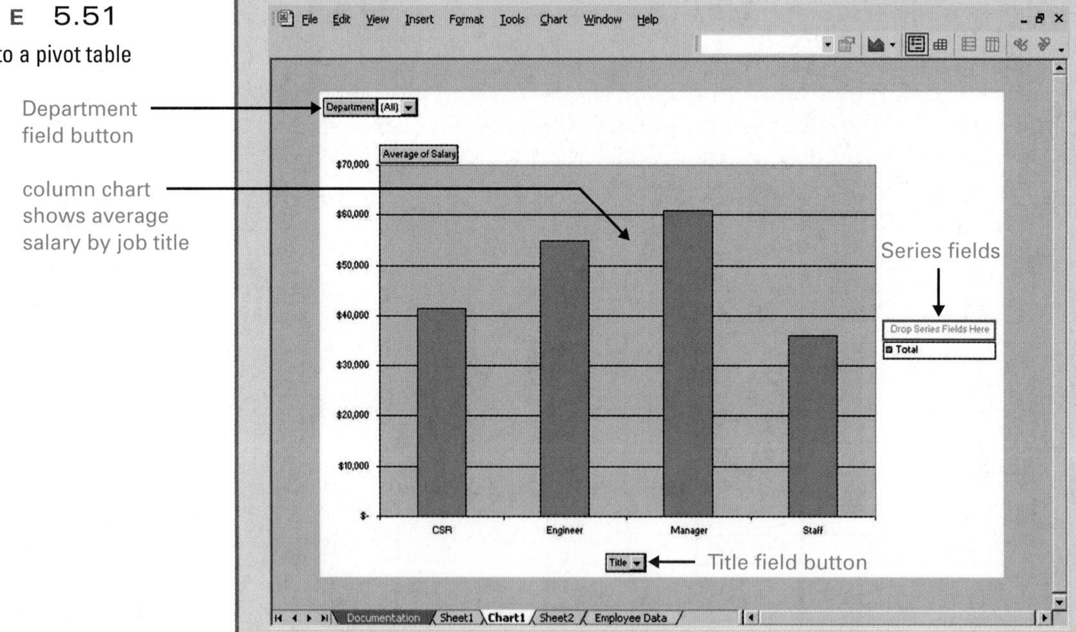

FIGURE 5.51

Chart linked to a pivot table

Department field button

column chart shows average salary by job title

5. Restore the toolbars by clicking **View** on the menu bar and then clicking **Full Screen**

6. Click the **Chart Wizard** [icon] button on the PivotTable toolbar. The first of four Chart Wizard dialog boxes appears

7. Click **Bar** in the Chart type list box, click **Clustered Bar** (top row, first column) in the Chart sub-type panel, and click the **Next** button. The *Chart Wizard - Step 3 of 4* dialog box appears

8. Double-click the **Chart title** text box to select all of its text, and then type **Average Salary by Department**

9. Click the **Category (X) axis** text box and type **Average Salary,** and then click the **Finish** button to complete the chart
   Notice that the bars display the average salary for the four job titles but that there is nothing in the chart that distinguishes between genders in that category. You will take care of that next

10. Click the **Show Field List** button on the PivotTable toolbar to open the PivotTable Field List, and then click and drag the **Gender** field from the PivotTable Field list to the *Drop Series Fields Here* area on the right side of the chart.

11. Click the **Hide Field List** button on the PivotTable toolbar to reveal more of the chart, right-click the PivotTable toolbar, and then click **PivotTable** in the list of toolbars to close it. Figure 5.52 shows the bar chart displaying average salaries by department

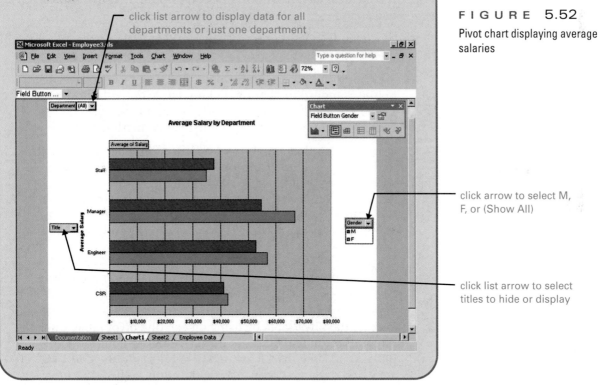

FIGURE 5.52

Pivot chart displaying average salaries

Finally, Alice wants you to print the entire workbook and save it.

Printing the Employee workbook and saving it:

1. Click the **Documentation** sheet tab, type your name in cell C6 to the right of the label Designer, and save the workbook

EXCEL

2. Click **File** on the menu bar to open the Print dialog box, click **Print,** click the **Entire workbook** option button in the *Print what* panel, and then click **OK** to print all worksheets in the Employee workbook

3. Close the **Employee3.xls** workbook and exit Excel

You show Alice your final workbook printouts. She is pleased with the results. Your pivot tables show the differences in average salaries by looking at different perspectives. The pivot table chart is an especially dramatic way to show the average salaries based on job titles and gender.

SESSION 5.3

making the grade

1. Fields such as ID, LastName, Sex, and YearInSchool usually end up as _____ fields in a pivot table.

2. A field such as Salary, CommissionAmount, and Age usually ends up as _____ fields in a pivot table.

3. The default function that calculates pivot table summary information is what?

4. You can format a pivot table data field using the Format menu on the Standard toolbar or clicking the Number button on the PivotTable Field dialog box. Both format pivot table entries. Discuss the major advantage of using one method over the other.

5. Open the **Employee3.xls** workbook and immediately save it under the new name **Employee3Modified.xls.** Modify the workbook in the following ways. Make the Employee Data worksheet active and create a new pivot table using the PivotTable Wizard. The pivot table will count the number of people with each type of clearance (or none at all) within each department.

   Do the following at each of the PivotTable Wizard dialog boxes. Create the pivot table from the Excel list. Accept the Excel-suggested cell range of A2:J29. Click **No** when the wizard displays a dialog box asking if you want to conserve space while making the pivot table by using an existing pivot table. Click the **Layout** button and drag the **Department** field button to the ROW area. Drag the **Clearance** field button to the COLUMN area, and drag the **Clearance** field button to the DATA area. Click **OK** to close the Layout dialog box. Click the **Options** button to open the PivotTable Options dialog box. Clear the *Grand totals for rows* check box to eliminate row totals, place a checkmark in the *For empty cells, show* check box, click the text box to its right, type **0,** and click **OK.** Click the **Finish** button to complete the pivot table. On the sheet displaying the count of clearances by department, type your name in the worksheet header and print the worksheet. Open the Clearance column list box, clear the **N** and **C** check boxes, and click **OK.** Print the worksheet, save the workbook, and close Excel.

SESSION 5.4 SUMMARY

An Excel list is a collection of data arranged in columns and rows in which each column displays one particular type of data. A label at the top of each column of the list identifies each column. To prevent the column-top labels from scrolling out of sight as you scroll down a long list, execute the Freeze Panes command on the Window menu. Rows above the active cell and columns to the left remain in place when you scroll vertically or horizontally, respectively. Using a data form facilitates adding, searching, and modifying a list. With the worksheet cursor inside the list, execute Form on the Data menu to create a form that uses the column labels for list box names.

Sort a data list on one column by making any cell in the column and in the list active and then clicking the Sort Ascending button or Sort Descending button on the Standard toolbar. More complicated sorts involving multiple columns require you to use the Sort command on the Data menu. You can sort data on up to three columns—a primary sort column and two tie-breaker columns. Blank fields always sort the corresponding row to the bottom of the list.

Apply an AutoFilter to a list to display rows satisfying criteria you select for one or more columns. Selecting match criteria on more than one column means multiple criteria must be true simultaneously for a row to remain in view. Excel hides other rows—those not matching the selection criteria. Criteria available through the AutoFilter list boxes are exact match criteria. More complex criteria such as selecting values greater than or equal to a particular value require the use of custom AutoFilters.

When you maintain data lists in order by one or more columns, you can use the Subtotal command to group and summarize the values in a group. Subtotal functions allow you to sum, average, and count values in numeric columns, and you can produce counts of character data. Using the outline buttons, you can expand or reduce the detail information visible in individual groups. Printing long lists containing summarized information provided by Subtotals often requires that you specify column labels on the top of each page to identify each column. Print options provide a Row and columns check box on the Print tab of the Page Setup dialog box to specify columns to repeat on each page. Applying conditional formatting to selected rows and columns provides a convenient way to automatically highlight values that meet user-specified criteria. You can apply any of the format options available on the Format Cells dialog box to create conditional formats.

Pivot tables summarize lists by summarizing data based on one or more grouping criteria. You can choose from sum, average, count, and several other aggregate functions in the data item area to summarize data based on row, column, and page fields consisting of columns. For example, you can ask Excel to average the salaries of health care workers in Virginia. The pivot table row field is job title ("health care worker," for example), the column field is state abbreviation, and the data item field is salary. Pivot tables can reveal hidden information about groups of data in your lists. Pivot tables are also known as cross tabs or cross tab tables.

MOUS OBJECTIVES SUMMARY

- Freeze rows and columns (MOUS Ex2002e-3-2)
- Group and outline structured data (MOUS Ex2002e-7-3)
- Create subtotals (MOUS Ex2002e-7-1)

EXCEL

- Create and apply conditional formatting (MOUS Ex2002e-3-2)
- Create filters with AutoFilter (MOUS Ex2002e-7-2)
- Use worksheet labels and names in formulas (MOUS Ex2002e-4-1)
- Create a pivot table and pivot chart (MOUS Ex2002e-8-1)

task reference roundup

Task	Page #	Preferred Method
Freezing Rows and Columns	EX 5.6	• Select cell at upper-left corner
		• Click **Window**; click **Freeze Panes**
Adding a Record to a List Using a Data Form	EX 5.8	• Click list cell, click **Data**, click **Form**
		• Click **New,** type values in fields, press **Enter,** and click **Close**
Deleting a Record from a List with a Data Form	EX 5.12	• Click list cell, click **Data**, click **Form**
		• Click **Criteria** button, Click **Find Next** as needed, click **Delete,** and click **OK**
Sorting a List on One Column	EX 5.15	• Click cell in list
		• Click the **Sort Ascending** or **Sort Descending** button
Sorting a List on More Than One Field	EX 5.17	• Click list cell, click **Data,** click **Sort**
		• Specify Sort by and Ascending/Descending options
		• Repeat for up to two Then by fields
		• Click **OK**
Creating a Custom Sort Order	EX 5.19	• Click **Tools,** click **Options,** click **Custom Lists** tab
		• Click **NEW LIST,** type each new member of the list in order
		• Click the **Add** button and click **OK**
Filtering a List with AutoFilter	EX 5.24	• Click list cell, click **Data**
		• Click **list arrow** on filtering column, click filter value from list
Clearing All AutoFilter Filtering Criteria	EX 5.26	• Click **Data,** point to **Filter**
		• Click **Show All** to remove all existing filters
Subtotaling a List's Entries	EX 5.29	• Sort list by grouping column
		• Click a cell inside the list
		• Click **Data,** click **Subtotals**

task reference roundup

Task	Page #	Preferred Method
		• Choose group column, choose aggregate function
		• Click **OK**
Displaying Row or Column Headings on Each Page	EX 5.34	• Click **File**, click **Page Setup**, click the **Sheet** tab
		• Click **Collapse** dialog button on the **Specify Rows to repeat at top** or the **Specify Columns to repeat at left**
		• Specify row(s) or column(s)
		• Click **OK**
Applying a Conditional Format to Cells	EX 5.37	• Click cell range to conditionally format
		• Click **Format**, Click **Conditional Formatting**, specify criteria
		• Click **Format** button on the Conditional Formatting dialog box and specify formatting options
		• Click **OK**
		• Click **OK**
Creating a Pivot Table with the PivotTable Wizard	EX 5.43	• Click **Data**, click the **PivotTable and PivotChart Report**
		• Specify the data's location (worksheet, external list, etc)
		• Select the **PivotTable** option and click the **Layout** button
		• Design pivot table layout by selecting row, column, data, and page fields
		• Designate location for pivot table as separate page or object on worksheet
		• Click the **Finish** button
Selecting Pivot Table Fields	EX 5.46	• Click and drag selected field(s) to summarize to Data Items area
		• Click and drag field buttons to Column, Row, and Page fields
Formatting Pivot Table Fields	EX 5.48	• Select any cell in the pivot table data item area
		• Open the PivotTable toolbar, click **Field Settings,** and click the **Number** button
		• Select a format from the Category list and make associated format choices
		• Click **OK** to close the Format Cells dialog box and then click **OK** to close the PivotTable Field dialog box

EXCEL

CROSSWORD PUZZLE

Across

1. If you change the date in a list that is linked to a pivot table, you must do what to the pivot table?
3. _____ match criteria mean that a field value matches a particular value
5. Sort from low to high order is call _____ order
7. Pivot tables summarize _____ fields, not row, column, or page fields
9. The _____ criteria are values that a data form should match in specified data form fields
11. Sort form high to low order is called _____ order
12. Use a _____ table to develop an interactive table to summarize the data in a list
14. A collection of data arranged in columns and rows in which each column displays one particular type of data
16. You _____ a list to hide rows that do not match a criteria

Down

2. A _____ row is the first row in a data list
4. A _____ operator compares two values
6. A _____ sort field breaks ties a more significant sort field
8. Each row of a data list is called a _____
10. A _____ sorting series is an ordered list you create (Freshman, Sophomore, etc.)
12. The _____ key (or sort field) is required to sort a list
13. Each column of a list containing related information describing some characteristic of the object, person, or place
15. When one or more records have the same value for a field, a _____ exists
16. A dialog box displaying one row of a list in text boxes is called a data _____

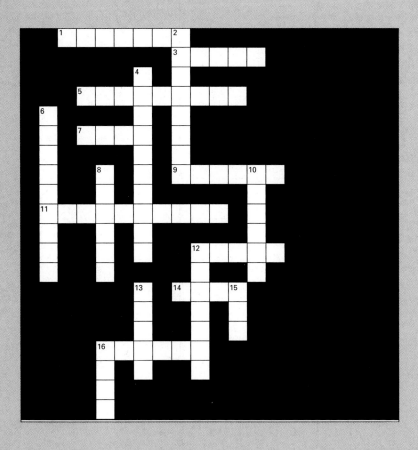

FILL-IN

1. Pivot table fields correspond to _____ in a worksheet.

2. A _____ sort key sorts the list on one column.

3. The easiest way to add a record to a long data list is to use a _____ _____, which you access from the Data menu.

4. Use _____ (on the Data menu) to display only rows that match a particular value that you select from a list of values in the column's label list box.

5. You can display record groups on separate pages by inserting _____ _____(s) following each group in a list.

6. Use _____ _____ to format values in a special way for any values that match criteria for the cell range. For example, you can use this technique to display blue text for values less than $2,000.

REVIEW QUESTIONS

1. What is a list field and how is it related to record?

2. You have a long list of sales information including sales amount, sales person, sale date, and customer city. What is a good way to create a worksheet showing total sales amount by city. Are there two different and equally good ways to approach this?

3. Explain why you must sort a list before using the Subtotals command. What would happen if you did not sort the list?

4. How is using a pivot table page field different from using a Row or Column field to select a particular value to summarize?

CREATE A QUESTION

For each of the following answers, create an appropriate, short question.

ANSWER	QUESTION
1. You have to sort the list first	_____
2. Click the Criteria button and type the field criteria	_____
3. Cells matching the criteria display with a special format	_____
4. Rows not matching the criteria are hidden	_____
5. Drag the field button to the Data Item area	_____
6. Drag the field button off of the pivot table	_____

practice

1. Filtering Fairmont Consulting's Charitable Contributions

Fairmont Consulting is a large computer consulting firm in Northern California. Charles Fairmont, the CEO and founder of the firm, is well known for his philanthropic efforts. He believes that many of his employees also contribute to nonprofit organizations and wants to reward them for their efforts while encouraging others to contribute to charities. He started a program in which Fairmont Consulting matches 50 percent of each donation an employee makes to the charity of his or her choice. The only guidelines are that the charity must be a nonprofit organization and the firm's donation per employee may not exceed $500 a year.

Charles' assistant, Saundra, started an Excel file to record the firm's donations. Included are the day the request for a donation was submitted, the employee's name and ID number, the name of the charity, the dollar amount contributed by the firm, and the date the contribution was sent. Saundra wants you to give the completed record for December 2002 to the firm's accountants in order for the donations to be included in Fairmont's tax filings for the year.

1. Open the workbook **ex05Fairmont.xls** and save the workbook as **Fairmont2.xls**
2. Add the following information:

Date Submitted:	**December 25, 2002**
Employee ID #:	**J24A**
Last Name:	**Greenburg**
First Name:	**Peter**
Organization:	**Leukemia Society**
Amount:	**$50**
Date Sent:	**December 29, 2002**
Date Submitted:	**December 27, 2002**
Employee ID #:	**1E5A**
Last Name:	**Taylor**
First Name:	**Steven**
Organization:	**Red Cross**
Amount:	**$200**
Date Sent:	**December 29, 2002**

3. Use the data form to determine how many organizations received single donations of over $100. Explain the steps you took.

4. Sort the list alphabetically by organization and then by employee's last name. Include your name in the custom footer and then print the sorted list.
5. Use the Subtotals command to total the contribution made per employee for the month of December. Print the sorted list.
6. Use the AVERAGE function to determine the average donation made.
7. Sort the list by donation value and compare these values to the average found in step 6. Include your name and print a list of all organizations that received a single donation above the average donation.

2. Using Sorting and Filtering to Determine Top Students

Everingham Elementary School is preparing for the sixth-grade graduation ceremony. Part of the ceremony gives a special award for top students. One award is given to each male and female student with the highest scores in each of Math, English, and Science. Mrs. Moore is the only sixth-grade teacher, and she volunteered to compile a list of her students with grades above 95 percent in these subjects. She started the list, but fell ill and is unable to finish the list in time to prepare the awards.

You have been asked to finish the list and are given her work. Mrs. Moore has gathered the data in a spreadsheet called **ex05Grades.xls.** Unfortunately, she also included all of her fifth-grade students with grades above 95 in these subjects.

1. Open the database **ex05Grades.xls,** save it as **Grades2.xls** and begin by sorting by grades.
2. Delete rows containing students in the fifth grade.
3. Sort the list in descending order by Subject.
4. Further sort the data within Subject by Grade in descending order. Include your name in a custom header and print the worksheet.
5. Use the AutoFilter command to include only students whose Grade values are above 95. Print the worksheet.

challenge

1. Filtering Soda Sales

Shores, Incorporated manufactures and bottles 10 different types of soda, three of which are citrus non-cola sodas. Shores decided a few years ago to focus on their citrus drinks division instead of colas, since their competition has been neglecting this area. Shores was expecting to capture a large portion of this market, but sales have not been strong in this area, and the company wants to focus its marketing efforts to further promote these drinks. The president of Shores feels that a factor in poor sales is that the firm has been spreading their efforts over the three different brands of citrus beverages. He wants to drop one of the brands. He has asked you to look at the drinks sales figures to help determine which drink of the three they should stop producing and which regions consume the most of Shore's non-cola sodas.

You are given data for the past three months. It is sorted by month, brand of soda, in which region sold, and number of cases sold in thousands. Open the workbook **ex05Shores.xls** and use the Save As command in the File menu to save the workbook under the name **Shores2.xls.** Improve the formatting of the data and bold the headers for each column. Sort the soda lists by product, within product by month, and within product and month by region. Use the Subtotals command to display total cases sold by brand of soda per region. Include your name in the custom header and print this list of subtotals. Sort the data by month and within month by region. The months should appear in order of March, April, and May. Print the list. Determine the firm's worst-selling brand of soda. Is this the brand that should no longer be produced? Determine which soda and region have the highest sales. Prepare a pivot table to provide you with this information. Summarize each month's sales using a pivot table. Use the Chart Wizard button on the PivotTable toolbar to create a bar chart of total cases sold by month. Print the pivot table and bar chart.

2. Analyzing Doctor's Information with Subtotals and Pivot Tables

Before choosing a doctor, several patients call Montgomery Hospital's Client Services office to get more information on the various doctors' backgrounds and experience. Since the hospital staff is overworked, the office manager, Alice Honeycutt, wants to prepare a database of information for quick reference in order to quickly answer questions. The most common questions from callers are about each doctor's specialty and the number of years that each doctor has been practicing medicine. Alice has compiled the necessary information, but needs help in making some corrections and summarizing the data. Open the workbook **ex05Doctors.xls** and use the Save As command in the File menu to save the workbook under the name **Doctors2.xls.** Freeze the column headings for last and first name row labels.

Use the data form to find Robert Gordon's information. Change his years of experience to **20.** Find the information for Charlie Maxwell and change his years of experience to **27.** Sort the data by Specialty and within Specialty by years of experience (most to least). Add your name to the custom header and print the list. Apply conditional formatting so that the Experience field for doctors with fewer than eight years of experience is boldface. Print all doctors with less than eight years of experience, sorted by specialty (Hint: Use AutoFilter.). Prepare a pivot table to summarize the average years of experience by specialty. Print the pivot table report. Format the average year's experience values to display two decimal places. Create a Clustered Bar chart showing the average years of experience by specialty (based on the pivot table you created). Place your name in the header and print the chart.

1. Analyzing California's Weather Patterns

Kevin Towers is the sales manager of the Kansas City office of a golfball manufacturing firm based in Michigan. For the past 18 months, his team has had record sales for their territory, and their sales were higher than any other offices. Management knows that Kevin's approach to teaching and motivating his staff has been greatly responsible for the phenomenal figures. To reward Kevin, and to hopefully spread his team's performance, he has been given the opportunity to spend four months in any of the firm's offices in California.

Kevin gladly accepts the offer and starts looking into where he wants to go. He decides he wants to be in a coastal city, and the firm has offices in San Diego, Los Angeles, and San Francisco. He will be in California from January 1 to April 30. Because he hasn't visited any of these three cities and wants to get in a lot of golf time, Kevin determines the main factor that will affect his decision is weather.

Begin by setting your browser to www. weather.com and locate the box in which you can enter the city or zip code for which you want information. Enter **San Diego, CA** and when the data appears, click the **Averages and Records** tab. Print this page and repeat this for Los Angeles and San Francisco. As Kevin is trying to predict the temperature and potential rainfall, focus on the Monthly Average and Records section on the top of the page. Do the following:

Create a spreadsheet to summarize the information you find. Record the temperature and rainfall in columns, and group the cities into four groups of rows labeled Average High, Average Low, Mean, and Average Precipitation. Fill in the appropriate data for each city and month. Because rain is Kevin's greatest concern, use conditional formatting to display the months with an average precipitation below 2.5 inches in blue and apply boldface. Place your name in a custom header and print the list. Prepare and format a pivot table summarizing total average precipitation by city. Print the pivot table. Print the new pivot table. Kevin also wants to be in the warmest weather possible while in California. Use conditional formatting to display the months with average high temperatures above 65 degrees in red

and apply boldface. Print this worksheet. Looking at the average high temperatures above 65 degrees and average precipitation below two inches, to which city do you think Kevin should relocate? Explain your answer.

2. Analyzing Differences in Salaries

Howard Parker has just completed his MBA and has been received several exciting job offers in the area of project management. He has lived in Austin, Texas, for most of his life and is looking to make a change. Since he received job offers from around the country, Howard has the opportunity to finally make a change and move to a new location. His problem is deciding which offer to take. All of his friends tell him to accept the job with the highest salary offer, but Howard knows it isn't that simple. Due to the great differences in cost of living, he knows he can't just look at the dollar figures, he must figure out which will give him the greatest standard of living. Howard decided that he must make the equivalent of a $65,000 salary in Austin—no matter where he moves.

Open **ex05Salaries.xls,** which contains information on the Howard's different job offers and save it as **Salaries2.xls.** Go to www.homefair.com and click on the **moving** tab at the top of the page. Click the link **the salary calculator**™ found under the heading *Browse Categories*. This tool will enable you to help Howard figure out the equivalent of a $65,000 salary in each of the cities where he was offered a job. Follow the prompts on the Web site to enter Austin, Texas, as where moving from with a $65,000 salary. Run a calculation for each of the cities in which he was offered a job. Be sure to include that he wants to own a home, not rent. Input all of the salary equivalents in the Austin Eq. column. Type **Difference** in cell E1 and then create formulas in column E that calculate the difference between his offered salary and desired salary for each state. Include your name and print this spreadsheet.

Use the AutoFilter command to display only those offers that have a difference of $5,000 or more. Based on this, if Howard's main desire is having the greatest standard of living, which offer should he accept?

e-business

1. Haller Electronics Online Store Initiative

Haller Electronics is an electronics manufacturer specializing in televisions, DVDs, and CD players. Haller Electronics targets the market of customers who know what they want to purchase and don't like the sales atmosphere of large electronics stores. Management decided to launch an online store for customers to buy their products. Brief descriptions and prices of each product would be included for a quick-and-easy purchasing experience. In attempt to stay truly web based, Haller Electronics' customer service department doesn't have a toll-free telephone number. Instead, customers can reach them through the firm's Web site or by sending e-mail to the department. Most customer service contacts are general inquiries. The manager of the customer service department, Todd Felks, wants to ensure that customers are receiving timely responses from his staff.

Todd has taken a sampling of the customer requests and is looking at those received Monday and Tuesday of last week. Included are the date received, type of product the customer is inquiring about, whether the customer used the e-mail address or the Web site, date a response was sent, number of days it took to send the response, and name of the customer service specialist that handled it. To encourage staff to quickly expedite responses, a bonus program was started that rewards staff based on how quickly they respond. These figures are also included in the worksheet. Begin by opening **ex05Service.xls,** which includes all of this information. Immediately save the worksheet as **Service2.xls** to preserve the original worksheet.

Todd needs you to help organize this data for a presentation he must make to the board of the firm. First, sort the list in ascending order by the *Sent By* column. Within *Sent By*, further sort the ties in descending order by *Days*, and then sort in ascending order by *Specialist*. Include your name in the header and print the list.

Re-sort the data, first in ascending order by *Days* and then in ascending order by *Specialist* for matching Days field values. From this, which method of inquiries is getting faster responses?

1. Analyzing Global Marketing Opportunities

Gretchen Kadletz had been a part-time tennis instructor for several years. As she had grown frustrated with the tennis equipment available in the market, she started her own company. With the aid of her attorneys and investors, she founded ProSwing to design tennis equipment and apparel.

Gretchen was able to develop a strong product line and was becoming successful in the United States. The area in which she was having trouble was the firm's international marketing strategy. One of her close friends, Susan Rawlings, suggested that Gretchen advertise the most effective way—by getting players to use and wear her products. While this was a good idea, Gretchen was not quite satisfied. She wanted to be sure that the players using her line were the players followed by the fans (her target market). She knew that this would bring ProSwing attention from tennis players around the world. She decided to concentrate on the tennis players with the highest current winnings, since they were likely to be very popular and visible to the fans. She would approach the top 25 international men and women players about using ProSwing products. She would then additionally advertise during tennis matches in the four countries most represented by the top 50 players in order to represent both the men and women top players.

Gretchen's assistant prepared a spreadsheet after finding recent sport statistics on the Web and compiled data on the top players. Included in the spreadsheet are the player's name, country of residence, most recent winnings, and gender. Currently, this database isn't very helpful to Gretchen and she needs your help to organize the data to plan her international strategy.

Begin by opening **ex05Tennis.xls** and then saving it as **Tennis2.xls.** Sort the data in descending order by Winnings. Select and bold the data for the 25 players with the highest winnings. These are the players Gretchen will approach to use and wear ProSwing products. Include your name and print the data. Include your name in the worksheet header and print the worksheet. Remove bold from the 25 highest winners.

Next, sort the data in ascending order by Country and then in descending order by Winnings within each Country. Change the order of the columns so that Country is the first column, followed by Winnings, and then Player. Print the worksheet.

Use the Subtotals command to compute the total winnings for country. Collapse the subtotals so that only the country names and their totals appear, not the individual players or their genders. Ensure that all columns are wide enough. Print the Subtotaled worksheet.

running project

Pampered Paws

Grace Jackson has obtained data from the cash registers showing sales for the months of October and November of cat and dog food products. She wants you to produce and print reports as described in the following paragraphs.

The first report is a pivot table listing total sales of all products broken out by Item Name and Animal. The data item is the sum of the Total Sale column. The Row field is Item Name, and the Column field is either cat or dog (Animal). Format the sums to display the currency symbol and two decimal places. Do not produce row totals, but do produce column totals for the two animals—cat and dog. Place your name in the worksheet header and print the worksheet in landscape orientation.

The second report, also a pivot table, displays the sum of the Total Sale field for each product and each weight size. Place the Item Name in the Row field, the Size (lb) in the pivot table column field, and place Animal in the Page field. Do not produce row totals in the pivot table, but allow column totals. Format the sums with currency symbols and two decimal places. Place your name in the worksheet header and print the worksheet in landscape orientation.

For the third report, Grace wants a list of all products in ascending order by Animal (1st), Item Name (2nd), and Date (3rd). Produce sums (Subtotals) for each unique Item Name, and ensure that each printed page prints the header row, which contains the column names. Place your name in the worksheet header and print the page in landscape orientation.

For the fourth report, use the Outline buttons to display only the subtotals by Item Name. Print the summary report in landscape orientation. Based on this third report, which item has the largest dollar sales volume?

did you

know?

famed *chef Wolfgang Puck chose the Italian word Spago as the name for his popular chain of restaurants. In Italian, spago means "string" or "twine," which is slang for spaghetti.*

the *Ross Ice Shelf, a very small portion of Antarctica, is hundreds of feet thick and about the same size in land area as France.*

in *the United States before 1933, the dime was legal as payment only in transactions of $10 or less. In that year, Congress made the dime legal tender for all transactions.*

since *the Lego Group began manufacturing blocks in 1949, more than 189 billion pieces in 2,000 different shapes have been produced. This is enough for about 30 Lego pieces for every living person on Earth.*

the *world's longest suspension bridge near Kobe, Japan, opened to traffic on April 5, 1998. The 3,911-meter (12,831-foot) Akashi Kaikyo Bridge is called a three-span, two-hinged truss-stiffened suspension bridge.*

you *can replace absolute cell references in expressions with what? Find out how in this chapter.*

Chapter Objectives

- Develop separate assumptions and output sections of a worksheet
- Use Insert Function to help write worksheet functions
- Provide data validation for selected worksheet cells—MOUS Ex2002-7-4
- Define and use names in functions in place of cell references—MOUS Ex2002-4-1
- Investigate the logical function IF
- Learn about index functions and write the index function VLOOKUP—MOUS Ex2002-4-2
- Write financial functions including PV, PMT, PPMT, and IPMT—MOUS Ex2002-5-2
- Write and apply the NOW date function—MOUS Ex2002-5-2
- Add, delete, move, and rename worksheets—MOUS Ex2002-4-1, MOUS Ex2002-4-2
- Apply worksheet protection—MOUS Ex2002-9-1

Cal Whittington Automobiles

Cal Whittington, owner of Cal Whittington Automobiles or "Cal's Cars," has a medium-sized automobile dealership in Muncie, Indiana. Cal's reputation for honesty and integrity is known throughout Indiana, and his funny (some say, silly) television advertising has helped spread the word about his automobiles. People from bordering states even venture over to Cal's dealership to deal for their next car. Cal has a trained staff of salespersons and sells both new and used automobiles. Each salesperson's desk contains a personal computer that the salespersons can use to request credit histories of customers, do worksheet calculations using Excel, and search a car database listing cars both on their lot and in neighboring cities. Having an Internet connection is handy for the salespersons, because they can locate a requested make and model of just about any car or truck from a network of dealerships that work together to provide cars to each other. Using the cooperative dealership network, a salesperson can search for a customer-requested car within the network whenever Cal does not have a particular model in his stock.

In addition to selling automobiles, Cal's dealership also provides financing for both the new and used vehicles they sell. By having their own financing within the dealership, Cal's makes a small profit through their increased interest rates and provides convenient, no-hassle financing for customers who might have difficulty obtaining a consumer loan elsewhere. Whenever a customer requests Cal's dealership to provide financing, the salesperson asks the customer to fill out a form and then the salesperson obtains the customer's credit history and rating from credit reporting agencies such as Equifax (www.Equifax.com), TransUnion (www.transunion.com), or Experian (www.experian.com). Then, the salesperson fills out an online form with the finance details including the customer's down payment, car purchase price, and loan information and electronically transmits the information to another location for processing. It takes as much as 20 minutes to receive the loan information results back from the processing center.

The report shows loan details such as the customer's name, loan amount, and interest rate. In addition, it contains a loan payment and amortization schedule showing details about each loan payment throughout the life of the loan. The report helps the customer understand all the loan repayment details. Cal's salespersons want to provide the loan information more quickly and have asked Cal to look into eliminating the step of submitting information to the processing center and instead

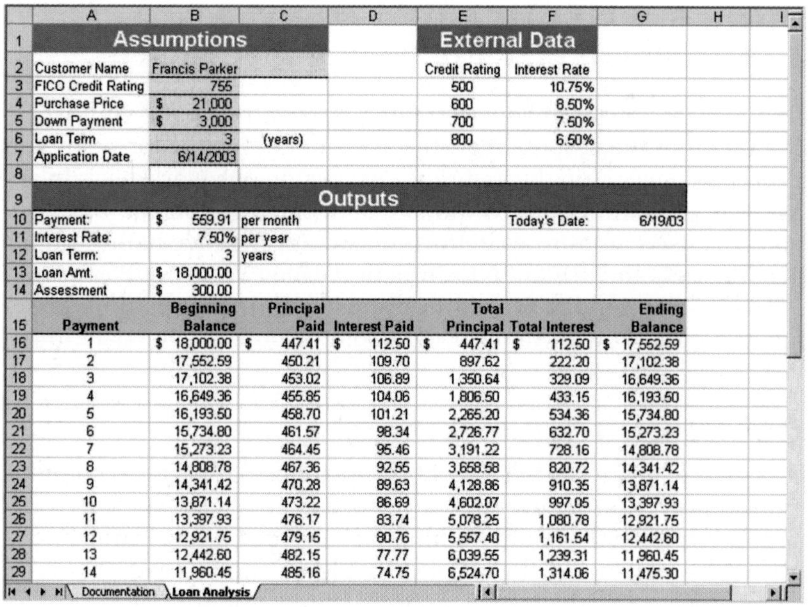

FIGURE 6.1

Completed loan analysis worksheet

	A	B	C	D	E	F	G	H
1	Assumptions				External Data			
2	Customer Name	Francis Parker			Credit Rating	Interest Rate		
3	FICO Credit Rating	755			500	10.75%		
4	Purchase Price	$ 21,000			600	8.50%		
5	Down Payment	$ 3,000			700	7.50%		
6	Loan Term	3	(years)		800	6.50%		
7	Application Date	6/14/2003						
8								
9	Outputs							
10	Payment:	$ 559.91	per month			Today's Date:	6/19/03	
11	Interest Rate:	7.50%	per year					
12	Loan Term:	3	years					
13	Loan Amt.	$ 18,000.00						
14	Assessment	$ 300.00						
15	Payment	Beginning Balance	Principal Paid	Interest Paid	Total Principal	Total Interest	Ending Balance	
16	1	$ 18,000.00	$ 447.41	$ 112.50	$ 447.41	$ 112.50	$ 17,552.59	
17	2	17,552.59	450.21	109.70	897.62	222.20	17,102.38	
18	3	17,102.38	453.02	106.89	1,350.64	329.09	16,649.36	
19	4	16,649.36	455.85	104.06	1,806.50	433.15	16,193.50	
20	5	16,193.50	458.70	101.21	2,265.20	534.36	15,734.80	
21	6	15,734.80	461.57	98.34	2,726.77	632.70	15,273.23	
22	7	15,273.23	464.45	95.46	3,191.22	728.16	14,808.78	
23	8	14,808.78	467.36	92.55	3,658.58	820.72	14,341.42	
24	9	14,341.42	470.28	89.63	4,128.86	910.35	13,871.14	
25	10	13,871.14	473.22	86.69	4,602.07	997.05	13,397.93	
26	11	13,397.93	476.17	83.74	5,078.25	1,080.78	12,921.75	
27	12	12,921.75	479.15	80.76	5,557.40	1,161.54	12,442.60	
28	13	12,442.60	482.15	77.77	6,039.55	1,239.31	11,960.45	
29	14	11,960.45	485.16	74.75	6,524.70	1,314.06	11,475.30	

Documentation \ **Loan Analysis** /

using an Excel template on each salesperson's computer to speed report production. Cal agrees that doing so would be a great time saver.

Jessica Allison, Cal's financial manager, has asked you to produce a simple loan information and amortization worksheet that salespersons can use to show customers details about their loans whenever Cal's company provides the financing for a sale. Jessica has dubbed it the Loan Analysis worksheet. Figure 6.1 shows an example of a completed Loan Analysis worksheet. Use that as a guideline as you create the report and enhance it by following the steps in this chapter.

Chapter 6 covers more Excel functions. Earlier chapters described a few mathematical functions such as SUM, AVERAGE, MIN, and MAX. Excel has several hundred functions, and it would be boring and difficult to cover all of them in this textbook. In this chapter, you will use several of the most common and important Excel functions including the financial functions, lookup functions, the NOW date function, and logical functions. In addition, you will learn how to create and use names and labels in formulas in place of cell references.

The chapter case makes heavy use of financial functions, but you will also create and use other nonfinancial functions that support the financial calculations. You will find many other uses for the many functions presented in this chapter, and you should spend time developing your own worksheets and experimenting with them. The end-of-chapter exercises will reinforce your understanding of these functions

CHAPTER OUTLINE

6.1 Using Data Validation, Names, and IF and Index Functions

6.2 Using Financial Functions

6.3 Maintaining and Protecting Worksheets and Using Date Functions

6.4 Summary

SESSION 6.1 USING DATA VALIDATION, NAMES, AND IF AND INDEX FUNCTIONS

In this section, you will learn how to create a data entry area of your worksheet separate from the output area—the area containing the formulas and calculations that depend on the assumptions portion of a worksheet. In addition, you will write functions to validate data entries to ensure that they are reasonable, use names to write formulas that reference names rather than cell addresses, and use an index function called VLOOKUP to search a table. This session emphasizes both the use and understanding of selected functions and how to validate data before you enter the data into a worksheet.

INTRODUCTION TO FUNCTIONS

Worksheet functions are special Excel built-in tools that perform complex calculations quickly and easily. Similar to special keys such as SQRT on a calculator, Excel functions compute square roots, loan amortizations, and a wide variety of statistical calculations. Excel has more than 240 built-in functions that perform calculations ranging from computing the absolute value (ABS) of a number to returning the two-tailed P-value of a z-test (ZTEST) and everything in between. Each Excel function is a member of one of several function groups. Figure 6.2 lists the function categories and briefly describes them. You are not going to learn about the 200 plus functions in this chapter. Instead, you will learn about some very important and often-used functions.

When you want to use a function with which you are not familiar, you can use Insert Function to select the function you need and simultaneously learn about the function and its arguments in the Wizard's steps. Alternatively, you can search for an appropriate function by typing a brief description of what you want to do. Excel then returns a list of function names and descriptions that you can browse.

FIGURE 6.2

Excel's function categories

Function Group	Description
Database	Analyze data stored in lists or databases
Date and Time	Manipulate dates and times
Financial	Present value, amortization, and interest-related functions
Information	Determines the type of data in a cell (blank, numeric, empty)
Logical	AND, OR, NOT functions to calculate yes/no answers
Lookup and Reference	Search tables and return answers, determine row or column number of a cell
Math and Trigonometry	LOG, MOD, PI, COS, and other common math and trig functions
Statistical	Standard statistical functions including average, max, and standard deviation
Text	Character extraction, manipulation, and counting functions for text (labels)

WORKING WITH FUNCTIONS

Recall that worksheet functions have two parts. The first part is the name of the function. The second part is a list of zero or more function *arguments* enclosed in parentheses, which are sometimes called *argument lists.* Of course, if a function is the first thing you write in an expression, it is preceded by an equal sign. Function names such as PMT describe, very briefly, what the function does (PayMenT, for example). Arguments specify the values, cells, or expressions that the function uses as input to compute its final value. All functions return a single answer—the value of the function's evaluation. While most Excel functions have arguments, a few do not. Normally, a function without any arguments would be doomed to return the same value over and over because there are no input values (arguments) from which the function can compute a different answer. However, the few functions that have no arguments return different values each time they are used because they rely on outside values such as an ever-changing clock value or a random pattern to create a unique answer each time. Functions have the general form

function-name (argument list)

where "function name" is the function's name and "argument list" is zero or more arguments separated by commas forming the list placed inside of parentheses. Functions that have no arguments still must have opening and closing parentheses. The NOW() and RAND() functions are two examples. NOW returns the current date and time, but it has no argument list. Similarly, the RAND function returns a random number in the range of zero to one. NOW receives its input from your computer's clock, and RAND generates a random number from an internal calculation without the need for an argument value. If you were to accidentally omit the parentheses from any function that has no arguments, Excel would misinterpret your entry as a special user-defined name (discussed in this chapter) rather than a function name. Excel probably would not find a name such as RAND in its list of user-defined names within a worksheet and consequently would display an error message. Therefore it is important to always use parentheses following a function's name—either with or without arguments as required by the function.

Most functions have a particular number of arguments arranged in a particular order. An example is the date-category function DATE, which returns a number that represents, within Excel, a date and time. The function has the general form

DATE(year, month, day)

What is important to understand at the moment is that DATE always has three arguments in a particular order. If you were to enter month information as the first argument, then the DATE function would return a spurious answer. Arguments like these are called *positional arguments* because their position in the argument list is important and inflexible. Other functions such as SUM, a function with which you are already familiar, have a maximum of 30 arguments. The arguments in the SUM function list are not positional. That is, the first argument has no particular significance different from any other arguments in the list. In other words, you can enter arguments into the list in any order that suits you. While 30 arguments may seem rather restrictive, one or more arguments can be a cell range and thus extend the total number of cells involved in the function. With the SUM function, for example, it is just as easy to sum 300,000 cells as it is to sum 30 in a single function. The trick is to use large cell ranges as individual arguments.

ORGANIZING A WORKSHEET INTO SECTIONS

For uncomplicated worksheets, it is common to divide them into at least two sections. More complex worksheets often consist of multiple worksheet pages woven together. For Cal's worksheet, it is helpful to divide the worksheet into sections. Doing so reduces or eliminates confusion about where a worksheet user is to enter values unique to each new customer. Cal's financial manager, Jessica Allison, has divided the *prototype* (a proposed model) worksheet into three sections called Assumptions, External Data, and Outputs. The Assumptions section contains input information unique to each customer and used by all the other formulas in the worksheet. They are called assumptions because the results of the worksheet in the output section depend upon the values of the assumptions. The external data section contains interest rate information, also used by formulas in the worksheet, whose values fluctuate based on the prime lending rate and other external factors. The outputs section performs calculations using the assumptions values and displays the results. Almost all of the values in the output section are formulas, with few exceptions. They reference, and thus depend upon, values stored in cells in the assumptions section. Change one or more values in the assumptions section and the outputs section values change automatically.

A well-designed worksheet divided into sections provides the benefits of providing the user with a clearly labeled input-only area, and the worksheet user need not change any formulas in the outputs section when input values change. The latter is a characteristic of formulas informally called "bullet-proof," because they need no subsequent modification.

PROVIDING AN ASSUMPTIONS FRAMEWORK

Begin constructing the loan worksheet by opening the prototype worksheet that Jessica has constructed. Jessica has preformatted several worksheet cells to allow you to concentrate on the constants, formulas, and functions in the Loan Analysis worksheet that comprises what you are learning.

Opening the Loan Analysis worksheet and saving it under a new name:

1. Start Excel

2. Open the workbook **ex06Loan.xls** and immediately save it as **Loan1.xls** to preserve the original workbook in case you want to revert to that version. Review the documentation worksheet, called Sheet1, briefly

3. Click the **Sheet3** tab to switch to that worksheet. The worksheet is empty. Depending on your settings, Excel automatically creates a certain number of worksheets when you create a new worksheet

4. Click the **Sheet2** worksheet tab to display the loan analysis details (see Figure 6.3). The worksheet displays the three sections with white characters on a blue background, and the Outputs section displays labels followed by several column labels on a light blue background

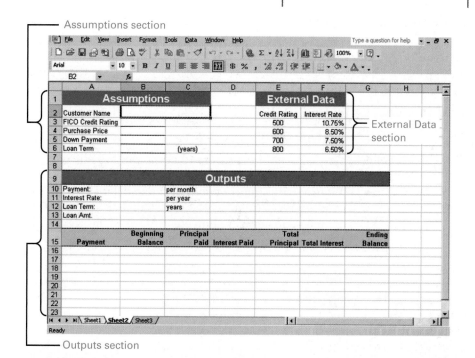

FIGURE 6.3

Main loan analysis worksheet

FIGURE 6.4

Initial Assumptions values and their meanings

Assumptions Cell	Description/Use	Value
B2	Customer's name	Francis Parker
B3	Credit rating number (obtained from credit report)	755
B4	Vehicle purchase price (negotiated)	21000
B5	Customer's down payment	3000
B6	Loan duration in years	3

Assumptions Data

With the general structure of the loan analysis worksheet in mind, you can enter the assumptions information—example data—that you will use to test the worksheet. In Session 6.2, you will add formulas to the Outputs section of the worksheet that depend on the assumptions values you are entering next. Later, when you are convinced that the worksheet works properly, you can erase the entries in the Assumptions section and save the workbook so that others can use it without erasing the data you have entered. Figure 6.4 lists the first set of values you will enter and briefly describes them.

Entering input values in the Assumptions area:

1. Click cell **B2** and type **Francis Parker**

tip: *You can press the down arrow key to move directly to the next cell. This allows you to keep your hands on the keyboard and move the mouse too.*

2. Click cell **B3** and type **755**

3. Click cell **B4** and type **21000**

4. Click cell **B5** and type **3000**

5. Click cell **B6,** type **3,** and press **Enter** to complete the entry. Notice that the values in cells B4 and B5 display currency symbols (see Figure 6.5). That means that those cells are already formatted. Indeed, much of the worksheet is preformatted so that you can concentrate on formulas rather than on formatting

FIGURE 6.5

Completed Assumptions section

assumptions filled in

	A	B	C	D	E	F	G	H	I
1	Assumptions				External Data				
2	Customer Name	Francis Parker			Credit Rating	Interest Rate			
3	FICO Credit Rating	755			500	10.75%			
4	Purchase Price	$ 21,000			600	8.50%			
5	Down Payment	$ 3,000			700	7.50%			
6	Loan Term	3	(years)		800	6.50%			
7									

External Data

The External Data section contains two completed columns of data. What do those represent? They are data that have been generated from external sources and entered here. The first column contains four values that the credit industry uses to report consumers' creditworthiness. The four values represent arbitrary groups of values. The first value, 500, is the lower limit of values ranging from 500 to 599. Second in the list, the value 600 is the lower limit of a range of values from 600 to 699. The third value, 700 is the smallest value in the range of values from 700 to 799. Finally, the value 800 represents any values from 800 up to infinity. While these credit ratings are similar to those used throughout the United States, they may not correspond to the lowest or highest possible credit rating scales or match current interest rates for the given credit rating range.

The second column in the External Data section represents interest rates that correspond to different credit rating groups. A person whose credit report shows a creditworthiness rating of 654 can qualify for a loan interest rate of 8.50 percent, because 654 falls in the category 600 to 699. Because a higher credit rating represents a lower risk that the consumer will default on the loan, higher credit ratings receive lower interest rates. In a similar way, someone with a poorer credit rating, say 550, would be a higher loan risk and thus assigned a higher interest rate. Values in both columns of the External Data table will fluctuate both with changing prime interest rates and subjective opinions about the meaning of a credit rating value. Values in this worksheet merely illustrate the notion that interest rates vary with consumers' credit ratings. You will later use the table to locate and assign a consumer a particular interest rate. The rate will be based on the consumer's reported credit rating obtained from one of the credit reporting agencies mentioned previously.

SUPPLYING DATA VALIDATION

As a worksheet designer, you should always be aware that anyone using your worksheet could accidentally type the wrong data into the one of the several input cells in the Assumptions area of your worksheet. Invalid entries include mistakes like entering text instead of a value or a value that is incorrect because it is too large or too small. Called *range errors,* values that are either too large or too small (negative or too close to zero, for example) do not make sense in the context of the application. For example, typing 50 in cell B6, the loan term duration in years, would be incorrect. Similarly, a negative value in cell B6 is incorrect. A credit rating value that is negative or larger than 800 is also incorrect. How can you detect or prevent range errors?

Excel provides an elegant solution with its data validation feature. By specifying criteria, you can apply rules about the range of values and type of data that are allowed for one cell or a range of cells. Specifying data validation for individual cells allows you to restrict the type and value of information users enter into a worksheet. For example, you can specify that users must enter values in the range of 1 to 5 (years) in cell B6, the loan length in years. Similarly, you can restrict the values in cell B3 to values from 500 to 899. Seldom do you place text value restrictions on cells, such as cell B2 containing a customer's name, because it is very difficult—impossible, really—to express the valid range of legitimate names. In addition to providing criteria restricting values a user may type into cells, you can attach to a cell a helpful reminder message stating the range of acceptable values. Excel data validation features allow you to stipulate an error alert message that appears if the user enters data that is not allowed. You will use each of these features in the steps that follow to protect selected cells from incorrect user input.

Specifying Valid Data Value Ranges

Jessica wants you to restrict the value that a user can type into loan term cell, B6, to values in the range of 1 to 5. Cal's does not offer loans for less than one year or more than five.

> ### Restricting data values to a specific range and data type:
>
> 1. Click cell **B6** to select the cell to which you will apply data validation
>
> 2. Click **Data** on the menu bar and then click **Validation** to open the Data Validation dialog box. In the Data Validation dialog box, you specify the data range information and the messages that appear when the user enters information into the cell or when Excel detects that the user has entered an invalid value
>
> 3. Click the **Settings** tab, if necessary, click the **Allow** list box to reveal the list of values, and click **Whole number.** The dialog box reveals several new text boxes, which depend on the value you select in the Allow list box (see Figure 6.6). Next, you will specify the valid value ranges for the loan term

EXCEL

FIGURE 6.6

Partially completed Data
Validation dialog box

select data type
restriction from
this list

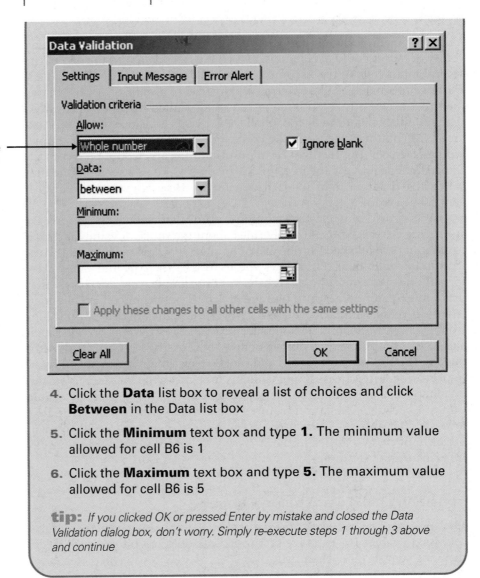

4. Click the **Data** list box to reveal a list of choices and click
   Between in the Data list box

5. Click the **Minimum** text box and type **1.** The minimum value
   allowed for cell B6 is 1

6. Click the **Maximum** text box and type **5.** The maximum value
   allowed for cell B6 is 5

tip: *If you clicked OK or pressed Enter by mistake and closed the Data
Validation dialog box, don't worry. Simply re-execute steps 1 through 3 above
and continue*

Providing a Data Entry Message

With the data type (whole number) and value range established for cell B6,
you can proceed to specify the message to display as someone begins to enter information into cell B6. The Data Validation dialog box should still be
open as you do the following steps.

*Entering an informative Data Validation
input message:*

1. Click the **Input Message** tab in the Data Validation dialog box,
   and ensure that the *Show input message when cell is selected*
   check box is checked

2. Click the **Title** text box and type **Valid Loan Term Value**

3. Click the **Input message** text box and type **Loan term must
   be from 1 to 5.** The message appears when cell B6 is selected

Whenever anyone clicks cell B6, the Data Validation input message appears automatically. It will help reduce the risk that a user will enter an invalid value for the loan term. Still, errors can occur. The final procedure in completing the Data Validation dialog box is to specify an error message to adequately warn a user if he or she does make an invalid entry in the cell.

Giving Data Entry Error Feedback

The Data Validation dialog box provides a third tab in which you can optionally specify an error message that Excel displays if the data in the cell do not meet the criteria specified on the Settings tab. Short of ringing a bell (which you can do with Visual Basic code), this is the best way to bring data entry errors to a user's attention. You complete the Data Validation dialog box with an error message, called an error alert message, next.

Entering an error alert message:

1. Click the **Error Alert** tab in the Data Validation dialog box, and ensure that the *Show error after invalid data is entered* check box is checked

2. Click the **Style** list box and click **Stop** (if necessary). Three levels of alert are available: Information, Warning, and Stop. The action each of the three alert levels cause appears in Figure 6.7

Type	Button Label	Action If Button Is Clicked
Information	OK	Value entered into the cell; processing continues normally
	Cancel	Value is not entered into the cell
Warning	Continue Yes	Value entered in cell; processing continues normally
	ContinueNo	Value placed in cell; Excel stops, waiting for you to enter another value
	Cancel	Value is not entered into the cell
Stop	Retry	Value remains; Excel stops and waits for you to enter another value
	Cancel	Value is not entered into the cell

FIGURE 6.7

Error Alert Style messages and actions

3. Click the **Title** text box and type **Error!** What you type in the Title text box appears at the top of the error message when Excel detects a data input error

4. Click the **Error message** text box and type **Loan term must be between 1 and 5. Your entry is incorrect. Please enter a correct value.** The message appears when Excel detects an invalid value in the cell

5. Click the **OK** button to close the Data Validation dialog box and finalize your settings

Testing Data Validation

After the Data Validation dialog box closes, you notice that the input message appears. That is because cell B6 is active. With the data validation rule intact, you can test it to ensure that invalid entries do not escape Excel's attention.

Testing data validation rules for cell B6:

1. Click cell **B5** to make it active momentarily, then click cell **B6**. The Data Validation input message appears indicating the range of valid data for the loan term (see Figure 6.8)

FIGURE 6.8
Input message display

input message appears whenever the cell selected is active

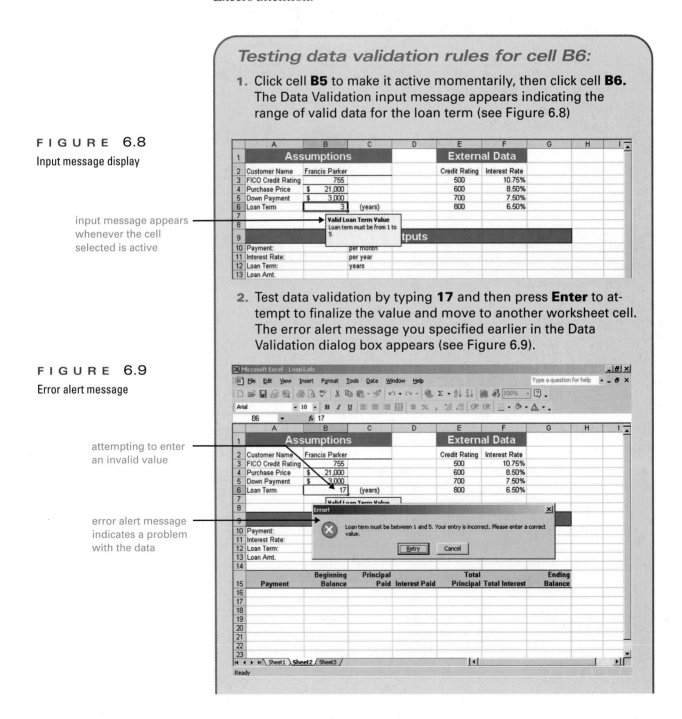

2. Test data validation by typing **17** and then press **Enter** to attempt to finalize the value and move to another worksheet cell. The error alert message you specified earlier in the Data Validation dialog box appears (see Figure 6.9).

FIGURE 6.9
Error alert message

attempting to enter an invalid value

error alert message indicates a problem with the data

You can click **Retry** to correct the mistake or you can click **Cancel** to erase your incorrect entry. Clicking Cancel restores cell B6 to the value it had prior to your incorrect entry

3. Click the **Retry** button. Excel highlights cell B6, making it ready for you to re-enter a value

4. Type **3** and press **Enter.** Because this value is within the specified range of 1 to 5, Excel permits the entry and then makes cell B7 active

DEFINING NAMES

Until now, you have referenced cells using their addresses. In larger worksheets, it is easy to forget which cells contain particular values. When you are enhancing a worksheet someone else developed, you will likely examine the formulas to determine what calculations various parts of the worksheet are performing to better understand its flow and structure. Formulas such as =B4*C5−A7−C42 provide little information about the purpose of the expression. An alternative expression such as hoursworked*hourlyrate−statetax−federaltax is much easier to understand because the formula is built with names that infer their purpose. Excel provides an extremely helpful feature that allows you to assign a name to a cell or cell range and then use the name anywhere you would use the cell address. A ***name*** (also known as a ***range name***) is a name that you assign to a cell or cell range that can replace a cell address or cell range in expressions or functions. Names provide several benefits over using cell addresses.

- Names are easier to remember than cell addresses as you create formulas referencing cells
- Names provide documentation because the name reveals the purpose of the cell and clarifies formulas that contain names
- Excel treats names in copied formulas as though they are absolute cell references, which is an advantage when you clone a formula that you want to refer to a fixed location or cell

Names must be named in a particular way. Rules for names are the following:

- Names must begin with a letter or an underscore character
- The remaining characters in the name can be letters, numbers, periods, and underscore characters
- The maximum length of a name is 255 characters, although short and meaningful names are better
- Capitalization is ignored in names. (Excel considers the names "Payment" and "payment" as identical)
- Names can be words, but spaces are not allowed. Instead, use the underscore character in place of a space for multi-word names. (Gross_Pay is a legitimate name)
- Names can be single letters, with the exception of the letters R and C

EXCEL

- Names that resemble cell references cannot be used. (IR42 is not allowed)
- Simply stated, define names using six or more characters that contain letters and numbers and that are meaningful words

---

task reference

Naming a Cell or Cell Range

- Select the cell or cell range you want to name
- Click the **Name box** in the formula bar
- Type the name and press **Enter**

An alternative way to assign a name to a cell or cell range is to execute Insert, Name, Define, and type the name. You can use either method.

Defining a Name with a Menu Bar Command

Jessica wants you to assign names to key cells and cell ranges to make creating formulas easier. She suggests you define names for cells containing the purchase price, down payment, loan term, and the table containing the FICO (Fair, Isaac and Company) credit ratings and interest rates. (see www.fairisaac.com.) Defining names to key assumptions will make it easier to write formulas in the Outputs area that reference the cells in the Assumptions section of the worksheet. Specifically, you will define names for cells B3, B4, B5, B6—key input values—the cell range E3:F6, which is the table with credit rating and interest rate information, and cells B10, B11, B12, and B13 in the Outputs section.

Defining a name:

1. Click cell **B3,** the cell for which you want to define a name

2. Click **Insert** on the menu bar, point to **Name,** and click **Define** to open the Define Name dialog box in which you define and delete names. Excel suggests the name FICO_Credit_Rating, which appears in the *Names in workbook* text box, because the label appears to the left of the selected cell

3. Type **CreditRating** (no spaces) in the *Names in workbook* text box to name cell B3 (see Figure 6.10), and then click **OK** to close the Define Name dialog box and finalize your choice

4. Repeat steps 2 and 3 to name the following cells with the following names (Remember: Do not use spaces anywhere):

B4	**PurchasePrice**	B10	**PeriodicPayment**
B5	**DownPayment**	B11	**InterestRate**
B6	**LoanTerm**	B13	**LoanAmount**

With cell B13 still selected, look at the **Name box** located at the left end of the Formula bar. Notice that it displays the name you assigned cell

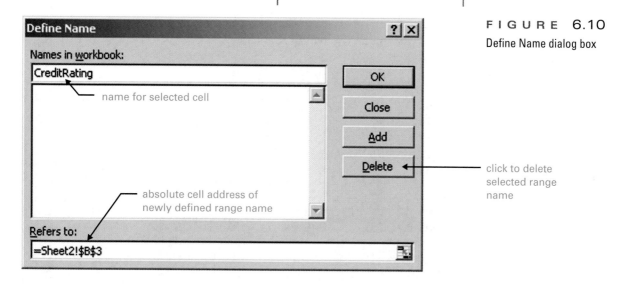

FIGURE 6.10
Define Name dialog box

B13—*LoanAmount*. Whenever you select a cell or cell range that has a defined name, the name appears in the Name box.

Note that when you define a name, the worksheet name is part of the definition and the cell reference is absolute. The name defined for cell B13, for example, is assigned to cell Sheet2!$B$13. Sheet2 is part of the name because it identifies the sheet on which the name is found—a true three-dimensional name.

Defining a Name Using the Name Box

The most convenient way to assign a name is to use the Name box located on the left end of the formula bar. You can use the Name box either to define a name or to go to a named cell or cell range. A name defined in one worksheet is available to all worksheets in the workbook. If you have a large worksheet, clicking a name in the Name box list of names is a convenient way to move directly to a cell. For example, you could name the entire Assumptions area of the worksheet with the name Assumptions. Then, when you click the name Assumptions in the Name box, Excel goes to that section of the worksheet and highlights the name. In fact, whenever you want to know which cell or cell range is assigned a particular name, simply select the name from the Name box list.

Next, you will define a name for the External Data cell range containing columns for credit rating values and corresponding interest rates. Later, you will find it very convenient to use a name rather than a cell range to refer to the table.

*another*word

. . . on Names

Normally, names you define are **workbook-level names.** A workbook-level name (range name) is a name you define that is available for use in formulas from *any* worksheet in a workbook. You can create a *worksheet-level name,* which is a name that is available only on the worksheet in which it is defined. To define a worksheet-level name, precede the name with the name of the worksheet followed by an exclamation point. For example, you could define a worksheet-level name SalePrice on the worksheet Sheet12 by typing Sheet12!SalePrice as you define the name.

Using the Name box to define a name:

1. Select cell range **E3:F6,** the cell range to which you want to assign a name

2. Click inside the Name box, type **CreditTable** (see Figure 6.11), and press **Enter**

tip: *If you accidentally enter the name in cell E3, then press the **Esc** key to nullify your action. Select cell range **E3:F6** again and be sure to click inside the Name box, which is on the left end of the Formula bar. If you pressed **Enter** before discovering the mistake, click **Edit,** Undo and repeat Steps 1 and 2*

FIGURE 6.11

Defining a name with the Name box

Name box ——

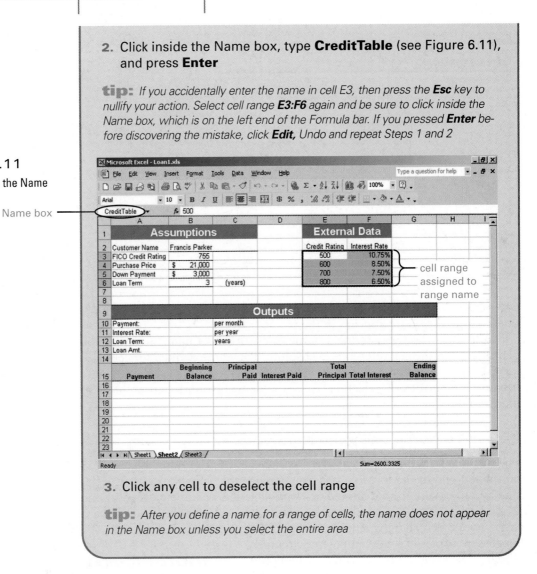

3. Click any cell to deselect the cell range

tip: *After you define a name for a range of cells, the name does not appear in the Name box unless you select the entire area*

Now that key data input cells in the Assumptions and External Data areas have defined names, you can refer to cells by their names rather than their cell addresses. Using names in expressions is usually a better alternative than using cell references.

USING NAMES IN FORMULAS

The purpose of worksheet and workbook names is so that you can use them instead of cell addresses in formulas that you create to complete the loan analysis worksheet. When you use a name, Excel treats it like an absolute cell reference. You begin by writing the formula for cell B13 to compute the loan amount.

Creating a formula containing names:

1. Select cell **B13,** the cell that will contain the loan amount. Loan amount is the vehicle's purchase price minus the down payment

2. Type **=PurchasePrice-DownPayment** and press **Enter**. The loan amount, $18,000.00, appears in cell B13

3. Click cell **B13** to make it active again and press the **F2** function key to edit the formula. Notice the names appearing in the formula (see Figure 6.12). They are color-coded to match the outlines around the independent cells that the formula references

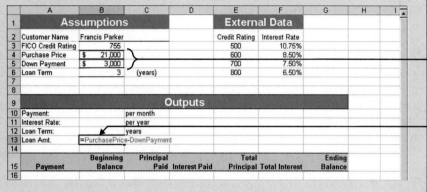

FIGURE 6.12

Names appear in the formula

color coding shows cells referenced in formula

formula contains names with colored outlines to identify referenced cells

4. Press the **Esc** key to cancel the edit cell request

You will use the other names in formulas you create in this chapter.

---

task reference

Deleting a Name

- Click **Insert,** point to **Name,** and then click the **Define** button

- Click the name in the *Names in workbook* list that you want to delete

- Click the **Delete** button and then click the **OK** button

---

Next, you need to enter formulas for Loan Term in the Outputs section (which is the same value as Loan Term in the Assumptions section), the loan interest rate, and a special assessment fee Jessica just mentioned to you.

USING IF AND INDEX FUNCTIONS

Making Alternative Choices with the IF Function

Last month, Cal's Cars began charging a special fee to any customer whose loan is over 80 percent of the purchase price of a car. Cal's management created the special assessment to cover the cost of insuring loans. The special assessment is $300. History has shown Cal and his managers that there is a much higher loan default rate among customers who finance more than 80 percent of a vehicle's purchase price than among those who do not. The special assessment, which Cal calls a "processing fee," will reduce Cal's risk with insurance to cover the balance of a loan should a customer simply quit making loan payments (default) on the loan. There is no special assessment for customers who finance 80 percent or less of their vehicle's purchase price.

Writing a formula to capture the preceding business rule requires a new statement—one in which there is one outcome from two possible choices. The two possible outcomes are a $300 fee for loans in which the ratio of loan amount to purchase price is greater than 0.8 or no fee for ratios less than or equal to 0.8. You will encounter many situations in which the formula you write in a cell can have two or more possible outcomes from which to choose depending on another cell or cells' value(s). Excel anticipates this and provides the function IF, belonging to the logical function category. The IF function has the following form:

IF(conditional test, expression if true, expression if false)

A *conditional test* is an equation that compares two values, functions, formula labels, or logical values. Every conditional test equation must include a *relational operator,* which compares two parts of a formula. The result of the comparison is either true or false. For example, in the conditional test A1>B2, the greater than symbol (>) relational operator compares the values in cells A1 and B2. IF A1 is greater than B2, then the result of the conditional test is true. Otherwise, it is false. Figure 6.13 shows a complete list of Excel's relational operators.

The second and third arguments of the IF function can be constants or arbitrarily complex expressions. The IF function displays the computed value of only one of the two argument expressions, depending on the evaluation of the conditional test. If the conditional test is true, Excel calculates and displays the value of the second argument. Otherwise (if the test is false), Excel calculates and displays the value of the third argument. Thus, you can create a formula whose output depends on a condition—a value in another cell.

In the loan analysis worksheet, the conditional expression you will write examines the ratio of the loan amount to the purchase price. You create a ratio simply by dividing one value by another. If the ratio is greater than 0.8, then the special assessment is $300. Otherwise, the special assessment is $0. Figure 6.14 shows the IF function and the logic of the expression.

Now you are ready to enter the IF function to determine whether the customer must pay the special assessment of $300 or

FIGURE 6.13

Excel's relational operators

Relational Operator	Meaning
<	Less than
>	Greater than
=	Equal to
<=	Less than or equal to
>=	Greater than or equal to
<>	Not equal to

FIGURE 6.14

Logic of the IF function

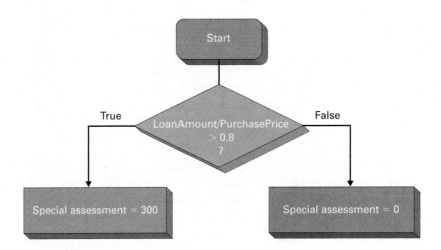

not. In addition to the special assessment, you should conditionally display the label "Assessment" in cell A14 when processing fee appears in cell B14.

Writing an IF function:

1. Click cell **A14,** the cell that will display *Assessment* if the ratio of loan amount to purchase price is greater than 0.8—the same criteria for displaying (or not) an assessment fee of $300

2. Type **=IF(LoanAmount/PurchasePrice > 0.8, "Assessment", "")** and press **Enter.** The cell displays *Assessment* because the loan-to-price ratio is 0.875. Otherwise, nothing is displayed ("")

tip: *Notice that the third argument contains two quotation marks in a row without a blank between them. The IF function can display character string expressions such as "Assessment" as well as numeric expressions.*

When you are unsure of a function and want help writing it, use the Insert Function command. Executing Insert Function opens a dialog box that lists functions by categories and helps you build the function. Next, you will use the Insert Function to build the second IF function to display the special assessment amount.

Using the Insert Function command to write an IF function:

1. Click cell **B14** to make it active

2. Click **Insert** on the menu bar, and then click **Function** to open the Insert Function dialog box

3. Click the **Or select a category** list box to display its list of function categories

4. Click **Logical** in the list of function category choices, click **IF** in the Select a function list box, and then click **OK.** The Function Arguments dialog box opens (see Figure 6.15)

5. Click the **Logical-Test** text box and type **LoanAmount/PurchasePrice>0.8** (no spaces in this line). Notice that the moment you type 0.8, the label TRUE appears to the right of the value. That indicates the current value of the expression based on the condition you just completed

6. Click the **Value_if_true** text box and type **300,** which is the value to return if the condition is true

7. Click the **Value_if_false** text box and type **0,** which is the value to return if the condition is false (see Figure 6.16)

8. Click **OK** to complete the function. Excel places the completed IF function into cell B14, calculates the value of the function, and displays $300.00 because the ratio of the down payment to the purchase price is greater than 0.8

EXCEL

F I G U R E   6.15

The Function Arguments dialog box

three text boxes represent the IF function's three arguments

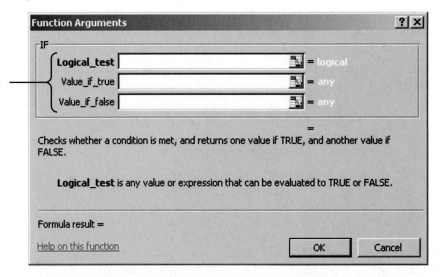

F I G U R E   6.16

Completed Function Arguments dialog box

value of the entire IF function

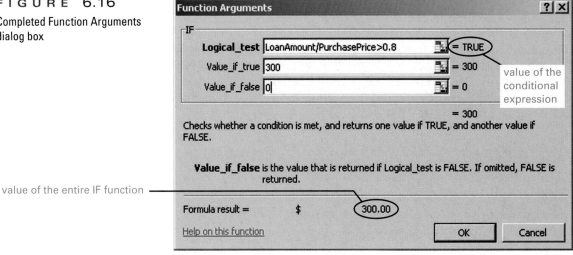

Testing an IF Function

Just to make sure that the IF function is working properly, you will temporarily increase the down payment value in cell B5 so that it reduces the loan amount to purchase price ratio below 0.8. Then, observe cell A14 to ensure that it does not display a label and that cell B14 displays a currency symbol and a hyphen, which indicates the value zero for the special assessment.

Testing IF functions by altering the down payment value:

1. Click the **Name box list arrow** and then click **DownPayment** in the list. Excel makes cell B5 active

2. Type **12345** and press **Enter.** Notice that cell A14 appears empty and cell B14 displays a currency symbol and a hyphen, symbolic of the value zero under the Accounting format

3. Click **Edit** in the menu bar and then click **Undo Typing '12345' in B5.** Excel restores the value $3,000 in cell B5. The IF function works just the way you want it to. It returns one of two possible values depending on a condition you specify

You can now enter the function into cell B11 that determines the appropriate interest rate to charge the customer based on his or her credit rating. You will do that with one of the Index category of functions called Lookup functions.

Using the VLOOKUP Function

You will encounter many situations in which you need to look up an answer from a table of possible answers. These needs arise frequently in Excel worksheet applications. For example, an instructor needs a convenient way to look up letter grades that correspond to students' percentage values. An express shipping company determines shipping prices by a package's weight and the location to which it will be shipped. Or, a tax consultant finds it convenient to look up the state or federal tax rate for a client using the client's gross income and number of dependents.

Situations like the preceding ones call for a special class of functions called lookup functions, also known as table lookup functions. Excel provides several *lookup functions,* which use a search value to search a table—a range of cells—for a match or close match and then return a value from the table as a result. The table that a lookup function searches is called the *lookup table,* and the value being used to search the lookup table is called the *lookup value.* With Excel lookup functions, you specify the value or cell address of the lookup value, the cell range of the lookup table, and the column or row that contains the values you want to return as an answer.

Excel provides two lookup functions: HLOOKUP and VLOOKUP. You use the HLOOKUP function, which stands for horizontal lookup, for lookup tables in which the lookup column is in the first row of a multi-row table. You use the VLOOKUP function, which stands for vertical lookup, for a vertical lookup table—one in which the search values are in the first column of the table. For either lookup function to work properly, the horizontal or vertical table must be sorted from low to high on the values in the first row (HLOOKUP) or first column (VLOOKUP). Otherwise, either function returns spurious results.

The VLOOKUP function has the general form shown in Figure 6.17. Before you apply the VLOOKUP function to the loan analysis worksheet, examine its parts for a better understanding of how it works.

The first argument of the function is the lookup value. The VLOOKUP function uses that value to search the lookup table. The second argument is the lookup table, which is the cell range or name specifying the lookup table's location. The third argument is the column containing the data you want VLOOKUP to retrieve. Finally, the fourth argument can be FALSE, TRUE, or omitted. If it is FALSE, VLOOKUP will look for an exact match in the lookup table. If it does not find a value in the first column exactly matching the lookup value, VLOOKUP returns #N/A error value. If the argument is TRUE or omitted (most people omit the argument), then

FIGURE 6.17

VLOOKUP function syntax

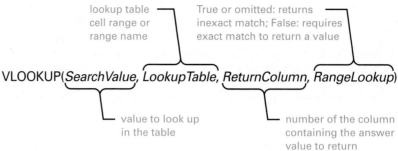

FIGURE 6.18

VLOOKUP function searching a lookup table

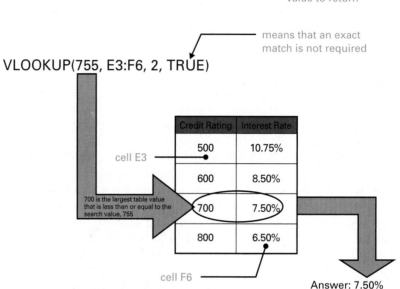

VLOOKUP searches the first column looking for the largest value in the first column that is less than or equal to the search value. You can better understand this function by applying it to the loan analysis worksheet.

Cal's loan analysis worksheet can use a lookup function in cell B11 (which holds the loan interest rate) to retrieve the interest rate by searching the table you named CreditTable (cells E3 through F6) using the FICO Credit Rating value in cell B3 as the lookup value. The CreditTable cell range is arranged in columns, and it is sorted in ascending order on the first column—Credit Rating. With the lookup table arranged in this way, you will use the VLOOKUP function because the search values are in the first column. Figure 6.18 shows a graphical example of the VLOOKUP function and how it searches the lookup table and returns an applicable interest rate based on a customer's credit rating number.

---

task reference

Using the VLOOKUP Function

- Create a lookup table and sort the table in ascending order by the leftmost column

- Place in columns to the right of the search columns values you want to return as answers

- Write a VLOOKUP function referencing a cell containing the lookup value, the lookup table, and the column containing the answer

Jessica asks you to write a function in cell B11 that will use the customer's credit rating in the Assumptions section, cell B3, and look up and return the interest rate from the lookup table. Because the table is arranged with ranges of credit ratings corresponding to individual interest rates, the VLOOKUP table search will locate the credit rating value range that the lookup value falls into. For example, Francis Parker's credit rating (cell B3) of 755 falls into the third group in the table—the row containing the values 700 and 7.50%. A credit rating of 723 or 799 would also fall into that range and return the same interest rate. Write the VLOOKUP formula in the steps that follow by using the Insert Function command to help you build the function.

Writing a VLOOKUP function:

1. Click cell **B11** (named InterestRate) to make it the active cell

2. Click **Insert** on the menu bar, and then click **Function** to open the Insert Function dialog box

3. Click the **Or select a category** list box to display its list of function categories

4. Click **Lookup & Reference** in list of choices, scroll to the bottom of the *Select a function* list, click **VLOOKUP,** and click **OK.** The VLOOKUP function dialog box opens

5. Type **CreditRating** in the Lookup_value text box and press the **Tab** key

6. Type **CreditTable,** which is the name of the lookup table, and press the **Tab** key

7. Type **2** in the Col_index_num box because you want VLOOKUP to return an answer from the second column of the lookup table. Because you do not want an exact-match table search, you can omit the fourth argument (see Figure 6.19)

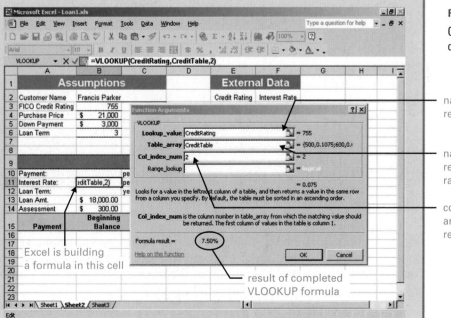

FIGURE 6.19

Completed VLOOKUP function dialog box

name CreditRating refers to cell B3

name CreditTable refers to cell range E3:F6

column 2 holds answers to be returned

result of completed VLOOKUP formula

Excel is building a formula in this cell

EXCEL

8. Click **OK** to complete the function definition and close the VLOOKUP function dialog box. The function returns and displays the value 7.50%, which is the interest rate corresponding to the credit rating of 755

anotherword

. . . on the Lookup Table Col_index_num argument

The third argument of the VLOOKUP function, the column index, is the number of the answer column—the table column holding the values to return. The number is always relative to the first column of the lookup table as specified within the function. The first column of a lookup table, the column searched by VLOOKUP, is column 1. Columns to the right are numbered consecutively: 2, 3, and so on up to the last column specified in the second argument of the lookup function.

The last activity before ending this session is to write a simple formula in cell B12 that displays the loan term. While the loan term used in calculations is found in the Assumptions area, a second copy of it is handy to place in the Outputs section. That way, the vehicle salesperson can print the Outputs section of the worksheet for the customer and it will contain a complete record of the proposed loan details. Because the value in cell B12 should always be identical to the input value in cell B6, you will write a simple formula that refers to cell B6 from cell B12.

Writing the loan term "copycat" formula:

1. Click cell **B12** to make it the active cell

2. Write **=LoanTerm,** the name for the Assumptions area cell containing the loan term, and press **Enter.** Cell B12 displays 3, a formula that automatically changes whenever a worksheet user changes the value in cell B6

You have done a lot of work on the loan analysis worksheet in this session. Always save a worksheet before going on to the next session.

Saving the loan analysis worksheet:

1. Click **Save** button on the Standard toolbar to save **Loan1.xls** and preserve the work you completed in this session

2. Click **File** on the menu bar and click **Exit** to close the worksheet and exit Excel

Congratulations. You have learned a great deal about several important functions. In the next section, you will write several financial functions to produce a schedule of loan repayments that indicate how much you pay each month and how much of the payment reduces the loan balance and how much pays each month's interest.

making **the grade**   **SESSION 6.1**

1. Enclosed in parentheses following a function's name are one or more _____.

2. The _____ section of a worksheet contains input values used by other formulas in the worksheet.

3. You can use data _____ to restrict the information being entered into a worksheet cell.

4. You provide error messages with data validation techniques by specifying an error _____ message in the Data Validation dialog box

5. Open the worksheet you saved as **Loan1.xls** and save it as **Loan11.xls.** Then, make the following changes to it. Click cell **B3** and, using Data Validation, ensure that the only values a user can enter in the cell are **whole numbers** from **350** to **900.** The data validation should provide an informative input message stating that the **Valid values are in the range 350-900** (title is **Input Value Information**). Provide an error alert message that tells the user the correct range of values for the cell. Use the title **Error!** for the error alert message and select the **Warning** style. Define the name **Assessment** for cell B14. Name the range E1:F6 **ExternalData**. Apply data validation to the DownPayment cell (B5) so that a user must enter a Whole number in the range of **100** up to and including the value in cell **B4** (PurchasePrice). (Hint: When choosing the values for the Maximum text box, click the Collapse button and click cell B4.) Supply an input message and an error alert message similar to the preceding ones. Write an IF function in cell C14 that displays the value of LoanAmount/PurchasePrice if it is above 80 percent. If the ratio is not greater than 80 percent, display nothing in cell C14. Format cell C14 to display a percentage to two decimal places. Place your name in the worksheet header. Print the worksheet. Type **12000** in cell B5 and print the worksheet again. Save the changed workbook and then exit Excel.

SESSION 6.2 USING FINANCIAL FUNCTIONS

In this section, you will learn how to write several financial functions including PMT, PPMT, IPMT, and PV. You will use AutoFill to copy an ascending series of values in a column and, later, to create several families of related formulas throughout your worksheet.

USING FINANCIAL ANALYSIS FUNCTIONS

Excel's financial functions allow you to extend your proficiency beyond the simpler functions of SUM, MIN, and MAX. You can use the financial and date functions to perform quite sophisticated financial and date calculations without the need to know the theory behind the functions. This chapter provides you with both the understanding of financial and date

EXCEL

functions and experience using them in worksheets to see how they work. Excel's financial functions allow you to take control of many important monetary calculations such as the amount of a monthly payment of a mortgage, the present value of a future steady flow of revenue, or the amount of a loan payment that goes to pay off the principal and the amount that pays the periodic interest.

Financial functions can seem somewhat daunting. Sometimes it is difficult to remember the order and type of arguments to a particular financial function. To complicate matters, some financial functions such as PMT, IPMT, and PPMT have similar names. Others have up to seven arguments. Remember that you can use a function wizard to help you build the more complicated functions. Click Insert on the menu bar and then click Function to summon the function wizard, select the function category and function name, and then step through building the function.

The financial functions you will encounter in this session all have a common basis. Each of the functions is in a family of functions that calculates basic rates of return and payment amounts. A fundamental concept in finance is the *time value of money*. In its simplest form, the **time value of money** means that receiving $100 today is more valuable than receiving it next year. Why? Because you could put the $100 in a bank and earn interest for a year and end up with more than $100 next year—perhaps $105 or $110. Furthermore, if you decide you do not need the $100 and leave it in the bank or other investment, the interest compounds. That is, you earn interest on the interest. Financial functions answer questions such as this one: "How much money do I have to place in an investment that pays 5 percent per year in order to accumulate $10,000 in 10 years?" Other Excel financial functions answer the question "How much is my monthly payment for a $6,000 loan at 8 percent per year for three years?" The similarity between these examples is that they both affirm that time is money.

Using the Payment Function, PMT

PMT is one of the Excel functions that calculates payments for a loan or investment that pays a fixed amount at a periodic rate. PMT, which stands for payment, is the most commonly used payment function. The PMT function calculates the periodic payment given three values: the loan amount, the periodic interest rate, and the loan duration. Loan payments are amortized. **Amortization** is the process of distributing periodic payments over the life of a loan. The amount borrowed is the **principal.** The interest percentage is called the **rate,** and the time period over which you make periodic payments is the **term.**

A periodic payment is a fixed payment that you make on a regular basis—once every year, every month, every day, and so on. Commonly, periodic payments are made month-to-month, though high-risk loans may require a payer to make weekly payments. Loan repayments are an example of periodic payments. Each month, the loan recipient pays the same amount to the lending institution. Part of the payment covers the interest on the loan and part of the payment covers repaying the loan (principal). After the final loan payment, the loan's balance is zero—it is paid off. Over the life of a loan repayment, more of each monthly payment goes toward reducing the loan amount and less goes toward paying interest on the loan. The general form of the payment function, PMT, is shown in Figure 6.20.

Jessica wants you to work on the periodic payment function that will compute the monthly payment amounts for each customer and display that value in cell B10. The PMT function references the InterestRate (cell

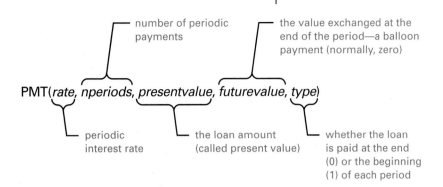

FIGURE 6.20
PMT function syntax

B11), LoanTerm (cell B6), and LoanAmount (cell B13). All of Cal's customers make monthly payments. For example, in a three-year loan, a customer will make 36 payments—one per month. The frequency of the payment affects the interest rate. When you are dealing with *monthly* payments, remember to divide the annual interest rate by 12 (months) to yield a monthly interest rate.

Begin modifications to the loan analysis worksheet by opening Excel and loading the worksheet.

Opening the loan analysis worksheet:

1. Start Excel

2. Open the loan analysis workbook **Loan1.xls**

3. Immediately save workbook as **Loan2.xls** to preserve the original workbook in case you want to revert to the final version you saved in Session 6.1

Now you can write the formula for the monthly payment.

Writing the PMT function:

1. Click the **Name box list arrow** on the left end of the formula bar and click **PeriodicPayment** to make cell B10 active

2. Click **Insert** on the menu bar, click **Function,** type **periodic payment** in the *Search for a function* text box, click the **Go** button, ensure that **PMT** is highlighted in the *Select a function* list box, and click **OK.** The PMT function dialog box opens

3. If necessary, click the **Rate** text box and then type **InterestRate/12.** Because each customer makes monthly payments, you must divide the annual interest by the number of payments per year. (You can write an arithmetic expression as a function argument)

4. Click the **Nper** text box and type **LoanTerm*12.** Making monthly payments means that you must multiply the number of years (in the cell named LoanTerm) by the number of payments per year (12)

---

5. Click the **Pv** text box and type **-LoanAmount.** The minus sign preceding LoanAmount reverses the sign of the function's result. Normally, the PMT function reports a negative value—an outflow. The negative sign makes the result positive. Excel calculates the periodic (monthly) payment and displays it in the dialog box (see Figure 6.21)

FIGURE 6.21

Completed PMT function dialog box

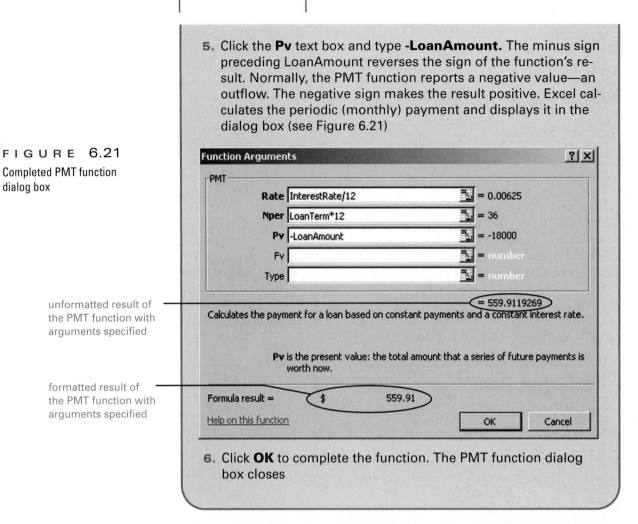

unformatted result of the PMT function with arguments specified

formatted result of the PMT function with arguments specified

6. Click **OK** to complete the function. The PMT function dialog box closes

The LoanAmount cell displays $559.91, which is the monthly payment on a loan of $18,000 for three years at 7.5 percent annual interest. The calculated result is not precise to the penny. Examine Figure 6.21 and you will see that the answer is actually 559.9119269 to seven decimal places. Formatting visually rounds that number to $559.91. Such a small difference will not affect what you do here, but you will learn to use the ROUND function in this session to counteract any cumulative affects such a number would have on a long-term loan or other investment.

Building a Loan Amortization Schedule

Jessica thinks that customers will want to know exactly how much of their loan payment is going toward repaying the loan and how much is going toward interest. She wants you to build a complete month-by-month amortization schedule. An *amortization schedule* lists the monthly payment, the amount of the payment applied toward reducing the principal (loan amount), and the amount of the payment that pays the interest due each month. In addition, she wants you to display, each month, the beginning balance of the loan amount, the total paid so far toward the principal, and the total paid so far in interest charges. The column labels that appear in row 15 are the beginning of the amortization schedule. They label the contents of each column of the schedule. The remaining work to complete the loan analysis worksheet is to create the formulas and constants that comprise the rows in the amortization schedule.

There will be 36 rows of information in the amortization schedule for this example because it will take 36 payments to pay off the loan. Each row represents a month in the 36-month payout schedule. It would be nice if you could automatically allocate 12, 24, 36, or 48 rows in the amortization schedule based on the value in the LoanTerm cell. Unfortunately, that requires using programming called VBA (Visual Basic for Applications). You have not learned that skill in these first six chapters. Therefore, you will have to create the amortization schedule by manually filling in the correct number of rows. That's not a terrible restriction. Just remember to change the number of rows in the amortization schedule to match a changed LoanTerm value when necessary.

Creating a Series of Constants with the Fill Handle

The Payment column is designed to hold the payment number beginning at 1 and ending, in this case, at 36. Although you could enter the values in cells A16 through A51 one at a time, it is much faster to enter the initial two values and then clone the remaining 34 values using the fill handle.

Creating and formatting an ascending number series:

1. Click cell **A16,** the topmost cell in the column labeled Payment, and type **1**

2. Click cell **A17,** type **2,** and press **Enter**

3. Click and drag the mouse through the cell range **A16:A17** and release the mouse. The first two cells under the Payment heading are selected

4. Hover the mouse over the fill handle in the lower-right corner of cell **A17,** click and drag the fill handle down through cell **A51,** and release the mouse. The values 1 through 36 fill cells A16 through A51, and Excel displays the AutoFill Options smart tag

5. With cell range A16:A51 still selected, click the **Center** alignment ☰ button on the Formatting toolbar to center the numbers in their cells

6. Click cell **B16** to deselect the cell range and prepare for the next series of steps (see Figure 6.22)

You will be creating formulas and expressions in the first row of the amortization schedule. Then you will create the second row of the schedule. Finally, you will copy the second row of carefully crafted formulas and expressions down through the remaining 34 rows of the amortization schedule.

Writing a PV Function

The next formula you will write will appear in cell B16, the first of 36 that will display the beginning balance each month. The beginning balance is the amount of the loan left to pay after making the previous month's

EXCEL

F I G U R E   6.22

Payment column completed

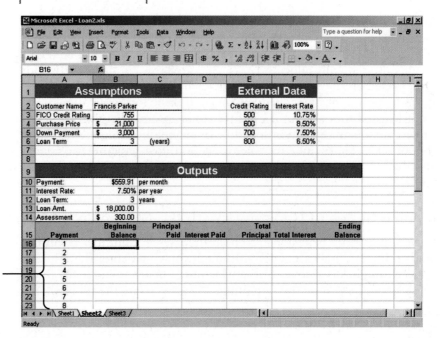

Payment column displaying some of the ascending numbers

payment. The first month, the beginning balance is equal to the full loan amount. The beginning balance the second month is the original loan amount minus the amount of the payment applied in month one to pay off the loan. Although you could simply write the formula =LoanAmount (or the equivalent formula, =B13) in cell B16, you will use the present value function, PV, as a test to ensure the PMT formula computed the correct answer. Using the PMT value, interest rate, and loan term as arguments, the PV function should return the original loan amount as its computed result. If it does, that proves the periodic payment in cell B10 is correct. Otherwise, something is wrong.

Writing a PV function to compute the Beginning Balance:

1. If necessary, click cell **B16** to make it the active cell

2. Type the formula **=PV(InterestRate/12,LoanTerm*12,-PeriodicPayment)** and press **Enter.** Remember to not include any spaces in the formula. Excel displays $18,000

tip: *One of the tricky things about financial functions, something mentioned earlier, is the sign of the resulting number. A negative sign means the money is flowing out of your pocket, and a positive sign means the money is flowing into your pocket. Because you want a positive value for the loan balance, be sure to type a minus sign preceding PeriodicPayment.*

Because the present value matches the loan amount, the PMT function is correct. The present value of a series of mortgage payments should equal the loan amount, because it represents the current value of a loan—far less than its value in the future as it collects interest. Did you notice that Excel was clever enough to format the cell with a currency symbol and two decimal places? It realizes that financial functions deal in money and

FIGURE 6.23

PPMT function syntax

PPMT(*rate*, period #, *nperiod*, *presentvalue*, *futurevalue*)

- payment period number
- value of the loan today
- periodic interest rate
- number of periodic payments
- residual value of the loan at the end of the term (optional argument)

consequently provides a default format. While it is not the same as the Accounting format applied to other cells in the worksheet, you can change the formatting later.

Writing a PPMT Function

The amount of each loan payment that is applied to reduce the principal— eventually making it zero—varies throughout the term of the loan. For example, you will soon find out that the amount of the $559.91 monthly payment that goes toward paying off the loan (the principal) is $447.41 the first month. The remainder of the payment, $112.50, is the interest on $18,000 for one month. When the last payment is due, the amount of the loan payment going toward paying off the loan is $556.43, whereas only $3.48 is due in interest. Thus, over the term of a loan, the payment toward reducing the loan increases, and the payment toward interest decreases.

Excel provides the PPMT function to compute the amount of a fixed periodic payment that goes to reduce the principal. Another function, IPMT, computes the interest portion of a payment, and you will learn about it after you investigate the PPMT function.

The PPMT function requires four arguments: the periodic interest rate, the particular period this payment is for, the total number of payments, and the present value of the loan. The fourth required argument, present value of the loan, is the total amount that a series of future payments is worth now—the loan principal. When creating a series of these formulas in a loan amortization schedule, the only argument of the four that changes is the second one. For the first period payment, it is 1; for the second period payment, it is 2 (or references a cell containing 2), and so on. The general form of the PPMT function appears in Figure 6.23.

Jessica wants each row of the amortization schedule to display the portion of the $559.91 payment that goes to pay off the loan. You code the function next.

> *Writing a PPMT function to compute the principal reduction amount:*
>
> 1. Click cell **C16** to make it the active cell
>
> 2. Type **=PPMT(InterestRate/12,A16,LoanTerm*12,–LoanAmount)** and press **Enter.** Excel displays $447.41, which is the portion of the payment that reduces the principal this month

Be careful to place a minus sign just before typing LoanAmount in the fourth argument so Excel computes and displays a positive value.

Notice that Excel formats the cell to display the currency symbol and two decimal places. Recall that using a name is the same as using the absolute reference of the cell address. This is particularly important because you will copy this formula and others down through the 35 other rows of the loan amortization schedule. You want all cell references to point to the original interest rate, loan term, and loan amount values throughout the amortization schedule. Using names instead of cell addresses guarantees that Excel will not change the references or adjust them in any way. The only cell reference that Excel will adjust when the formula is copied is the second argument, A16. Because you want the second argument to reference each of the individual payment numbers in column A, allowing the reference to remain a relative reference is perfect. Excel will adjust that reference as it copies the formula down through the amortization schedule rows.

Writing a IPMT Function

Cell D16 will contain a formula that computes the amount of the payment that is applied to pay the current month's interest. As you read above, the interest payment varies each month, depending on the payment number. It is higher in the first payment than the last. You will use the IPMT (Interest Payment) function to compute the interest payment. With this first formula as a guide, you will copy it down through all 36 months in the schedule in later steps. The general form of the IPMT function is similar to PPMT. Simply use the same form as PPMT but substitute IPMT for the function name preceding the opening parenthesis starting the function list.

Writing an IPMT function to compute the period's interest:

1. Click cell **D16** to make it the active cell

2. Type
   =IPMT(InterestRate/12,A16,LoanTerm*12,–LoanAmount)
   and click the **Enter** button on the left end of the formula bar to complete the formula and keep cell D16 the active cell. Excel displays $112.50—the interest portion of the current payment (see Figure 6.24)

BUILDING TOTAL PRINCIPAL, TOTAL INTEREST, AND ENDING BALANCE FORMULAS

You have three formulas to build before the first row of the loan amortization schedule is complete. Once that line is done, the remaining 35 lines of the schedule will be simple to create. The Total Principal column holds a running sum of the payments to reduce the loan. The Total Interest column holds the sum of all the interest payments up to and including the current payment. In the last column is the Ending Balance. It is the amount of the principal left to pay. It is equal to the beginning balance for the month minus the Principal Paid amount. You will create these simple formulas in the next steps.

FIGURE 6.24

Worksheet with PPMT and IPMT functions

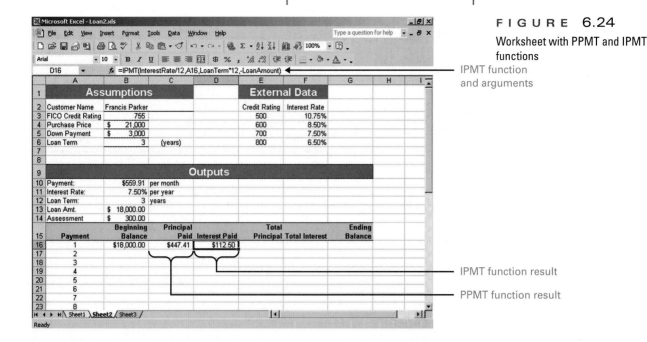

Writing Total Principal, Total Interest, and Ending Balance formulas:

1. Click cell **E16,** type **=C16**

2. Click cell **F16** and type **=D16**

3. Click cell **G16,** type **=B16-C16,** and press **Enter.** The value $17.552.59 appears and is the unpaid loan balance after the first payment is made

Cell E16 shows that of the $559.91 monthly payment, $112.50 is this month's interest payment and $447.41 reduces the loan balance. Each month, the sum of these two numbers is always the same—the monthly payment amount.

If creating formulas required you to write 36 rows of six formulas each, you'd be in for a lot of work. Thankfully, that is not the way worksheet products are designed. You can create a series of formulas that are unique and, often, clone them down or across worksheet cells to create an entire family of related but slightly different formulas. That is what you will do with the amortization schedule. Fortunately, the real work remaining in the schedule is to create a representative set of formulas in the second amortization schedule row and then clone the remaining 34. The first and second rows are unique and require hand crafting though.

Jessica tells you that you can create a unique formula for the beginning balance for the second payment and then clone the remainder of the first payment's formulas to the second payment row. With a few adjusting tweaks to selected second payment row formulas, you will have a model row that you can then copy to payment rows 3 through 36. Next, create the general formula for the beginning balance that will be correct for any payment row. The beginning balance of any payment period is the ending balance of the previous payment period. How simple!

EXCEL

> ### Writing a general-purpose Beginning Balance formula:
>
> 1. Click cell **B17**
>
> 2. Type **=G16,** and press **Enter.** The value $17552.59 appears in cell B17

The quickest way to create the formulas for the remainder of the second payment's row is to copy the corresponding formulas from the first payment's row and then make a couple of minor formula adjustments.

> ### Using the fill handle to clone and then adjust selected formulas for the second payment row:
>
> 1. Select the cell range **C16:G16**
>
> 2. Click the **fill handle,** drag the mouse down one row until the AutoFill outline highlights the cell range C17:G17, and then release the mouse. Excel copies the formulas and makes cell reference adjustments
>
> 3. Click cell **E17,** the Total Principal cell for the second payment, type **=C17+E16,** and press **Enter.** Excel displays $897.62—the total paid to reduce the loan after the customer makes the second loan payment
>
> 4. Click cell **F17,** the Total Interest cell for the second payment whose formula you are going to replace with a new one, type **=D17+F16,** and press **Enter.** Excel displays $222.20—the total interest paid after the customer makes the second loan payment (see Figure 6.25)

FIGURE 6.25

Amortization schedule with second payment's row completed

	A	B	C	D	E	F	G	H	I
1		**Assumptions**			**External Data**				
2	Customer Name	Francis Parker			Credit Rating	Interest Rate			
3	FICO Credit Rating	755			500	10.75%			
4	Purchase Price	$ 21,000			600	8.50%			
5	Down Payment	$ 3,000			700	7.50%			
6	Loan Term	3	(years)		800	6.50%			
7									
8									
9				**Outputs**					
10	Payment:	$559.91	per month						
11	Interest Rate:	7.50%	per year						
12	Loan Term:	3	years						
13	Loan Amt.	$ 18,000.00							
14	Assessment	$ 300.00							
15	Payment	Beginning Balance	Principal Paid	Interest Paid	Total Principal	Total Interest	Ending Balance		
16	1	$18,000.00	$447.41	$112.50	$447.41	$112.50	$17,552.59		
17	2	$17,552.59	$450.21	$109.70	$897.62	$222.20	$17,102.38		
18	3								
19	4								
20	5								
21	6								
22	7								
23	8								

H ◄ ► H\ Sheet1 \ **Sheet2** / Sheet3 /

Ready

Format the first row so that it displays accounting-style currency symbols and then format the second payment row so that it does not display currency symbols at all. Once the second row is formatted properly, you can copy it to the remaining 34 rows. Whenever you copy cells, Excel copies their formatting too. You will also format cell B10 containing the periodic payment to match formatting in other cells.

Formatting cells with the Format Painter:

1. Click cell **B13** containing the loan amount. Cell B13 has the format you want to duplicate in other cells

2. Double-click the **Format Painter** button on the Standard toolbar to copy the format of cell B13. Double-clicking the Format Painter button turns it on until you click it again to turn it off. This allows you to paint a cell's format onto more than one cell or cell range

3. Click cell **B10.** Excel changes the format so that the currency symbol is aligned on the left side of the cell

4. Click and drag the cell range **B16:G16** and release the mouse. The first row takes on the same currency format as cell B13 from which the format is copied: a left-aligned, accounting-style currency symbol and two decimal places

5. Click the **Format Painter** button to deactivate it. The Format Painter button pops out to indicate it is no longer active

6. Click and drag the cell range **B17:G17,** click **Format** on the menu bar, click **Cells,** and click the **Number** tab if necessary.

7. Click **Currency** in the Category list box, click the **Decimal places spinner control** until it displays 2, and click the **Symbol list box** and click **None**

8. Click **OK** to finalize your decisions and close the Format Cells dialog box. Excel displays numbers in row 17 whose formats match those in row 16 except that the currency symbol is omitted (see Figure 6.26).

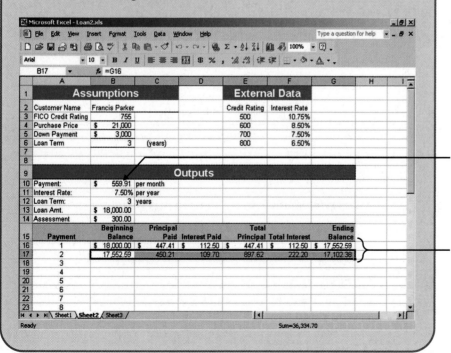

FIGURE 6.26

Formatted rows of the amortization schedule

modified formatting

formatted amortization schedule rows

The result of formatting the first two payment rows is that the first payment row displays currency symbols and the second row does not. This is a format many people prefer.

Jessica examines your results and comments that the only work left to complete the loan amortization schedule is to copy row 17 to rows 18 through 51. Because you carefully crafted formulas for the second payment row (row 17), you can copy those formulas to the remaining 34 rows of the amortization schedule and make no further changes. Excel will take care of the rest by making appropriate cell reference adjustments.

USING AUTOFILL TO COMPLETE A SERIES OF RELATED FORMULAS

Completing the amortization schedule will be surprisingly simple. Because you have created a model row—row 17—whose formulas contain cell references that use both absolute references (names) and relative references in the appropriate way, the row is a model row for the remaining rows. A **model row** contains distinct formulas that you can copy to other rows and not have to modify any copied cell formulas afterwards.

You are ready to copy row 17 to rows 18 through 51.

Using the fill handle to copy formulas and complete the loan amortization schedule:

1. If necessary, select the cell range **B17:G17**

2. Move the mouse to the fill handle near the lower-right corner of cell **G17.** The mouse pointer changes to a small plus symbol ⊞

3. Click the mouse and slowly drag the fill handle down through row 51 so that Excel highlights the range **B17:G51** and then release the mouse. Excel copies the formulas from cells B17 through G17 to the highlighted cell range, adjusts cell references in copied formulas, displays the AutoFill Options smart tag, and displays the completed loan amortization schedule (see Figure 6.27)

tip: *If you fill up too few rows, click and drag the fill handle to fill the remaining rows of the amortization schedule. If you fill up too many rows, delete the extra rows*

4. Scroll down the worksheet until you reach row 51. Notice that the final loan payment reduces the ending balance to zero. In other words, the last payment is just enough to pay off the remaining balance of $556.43 and pay the last month's interest of $3.48.

5. Click **Ctrl+Home** to deselect the cell range and make cell A1 active

6. Click **Save** button on the Standard toolbar to save the **Loan2.xls** workbook and preserve the work you completed in this session

7. Click **File** on the menu bar and then click **Close** to close the workbook

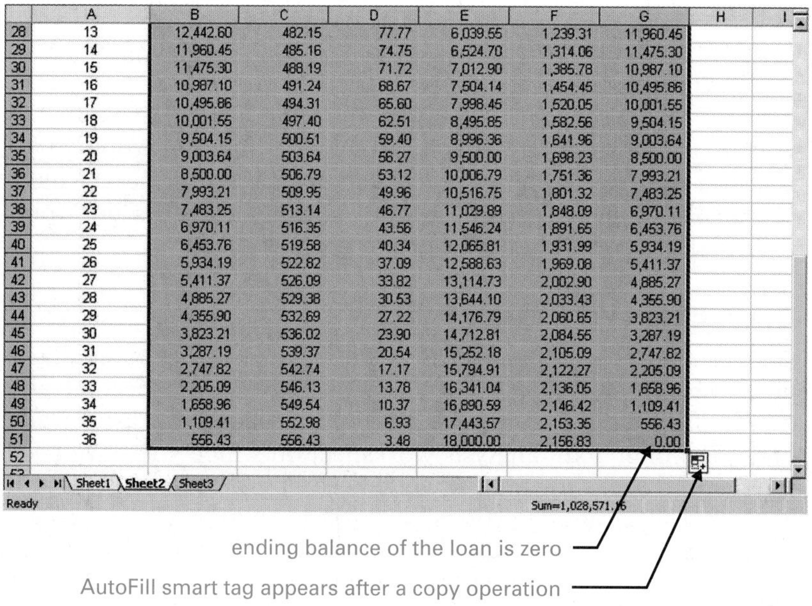

FIGURE 6.27
Completed amortization schedule

	A	B	C	D	E	F	G	H	I
28	13	12,442.60	482.15	77.77	6,039.55	1,239.31	11,960.45		
29	14	11,960.45	485.16	74.75	6,524.70	1,314.06	11,475.30		
30	15	11,475.30	488.19	71.72	7,012.90	1,385.78	10,987.10		
31	16	10,987.10	491.24	68.67	7,504.14	1,454.45	10,495.86		
32	17	10,495.86	494.31	65.60	7,998.45	1,520.05	10,001.55		
33	18	10,001.55	497.40	62.51	8,495.85	1,582.56	9,504.15		
34	19	9,504.15	500.51	59.40	8,996.36	1,641.96	9,003.64		
35	20	9,003.64	503.64	56.27	9,500.00	1,698.23	8,500.00		
36	21	8,500.00	506.79	53.12	10,006.79	1,751.36	7,993.21		
37	22	7,993.21	509.95	49.96	10,516.75	1,801.32	7,483.25		
38	23	7,483.25	513.14	46.77	11,029.89	1,848.09	6,970.11		
39	24	6,970.11	516.35	43.56	11,546.24	1,891.65	6,453.76		
40	25	6,453.76	519.58	40.34	12,065.81	1,931.99	5,934.19		
41	26	5,934.19	522.82	37.09	12,588.63	1,969.08	5,411.37		
42	27	5,411.37	526.09	33.82	13,114.73	2,002.90	4,885.27		
43	28	4,885.27	529.38	30.53	13,644.10	2,033.43	4,355.90		
44	29	4,355.90	532.69	27.22	14,176.79	2,060.65	3,823.21		
45	30	3,823.21	536.02	23.90	14,712.81	2,084.55	3,287.19		
46	31	3,287.19	539.37	20.54	15,252.18	2,105.09	2,747.82		
47	32	2,747.82	542.74	17.17	15,794.91	2,122.27	2,205.09		
48	33	2,205.09	546.13	13.78	16,341.04	2,136.05	1,658.96		
49	34	1,658.96	549.54	10.37	16,890.59	2,146.42	1,109.41		
50	35	1,109.41	552.98	6.93	17,443.57	2,153.35	556.43		
51	36	556.43	556.43	3.48	18,000.00	2,156.83	0.00		
52									

H ◄ ► ►I \ Sheet1 \ **Sheet2** \ Sheet3 /

Ready   Sum=1,028,571.06

ending balance of the loan is zero

AutoFill smart tag appears after a copy operation

You have completed a lot of work on the loan amortization workbook and learned about several more important financial functions. In the next section, you will complete the loan analysis worksheet by renaming worksheets, adding and deleting worksheets, using date functions, and protecting worksheet cells and worksheets.

making the grade   SESSION 6.2

1. The process of distributing periodic payments over the life of a loan is called _____.

2. The Excel built-in function that computes the periodic payment is called _____.

3. A periodic payment includes money to repay the loan and money for _____ on the outstanding loan amount.

4. The _____ function computes today's value of a future series of cash flows. Today's value of the cash flow is called its _____ value.

5. Open the worksheet **Loan2.xls** and save it as **Loan22.xls.** Then make the following changes to it. Click **B2** and type **Alice Honeycutt.** Select the cell range **B3:B5,** press the **Delete** key to delete the data in the range. With the cell range still selected, type the following values and press the **Enter** key after you type each value: **500, 15500, 4000.** Click and drag the cell range **F3:F6.** Change the interest rates in cells F3 through F6 to the following values, respectively: **12%, 10%, 8%,** and **6%.** (Press **Enter** after typing each entry to move to the next cell in the range.) Click the **Sheet1** sheet tab, click cell **B5,** and type your name. Click cell **D7,** type today's date (to indicate a third modification date), and press **Enter.** Save the workbook, print both worksheets, and exit Excel.

SESSION 6.3 MAINTAINING AND PROTECTING WORKSHEETS AND USING DATE FUNCTIONS

In this session, you will learn about the NOW date function. You will rename worksheet tabs and learn how to delete unneeded worksheets from a workbook. Finally, you will learn how to protect worksheet cells and worksheets so that selected cells cannot be deleted or modified.

MAINTAINING WORKSHEETS

Jessica notices that the loan analysis workbook has three worksheets called Sheet1, Sheet2, and Sheet3. She clicks the Sheet1 worksheet tab and sees that it contains documentation. Clicking the Sheet2 worksheet tab, Jessica opens the main loan analysis worksheet on which you have been working. When she clicks the Sheet3 worksheet tab, she comments that it is an empty worksheet and questions why you have included it. You explain to her that you have set up Excel so that it automatically creates three worksheets whenever you create a new workbook. Jessica asks how you control the number of worksheets. First, save your workbook under a new name to preserve the work you finished in Session 6.2.

Save the Loan2 workbook under a new name, Loan3.xls:

1. Open the workbook **Loan2.xls**

2. Click **File** on the menu bar, click **Save As,** type **Loan3** in the File name text box, and click the **Save** button. Excel saves the workbook under its new name

---

Setting the Number of Worksheets Created for a New Workbook

You explain to Jessica that by setting a value in an Excel menu, you set the number of worksheets that Excel creates when you click New in the File menu, or click the Blank Workbook entry in the task pane, or click the New button on the Standard toolbar. Jessica asks you to set the default number of worksheets to two so that each new workbook you create on your computer will contain two worksheets. You explain to Jessica that changing the number of worksheets does not alter any open worksheets in any way.

Setting the number of worksheets in a new workbook:

1. With Excel active, click **Tools** on the menu bar, click **Options** to open the Options dialog box, and then click the **General** tab to display the general Excel settings

2. Drag the mouse across the value currently in the **Sheets in new workbook** spin control, and then type **2** (see Figure 6.28)

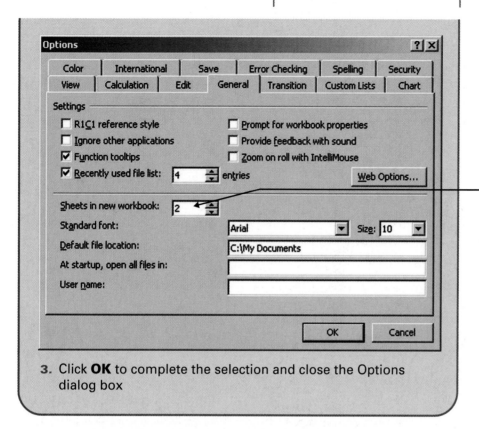

FIGURE 6.28

Setting the number of worksheets in a new workbook

number of sheets created in a new workbook

3. Click **OK** to complete the selection and close the Options dialog box

Test the new setting by creating a new workbook. When you create a new workbook, Excel will create only two worksheets.

Testing the new worksheet number setting:

1. Click the **New** button on the Standard toolbar to create a new workbook. Notice that the new workbook has two worksheets, Sheet1 and Sheet2

2. Click **File** on the menu bar and then click **Close** to erase the newly created workbook. The loan analysis workbook reappears

Deleting, Adding, and Moving Worksheets

Now that you have experimented with setting the number of worksheets Excel creates in a new workbook, you still have the extra worksheet, Sheet3, in the loan analysis workbook. Jessica asks you to delete that empty worksheet.

task reference

Deleting a Worksheet from a Workbook

- Right-click the worksheet tab of the worksheet you want to delete

- Click **Delete** on the shortcut menu

EXCEL

FIGURE 6.29

Sheet tab shortcut menu

Deleting a worksheet from a workbook:

1. Right-click the **Sheet3** worksheet tab. A shortcut menu appears (see Figure 6.29)

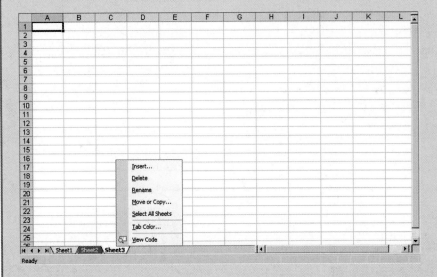

2. Click **Delete** to remove the worksheet from the workbook. Excel deletes Sheet3 and displays Sheet2

tip: *If Excel displays the warning message "Data may exist in the sheet(s) selected for deletion. To permanently delete the data, press Delete," that means you typed a value on the empty worksheet Sheet3 at some point. Click **Delete** to delete the worksheet.*

Adding a worksheet to an existing workbook is equally easy.

task reference

Adding a Worksheet to a Workbook

- Click the worksheet tab before which you want to add a worksheet
- Click **Insert** on the menu bar and then click **Worksheet**

Adding a worksheet to a workbook:

1. Click **Sheet2,** if necessary, to make that worksheet active

2. Click **Insert** on the menu bar and then click **Worksheet.** Excel inserts a worksheet called Sheet3 ahead of Sheet2, the previously active worksheet, and makes Sheet3 the active worksheet (see Figure 6.30)

FIGURE 6.30

Inserting a new worksheet

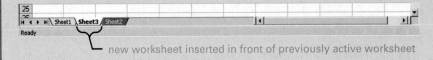

new worksheet inserted in front of previously active worksheet

tip: *If you have added worksheets to this workbook previously, Excel will name the newly inserted worksheet with a higher number (Sheet4 or Sheet8, for example), depending on the number of worksheets you may have already added.*

If you want to change the order of worksheets in a workbook, simply move a worksheet to a new position by dragging its worksheet tab.

---

task reference

Moving a Worksheet to a New Position Within a Workbook

- Click the worksheet tab of the worksheet you want to move

- Drag the worksheet to its new position indicated by the down-pointing arrow and release the mouse

---

Moving a worksheet within a workbook:

1. If necessary, click the **Sheet3** worksheet tab to make the worksheet active

2. Click and drag the **Sheet3** worksheet tab to the right of the sheet tab labeled Sheet2 (see Figure 6.31)

arrow indicates proposed new location of the page

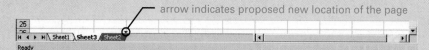

3. Release the mouse to drop the sheet into its new location following Sheet2

tip: *If Sheet3 does not change positions, try it again. Be sure to watch the down-pointing arrow and release the mouse only when the arrow is on the right end of Sheet2. That indicates the position of the worksheet if you release the mouse.*

FIGURE 6.31

Dragging a sheet to its new position

Well, your workbook is back where it started—with an extraneous worksheet called Sheet3. Go ahead and delete Sheet3, the empty worksheet, to remove it once and for all from the loan analysis worksheet.

Deleting Sheet3 again:

1. Right-click the **Sheet3** worksheet tab

2. Click **Delete** to remove the worksheet from the workbook

Renaming Worksheets

Jessica is happy that you eliminated the extra worksheet from the workbook. Now she would like you to give the worksheets more meaningful names. She would like you to rename Sheet1 to Documentation to reflect its purpose. She wants you to rename the second sheet, which contains the bulk of the loan analysis information, to Loan Analysis.

task reference

Renaming a Worksheet

- Right-click the worksheet tab of the worksheet you want to rename
- Click **Rename** on the shortcut menu
- Type the new worksheet name and press **Enter**

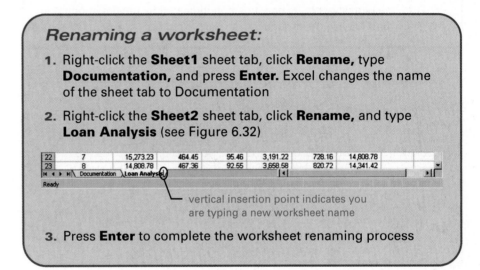

FIGURE 6.32

Renaming a worksheet

Renaming a worksheet:

1. Right-click the **Sheet1** sheet tab, click **Rename,** type **Documentation,** and press **Enter.** Excel changes the name of the sheet tab to Documentation

2. Right-click the **Sheet2** sheet tab, click **Rename,** and type **Loan Analysis** (see Figure 6.32)

vertical insertion point indicates you are typing a new worksheet name

3. Press **Enter** to complete the worksheet renaming process

The loan analysis worksheet is in great shape. There are only a few more details to attend to before calling the workbook complete.

WORKING WITH DATE FUNCTIONS

Excel has 14 date and time functions available. When you enter a date manually, you simply type it in one of several acceptable forms. Excel recognizes that the information is a date and stores it in a special form. For example, if you type into a cell *10/17/2003* without an equal sign preceding it, Excel assumes you are entering the date October 17, 2003 and stores the date in a special date-valued form. The preceding form is called a **_date constant._** Similarly, you can type *October 17, 2003* and Excel will recognize the entry as a date and store it in the same, date-valued form. However, Excel recognizes *=10/17/2003* as an expression whose value is 0.000294, rounded to six decimal places.

There are occasions when you cannot or do not want to enter a fixed date either because it is unknown at the time or it varies with time. For instance, you might want to label a worksheet with the current date. If you type 6/14/2003 into a worksheet cell, the date is static—it never changes. If you want a date that is always current, you can use the Excel function NOW.

Jessica wants you to document the worksheet by adding two dates to the Outputs section of the worksheet: the date that the customer applied for the loan (the application date) and the current date each time the worksheet is printed. The former date is simply a date-valued expression such as 10/17/2003 whereas the latter date uses the NOW function to pick up the current date from the computer's internal clock/calendar. The loan application date requires a label as well as the date constant. Because the application date is an input value, you will place it in the Assumptions section.

Entering a date constant into a worksheet cell:

1. Click cell **A7**, type **Application Date,** and press **Enter.** Because you want to place an underline in cell B7 displaying the application date, you can copy the format from an existing cell, B6

2. Click cell **B6,** click the **Format Painter** button on the Standard toolbar, and click cell **B7.** Excel copies the format from cell B6 to cell B7. An underline displays in cell B7

tip: *If you accidentally paint the format on the wrong cell, simply click Undo Paste Special in the Edit menu to reverse the last action.*

3. With B7 active, type **6/14/2003** and press **Enter.** Excel displays the date in cell B7. The underline in cell B7 emphasizes that it contains an input value—something an employee must type

4. If cell B7 displays a two-digit year, then execute step 5. If cell B7 displays a four-digit date, then skip step 5

tip: *If the date in cell B7 displays only two digits for the year, then the default date set for your machine may be set to show two years. You can change the date format by executing step 5.*

5. Click cell **B7,** click **Format** on the menu bar, click **Cells,** click the **Number** tab, click **Date** in the Category list, scroll the Type list box until you locate the example date format 3/14/2001, click **3/14/2001,** and click **OK** to format cell B7 so it displays a four-digit year (see Figure 6.33)

	A	B	C	D	E	F	G	H	I
1		**Assumptions**				**External Data**			
2	Customer Name	Francis Parker			Credit Rating	Interest Rate			
3	FICO Credit Rating	755			500	10.75%			
4	Purchase Price	$ 21,000			600	8.50%			
5	Down Payment	$ 3,000			700	7.50%			
6	Loan Term	3	(years)		800	6.50%			
7	Application Date	6/14/2003							
8									
9			**Outputs**						
10	Payment:	$ 559.91	per month						
11	Interest Rate:	7.50%	per year						
12	Loan Term:	3	years						
13	Loan Amt.	$ 18,000.00							
14	Assessment	$ 300.00							
15	Payment	Beginning Balance	Principal Paid	Interest Paid	Total Principal	Total Interest		Ending Balance	
16	1	$ 18,000.00	$ 447.41	$ 112.50	$ 447.41	$ 112.50	$ 17,552.59		
17	2	17,552.59	450.21	109.70	897.62	222.20	17,102.38		
18	3	17,102.38	453.02	106.89	1,350.64	329.09	16,649.36		
19	4	16,649.36	455.85	104.06	1,806.50	433.15	16,193.50		
20	5	16,193.50	458.70	101.21	2,265.20	534.36	15,734.80		
21	6	15,734.80	461.57	98.34	2,726.77	632.70	15,273.23		
22	7	15,273.23	464.45	95.46	3,191.22	728.16	14,808.78		
23	8	14,808.78	467.36	92.55	3,658.58	820.72	14,341.42		

formatted date constant

Documentation \ Loan Analysis /

Ready

FIGURE 6.33
Entering a date constant

Using the NOW Function

Several date functions examine your computer's clock to determine the current date and time. The NOW function is the most commonly used of these functions. It is one of the Excel functions that has no arguments, but you must be sure to write it with both the opening and closing parentheses immediately following its name. Its form is simply

NOW()

If you forget the parentheses and type, instead, *=NOW* in a cell, Excel will generate and display the error message "#NAME?" The error message occurs because Excel thinks you are using a name called NOW, but you have not created that name. If you omit the pair of parentheses when you type the NOW function, simply edit the cell and include the opening and closing parentheses side by side.

Jessica wants the current date displayed in the Outputs section of the worksheet. The current date is a formula, not a value that a worksheet user would type.

Writing the NOW function:

1. Click cell **F10,** type **Today's Date:** and then press the **Tab** key

2. In cell G10, type **=NOW()** and press **Enter.** Depending on the exact width of column G, cell G10 either displays pound signs (#) or the date and time side by side in the cell

---

Regardless of which form displays in your worksheet (pound signs or the date and time), you will format the cell so that it displays the date but not the time in the next set of steps.

Formatting Date-Valued Cells

By default, the NOW function determines and displays both the current date and the current time. Jessica tells you that the time is unnecessary and distracting. She asks you to format the cell so that it displays the current date and omits the current time. To display the date only, you simply use one of the available date formats to exclude the time of day.

Formatting a date-valued cell to display only the date:

1. Right-click cell **G10.** A shortcut menu appears

2. Click **Format Cells** on the shortcut menu

3. If necessary, click the **Number** tab

4. Click **Date** in the Category list box,

5. Scroll the Type list to locate the example format 3/14/01, and click **3/14/01** in the Type list box (see Figure 6.34)

---

*another*way

. . . to Display the Format Cells Dialog Box

Right-click the cell or cell range to be formatted

Click **Format Cells** in the shortcut menu

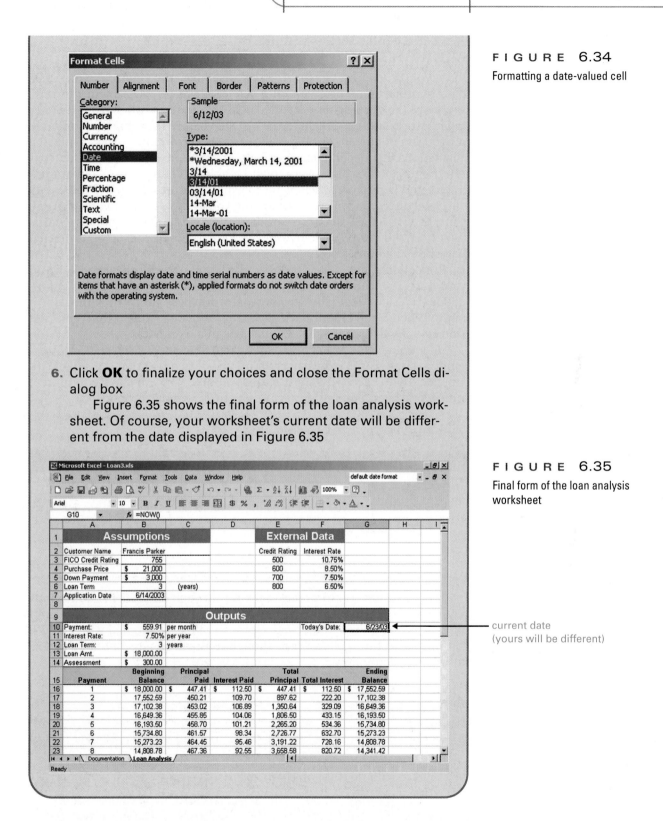

FIGURE 6.34
Formatting a date-valued cell

FIGURE 6.35
Final form of the loan analysis worksheet

current date
(yours will be different)

6. Click **OK** to finalize your choices and close the Format Cells dialog box

Figure 6.35 shows the final form of the loan analysis worksheet. Of course, your worksheet's current date will be different from the date displayed in Figure 6.35

You show your final design to Jessica. After a few quiet moments, Jessica asks you what would happen if a salesperson were to type in the Outputs section. Jessica suggests that you protect the worksheet. She asks you to allow data entry only in the Assumptions area of the worksheet.

PROTECTING WORKSHEET CELLS AND WORKSHEETS

When you *protect* a worksheet, Excel disallows any changes to any cells that are protected. A user cannot delete columns or rows, change format, or change the contents of protected cells. Normally, a worksheet designer applies worksheet protection as the last step before releasing the workbook to the users or customers. Typically, worksheet formulas—cells displaying calculations that depend on other cells—receive protection. Cells that contain input values, which users must be able to change, must remain unprotected. Therefore you will want to explicitly unprotect those cells.

Excel offers many features allowing you to protect your work. You can protect a worksheet, an entire workbook, individual cells, graphics, charts, scenarios, and more. You can allow specific types of editing on protected worksheets and other objects.

Protection is a two-step process. First, you unlock cells for which you want users to be able to type in new data. Second, you enforce Excel protection rules by explicitly turning on worksheet protection through a menu. When a cell is *unlocked,* it is not protected. Only locked cells are protected. By default, Excel locks *all* cells in a workbook.

After you enable protection, you cannot change a locked cell. If you attempt to do so, Excel issues an error message. As protection is available independently to each worksheet in a workbook, you can choose to protect some worksheets and not protect others in the same workbook.

Locking Worksheet Cells

---

task reference

Locking Cells

- Select the cells you want to be unprotected (unlocked)

- Click **Format,** click **Cells,** and then click the **Protection** tab

- Click the **Locked** check box to clear its checkmark and click **OK**

Jessica wants you to unlock cells B2 through B7 in the Assumptions section so that anyone can type in new values in the assumptions area. All other cells should remain locked. Because cell B2 is merged with cell C2, you must select the cell range as though it were two noncontiguous areas in the steps that follow.

Unlocking cells:

1. Click cell **B2.** Excel highlights the merged cell pair, B2:C2

2. Press and hold the **Ctrl** key as you select the cell range **B3:B7,** release the mouse, and release the **Ctrl** key

3. Click **Format** on the menu bar, click **Cells** to open the Format Cells dialog box, and then click the **Protection** tab. Notice that the Locked check box contains a checkmark. By default, all workbook cells are locked (see Figure 6.36)

4. Click the **Locked** check box to clear it

5. Click **OK** to close the Format Cells dialog box

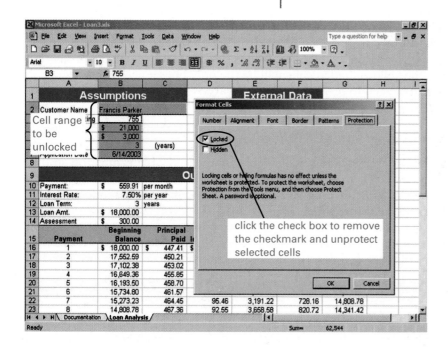

FIGURE 6.36
Locked is the default for all cells

Although nothing appears to happen to the worksheet, you have re-moved the locks on the six input cells. Excel does not provide any visual on-screen clues that indicate which cells are locked and which are not. It is a good idea to provide the user with a hint by formatting unlocked cells with a background color or a border color. You do that next.

Color-coding unlocked (input) cells:

1. With cells B2:C2 and B3:B7 still selected, click the **Format** on the menu bar, click **Cells,** and click the **Patterns** tab

2. Click the **Yellow** color square (fourth row from the top, third column), and click **OK**

3. Click any cell to deselect the cell range (see Figure 6.37)

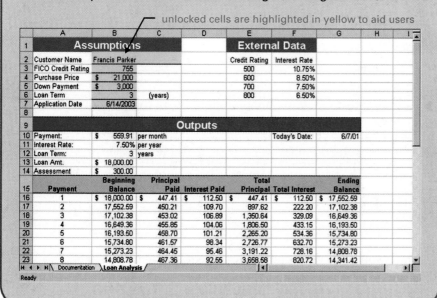

FIGURE 6.37
Applying color to unlocked cells

EXCEL

The yellow color reminds users that the cells are unlocked and available for input. Anyone wishing to use the worksheet will be alerted to the cells by their vibrant color. Later in this session, you will enable protection so that the yellow-shaded cells will be the only ones a user can select.

The next step to protect the Loan Analysis worksheet is to tell Excel to enforce worksheet cell protection.

Enabling Worksheet Protection

Once you have unlocked selected cells, you can enable protection so that every locked cell is protected from modification. In addition, you will set a parameter so that the only cells that the user can click are unlocked cells in the protected worksheet. This means that if you later choose to make changes to your worksheet, you will have to turn off worksheet protection before making those modifications. If you do so, remember to enable protection again before releasing the modified worksheet for general use.

---

task reference

Enabling Worksheet Protection

- Click **Tools,** point to **Protection,** and click **Protect Sheet**

- Optionally enter (and remember) a password twice and click **OK**

Even though you have unlocked selected cells, anyone who opens the workbook can make changes to any cell in the Loan Analysis worksheet. You must tell Excel to enforce the protection by enabling protection for the Loan Analysis worksheet. Each worksheet in a workbook is independently protected, so you can enable protection for one or more worksheets in a given workbook and leave other worksheets unprotected in the same workbook. For example, no worksheet protection is enabled for the Documentation worksheet, even though all of its cells are locked (by default). A user can change any cell in the Documentation worksheet, but not all cells in the Loan Analysis worksheet. Excel also provides password protection so that anyone attempting to reverse worksheet-enabled protection must know the password you assigned before he or she can proceed to disable worksheet protection.

Enabling protection:

1. Click **Tools** on the menu bar, point to **Protection,** and click **Protect Sheet.** The Protect Sheet dialog box appears (see Figure 6.38). Several detailed options, in the form of checkboxes, are available. Two are checked by default. You can assign a password so that a password is required to make protection changes

2. Click **OK.** If you had entered a password, a Confirm Password dialog box appears in which you retype the password to confirm it

Once you have protected a worksheet, you can press the Tab key to move between unprotected cells. In other words, Excel will not allow a locked cell to become active. Try it.

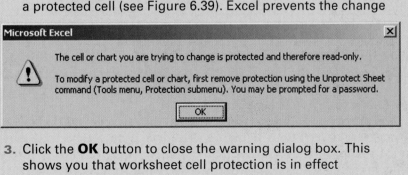

F I G U R E   6.38
Protect Sheet dialog box

type an optional password to prevent unauthorized protection changes

Using the Tab key to move between unlocked cells:

1. Click cell **B3,** one of the unlocked cells, and press **Tab.** Cell B4 becomes active

2. Press the **Tab** key four more times, slowly. Notice that cells B4, B5, B6, B7, and then B2/B3 become active, in turn. That's a handy feature of unlocked cells in protected worksheets

What happens when you try to change a locked cell?

Testing worksheet protection:

1. Click cell **B10,** one of the protected cells in the Outputs section

2. Type **888.** The moment you type the first character, a warning dialog box appears indicating that you are attempting to alter a protected cell (see Figure 6.39). Excel prevents the change

F I G U R E   6.39
Testing worksheet protection

Microsoft Excel

The cell or chart you are trying to change is protected and therefore read-only.

To modify a protected cell or chart, first remove protection using the Unprotect Sheet command (Tools menu, Protection submenu). You may be prompted for a password.

OK

3. Click the **OK** button to close the warning dialog box. This shows you that worksheet cell protection is in effect

A better protection mechanism would be one in which the end user never has to encounter the seemingly intimidating protection message shown in Figure 6.39. Excel provides a way to prevent a user from making

EXCEL

a locked cell active. When that particular protection feature is enforced, clicking a locked cell has no effect. The active cell cannot be changed. Only unlocked cells are accessible and protection error messages will not occur as a result. You fine tune your worksheet protection next.

Preventing users from selecting locked cells:

1. Click cell **B10** to make it active. Keep your eye on the active cell indicator when you complete these steps

2. Click **Tools** on the menu bar, point to **Protection,** and click **Unprotect Sheet**

3. Click **Tools** on the menu bar, point to **Protection,** and click **Protect Sheet.** The Protect Sheet dialog box opens (see Figure 6.38)

4. Click the **Select locked cells** check box to clear its check mark (see Figure 6.40)

FIGURE 6.40

Protecting locked cells from being selected

clear this check box to prevent locked cells from being selected

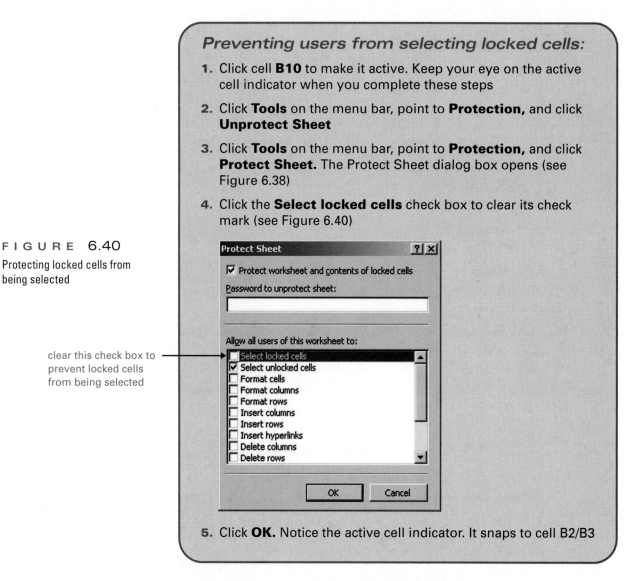

5. Click **OK.** Notice the active cell indicator. It snaps to cell B2/B3

Try clicking any cell except the one highlighted in yellow. You cannot make any other cell active. It is as though there is a protective invisible shield covering all the cells except the ones that are unlocked. This type of protection prevents users from even accessing parts of a worksheet where they cannot alter a cell's contents.

You are happy with your work. You tell the salespersons that changing the loan term in cell B6 will require assistance from you because the loan amortization schedule must be recreated for longer or shorter terms—a design decision made earlier. Now that the workbook is complete, save it.

Saving the completed loan analysis workbook:

1. Click the **Documentation** worksheet tab, click cell **B5,** and then type your first and last names

2. Click cell **B3** and type the current date

3. Click cell **E3,** type **=NOW()**

4. Format cell E3 to display only the date, not the date and the time, showing a four-digit year

5. Press **Ctrl+Home** to make A1 the active cell

6. Click the Standard toolbar **Save** button to save the completed workbook **Loan3.xls**

7. Click **File** on the menu bar, click **Print,** click the **Entire workbook** option button, and click **OK** to print both worksheets

8. Click **File** on the menu bar and then click **Exit** to close Excel

making the grade

SESSION 6.3

1. The _____ function returns the current date and time.

2. By default, all workbook cells are _____ and those cells cannot be modified in any way as long as you enable worksheet protection.

3. To prevent users from unprotecting worksheets, you can type an optional _____.

4. Press the _____ key to move from one unlocked cell to another in a protected worksheet.

5. Open the worksheet **Loan3.xls** and save it as **Loan33.xls.** Then make the following changes to it. First, disable worksheet protection: Click **Tools** on the menu bar, point to **Protection,** and click **Unprotect Sheet.** Unlock cell range **F3:F6.** Apply to cell range F3:F6 the same yellow background color you applied for the other unlocked cells. Open the Protect Sheet dialog box to apply worksheet protection to the Loan Analysis worksheet, but check the Select locked cells so that users can select any cell in the worksheet. Enter the password **sherlock** in the *Password to unprotect sheet* text box. Click OK to open the Confirm Password dialog box and type **sherlock** again in the text box. Then click OK to close the Confirm Password and Protect Sheet dialog boxes. Unprotect the worksheet again by clicking Tools, pointing to Protection, and clicking Unprotect Sheet. Type an incorrect password in the Unprotect Sheet dialog box and click OK. Unprotect the worksheet again, but supply the correct password when prompted. Print both worksheets, save the workbook again, and then exit Excel.

SESSION 6.4 SUMMARY

Excel functions are built-in tools that perform calculations quickly and easily. Excel's over 320 functions are grouped by type. Most Excel functions have one or more arguments enclosed in parentheses following the function name. A select few functions have no arguments, but you must write them with the opening and closing parentheses. Otherwise, Excel will mistake the function for a name. A function operates on the input values and expressions in its argument list enclosed in parentheses and it returns a single value. Most functions have positional arguments that must be arranged in a particular order.

It is often helpful to arrange worksheets into distinct input (or assumptions) and output sections so worksheet users are clear about where worksheet users enter data and where they see results. Creating worksheets used by others often requires that you provide built-in tests for input data to ensure that they are reasonable and within range. Excel's data validation provides automatic input data checking and allows you to specify the range of allowed values in an input value, an input (help) message, and an error message. When a user enters an incorrect value into a cell, data validation can allow the error to stand or disallow its entry completely and force the user to re-enter correct data.

Names allow you to assign a name to a cell or range of cells. They have an advantage over cell references because you can assign a meaningful and memorable name; you can remember names as you write expressions referencing the named cells. Secondly, names function as absolute cell references, making it simpler to copy formulas that reference named ranges.

The IF function allows you to create alternative expressions based on a condition. IF evaluates a condition, which is its first argument, and calculates and displays one expression's value if the condition is true or displays the other expression's value if the condition is false.

VLOOKUP is one of several index functions that does a table search with a search value and returns an answer from the table lookup operation. The two most popular lookup functions are VLOOKUP and HLOOKUP. Both are identical in function except for the arrangement of the lookup table—one uses a vertical lookup table and the other uses a horizontal lookup table.

Financial functions including PMT, PPMT, IPMT, and PV are all related. Each function operates on the theory of the time value of money: Money today is worth more than the same amount of money tomorrow. PMT computes a periodic payment given the interest rate, principal amount, and period. PPMT and IPMT compute the amount of the periodic payment for a particular period that pays off the principal (PPMT) and the amount that pays the interest due on the principal (IPMT). PV, or present value, computes today's value of a future steady stream of cash flows.

Worksheet date functions work with date-valued cells. The NOW function displays the current date and time. Special formats are available for formatting the NOW cell to display various forms of the date or to display various forms of the time. NOW obtains its information from the system clock, which also contains a calendar.

Providing worksheet cell protection is vital when you are sharing a worksheet with others. By default, all worksheet cells are locked. Protection is not enforced, however, until you turn on protection by executing the command Protect Worksheet found in the Tools menu. To allow users to enter data into unprotected cells, you must unlock them. All protected cells display an error message when a user attempts to alter them in any way. Check the I-Series Web site for more information at www.mhhe.com/i-series.

MOUS OBJECTIVES SUMMARY

- Provide data validation for selected worksheet cells—MOUS Ex2002-7-4
- Define and use names in functions in place of cell references—MOUS Ex2002-4-1
- Write financial functions including PV, PMT, PPMT, and IPMT—MOUS Ex2002-5-2
- Learn about index functions and write the index function VLOOKUP—MOUS Ex2002-4-2
- Write and apply the NOW date function—MOUS Ex2002-5-2
- Add, delete, move, and rename worksheets—MOUS Ex2002-4-1, MOUS Ex2002-4-2
- Apply worksheet protection—MOUS Ex2002-9-1

task reference roundup

Task	Page #	Preferred Method
Naming a Cell or Cell Range	EX 6.14	• Select the cell or cell range you want to name
		• Click the **Name box** in the formula bar
		• Type the name and press **Enter**
Deleting a Name	EX 6.17	• Click **Insert,** point to **Name,** and then click the **Define** button
		• Click the name in the *Names in workbook* list that you want to delete
		• Click the **Delete** button and then click the **OK** button
Using the VLOOKUP Function	EX 6.22	• Create a lookup table and sort the table in ascending order by the leftmost column
		• Place in columns to the right of the search columns values you want to return as answers
		• Write a VLOOKUP function referencing a cell containing the lookup value, the lookup table, and the column containing the answer
Deleting a Worksheet from a Workbook	EX 6.39	• Right-click the worksheet tab of the worksheet you want to delete
		• Click **Delete** on the shortcut menu
Adding a Worksheet to a Workbook	EX 6.40	• Click the worksheet tab before which you want to add a worksheet
		• Click **Insert** on the menu bar and then click **Worksheet**
Moving a Worksheet to a New Position Within a Workbook	EX 6.41	• Click the worksheet tab of the worksheet you want to move
		• Drag the worksheet to its new position indicated by the down-pointing arrow and release the mouse
Renaming a Worksheet	EX 6.42	• Double-click the worksheet tab of the worksheet you want to rename

EXCEL

task reference roundup

Task	Page #	Preferred Method
		• Type the new worksheet name and press **Enter**
Locking Cells	EX 6.46	• Select the cells you want to be unprotected (unlocked)
		• Click **Format**, click **Cells**, and then click the **Protection** tab
		• Click **Locked** check box to clear its checkmark and click **OK**
Enabling Worksheet Protection	EX 6.48	• Click **Tools**, point to **Protection**, and click **Protect Sheet**
		• Optionally enter (and remember) a password twice and click **OK**

CROSSWORD PUZZLE

Across

1. An error in which a value is either too large or too small
4. An equation that compares two values is a _____ test
6. An operator that compares two parts of a formula
7. A proposed worksheet model
9. The _____ value of money states that $10 today is worth more than $10 tomorrow
10. One class of functions, called _____ functions, searches a table and returns a value
13. An amortization _____ lists the monthly payment and the amount of payment applied to pay down a loan
14. A constant such as 10/14/02 is formated as what?

Down

2. _____ is the process of distrubuting periodic payments over the life of a loan
3. Arguments that must be written in a special order are called _____ arguments
5. A list of zero or more items enclosed in parentheses following a function name
8. When you click _____ Sheet, Excel enforces worksheet protection
11. _____ cells that you do not want Excel to protect when you apply worksheet protection
12. The lookup _____ is used to search a table for a match
15. VLOOKUP searches a _____ table for a match

FILL-IN

1. It is convenient to divide a worksheet into a(n) _____ section and an output section.

2. Use data _____ to ensure that a worksheet user enters an appropriate value into a cell or cell range.

3. A _____ name acts like an absolute cell reference when you copy a formula containing it to other cells.

4. The _____ function has three arguments: a conditional expression and two alternative expressions. One of the expressions displays if the condition is true, and the other displays otherwise.

5. Some functions have no arguments. An example is the _____ function, which returns the date and time.

6. To compute a periodic payment, use the PMT function. Its arguments are the _____, the number of periods, and the present value or loan amount.

7. You must execute a command to _____ worksheet cells in order to unprotect them.

REVIEW QUESTIONS

1. Discuss how cell protection differs from data validation.

2. Suppose you want to write an expression in cell B7 that guarantees that a value a user enters into cell A1 is positive. Discuss how you would use an expression involving the IF function in cell B7 to return the positive value of any value entered in cell A1.

3. Describe the meaning of "the time value of money" and provide a concrete example using a savings account.

4. Explain the difference between these two expressions: **=7/21/2002** and **7/21/2002.**

5. Describe what happens if you type **=NOW** into a worksheet cell and press Enter. Assume that today's date is January 14, 2002.

6. Explain why locking or unlocking worksheet cells is not sufficient to protect or unprotect them.

CREATE THE QUESTION

For each of the following answers, create an appropriate short question.

ANSWER	QUESTION
1. It displays an error alert message.	_____
2. The first argument of an IF function.	_____
3. The greatest value that is less than or equal to the search value.	_____
4. The Name box is the fastest way.	_____
5. The IPMT function calculates and displays that value.	_____
6. Double-click the tab, type a new name, and press Enter.	_____

1. Determining Savings Match with Data Validation

Shelly Mueller has been studying German since her freshman year in high school. This summer, she has decided to participate in a study-abroad program sponsored by the German Club at her school. Her parents feel this will be a good learning experience for her and have agreed to pay for the cost of the program. In order for her to share in the cost, they have told Shelly that she needs to save for the spending money she will need while she is in Germany.

Shelly has a part-time job at a nearby stationery store where she earns $125 a week. She has two full months to save money for the trip before she leaves on the first of June. To encourage and help her with her savings, her grandfather has agreed to contribute to her savings. Since her grandfather lives in another state, he has asked her to send an e-mail that summarizes her savings and what his contribution should be for the eight weeks. Shelly has kept track of her savings for each week and needs to send the summary to her grandfather. Since her grandfather is matching her savings, Shelly has decided to put in equal amounts for the "Match" row as she entered in the Savings row.

1. Open the workbook **ex06Savings.xls** and save it as **Savings2.xls**
2. Click cell **A5** and type **Match.** Click cell **B5** and enter the formula **=B4.** Using the fill handle, copy this formula into the cell range **C5:I5.** Include your name in a custom header and print this sheet
3. Her father reminded Shelly that her grandfather agreed to match her savings, but only up to $50 a week. Shelly needs to make sure no amount over $50 will be in the Match row. Delete the formulas in the cell range **B5:I5.** Click cell **B5,** click **Data** and then click **Validation** to activate the Data Validation dialog box. Use the data validation tool to ensure that no amount greater than $50 or less than $1 will be entered for the Match value.
4. Type the title **Valid Amount** and type the input message **Valid amounts are less than or equal to $50**

5. Type an error alert message titled **Invalid Amount** and type the message **The amount you entered is greater than $50.** Use the stop style for this alert
6. Test the data validation by entering **$75** for the match value of cell B5. What happens?
7. Using the fill handle, copy these validation terms in cells **C5:I5**
8. Enter the correct match values, using the values in the Savings row and the $50 match limit as your guide
9. After the values for the fourth week of May, create a column titled **Totals.** (Type **Totals** in cell **J2.**) Write a SUM function in cell J4 to total the Savings row for both months
10. Using the fill handle, copy the formula into cell **J5** so that it includes the total matching contribution for her grandfather
11. Click cell **J6,** and then write a formula that displays the grand total amount Shelley will have for her trip. Label it **Grand Total** and adjust the cell widths, heights, and colors so that the worksheet is attractive
12. Delete the worksheets called **Sheet2** and **Sheet3** from the **Savings2.xls** workbook
13. Include your name in the custom header, save the workbook, and print the worksheet

2. Deciding between Loan Options by Total Payment

James Thomas has been out of college for three years. Now that he has had the chance to put aside some of his income, he would like to look for a new car. He has been able to save $4,000 and has decided that he would like a car that is two years old with no more than 20,000 miles on it. He found a car that meets his criteria. The current owner wants $10,500 for the car. James will apply his savings to the purchase, but needs a loan for the remaining $6,500. He went to several local banks to find the best loan offer.

ABC Bank has a loan available at 9.5 percent interest for two years. The interest compounds monthly and James' payments would be due at the end of each month. XYZ Bank has a loan available at 9 percent interest for 2½ years. This loan also compounds monthly with payments due at the end of each month.

James needs your help to determine which loan alternative is best. He wants to determine which loan has the lowest monthly payment. He has entered each bank's offer in the worksheet called **ex06CarLoan.xls.**

1. Open **ex06CarLoan.xls** and save it as **CarLoan2.xls** to preserve the original worksheet
2. Click cell **A6** and type **Periodic Payment**
3. Click cell **B6,** click **Insert** on the menu bar, and then click **Function**
4. Click **Financial** in the *Or select a category* list box, click **PMT** in the *Select a function* list box, and click **OK**
5. Based on the information given for ABC Bank, in the **Rate** text box write a formula referencing the interest rate cell, cell B4. Remember to divide the interest rate by the number of payments per year
6. Click the **Nper** text box and type the formula for the total number of payments you will make for the entire life of the loan. Remember to multiply the loan duration in years (a reference to the cell containing it) by the number of payments per year
7. Click the **Pv** text box, type − (minus) followed by the cell address containing the principal amount, **B3,** and then click **OK**
8. Copy the formula in cell **B6** to cell **C6** to also create the PMT function for the loan from XYZ Bank

9. Based on the monthly payment figures alone for each bank, which appears to be the better loan for James? Highlight this bank's information with a Light Green fill color. (Click the Fill Color list arrow on the Formatting toolbar and click the color **Light Green**)
10. Place your name in your worksheet's header, save the workbook, and print the CarLoanData worksheet
11. After examining your results, you decide to determine the total payments that James will make to each bank for their loan to make sure he chooses the right loan for his car. Title the row below Monthly Payments **Total Payments.** In cell **B7,** create a formula to multiply the monthly payment in B6 by the number of months in ABC Bank's loan term
12. Create a similar formula in cell **C7** using the monthly payment and months in the loan for XYZ Bank. Be sure the Total Payments display positive values
13. Based on the total payments, which loan should James take? Highlight the information for this bank and print the worksheet
14. Delete the worksheet called **Sheet2** and save the workbook

hands-on
projects

challenge

1. Forecasting Interest Expense Using Amortization Schedules

Sharon Crowley has always wanted to blend her business savvy with her love of cooking. After college, she attended culinary school for two years specializing in pastries and desserts, and she decided to fulfill her lifelong dream to open her own dessert shop. After carefully searching, Sharon found a nearby location that would be perfect for the shop. She spent the next few weeks carefully determining which machines and supplies she would need for her business.

Sharon was able to qualify for a small business loan through her local credit union that would cover the costs of needed machinery and supplies and the first few payments of her lease for a total of $25,000. The loan rate is 8.75 percent and is to be paid monthly over a four-year period. Shelly wants to be able to forecast what her interest expenses will be for tax purposes. She has asked you to create an amortization schedule to detail the loan over its term. Do the following. Open **ex06Desserts.xls** and save the workbook as **Desserts2.xls.** Sharon has already figured out what her monthly payment would be using the PMT function, but she input the wrong rate for the loan. Change the interest rate in cell B4 to 8.75 percent. What happens to her monthly payment after the rate is adjusted? Enter the dates that each payment is due under the Date heading (cell A14), with the first payment due on March 31, 2003, in cell A15. Use the AutoFill feature to complete the sequential series April 30, 2003 through February 28, 2007. To represent the payment numbers, type **1** in cell B15 and **2** in cell B16. Use the AutoFill feature to complete the sequential series 3 through 48 in the Payment Number column. In cell C15, type the formula **=B3** to display the initial unpaid loan balance.

Click cell **D15,** click **Insert** on the menu bar, click **Function,** type **payment** in the *Search for a function* text box, click the **Go** button, and then click **PPMT** in the Function name. Enter the necessary information by typing cell references in each list box for the function. *Important:* Be sure to make cell references in the Rate, Nper, and Pv text boxes absolute references. The cell reference in the Per text box must be relative (e.g., B15 but not $B$15). This is so that the formulas will copy correctly. Fill in the remaining information for Per (relative cell reference), Nper (absolute cell reference), and Pv (absolute cell reference), and then click **OK.** Change the formula, if necessary, so that the result is a positive number. Click cell **E15,** and write the formula

```
=-IPMT($B$4/12,B15,$B$5*12,$B$3)
```

To complete the information for the first payment due on March 31, 2002, the ending balance must be determined. Create a formula for cell **F15** that subtracts the Repayment of Principal from the Beginning Balance (cell **C15**). Create a formula for the Beginning Balance for cell C16 (payment 2) by referencing the Ending Balance of the previous month (using all relative references). Copy the remaining formulas from payment 1 (cells **D15:F15**) to the cells for payment 2 (to cells **D16:F16**). Now copy the formulas in cell range **C16:F16** to the cell range **C17:F62** to complete the schedule. What is the Ending Balance for payment 48? Include your name in the worksheet header and print the worksheet. Delete any unused worksheets.

on the web

1. Using Future Values to Choose a Savings Vehicle

When Anthony Tallarico and his wife Sheila had their first child, they immediately started investing for his college education. Since they knew that the investments would be held for almost 18 years, the Tallaricos took the risk of investing in various stocks and mutual funds. The Tallaricos' oldest son will be starting college in a little over a year. Since the tuition will be due at that time, they have decided to pull some of their money out of the stock market and invest in very conservative savings vehicles. They feel that they don't want to take any risks with this money. It must be available to pay for college. The first year's tuition will be approximately $24,000 and this is the amount for which the Tallaricos want an alternative investment.

Anthony has narrowed the options for the $24,000 down to two conservative short-term investments. These are an interest-bearing checking account and a money market account. He has asked you to help him find the most recent interest rates on these accounts so that he can determine which will give him the best rate of return.

Open **ex06Conservative.xls** and save the workbook as **Conservative2.xls.** First define the appropriate cells with the names **Rate, Years, Payment,** and **FutureValue,** as the columns are labeled. You have decided to go to www.bankrate.com to get the latest rates for each of these investments. When the Web page opens, click the **Rates** tab. In the box labeled **Overnight Averages,** click **Today's averages.** Once that page appears, scroll down until you see the Rates for Savings investments. Input these rates into the worksheet and input the information for Years and Payment. Remember that each investment will be for one year. For the money market account and checking account, Mr. Tallarico will make monthly contributions of $2,000 for the year period.

For the Future Value column, click cell **E5** and then click **Insert,** click **Function,** and locate the **Future Value** function. Use the given information to input the Future Value formula. Remember that the money market and checking accounts pay interest monthly. Once this is computed, use the fill handle to drag the formula into the needed cells in the Future Value column. Which savings vehicle should Mr. Tallarico use to invest $20,000? Include your name in the header, print the worksheet, and save it.

2. Selling or Holding Stocks Using Lookup Tables

Professor Pasquale is a finance professor at the Stockdale City University. He started trading his own stocks a few years ago to illustrate how the stock market works for his class lectures. What started out as an experiment has become a hobby for the professor and he has his own online account in which he can place all of his trades and get any data on the stock market that he may need. This semester, he has had little time to monitor his stock portfolio since he is teaching two additional classes that take up most of his day. He has asked you to help him determine how his stocks are performing. He would like you to create a worksheet illustrating how each stock has performed for him, which he will use as an illustration in his finance class.

Open **ex06Stocks.xls** and save the workbook as **Stocks2.xls.** Professor Pasquale has already set up how he would like the worksheet to be constructed. He has given you the name of each stock and its ticker symbol. He wants you to look up the price of each stock on the day it was purchased, February 10, 2003, and its price today. He then wants you to write formulas to calculate each stock's net change in price.

First, enter the date 2/10/2003 in cell C4, and then copy it down through the cell range C5:C1. Next, ensure that the Date of Purchase and

Current Date columns display dates with four-digit years by formatting them, if needed. Use your favorite browser and go to finance.yahoo.com (do not type www before finance). Under Research & Education, click the Historical Quotes link. For each stock, enter the ticker symbol, date of purchase, and today's date. The Web site will give you the price of the stock for each day during this period. Retrieve the closing price on the date of purchase and today's date and input this data into the worksheet for each stock. Write formulas in the Net Change column to subtract the purchase price from the current price.

Professor Pasquale wants to use this worksheet throughout the semester, updating the current stock prices and net change per stock each week. To avoid deleting the purchase date and base price by mistake, unlock cells E4 through F10 and then protect the worksheet so that no other cells can be changed and no other cells can be made active. Delete unused worksheets from the workbook. Include your name in the worksheet header. Change the worksheet printing orientation to Landscape so that it prints on one page, print the worksheet, and save the workbook.

e-business

1. Deciding between Investment Opportunities Using Payment

Jonathan Leitman owns a small, yet successful, custom furniture company. For the past few years, he has done little marketing since current customers refer most of his new customers to him. This past year, his business has greatly increased and he has decided to grow the business. He has already looked into opening a larger production facility, purchasing new machines and tools, and hiring a few carpenters to assist him. The initial cost of expanding the business will be $225,000, and Jonathan knows he will be able to raise this initial capital. Jonathan's problem is that he doesn't know how he should market his company.

A business consultant has recommended two options to him. The first option is that Jonathan hires a Web designer to create a Web site for the firm. The consultant feels this would be the best marketing opportunity since he could include pictures, dimensions, costs, and anything else a potential customer would want to know. The greatest advantage of the Web site is that orders could be placed directly through the Web site. The second option is to hire an advertising agency to design and implement a marketing campaign for the company. The main advantage of the advertising campaign option is that it would give the company exposure to a lot of potential customers that would not otherwise hear about the company's products.

Jonathan's consultant has estimated the additional initial cost for each of the options. The Web site will incur an additional initial cost of $250,000. Hiring an advertising agency will require an initial cost of $325,000. After meeting with his loan officer, Jonathan was approved for an additional $325,000 for his loan at a rate of 9.5 percent for three years with payments due monthly. In addition, the advertising agency has a relationship with the bank that would result in a reduction of the annual interest rate to 4.5 percent if Jonathan hires the agency.

Jonathan has asked you to help him decide which he should invest in—a Web site, or an advertising campaign. He can choose only one of the options due to capital restraints. Create a worksheet, titled **Payments,** that summarizes the initial cost and loan terms for each option. Remember to include in the initial cost the total of the initial costs of each investment and the initial cost of the facility, tools, and new carpenters. Using the Payment Function, determine the monthly payment and total payments for each investment option. Jonathan wants to compare interest and principal payments for each option since both the interest rates and principal amounts are different. He does not want to look at all 36 months, but has asked you include in your worksheet a breakdown of the interest, principal, and total payments for the first and second month. If Jonathan's goal is to pay as little interest as possible, which option should he choose based on these results?

Improve the worksheet's appearance and make all payment amounts appear in red. Add a worksheet titled **Documentation** and, in row 4, enter Investment and Loan Options. In cell **B7,** enter **Prepared by: Jonathan Leitman.** In cell **B9** enter **Analyzed by:** followed by your name. Click in cell **B11** and enter **Date:** followed by the current date. Make the appearance of the documentation sheet similar to the payments worksheet in font and color. Save the workbook again to preserve your work and print it.

around the world

1. Comparing Semester Abroad Costs

Karen's university has a very strong study abroad program for the students. The university has developed relationships with many well-respected schools around the world and offers semester-length programs with course work completed at these schools. Karen is graduating next year and wants to spend the next semester in Europe. She has studied French and Spanish extensively and would like to spend the semester abroad in order to improve her foreign language skills. Because she will need to take out more loans to participate in any of the programs, the total cost of each program will be the deciding factor for which country she chooses to live in for the semester.

You work in the office for study abroad programs and are friends with Karen. She has asked you to help her summarize the costs associated with each program so that she can make a decision. You need to design a worksheet for her and keep in mind that it needs to be clear and accurate. The program in Spain has the following costs: tuition $8,500, room and board $3,000, and airfare of $750. The France program has the following costs: tuition $7,200, room and board $4,500, and airfare of $975. The England program has the following costs: tuition $11,000, room and board $2,800 and airfare of $895. Karen has determined that she wants to also take $2,000 with her for spending money, no matter which program she chooses. Input these costs into a worksheet and label the worksheet Abroad

Costs. Create a column titled Total Costs and create the appropriate formula so the total cost of each program is included on the worksheet.

Based on your results, Karen has decided she must choose between Spain and France. This decision will be based on how much her loans will cost per program. A local French Club has a loan program for students wanting to further their education in France. They will loan Karen the full amount needed at an interest rate of 8.75 percent. She will need to make monthly payments on the loan for 10 years. For the Spanish program, she would take out a loan from the university at an interest rate of 9 percent. She would also have to make monthly payments on this loan, but for a total of seven years. Summarize this information on the next sheet and title it Loan Costs. Create a column titled Monthly Payment and use the Payment function to calculate the monthly payment for each loan. Karen decides that she will choose the program with the lowest monthly payment because she feels it will cost her less overall. You think this way of thinking is incorrect and illustrate by showing her the Future Value of each loan, which is how much she really pays for each. Create a column for this information and input the appropriate financial formula to give the future value of each loan. Based on future value, which program should Karen choose? Was her rationale correct? Include your name in the header of both worksheets and print them both. Save your workbook.

running project

Pampered Paws

Grace is worried about her cash flow this month. Each month she places her order for supplies and feed by the fifth of the month to ensure delivery for the next month. January and February have been lean months this year and she will need to order over $10,000 in pet food to carry her through next month. She has put together a worksheet containing her estimate of all the pet food she will need to purchase from her wholesale distributor. The wholesale price, the price she pays, totals $10,932.60. She has calculated that she will be able to pay $2,000 cash, but she wants to obtain a loan for the balance to help her cash flow. She reasons that by financing her inventory for one year, she will have enough cash and sales to pay off the loan and remain financially stable. She asks you to put together a loan amortization schedule for the proposed loan's 12 payment periods beginning on March 1.

Begin by loading **ex06Paws.xls** and save it with a different name. Next, add a new worksheet to the workbook and move it to the first position in the workbook. Change the name of this worksheet to **Documentation.** Type some documentation information on this sheet such as the creation date, the author's name, the modification date, and the store's name.

The sheet following Feed Purchases is called Sheet2. Rename it to **Loan Amortization.** Create the loan amortization information on this sheet. Model the worksheet after the loan analysis worksheet you created for this chapter, except omit the External Data section and use labels in the Assumptions area that are appropriate for her business. (Use "Inventory Total Price" instead of "Purchase Price.") Omit the FICO Credit Rating in-

formation. For the Application Date, write a function to display today's date. Assume the annual interest rate is 9.75 percent (inventory financing is more risky than automobile financing). Create the same columns in the amortization section as in the chapter case problem: Payment, Beginning Balance, Principal Paid, Interest Paid, Total Principal, Total Interest, and Ending Balance. The value in the Inventory Finance Amount should be the total order value (see sum on the Feed Purchases worksheet). The loan amount value is the Inventory Total Price minus $2,000 (cash that Grace will pay as a down payment on the feed purchase). Create names for the value for Inventory Total Price, Down Payment, Loan Term, Periodic Payment, Interest Rate, and Loan Amount. Move the Interest Rate label and the interest rate up into the Assumptions section, since it is now a user-input value. Unlike the chapter example, there is no special assessment fee. Protect the cell containing the value of the Inventory Total Price so that a user can enter values only in the range of $0 through $25,000. Format all the worksheet cells in an attractive way.

Color the Documentation sheet tab green, color the Feed Purchases sheet tab yellow, and color the Loan Amortization sheet tab blue. Protect the worksheet so that only the Assumptions area values are unlocked (but lock the Loan Term value) and only they can be selected. Write your name in each worksheet's header and print all three worksheets when you are done. Print the formulas for the Loan Amortization worksheet to demonstrate your use of names. Remember to save your finished workbook.

did you know?

zebras, *like other equines, have three gaits: walk, trot, and gallop.*

swimming *pools in the U.S. contain enough water to cover the city of San Francisco with a layer of water about 7 feet deep.*

Attila *the Hun died of a nosebleed on his wedding night in A.D. 453.*

Gene *Simmons, of the shock-rock group Kiss, earned a B.A. in education and speaks four languages.*

orchids *have the smallest seeds. It takes more than 1.25 million seeds to weigh 1 gram.*

office *products can interact with each other via embedding, pasting, and _____. Find the third way by reading this chapter.*

Chapter Objectives

- Link an Excel object into a Word document

- Design document that integrates several Excel objects with Word

- Modify a linked Excel worksheet from within Word

- Embed an Excel object within a Word document—MOUS Ex2002e-1-2

- Create a mail merge letter obtaining its variable data from an Excel worksheet list

- Print merged documents

CHAPTER

7

seven

Integrating
Excel and
Office Objects

chapter case
Avicon International Art Treasures

Avicon International Art Treasures is an e-commerce company having no storefront besides its Web site. Avicon is called a pure-play company because its store has no counterpart brick-and-mortar store. Avicon specializes in discovering, marketing, and making available to the public art that is produced by artisans located in difficult-to-reach corners of the world. Avicon agents and buyers trek remote locations from the Andes Mountains to the rain forests of Africa seeking isolated villages—especially communities where artisans produce high-quality objects that have very narrow distribution.

While artists in isolated communities have always been able to sell their goods in small quantities to local residents, they have never been able to gain wider exposure for their goods. Shipping goods to other countries has been a problem for most artists in difficult-to-reach locations because they are not close to mass transportation. Some villages rely on horses or mules to deliver their few goods to larger towns often hundreds of miles away. Occasionally an adventurous tourist would stumble onto a village producing a particular type of art, purchase and transport the artwork out of the country, and tell friends about the wonderful art he or she found. Typically, such art cannot be shipped to others without personally contacting the artists, so visiting the village in person has

been the only way to purchase locally made art objects—until recently.

Avicon and other companies like it are filling the void between local producers and world consumers. They arrange to purchase art objects from over a dozen regions around the world that produce extraordinary art in villages at a reasonable price. Avicon arranges to pick up and ship objects to consumers who view and order art from the Avicon online Web site. Shipping typically takes three to four weeks after a consumer orders one or more objects online because Avicon must arrange to transport the art from the village to a larger city with a transportation infrastructure. In Chile, for example, some objects made high in the Andes must travel to villages far down the mountain, then to a central hub city where normal UPS-style shipping exists. The first part of an art object's journey is the longest. Once the object reaches a large city, it's a matter of a week or less before it reaches the consumer.

Avicon can compete in the marketplace because they are able to deliver products to consumers for far less than large chain department stores can, they provide worldwide exposure to artists whose exposure is otherwise very limited, and they provide a good profit for the artisans producing the artwork. Bigger stores find it expensive to compete in this niche. For example, not long

FIGURE 7.1

Avicon letter integrating elements from Excel

1224 5th Avenue, San Diego, CA 92110 • (619) 555-1224

Robert Choate
150 Marcus Boulevard
Hauppauge, NY 11788

October 17, 2002

Dear Robert Choate,

This letter introduces you to some of the products featured this month. As you know, we offer our products only through the Internet. The purpose of this letter is to introduce new customers to a sampling of our products and showcase selected special sale items to existing customers. We at Avicon appreciate your interest, Robert Choate. Avicon's mission is to provide you with access to hard-to-find items at great prices available through the cost-saving Internet and to create a link from you to the many talented artisans around the globe. Unlike department stores, we want you to know the artist from whom you are buying your art, and we want you to feel closely linked to the person whose hands created the art. We feature products from eleven regions, each with a regional fulfillment office staffed by locals who carefully pack and ship each order. We have over 2,400 artisans who regularly produce art for sale through Avicon.

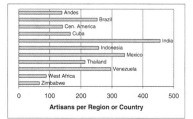

Avicon follows a special law of product pricing based on two simple rules: 1) Clients must pay less than their prevailing local prices, and 2) Artisans must make more than they would selling at their local market prices.

In addition to the products featured on our Web site, we are proud to display this month's special values available for quick shipment from our regional fulfillment centers.

ago, a large upscale New York department store sold vases produced by artisans in San Pedro, Peru. Although the vases typically sell for approximately $350 through the department store, Avicon and stores like it have sold the same type of vase for $11 (plus shipping). What's more, the San Pedro producers make more profit from the $11 sale than they do from the $350! That's exactly where Avicon flourishes. By *disintermediation*—eliminating the often-expensive "middleman"—everyone can benefit.

Occasionally, Avicon mails out letters to previous customers and Web site visitors who have indicated an interest. The monthly letters describe some special purchase items they have recently acquired. Though the Web is the most cost-effective way to advertise, the monthly mailings have proven to be a good way to acquire new customers. Bill Freitag is Avicon's marketing manger. He has proposed creating a letter to mail to customers and prospects (see Figure 7.1). This letter integrates information from Excel into the Word document. In addition, Bill wants to produce a Web version of the document to post on their Web site.

Chapter 7 covers Office integration—using more than one Office product to produce a document containing elements of one or more Office products. In particular, you will insert an Excel graph and part of a worksheet into a simple Word document to send to customers. The letterhead is the company logo pasted into the Word document, and the inside address is a link, or pointer, to an Excel list containing customer name and address data. You will create an Excel worksheet, launch Word, and insert Excel objects into the Word document using three techniques: pasting, linking, and embedding. Finally, you will insert hyperlinks into a document and publish it to the Web.

SESSION 7.1 LINKING EXCEL AND WORD

In this section, you will learn how to insert elements from Excel into a simple Word document. You will learn about object linking and embedding, or OLE, and the differences between pasting, linking, and embedding objects.

INTRODUCTION

Bill has designed the way he wants the advertising letter to look and has picked out a list of customers he thinks will be receptive to the letter. Bill's design shows the company logo at the top of the letter, pasted there with a simple paste operation. The inside address, which contains the name and address of the recipient, is actually a mail merge field that obtains individual name and address information from a customer list maintained in Excel. Each customer's name and address information is in a separate row, and columns identify elements such as the first and last names, street number, street name, city, state, and postal code. The body of the letter describes, in a few sentences, this month's special items and contains a graph showing the number of art objects sold last month from various areas of the world. Near the bottom of the letter is part of an Excel worksheet containing a sampling of art objects available, their country of origin, unit price, and estimated shipping time and cost. Figure 7.2 shows Bill's hand-sketched design of the letter's layout with notes indicating where Excel information is incorporated into the letter.

Bill will need your help in building the integration between the Word document and the Excel files. He will draft the marketing letter and place tags in the letter where he wants you to insert content from Excel. First, he goes over several ways to incorporate information from another Office product into an existing one.

INTEGRATING INFORMATION FROM DIFFERENT PRODUCTS

You will find several occasions when you need to draw data from several sources to produce a *compound document.* For example, different parts of a document may have come from any of the office products including Word, Excel, or Access. A letter created in Word can contain a selected group of cells from an Excel worksheet as well as a chart and the latest customer information from an Access database.

Microsoft software developers have designed the suite of Office programs so that they work well together. While there are many combinations of programs you can purchase among the Office suite of programs, the suite includes Word, a word processing program; Excel, the spreadsheet program; Access, a relational database program; PowerPoint, a presentation program; and Outlook, a personal information manager (PIM). You

FIGURE 7.2

Sketch of the letter's design

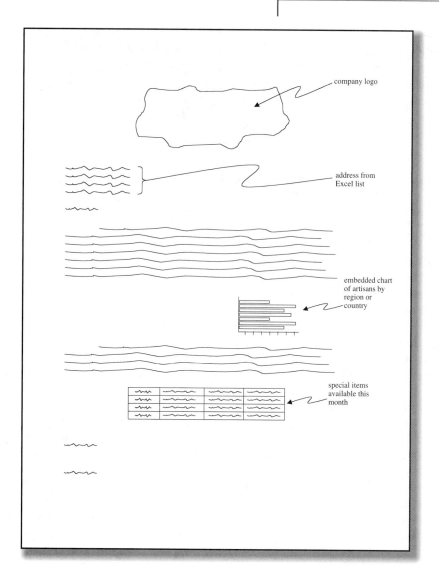

will experience the smooth interaction between two of these programs—Excel and Word—in this chapter.

As you work with Microsoft Excel, you may need to transfer data from Excel to Word or vice versa. Office provides three main ways to transfer information from one Office product to another, and all use the Clipboard as an intermediary. These methods are pasting, linking, and embedding. (Although a product sometimes will allow you to save data in the format of another product, doing so does not facilitate integration of two programs' data.) Each method has advantages and disadvantages, but the end result is the same: a single document containing data from different programs. Figure 7.3 briefly compares the differences between these three methods. Sections that follow will explain these differences fully.

Pasting Data from Another Office Program

The simplest way to grab information maintained by one program and place it into a document maintained by another is to use the ***paste*** method. You can copy and subsequently paste a worksheet cell or cell range into a Word document, or you can paste a document or part of a document into an Excel worksheet. (In this chapter, the term *document* is not restricted to

FIGURE 7.3

Pasting, linking, and embedding compared

Integration Method	Description
Copy/Paste	Places a copy of the data on the Clipboard (copy) and then places it in the document (paste)
Linking	Displays the object in the document, but the original object is stored elsewhere
Embedding	Displays and stores a copy of the object in the document, disconnected from the original object's source

a Word document. It means any recipient container into which you place information from another source—a worksheet, a Word document, or a PowerPoint slide, for example.)

When you paste information into a document, you paste a copy of that information. The copy is not affected by any subsequent changes to the source information from which you copied it. In other words, the copied information is no longer associated with or connected to the source information. For instance, suppose you copy a group of six cells from an Excel worksheet into a Word document. You can change the values of the pasted information within Word, but the changes have no effect on the original six cells in the Excel worksheet and vice versa. If you discover a mistake in the Excel information you copied, you can change the original Excel worksheet and recopy it into the Word document to change the data in both locations. On the other hand, if you copy the worksheet information into 10, 50, or even 100 different documents, discovering a mistake in the original Excel worksheet gives rise to a lot of unnecessary work of pasting the changes to all affected documents. In situations where source data is likely to change frequently, a better solution is to use either of the other two integration methods of linking or embedding.

Linking or Embedding Data Produced by Another Office Program

When you decide that pasting an object into Excel or another Office product does not provide the power and versatility you are seeking, Microsoft has two more powerful alternatives. Like all Office products, Excel supports this more powerful technology that Microsoft calls **Object Linking and Embedding** (abbreviated OLE and pronounced "oh-lay"). In short, OLE allows you to paste an object from one application into another application in the Office suite so that it maintains a linkage between the pasted object and the original object from which it is copied. Examples include pasting an Excel worksheet cell range into a PowerPoint slide, pasting a Word document paragraph into an Excel worksheet, or pasting an Excel chart into a Word document.

Using the OLE technology, you exchange information between two programs and the data files they are displaying. The program from which you copy information is called the **server** or **source program.** The program that receives the information is called the **client** or **container program.**

You can share data between programs by embedding. **Embedding,** one of two OLE techniques, allows you to store the data from one program (Excel, for example) in another program such as Word. Examples of objects that you can embed include a worksheet, graphic, chart, clip art, movie, or sound file. When you embed information from one program into another program's data file, you create a copy of the original data that is a separate file within the client data. You can make changes directly to the embedded data within the container object. Because the copied data has no link or association with the original source from which it has been copied, changes to the embedded copy do not change the original source document data. Similarly, changes you make to the original source data do not affect the copied data within the container.

When you create a *link* to a data file within another file, there is no actual copy and source data as there is with embedded files. There is only one file, the source, which is also displayed in the container document—a kind of virtual copy of the source document. The linked object and the source data are one file. The container document stores a link to the source document. The link or *reference* to the data describes the data filename and its location on your computer. When you display the container document along with the linked object data, the container tracks down the reference and displays the linked file's current value within the container document. Think of the linked document as a window through which you view the actual data file referenced in the container document. A linked object behaves differently from an embedded object in one significant way. If you make changes to the original document, changes simultaneously appear in the document containing the link to the source. Similarly, if you make a change to the data in the container document containing the link to the source data, a change occurs to the source data. That change also affects all other documents linked to the source document. That is both the power and danger of using linking instead of embedding. Changes to a linked document can have far-reaching effects, whereas changes to an embedded document affect only the document within which it is embedded. The key differences between a linked object and an embedded object are:

- Linked objects are dynamic, changing whenever data in the source document changes. Data in embedded objects is static and does not change when the source data changes.

- Only information needed to sustain a link to the source data file is stored in the container object. On the other hand, an embedded object stores all of its data within the container object. Containers with embedded objects are typically much larger than the same container document containing a link to the same object source object.

In this chapter, you will use all three forms of data sharing: pasting, embedding, and linking.

Comparing Embedding, and Linking

When you compare them visually, linked objects and embedded objects appear to be identical. However, each of the two forms is useful in different situations. It is best to use a linked object rather than an embedded object if the source data change frequently. For example, a document displaying this hour's sales figures should be linked to the sales data. Embedded data is out of date and quickly useless. On the other hand, if the source data is stored on removable media such as a floppy disk, then linking to the data is impractical—particularly if you plan on distributing the document containing the link to a widely dispersed audience. In this case, each report recipient would also have to receive a copy of the source floppy disk.

EXCEL

In contrast, you will want to use an embedded object rather than a linked object if you want control over the server data that each container document displays. In other words, if you want to disallow changes to very important worksheet data, do not create documents with links to the data. Otherwise, anyone with a container document can change the central source data quickly and without realizing the potential for damage. Embedded data is a good choice for data that does not change frequently—employee name and address information or a listing of this month's high and low stock prices.

DESIGNING AN INTEGRATED DOCUMENT

Bill has designed the letter he wants to send out to customers and written the body of the letter using Microsoft Word. There are special document tags such as "[insert inside address]" or "[insert logo]" where Bill wants you to insert special elements into the letter. Figure 7.4 shows a printout of the letter with the special tags. You will replace the special tags in the letter with pasted elements such as the company logo, customer addresses, a graph, and an Excel worksheet as you complete exercises in this chapter.

FIGURE 7.4

Design of the customer letter

[insert logo]

1224 5th Avenue, San Diego, CA 92110 • (619) 555-1224

[insert inside address]

October 17, 2002

[insert greeting]

This letter introduces you to some of the products featured this month. As you know, we offer our products only through the Internet. The purpose of this letter is to introduce new customers to a sampling of our products and showcase selected special sale items to existing customers. Avicon's mission is to provide you with access to hard-to-find items at great prices available through the cost-saving Internet and to create a link from you to the many talented artisans around the globe. Unlike department stores, we want you to know the artist from whom you are buying your art, and we want you to feel closely linked to the person whose hands created the art. We feature products from eleven regions, each with a regional fulfillment office staffed by locals who carefully pack and ship each order. We have over 2,400 artisans who regularly produce art for sale through Avicon.

[insert graph of regions/artists per region]

Avicon follows a special law of product pricing based on two simple rules: 1) Clients must pay less than their prevailing local prices, and 2) Artisans must make more than they would selling at their local market prices.

In addition to the products featured on our Web site, we are proud to display this month's special values available for quick shipment from our regional fulfillment centers. They are:

[insert Excel worksheet with products, country, artists' names, and prices]

Once you place your order through our convenient, toll-free number, our regional office will process, pack, and ship your order within 10 days. All goods are insured for their full value, and you can return any unsatisfactory item up to 90 days after you receive it.

Thank you for supporting Avicon.

Sincerely,

Bill Freitag,
Marketing Manager

In addition to the customer letter, Bill has designed an informal worksheet containing the specials sales for the month that he will circulate among the staff at headquarters. Because it is designed for internal use, it is less polished than the customer letter. Figure 7.5 shows the architecture of both the internal memo and the customer letter along with a graphical representation of objects that you will help Bill paste into both documents. Bill has chosen to use a beveled glass rectangle in both the internal document and the customer letter to add a splash of color and interest.

Bill wants to paste the logo into the top of the internal worksheet memo and the letter. The graph depicts the number of artisans in various countries, a number that is relatively stable. Therefore Bill plans on embedding the graph in the customer newsletter. The worksheet contains representative samples of art on sale this month. The precise cost of each of these is not finalized yet, so Bill wants to link the worksheet displayed in the customer letter to the stand-alone Excel worksheet. That way, when Bill receives the final prices, he can change the worksheet and the customer letter will automatically display the changed worksheet. Linking provides the kind of dynamic connection that facilitates making last-minute changes and rippling them throughout all documents linked to the single source.

FIGURE 7.5

Combining elements of Excel and Word

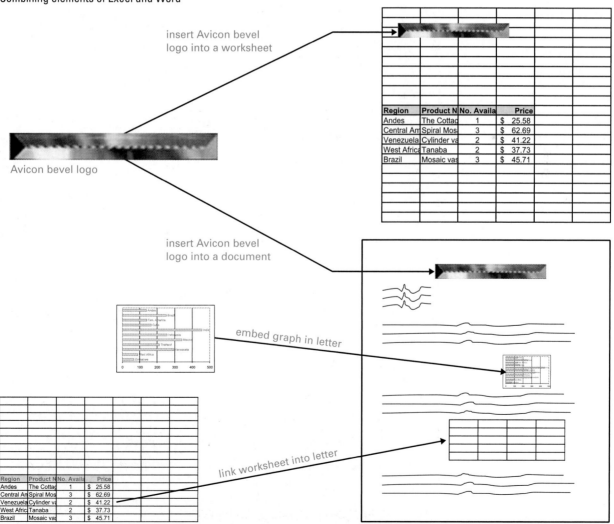

PASTING AN OBJECT INTO AN EXCEL WORKSHEET

First, Bill wants you to paste the bevel glass logo into a worksheet page. Then you will print the page for Bill and e-mail it as an attachment to selected Avicon regional managers. To get started, you launch Excel and open a worksheet.

Opening the Avicon worksheet and saving it under a new name:

1. Start Excel as usual

2. Open the workbook **ex07Avicon.xls** and immediately save it as **Avicon2.xls** to preserve the original workbook in case you ever want to revert to it. Review the Cover Sheet worksheet and observe that it contains a pasted object—one of the vases Avicon sells

3. Click the **Artisans by Region** worksheet tab. It lists the latest count of artisans by country or region. A bar graph shows the numbers graphically

4. Click the **Sale Items** worksheet tab. The worksheet contains a list of special sale items from their collection. The list shows the object's region of origin, the product name, the number of items available, and the price of each object (see Figure 7.6)

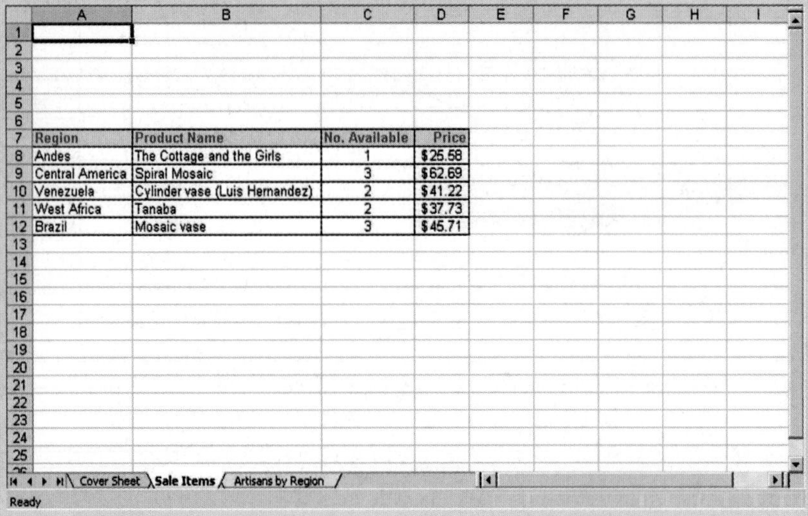

FIGURE 7.6

Sale Items worksheet

	A	B	C	D
7	Region	Product Name	No. Available	Price
8	Andes	The Cottage and the Girls	1	$25.58
9	Central America	Spiral Mosaic	3	$62.69
10	Venezuela	Cylinder vase (Luis Hernandez)	2	$41.22
11	West Africa	Tanaba	2	$37.73
12	Brazil	Mosaic vase	3	$45.71

Cover Sheet \ **Sale Items** / Artisans by Region /

Ready

With the Sale Items worksheet open, you are ready to paste an object into an Excel worksheet.

Inserting the Avicon graphic into a worksheet:

1. Press **Ctrl+Home** to select cell A1, if needed

2. Click **Insert** on the menu bar, point to **Picture,** and click **From File.** The Insert Picture dialog box opens

3. Click the **Look in** list box and navigate to the folder containing the file **ex07Bevel.jpg**

4. Click **ex07Bevel.jpg** from the list of files and then click the **Insert** button to paste the logo into the worksheet. The Picture toolbar appears—either floating or docked—on-screen

5. Move the mouse inside the graphic until it changes shape to a four-headed arrow, then click and drag the graphic down and to the right until the upper-left corner of the bevel aligns with the upper-left corner of cell **B3** (see Figure 7.7)

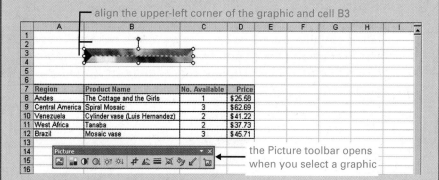

align the upper-left corner of the graphic and cell B3

the Picture toolbar opens when you select a graphic

F I G U R E   7.7

Pasting a graphic inside an Excel worksheet

tip: *Press and hold the **Alt** key as you drag the graphic to snap the upper-left corner to cell gridlines.*

6. Click anywhere outside the graphic to deselect it

7. Save the worksheet

8. Click the **Print Preview** button on the Standard toolbar to preview the worksheet and then click the Print Preview toolbar **Close** button

"Simple but to the point" are Bill's words when you show him the worksheet. He asks you to go ahead and e-mail the workbook to the regional managers with a short note that these prices are tentative.

MAILING A WORKBOOK AS AN E-MAIL ATTACHMENT

You get the names of Avicon's regional managers from Bill and prepare to e-mail them the Excel workbook. You can use Excel's available e-mailing capabilities as long as you have an installed e-mail package for Excel to use—a package such as Outlook Express, Outlook, Lotus cc:Mail, or Eudora.

task reference

Mailing a Workbook as an E-Mail Attachment

- Open the Excel workbook you want to send as an e-mail attachment
- Click **File** on the menu bar, point to **Send To,** and then click **Mail Recipient (as Attachment)**
- Enter the recipient's e-mail address in the **To** text box
- Click the **Send** button

If you have an e-mail program installed on the computer you are using, execute the steps that follow to e-mail the workbook to yourself. Otherwise, if you are not sure whether you have an e-mail program installed, skip the next exercise.

Mailing an Excel workbook as an e-mail attachment:

1. With **Avicon2.xls** open, click **File** on the menu bar, point to **Send To,** and click **Mail Recipient (as Attachment).** Your installed e-mail program opens. Figure 7.8 shows the screen that appears if you have Outlook Express installed. Your e-mail program's compose screen may vary slightly

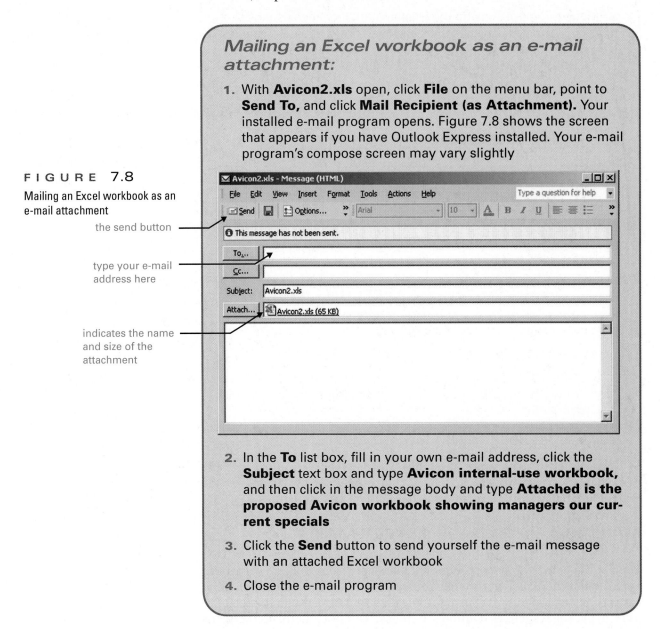

FIGURE 7.8

Mailing an Excel workbook as an e-mail attachment

the send button

type your e-mail address here

indicates the name and size of the attachment

2. In the **To** list box, fill in your own e-mail address, click the **Subject** text box and type **Avicon internal-use workbook,** and then click in the message body and type **Attached is the proposed Avicon workbook showing managers our current specials**

3. Click the **Send** button to send yourself the e-mail message with an attached Excel workbook

4. Close the e-mail program

When you open your e-mail, you will find that the preceding e-mail message has an icon with the name **Avicon2.xls.** Double-click the icon to open the workbook.

PASTING AN OBJECT INTO A WORD DOCUMENT

Bill wants you to place the bevel graphic at the top of the customer letter. He tells you to follow the same steps that you performed to insert the graphic in the Excel worksheet.

Pasting a graphic into the customer letter:

1. Click the **Start** button on the taskbar, point to **Programs,** and then click **Microsoft Word** to start the word processing program

2. Click the **Open** button on the Standard toolbar. Using the **Look in** list box, navigate to the folder containing **ex07Letter.doc**, and then click **ex07Letter.doc** in the Open dialog box. Click the **Open** button to open the document

3. Press and hold the **Ctrl** key, click anywhere inside the tag **[insert logo],** and then release the **Ctrl** key. Word highlights the entire tag (see Figure 7.9)

select the [insert logo] tag to replace it with a graphic

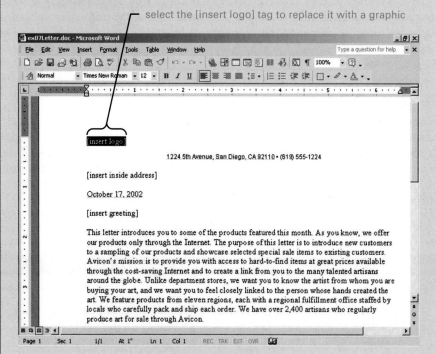

FIGURE 7.9
The customer letter

4. Click **Insert** on the menu bar, point to **Picture,** and click **From File.** The Insert Picture dialog box opens

5. Click the **Look in** list box and navigate to the folder containing the file **ex07Bevel.jpg**

6. Click **ex07Bevel.jpg** from the list of files and then click the **Insert** button to paste the logo into the worksheet. The document displays in Print Layout View

7. Click the graphic to select it. Selection handles appear around the graphic

8. With the graphic still selected, click the **Format Picture** button on the Picture toolbar. The Format Picture dialog box opens

9. Click the **Layout** tab of the Format Picture dialog box. The Layout panel appears

EXCEL

10. Click **In front of text** in the Wrapping style panel, click the **Center** option button in the Horizontal alignment panel, and click **OK** to complete the task of horizontally centering the graphic

11. Click **File** on the menu bar, click **Save As,** type **Letter2.doc** in the File name text box, and click the **Save** button. This preserves the original letter in case you want to go back to it later. Leave Word running, because you will continue to use it together with Excel

Now the letter contains the bevel logo at the top, in the letterhead area just above Avicon's address. Next, you will insert a graphic into the letter using a slightly different technique to provide added functionality to the graphic.

EMBEDDING AN EXCEL CHART INTO A WORD DOCUMENT

Bill wants to provide customers with a chart showing the number of artisans who are producing art for Avicon throughout the world. This will give customers a sense of the diverse cultural and artistic backgrounds of the artisans who produce the wonderful art objects. Although the data may change in small ways, Bill thinks that embedding the object in the letter rather than linking it to the source chart is sufficient.

The chart that Bill wants you to include in the customer letter is located in the Artisans by Region worksheet of the **Avicon2.xls** workbook.

task reference

Embedding an Object

- Start the source program, open the source document, select the object you want to copy, and click the **Copy** button on the Standard toolbar

- Start the container (destination) program, open the container document that will contain the embedded object, and place the insertion point at the destination point in the container document

- Click **Edit,** click **Paste Special,** click the **Paste** option button, click an option in the **As** list box, and click **OK**

Next, embed the bar chart found in the Artisans by Region worksheet of the **Avicon2.xls** source document into the container document **Letter2.doc.**

Embedding an Excel chart in a Word document:

1. With both **Letter2.doc** and **Avicon2.xls** open, click the **Microsoft Excel** button on the taskbar to make that task active and display the **Avicon2.xls** workbook

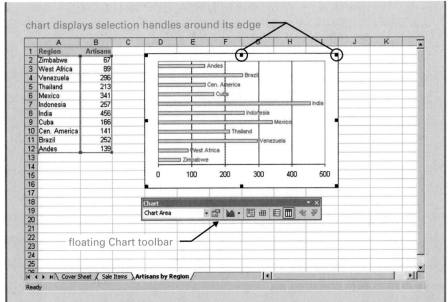

chart displays selection handles around its edge

floating Chart toolbar

F I G U R E 7.10

Selecting a chart in the source worksheet

2. Click the **Artisans by Region** worksheet tab to make that worksheet active, and click the **Chart Area** to select the chart. Selection handles surround the chart object (see Figure 7.10)

tip: *Your worksheet may not display the Chart toolbar. That is okay, because you will not use it anyway. If your Chart toolbar is visible, be sure to move it so it does not cover any part of the chart.*

tip: *If you have trouble selecting the entire chart, click just inside the outer border near the top-left portion of the chart area.*

3. Click **Edit** on the menu bar and click **Copy.** A dashed marquee appears around the chart object and Excel copies the chart to the Clipboard. It is ready to be pasted into the container you select

4. Click the **Letter2.doc - Microsoft Word** button on the taskbar to make Word and the letter active

5. Scroll down the letter past the first paragraph, locate the tag, press and hold the **Ctrl** key, click anywhere inside the text **[insert graph of regions/artists per region],** and then release the **Ctrl** key to position the cursor over the marker text that you will replace with the Excel chart (see Figure 7.11)

6. Press the **Delete** key to delete the chart insertion tag

7. Click **Edit** on the menu bar and then click **Paste Special.** The Paste Special dialog box appears

8. Click the **Paste** option button, if necessary, and (if necessary) click the **Microsoft Excel Chart Object** in the **As** list box (see Figure 7.12)

9. Click **OK.** Excel embeds the object in your document (see Figure 7.13) and displays the Paste Options smart tag

10. Click the **Save** button on the Word Standard toolbar to save the altered document containing the embedded Excel chart

EXCEL

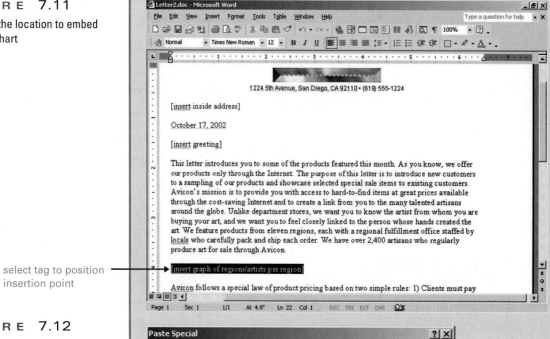

select tag to position
insertion point

click the paste option

select Microsoft Excel
Chart Object

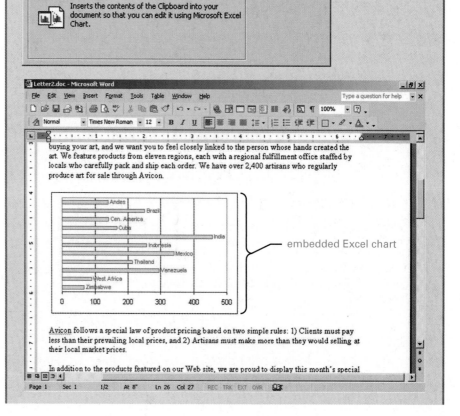

embedded Excel chart

11. Make the Microsoft Excel worksheet active by clicking the **Microsoft Excel** button on the toolbar, and then click anywhere outside the chart area to deselect it

12. Click **File** on the Excel menu bar and then click **Exit.** Click **No** when asked if you want to save your changes to **Avicon2.xls.** Do not close the Word document, as you will be making changes to it shortly

Bill reviews the customer letter containing the newly inserted Excel chart and asks if you could make a change to the chart in the letter. He would like you to add an explanatory label along the Y-axis. He would like you to make the Y-axis values the same dark brown as other elements of the chart. He cautions you not to alter the source chart in the **Avicon2.xls** Excel worksheet.

Altering an Embedded Excel Chart

Whenever you change an embedded object, the changes occur to the object within the container but not to the original source document. Recall that an embedded object is an island of information that is separated logically from the source from which it is copied. This means you can make changes to an embedded object without worrying about the change affecting another document—it won't.

You make changes to an embedded object by double-clicking it. When you do, the menu bar and toolbars change to those of the program that created the embedded object. In other words, if you double-click an Excel chart that is embedded within a Word document, Excel's menu bar and toolbars replace Word's menu bar and toolbars.

With the Excel chart within the Word container now, you can double-click the chart to automatically launch Excel and make Excel-only changes to the chart. Click outside the area of the embedded chart and Word toolbars and the Word menu bar reappear.

Altering the Excel bar chart from within the Word document:

1. Click the **Letter2.doc - Microsoft Word** button on the taskbar, if necessary, to make Word active and to display the customer letter

2. Double-click the bar chart. Within a few seconds, a border appears around the edge of the chart area and the Excel chart toolbar appears at the top of the Word window (see Figure 7.14)

3. Click **Chart** on the menu bar and click **Chart Options.** The Chart Options dialog box opens

tip: *Make sure the Chart toolbar is visible. If not, click **View** on the menu bar, point to **Toolbars,** and click **Chart** to display the Chart toolbar*

4. Click the **Titles** tab on the Chart Options dialog box, click the **Value (Y) Axis** text box, type **Artisans per Region or Country,** and click **OK.** Excel adds a Value axis title to the chart

EXCEL

FIGURE 7.14

Double-clicking the embedded chart

Excel menu bar and toolbars and formula bar appear

striped border indicates Excel is active

your temporary chart name may be different

Excel Chart toolbar

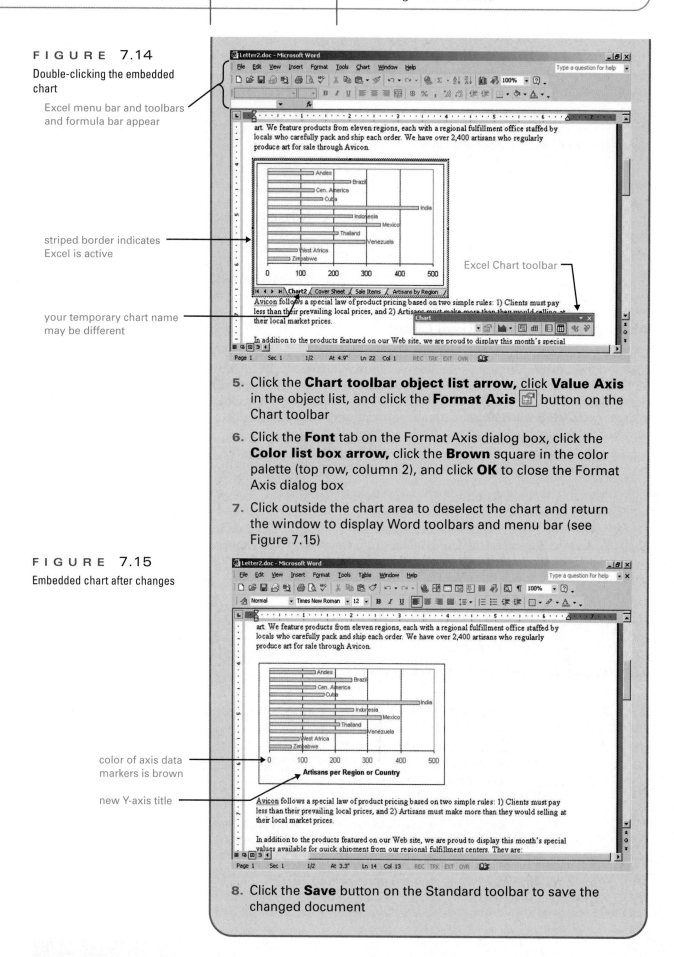

5. Click the **Chart toolbar object list arrow,** click **Value Axis** in the object list, and click the **Format Axis** button on the Chart toolbar

6. Click the **Font** tab on the Format Axis dialog box, click the **Color list box arrow,** click the **Brown** square in the color palette (top row, column 2), and click **OK** to close the Format Axis dialog box

7. Click outside the chart area to deselect the chart and return the window to display Word toolbars and menu bar (see Figure 7.15)

FIGURE 7.15

Embedded chart after changes

color of axis data markers is brown

new Y-axis title

8. Click the **Save** button on the Standard toolbar to save the changed document

LINKING AN EXCEL WORKSHEET AND A WORD DOCUMENT

Bill wants to include a sample of this month's special values in the customer newsletter. The information he wants to include is in an Excel worksheet, which is one of the worksheets in the **Avicon2.xls** workbook. Because the number of items available changes and the prices are not yet firm, Bill wants to ensure that the special values listed in the worksheet are as current as possible. While it is difficult to display prices that are only hours old in a letter mailed to customers, Bill wants to be able to send the same letter to customers next month too. In order to include a different group of monthly specials in the letter, Bill decides that the most efficient way is to dynamically link the worksheet information to the letter. Simply pasting the worksheet into a letter makes the process more difficult the next time Bill wants to send out a new letter, because he has to open the letter and then cut and paste in the newest values. By linking the worksheet to the letter, changing the monthly specials in the letter involves simply changing the contents of the worksheet. The next time he opens the customer letter, Word will automatically update the list of special values.

---

task reference

Linking an Object

- Start the source program, open the source document, select the object you want to link, and click the **Copy** button on the Standard toolbar

- Start the container (destination) program, open the container document that will contain the linked object, and place the insertion point at the destination point in the container document

- Click **Edit,** click **Paste Special,** click the **Paste link** option button, click an option in the **As** list box, and click **OK**

The customer letter, **Letter2.doc,** is open, but the workbook containing this month's special values is not open. You will open the worksheet and link selected cells into the Word document.

Linking Excel worksheet cells to a Word document:

1. Start Excel and open the **Avicon2.xls** worksheet. Buttons representing the worksheet and the customer letter appear on the taskbar

2. With the **Avicon2.xls** worksheet displayed, click the **Sale Items** tab to make that worksheet active

3. Select the cell range **A7:D12,** which lists this month's special values

4. Click the **Copy** button on the Standard toolbar to place the cell range on the Clipboard. Excel displays a marquee around the selected cells indicating they are on the Clipboard

5. Click the **Letter2.doc** button to bring Word to the foreground and display the customer letter

EXCEL

6. Click **File** on the menu bar, click **Save As**, type **Letter2Link** in the File name text box, and click the **Save** button to save the letter under a new name. That way, if you make a mistake, you can always revert to the previous version of the letter and try it again

7. Scroll down the document, locate the phrase *[insert Excel worksheet with products, country, artists' names, and prices]*, press and hold the **Ctrl** key, click anywhere inside the text **[insert Excel worksheet with products, country, artists' names, and prices]**, and then release the **Ctrl** key. Word highlights the entire tag

8. Press the **Delete** key to remove the entire tag. This action also moves the Word insertion point to the place where you want to link to the worksheet (see Figure 7.16)

FIGURE 7.16

Selecting the location to link an Excel cell range

temporary tag marking the location to paste the worksheet link

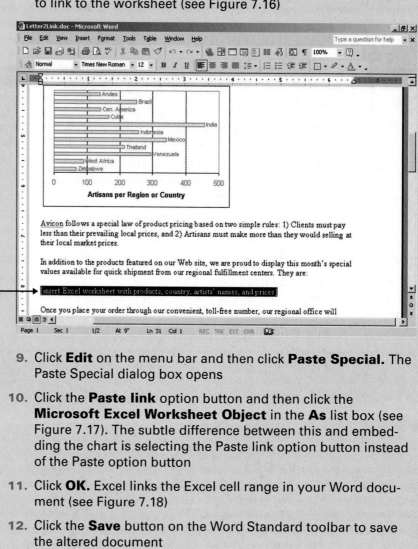

9. Click **Edit** on the menu bar and then click **Paste Special.** The Paste Special dialog box opens

10. Click the **Paste link** option button and then click the **Microsoft Excel Worksheet Object** in the **As** list box (see Figure 7.17). The subtle difference between this and embedding the chart is selecting the Paste link option button instead of the Paste option button

11. Click **OK.** Excel links the Excel cell range in your Word document (see Figure 7.18)

12. Click the **Save** button on the Word Standard toolbar to save the altered document

The linked worksheet looks about the same as the embedded chart. Both are objects from an Excel workbook and both first appeared with selection handles around their perimeters. The big difference between

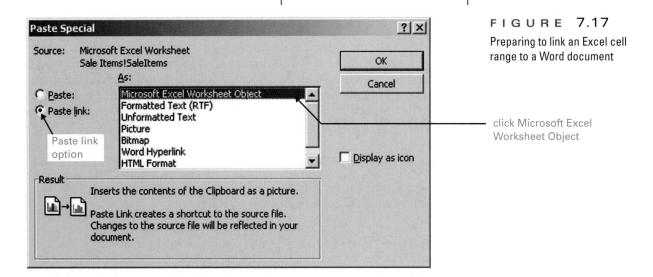

FIGURE 7.17

Preparing to link an Excel cell range to a Word document

click Microsoft Excel Worksheet Object

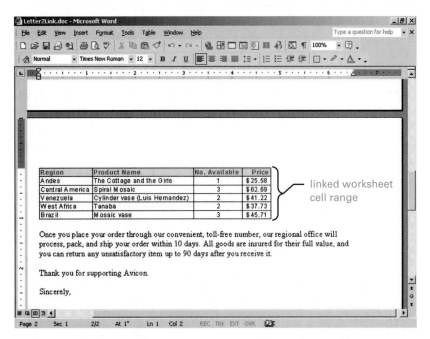

FIGURE 7.18

Linked Excel cell range in the customer letter

linked worksheet cell range

them is that the embedded object is a self-contained chart that has no connection to the original workbook chart. The linked Excel worksheet cells you just pasted into the customer letter are different. They are a live link to the real worksheet, not a copy of the cells.

The way linked worksheet cells behave in a Word document is similar to the behavior of a television and a television studio. You can think of the cells appearing in the Word document as the television set. It displays a picture of the worksheet cells. A television camera is trained on the worksheet cells in the workbook. Any time someone changes one or more of the worksheet cells, the television camera transmits that change to the television set in the Word document.

In the previous exercise, both the Word document (customer letter) and the Excel workbook (**Avicon2.xls**) are open as you link them. You might wonder what would happen if you made changes to the Excel workbook cells and the Word document were not open. Would the Word document somehow know about the Excel worksheet changes, or would it display stale information? The best way to find out is to experiment.

EXCEL

Modifying a Linked Excel Worksheet

When you make changes to a document—a Word document, Excel worksheet, or PowerPoint slide—you do not need to open the container document containing the link to the source. Whenever you open a document containing a link, the program automatically refreshes the link by examining the file containing the source data and loading it into the container document.

Refreshing Linked Information

Bill wants you to make three changes to the linked worksheet cells containing this month's special values as follows:

- Change the value of the number of available vases called *The Cottage and the Girls* to 4. (Bill's assistant read the quantity incorrectly when he entered the original information.)
- Change the value of the number of available vases called *Spiral Mosaic* from 3 to 2.
- Change the price of the product called *Tanaba* from $37.73 to $42.55.

You will make the first change listed above while both the customer letter and the worksheet are open. You will make the second and third changes after you close the customer letter. That way, you can observe whether or not Word refreshes the link when you reopen the document after making changes in the Excel source data.

Altering Excel source data linked to a Word document:

1. Click the **Microsoft Excel** button on the taskbar to make **Avicon2.xls** active

2. Press **Esc** to remove the copy border from around the cell range

3. Click cell **C8,** type **4,** and press **Enter** to complete the quantity change for the vase titled *The Cottage and the Girls*
   Next, go to the Word document to see if the value changed in the linked version displayed in the customer letter

4. Click the **Letter2Link.doc** button on the taskbar to switch to the Word document. Notice that the Word document updates automatically (see Figure 7.19)

5. Click the **Save** button on the Standard toolbar to save the changed customer letter

---

To answer the question, "What happens when I make a change when the container document is closed?," you will do exactly that. First, you will close the customer letter and then you will make changes to the source data that is linked to the document and save the worksheet. Then you will close the Excel worksheet and open the customer letter to see if it is updated.

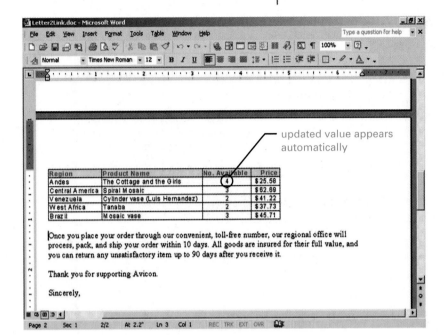

FIGURE 7.19
Updated value in customer letter

Altering Excel source data linked to a closed Word document:

1. Click **File** on the Word menu bar and click **Close** to close the customer letter but leave Word open. Click **No** if a dialog box appears asking if you want to save your changes

2. Click the **Microsoft Excel** button on the taskbar to switch back to the **Avicon2.xls** worksheet

3. Click cell **C9**, type **2**, and press **Enter**

4. Click cell **D11**, type **42.55**, and press **Enter**. That completes the changes to the worksheet

5. Click the **Save** button on the Standard toolbar to save the changes to Avicon2.xls and then click **File** on the menu bar and click **Exit** to close Excel
    Next, open the customer letter to verify that the changes you made appear in the customer letter

6. Click the **Microsoft Word** button on the taskbar to make Word active. No document is open

7. Click the **Open** button on the Standard toolbar, navigate to the folder containing **Letter2Link.doc,** click **Letter2Link.doc** , click **Open,** and scroll down to the linked worksheet. Notice that the values in the Word document are current. The linkage between Word and Excel automatically refreshed the changes so that they appear in the letter (see Figure 7.20)

8. Click the **Save** button on the Standard toolbar to save the document **Letter2Link.doc**

9. Click **File** on the menu bar and click **Exit** to close Word

EXCEL

F I G U R E   7.20

Document with all changes
refreshed

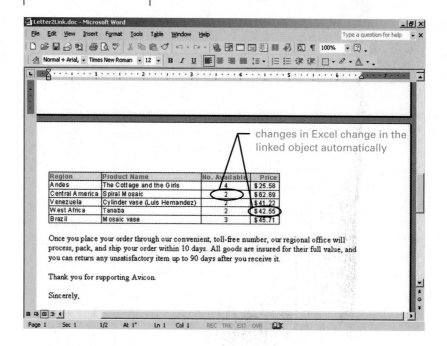

Bill is pleased with the customer letter. It contains the company logo, an embedded chart, and a linked worksheet that responds instantly to changes in the source Excel document.

SESSION 7.1   *making* **the grade**

1. If you want to display data in many different documents and you want to ensure that each document displays the same information, you should _____ the object into the documents.

2. You link or embed objects into your document by first copying them to the _____.

3. Use the _____ command in the Edit menu to create a linked or embedded object in the container document.

4. OLE stands for _____ _____ and _____.

5. Make the following modifications to the letter **Letter2Link.doc.** Open **Letter2Link.doc** and save it as **Letter22Link.doc.** Scroll down to the embedded chart, double-click it to launch Excel, and change the Value Axis title color by doing the following. Click the **Value Axis Title** *Artisans by Region or Country.* Click the **Format Axis Title** button on the Chart toolbar, click the **Font** tab, click the **Color list box arrow,** and click the **Brown** color square (top row, column 2). Click **OK** to close the Format Axis Title dialog box. Click **Chart** in the menu bar, and then click **Chart Options.** Click in the **Chart title** text box, type **November 2002,** and click **OK.** Click outside the chart to deselect it. Scroll down farther into the customer letter to the Excel worksheet. Double-click the worksheet and change the price of the Cylinder vase (by Luis Hernandez) to **$56.75.** Save the Excel workbook and exit Excel. Click outside the worksheet area in the Word document. Save, print, and close the customer letter. Exit Word.

SESSION 7.2 MERGING AN EXCEL LIST INTO A WORD DOCUMENT

In this section, you will learn how use mail merge, another form of object linking and embedding, to fill in selected fields of a Word document with information stored in an Excel worksheet. You will see how to forge cooperation between two programs in which the container program requests data from the source program one data record at a time. Finally, you will learn how to publish an Excel worksheet as a World Wide Web page.

DESIGNING AND CREATING A LETTER LINKED TO AN EXCEL LIST

Organizations frequently have quite an extensive customer list containing all sorts of useful information. Large lists are stored in a database and accessed with a database product such as Microsoft Access. Typically, the customer database contains fields for customer name, address (street, city, state, and postal code). In addition, the customer database often contains other handy data that the marketing department uses to send out fliers to a specific subset of their audience—data such as the age range of the customer, whether or not the customer has small children, and the largest order amount.

Much of the customer data is available through sources such as information the customer supplies through order forms. A company can obtain a lot of information by drawing inferences from the types of products each customer purchases and the frequency of those item purchases. Several grocery chains employ a very simple way to track consumer spending habits—the discount card, sometimes called the club card. The card provides discounts for selected transactions when you present it at the grocery checkout counter. Grocery club card discounts provide a significant incentive for a customer to give up a bit of information. What is the information? It is the exact identity of all grocery items you purchase each time you go to the store. Customer information and the data associated with customers is valuable information.

Avicon does not have a club card, but they do have a customer list. Part of the customer list is stored in an Excel worksheet—data that Bill requested be extracted from the database. Another part is saved in a database. The customer list in the Excel worksheet is stored in a separate workbook away from other information. Bill does not want the customer list stored in the same Excel worksheet as the other Avicon information. In particular, he does not want the customer list to be mailed by accident along with the Avicon worksheet.

Designing a Letter for Mail Merge

Bill wants to mail out the letter you worked on in Session 7.1 to a select group, or target group, of customers. The target group has a history of purchasing the vases of the type and origin listed in this month's specials on the **Avicon2.xls** worksheet. Bill would like you to customize the customer letter by filling in the names and addresses of all customers who live in two ranges of postal codes and who fit certain profiles. He tells you that he has already asked the database administrator to extract the names and addresses of the customers fitting a particular purchasing profile and to place that customer data into an Excel workbook. Because the entire customer list is over 128,500 customers and climbing, Bill explains that handling the entire customer list in an Excel workbook would be

EXCEL

cumbersome. He wants you to merge the customer names into the letter and print the letters. When you get ready to merge the list, he will provide details about how to select the customers from the list by postal code. Bill wants you to use Word's Mail Merge facilities to merge the Excel customer list data into the appropriate places in the letter's inside address. He also wants you to add a new sentence to the letter making it a little more personalized by including the customer's first and last names.

Before you start the process of merging the customer name and address list to produce multiple copies of the letter, you want to make sure that the letter's design is okay. In addition, you want to examine an overview of the merging process itself. Figure 7.21 shows a diagram of the mail merge process with the Excel data flowing into the Word letter at specific locations.

Using instructions available in Word, you will locate the data fields in the Excel list containing information to merge into the letter—Excel-named columns such as FirstName, LastName, City, State, and ZipCode. In the form letter, you select from a list of available Excel fields and place these symbolic field names anywhere you want an actual customer name or address value to appear. A named Excel field can appear in more than one location in the form letter.

Modifying the Letter for Mail Merge

The letter that Bill wants to modify so that it will contain customer names and addresses is the one you saved in Session 7.1. The latest version of it containing the logo, embedded graphic, and linked worksheet is called **Letter2Link.doc** ("link" in the name reminds you that it contains links to other files).

F I G U R E   7.21

Designing a document for mail merge

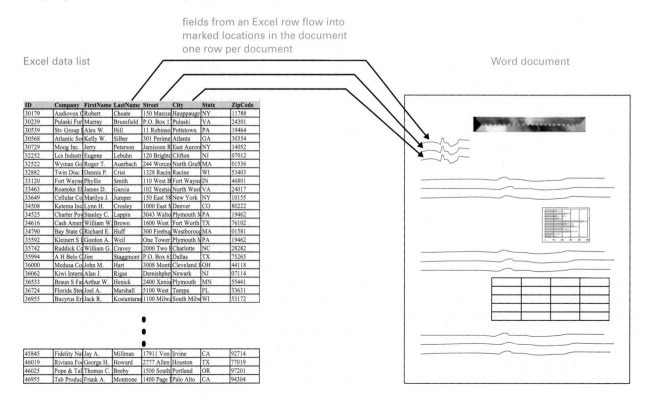

You begin by opening the letter in Word and saving it under a new name. That way, you preserve the letter's latest version from Session 7.1. In addition, you will position the insertion point where the customer's name and address is to appear—in the inside address. Conveniently, Bill has marked the model letter with a special tag.

Creating a new document and positioning the cursor:

1. Start Word by clicking the **Start** button on the task bar, pointing to **Programs,** and clicking **Microsoft Word** in the Programs menu. Word opens and displays a blank document

2. Click the **Open** button on the Standard toolbar, click the **Look in list box arrow** and go to the folder containing the file **Letter2Link.doc,** click **Letter2Link.doc** in the Open dialog box, and click the **Open** button to open the file. The letter you modified in Session 7.1 opens

tip: *Remember that you also can double-click the file name to open the file. You may find that method more convenient.*

3. Click **File** on the menu bar, click **Save As,** type **Letter3Merge.doc** in the File name list box, and click the **Save** button in the Save As dialog box. Word saves the document under its new name

4. Scroll to the top of the document, if necessary, so that the logo, company address, and the tag [insert inside address] are visible, move the mouse pointer to the left of the tag, and click the mouse to position the insertion point in the Word document (see Figure 7.22)

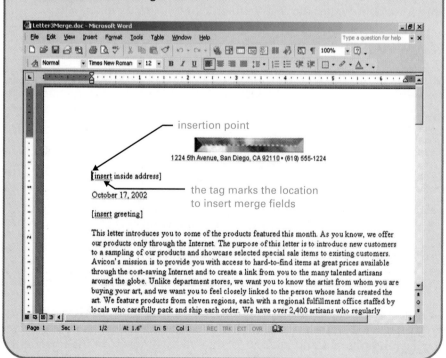

FIGURE 7.22

Positioning the insertion point

> **tip:** *If your document contains paragraph symbols, you can turn off their display by clicking the **Show/Hide** ¶ button on Word's Standard toolbar. Your display may be different from Figure 7.22 if Word is displaying your document in Normal View. To match the view in Figure 7.22, simply click **View** on Word's menu bar and then click **Print Layout**.*

Now you have established the insertion point for the customer's address information. If you were creating a typical customer letter, you would simply type in the customer name, street number, street name, city, state, and postal code to complete the inside address. But that would be impractical for a large list of customers and their addresses. That is exactly the type of situation where you can take advantage of Word's mail merge capabilities. Instead of typing each customer's name and address into new copies of a form letter, you can insert name and address "variables," called *merge fields,* as placeholders in the letter. When all the merge fields are in place in a form letter, you ask Word to produce merged documents. Word substitutes into the merge fields the corresponding data field one customer row at a time. It then produces as many copies of the letter as there are rows in the customer list with real customer data substituted for the merge field names for each unique letter. Word can perform this operation for hundreds or thousands of names in a matter of seconds. If you discover an error in the letter or the data, you can save the document containing the merge fields and make corrections. Then you can perform the mail merge again. When the result is good, you simply print out the merged documents.

MERGING SOURCE DATA INTO THE CONTAINER DOCUMENT

Next, you will use a handy Mail Merge Helper dialog box to step through the process of selecting mail merge fields and placing them into the form letter. Locating the merge fields requires the cooperation of Excel to open and examine fields in the Excel list containing customer data. The first step is to identify the source document, your customer letter.

Identifying the Merge Field Source Data File

> *Identifying the container document to hold mail merge fields:*
>
> 1. With the customer letter, **Letter3Merge.doc,** open in Word, click **Tools,** point to **Letter and Mailings**, and then click **Mail Merge Wizard.** The Step 1 of 6 of the Mail Merge Wizard task pane opens (see Figure 7.23)
>
> 2. Ensure that the **Letters** option at the top of the task pane is selected, then click **Next: Starting document** at the bottom of the task pane to continue. The Mail Merge Step 2 of 6 task pane appears

You have identified the container document, **Letter3Merge.doc,** to Word. The next step is to locate the source file that contains merge fields, the customer names and addresses, that you will insert in the form letter

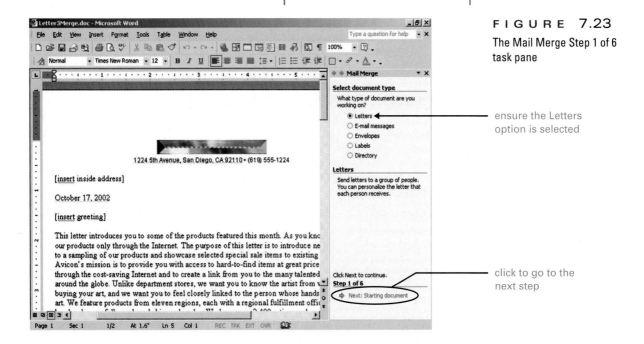

FIGURE 7.23

The Mail Merge Step 1 of 6
task pane

in the appropriate places. Bill explains that you first identify the file containing the data that constitutes the name and addresses to merge into the letter. The data file can be another Word document, an Excel worksheet, an Access database, or several other structured data file formats. If a Word document is the source data file, Mail Merge expects the data to be in a Word table. In this case, the data is an Excel worksheet, which automatically provides a tablelike structure consisting of Excel rows and columns.

Identifying the source file and selecting merge fields:

1. Ensure that the **Use the current document** option is selected in Mail Merge Step 2 of 6 and then click **Next: Select recipients** to continue creating your mail merge letter. The Mail Merge Step 3 of 6 appears (see Figure 7.24)

2. Ensure that the **Use an existing list** option in the Select recipients panel is selected, then click the **Browse** link in the Use an existing list panel. The Select Data Source dialog box opens

3. Click the **Look in** list box, navigate to the disk drive and folder containing the file ex07Customers.xls, click **ex07Customers.xls,** and click the **Open** button. Word opens the Select Table dialog box (see Figure 7.25)

4. Click **Database** in the list of choices in the Name column, ensure that the check box labeled *First row of data contains column headers* contains a checkmark, and then click **OK**. The Mail Merge Recipients dialog box opens (see Figure 7.26). The dialog box lists all rows and columns that comprise the list of customers found in an Excel worksheet

EXCEL

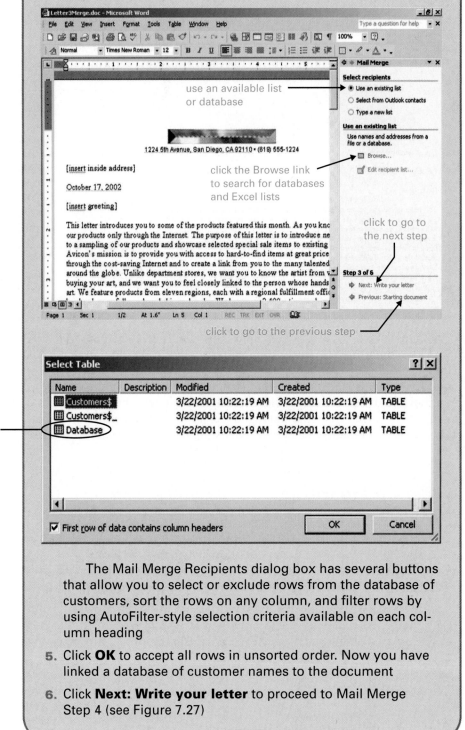

Excel worksheet named cell
range containing customer
names and addresses

The Mail Merge Recipients dialog box has several buttons
that allow you to select or exclude rows from the database of
customers, sort the rows on any column, and filter rows by
using AutoFilter-style selection criteria available on each column heading

5. Click **OK** to accept all rows in unsorted order. Now you have
   linked a database of customer names to the document

6. Click **Next: Write your letter** to proceed to Mail Merge
   Step 4 (see Figure 7.27)

Things look just about as they did before you executed the Tools, Mail
Merge command. Now that you have associated a database with the form
letter, you can place field names from the Excel database list in the form
letter. Later, Word will merge data rows, one by one from the Excel list,
and create many personalized letters with unique customer name and
address information in each one.

click field name to sort rows by that field

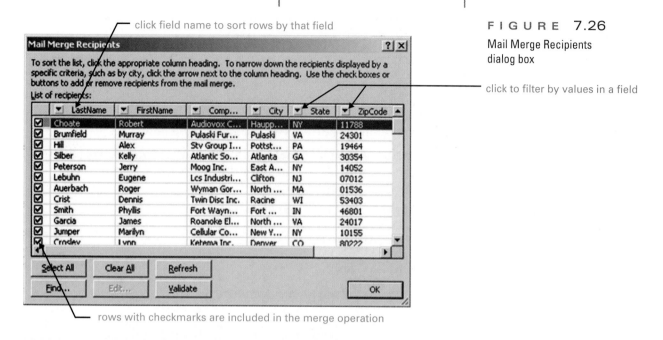

F I G U R E   7.26

Mail Merge Recipients
dialog box

click to filter by values in a field

rows with checkmarks are included in the merge operation

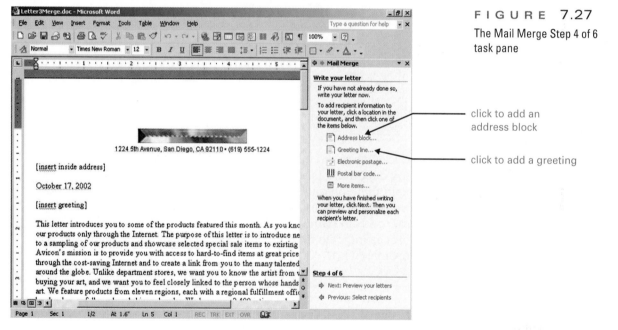

F I G U R E   7.27

The Mail Merge Step 4 of 6
task pane

click to add an
address block

click to add a greeting

Inserting Merge Fields

Now you are ready to place merge fields in the letter's inside address and
other locations within the letter. Inserting merge fields means you are
inserting into the container document special markers that are linked to the
data source and identify the data field by name. You can think of merge
fields as variables—generic names—that Word and Excel work together to
fill in with real values from each customer record or other data source.

EXCEL

F I G U R E   7.28

Insert Address Block dialog box

Inserting a merge field into the customer letter:

1. Click and drag across the tag **[insert inside address]** to select it, but do not select the space following the right bracket, and press **Delete** to remove the tag and position the insertion point at the inside address location in the letter

2. Click the **Address block ...** link in the Write your letter panel of the task pane. The Insert Address Block dialog box opens (see Figure 7.28)

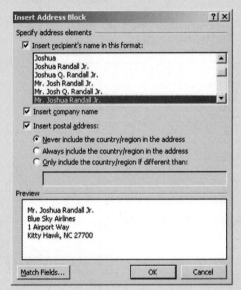

3. Click **OK.** Word inserts the merge field {{Address Block}} into the document (see Figure 7.29). The Address Block is a special field that contains fields such as name, address, and zip code from the Excel list. Opening and closing braces enclose the merge field name and the entire string is the merge field. The braces indicate that the enclosed text is a merge field and not ordinary text

Next, insert the greeting, sometimes called the salutation: "Dear ..." in place of the "[insert greeting]" tag.

Inserting the greeting:

1. Select the **[insert greeting]** tag by dragging the mouse across it, and then press the **Delete** key to delete the tag in preparation for substituting merge fields

2. Click the **Greeting line** link (see Figure 7.27) in the Write your letter panel of the Mail Merge task pane. The Greeting Line dialog box appears (see Figure 7.30)

3. Click **OK** to close the Greeting Line dialog box. Word places the field {{GreetingLine}} in the letter

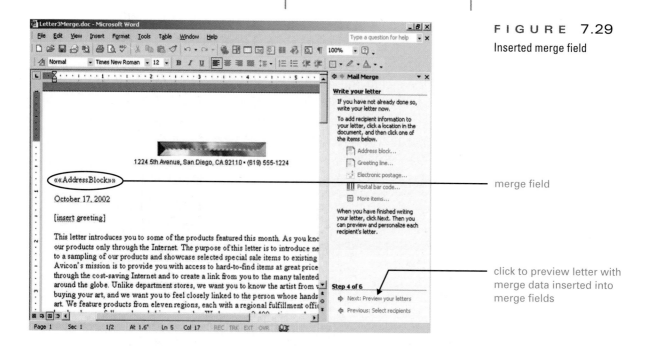

FIGURE 7.29
Inserted merge field

merge field

click to preview letter with merge data inserted into merge fields

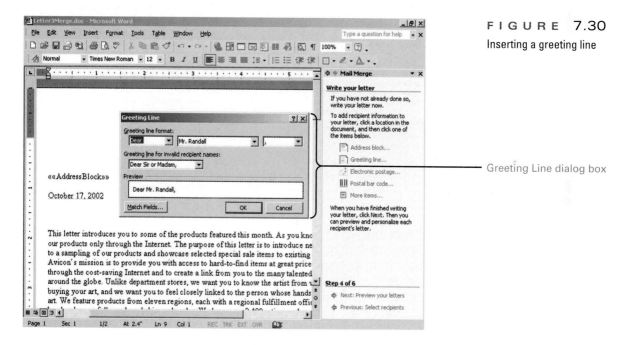

FIGURE 7.30
Inserting a greeting line

Greeting Line dialog box

You inspect the two merge fields you have inserted into the Word document. They are all in the correct position, although Word provides no clue whether or not the actual customer names and addresses will be correct.

PREVIEWING MERGED DATA

Bill looks at the letter's merged fields and overall design. Like you, Bill is concerned about whether real customer information will look good in the letter. He asks you to display a sample of a customer letter before going any further.

EXCEL

FIGURE 7.31

Previewing merge fields

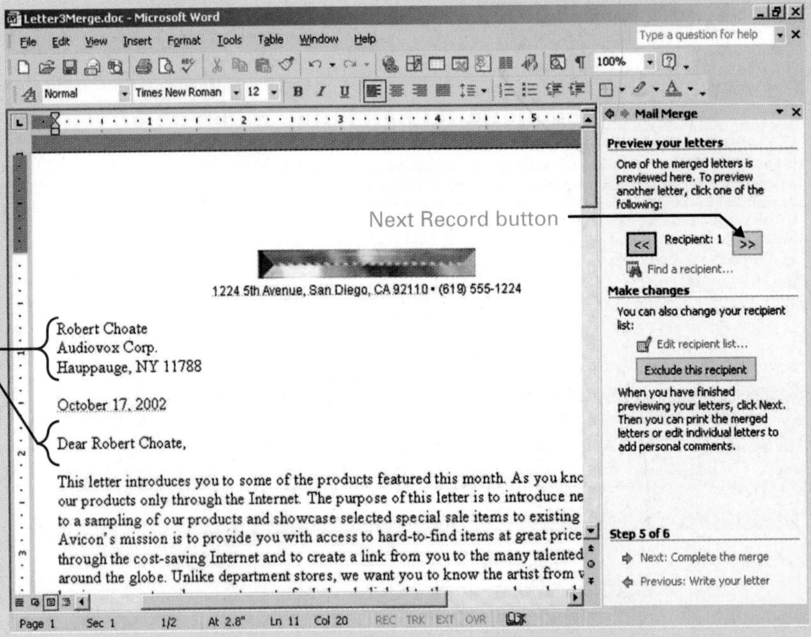

Previewing merged data:

1. Click the **Next: Preview your letters** link (see Figure 7.29). The inside address displays the first customer record, Robert Choate, Audiovox Corp. in Hauppauge, NY (see Figure 7.31).

2. Click the **Next Record** button (see Figure 7.31) in the Mail Merge task pane to display the next customer's information in the merge fields.

preview of customer data inserted in merge fields

Next Record button

3. Click the **Previous: Write your letter** link to prepare to add more merge fields to your form letter

Bill is happy to see the records. He does not want customers' records from states other than Ohio or Pennsylvania merged into the letter, and you assure him that you will filter the source data so that only records matching Bill's criteria appear in the merged set of letters.

Looking at the mail merge preview, Bill notices that the customer street address is missing. He asks you to look into why the Address Block field does not contain this vital information and to correct it. He wants you to remove the company name from the Address Block also.

Adding a merge field and removing one in the Address Block field:

1. Click the **Address Block** merge field. The merge field darkens to indicate that you have selected an entire field, not an ordinary bit of text

2. Right-click the **Address Block** merge field. A shortcut menu appears

3. Click **Edit Address Block.** The Insert Address Block appears (see Figure 7.28)

4. Click the **Match Fields** button at the bottom of the dialog box. The Match fields dialog box opens. You can add fields to the Address Block collection of fields by indicating which of your field names correspond to address information

5. Click the **list box arrow** to the right of the Address 1 name in the Required Information list, move the mouse to the Street field (a column name in the Excel data list) (see Figure 7.32), and click Street. "Street" appears in the field corresponding to Address 1

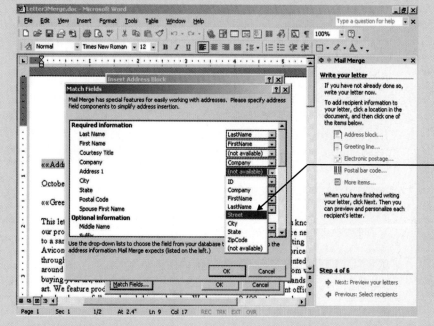

FIGURE 7.32
Match Fields dialog box

select Street to correspond to Address 1

6. Click **OK** to close the Match Fields dialog box. The Insert Address Block dialog box reappears

7. Click the **Insert company name** check box to remove its checkmark. With the check box cleared, the company name will not be part of the Address Block

8. Click **OK** to finalize your Address Block modifications and close the Insert Address Block dialog box

Though you do not need to delete any merge fields here, you ought to know how to do it in case you add a field by mistake and want to remove it.

task reference

Deleting a Mail Merge Field

• Click the mail merge field you want to delete

• Press the **Delete** key

ADDING MERGE FIELDS IN OTHER LOCATIONS IN THE DOCUMENT

Bill wants you to add another sentence to the letter following the third sentence of the first paragraph. That sentence will personalize the letter by adding each customer's first and last names in the body of the letter. The sentence you are to add is: "We at Avicon appreciate your interest, [customer name]." The FirstName and LastName merge fields replace "[customer name]" in the added sentence.

FIGURE 7.33

Insert Merge Field dialog box

available merge fields (column labels in the Excel data list)

> *Inserting a merge field in the body of the customer letter:*
>
> 1. Click to the right of the third sentence, which ends with "... sale items to existing customers"—immediately after the blank that follows the period ending the sentence. (You may want to use the document's horizontal scroll bar to move to view the right side of the letter)
>
> 2. Type **We at Avicon appreciate your interest,** type **,** (comma), and press the **Spacebar**
>
> 3. Click the **More items** link in the Mail Merge panel to display the available merge field names. The Insert Merge Field opens (see Figure 7.33)

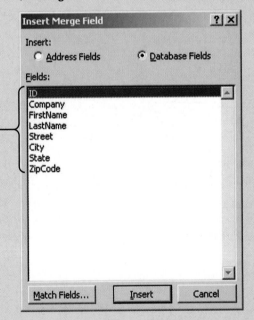

> 4. Ensure that the **Database Fields** button is selected, click **FirstName,** click the **Insert** button, click **LastName,** click the **Insert** button, and click the **Close** button to close the dialog box
>
> 5. Press the **left arrow** key to move the Word insertion point between the newly created fields, press **Spacebar,** move the insertion point just after the LastName field, type **.** (period), and press the **Spacebar** to complete the newly added sentence. Figure 7.34 shows the letter with the added merge fields FirstName and LastName

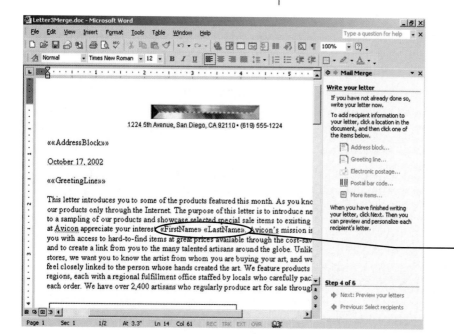

FIGURE 7.34
Letter with all customer merge fields inserted

FirstName and LastName merge fields in the letter body

FILTERING AND SORTING SOURCE RECORDS

Recall that Bill wants to produce letters for customers in selected zip codes that correspond to a few cities in Pennsylvania and Ohio. He specifically does not want all the customers in the Excel worksheet to be included in the mailing.

A very handy database-like feature provided by mail merge is record filtering. A *filter*, or *query*, constitutes the criteria that select a subset of the available records from the source data file. When you filter records for mail merge, only those records that match the criteria appear in merged fields in the container document. Filtering is used frequently. Realtors tailor their listings of recent real estate sales by zip code; credit card companies filter their mailed advertisements to people in a particular age bracket or income level, and so on.

You have viewed a few of the records and realize that they are from customers around the United States. If you were to perform a mail merge operation without using a filter, 75 customers would receive it, far more than the intended circulation this month. Recall that Bill wants zip codes from 19400 to 19499 (selected Pennsylvania communities) and from 43000 to 45800 (selected Ohio communities).

Sorting, another handy feature of mail merge, sorts merged records into order. You can select any of the source file field names as the sort key, and data are delivered to mail merge in either ascending or descending order on the sort field(s) you select. Similar to the Sort command available in the Data menu, the Sort Records option lets you supply up to three sort fields.

Establishing a source-data mail merge filter:

1. Click the **Next: Preview your letters** link on the Mail Merge task pane. The Mail Merge Step 5 of 6 task pane opens

2. Click the **Edit recipient list** link in the Make changes panel of the task pane. The Mail Merge Recipients dialog box opens (see Figure 7.26)

3. Scroll to the right side of the database list so that the ZipCode field is visible in the Mail Merge Recipients dialog box

4. Click the **ZipCode column heading list arrow,** and then click **(Advanced ...).** The Filter and Sort dialog box opens

5. Click the **Field** list box, drag the **Field scroll box** down to scroll the list until ZipCode appears, and click **ZipCode,** which is the field you will use to filter the customer records

6. Click in the topmost **Comparison** list box and then click the **Greater than or equal** in the list

7. Click the **Compare to** text box, type **19400,** and press the **Tab** key to move to the logical operator list box
    So far, you have established one of the criteria that make up the filter. Next, you specify the remaining filters

8. Ensure that **And** appears on the left end of the second row. And is a logical operator. Click the **Field** list box in the second row, locate and click **ZipCode** in the Field text box, click the **Comparison** list box, and select **Less than or equal,** click the **Compare to** text box, and type **19499**

9. Using Figure 7.35 as a guide, continue as you have in the preceding steps and complete the Filter and Sort dialog box. Do not click the OK button yet. You will be making one more modification in the Query Options dialog box

FIGURE 7.35
Completed Filter Records panel

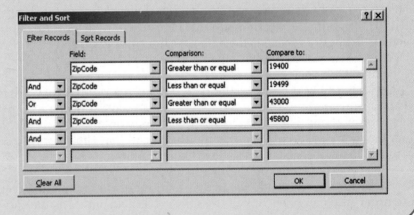

Here's how the filter you created above works (study Figure 7.35). First, the condition written in the first row—ZipCode >= 19400—must be true, along with the condition written in the second row—ZipCode<= 19499—for a customer row to appear in the mail merge letter. The third and fourth rows have a similar structure: Both the condition in the third row *and* the fourth row must be true (simultaneously) for a customer row to appear in the mail merge letter. Because the Or condition appears in the third row, a customer's data can satisfy either the first two rows' conditions or the third and fourth rows' combined conditions to appear in the mail merge letter. In other words, a customer's ZipCode value can satisfy either pair of conditions in order to be merged into the data.

Because you can reduce postage costs when you sort the envelopes to be mailed in order by zip code, Bill asks you to print the letters in ascending order by their zip codes. While there may not be enough records to qualify for a discount, it is a good idea to sort the letters just in case mail merge produces a large number of customers in the specified zip codes now or in the future. Mail merge does not sort the source file records. Instead, mail merge sorts the records into a temporary file after they are extracted from the source data file.

Establishing a mail merge sort order:

1. Click the **Sort Records** tab of the Filter and Sort dialog box

2. Click the topmost **Sort by** list box to reveal the list of field names from the source data file. You can sort the records by any of the fields listed

3. Type **Z** to zoom the scroll list to the ZipCode entry, press **Enter** to select **ZipCode,** and ensure that the **Ascending** option button to its right is selected (see Figure 7.36)

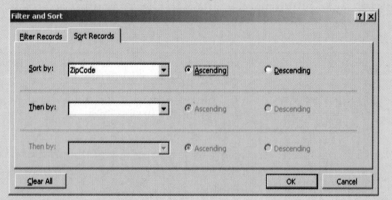

4. Click **OK** to save all of the Filter and Sort options—both the Filter Record options and the Sort Records options. The Mail Merge Recipients dialog box reappears. Notice that the filtered list contains six entries. Scroll to the list so that you can see the ZipCode field and can see that the records are in ascending order by ZipCode (see Figure 7.37)

5. Click **OK** to close the revised mail merge list of recipients

FIGURE 7.36
Completed Sort Records panel

With query options specified, you can merge in the records. The query options ensure that only customer records matching the specified zip code ranges appear in the merged letters and that the customer records appear in ascending order by zip code.

CREATING AND PRINTING MERGED DOCUMENTS

The customer letter is linked to the customer data in the workbook **ex07Customers.xls,** and you have set up both selection criteria (a filter) and sorting criteria. All that is left is to perform the merge operation, preview and approve the merged documents, and print them.

EXCEL

FIGURE 7.37

Revised Mail Merge
Recipients list

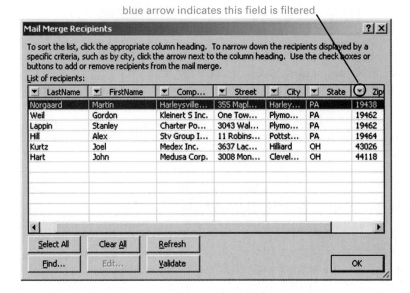

Creating Mail Merge Documents

Bill wants you to go ahead and perform the merge operation, but he wants to review some of the merged letters to check them for accuracy before you print them.

Previewing the filtered list of recipients:

1. In the Mail Merge Step 5 of 6 task pane, click the **>>** and **<<** buttons to preview the addressee fields in the letter for each of the six customers

2. Click the **Next: Complete the merge** link at the bottom of the task pane. The Mail Merge Step 6 of 6 task pane opens (see Figure 7.38)

FIGURE 7.38

The Mail Merge Step 6 of 6
task pane

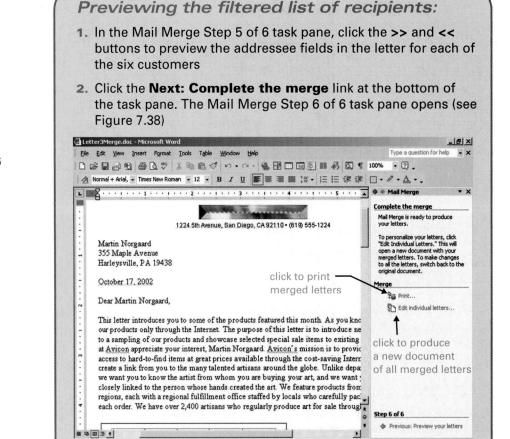

3. Click the **Save** button on the Standard toolbar to save all the work you have done

Printing Mail Merge Documents

Bill looks over your shoulder as you preview the merged letters. Mail merge produced six customer letters matching the filter criteria you established. He gives the okay to print them. Because you are experimenting with mail merge, you will print only two of the letters instead of the entire set.

Printing the customer letters:

1. Click **View** on the menu bar, click **Header and Footer,** and type your first and last names in the Header

2. Click **Close** on the Header and Footer toolbar to close it. Step 1 will identify your output

3. Click the **Print** link on the Mail Merge task pane (see Figure 7.38). The Merge to Printer dialog box opens

4. Click the **From** option button, type **1** in the leftmost text box, press **Tab,** type **2** (you will print only the first two of the two-page letters). Figure 7.39 shows the completed Merge to Printer dialog box

5. Click **OK** to close the Merge to Printer dialog box and click **OK** to print the merged letters and close the Print dialog box

FIGURE 7.39
Completed Merge to Printer dialog box

SAVING CRUCIAL FILES AND DELETING UNNEEDED ONES

Bill looks at your output and is very pleased. Had you printed all six of the two-page customer letters, you would have no further use for the letters. The important file is the original mail merge document containing mail merge fields. Called the ***main document,*** this document contains all the information you need to create another set of mail merge documents using different filtering and sorting criteria. Your main document is called **Letter3Merge.doc.** If you had clicked the Edit individual letters link (see Figure 7.38), Mail Merge would produce a new document containing the merged customer letters. You could delete that document because it is generated from the main document, Letter3Merge.doc in this case. It is time to close the main mail merge document and save it for future mass mailings.

At any time, you can change the Mail Merge filter so that you include other customer groups, just as long as you save the main document.

> ### Saving the form letter and exiting Word:
> 1. Click the **Save** button on the Standard toolbar to save the letter in its final form called **Letter3Merge.doc**
> 2. Click **File** on the menu bar and click **Exit** to close Word

You have created a very interesting document that contains a pasted object, an embedded object, and a linked object. In addition, the letter contains merge fields into which Excel data are inserted upon request. Bill is pleased with the results and sends out the letters. He wants to send out mailers to a larger audience in two states, but he is content to wait until next week to do that.

SESSION 7.2   making the grade

1. You can use Word's _____ _____ facility to merge customer addresses from an Excel list of addresses into a Word document.

2. Instead of typing each of 500 customers' names into the inside address of a form letter, you can insert _____ fields as placeholders.

3. In the example illustrated in this chapter, the Excel customer list is called the _____ file or document and the Word letter into which the information is merged is called the _____ file or document.

4. To merge an Excel list of names and addresses into specific places in a form letter, the Excel list must have unique _____(s) at the top of each column identifying the column's data.

5. Make the following modifications to the Word letter, **Letter3Merge.doc.** Open **Letter3Merge.doc** and save it as **Letter33Merge.doc.** Make the Mail Merge toolbar visible by clicking **View** on the menu bar, pointing to **Toolbars,** and clicking **Mail Merge.** Add a new mail merge field to the letter by placing the Word insertion point just above the AddressBlock field in the inside address. Then type **Cust. ID:** and press the **Spacebar** to insert a blank after the colon. Click the Insert Merge Fields button on the Mail Merge toolbar to insert the ID mail merge field after the blank space following Cust. ID. Click the Mail Merge toolbar **Mail Merge Recipients** button and then make these changes: Create a filter to select only customers in Alabama (AL), Arizona (AZ), and Arkansas (AR). Sort the customers by their last names. Add your name to the Word Header (click **View, Header and Footer,** and enter it just as you do in Excel.) Now, print the merged letters (there are not many of them) by clicking the **Merge to Printer** button on the Mail Merge toolbar. Save **Letter33Merge.doc** and then close Word. If either Excel or Word asks if you want to save changes, click **No.**

SESSION 7.3 SUMMARY

Microsoft OLE technology allows information from one program to be pasted into another program's data file. There are three ways to paste information from one document into another, and all three methods involve the Clipboard as an intermediary. Copying information from a source document and pasting it into a container document provides a picture of the data. Copying information and then embedding it in a container provides a copy of the original data that you can edit using the embedded object's original program, even if the original source is no longer available. The third way to paste data is to paste a link to the original source file. When you double-click the linked object in the container document, the original program that created the data file loads the file. Changes that you make from within the container document to the object are actually changes to the single source document. Linking allows one source program's data to be altered by any files in which they are linked, but it also means anyone can change the single copy of source data. Embedded data allows independence from the source and dynamic editing simultaneously. Microsoft Office suite programs all can act as either clients—recipient documents in which other objects reside—or servers—providers of information linked or embedded in other files. For example, Excel can supply charts or worksheet cell information to Word documents or PowerPoint slides. Similarly, Word can provide text to Excel worksheets or Access database fields.

Mail merge provides a convenient way to bring together a fixed component, such as a letter, and a variable component, such as customer names and addresses, to produce multiple copies of a document. Merging information requires a source data file containing data and a container document that contains symbolic merge fields that receive actual data when the merge operation occurs. Merge fields are special tags in the main document that indicate where the associated source document data fields are placed. A document can contain multiple occurrences of the same merge field, and you can format merged data by formatting their merge fields.

When merging a large database or Excel list into a document, you may wish to restrict the records that are merged by supplying a filter. Using the Query Options button of the Merge dialog box, you can specify up to three sort fields. Executing Mail Merge produces a single document containing as many Word sections as there are unique letters produced for each unique group of merge field records. For 100 customers' addresses in a merge operation, for example, a 100-section document results. Once you have printed the merged document, you can delete it, saving only the main document and the source data file (Excel workbook in this chapter). The main document and the source data file are all that are required to generate mail merge documents when needed.

MOUS OBJECTIVES SUMMARY

- Embed an Excel object within a Word document—
  MOUS Ex2002e-1-2

task reference roundup

Task	Page #	Preferred Method
Mailing a workbook as an e-mail attachment	EX 7.11	• Open the Excel workbook you want to send as an e-mail attachment
		• Click **File** on the menu bar, point to **Send To,** and then click **Mail Recipient (as Attachment)**
		• Enter the recipient's e-mail address in the To text box
		• Click the **Send** button
Embedding an object	EX 7.14	• Start the source program, open the source document, select the object you want to copy, and click the **Copy** button on the Standard toolbar
		• Start the container (destination) program, open the container document that will contain the embedded object, and place the insertion point at the destination point in the container document
		• Click **Edit,** click **Paste Special,** click the **Paste** option button, click an option in the **As** list box, and click **OK**
Linking an object	EX 7.19	• Start the source program, open the source document, select the object you want to link, and click the **Copy** button on the Standard toolbar
		• Start the container (destination) program, open the container document that will contain the linked object, and place the insertion point at the destination point in the container document
		• Click **Edit,** click **Paste Special,** click the **Paste link** option button, click an option in the **As** list box, and click **OK**
Deleting a mail merge field	EX 7.35	• Click the mail merge field you want to delete
		• Press the **Delete** key

CROSSWORD PUZZLE

Across

1. The act of pasting a copy of an object into another document
5. The program or document that receives a pasted object is called a _____
7. The program from which you copy information is called a _____ program
8. Another word for a container program is a _____ program
9. The simplest way to place information from one data source into another
10. A pointer to an object from its location in the container document is a _____
11. The _____ document contains all the information you need to create another set of mail merge documents

Down

2. Eliminating an intermediary
3. A _____ document draws data from several sources
4. Another name for a link to a file that describes the location of the data file
6. The criteria collectively known as a _____ determines what subset of the data is merged into a container document

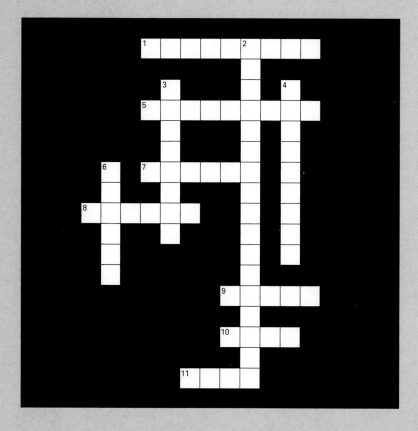

FILL-IN

1. A _____ document contains data that are pasted from one or more sources.

2. The Microsoft technology abbreviated _____ supports embedding and linking objects.

3. When you _____ an object, you can change it by double-clicking the object. Changing it does not affect the source document.

4. When you _____ an object in a document, changing the object changes its original source. The document containing the object has the file name and location on the computer of the object.

5. If you want container documents to always have the latest version of an Excel worksheet of sales figures, the best approach is to _____ the workbook to the documents.

6. Word's _____ _____ toolbar contains commands to insert merge fields into a Word document, start the merge process, or preview the results of a merge operation before you execute it.

REVIEW QUESTIONS

1. Explain the advantage(s) of linking an Excel worksheet into a letter versus pasting (not embedding) it.

2. Why might you want to name an Excel worksheet range before you paste that range into another document?

3. Discuss what, if anything, would happen if you formatted one of the Excel customer names and addresses with a font different from the others and then merged the data into a letter.

4. Discuss this statement: It is better to embed an object in a document than link to it from the container document.

CREATE A QUESTION

For each of the following answers, create an appropriate short question.

ANSWER

1. In Word, click Edit, click Paste Special, click the Paste option button, and then click Microsoft Excel Worksheet Object.

2. In Word, click Edit, click Paste Special, click the Paste link option button, and then click Microsoft Excel Worksheet Object.

3. Because you can update the object in all pasted documents by changing the object in its original location.

4. Mail merge provides filtering and sorting to accomplish this.

5. Select Paste, not Paste Special, from the Edit menu.

6. Click the Insert Merge Field button on the Mail Merge toolbar.

QUESTION

_____

_____

_____

_____

_____

_____

1. Prospecting with Excel Data and Merge Fields

SAT Savvy has been helping students prepare for the Scholastic Aptitude Test (SAT) exam for six years. Even though many students enroll each year in their courses, the SAT Savvy team feels that there are more students who need their help in preparation for the exam. SAT Savvy believes the SAT is the most important test students take before entering college since this is the one score most college admissions boards review and use to judge the student.

Jason Freeman was recently hired at SAT Savvy, and his manager wanted him to come up with a new way to attract parents to the company and the services they offer. SAT Savvy needed some type of proof that their courses helped students prepare for the test and get good scores. Jason decided that the best way to do this was to get information on all of the local high schools, calculate their average SAT scores, and determine what percentage of students attended one of SAT Savvy's courses.

Jason drafted a letter he will send to parents, **ex07SatLetter.doc.** In this letter, he wants to incorporate the data he has compiled in an Excel worksheet, **ex07SatScores.xls**

1. Click the **Start** button on the taskbar, point to **Programs,** click **Microsoft Excel,** and then locate and open the workbook **ex07SatScores.xls**
2. Click the **Start** button on the taskbar, point to **Programs,** click **Microsoft Word,** locate and open the Word document **ex07SatLetter.doc,** and save it as **SatLetter2.doc**
3. Scroll the document until you see the tag "[insert SAT worksheet here]"
4. Press and hold the **Ctrl** key, click anywhere inside the tag **[insert SAT worksheet here]**, and then release the **Ctrl** key to highlight the entire tag
5. Click the **Microsoft Excel – ex07SatScores.xls** button on the taskbar, click the **Name box list arrow,** click the name **SATdata,** and click the **Copy** button on the Standard toolbar

6. Click the **SatLetter2.doc** button on the taskbar to return to the word document, click **Edit** on the menu bar, click **Paste Special,** click the **Paste link** option, click **Microsoft Excel Worksheet Object,** and click the **OK** button
7. Ensure that only one blank line appears before the pasted worksheet and only one line appears after it

   Jason has just received some updated figures from students who took the SAT last month. The new average SAT score for Highland High is 790, Dingmann High is 1192, and Presidio High is 1410.
8. Click the **Microsoft Excel** button on the taskbar and update the Excel data with these new values, press the **Esc** key to remove the marquee from around the worksheet data, click cell **C4** and type **790,** click cell **C6** and type **1192,** click cell **C8** and type **1410,** and press **Enter**
9. Save and close **ex07SatScores.xls,** and then click the **SatLetter2.doc** button on the taskbar and observe the linked spreadsheet. Did the numbers in the Word Document also change? The letter Jason has drafted is to a particular parent. Insert merge fields into the letter so that he can quickly print several letters to different parents. You will use the worksheet **ex07SatAddresses.xls** to produce merge fields
10. Scroll to the top of the letter and locate the inside address tag "[Recipient address block]"
11. Click **Tools,** point to **Letters and Mailings,** click **Mail Merge Wizard,** click the **Next: Starting document** link in the task pane, and click the **Next: Select recipients** link in the task pane
12. Click the **Browse** link in the task pane, navigate the Look in list box to the disk and folder containing the workbook ex07SatAddresses.xls, click **ex07SatAddresses.xls,** and click the **Open** button

13. Click **MergeData** from the *Name* list box of the Select Table dialog box, click **OK** to close the Select Table dialog box, and click **OK** to close the Mail Merge Recipients dialog box

14. Click the **Next: Write your letter** link in the task pane

15. Click and drag across the tag **[Recipient address block]** in the letter to select it, click the **Address block** link in the Mail Merge task pane, and click **OK** to close the Insert Address Block dialog box

16. Select the entire tag **[First Name],** click the **More items** link in the Mail Merge task pane, click **First Name** in the Fields list, click the **Insert** button, and click the **Close** button

17. Select the entire tag **[student],** click the **More items** link in the Mail Merge task pane, click **Student** in the Fields list, click the **Insert** button, and click the **Close** button

18. Click **View** on the menu bar, click **Header and Footer,** type your first and last names in the header, and click the **Close** button on the Header and Footer toolbar

19. Click the **Next: Preview your letters** link on the Mail Merge task pane, click the **Next: Complete the merge** link, click the **Print** link in the task pane, and print two letters by specifying from **1** to **2** in the Merge to Printer dialog box, click **OK,** and then click **OK** in the Print dialog box to print the two letters

20. Save the changed **SatLetter2.doc** letter and close Word. Respond **No** if you are asked if you want to save the changed documents

2. Creating a Fax to Send to Amalgamated Holdings Board Members

Philip Hurd, the Chairman of the Board of Amalgamated Holdings, wants to hold a special meeting of the board members in Humble, Texas. He has created a letter requesting that selected board members convene at corporate headquarters on August 12. He asks you to send letters to all board members. In the letter, he wants you to include a chart of the company's stock prices for the preceding year. Philip has placed special tags in the letter indicating where

to insert address information, the member's name, and the chart. He asks you to use Mail Merge to insert the members' names in the letter and to place a copy of the chart in the letter. Because Philip may want to make last-minute formatting changes to the chart, he asks you to insert it so that the chart in the letter is linked to the workbook containing the chart. The Board of Directors member names are listed in a workbook named **ex07Amalgamated.xls.** The form letter is a Word document called **ex07Amalgamated.doc.**

1. Open the worksheet **ex07Amalgamated.xls** and click each sheet tab in turn to examine the structure and content of the data. The workbook contains data that you will merge into the form letter and a chart that you will link into the form letter

2. Click the **Common Stock Information** worksheet tab in preparation to copy the chart

3. Open in Word the document called **ex07Amalgamated.doc**

4. Save the document as **Amalgamated2.doc** so that you can preserve the original one

5. Press **Ctrl**, click **[insert chart here]** to select the text, release the **Ctrl** key, and press the **Delete** key to delete the text

6. Click the **Microsoft Excel** button on the taskbar to display to the worksheet, click the **Chart Area** of the chart object so that selection handles surround the entire chart, and then click the **Copy** button on the Standard toolbar to copy the chart to the Clipboard

7. Click the **ex07Amalgamated2.doc** button on the taskbar, click **Edit**, click **Paste Special**, click the **Paste link** option button, and click the **OK** button to paste (link) the chart

8. Scroll to the top of the document, press **Ctrl**, click **[insert member's address]** to select the text, release the **Ctrl** key, and press the **Delete** key to delete the text. Next, you will use Mail Merge to set up the remainder of the letter

9. Click **Tools**, point to **Letters and Mailings**, click **Mail Merge Wizard,** click the **Next: Starting document** link in the task pane, and click the **Next: Select recipients** link in the task pane

10. Click the **Browse** link in the task pane, navigate the Look in list box to the disk and folder containing the workbook ex07Amalgamated.xls, click **ex07Amalgamated.xls,** and click the **Open** button

11. Click **BoardMembers** from the *Name* list box of the Select Table dialog box, click **OK** to close the Select Table dialog box, and click **OK** to close the Mail Merge Recipients dialog box

12. Click the **Next: Write your letter** link in the task pane

13. Ensure that the Word insertion point is above the greeting and then click the **Address block** link in the Mail Merge task pane, and then click **OK** to close the Insert Address Block dialog box

14. Delete the text **[insert member's name]** in the salutation, click the **More items** link, and then insert the following merge fields in one line: **Title, FirstName,** and **LastName.** After inserting the fields, click Cancel to close the Insert Merge Field dialog box and then insert a space between each field in the greeting line

15. Insert your name in the document header

16. Click the **Next: Preview your letters** link on the Mail Merge task pane, click the **Next: Complete the merge** link, click the **Print** link in the task pane, and print two letters by specifying from 1 to 2 in the Merge to Printer dialog box (click **OK** to print)

17. Save the changed **Amalgamated2.doc** letter, close Word and Excel windows, and respond **No** if you are asked if you want to save the changed documents

challenge!

1. Sending a Fax to Multiple Recipients

Wayne Fisher is a consultant to the cattle industry and writes a monthly newsletter about cattle ranching. In addition to mailing newsletters out to over 200 subscribers around the United States, Wayne also maintains an elite clientele of customers who want to know his latest thinking on beef cattle nutrition on a weekly basis. He calls this elite group his Tier One clients. To provide weekly updates to his two dozen Tier One clients, he uses Word to compose his weekly hot sheets, which he faxes to the clients using the fax/modem attached to his computer. He uses mail merge to personalize and create his weekly facsimile. Name and address information for all of his clients—both Tier One clients and his monthly newsletter customers—are in one Excel list. The Tier One clients each have a "T1" in the ClientType column of the worksheet. Other clients have a "T2" in that column to distinguish the two groups.

Using Mail Merge, the form letter **ex07CattleNews.doc** and the Excel list of clients in the file **ex07CattleClients.xls,** create a custom letter. The bracketed tags inside the letter indicate which fields you should merge into the letter. Be sure to select only clients who are Tier One members (ClientType = T1) to merge into the letter, and sort the merged letters in ascending order by the Fax number (in the Merge options). Insert the merge fields indicated in the letter. Identify the letter as yours by placing your name in the document's header. Print a copy of the Main Document showing the merge field names, and print a copy of the first customer letter and the twelfth custom letter. Save the main mail merge document after you complete it.

2. Composing a Generic "Real Estate for Sale" Mailer

Sharon Grundies operates a small real estate office in Tucson, Arizona. Periodically, she produces a one-page brochure that her assistant delivers by hand to homes in selected areas. This month, she is prospecting in the zip code 92015 and wants to list properties on the ad piece that are similar in price to those in her prospect area. The letter she has composed is called **ex07Realtor.doc.** The workbook containing properties for sale is called **ex07Realtor.xls.** You are to link the section of the worksheet listing properties in 92015 to the letter. In particular, select only properties in the price range from $210,000 through $230,000—no higher and no lower—and place the linked cells just below the labels Parcel, Zip, Sqft, and Price.

Begin by opening **ex07Realtor.xls** and sorting the data by Zip and then by price within matching Zip values. Then open the letter (**ex07Realtor.doc**) and *link* (Edit, Paste Special) the section of the worksheet in the target zip code and price into the worksheet just below the labels. Place your name in the document header, print the document, and save both the document and the sorted worksheet.

1. Creating a Snappy Brochure for a Coffee Merchant

Create an advertising brochure that you pass out to residents near your coffee store. Located in a small shopping mall, Coffee Merchant serves espresso-style drinks and sells coffee beans. You want to advertise that your coffee bean prices are the lowest in the area. In order to back up your low-price claim, you go to the Web and search for coffee bean prices from four companies on the Web. Start by creating an Excel worksheet listing the price of one pound of these three coffee bean types: Yemen, Kenya AA, and Kona. List the preceding coffee names in cells B1 through D1. In cells A2 through A5, list Store 1, Store 2, Store 3, and Store 4. In the 12-cell range B2:D5, list the prices per pound of the four coffees from any four stores you locate on the Web. Save the completed worksheet as **CoffeePrices2.xls.** Then open **ex07CoffeeBrochure.doc** and embed the coffee prices worksheet cells in the indicated location. Near the top of the letter, in the indicated position, paste the logo that is stored in the file **ex07CoffeeLogo.jpg.** Place your name in the header of the Word document and print it. Save the document and worksheet.

To locate coffee prices, you can use a search engine such as the one at www.hotbot.com or at www.google.com. Type in "coffee beans" in the search text box, and then select one of four of the returned links to locate prices of the selected coffee beans. Here are some other links you can try: www.seattlesfinest.com, www.beanusa.com, www.coffeetraders.com/store.html, www.cafemoto.com/

2. Managing a CPA Firm's Clients

Christopher Hines has been a CPA for 16 years. He has noticed a shift in how educated clients are about their taxes and how involved clients want to be with their taxes. Clients are always expecting him to find new ways to ease their tax burdens. Fortunately, Christopher's clients are also increasingly getting more involved in the tax filing process. Clients want to have a deeper understanding of the process and the tax system. Many of them want to work with Christopher year-round to ensure that they are doing all they can to lower their taxes.

A few years ago, Christopher started sending monthly letters to all of his clients with updates, new ideas, and tax tips. The more informed his clients are, the less time he spends on explaining processes, giving him more time to spend on tax work. Christopher wants his clients to start preparing documents for his annual meeting with each of them. This month's letter will focus on what they should bring to the meeting. He also wants to help them become resourceful and use the Internet to answer their tax questions.

Open the Word document **ex07Tax.doc** and save as **Tax2.doc.** This is the letter Christopher will send his clients. First, embedded in the letter is the list of items that he wants his clients to bring to the meeting. Specifically, embed the Excel file **ex07TaxList.xls** in the client letter following the last paragraph. Be sure the embedded list is the same font (Times New Roman) and point size (12 pt) as the letter. Remember that the Excel data are embedded. Therefore, you can edit the data through the Word document.

Next, Christopher wants you to search the Web for helpful tax sites for his clients to reference. Go to the World Wide Web and access a search engine site such as www.google.com or www.yahoo.com to locate Web sites containing useful and practical tax help and tips. Be sure to only use sites on American tax returns and non-city-specific sites. Write an introductory paragraph explaining the usefulness of these sites and list a few of them for clients to reference.

The last thing Christopher wants you to do is create two graphs to illustrate how his clients find out about his services. Open **ex07TaxClients.xls,** which contains data on where Christopher's clients came from over the past two years. For each year, create an embedded pie chart illustrating the different percentages. Do not include a legend, but display the percentage and label above or near the pie slice. Embed the two graphs into the letter. Beneath the data, in the Excel worksheet **ex07TaxClients.xls,** Christopher accidentally embedded the closing paragraph for the letter. Copy the text and embed it into the letter. Print the letter with a salutation. Be sure to type Christopher's name following "Sincerely" and include your name in the Word document header. Print the letter. Close and save all files.

e-business

1. Billing Clients with Excel Invoices

Flora Style has been servicing the New Jersey area for four years. The owner, Desiree Monroe, spent several years studying botany and decided that opening her own floral service would be a fun way to use her knowledge. Flora Style is different from most floral shops because Desiree does not arrange individual bouquets or other small orders. Her expertise is in large arrangements and she makes them mainly for corporate offices, estates, parties, and special events. The first year of the store's operation, Desiree advertised with brochures and flyers with colored photographs of some of her arrangements, services available, and prices. In an effort to expand her business to surrounding areas, she has hired a Web designer to create a Web site for Flora Style. Desiree wants the Web site to have many large photographs of arrangements she has made and updated lists of services available, prices, and references. She wants clients to be able to search her site for the exact arrangement they want and fill out an order form online. This order form would be sent to Desiree electronically, reducing paperwork and time.

The Web site has been very successful for Flora Style and the online ordering has proved to be useful to Desiree and her clients. She wants to become even more Web-based by changing her method from billing by mail to sending invoices by e-mail. Open **ex07FloraInvoice.xls** and save as **Invoice2.xls.** This is the invoice Desiree has designed to use for her billing. She wants to send her first electronic invoice to a client she made three arrangements for last week. On June 12, she delivered a two-foot orchid arrangement and on June 15, she delivered one each of a one-foot and a three-foot bird of paradise arrangement. The prices for these arrangements can be found in **ex07FloraPrices.xls.**

Fill out the invoice with the appropriate dates of delivery and the names of the arrangement(s) that were delivered. Since Desiree has yet to be billed by the company that provides her flowers, she expects that their prices will be increasing. Because of this, she wants to link the prices from the spreadsheet to the invoice. This way, if her supplier's prices change, any change in what she charges will be reflected in the invoice. Be sure to create a formula for the cell that reflects the total amount to be billed. Include your name and print the invoice.

The bird of paradise prices did increase and Desiree needs to update her prices. The new prices are as follows: 1 Foot $260, 2 Feet $510, 3 Feet $785, and 4 Feet $960. Update the prices in the price spreadsheet and be sure the price changes are reflected on the invoice. Now Desiree is ready to e-mail the invoice to her client. Access an e-mail account and address the e-mail to billing@johnson.com. In the subject box, type **Invoice for June Arrangements.** In the body of the e-mail, attach the correct invoice from Excel. Include your name and print the invoice.

around the world

1. Reporting New Accounts for Shoemann's International Investments

Michael Kelleher is the new accounts manager for Shoemann's International Investments. His department receives all new account applications and is responsible for reviewing all new account information. Department members look for things such as suitability of investments, proper beneficiary designations, and complete document information. After an application is approved, the account is set up and brokers may begin to place trades for their accounts.

The recent international market volatility has created great amounts of new account openings. Michael's supervisor is concerned that some brokers may be choosing investments that are not suitable for their clients and are opening an excessive number of new accounts. He has asked that Michael prepare a memo once a week to present to the management team. This memo is to include the total number of applications per week, sorted by account type. His supervisor feels that this will help determine if brokers are opening a greater number of a particular type of investment account. If it is found that many new account applications are concentrated among one or more types of accounts, all account applications for those accounts must be re-evaluated.

Open **ex07NewAccounts.xls** and save as **NewAccounts2.xls.** This is Michael's nearly completed data for the past week's new account applications. Create a row for the totals of number of applications, accepted, and rejected. Create a formula for this row to calculate the correct numbers and save the worksheet. Open the Word document **ex07NewAccountsMemo.doc** and save it as **NewAccountsMemo2.doc.** Link (Paste Special, Link) the worksheet to the memo. Include your name in the document's header and print the memo.

Michael's supervisors shared in his concern regarding the types of accounts being opened. Before deciding to re-evaluate those applications, they want to compare the figures to the number of applications received the week before for only variable annuity, limited partnership, and unit investment trust accounts. The figures are as follows for the number received, rejected, and accepted (respectively): variable annuity **115, 80,** and **35**; limited partnership **85, 46,** and **39**; unit investment trust **39, 8,** and **31.** Change the Excel worksheet to reflect this new information and delete the information for the other types of accounts. Update the memo by replacing **RE** with **Previous week's application figures.** Next, change the text of the memo to indicate that Michael is simply sending these figures, which also give him cause for concern about these accounts. Link in the new spreadsheet, include your name, and print the document.

running project

Pampered Paws

Last month was a slow one for Pampered Paws. Grace Jackson wants to spark some customer interest by sending out a mailer listing some of the products that are on sale this month. In addition to some marketing hype, the letter will contain a coupon for 20 percent off of any purchase over $75. To redeem the coupon, the customer must bring in the letter containing the coupon and spend at least $75 in the store.

Grace does not know how to do mail merge, but she knows you do. She asks you to merge in the names of all customers living in the city of San Diego, California. Although her customer list also includes people from other cities in California and from out of state, she realizes it would be futile to send the mailing to that group.

The customers' names and addresses are in the worksheet **ex07PawsCustomers.xls.** The letter you are to modify is called **ex07PawsLetter.doc,** and the Excel worksheet containing the items on sale this month is called **ex07PawsItems.xls.** Merge the customer names and addresses into the letter's inside address as you did in this chapter. Include merge fields for the first and last names in the salutation, replacing the tags [*insert first name*] and [*insert last name*]. Embed the Excel worksheet cell range called *SaleItems,* found in the worksheet **ex07PawsItems.xls,** in place of the tag [embed SaleItems named range here], which is found near the bottom of the letter. Replace Grace Jackson's name with your own name to identify the letters. Specify filter criteria to select San Diego customers, perform mail merge, and print all merged letters (there won't be a lot, honest). Save the main Word document, but do not save the merged documents when you have printed them.

EXCEL

did you
know?

the *game of a cat's cradle—two players alternately stretch a looped string over their fingers to produce different designs—has been around since about 1760.*

there *are 110 calories per hour consumed during an hour of typing—only 30 more than those used while sleeping.*

Cleveland *spelled backwards is "DNA level C."*

as *of January 1998, American Express had not issued a single credit card with an expiration date past December 1999. The company hoped to protect cardholders from Y2K problems.*

you *can reference worksheet cells that are stored on disk but not currently open. Learn more about this in the chapter.*

Chapter Objectives

- Understand when using multiple worksheets and workbooks is handy or essential

- Design a multiple-sheet workbook

- Group worksheets in a workbook

- Consolidate and summarize data using three-dimensional formulas—MOUS ex2002-4-3

- Use link formulas to reference cells in other workbooks

- Maintain and update linked workbooks

CHAPTER

8

eight

Developing Multiple Worksheet and Workbook Applications

chapter case

Bridgewater Engineering Company (BECO)

Bridgewater Engineering Company (BECO) builds industrial tools and machines for heavy industry. Jack Leonard established the firm in 1951 in Somerville, New Jersey. After Jack retired, Stirling Leonard, Jack's son, took over as CEO. In addition to the plant in Somerville, BECO has plants in two other locations: Van Buren, Arkansas, and West Lafayette, Indiana.

The three plants collectively employ 175 people and 9 administrators. The workforce consists of trained, versatile mechanics led by professional engineers. BECO is experienced and equipped to build special machinery and equipment of all kinds including the installation of electrical, hydraulic, and pneumatic power components and their controls. Each spacious plant has over 10,000 square

feet of workspace with 28 feet of headroom in all manufacturing areas. BECO's own facilities include lathes, vertical and horizontal boring mills, planers, and assorted machinery for milling, drilling, welding, and control assembly. BECO builds all machinery from scratch, using steel rods, sheet steel, and other sheet metals to fashion the custom-built machinery that customers order. Examples of machinery that BECO builds include lathes, surface grinders, drill presses, boring mills, band saws, and Turret mills—all products used in heavy manufacturing.

Stirling was slow to embrace computing, but two years ago he finally converted many of BECO's financial and job-bidding systems over to computer professionals who designed automated systems

FIGURE 8.1

Summary of BECO machine sales

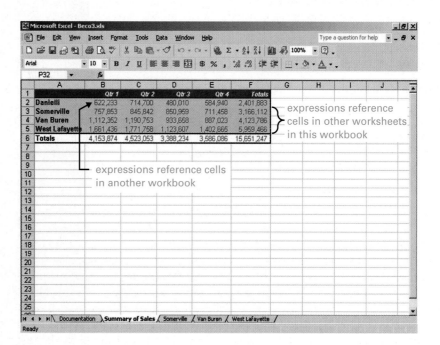

for him. He has maintained control and interest in tracking sales of machine tools and machines that BECO manufactures to give him a good overview of sales by machine type. He wants a summary of sales of machinery by all three plants in a handy, simple, easy-to-read format. Your job is to first study the three manufacturing plants' workbooks and then devise a workbook or workbooks that merge the data from the three plants together into a single overview worksheet. Figure 8.1 shows an example of the summary worksheet displaying total sales of the three BECO plants.

Chapter 8 covers writing formulas that reference other worksheets in the workbook and other workbooks stored on your computer. In particular, you will learn about the benefits of using multiple worksheets to organize related data and how to create *three-dimensional formulas (3-D)* formulas—formulas that reference other worksheets in the current workbook. When you create formulas that reference cells in other worksheets, you link the referenced workbooks to the worksheet containing the reference to other workbooks. When you have completed this chapter, you will understand three-dimensional formulas and link formulas thoroughly.

SESSION 8.1 WORKING WITH MULTIPLE WORKSHEETS

In this section, you will learn why it is advantageous to keep related data in separate worksheets of a workbook, and you will write formulas that reference information on other worksheets in the same workbook. You will learn the benefits of grouping worksheets before formatting them or typing text and values common to all grouped worksheets.

USING MULTIPLE WORKSHEETS

Using more than one worksheet in a workbook is one of the best ways to organize your data. Almost all of the Excel applications you have examined in the first seven chapters of this textbook consisted of one worksheet with a few small exceptions. There are several advantages to storing data on separate worksheets of a workbook.

Why Multiple Worksheets Are Useful

Using multiple worksheets to store distinct, related information on separate worksheets makes sense for several reasons. Consider, for example, the Pampered Paws case that appears in each chapter. Suppose that Grace Jackson wanted to keep the sales of dog products—food, toys, and other items—separate from the sales of cat products. The simplest way to maintain a logical separation between product categories is by placing each on its own worksheet. Because each worksheet can have its own margin settings, unique page header and footer, print area, and other worksheet-specific settings, you can tailor print characteristics of each worksheet independently of other worksheets. Another advantage multiple worksheets provide is that you can protect individual worksheets in a workbook independently from others.

Employing individual worksheets in a workbook is analogous to using physical folders to store related information in an office filing cabinet. Using folders in an office cabinet allows you to place related correspondence in one folder, tax information in another folder, and so on. You can click a worksheet tab and immediately open a particular worksheet of a workbook and examine or print its contents.

Designing a Multiple-Sheet Workbook

The BECO workbook, **ex08Beco.xls,** contains a documentation worksheet, which is the first worksheet in a workbook. Following the documentation worksheet is a worksheet containing sales data for BECO's Somerville plant. The worksheet lists the most recent four quarters of sales broken down by machine type (see Figure 8.2).

Sales information for BECO's other two plants is kept in separate workbooks. Sales data for the Van Buren plant are stored in the Excel workbook **ex08VanBuren.xls,** and sales data for the West Lafayette plant are in **ex08WestLafayette.xls.** When complete, the BECO workbook will contain worksheets from all three plants in one workbook. In addition to the detail worksheets, the workbook will contain a summary worksheet. A *summary worksheet,* sometimes called a *consolidation worksheet,* contains a digest or synopsis of the information contained in the individual worksheets. Similar to an executive summary or abstract in a written proposal, a summary worksheet provides an outline listing the total sales for the year or the total sales by quarter. A summary is often the only page an executive reads, because he or she is so busy running the company. The summary worksheet can be placed anywhere in a workbook. Its placement is often dictated by how the summary worksheet is used by worksheet readers. Frequently, the summary worksheet appears at the front of the workbook, either before the documentation worksheet or immediately

FIGURE 8.2

Somerville sales information

sales for each machine type by quarter

machines manufactured in Somerville

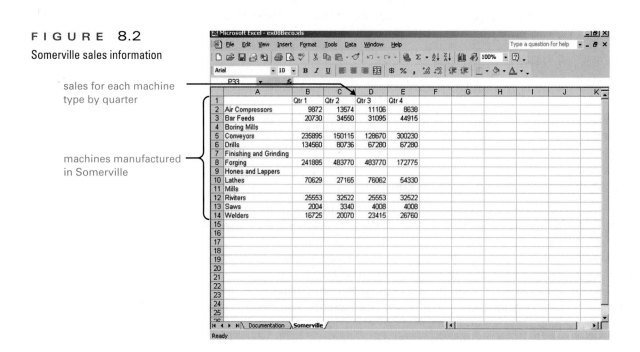

after it. Some people prefer the summary worksheet as the last worksheet in the workbook—like a final chapter in a book summarizing its plot or the summary paragraph in a document. Figure 8.3 depicts the overall structure of the BECO workbook containing three plants' worksheets, a summary sheet, and a documentation sheet—all in one workbook.

Stirling asks you to help him with the BECO workbooks. First, he wants the worksheets from each of the three manufacturing plants in one workbook so that he can refer to each plant, or division, easily. Second, he would like you to create a summary worksheet to illustrate total sales by machine type for each quarter. That way, he can easily see which machines are selling the best and which aren't without examining the sales details for each manufacturing location.

COMBINING MULTIPLE WORKSHEETS INTO ONE WORKBOOK

One of BECO's administrators created the two-worksheet workbook containing the documentation worksheet and sales information about the Somerville plant for four quarters and several machine types (see Figure 8.2). Data for the other two plants are in separate workbooks. Your first task is to open all three workbooks and then combine the three workbooks into one workbook.

Because Stirling wants you to combine all three workbooks into one workbook, you will open the Van Buren workbook and then copy the worksheet into the main BECO workbook by dragging the worksheet's tab.

FIGURE 8.3

Structure of the BECO workbook

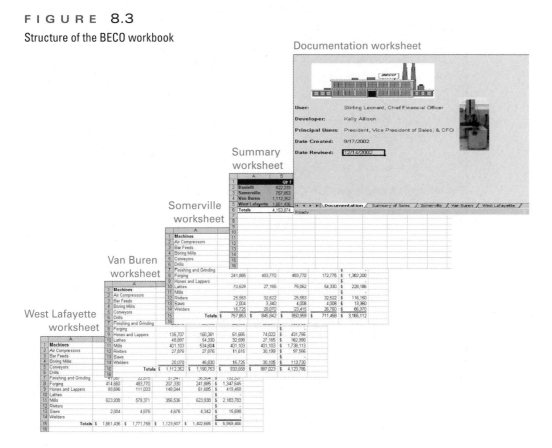

EXCEL

---

task reference

Copying Worksheets from Other Workbooks

- Open the master workbook—the workbook into which you want to copy worksheets from other workbooks

- Open all other workbooks containing worksheets you want to copy to the master workbook

- In any of the open Excel workbooks, click **Window,** click **Arrange,** click the **Tiled** option button, and click **OK**

- Press and hold the **Ctrl** key, and then click and drag to the master workbook the tab of the worksheet you want to copy

- Release the mouse when the down-pointing arrow is in the correct tab location in the master workbook, and then release the **Ctrl** key

---

Copying the Van Buren worksheet to the BECO master workbook:

1. Start Excel as usual

2. Open the workbook **ex08Beco.xls** and immediately save it as **Beco2.xls** to preserve the original workbook

3. Review the Documentation worksheet. Because all Documentation worksheet cells except B18 are locked, worksheet protection prevents you from selecting any cell except B18

4. Click **File** on the menu bar, click **Open,** use the Look in list box to navigate to the workbook **ex08VanBuren.xls,** and double-click **ex08VanBuren.xls** to open the file. The Van Buren workbook opens, replacing **Beco2.xls** as the active workbook

5. Click **Window** on the menu bar, click **Arrange,** click (if necessary) the **Tiled** option button in the Arrange Windows dialog box, and click the **OK** button. The active worksheets of both workbooks appear side by side

6. Press and hold the **Ctrl** key, click and drag the **Van Buren worksheet tab** to the **Beco2.xls,** and release the mouse when the worksheet position indicator, a down-pointing arrow, appears to the right of the Somerville tab (see Figure 8.4)

7. Release the **Ctrl** key. Excel copies the Van Buren worksheet to the Beco2 workbook and makes Van Buren the active worksheet

8. Click the title bar of the **ex08VanBuren.xls** workbook, click **File** on the menu bar, and click **Close** to close the workbook

tip: *If you attempt to close **Beco2.xls** by mistake, Excel will ask you if you want to save your changes. Click the **Cancel** button to leave **Beco2.xls** open. Then repeat step 8*

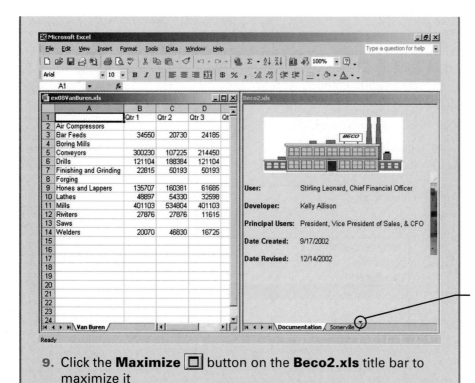

FIGURE 8.4
Copying the Van Buren worksheet

arrow indicates the new position of the dragged worksheet—following Somerville

9. Click the **Maximize** ☐ button on the **Beco2.xls** title bar to maximize it

another word

. . . on dragging a worksheet tab to another workbook

When you press and hold the Ctrl key before you drag a worksheet tab to another workbook, you are copying it. If you simply drag a worksheet tab to another open workbook, the worksheet is cut from the original workbook and pasted into the destination workbook. If the worksheet you cut from a workbook is its only worksheet, Excel closes that workbook.

Next, you copy the West Lafayette worksheet into the **Beco2.xls** workbook to complete the two-worksheet copy operation. This time, you will use a different method to copy the worksheet.

Copying the West Lafayette worksheet to the BECO master workbook:

1. Click **File** on the menu bar, click **Open,** use the Look in list box to navigate to the workbook **ex08WestLafayette.xls,** click the filename, and click **Open.** The West Lafayette workbook opens and becomes the active workbook

2. Click **Edit** on the menu bar and click **Move or Copy Sheet.** The Move or Copy dialog box opens

3. Click the **To book** list box to display the list of workbooks and click **Beco2.xls** from the list of workbook choices

EXCEL

4. Click the **(move to end)** choice in the *Before sheet* list box and click the **Create a copy** check box to *copy* the worksheet, making it the last worksheet in the destination workbook **Beco2.xls** (see Figure 8.5)

FIGURE 8.5
Move or Copy dialog box

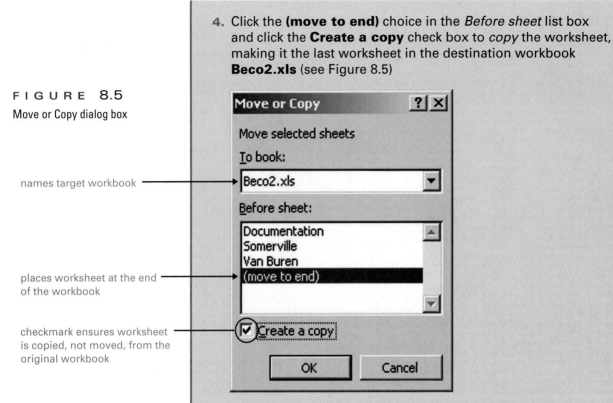

names target workbook ──────→

places worksheet at the end ──────→
of the workbook

checkmark ensures worksheet ──────→
is copied, not moved, from the
original workbook

5. Click **OK.** Excel copies the worksheet to **Beco2.xls** and makes it the active worksheet (see Figure 8.6)

FIGURE 8.6
Workbook with copied
worksheets

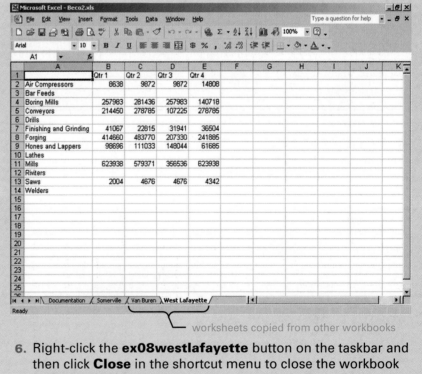

worksheets copied from other workbooks

6. Right-click the **ex08westlafayette** button on the taskbar and then click **Close** in the shortcut menu to close the workbook **ex08WestLafayette.xls**

7. Click the **Save** button on the Standard toolbar

Now the BECO workbook contains four worksheets: Documentation, Somerville, Van Buren, and West Lafayette. The latter three worksheets contain sales information about all three BECO plants in one workbook.

ADDING A WORKSHEET TO A WORKBOOK

Remembering that Stirling wants to summarize BECO's sales in a single worksheet that displays sales by machine across all three plants, you realize you will have to add a new worksheet to the BECO workbook. You will do that next.

Adding a new worksheet to a workbook:

1. With the West Lafayette worksheet of the **Beco2.xls** workbook active, click **Insert** on the menu bar

2. Click **Worksheet.** Excel adds a worksheet called Sheet1 in front of the West Lafayette worksheet. It makes the newly added worksheet active

tip: *If you practiced inserting a new worksheet more than once with an open workbook, the inserted worksheet name may be a different name such as Sheet2 or Sheet3, for example*

Moving the Worksheet

Because the worksheet will summarize the values in the three sales worksheets, you ask Stirling where he would like you to place the summary worksheet. Stirling tells you he prefers having the summary worksheet precede all the detail worksheets, but he wants the Documentation worksheet to remain the first worksheet in the workbook.

Move the new worksheet between the Documentation and Somerville worksheets:

1. With the newly added worksheet, Sheet1, active, click **Edit** on the menu bar, and then click **Move or Copy Sheet.** The Move or Copy dialog box appears

2. Click **Somerville** in the *Before sheet* list box, and ensure that the Create a copy check box is cleared. (You do not want to create a copy of the worksheet. Rather, you want to move it)

3. Click **OK** in the Move or Copy dialog box. Excel moves the worksheet to its new position between the Documentation and Somerville worksheets

---

anotherway

. . . to insert a new worksheet

Right-click the worksheet in front of which you want to insert a new worksheet

Click **Insert** on the pop-up menu

Ensure that the Worksheet icon is selected in the General tab and click the **OK** button

---

Renaming a Worksheet and Coloring a Worksheet Tab

The summary worksheet is an important one, and Stirling wants it to stand out. He asks you to rename the worksheet to Summary of Sales and to change the color of the tab to bright yellow.

EXCEL

Renaming a worksheet and coloring its worksheet tab:

1. Double-click the worksheet tab of the newly added worksheet (the tab name darkens), type **Summary of Sales,** and press **Enter.** Excel renames the worksheet

2. Right-click the **Summary of Sales** worksheet tab. A shortcut menu appears (see Figure 8.7)

FIGURE 8.7

Worksheet tab shortcut menu

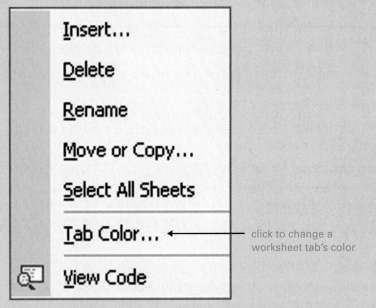

click to change a worksheet tab's color

3. Click **Tab Color.** The Format Tab Color dialog box appears

4. Click the **Yellow color well** (fourth row from the top, third column) (see Figure 8.8)

FIGURE 8.8

Selecting a worksheet tab color

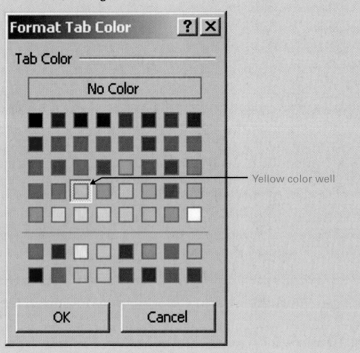

Yellow color well

5. Click **OK.** The dialog box closes and a fringe of yellow appears at the bottom of the Summary of Sales tab

6. Click the **Somerville** worksheet tab to make that worksheet active and notice the Summary of Sales tab—it is bright yellow (see Figure 8.9)

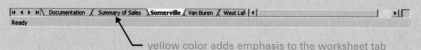

Ready

yellow color adds emphasis to the worksheet tab

7. Click the **Summary of Sales** tab to make that worksheet active again

FIGURE 8.9
Brightly colored worksheet tab

With all the worksheets in place, including the empty summary worksheet, you are ready to create formulas that reference cells and cell ranges in other worksheets and to work with multiple worksheets as a group.

GROUPING WORKSHEETS

When you need to enter the same labels or formulas in several worksheets within a workbook, you can save a lot of time by grouping worksheets and then entering information common to multiple sheets in one operation. For instance, neither the summary worksheet nor any of the three other sales information worksheets have a column label identifying the contents of column A—machines. While you could type "Machines" in cell A1 in each worksheet separately, it saves time to group the worksheets and then type the label once. Grouping worksheets is also beneficial when you want to insert or delete rows common to all grouped worksheets or format cells, rows, or columns of all grouped worksheets in the same way.

Entering Text into Worksheet Groups

Although the three sales worksheets contain the labels Qtr 1, Qtr 2, Qtr 3, and Qtr 4 to indicate sales in each of the four calendar quarters, the summary worksheet does not. Whenever you want to modify several worksheets simultaneously, you must first group them.

task reference

Grouping Contiguous Worksheets

- Click the worksheet tab of the first worksheet in the group

- Use the tab scrolling buttons, if necessary, to bring the last worksheet tab of the proposed group into view

- Hold down the **Shift** key and click the last worksheet tab in the group

Grouping Noncontiguous Worksheets

- Click the worksheet tab of the first worksheet you want in the group

- Press and hold the **Ctrl** key and then click each worksheet you want to include in the group

- When you are done, release the **Ctrl** key

Stirling wants you to type "Machines" in cell A1 of each of the three manufacturing plants' worksheets. If you first group the worksheets into which you want to enter the label and then type it in one of them, Excel places the label in all worksheets in the group. Worksheet users sometimes call this ***drilling down,*** because it changes several layers—grouped worksheets—in a workbook.

FIGURE 8.10

Grouped worksheets

Grouping worksheets and entering a label in all of them at once:

1. Click the **Somerville** worksheet tab, press and hold down **Shift,** click the **West Lafayette** worksheet tab, and release the **Shift** key. Excel indicates the grouped worksheets by coloring their tabs (temporarily) white (see Figure 8.10)

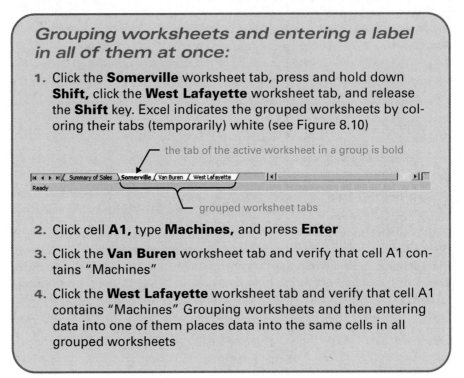

the tab of the active worksheet in a group is bold

grouped worksheet tabs

2. Click cell **A1,** type **Machines,** and press **Enter**

3. Click the **Van Buren** worksheet tab and verify that cell A1 contains "Machines"

4. Click the **West Lafayette** worksheet tab and verify that cell A1 contains "Machines" Grouping worksheets and then entering data into one of them places data into the same cells in all grouped worksheets

Notice that the name of the active worksheet of a grouped set is bold. Clicking any of the worksheet tabs in the grouped set makes the worksheet active, but it does not ungroup them. This happens because there is at least one worksheet in the workbook that is not part of the worksheet group.

task reference

Ungrouping Worksheets

*   Right-click any worksheet tab and click **Ungroup Sheets** from the shortcut menu

Ungroup the worksheets so that you can work independently on each worksheet.

Ungrouping worksheets:

1. Right-click the **West Lafayette** worksheet tab

2. Click **Ungroup Sheets** in the shortcut menu. Excel ungroups the worksheets, leaving West Lafayette active

Now you are ready to enter formulas into worksheet groups. Not only can you enter text or a formula into a cell of every grouped worksheet, you can also create the values in a single sheet, group the worksheets, and then copy the values to other worksheets in the group.

Copying Formulas and Data into Worksheet Groups

Stirling tells you there are several ways to copy formulas from one worksheet to other worksheets. If you want to copy one or more formulas to more than one worksheet, the most efficient way is to copy the formulas to grouped worksheets rather than copying to individual sheets, one sheet at a time. In the next series of steps, you will create the sum of the columns for each quarter's sales and place the sums at the bottom of each column. You begin by creating a summation for sales at the Somerville plant. Then you will copy those formulas to the same cells in the Van Buren and West Lafayette worksheets.

Writing summation formulas in the Somerville worksheet:

1. Click the **Somerville** worksheet tab and then select the cell range **B2:E15**

2. Click the **AutoSum** $\boxed{\Sigma \cdot}$ button on the Standard toolbar. Excel places four SUM functions in the cell range B15:E15, which sum their respective columns

3. Click cell **B15** to deselect the selected range and display the newly created sum function in the formula bar (see Figure 8.11)

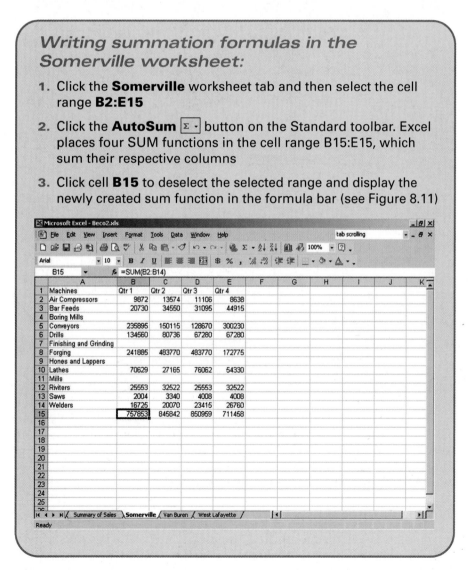

FIGURE 8.11

Sum functions totaling sales columns

With the summation formulas in place, you will first group the three sales worksheets together and then use the Excel Fill Across Worksheets command to complete the same process in two other workbooks.

Copying formulas to other worksheets in a workbook:

1. Select the cell range **B15:E15,** which contains four SUM functions

2. Press and hold the **Shift** key and click the **West Lafayette** worksheet tab, and then release the **Shift** key. Excel groups the three sales worksheets

3. Click **Edit** on the menu bar, point to **Fill,** and click **Across Worksheets.** The Fill Across Worksheets dialog box appears (see Figure 8.12)

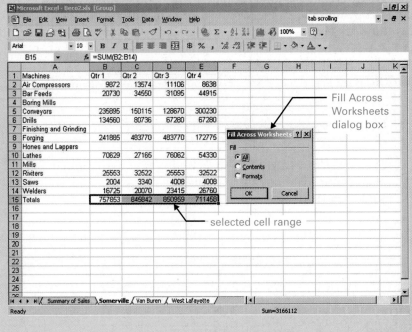

4. Click the **All** option button and then click **OK**

5. Click cell **A15** to deselect the cell range

6. Right-click any worksheet in the group and then click **Ungroup Sheets** in the shortcut menu. Excel ungroups the worksheets

The Fill Across Worksheets command copies the selected cells to all other worksheets in the group to exactly the same cell range as the source cells. The All option copies both cells' contents and their formatting. Alternatively, you can choose to copy only contents or only formatting by selecting either Contents or Formats, respectively.

Writing Formulas and Data into Worksheet Groups

An alternative way to enter formulas and data into grouped worksheets is to group the worksheets first and then write the formulas and data. As you press Enter to complete a formula or execute a copy operation on one worksheet, Excel automatically copies formulas and data to other members of the worksheet group.

Stirling wants row totals for each machine sale so that he can determine the total sales for lathes, for example. In addition, he wants you to place the label "Totals" in cells A15 and F1 to label the sums.

Writing formulas and labels to grouped worksheets:

1. Click the **Somerville** worksheet tab, hold down the **Shift** key, click the **West Lafayette** worksheet tab, and release the **Shift** key to group the three worksheets

2. Type **Totals** in cell A15

3. Click cell **F1** and type **Totals**

4. Click cell **F2,** type **=SUM(B2:E2),** and click the **Enter** checkmark (see Figure 8.13) on the formula bar to enter the formula and keep cell F2 active

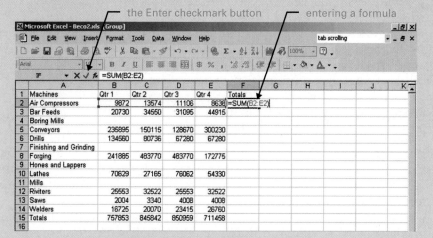

FIGURE 8.13
Entering a formula in three worksheets simultaneously

5. Move the mouse to the fill handle in the lower-right corner of cell **F2,** drag it down through cell **F15,** and release the mouse. Excel fills in cells F3 through F15 with row totals. Cell F15 is a grand total because it sums cells B15 through F15, which are column totals

6. Click cell **F2** to deselect the cell range (see Figure 8.14) and make that cell active so that you can inspect its formula

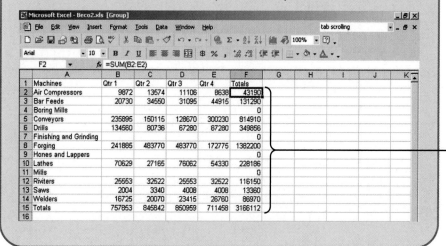

FIGURE 8.14
Drill-down formulas completed

EXCEL

Verify that the group formulas are correct.

Verifying copied formulas:

1. Click the **Van Buren** worksheet tab to make that worksheet active

2. Examine the Formula bar and notice that the formula in cell F2 is =SUM(B2:E2)

3. Click and drag the cell range **F2:F14** and observe that 4123786, the sum of the selected cells, appears in the lower-right corner of the status bar and matches the sum in cell F15

4. Click cell **A1** and then click the **Somerville** tab to make that worksheet active

---

Grouping similar worksheets and writing common functions and then formulas once saves a lot of time.

Next, you will investigate formatting worksheet groups. If you can save time by writing formulas and expressions simultaneously for multiple worksheets, it seems logical that you can save time formatting by grouping worksheets and then formatting them all at once.

Formatting Worksheet Groups

Formatting a cell or cell range in the active worksheet of a group of worksheets also formats the same cell or cell range in *all* group members. That is particularly handy when you want several worksheets to have the same appearance, helping to convey the message that similarly formatted worksheets are related to one another.

Stirling wants you to make several format changes to the three sales worksheets—Somerville, Van Buren, and West Lafayette. Because each of the three worksheets will be formatted in the same way, you will format the grouped worksheets and save time. By carefully selecting cell ranges, you can combine some of the preceding formatting steps to include more cells.

Formatting sales values with the accounting format:

1. With the three worksheets still grouped, click the **Somerville** worksheet tag, and then click and drag cell range **B2:F15**

2. Right-click anywhere inside the selected cells, click **Format Cells** on the shortcut menu, and click the **Number** tab (if necessary)

3. Click **Accounting** in the Category list, type **0** in the Decimal places spinner control, click the **Symbol** list box, click **None,** and click **OK**

4. Click and drag the cell range **F2:F15**

5. Press and hold the **Ctrl** key, click and drag the cell range **B15:E15,** and release the **Ctrl** key. Excel highlights the two cell ranges F2:F15 and B15:E15, the totals column and row

6. Right-click any cell within the selected ranges, click **Format Cells** on the shortcut menu, and click the **Number** tab (if necessary)

tip: *If you right-click outside the range of selected cells, press* **Esc,** *reselect the two cell ranges, and repeat step 6*

7. Click the **Symbol** list box, click **$,** and click **OK**

   Excel formats all three grouped worksheets exactly the same way

8. Click cell **A1** to deselect the cell ranges and to prepare for the next steps (see Figure 8.15)

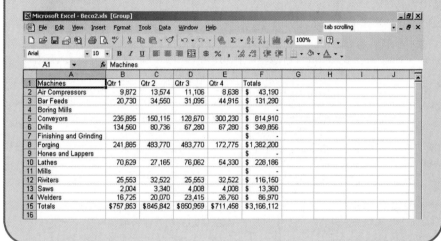

FIGURE 8.15

Applying the accounting format to grouped worksheets

Next, you will right-align and boldface labels in cells B1 through F1 and the "Totals" label in cell A15, and you will boldface the label "Machines" in cell A1.

Right-aligning and bolding labels in grouped worksheets:

1. With the three worksheets still grouped and the Somerville worksheet active, select cell range **B1:F1**

2. Press and hold the **Ctrl** key, select cell **A15,** and release the **Ctrl** key

3. Click the **Align Right** button on the Formatting toolbar. Selected labels snap to right alignment

4. Press and hold the **Ctrl** key, select cell **A1,** and release the **Ctrl** key. Cell A1 is added to the group of selected cells

5. Click the **Bold** button on the Formatting toolbar. Excel applies boldface to the 21 selected cells (seven cells in each of three worksheets comprising the grouped worksheets)

6. Click any cell to deselect the cell ranges

The last few formatting changes Stirling wants you to make are to place a double underline under the cell range B14:F14 to mark the bottom of the sales columns and then to widen columns B through F to 13 characters to accommodate the row totals and make the columns easier to distinguish from one another.

Applying underlining and increasing column widths:

1. Select the cell range **B14:F14**

2. Click **Format** on the menu bar and click **Cells.** The Format Cells dialog box opens

3. Click the **Font** tab, click the **Underline** list box (see Figure 8.16), and click **Double Accounting.** The Preview text box displays a facsimile of the double underline. Notice that vertical space is added between the bottom of the value and the double accounting underline

F I G U R E   8.16

Applying Double Accounting underline to selected cells

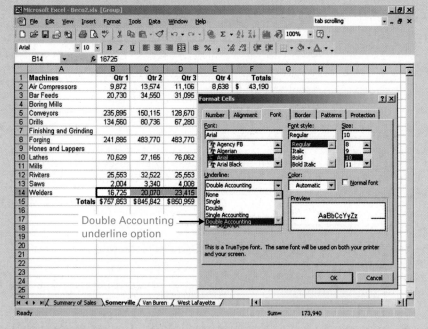

4. Click **OK** to apply the formatting changes and close the Format Cells dialog box

5. Select columns **B** through **F** by dragging the mouse through their column labels, right-click anywhere within the selected columns, click **Column Width,** type **13** in the Column Width text box, and click **OK.** Excel expands columns B through F on the three worksheets in the group to 13 characters in width

6. Click cell **A1** to deselect the column range (see Figure 8.17)

Satisfy yourself that the three worksheets all contain the same format changes by clicking the Van Buren and West Lafayette worksheet tabs and viewing their formats.

Establishing Worksheet Page Settings

After you format the worksheet, you give Stirling a copy of it on disk. He opens it and examines the worksheets over the weekend. Monday morning, he stops by your office and comments that some of the sales worksheets print on multiple pages and that the three plants' worksheets all have different print margins. He asks you to make all the sales worksheets page layouts uniform, including the print margins and page layout. In addition, he would like you to place each worksheet's name (Somerville, Van Buren, or West Lafayette) in the left section of the footer so that each worksheet is identified by its tab name. Looking ahead, you decide to include the Summary of Sales worksheet in the worksheet grouping so that it will have the same page setup as the sales worksheets that it summarizes.

The best way to take care of the page setup and footer details Stirling requests is to work with grouped worksheets. You begin by adding the Summary of Sales worksheet to the group of three plant worksheets. Then you will ensure that all four worksheets have the same page setup.

Adding a worksheet to an existing worksheet group:

1. With the three plants' worksheets grouped, press and hold the **Ctrl** key

2. Click the **Summary of Sales** worksheet tab to include it in the worksheet group and release the **Ctrl** key. Excel highlights the Summary of Sales worksheet white and includes it in the existing worksheet group. Notice that the Somerville worksheet is still active (the tab is bold)

With the enlarged worksheet group consisting of four of the five worksheets, you are ready to modify page setup details in all four worksheets at once.

Establishing page setup settings for grouped worksheets:

1. Click **File** on the menu bar and click **Page Setup.** The Page Setup dialog box opens

2. Click the **Margins** tab, double-click the **Left** margin spin control to select its current value, and type **0.75**

3. Double-click the **Right** margin spin control, and type **0.75**

4. Click the **Header/Footer** tab and click the **Custom Footer** [Custom Footer...] button. The Footer dialog box appears

5. Click the **Center section** text box, type **Worksheet:,** press the **Spacebar,** and click the **Tab Name** ▢ button. The Tab Name button displays "&[Tab]" because it is a variable—Excel fills in each unique worksheet tab name depending on which worksheet is printed (see Figure 8.18)

FIGURE 8.18

Setting the page footer for each worksheet in the group

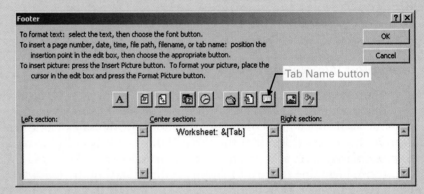

6. Click **OK** to apply your page setting choices and close the Footer dialog box, and then click **OK** to close the Page Setup dialog box.

You probably notice that a dashed line appears to the right of column F on the active worksheet. The line is a page break indicator. It appears when you modify any of the page setup values such as the left or right margins. You can remove the page breaks by clicking Tools, clicking Options, clicking the View tab, and clearing the Page breaks check box in the Window options pane. Then click OK to apply your worksheet options.

Because you have completed your work with the worksheet group, you can ungroup them.

Ungrouping worksheets:

1. Right-click any of the worksheet tabs in the grouped worksheets. A shortcut menu appears

2. Click **Ungroup** Sheets. Excel ungroups the four-worksheet group

NAMING CELL RANGES TO SPEED WORKSHEET ACCESS

When you work with a workbook containing many worksheets, it is somewhat difficult to access a sheet that is, say, 29 sheets to the right of the current one. If you maintain well-organized workbooks in which you give logical and meaningful names to worksheets, then you can use a trick to make accessing a particular page much easier: Name a cell in each worksheet with the name of the worksheet. You will learn what this means by putting the tip into practice.

Even though your BECO workbook contains only five worksheets, it is still useful to learn a technique that you can use to access any individual worksheet quickly. You can apply the technique to other workbooks that contain even more worksheets than the BECO workbook. The technique is this: Assign the sheet range name (without spaces) to cell A1 of each worksheet you want to access quickly. Then when you want to access one of these worksheets, select its name from the Name box located on the left of the Formula bar. Assign names to each worksheet.

Assigning a range name to cell A1 of each worksheet:

1. Click the **Summary of Sales** worksheet tab, click cell **A1,** click the **Name** box, type **Summary,** and press **Enter**

2. Click the **Somerville** worksheet tab, click cell **A1,** click the **Name** box, type **Somerville,** and press **Enter**

3. Click the **Van Buren** worksheet tab, click cell **A1,** click the **Name** box, type **VanBuren** (one word, no spaces), and press **Enter**

4. Click the **West Lafayette** worksheet tab, click cell **A1,** click the **Name** box, type **WestLafayette** (one word, no spaces), and press **Enter**

Because the Documentation worksheet is protected, you will first have to unprotect it, name cell A1, and then protect the worksheet again.

Assigning a range name to cell A1 of a protected worksheet:

1. Click the **First Worksheet tab scroll** button (see Figure 8.17), to the left of the worksheet tabs, to bring the Documentation worksheet tab into view

2. Click the **Documentation** worksheet tab, click **Tools** on the menu bar, point to **Protection,** and click **Unprotect Sheet**

3. If necessary, click cell **B18,** then click the **Name** box, type **Documentation,** and press **Enter**

4. Click **Tools** on the menu bar, point to **Protection,** click **Protect Sheet,** and click **OK**

Experiment with the newly minted names to switch from one worksheet to another. The cell-naming technique pays off in big ways for workbooks with large numbers of worksheets. Try switching from one worksheet to another by following the next exercise.

FIGURE 8.19

Clicking a range name to activate a worksheet

names used to speed access to worksheets

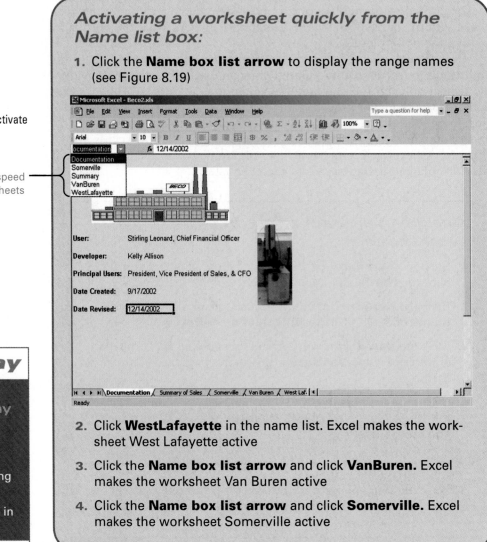

Activating a worksheet quickly from the Name list box:

1. Click the **Name box list arrow** to display the range names (see Figure 8.19)

2. Click **WestLafayette** in the name list. Excel makes the worksheet West Lafayette active

3. Click the **Name box list arrow** and click **VanBuren.** Excel makes the worksheet Van Buren active

4. Click the **Name box list arrow** and click **Somerville.** Excel makes the worksheet Somerville active

another way

. . . to quickly make active any worksheet in a workbook

Right-click any worksheet tab scrolling button

Click a worksheet tab in the shortcut menu

CONSOLIDATING AND SUMMARIZING DATA WITH 3-D FORMULAS

Until now, you have written *two-dimensional formulas,* which are formulas that reference cells that are on the same worksheet. Now that you have information about the three BECO plants in multiple worksheets of a single workbook, you can create formulas on one worksheet that summarize the information found on three other worksheets. Formulas that reference cells in other worksheet cells are called three-dimensional (or 3-D) formulas. Each worksheet of a workbook is analogous to the board of a tic-tac-toe game.

Three-dimensional formulas can consolidate data from multiple worksheets. When you *consolidate* information, you are summarizing data from multiple worksheets. For example, you could write a formula in the

FIGURE 8.20

Consolidating sales information

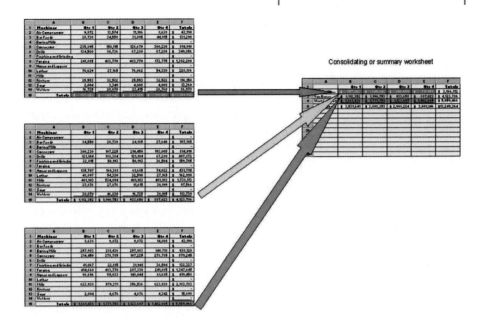

Consolidating or summary worksheet

Summary worksheet that is the sum of all sales by all divisions. Or, you could write a function to average sales for the first quarter (Qtr 1) for all machines manufactured by all three plants. Consolidating information presents a simplified picture to someone who does not necessarily want to know all the details—a division manager or the president of a company, for example.

Figure 8.20 shows a graphical example of how you might summarize the sales worksheets for Bridgewater Engineering Company. The summary provides Stirling with a clear picture of sales by each of the plants without confusing details.

Before you write formulas that reference other worksheets' cells, look at the general form of a three-dimensional reference. It is

```
'sheetname'!cell-range
```

Sheetname is the name of the worksheet, and *cell-range* is the cell or cell range in the referenced worksheet. The exclamation point (called "bang" by programmers) separates the worksheet name from the cell range. When a worksheet name contains a space, such as *Van Buren* and *West Lafayette*, then the sheet name is enclosed in apostrophes. For example, suppose you want cell B4 on the Summary of Sales worksheet to reference the sum of all first quarter sales at the Van Buren plant—cell B15 in the Van Buren worksheet. That 3-D formula is:

```
='Van Buren'!B15
```

To refer to cell B5 in the Somerville worksheet from another worksheet, you can omit the apostrophes because the sheet name does not contain spaces:

```
=Somerville!B5
```

How would you write a formula in the Summary of Sales worksheet to total the sales of all machines manufactured and sold by the West Lafayette plant? The West Lafayette plant's sales values are stored in the cell range B2:E14 on the West Lafayette worksheet. The summary worksheet would refer to that cell range as an argument of the SUM function this way:

EXCEL

```
=SUM('West Lafayette'!B2:E14)
```

Naturally, whether you refer to a single cell or a cell range in a three-dimensional reference, that reference must make sense in the formula in which it is used. Otherwise, Excel will display an error in the cell. For example, the preceding reference to a range of cells in the West Lafayette plant makes sense if it is an argument of a function that allows a range specification—a function such as SUM or AVERAGE. Thus, you could write in the Summary of Sales worksheet the expression containing a 3-D reference

```
=SUM('West Lafayette'!B2:E14)
```

However, that would be illegal in an expression that does not allow a cell range—an expression such as

```
='West Lafayette'!B2:E14/52
```

You can specify a range of worksheets in a three-dimensional reference just as you can specify a range of cells in a two-dimensional reference. A reference to a range of sheets must include the first and last names of the worksheets in the range, and no other, separated by a colon, followed by an exclamation point, and then followed by a cell or cell range. For example, the 3-D reference 'Somerville:West Lafayette'!B10 refers to cell B10 found in each of three worksheets from Somerville through West Lafayette.

When would you ever use a sheet range in an expression? There are several cases where that type of 3-D reference is handy. Suppose you want to write an expression in a summary worksheet that is the sum of the first quarter sales for each of the three plants—a single value that is a range of cells in a range of worksheets. The first quarter sales for each plant, conveniently, are found in the cell range B2:B14 on three worksheets (Somerville, Van Buren, and West Lafayette). You refer to the "silo" of cells in that 3-D range with the notation within the SUM function this way:

```
=SUM('Somerville:West Lafayette'!B2:B14)
```

When you include several worksheets in a sheet range, you do not enclose each worksheet name in its own apostrophes, even if some worksheet names contain spaces. Instead, enclose the entire range—the first worksheet name, the colon, and the final worksheet name—in apostrophes and follow the worksheet range with an exclamation point to mark the end of the worksheet range.

Writing 3-D Formulas

Happily, you have two choices when writing 3-D cell references. You can manually type the references, or you can use Excel's point mode to create a cell range expression automatically. If you use point mode, you must first select the *worksheet* range before you select the *cell* range, not the other way around.

You will make changes to the Summary of Sales worksheet by entering formulas in it. The worksheet will display four columns and three rows. The columns contain a sum of sales for the entire quarter by plant name. The plant names are in the left column. First, you will create labels to identify the rows and columns of information.

task reference

Writing a Formula Containing a 3-D Reference

- After clicking the cell where you want the formula to appear, type **=,** type a function name, and type **(.** However, if you are not writing a function, then simply type **=**

- Click the sheet tab of the worksheet containing the cell or cell range you want to reference

- If a worksheet range is needed, then press and hold the **Shift** key and click the last worksheet tab in the range

- Click the cell or cell range you want to reference

- Complete the formula (type a concluding right parentheses for a function, for instance), and then press **Enter**

Placing formulas and labels in the summary worksheet:

1. Click the **Name** box arrow and then click **Summary.** The Summary of Sales worksheet becomes active

2. Click cell **B1,** type **='Somerville'!B1,** and press **Enter** to reference the Qtr 1 label on the Somerville worksheet. Naturally, you could type the label Qtr 1 too. Using a reference is better. If the label on the summary worksheet changes, then the label on the Summary of Sales automatically changes too

3. Click cell **B1,** drag its fill handle, and drag through the cell range **C2:F1.** The labels Qtr 2, Qtr 3, Qtr 4, and Totals appear in the cell range

4. Select the cell range **A2:A5**

5. Type **Somerville,** press **Enter,** type **Van Buren,** press **Enter,** type **West Lafayette,** press **Enter,** type **Totals,** and press **Enter**

6. Click the **column A heading** button, click **Format** on the menu bar, point to **Column,** and click **AutoFit Selection.** Excel resizes the column to fit the widest entry

7. Drag column heading buttons **B** through **F** to select the columns, right-click anywhere *within* the selected columns, click **Column Width,** type **13** in the Column width text box, and click **OK** to resize columns B through F

8. Click cell **B1** to deselect the column range and display the 3-D formula in the formula bar (see Figure 8.21)

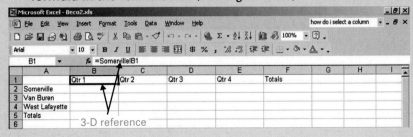

FIGURE 8.21

Summary worksheet with 3-D formulas

EXCEL

Now you are ready to write consolidating formulas. First, you will write a formula to sum the first quarter sales for the Somerville plant. Although the sum of Qtr 1 sales is in cell B15 on the Somerville worksheet, you prefer to write your own formula using a cell range in a 3-D reference as a double-check.

Writing formulas referencing other worksheets:

1. Click cell **B2** and type **=SUM(**

2. Click the **Somerville** worksheet tab

3. Click and drag the cell range **B2:B14,** type **)** and press **Enter.** Excel returns to the active worksheet, Summary of Sales, and displays the value 757,853 in cell B2

4. Click cell **B2,** drag the fill handle to cell **E2,** and release the mouse. Excel fills in the remainder of the Somerville total sales for each quarter, and it automatically adjusts the cell references (even for 3-D references) to reflect their location (see Figure 8.22)

FIGURE 8.22

Copied 3-D cell references

3-D reference ————

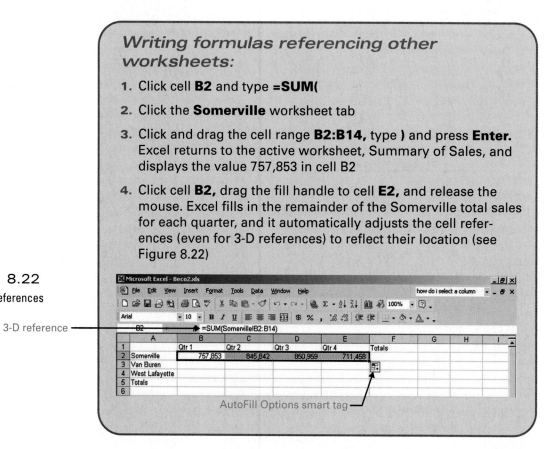

AutoFill Options smart tag ——

Filling in the remaining SUM formulas is the same process as above. This time, however, you will create the first-quarter sum formulas for the Van Buren and West Lafayette plants. Then you will copy that pair of formulas across their rows to save time.

Writing and copying the remaining 3-D SUM formulas:

1. Click cell **B3** and type **=SUM(**

2. Click the **Van Buren** worksheet tab. (You may have to scroll through the worksheet tabs to locate it)

3. Drag the mouse through the cell range **B2:B14,** type **)** and press **Enter.** Excel returns to the active worksheet, Summary of Sales, and displays the value 1,112,352 in cell B3

4. Click cell **B4** and type **=SUM(**

5. Click the **West Lafayette** worksheet tab. (You may have to scroll through the worksheet tabs to locate it)

6. Drag the mouse through the cell range **B2:B14,** type **)** and press **Enter.** Excel returns to the active worksheet, Summary of Sales, and displays the value 1,661,436 in cell B4
   You can complete the Van Buren and West Lafayette rows by selecting the two Qtr 1 formulas and then dragging their fill handle

7. Select the cell range **B3:B4,** drag the cell pair's fill handle from cell **B4** to cell **E4,** and release the mouse. Excel copies the formulas and adjusts all cell references

Totaling Formulas Containing 3-D References

You can sum cells containing references to other worksheets just as you can any other cells. Now that you have summarized the sales from three other worksheets by calendar quarter and company, you can form row and column totals and compute a grand total. The row totals will appear in cells F2 through F4 of the summary worksheet, and column totals will appear in cells B5 through E5. The grand total will appear at the intersection of the row totals and the column totals, in cell F5.

Using Excel's AutoSum button to write SUM functions:

1. On the Summary of Sales worksheet, click and drag the cell range **B2:F5**

2. Click the **AutoSum** button on the Standard toolbar. Row totals, column totals, and a grand total appear

3. Click any cell to deselect the range (see Figure 8.23)

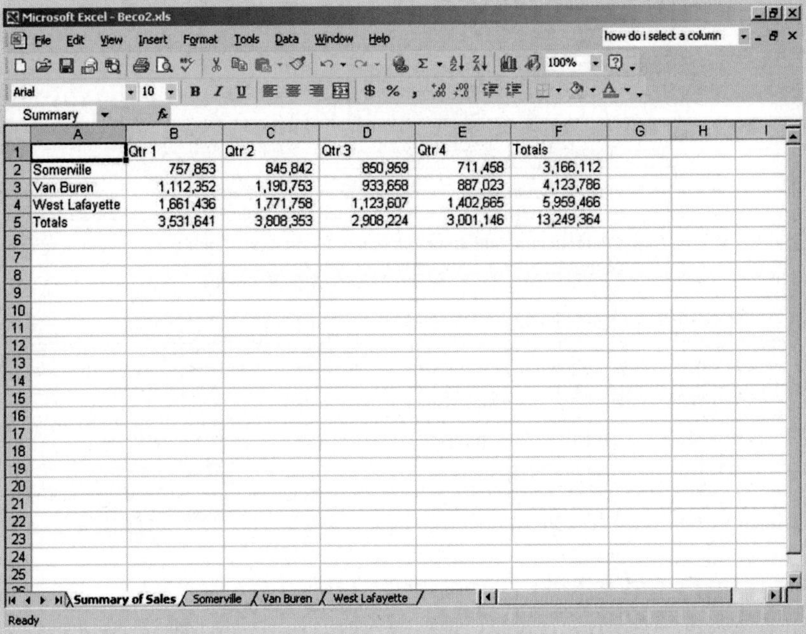

	A	B	C	D	E	F
1		Qtr 1	Qtr 2	Qtr 3	Qtr 4	Totals
2	Somerville	757,853	845,842	850,959	711,458	3,166,112
3	Van Buren	1,112,352	1,190,753	933,658	887,023	4,123,786
4	West Lafayette	1,661,436	1,771,758	1,123,607	1,402,665	5,959,466
5	Totals	3,531,641	3,808,353	2,908,224	3,001,146	13,249,364

FIGURE 8.23

AutoSum creates totals and a grand total

EXCEL

You are pleased with your worksheet and understand how to write formulas that reference other worksheets. You show the summary worksheet to Stirling. He, too, is happy with your work. He asks you to format the worksheet because he wants to present it in a PowerPoint slide show to some of the managers.

Formatting the Summary Worksheet

With the summary formulas complete, you are ready to format the summary worksheet for Stirling and the managers. You have already formatted the supporting worksheets by performing a series of format operations on them. (**Supporting** worksheets are worksheets that are referenced by other worksheets and thus support those worksheets.) Recall that you can use Excel's AutoFormat command to format a range of cells.

> ### Formatting the summary worksheet cells with AutoFormat:
>
> 1. Click and drag the cell range **A1:F5**
>
> 2. Click **Format** on the menu bar and then click **AutoFormat**. The AutoFormat dialog box appears
>
> 3. Drag the scroll button down until you see Classic 3 (see Figure 8.24)

FIGURE 8.24

Selecting an AutoFormat

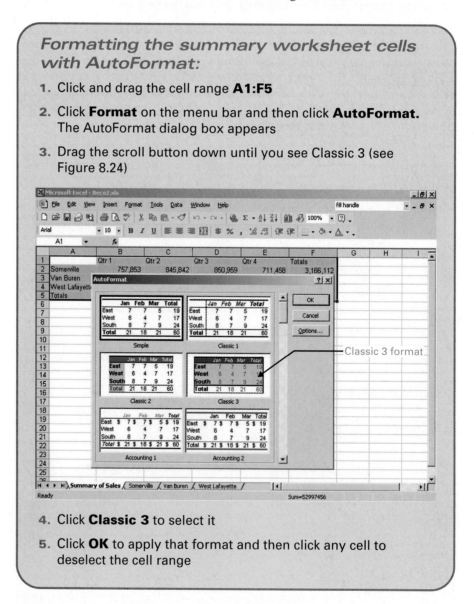

> 4. Click **Classic 3** to select it
>
> 5. Click **OK** to apply that format and then click any cell to deselect the cell range

PRINTING MULTIPLE WORKSHEETS

Stirling would like you to print out the Summary worksheet and the three sales worksheets, but not the Documentation worksheet. Previously, when you printed out a worksheet that was part of a workbook of several worksheets, you simply clicked File, Print, and OK to print the worksheet. Printing more than one worksheet is just as easy. The only additional step is that you must first select (group) the worksheets and then print them.

---

task reference

Printing Multiple Worksheets

- Group the worksheets you want to print by pressing **Ctrl** and then clicking the worksheet tabs or by pressing **Shift** and clicking the first and last worksheets in a contiguous group

- Click **File,** click **Print,** ensure that the **Active sheet(s)** option button is selected, and click **OK**

You print the worksheets for Stirling—all sheets except the Documentation worksheet.

Printing multiple worksheets:

1. Click the **Summary of Sales** worksheet tab, press and hold the **Shift** key, click the **West Lafayette** worksheet tab, and release the **Shift** key. Excel groups the four worksheets

2. Click **File** on the menu bar, click **Print,** ensure that the **Active sheet(s)** option button in the *Print what* panel is selected, click the **Preview** button, click the **Next** button repeatedly to examine each of the four pages, and then click the **Print** button. Excel prints four worksheet pages. Notice each worksheet page contains a centered footer containing the worksheet name

3. Right-click the **Summary of Sales** worksheet tab and then click **Ungroup Sheets** from the shortcut menu

---

Whenever you want to print *all* the worksheets in a workbook, you do not need to group the worksheets. Instead, click the *Entire workbook* option in the *Print what* panel. That option directs Excel to print all of a workbook's worksheet.

You have made a lot of changes to your workbook. Save it in case you want to take a break or return to work on the workbook another time.

Save the BECO workbook and close Excel:

1. Click the **Name box list arrow,** click **Documentation,** and edit the Date Revised value to today's date

2. Click the **Save** button on the Standard toolbar to save the completed work

3. Click **File** on the menu bar, click **Save As** and type **Beco3.xls,** and then click the **Save** button to save an identical copy under a new name in preparation for Session 8.2

4. Exit Excel by clicking **File** on the menu bar and then click **Exit.** Excel closes

SESSION 8.1   *making* **the grade**

1. You can view multiple workbooks on screen by clicking Window and then clicking the _____ command.

2. Group contiguous worksheets together by clicking the first worksheet tab, pressing the _____ key, and clicking the last worksheet tab in the series of tabs.

3. By default, a worksheet you add to a workbook appears where in the workbook?

4. Enter the same value in grouped worksheets by typing the expression and pressing Enter. That is also known as _____ down.

5. Open **Beco2.xls** and immediately save it as **Beco21.xls.** Then make the following modifications to the workbook. Insert a new worksheet and move it to the last position in the workbook—following the West Lafayette worksheet. Rename the worksheet tab **Madison.** Click cell **A1** and type the 3-D formula **='West Lafayette'!A1** and copy the expression using the cell's fill handle to the cell range **A2:A14.** Copy cell **A1** through the cell range **B1:E1.** In cell B2, write a 3-D expression to compute 1.5 times the value in West Lafayette's cell B2. Copy that cell through the cell range **B2:E14.** Format the worksheet so that all entries match the West Lafayette worksheet formats—numbers, labels, and column widths. Insert a new row 5 in the Summary of Sales worksheet. Type **Madison** in cell **A5** and write 3-D formulas that display Qtr 1 through Qtr 4 totals for Madison. Write the row total formula (or copy it from cell F4). Correct the column total formulas because they do not include the newly added row. Group the Summary of Sales and the Madison worksheets, insert your name in the header, and create a footer that displays "Worksheet" followed by the worksheet tab name, Madison. Save the workbook and print the grouped worksheets, Summary of Sales and Madison, in one print operation.

SESSION 8.2 WORKING WITH MULTIPLE WORKBOOKS

In this section, you will learn how to write formulas that reference another workbook. You will learn how to instruct Excel to locate and retrieve information from another workbook stored on your computer, even though the referenced workbook is not open. You will create an Excel Workspace to preserve the on-screen relationship between open workbooks and worksheets.

RETRIEVING DATA FROM OTHER WORKBOOKS

In the previous session, you created 3-D formulas that referenced cells from other worksheets within the same workbook. Excel allows you to extend the concept of three-dimensional references to include other workbooks on your computer. For example, you could write a formula in the Summary or Sales worksheet in the BECO workbook that averages or totals a cell group in the Avicon workbook you worked on in Chapter 7.

Linking Workbooks

A three-dimensional reference to a cell in another workbook resembles a three-dimensional reference to another worksheet in the same workbook. The only difference is that any 3-D reference to another workbook must contain the workbook's location and name in addition to the worksheet name and cell address or cell range. The general form of a 3-D reference to another workbook—also called a **link,** a **dynamic link,** or an **external reference**—is this:

```
'Location[workbook-name]worksheet-name'!cell-range
```

Location is the disk drive and folder name that contains the workbook. The folder may be within other folders, and the disk drive and folders that lead to the workbook are known as the **path.** Enclose a workbook name in brackets to distinguish the workbook name from both the path preceding it and the worksheet name that follows it. The location, workbook name, and worksheet name or name range are enclosed in apostrophes. Following the worksheet name is an exclamation point and the cell reference, cell range, or cell name.

You notice that each part of the link becomes more specific from left to right. For example, suppose you are working on the Summary of Sales worksheet in the BECO workbook and you want to display the value of a cell in another workbook. The workbook you want to link to is on the drive and path C:\My Documents\SalesWorksheets\, the workbook name is **BritishSales.xls,** the worksheet name is 2002, and the cell containing the value you want to reference is C42. You would write the link reference to the cell as shown in Figure 8.25

You notice that apostrophes enclose the Location[workbook-name]worksheet-name part of the 3-D cell reference. This is required when the location, workbook name, or worksheet name contain spaces. If there are no spaces in the location, workbook name, or worksheet name, you can omit the apostrophes. You can drop the location portion of the 3-D reference if the workbook to which you are linking is in the same folder as the active workbook in which you are typing the link expression.

An alternative is to point to the cell or cell range in the external worksheet and let Excel write the properly formatted link reference for you. This is far less error-prone than typing a reference.

In this chapter, you will practice both typing external references and pointing to external references to see which works best for you.

Advantages of Linked Workbooks

Workbook links are also called dynamic links because a change in a cell linked to another workbook automatically propagates to any expression that references the changed cell. This happens for links in open workbooks as well as workbooks that are not currently open or loaded. When you

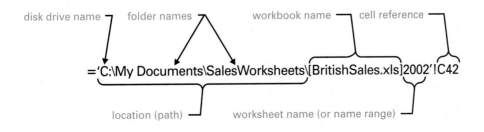

FIGURE 8.25

Link workbook reference

EXCEL

---

task reference

Building Link References by Pointing

- Open the supporting workbook containing the cell or cells you will reference in another worksheet and workbook

- Make the workbook containing the link reference active and click the cell to contain the link reference

- Type the formula up to the point in which you reference the cell or cell range in another workbook

- Click the taskbar button corresponding to the supporting workbook to make it active

- Click the worksheet tab containing the cell or cell range to reference

- Click the cell or drag the cell range of the cell(s) you want to reference and press **Enter**

---

open a workbook containing a link to another workbook, Excel informs you that the worksheet contains dynamic links. If you approve, Excel opens referenced workbooks, inspects referenced cells, updates formulas containing the references to other worksheets' cells when necessary, and then closes the referenced workbooks. A workbook containing a worksheet to which a link formula refers is called a *supporting workbook.* A workbook containing a link to a supporting worksheet is called a *dependent workbook,* because one or more of its cells' value depend on the value stored in another workbook.

Creating a series of linked workbooks is often a better alternative than creating and using one larger workbook containing worksheets from all the referenced workbooks for several reasons. One of the most important advantages is that linked workbooks require less memory than an equivalent multisheet workbook. Smaller workbooks containing dynamic links to other workbooks load and open faster than equivalent larger work books containing all the referenced worksheets. Linking workbooks allows a high degree of independence among worksheet developers. A workbook that consolidates information from several company divisions can refer to key values on divisional workbooks through workbook link references. Simultaneously, company division managers are free to use and modify their own divisional workbooks independently of other workbook developers.

Creating and Maintaining Linked Workbooks

Over the weekend, Stirling Leonard and members of the BECO's board completed the paperwork to acquire Danielli, Incorporated. Danielli is a small company that was a BECO competitor and manufactures some of the same types of machinery as BECO. While Stirling is busy with details of the merger, he wants you to incorporate some of the gross sales information Danielli keeps in their Excel workbook with the sales information in the BECO workbook. Danielli management wants to maintain physically separate workbooks for at least six months. To provide that separation, Stirling asks you to link to the Danielli workbook in order to summarize their sales in the BECO workbook. Both Stirling and Danielli's former CEO, Larry Sweet, agree that this is the best way to maintain a logical separation and yet have a consolidated sales statement.

Opening the Danielli Workbook:

1. If you closed Excel at the end of the previous session, then start Excel

2. Click **File** on the menu bar, click **Open,** navigate to the folder containing the Danielli workbook **ex08Danielli.xls** using the Look in list box of the Open dialog box, and click **Open.** The Danielli workbook opens and displays the Information worksheet (see Figure 8.26)

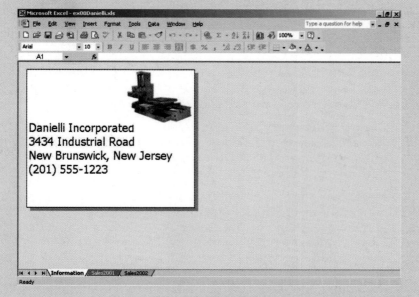

FIGURE 8.26
Danielli Information worksheet

Danielli Incorporated
3434 Industrial Road
New Brunswick, New Jersey
(201) 555-1223

3. Save the worksheet as **Danielli3.xls** so that you leave the original one undisturbed. (There is no **Danielli2.xls** worksheet, but the digit *3* in the name will keep the worksheet synchronized with the BECO worksheet version 3)

4. Click the **Sales2001** worksheet tab and briefly review the worksheet's contents

5. Click the **Sales2002** worksheet tab and briefly review the worksheet's contents. Both sales worksheets contain names that correspond to cell ranges for the four quarters' individual machine sales

6. Click the **Name Box list arrow** and then click the name **Qtr2** from the list. Notice the name refers to the cell range C5:F5

7. Click the **Name box list arrow** and then click the name **Qtr4** from the list. Notice the name refers to the cell range C7:F7

You notice that the Danielli worksheet arranges sales in a manner different from BECO. Danielli's quarters are arranged in rows and products run across columns. BECO's quarter sales are in columns and products are stored in rows. This is a problem if you want to copy a link formula either down or across in the BECO worksheet. However, Danielli's workbook creator assigned names to each quarter to facilitate referencing the product sales values by a name rather than by a cell range.

With the Danielli supporting worksheet open, you are ready to write your first external or link formula. Stirling wants you to summarize sales of Danielli for the four quarters and include the summary in the Summary of Sales worksheet of the **Beco3.xls** workbook. The plant's names are listed in alphabetical order in the Summary of Sales worksheet, so Stirling wants Danielli listed at the top of the list—just above the Somerville summary row.

Next, you open the BECO worksheet and point to create a link formula for the first quarter.

> ### Opening the BECO workbook and entering a link formula:
>
> 1. Click **File** on the menu bar, click **Open,** and navigate in the Look in list box to the disk and folder containing **Beco3.xls.** Then click **Beco3.xls** and click the **Open** button
>
> 2. Click the **Summary of Sales** worksheet tab, right-click cell **A2,** click **Insert** on the shortcut menu, click the **Entire row** option button, and click **OK** to insert a new row 2. Excel adds a new row and displays the Insert Options smart tag icon
>
> 3. Hover over the Insert Options smart tag until a list arrow appears, click the **Insert Options list arrow** (see Figure 8.27) and then click the **Format Same As Below** option button. Excel formats the newly added row the same as the other sales summary rows, not the header row

FIGURE 8.27

Formatting the new sales summary row

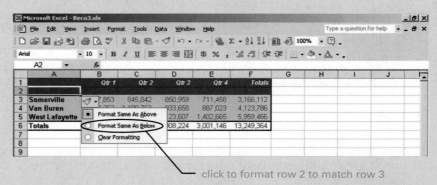

click to format row 2 to match row 3

> 4. Click cell **A2,** type **Danielli,** and press the **Tab** key to make cell B2 active
>
> 5. In cell B2, type **=SUM(**
>
> 6. Click **Window** on the menu bar, click **Danielli3.xls** in the list of open workbooks, click the **Sales2002** worksheet tab, drag the mouse through the cell range **C4:F4** (see Figure 8.28), and press **Enter** to complete the formula. The value 622,233 displays in cell B2 of the Summary of Sales worksheet
>
> 7. Click the **Danielli3.xls** button on the taskbar to make that worksheet active, click **File** on the menu bar, and click **Close** to close **Danielli3.xls.** Excel makes BECO the active workbook again

FIGURE 8.28

Selecting a cell range in an external workbook

dashed line outlines selected range

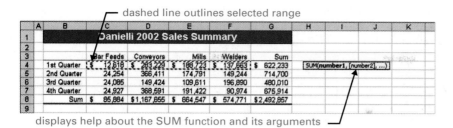

displays help about the SUM function and its arguments

You may be tempted to create the remaining Danielli formulas to be placed in cells C2 through E2 by copying the formula in cell B2. Unfortunately, the cells in the Danielli workbook are not arranged to accommodate a left-to-right copy as you did for the other BECO worksheets. Instead, you will have to build the remaining three link formulas by hand. In addition, you want a row total in cell F2, which you can copy from cell F3. Use the names Qtr2, Qtr3, and Qtr4 in the link formulas. The previous names are defined in the **Danielli3.xls** workbook for the three remaining cell ranges. Using names greatly simplifies your work because you do not need to worry about how the Danielli worksheet designer may have redesigned the worksheet—just as long as the names remain intact. That's why some worksheet designers call worksheets that use names "smart worksheets."

Creating the remaining three link formulas by typing the link references:

1. Click cell **C2** in the Summary of Sales worksheet, type **=SUM('** (be sure to type the apostrophe following the left parenthesis)

2. Type the path to *your* Danielli worksheet, then type **[Danielli3.xls]Sales2002'!Qtr2),** and press **Enter.** Excel displays the sum of Danielli's second quarter sales, 714,700

tip: *If you make a mistake in typing the link reference, Excel will display an error message such as "That name is not valid." If so, press the **Esc** key to go into edit mode, check the link formula very carefully, use your arrow keys to move to the mistake, correct it, and press **Enter.***

You can create the next formulas by copying the long complicated formula in cell C2 to cells D2 and E2. Then you can edit the cloned cells by making a very simple change.

3. Click cell **C2,** click the **Copy** button on the Standard toolbar to place the formula on the Clipboard, click and drag the cell range **D2:E2,** and click the **Paste** button on the Standard toolbar to paste in the two formulas

4. Click cell **D2,** press the **F2** function key to edit the cell, press the **Backspace** key twice to erase the last two characters in the formula, type **3),** and press **Enter** to save the edited formula. Excel displays the value 480,010.

5. Click cell **E2**, press the **F2** function key to edit the cell, press the **Backspace** key twice to erase the last two characters in the formula, type **4),** and press **Enter** to save the edited formula. Excel displays the value 675,914

6. Click cell **F2** and then click the **AutoSum** button on the Standard toolbar, and press **Enter** to approve the AutoSum-suggested cell range and complete the formula (see Figure 8.29)

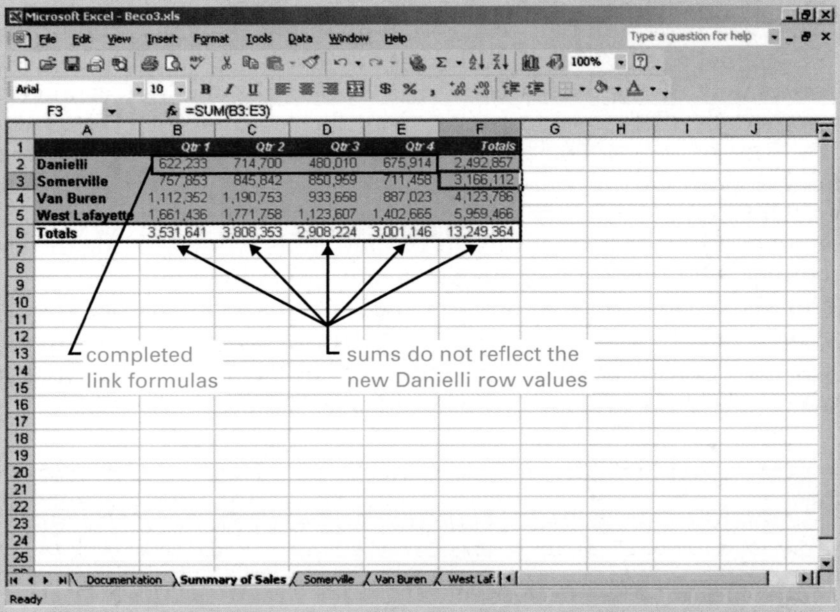

FIGURE 8.29

Worksheet after entering four link formulas

At first glance, all the values seem to be fine. However, you probably noticed that the totals in row 6 are unchanged. That is because Excel did not adjust the SUM functions in those rows after you added the Danielli row. Because the newly added row is out of range of the SUM functions in row 6, Excel does not know to automatically adjust the cell references to include the new row. Therefore, you need to fix those formulas before going on.

Modifying quarter summation formulas:

1. Select the cell range **B2:F6,** which includes the incorrect SUM functions in row 6 and the totals in column F

2. Click the **AutoSum** button on the Standard toolbar. Excel places updated SUM functions in cells B6 through F6

tip: *If any of the cells displays ######, widen the column in which the pound signs appear. Simply double-click the right border of the column heading button to widen it to an optimal width*

3. Click cell **A1** to deselect the range

Updating Linked Workbooks

When you save a dependent workbook containing links to other workbooks, Excel stores the most recent calculation of those results. If you later open a supporting workbook after closing the dependent workbook and make changes to various cells, the values of the dependent workbook are not updated and do not jibe with the supporting worksheet's newly updated cells. However, Excel takes care of that disparity when you open a dependent workbook. Excel recognizes that the workbook contains formulas that are dependent on workbooks that are closed and asks if you want to update the links. If you click the Update button on the information dialog box, Excel locates the supporting workbook, reads the link cell values from it, and updates the dependent workbook. If you click the Don't Update button because you do not need current values for your work at the moment, the workbook opens without updating the linked cells. In that case, dependent formulas retain their values from the last time the workbook was saved.

Erik Gepetti, Danielli's manager, just discovered an error in the **Danielli3.xls** workbook. The value in cell F7 (total sales of welders in the fourth quarter) is incorrect. Instead of $90,974, the value should be zero. Danielli did not make or sell any welders in the fourth quarter. He asks you to make the change for him because he is concerned that his changing the workbook independently might cause an error. You agree to make the change and ensure that Excel automatically updates the link value in the dependent workbook **Beco3.xls.**

---

task reference

Opening a Supporting Workbook from a Dependent Workbook

- Open the dependent workbook containing the link reference
- Click **Edit** and then click **Links**
- Click the name of the supporting workbook you want to open from the Links list
- Click the **Open Source** button

Modifying values in a supporting workbook:

1. Click **Edit** on the menu bar and click **Links.** The Edit Links dialog box appears (see Figure 8.30)

2. With the **Danielli3.xls** workbook name in the Edit Links list selected, click the **Open Source** button to open the selected workbook. Excel opens **Danielli3.xls** and makes it active

3. Click the **Sales2002** worksheet tab (if necessary), click cell **F7** and type **0** (zero), and press **Enter** to indicate no sales of welders in the fourth quarter

FIGURE 8.30
Edit Links dialog box

Danielli3 is the only supporting workbook for Beco3

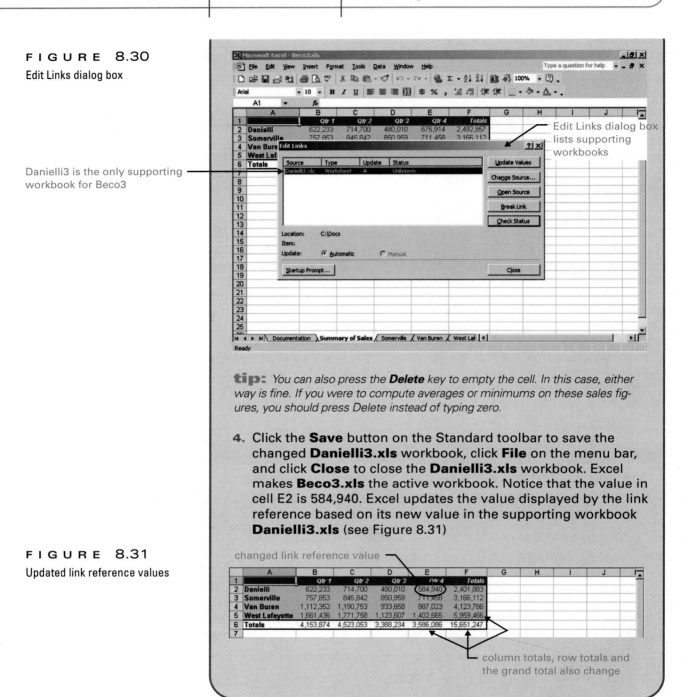

Edit Links dialog box lists supporting workbooks

tip: *You can also press the **Delete** key to empty the cell. In this case, either way is fine. If you were to compute averages or minimums on these sales figures, you should press Delete instead of typing zero.*

4. Click the **Save** button on the Standard toolbar to save the changed **Danielli3.xls** workbook, click **File** on the menu bar, and click **Close** to close the **Danielli3.xls** workbook. Excel makes **Beco3.xls** the active workbook. Notice that the value in cell E2 is 584,940. Excel updates the value displayed by the link reference based on its new value in the supporting workbook **Danielli3.xls** (see Figure 8.31)

FIGURE 8.31
Updated link reference values

changed link reference value

	A	B	C	D	E	F	G	H	I	J	
1		*Qtr 1*	*Qtr 2*	*Qtr 3*	*Qtr 4*	*Totals*					
2	**Danielli**	622,233	714,700	480,010	584,940	2,401,883					
3	**Somerville**	757,853	845,842	850,959	711,458	3,166,112					
4	**Van Buren**	1,112,352	1,190,753	933,658	887,023	4,123,786					
5	**West Lafayette**	1,661,436	1,771,758	1,123,607	1,402,665	5,959,466					
6	**Totals**	4,153,874	4,523,053	3,388,234	3,586,086	15,651,247					
7											

column totals, row totals and the grand total also change

Saving Linked Workbooks

You can choose to save the dependent workbook, **Beco3.xls,** and the supporting workbook, **Danielli3.xls,** under names different from their original names by executing the Save As command in the File menu. For example, Stirling may want to save the supporting workbook **Danielli3.xls** under a name such as **Danielli2002.xls** or **DanielliPlant.xls.** Nothing prevents you or someone else from saving either workbook under a new name, but you must be careful when saving a supporting workbook under a new name.

Because these are common scenarios, Stirling wants to make sure both you and he know how to deal with them. Three cases highlight the different scenarios that arise based on which workbooks are open or closed:

1. Both **Bec03.xls** and **Danielli3.xls** are open and you save the *supporting* workbook, **Danielli3.xls,** under a different filename

2. Both **Bec03.xls** and **Danielli3.xls** are open and you save the *dependent* workbook, **Beco3.xls,** under a different filename

3. **Bec03.xls** is closed and **Danielli3.xls** is open and you save the *supporting* workbook, **Danielli3.xls,** under a different filename

What happens to all the links in the dependent workbook when you save (and optionally close) **Danielli3.xls** under a different name? Excel automatically and without notification alters all link formulas to reflect the new name under which you save a supporting workbook. For example, if you choose to save **Danielli3.xls** as **Acquisition2002.xls** after you execute File, Save As to save the supporting workbook, Excel changes all the links in cells B2:E2 to reflect that change. The link formula in cell B2, for example, becomes:

```
=SUM([Acquisition2002.xls]Sales2002!Qtr1)
```

Excel makes the change because the dependent workbook is open and available for change.

In case 2, nothing happens to the links in the dependent workbook. After all, you are changing the name of a workbook that is not a supporting workbook. All formulas remain the same.

Case 3 is the most interesting one. If you change the name of a supporting workbook when the dependent workbook to which it is linked is closed, then Excel cannot make changes to the links in the closed dependent workbook. When you later open **Beco3.xls,** the dependent workbook, Excel searches for **Danielli3.xls.** If you saved **Danielli3.xls** under the new name, **Acquisition2002.xls,** Excel will update **Beco3.xls** based on the old worksheet values stored in **Danielli3.xls,** not the new workbook **Acquisition2002.xls.** Worse yet, if you deleted **Danielli3.xls** after saving it under its new name, Excel will not be able to locate the workbook and thus will not be able to update link reference values in the dependent workbook. In this case, Excel issues an error message. Because you need to know how to handle this case—someone changes the names of one or more supporting workbooks—you will experience it firsthand.

In the steps that follow, you will experience just such a situation. It shows you that if you rename a supporting workbook or move it to another drive or directory, you must tell Excel the new name of the supporting workbook or where you moved it so that Excel can modify the link references, which is not the same as updating the *values* in a link reference.

Redirecting link references to a renamed supporting workbook:

1. Click **File** on the menu bar, click **Close,** and click **Yes** when asked if you want to save your changes to **Beco3.xls. Beco3.xls** closes, but Excel remains running

2. Click the **Open** button on the Standard toolbar. The Open dialog box opens

EXCEL

3. Use the Look in list box to navigate to the disk drive and folder containing the supporting workbook **Danielli3.xls,** right-click the filename in the Open dialog box, click **Rename** in the shortcut menu. Excel highlights the name **Danielli3.xls** in edit mode in the Open dialog box

4. Type the new name **Acquisition2002.xls,** press **Enter** to complete the file renaming process, but do not open the renamed dependent workbook

5. With the Open dialog box still displayed, use the Look in list box to navigate to the disk and folder containing **Beco3.xls** workbook and then double-click **Beco3.xls** to open the workbook. Excel opens the workbook and displays a dialog box asking if you want to update links

6. Click the **Update** button. Excel displays an alert box indicating it cannot update links (see Figure 8.32)

FIGURE 8.32

Update links error dialog box

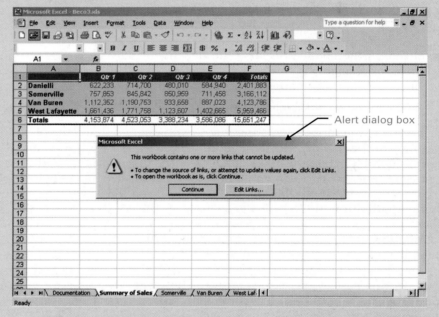

7. Click the **Edit Links** button so that you can help Excel find the renamed supporting workbook. The Edit Links dialog box appears (see Figure 8.33)

8. Click the **Change Source** button in the Edit Links dialog box. The Change Source dialog box opens. It resembles the Open dialog box

9. Using the Look in list box, go to the folder containing the **Acquisition2002.xls** workbook, click the **Acquisition2002.xls** filename in the Change Source list of files and folders, and click the **OK** button. The Edit Links dialog box reappears and displays OK in the Status list (see Figure 8.34)

10. Click the **Update Values** button, and then click the **Close** button to close the Edit Links dialog box

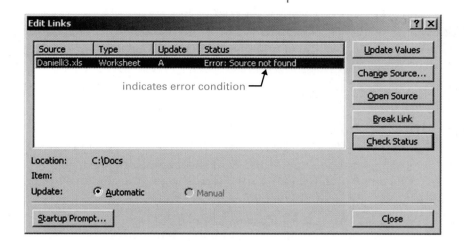

FIGURE 8.33

Edit Links dialog box

FIGURE 8.34

Edit Links dialog box with updated link locations

You have done a lot of work and completed the workbook. Stirling is pleased. Save the workbook and exit Excel.

Saving your final BECO workbook and closing Excel:

1. Click the **Save** button on the Standard toolbar to save your changed **Beco3.xls** workbook

2. Click **File** on the menu bar and then click **Exit** to close Excel

Stirling is pleased to have the linked references in a summary worksheet, and he is particularly glad to know that he can reference cells in other workbooks—even if the workbooks are not open.

making **the grade**

1. A reference to a cell in another workbook is called a _____, a dynamic _____, or a(n) _____ reference.

2. The disk drive and folders that lead to a workbook are known as the _____.

3. In an external reference, the workbook name is always enclosed in _____, even if it does not contain spaces.

4. The path, workbook name, and worksheet name of an external reference in which the path or the worksheet name contains a blank must be enclosed in what?

5. Make the following modifications to the BECO workbook, **Beco3.xls,** and its supporting workbook, **Acquisition2002.xls.** Open **Beco3.xls,** update its links, and save it as **Beco4.xls.** Click **Edit** and then click **Links,** and click **Open Source** to open **Acquisition2002.xls.** Save the file under the name **Danielli4.xls.** Click the **Sales2002** worksheet tab. Insert a new column in **Danielli4.xls** between existing columns **E** and **F** (between Mills and Welders). Click **F3,** type **Saws** and type the following values in cells **F4** through **F7**: **123400, 222344, 34500,** and **99678.** Copy cell **E8,** a column sum expression, to cell **F8.** Type your name in the worksheet header, print the **Sales2002** worksheet of **Danielli4.xls,** save the workbook, and close it. Click the **Summary of Sales** worksheet tab in the **Beco4.xls** workbook, type your name in the worksheet header, print the **Summary of Sales** worksheet, save the **Beco4.xls** workbook, and exit Excel.

SESSION 8.3 SUMMARY

Three-dimensional formulas reference cells in other worksheets of a workbook. The cell references include the worksheet name enclosed in square brackets, an exclamation point, and a cell or cell range. A 3-D or link reference acts like any other cell reference.

You can combine worksheets from other workbooks into one workbook by opening all workbooks, clicking Window and then Arrange to display all workbooks on one screen. Then click and drag a worksheet tab from one window to a workbook in another window to cut and paste a worksheet. To copy a worksheet, press and hold Ctrl and then click and drag a worksheet tab to a workbook in another window. Alternatively, you click Edit, Move or Copy Sheet, and designate a target workbook to which you want to copy or move a worksheet. Move a worksheet to a new location in a workbook by clicking and dragging its tab to the new position. Double-click a worksheet tab and type a new name to rename the worksheet and its tab.

You can group worksheets in a workbook by clicking the first worksheet tab and then shift-clicking (hold Shift and then click the mouse) the last worksheet of a contiguous set of worksheet tabs. Group noncontiguous worksheet tabs by Ctrl-clicking individual worksheet tabs. With grouped worksheets, you can type text in one worksheet cell and the text is placed in all grouped worksheets in the same cell location. Similarly, you can format entries in the same cell(s) on grouped worksheets at the same time by formatting one of the worksheets in the group. Grouping and then formatting saves time when dealing with similar worksheets. Grouping allows you to establish the same page-level settings for all worksheets in a group. For example, you can group worksheets and then assign the same worksheet header, footer, margins, or orientations for all worksheets in the group with one operation.

You can forge links between one workbook and a cell or cells of another workbook. Such cell references are called links, dynamic links, or external links. Workbooks containing external links are called dependent workbooks, and the workbooks to which they refer are called supporting workbooks. External links contain three parts: a path, a workbook name, and a cell or cell range. The combination of a path and a workbook name are enclosed in apostrophes if either the path or the workbook name contains spaces. If you rename a supporting workbook file, you have to reestablish the dependent program's link references to the renamed workbook. When one or more values in a supporting workbook change, the dependent workbook is updated with the new values the next time it is loaded.

MOUS OBJECTIVES SUMMARY

* Consolidate and summarize data using three-dimensional formulas—MOUS ex2002-4-3

task reference roundup

Task	Page #	Preferred Method
Copying Worksheets from Other Workbooks	EX 8.6	• Open the master workbook—the workbook into which you want to copy worksheets from other workbooks
		• Open all other workbooks containing worksheets you want to copy to the master workbook
		• In any of the open Excel workbooks, click **Window,** click **Arrange,** click the **Tiled** option button, and click **OK**
		• Press and hold the **Ctrl** key, and then click and drag to the master workbook the tab of the worksheet you want to copy
		• Release the mouse when the down-pointing arrow is in the correct tab location in the master workbook, and then release the **Ctrl** key
Grouping Contiguous Worksheets	EX 8.11	• Click the worksheet tab of the first worksheet in the group
		• Use the tab scrolling buttons if necessary to bring the last worksheet tab of the proposed group into view
		• Hold down the **Shift** key and click the last worksheet tab in the group
Grouping Noncontiguous Worksheets	EX 8.11	• Click the worksheet tab of the first worksheet you want in the group
		• Press and hold the **Ctrl** key and then click each worksheet you want to include in the group
		• When you are done, release the **Ctrl** key

task reference roundup

Task	Page #	Preferred Method
Ungrouping Worksheets	EX 8.12	• Click the worksheet tab of any worksheet not in the worksheet group
		• If all worksheets in the workbook are grouped, right-click any worksheet tab and click **Ungroup Sheets** from the shortcut menu
Writing a Formula Containing a 3-D Reference	EX 8.25	• After clicking the cell where you want the formula to appear, type =, type a function name, and type the left parenthesis. If no function is needed, then type =
		• Click the sheet tab of the worksheet containing the cell or cell range you want to reference
		• If a worksheet range is needed, then press and hold the **Shift** key and click the last worksheet tab in the range
		• Click the cell or cell range you want to reference
		• Complete the formula (type a concluding right parenthesis for a function, for instance) and then press **Enter**
Printing Multiple Worksheets	EX 8.29	• Group the worksheets you want to print by pressing **Ctrl** and then clicking the worksheet tabs or pressing **Shift** and clicking the first and last worksheets in a contiguous group
		• Click **File**, click **Print**, ensure the **Active sheet(s)** option button is selected, and click **OK**
Building Link References by Pointing	EX 8.32	• Open the supporting workbook
		• Make active the workbook to contain the link reference and the cell to contain the link reference
		• Type the formula up to the point in which you reference the cell or cell range in another workbook
		• Click the taskbar button corresponding to the supporting workbook to make it active
		• Click the worksheet tab containing the cell or cell range to reference
		• Click the cell or drag the cell range of the cell(s) you want to reference and press **Enter**
Opening a Supporting Workbook from a Dependent Workbook	EX 8.37	• Open the dependent workbook containing the link reference
		• Click **Edit** and then click **Links**
		• Click the name of the supporting workbook you want to open from the Links list
		• Click the **Open Source** button

CROSSWORD PUZZLE

ACROSS

4. Changing all the grouped worksheets by typing information in one is called _____ down
6. Describes the disk name and folder(s), in sequence, where another workbook is stored
7. Formulas that reference other worksheets in the current workbook are _____ dimensional formulas
8. Another word for a summary worksheet is a _____ worksheet

DOWN

1. A _____ worksheet contains a digest or synopsis of the information in other worksheets in the same workbook
2. A 3-D reference to another workbook is also called what?
3. A _____ workbook or worksheet contains cells referenced by another workbook or worksheet
4. A _____ workbook contains expressions that reference cells in other workbooks
5. Another term for a dynamic link is a(n) _____ reference

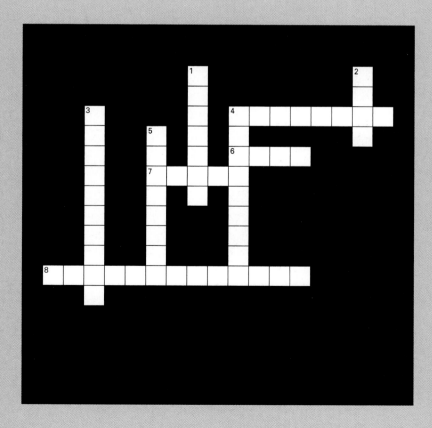

FILL-IN

1. A _____ worksheet is sometimes called a consolidation worksheet.

2. One way to copy a worksheet from one workbook to another is to display the source and target workbooks, press and hold the _____ key, and drag the worksheet from the source workbook to the target workbook.

3. Add a blank worksheet to a workbook by clicking Insert on the menu bar and then clicking _____.

4. When you press and hold the Ctrl key and then click two or more worksheet tabs in a workbook, you are _____ the worksheets.

5. In a workbook with many worksheets, you can speed up accessing worksheets by assigning a unique range _____ to cell A1 of each worksheet. Then you can access the _____ Box left of the formula bar to switch from one worksheet to another.

6. Worksheets that contain cells referenced by expressions in another workbook are called _____ worksheets.

REVIEW QUESTIONS

1. Discuss the fastest way to enter the text **Acme Consolidated** in cell A12 of seven worksheets.

2. What is the advantage of a summary or consolidating worksheet?

3. Discuss what, if anything, is wrong with the following expression (assuming that the workbook exists and contains the referenced worksheet):

   =SUM(C:\My Worksheets for Beco\[Danielli.xls]Sales!B4:B12)

4. What happens if you change the name of a supporting workbook when the dependent workbook is closed?

CREATE A QUESTION

For each of the following answers, create an appropriate short question.

ANSWER	QUESTION
1. Click Edit, click Links, and then click the Change Source button	_____
2. =[SalesDetail]Sales!C12	_____
3. Click the Qtr1 worksheet tab, press the Ctrl key, click the Qtr2 worksheet tab, click cell A1, and type Sales Information	_____
4. Click File on the menu bar and then click Save Workspace	_____
5. Click and drag the worksheet tab from where it is to another location	_____

practice

1. Summarizing Sales Data Using Reference Tools

Reed Lanterns makes specialty and custom lanterns and lamps. Their clients range from amusement parks to business buildings to private homebuilders. Reed currently has 11 sales representatives across the country to promote the firm and service their clients. Scott Reed, the owner of Reed Lanterns, has decided to promote one of the representatives to sales manager. Scott has asked you to help him determine which sales representative should be promoted to the management position. He would like you to summarize the sales reps' sales per quarter for the past two years in order to see which sales rep has sold the most.

Scott has reviewed the worksheets you have created and has given you some suggestions. He would like you to add a worksheet to summarize the sales representative's figures for the past two years. There are also some formatting changes he would like you to complete to improve the appearance of the worksheet.

1. Open **ex08ReedReps.xls** and save it as **ReedReps2.xls.** These two worksheets are what you have created for Scott
2. Insert a Documentation sheet so that it is the first worksheet in the workbook. Enter the workbook name, **Reed Sales Representative Report,** your name, and the date
3. Insert a worksheet at the end of the workbook titled **Sales Summary.** Create the following column titles and place them in the cell range A1:D1: **Sales Rep, 2001 Total Sales, 2002 Total Sales,** and **Total Sales**
4. Use 3-D references to place the reps' names in the Sales Summary worksheet, cells **A2** through **A12,** by referring to their cell addresses in the 2002 Totals worksheet
5. In the Sales Summary worksheet, type a 3-D cell reference in cells **B2** and **C2** referring to cell **F3** in the 2001 Totals and 2002 Totals worksheets, respectively. Select cells **B2:C2** and drag the fill handle down through the cell range **B12:C12** to complete columns B and C

6. For the Total Sales column, select cell range **B2:D12** and then use the AutoSum button to create SUM functions in column D. Be sure that all currency figures display two decimal places and the Accounting format with the currency symbol
7. To improve the appearance of the worksheets, do the following. In the 2001 and 2002 Totals worksheets, make the font of the top row 14 point, bold, and blue. In these worksheets and the Sales Summary worksheet, make the column headings' font bold and blue, and fill the cells in light yellow
8. Format the column headings in the summary worksheet so that the cells are bordered as in the 2001 and 2002 Totals worksheets
9. In the summary worksheet, determine which rep had the greatest sales and should be promoted to manager. Display this rep by filling his information with a light green background. Remove the on-screen gridlines from the Documentation worksheet. Place your name in the worksheet header of each worksheet, save the workbook, and print all sheets in the workbook

2. Producing a Consolidated Income Statement for Delzura Machinery

Delzura Machinery firm builds glass-beveling machinery for both professional and hobbyist customers. They produce and sell a small lathe-style glass-beveling machine with four stations for $1,350 up through a large industrial-model beveling machine for $14,000. With small manufacturing and sales offices in Hawthorne and Portland, sales of Delzura's custom-made machinery tops $450,000 per year and is rising rapidly. Each manufacturing location maintains its own workbook detailing net sales, cost of goods sold, operating expenses, and net income. Workbooks for both manufacturing sites are on the company's workstation located in Hawthorne, home of the executive offices.

Phyllis Dobkin, the executive vice president, wants you to create a one-page summary workbook that summarizes the key figures from each workbook. Each workbook contains a similar format as the same person created both of them. Both workbooks detail each quarter's net sales, cost of goods sold, operating expenses for several categories of expenses, and net income. Key figures Phyllis wants you to place on a summary workbook are Net Sales, Cost of Goods Sold, Gross Profit, Total Operating Expenses, and Net Income. You will create three of the five values by using link references to the Hawthorne and Portland workbooks. Gross Profit and Net Income are simple expressions that do not involve link references. After entering all formulas, you should format the workbook using the accounting format, zero decimal places, and currency symbols for numeric values.

1. Open the supporting workbooks **ex08DelzuraHawthorne.xls, ex08DelzuraPortland.xls,** and the main workbook you will alter and save called **ex08DelzuraMain.xls**

2. Make **ex08DelzuraMain.xls** active, save the workbook as **DelzuraMain2.xls,** click the **Summary** worksheet tab, and type the following labels in the indicated cells: A1: **Consolidated Income Statement;** A4: **Net Sales;** A6: **Cost of Goods Sold;** A8: **Gross Profit;** A10: **Total Operating Expenses;** A12: **Net Income;** B3: **Hawthorne;** and C3: **Portland**

3. Bold cells **B3** and **C3,** select cell **A1** and drag the mouse across the cell range **A1:C1,** click the **Merge and Center** button, and format the merged cells to **Bold** and 12 pt

4. Display portions of all three worksheets by clicking **Window** on the menu bar, click **Arrange,** click the **Tiled** option button, and click **OK**

5. In preparation for writing link formulas, click the **ex08DelzuraHawthorne.xls** title bar to make it active and then click the **Hawthorne** worksheet tab

6. Click the **ex08DelzuraPortland.xls** title bar to make it active, then click the **Portland** worksheet tab, and then click the **DelzuraMain2.xls** title bar to make it active

7. In the DelzuraMain2.xls worksheet, click cell **B4,** type **=SUM(,** click the **ex08DelzuraHawthorne.xls** title bar, drag cell range **B4:E4** in the Hawthorne workbook, type **),** and press **Enter.** (Excel displays the value $ 462,735 and formats the entry)

8. Click cell **C4,** type **=SUM(,** (don't type the comma) click the **ex08DelzuraPortland.xls** title bar, drag cell range **B4:E4** in the Portland workbook, type **),** and press **Enter.** (Excel displays the value $529,286 and formats the entry)

9. Click cell **B6,** type **=,** (don't type the comma) click the **ex08DelzuraHawthorne.xls** Title bar, click cell **F5** in the Hawthorne workbook, and press **Enter**

10. Click cell **C6,** type **=,** (don't type the comma) click the **ex08DelzuraPortland.xls** title bar, click cell **F5** in the Portland workbook, and press **Enter**

11. Click cell **B8,** type **=B4-B6,** press **Enter,** and copy cell **B8** to cell **C8**

12. Click cell **B10,** type **=,** click the **ex08DelzuraHawthorne.xls** title bar, click cell **F14** in the Hawthorne workbook, and press **Enter**

13. Click cell **C10,** type **=,** click the **ex08DelzuraPortland.xls** title bar, click cell **F14** in the Portland workbook, and press **Enter**

14. Click cell **B12,** type **=B8-B10,** press **Enter,** and copy cell **B12** to cell **C12**

15. Format the eight cells displaying values to accounting format, zero decimal places, and currency symbols

16. Close the **ex08DelzuraHawthorne.xls** and **ex08DelzuraPortland.xls** workbooks, and click **No** if you are asked if you want to save changes

17. Click the **Maximize** button on the title bar of **DelzuraMain2.xls,** click the **Comments** worksheet tab, fill in your name in the Developer text box, type in yesterday's date in the Date Created text box, and type in today's date in the Date Revised text box

18. Click the **Summary** worksheet tab of **DelzuraMain2.xls,** click **File,** click **Page Setup,** click **Header/Footer,** fill in your name in the header section, click **OK** to close the Page Setup dialog box, save the workbook, and print both worksheets of the workbook

challenge

1. Summarizing Contract Billing and Bonuses with Excel

Kelleher & MacCollum is an accounting firm that services large corporations in the Northeastern United States. The main role of the firm's consultants, however, is not examining financial statements during audits or tax season; instead, the consultants at Kelleher & MacCollum are highly regarded as accounting experts. They are hired by corporations to come into their accounting offices, analyze current policies and procedures, recommend changes and improvements, and consult management on the best way to implement the needed changes.

The last three firms that hired Kelleher & MacCollum to recommend changes to their accounting departments specifically asked for the team led by Aaron Cole. These were the most successful contracts in the firm's history. The gross billing for each company was over $100,000, far exceeding any past contracts. The CEO of Kelleher & MacCollum, Dennis Kelleher, wants to reward Aaron and his team members for their excellent work. He has decided to give each team member a bonus of 5 percent of their gross billing for these three contracts. In addition to this 5 percent, Aaron Cole will also receive an additional 5 percent bonus on the total amount billed to all three contracts.

Currently, the amount billed per contract is by consultant name, hours billed, and charge per hour. The total charge for each consultant and the total charge for the contract are also included. Each consultant's charge per hour is based on his or her levels of education, experience, and knowledge. Dennis Kelleher needs a summary of all three contracts' figures in order to determine the appropriate bonus amounts. He has asked you to create a summary worksheet of this information.

Open the workbook **ex08Kelleher.xls** and save as **Kelleher2.xls.** Insert a documentation worksheet, called *Documentation*, and enter the workbook name, your name, and the date in the first column. At the end of the workbook, insert a new sheet called **Total Billing.** Use the Fill Across Worksheets command in the Edit menu to copy the column titles from the Front & Leaf worksheet to the Total Billing worksheet and the con-

sultants' names from the Front & Leaf worksheet. In the Hours Billed column of the Total Billing worksheet, insert the sum for each consultant's hours from the corresponding cells of the three contract worksheets. From the Front & Leaf worksheet, use the Edit, Fill Across Worksheets command to copy the dollar amounts from the Charge per Hour column to fill in the same column in the Total Billing worksheet.

In the Total Billing worksheet, title column D **Total Billed.** For each cell corresponding to each person's row, create a formula that multiplies the Hours Billed by the Charge per Hour. At the bottom of the Total Billed column, sum the consultant Total Billed values. Title column E **Bonus.** In this column, create formulas that multiply the Total Billed per consultant by 5 percent to determine their bonus amount. Remember that Aaron Cole receives a 5 percent bonus of his total hours billed and 5 percent of all hours billed. Total this column and bold the total value at the bottom of the column. Save your changes. Include your name in the header of each worksheet and print the Total Billing worksheet.

2. Consolidating Information for a Toy Robot Seller

Elizabeth Brodkin is the Chief Financial Officer for Robotic Creations, a company that sells four categories of robot toys: educational robots, tin robots, transformers, and robot pets. She maintains two very simple workbooks. The main workbook contains four worksheets in which she keeps a summary of sales by quarter of three of the four categories of robot toys. Called **ex08Robot,** the workbook also contains a documentation worksheet on the front. The second workbook, called **ex08RobotPets,** tracks sales of the robot pet category of robots. She would like you to help her in two major ways. First, she wants you to copy the single worksheet in ex08RobotPets into the ex08Robot workbook and place it between the Tin Robots worksheet and the Transformers worksheet. Secondly, she wants you to insert a new worksheet after all the worksheets in the ex08Robot workbook. That worksheet should summarize the sales of each of the robot categories. You should apply an attractive

www.mhhe.com/i-series

format to the summary worksheet. The summary worksheet contains text with the four quarters listed in column A and labels in cells B1 through E1 containing the labels for the four categories of robots. Be sure to label each worksheet with your name in the header and the sheet name in the footer, and print all worksheets.

Begin by opening **ex08Robot.xls** and save the workbook as **Robot2.xls.** Then open **ex08RobotPets.xls.** Copy the Robot Pets worksheet to the **Robot2.xls** workbook. Add a new worksheet to the **Robot2.xls** workbook and rename it Sales Summary. Create link formulas to the other worksheets to summarize sales. Save your finished work and print all worksheets in the **Robot2.xls** workbook.

1. Analyzing and Selecting the Best Law Schools Using the Web

Roger Thornburg graduated from college three years ago. He has been working for his father's law firm and has decided to pursue his law degree. Since Roger plans on returning home after he graduates to continue working with his father, he wants to spend his law school career far away from home. For the three years he will be in school, Roger has picked two states on opposite ends of the country where he wants to go to school—California and New York. Fortunately, both states are home to several of the top-tier law schools. Since Roger is working six days a week, he has asked you to help him in his application process by finding information online regarding law schools in these two states.

Because Roger is only interested in schools among the top 25, he suggests you go to a web site that lists schools in order of ranking: www.usnews.com. When on the homepage, select **Best Grad Schools** under **Rankings and Ratings.** Under Best Graduate Schools, look at the section titled **Law.** You will be using Top Law Schools for your information. Open **ex08LawSchools.xls** and save as **LawSchools2.xls.** This is the workbook Roger has started in which you will record the information you find on the Web. He has created a worksheet for each state and created column headings to organize the criteria most important to him in choosing schools to apply to—each university's name, rank, overall score, average undergraduate GPA of incoming students, and the average LSAT score of those students. For each worksheet, use the information from the Web to fill in the appropriate data for the schools in each state that appear in the top 25.

After glancing at the results, Roger asks you to add a column titled Diversity. He knows that he will best benefit from going away to school if he is part of a diverse student body. Go back to the Best Graduate Schools page, look under the Law heading, and select Diversity Rankings. Use these figures to fill in the needed data. To further narrow down Roger's choice of schools, he wants you to highlight the information for the top two schools in each state. To do this, under each column heading (rank/score/etc.) highlight the two cells with the highest score or ranking. Determine which two schools from each state have the greatest number of highlighted cells.

Create a worksheet titled Summary. In the summary worksheet, include the same column headings as in the state worksheets. Consolidate the information for the top two universities from each state in this worksheet so that it reflects the data for the top four schools. Again highlight the two cells under each column with the highest score or ranking. Conclude which two universities have the greatest scores for Roger's criteria. Highlight the names of those two universities. Create a documentation worksheet and on it include your name, the date, and the title **Law School Rankings.** Group all the worksheets and then place your name in the worksheet headers and place the worksheet name in the worksheet footers. Print the entire workbook.

e-business

1. Summarizing Multiple Worksheets and Workbooks to Analyze Customer Base

Assist Insurance is a web-based insurance company. Assist Insurance (AI) has advertised throughout the southern states as their office is in Tennessee. AI is a site that the public uses to find the best health care insurance plans for their individual needs. They pride themselves on their excellent customer service and low prices. The CFO of AI feels that there is a market segment that AI could dominate—students. Since AI's prices are so low, their services are attractive to the typical student. After several meetings, the board decided that in order to get more student clients, they plan to open a few test locations in selected cities. Recent studies have shown that Web-based businesses that are also in front of students and easily accessible are more successful than those with Web-only services. The board has approved the opening of six test locations.

As an intern at AI, you have been assigned to the project of determining the areas where AI should open an office. AI wants these offices to be in the six cities with the greatest amount of student awareness. In other words, AI needs to determine in which cities they are currently best known. Your manager has already narrowed it down to three states, Florida, Georgia, and Louisiana. Each state's figures for the past four quarters have been recorded in an individual notebook. Open **ex08AIFlorida.xls** and save as **AIFlorida2.xls.** Do the same for the worksheets **ex08AIGeorgia.xls** and **ex08AILouisiana.xls**— save the workbooks as **AIGeorgia2.xls** and **AILouisiana2.xls,** respectively. For each state, the following statistics are available for each quarter: the number of hits the Web site received from that city, the number of hits that resulted in purchases, the average age of site visitor, and the number of hits received from students. For each state, you will need to create a summary sheet to summarize the past four quarters' figures. Once each workbook is summarized, the information will need to be incorporated into a single summary workbook.

The board is only concerned with the number of hits and the number of hits received from students. Create a summary sheet for each state so that column A contains the same information on each worksheet for each individual state. Title Column B **Hits** and column C **Student Hits.** For column D, create the title **Percent from Students.** Create formulas for columns B and C, using 3-D cell references, so that they total the corresponding figures for each city from each quarter. For column D, create a formula that will divide the number of student hits by total hits. This will give the percentage of hits that were received from students. Fill the formulas for each city. Format this column in percentages with one decimal point.

Create a new workbook and name it **AISummaryReport.** Create a documentation worksheet and place on it the title of the workbook, the names of three states summarized, your name, and the date. Create a summary worksheet, called AI Summary Report, grouped into distinct rows by state. Use a light green color to highlight the three state names, below which are the cities within the state. Include within each state's group of cities the information from each state's summary sheet. Create columns to include the total number of hits, number of hits received from students, and total percentage of hits from students. Improve the appearance of the worksheet (bold column headings, use *Wrap text* alignment, etc.) and use a light yellow background color to highlight the rows of the four cities with the greatest response from students. (Hint: Sort all cities on percent, note the highest values, and click Edit, Undo to restore the rows to their original order.) Type your name in the AISummaryReport header. Print the AISummaryReport workbook and follow the summary worksheet with the summary worksheet for each state.

1. Wilton Industries International Sales Consolidation Workbook

Wilton Industries International has sales offices in North America, Europe, the Pacific Basin, Latin America, and Asia. Jerry Parr keeps track of the sales in each region for each month. Currently he has collected sales, in millions of U.S. dollars, in a workbook named **ex08Wilton.xls.** Jerry's workbook contains seven sheets—a summary worksheet called Sheet1, and six worksheets, one for each month from January through June, called Jan, Feb, Mar, Apr, May, and Jun. Unfortunately, Jerry created the worksheets in a haphazard manner. Consequently, the worksheets are not in order by month. Your task is to use link formulas to summarize data from the individual month's sales in both the summary worksheet and two quarterly worksheets you will add to the workbook.

Open **ex08Wilton.xls** and save it immediately as **Wilton2.xls.** Next, add two new worksheets and rename them **Qtr1** and **Qtr2.** Rename the sheet called Sheet1 to **Summary.** Reorder the sequence of worksheets so that Summary is followed by these: Qtr1, Jan, Feb, Mar, Qtr2, Apr, May, and Jun. This way, each quarter precedes the three months it summarizes. Place the label **Quarter 1 Sales** in cell **A1** on the **Qtr1** worksheet. Place the label **Quarter2 Sales** in cell **A1** on the **Qtr2** worksheet. Merge and Center format the Quarter 1 and Quarter 2 labels across cells A1 and B1 in each worksheet and then apply bold-face to both labels. Write link formulas in cells A2 through A6 that will display the region labels on the Jan worksheet in cells A2 through A6. Do the same thing for the Qtr2 worksheet. On the Qtr1 worksheet in cells B2 through B7, write line formulas that sum the sales for each region in the first three months. Do the same thing for the Qtr2 worksheet: Write link formulas to sum sales for April through June by region. Group Qtr1 and Qtr2 and then format cell B2 with the Accounting format, display two decimal places, and display the currency symbol. Format cells B3 through B6 the same way, but omit the currency symbol. Click cell A1 and then ungroup the worksheets. Color the Qtr1 and Qtr2 worksheet tabs green. Color the Summary worksheet tab red.

The summary worksheet should summarize sales for the five regions for each quarter. Write link formulas that reference the total sales on the Qtr1 and Qtr2 summary worksheets for each region (e.g., =Qtr1!B3 for cell B4 on the summary worksheet). Remove the gridlines from the onscreen display of the Summary worksheet. Italicize the five region names on the Summary worksheet. Group all worksheets in the workbook, and then place your name in the header and place the worksheet names in the footer. Remember to use the code for the worksheet names so that you do not have to visit each worksheet and individually type the worksheet names. Save the workbook and print it.

(running project

Pampered Paws

Pampered Paws has tracked their sales of the cat and dog food portion of their business and captured the sales data in a workbook called **ex08Paws.xls.** It contains six worksheets, one for each month, listing sales in date order for the first six months of the year. Grace wants you to add three worksheets to the workbook, write link expressions to summarize the sales information, and print only the three worksheets you added. Two of the new worksheets are the quarterly summary worksheets. Label the first of these worksheets **Quarter 1** and the second one **Quarter 2.** Color the preceding worksheet tabs green. Place the worksheet Quarter 1 just before the January worksheet and place the worksheet Quarter 2 between the March and April worksheets. Quarter 1 should summarize both the total number of bags sold and the total sales amount for each month. Quarter 2 should be similar to Quarter 1, except that it summarizes sales for April through June.

The **Summary** worksheet should be the first worksheet in the workbook. Color its worksheet tab red. It displays four numbers and four labels. The numbers are the sum of quarter 1 bags sold, sum of quarter 1 total sales, sum of quarter 2 bags sold, and sum of quarter 2 total sales.

Start by loading **ex08Paws.xls** and save it as **Paws8.xls.** Insert the three new worksheets and move them into their locations among the worksheets. Rename the worksheet tabs as indicated above. Follow this model for both Quarter 1 and Quarter 2: Place the text **Total Bags** in **B1,** the text **Total Sales** in **C1,** the text **January** in **A2, February** in **A3,** and **March** in **A4.** Write link formulas in B2 to sum January's total bags sold and in C2 to sum January's total sales. Repeat these two formulas for February and March. Follow the same pattern for Quarter 2, but write the link formulas and month names for April through June. The Summary worksheet is simple: Place the label **Quarter 1** in cell **A2,** the label **Quarter 2** in cell **A3,** the label **Total Bags** in **B1,** and **Total Sales** in **C1.** Write four link formulas that sum quarter 1 total bags and total sales from the Quarter 1 worksheet and sum quarter 2 total bags and total sales from the Quarter 2 worksheet. Color the Summary worksheet tab red. Color both Quarter 1 and Quarter 2 worksheet tabs yellow. Format all three worksheets you added in an attractive manner, place your name in the worksheets' headers, save the workbook, and print only the three summary worksheets: Summary, Quarter 1, and Quarter 2.

CHAPTER

9

nine

Using Data
Tables and
Scenarios

did you know?

each year, 9 million tons of salt, more than 10 percent of all the salt produced in the world, is applied to American highways for road deicing. The cost of buying and applying the salt adds up to $200 million.

the first VCR, or videocassette recorder, was made in 1956 and was the size of a piano.

Rudyard Kipling, living in Vermont in the 1890s, invented the game of snow golf. He painted his golf balls red so that they could be located in the snow.

Denver has the nation's largest city park system, with more than 200 parks within city limits and 20,000 acres of parks in the nearby mountains—an area larger than all of Manhattan Island.

Queen Elizabeth I of England, using a diamond, scratched the following message on her prison window: "Much suspected of me, Nothing proved can be."

Excel data tables and scenarios are related. Find out how in this chapter.

Chapter Objectives

- Learn about the relationship between volume, cost, and profit

- Gain knowledge about break-even analysis

- Create and use a one-variable data table

- Create and use a two-variable data table

- Create charts based on one- and two-variable data tables

- Create Excel scenarios—(MOUS Ex2002e-8-3)

- Manage Excel scenarios with the Scenario Manager—(MOUS Ex2002e-8-3)

- View, add, edit, and delete scenarios—(MOUS Ex2002e-8-3)

- Create a scenario report—(MOUS Ex2002e-8-3)

chapter case

Artistic Furniture Corporation

Artistic Furniture Corporation ("Artistic") was founded in 1985 in El Cajon, California, by its president, Dave Messer. Artistic designs and manufactures high-quality home theater cabinetry in both oak and maple. Artistic Furniture Corporation is housed in a 4,800-square-foot facility in an industrial park that is close to a main thoroughfare—providing easy access for raw material delivery and finished product shipment. Paul Messer, Artistic's vice president and Dave's son, is a 50 percent owner of the privately held corporation and actively participates in all facets of the business.

Artistic is a wholesale business and sells its custom home theater cabinet systems to retailers—most of whom are located in California. Artistic sells its systems to both furniture dealers and electronics retailers who sell large-screen televisions and complete, expensive stereo systems. Although Artistic Furniture Corporation does not produce *custom* entertainment center cabinetry, it has an almost daunting number of combinations of cabinet dimensions, door panel styles (including glass), wood types, and stain and paint combinations. In a typical workweek, Artistic produces and ships eight home entertainment systems.

Artistic's typical home theater cabinet sells in the retail market for over $4,000. Retail customers with expensive entertainment systems often want attractive cabinets in which to house their equip-

ment. Thus, retail electronics and big-screen stores like to have at least two of Artistic Furniture Corporation's home theater cabinetry in the showroom.

In addition to a management function, Artistic's operation contains seven manufacturing departments: panel processing, lumber milling, assembly, pre-finishing, finishing, final assembly, and shipping. Artistic receives raw wood boards and panels at its receiving dock and sends the materials through each department, in turn, to produce a finished entertainment center. Panel processing and lumber milling prepare the panels, doors, and drawers for the cabinet from the blueprints. Assembly and pre-finishing departments build and sand the cabinet. Members of the finishing and final assembly departments (most employees work in at least three of the departments) are responsible for applying the finish coat of paint or lacquer and installing all hardware and glass. Shipping is responsible for placing the furniture in containers in preparation for pickup and shipment.

There are two major categories of costs in building the home entertainment systems: fixed costs and variable costs. Fixed costs include rent, taxes, and utilities. Variable costs include the cost of raw materials, labor, and supplies used to manufacture the systems. Dave and anyone else in a profitable business must be aware of both costs in order to make a profit. Figure 9.1 shows a worksheet displaying examples of both fixed and variable costs, the number of units produced, the revenue generated, and profit. You will be helping Paul Messer improve the worksheet and do sophisticated what-if analysis by using two Excel tools: data tables and scenarios.

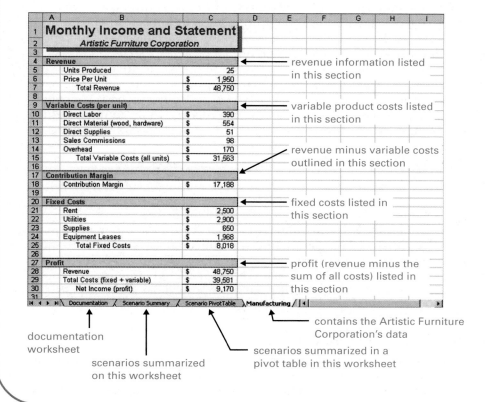

FIGURE 9.1
Artistic Furniture Corporation completed worksheet

revenue information listed in this section

variable product costs listed in this section

revenue minus variable costs outlined in this section

fixed costs listed in this section

profit (revenue minus the sum of all costs) listed in this section

contains the Artistic Furniture Corporation's data

documentation worksheet

scenarios summarized on this worksheet

scenarios summarized in a pivot table in this worksheet

Chapter 9 covers two very important what-if tools: one- and two-variable data tables and scenarios. In this chapter, you will learn how to use one-variable and two-variable tables to quickly and easily make changes and observe their effect on a series of values in a worksheet—changes to the profitability of a company, for example. You will consider the relationships among the important business terms of volume, cost, and profit. Called *Cost-Volume-Profit (CVP) analysis,* it examines the relationship between a product's expenses (cost), the number of units of the product produced (volume), revenue, and profit. Revenue, which is the total units produced multiplied by their sales price, determines profit. Profit, a value you always hope will be positive, is revenue minus total cost. CVP analysis helps managers make good decisions, including which products to make and sell, whether or not the company should change its pricing policy, and whether or not to purchase additional manufacturing facilities to increase productivity. Using CVP, managers focus on these five elements: production volume, product pricing, product mix, per unit variable costs, and total fixed costs.

CHAPTER OUTLINE

9.1 Creating and Using Data Tables

9.2 Creating and Using Scenarios

9.3 Summary

EX 9.3

EXCEL

In this chapter, you will make the simplifying assumption that the company is focusing on a single product and not attempting to determine the proper product mix for maximum profit. However, you will be using Excel to examine the remaining four elements in CVP.

A frequent problem in examining the effect of altering the sales price of a unit or another variable is keeping track of the various outcomes. Several worksheet cells aid in determining that all-important bottom line, profit. Frequently, business people want to examine several cases, or scenarios, each with a different combination of variables (unit cost, labor, volume, etc.) to observe the effect on profit. One solution is to create multiple worksheets, each with a different combination of variable values, and print out each sheet. A better solution, and one you will learn to use in this chapter, is to create several scenarios. Scenarios allow you to create sets of variable values you want to change as named groups. Then, you can invoke each scenario, in turn, on one worksheet and observe how it changes profit. Finally, you can produce a scenario report, which summarizes the different input sets and the values they affect in a concise, small report.

SESSION 9.1 CREATING AND USING DATA TABLES

In this section, you will learn about the relationships among product cost, volume, and profit. You will build a worksheet to aid Dave in making manufacturing decisions such as whether to reduce unit costs, produce more units, and determine how many units they must sell to reach *break-even*— when profit is zero. Break-even analysis is particularly important because it illustrates the effects on profit from cutting variable and fixed costs or raising prices.

CREATING AN INCOME STATEMENT

Paul wants to examine ways that Artistic can increase profits. To do so, he wants you to build an income statement that conveys the revenue and expenses, at a high level, so that he can look for ways to increase revenue or cut expenses to achieve higher profitability. Paul has started a monthly income statement worksheet, but he has become quite busy and wants you to complete the worksheet. Once you have created the worksheet showing revenue, expenses, and profit, then Paul and you will discuss ways to use a worksheet with data tables and scenarios to review the effect of changes in production units and expense reductions. By generating a data table, you will be able to display a series of revenues, expenses, and profits based on changes to a single worksheet cell—units produced—to locate any critical inflection points where Artistic's profitability changes dramatically. First, Paul explains the relationships between cost, volume and profit in general and then describes expenses that Artistic has when producing its line of entertainment center cabinets.

Paul wants you to investigate the relationships between Artistic's units produced, variable expenses, fixed expenses, and profit to help him find ways to increase their profit. Paul knows you want to learn more about how various business factors affect a business and agrees to discuss more details with you about Artistic's revenue and expenses. Because the business is small, understanding their business model will be simpler than understanding that of a large and more complex business. However, the principles that affect Artistic Furniture Corporation apply in the same way to larger businesses.

It is important for any manager to understand the relationships because she or he may have to decide whether it is better to cut costs, boost prices, or increase production to increase profitability. For example, do you know what will happen if Artistic's sales volume drops? If you suggest that Paul and Dave lower prices to increase demand for a product, how many more units will the company have to sell to make up for the lower per-unit sales price? Or, if you decide to get a business loan, what sales volume must the company attain to cover the added cost of the monthly loan payment? Paul knows that CVP analysis will help you answer these questions, and many more.

Revenue

One of the components of CVP analysis, *revenue*, is the money (or other items of value) that a company receives during a given period. Revenue can include sales, interest income, proceeds from the sale of a subsidiary, and so forth. In Artistic's case, revenue is the money that flows in whenever it sells an entertainment center to a wholesale customer. You will use monthly periods to measure revenue—the money that flows in each month. You will create the monthly income statement by building on the workbook that Paul created. Paul explains to you that the main source of revenue is, of course, wholesale sales of their entertainment centers. They sell for an average of $2,050 per unit. With its current pool of skilled labor, Artistic can produce up to 30 units per month. Paul asks you to continue his work by creating the revenue section of the income statement first, and he wants you to enter two values and a formula into three worksheet cells. One cell will display the number of units Artistic projects it will produce in a month and the second cell should contain $2,050—the sale price of each unit. In addition, Paul wants a formula to display total sales, which is the number of units times the price per unit. Because almost all values in the worksheet represent money, Paul wants you to format all worksheet cells with the accounting format with the currency symbol and zero decimal places. You can change the format of the number of units produced to not display the currency symbol, because it is not a currency value. You can apply other formatting as the need becomes apparent while you are developing the worksheet.

Opening the Artistic worksheet, entering revenue values and formulas, and applying a default numeric format:

1. Start Excel

2. Open the workbook **ex09Artistic.xls** and immediately save it as **Artistic1.xls** to preserve the original workbook in case you want to revert to that version. Review the documentation worksheet, called Documentation (see Figure 9.2)

3. Click the **Manufacturing** tab to switch to that worksheet. The Manufacturing worksheet contains preformatted rows under which you will create the body of the income statement (see Figure 9.3)

FIGURE 9.2

Artistic Furniture Corporation
Documentation worksheet

unlocked cell for
today's date

unlocked cell-pair for
your name

unlocked cell for
adding modification date

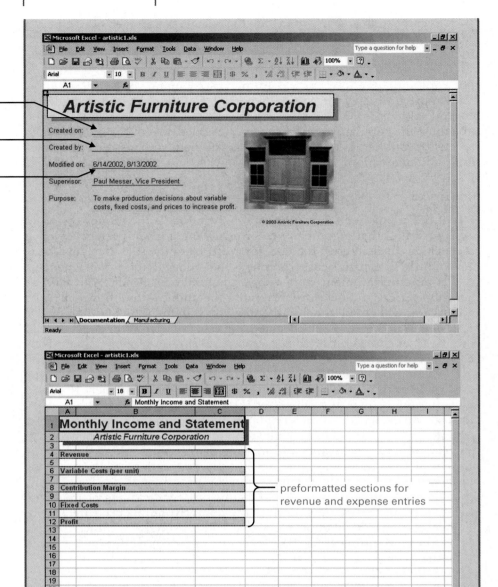

FIGURE 9.3

Monthly income statement
worksheet

preformatted sections for
revenue and expense entries

4. Set a default numeric format by pressing **Ctrl+A** to select all
   the worksheet's cells, click **Format** on the menu bar, click
   Cells, click the **Number** tab, click **Accounting** in the
   Category panel, type **0** in the Decimal places spin control box,
   click the **Symbol** list box, select **$** (if necessary) from the list
   of choices, and click **OK** to apply your choices and close the
   Format Cells dialog box

5. Select the cell range **A5:A7,** click **Insert** on the menu bar, and
   click **Rows.** Excel inserts three rows that are formatted to
   match row 4

6. Click the **Insert Options** smart tag to display the list of options, and click the **Format Same As Below** option. The smart tag Insert Options list closes, and Excel reformats the inserted rows to match row 8

7. Click cell **B5,** type **Units Produced,** click cell **B6,** type **Price Per Unit,** click cell **B7,** type **Total Revenue,** press **Enter,** click cell **B7** again, and click the **Increase Indent** button *twice* to indent the label (see Figure 9.4)

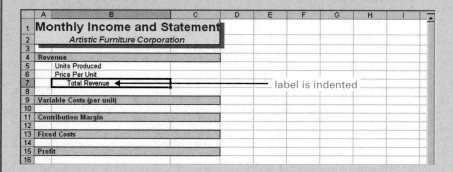

FIGURE 9.4

Partially complete revenue section

8. Click cell **C5,** click **Format** on the menu bar, click **Cells,** click the **Number** tab (if necessary), click **Accounting** in the Category panel, click the **Symbol** list box, click **None** in the list of choices, click **OK** to apply your choices and close the Format Cells dialog box, and type **3** in cell C5

9. Click cell **C6,** click the **Borders list box arrow** on the Formatting toolbar, click the **Bottom Border** button (row 1, column 2), and then type **2050**

10. Click cell **C7,** type **=C5*C6,** and press **Enter.** Excel computes the total revenue, which is the units produced times the price per unit, and displays the result (see Figure 9.5)

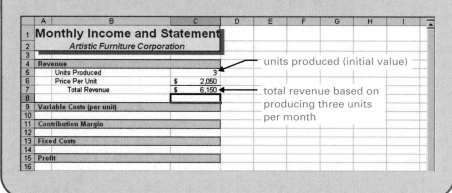

FIGURE 9.5

Computing revenue

You have completed Artistic's revenue formula. It is very simple because Artistic is a one-product company. Were it to shift to producing several, slightly different entertainment center cabinets, then the revenue section would list several pairs of values representing each product's projected number of units produced and the price. In that case, total revenue would simply be the sum of individual product revenues.

By changing cell C5, the number of units produced, you can conduct what-if analysis to project total revenue for various numbers of units. What-if analysis on this developing worksheet answers the question "How much revenue is generated if we produce x units per month?" Perform a few what-if examples to view the changes in revenue.

Performing what-if analysis of revenue:

1. Click cell **C5,** type **0,** and click the **Enter** ✓ button on the left end of the Formula bar. Excel displays a hyphen in cell C5, which is the representation of zero formatted with the Accounting format. If Artistic were to produce no cabinets, then it would generate zero revenue, of course

2. Type **20** in cell **C5** and click the **Enter** ✓ button found on the left end of the Formula bar. Excel computes total revenue of $41,000.

3. Type **10** in cell **C5** and click the **Enter** button on the left end of the Formula bar. Producing 10 units per month yields revenue of $20,500

If that were all there were to making money, businesses would hire lots of people and start producing products at maximum capacity. There's more to business than revenue, of course, because creating any product also involves costs.

Variable Costs

Artistic Furniture Corporation produces a home theater cabinet that costs a certain amount to produce. There are two categories of costs incurred when producing almost anything: variable costs and fixed costs.

A *variable cost* (or variable expense) is one that varies directly with the number of units of a product a company produces. If you increase the number of units you produce, variable costs increase. Decrease units produced, and the variable costs decrease correspondingly. Variable costs are sometimes called direct costs. Variable costs are zero if Artistic decides to not produce cabinets. For example, if all employees go on vacation in the first two weeks of August, then labor, a variable cost, is zero for the two-week vacation period.

Another variable cost at Artistic is direct material. The main direct material is wood. Artistic receives thousands of board-feet of wood each month (wood volume is measured in board-feet), which it uses to make its cabinets. Wood includes hardwood boards for face frames and doors of a cabinet and particleboard sheets for the backs and sides of the cabinets. Small amounts of hardware—hinges, door handles, and screws—make up part of the variable cost also. Labor, mentioned previously, is another significant variable expense. Labor simply means the wages paid to employees who work each day to produce cabinets.

Other variable costs that are directly tied to the number of cabinets Artistic produces include supplies (sand paper, drill bits, and other supplies that are consumed during production), overhead (utilities directly attributable to production, for example), and sales commissions. Paul wants you to add rows to the Variable Costs section of the worksheet so that you can enter five categories of variable costs and a line that totals all variable costs.

Adding rows to the Variable Costs section:

1. Select the cell range **A10:A15,** click **Insert** on the menu bar, and click **Rows.** Excel inserts six rows that are formatted to match row 9. The Insert Options smart tag appears

2. Click the **Insert Options** smart tag to display the list of options (see Figure 9.6), and click the **Format Same As Below** option. The smart tag Insert Options list closes, and Excel reformats the inserted rows to match row 16. (Notice that the smart tag remains visible until you type or edit data)

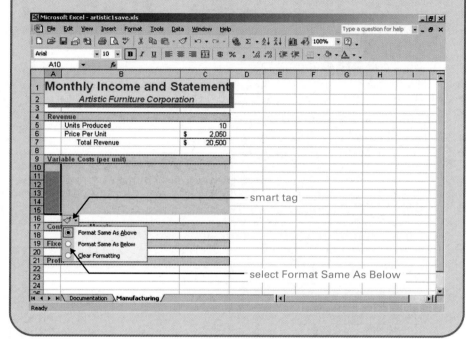

FIGURE 9.6
Insert Options smart tag

With ample room in the variable costs section of the worksheet, you can add the variable cost items and add a formula to subtotal the variable costs. Paul explains that the variable costs are each computed as a percentage of the wholesale price of each unit. He outlines the variable costs and the percentages of each one. Because the costs expressed as percentages are averages, Paul asks you to type in constants that correspond to these percentages of the price per unit. Direct labor, the cost of production workers, is approximately 20 percent of sales. Direct material (wood and hardware) is approximately 30 percent of sales. The value for direct supplies is approximately 2.5 percent of sales. Sales commissions are exactly 5 percent of sales, and overhead is approximately 9 percent of sales.

Entering variable cost values and formulas:

1. Click cell **B10,** type **Direct Labor,** click cell **B11,** type **Direct Material (wood, hardware),** click cell **B12,** and type **Direct Supplies**

2. Click cell **B13,** type **Sales Commissions,** click cell **B14,** type **Overhead,** click cell **B15,** type **Total Variable Costs (all units),** and press **Enter**

3. Click cell **B15** and click *twice* the **Increase Indent** 🔳 button on the Formatting toolbar to indent the label

4. Click cell **C10** and type **410**

5. Click cell **C11** and type **615**

6. Click cell **C12** and type **51**

7. Click cell **C13** and type **=5%*C6** (sales commissions vary directly with a sale and should be entered as a formula— in case the price changes)

8. Click cell **C14** and type **185**

   Next, you will write the total variable costs formula. Because the total variable costs are unit costs times the number of units, you can sum the variable costs and multiply the total by the number of units produced

9. Click cell **C15,** type **=SUM(C10:C14)*C5,** and press **Enter**

10. Click cell **C6,** click the **Format Painter** 🖌 button on the Standard toolbar, and click cell **C14** to copy the format to it. Excel copies the formatting from cell C6 to cell C14

11. Click cell **A18** in preparation for steps that follow (see Figure 9.7)

FIGURE 9.7

Completed Variable Costs section

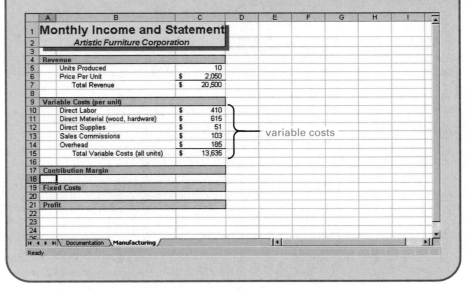

So far, the worksheet looks good and the company is taking in more money than it is spending in variable costs.

Contribution Margin

Paul describes the contribution margin, another important concept in any business. ***Contribution margin (CM)*** is the amount remaining from revenue after you deduct all variable costs. Managers use contribution margin to first cover fixed expenses. Any remaining amount goes toward profits. If CM is not large enough to cover fixed expenses, then there is a loss for the reporting period. Simply stated, CM is revenue minus variable expenses. Paul asks you to write a simple formula that displays the contribution margin and to place that formula in the Contribution Margin section. Begin by inserting a new row and then write the label and formula for the contribution margin.

Adding a row for contribution margin and writing the CM formula:

1. With cell **A18** selected, click **Insert** on the menu bar, and click **Rows.** Excel inserts one row whose format matches row 17. The Insert Options smart tag appears

2. Click the **Insert Options** smart tag to display the list of options, and click the **Format Same As Below** option. The smart tag Insert Options list closes and Excel reformats the inserted rows to match row 19

3. Click cell **B18** and type **Contribution Margin**

4. Click cell **C18,** type **=C7-C15,** and press **Enter.** Excel displays the value $6,865 for the contribution margin—based on the fundamental assumption that the company will produce 10 units per month (see Figure 9.8)

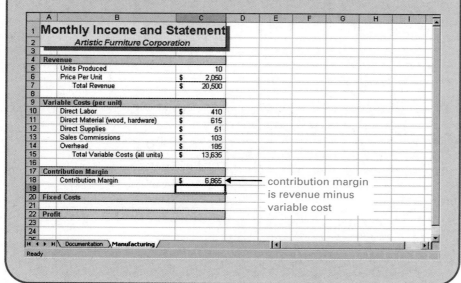

contribution margin is revenue minus variable cost

FIGURE 9.8
Contribution margin

The contribution margin in this example indicates that if the company produces 10 entertainment centers, then the company's fixed costs (as yet to be determined) must be less than $6,865. What are Artistic Furniture Corporation's fixed costs and how do they reduce the profitability of the company?

Fixed Costs

A *fixed cost* (or fixed expense) is one that remains constant no matter how many or how few goods or services you manufacture and sell. Paul tells you that fixed costs include the rent on the building, heating and lighting (utilities), equipment leases, and supplies. If all the Artistic employees go on vacation for two weeks, the company must still pay the building rent. Artistic incurs other fixed expenses such as supplies, computers, computer supplies, and communication equipment. No matter how many cabinets Artistic sells, it still needs a computer to help it make business decisions. The term fixed cost does not imply that the cost remains constant forever. Fixed costs do remain constant over the period you are studying, however. Paul lists the major fixed costs that Artistic must pay each month, regardless of its productivity. He asks you to add rows to the Fixed Costs section to hold the four fixed costs and the fixed cost total. The fixed costs are as follows. Rent is $2,500 per month; utilities average $3,280 per month; supplies are $845 per month, and equipment leases amount to $1,968 per month.

Adding rows for fixed costs, entering values, and totaling fixed costs:

1. Click the row selector button for row **22** and drag the mouse through row selector button **26.** Excel highlights rows 22 through 26

2. Click **Insert** on the menu bar and then click **Rows.** Excel inserts five rows before row 27

3. Type the following labels in the indicated cells, pressing Enter after typing each entry:

   B21: **Rent**

   B22: **Utilities**

   B23: **Supplies**

   B24: **Equipment Leases**

   B25: **Total Fixed Costs**

4. Click cell **B15,** click the **Format Painter** ☑ button on the Standard toolbar, and click cell **B25** to copy the format from cell B15 and apply it to cell B25

   tip: *If you select the wrong cell—either to copy the format from or paint the format to—then click **Undo Paste Special** in the Edit menu and execute step 4 again*

5. Enter the following values and a formula in the indicated cells. Press Enter after entering each value and the formula:

   C21: **2500**

   C22: **3280**

   C23: **845**

   C24: **1968**

   C25: **=SUM(C21:C24)**

   Excel displays the total fixed costs, $8,593, in cell C25

6. Click cell **C14,** click the **Format Painter** ✎ button on the Standard toolbar, and click cell **C24** to copy the format from cell C14 and apply it to cell C24 (see Figure 9.9)

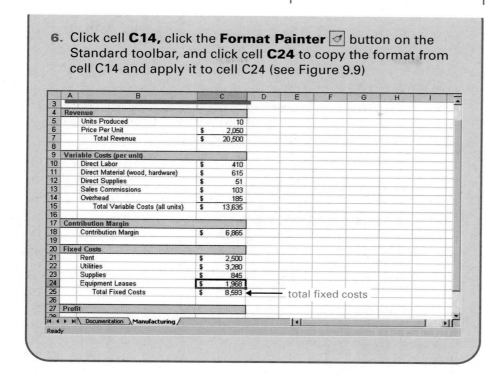

FIGURE 9.9
Fixed costs

Now that you have entered revenue, variable costs, and fixed costs, you can complete Artistic's financial snapshot by writing a formula for the all-important bottom line—profit.

Profit

Profit is revenue minus the sum of all costs—both fixed and variable, which is the same as the contribution margin minus total fixed costs. The case in which profit is zero is called the break-even point. Naturally, a healthy company sells enough units to generate profits above the break-even point.

Paul asks you to summarize revenue and total expenses and then write the formula for profit in the Profit section of the worksheet.

Entering labels and writing the profit formula:

1. Click cell **B28** and type **Revenue**

2. Click cell **B29** and type **Total Costs (fixed + variable)**

3. Click cell **B30** and type **Net Income (profit)**

4. Click cell **C28,** type **=C7,** and press **Enter.** Excel displays total revenue—the same value displayed in cell C7

5. In cell C29, type **=C15+C25**

6. Click cell **C30** and type **=C28-C29**

7. Click cell **C24,** click the **Format Painter** ✎ button on the Standard toolbar, and then click cell **C29**

8. Click cell **B25,** click the **Format Painter** button on the Standard toolbar, and then click cell **B30.** Cell C30 indicates that Artistic would lose money at the rate of $1,728 per month the way things stand now

9. To view more of the worksheet at once, click **View** on the menu bar and then click **Full Screen.** Excel displays more—perhaps all—of the active worksheet on the screen (see Figure 9.10)

FIGURE 9.10

Artistic loses money producing
10 units

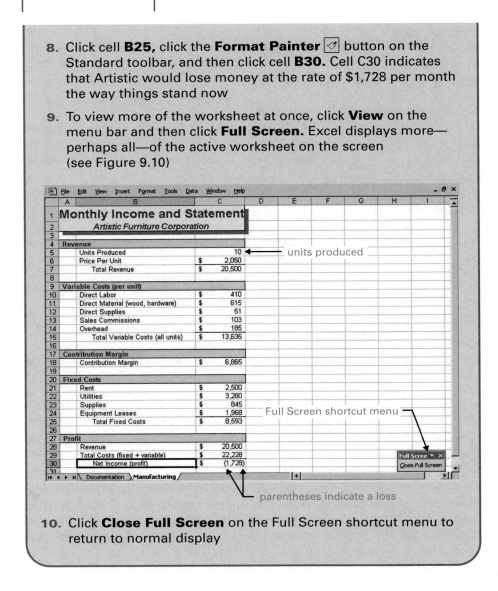

10. Click **Close Full Screen** on the Full Screen shortcut menu to return to normal display

DETERMINING THE BREAK-EVEN POINT

You show Paul the completed Monthly Income and Statement worksheet. While he is not surprised that Artistic would lose money manufacturing and selling 10 units per month, he'd like you to know more about how many units to produce. Perhaps Artistic Furniture Corporation could reduce its production and thereby reduce its variable costs. Alternatively, it could hire more people, produce more units per month, and see what that does to the bottom line—profit.

Paul wants you to produce a worksheet showing the different values for profit by changing the number of units from zero to their current maximum capacity of 30 units.

Break-Even Analysis Using an Equation

You have created an income statement that allows you to change several key values and observe their change on profit. Paul wants to know how many entertainment units Artistic must produce in order to generate a profit. Clearly, producing only 10 units per month is a losing proposition. Will producing 11 units be enough to create a profit?

Break-even analysis can help you find the point at which you generate a profit, because it takes into account the relationships among cost, volume, and profit (CVP). What-if variables that you can change include production and sales quantities—produce more (or fewer) entertainment center cabinets. Other variables you can alter include both individual variable costs and individual fixed costs (negotiate a better lease, lower your supplies usage, and so on). The formula below captures the relationship between volume, cost, and profit.

Profits = Revenue – (Variable expenses + Fixed expenses)

You can rearrange this equation into one that is widely used in CVP analysis to this:

Revenue = Variable expenses + Fixed expenses + Profits

Break-even occurs when profit equals zero. So, in the case of Artistic concepts, you can rewrite the equation using the number of units produced as a variable and solve for it. In other words, you rewrite the preceding equation using the variable U to stand for the number of units produced (found in cell C5, Figure 9.10):

$2,050U = $1,364U + $8,593 + 0

If you were to solve the preceding equation for the variable U—the number of units to produce—the break-even production point would be approximately 12.5 units.

Break-Even Analysis Using a Chart

Rather than solve the preceding equation, you can use Excel to create a line chart and then observe the break-even point by locating the point where the revenue and total cost lines cross. Figure 9.11 illustrates the relationship between revenue and costs. Units appear along the X-axis. Values appear on the Y-axis. Notice that revenue is less than total costs up to 12 units. Above the break-even point where the revenue and total costs curves cross, revenue is above the cost curve and thus the company generates a profit.

A spreadsheet approach to determining the break-even point is to perform what-if analysis by changing the value in cell C5 (see Figure 9.10),

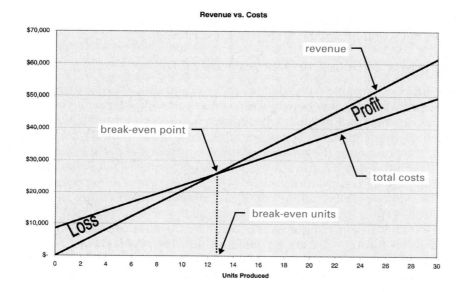

FIGURE 9.11

Relationship between revenue and costs

beginning at zero. That is, you could enter 0 in cell C5 and observe the value in cell C30. Then, type 5 into cell C5 and observe the value for profit. Continuing in this manner is both time-consuming and error-prone. A better approach is to create an Excel data table.

PERFORMING WHAT-IF ANALYSIS WITH A ONE-VARIABLE DATA TABLE

Paul wants you to take advantage of Excel's quick recalculation and what-if ability to generate a series of results, one after the other. There will be many situations where you will want to perform what-if analysis on a worksheet by varying one or more cells' values to see their effect on the entire worksheet. One approach, suggested above, is to type one or more values into worksheet cells and then print the resulting worksheet. Then, you can repeat the previous set by typing new values, observing the result, and printing the worksheet.

Excel provides a more efficient way to examine the results of multiple what-if analyses in a data table. A **data table** summarizes key input and output cell values of multiple what-if analyses in a single, rectangular cell range. Excel provides two types of data tables: one-variable data table and two-variable data table. A one-variable data table allows you to specify one input variable—a cell—that Excel changes automatically to produce the data table. As you can guess, a two-variable data table allows you to specify two distinct what-if variables and it generates a table of output values. Both types work in a similar fashion: You identify one or two key input variables and then indicate the range of values you want those key input variables to take on. The key input variable that you want Excel to change is called the **input cell.** You execute the Data Table command to create a compact table of results. When you do, Excel steps through each input value (or pair of values) and records in the data table how the value changes the output (dependent) formulas you have identified. The **result cell** holds the result that is affected by a change in the input cell. It is a value you want to study closely.

First, you will use a one-variable data table and designate the units produced as the input cell and examine the values for multiple result cells of revenue, cost, and profit. A one-variable data table allows you to identify a single input variable and an unlimited number of resulting formulas on which you want to see the results of your what-if analysis. Unlike a one-variable data table, a two-variable data table allows you to identify only a single output formula along with two input variables.

Examining a Simple One-Variable Data Table

Learn how a one-variable data table works by examining a simple example. Suppose you want to know how much revenue you will generate if you sell 2, 4, or more units of a product whose price is $24.50. Figure 9.12 shows a worksheet that illustrates a one-variable data table. Cell B4 contains =B2*B3, the product of the number of units purchased times the per unit price. The input cell is B2, the number of units produced. That is the value you will ask Excel to vary in increments of 2 to see the resulting purchase prices. The set of possible units produced, called the **input values,** are located in cells D3 through D12. Cell E2 contains the result cell, which is the formula =B4 because it references the formula in cell B4. Below the result cell, in cells E3 through E12 are the result values. The **result values** are the computed answer for each input value that Excel uses. The cell range D2:E12 is the one-variable data table, which contains the input values and resulting output or result values. Figure 9.12 shows an example of a data table. You can also construct a data table in two rows. In that case, the input values run along the first row and the result values appear in the second row. The input value must be placed in the first row or column.

While a one-variable data table can contain only one row or column of input values, you can specify several rows or columns of result values. You will see exactly how this works as you create a one-variable data table displaying several results for Artistic Furniture Corporation.

Creating a One-Variable Data Table

Paul wants you to create a one-variable data table in which you determine values for net income (profit) when varying the number of units produced from zero to 30 in increments of two units (0, 2, 4, etc.). When you create the data table, you will select C5 as the input cell, because it holds the number of units produced—the value that all other formulas in the Artistic worksheet depend on. The input values, mentioned above, will be placed in a column and range from 0 to 30. You are interested in observing the effect of changes in the input cell, units produced, on three result cells: Total Revenue (cell C28), Total Costs (cell C29), and Net Income (cell C30). The data table will have four columns: One column to hold the input values, and one column for each of the three result values (total revenue, total costs, and net income) (see Figure 9.13).

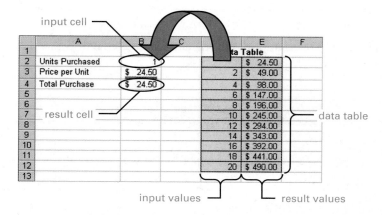

FIGURE 9.12

Simple example of a one-variable data table

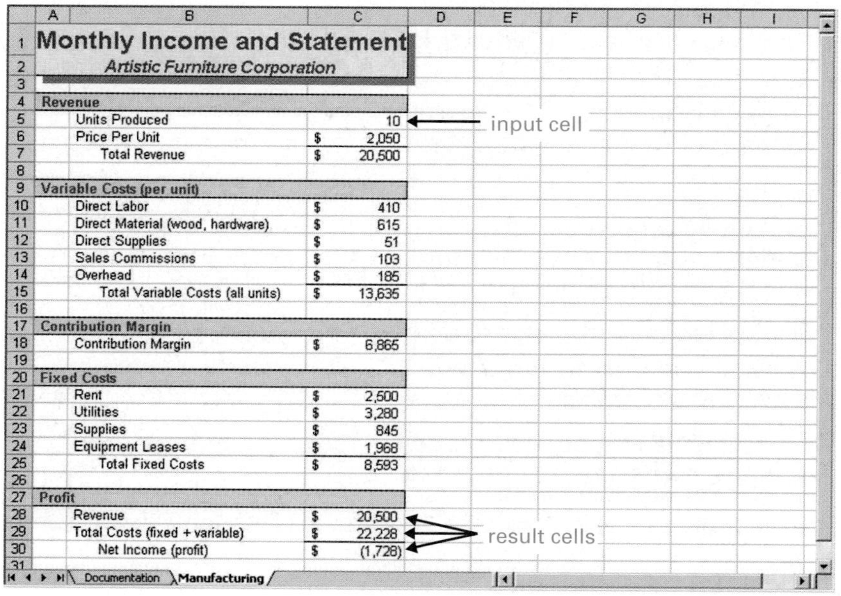

FIGURE 9.13

Key cells used to create a one-variable data table

task **reference**

Creating a One-Variable Data Table

- Decide whether you want values for the input cell to appear in a row or down a column

- If you arrange a data table in columns, then insert the input values in the first column beginning below the first row of the table and place a reference (a formula) to the result cell in the cell above and to the right of the column of input values

- If you arrange a data table in rows, then insert the input values in the first row beginning in the second column of the data table and place a reference (a formula) to the result cell in the cell below the input row and to its left

- Select the table, click **Data,** and then click **Table**

- Enter the cell reference of the input cell in the Row input cell box if input values are in a row or enter the cell reference of the input cell in the Column input cell box if the input values are in a column in the data table

- Click **OK**

You create a one-variable data table in the cell range E4:H20—near the top of the worksheet.

Entering an input values column and results formulas:

1. Click cell **E4** and type **Units**

2. Click cell **E5,** type **0,** click cell **E6,** type **2,** and press **Enter**

3. Select the cell range **E5:E6,** click **Format** on the menu bar, click **Cells,** click the Number tab (if necessary), click **Number** in the Category list box, and click **OK** to apply the formatting changes to the two cells

4. With cells E5 and E6 still selected, drag the fill handle down through cell **E20** and then release the mouse. Excel creates a series of ascending numbers from 0 to 30 in increments of 2

5. Click cell **F4** and type **=C28,** which is a reference to the revenue formula—one of the formulas for which you want to create a result values column

6. Click cell **G4** and type **=C29,** which is a reference to the total costs cell—another formula for which you want to create a series of result values

7. Click cell **H4** and type **=C30** (a reference to the profit formula) and press **Enter** (see Figure 9.14)

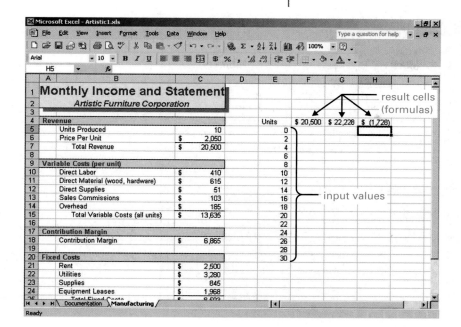

FIGURE 9.14
Input values and result cells in a
data table

Before you create the data table, you can format the result cells so that they look like labels. That little trick keeps the formulas intact and simultaneously supplies labels for the columns of the data table. Reformatting does not affect the results in the data table. It simply makes the results easier to read.

Formatting formulas in the top row of the data table to look like labels:

1. Click cell **F4**

2. Click **Format** on the menu bar, click **Cells,** click **Custom** in the Category list box, click the **Type text box,** press the **Home** key to move the insertion point to the first character of the Type entry, press and hold down the **Shift** key, press the **End** key, and release the **Shift** key. Excel selects the entire contents of the Type text box

3. Type **"Revenue"**—be sure to type both quotation marks (see Figure 9.15), and then click **OK** to apply the text format

4. Click cell **G4** and repeat steps 2 and 3, typing **"Costs"** (include the quotation marks) in step 3

5. Click cell **H4** and repeat step 2

6. Type **"Profit";"Profit"** and then click **OK** to apply the text format. You type the quoted string Profit twice, separated by a semicolon, so that Excel displays *Profit* for both positive and negative values. Notice the Formula bar shows that the cell contains the formula =C30, whereas the format displays a label (see Figure 9.16)

FIGURE 9.15

Applying a text format to a
formula

"Revenue" format

Custom

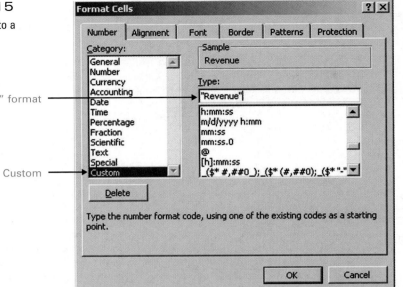

FIGURE 9.16

Completed text formats for
result cells

With the input values and result cells in place along the edges of the as-
yet imaginary table, you can create the data table to fill in result values for
all listed input values.

> ### Finishing the one-variable data table:
>
> 1. Select the cell range **E4:H20,** which is the data table
>
> 2. Click **Data** on the menu bar and then click **Table.** The Table
>   dialog box appears

3. Click the **Column input cell** box and type **C5,** which is the input cell value that Excel will replace temporarily with each value in the input values column (see Figure 9.17)

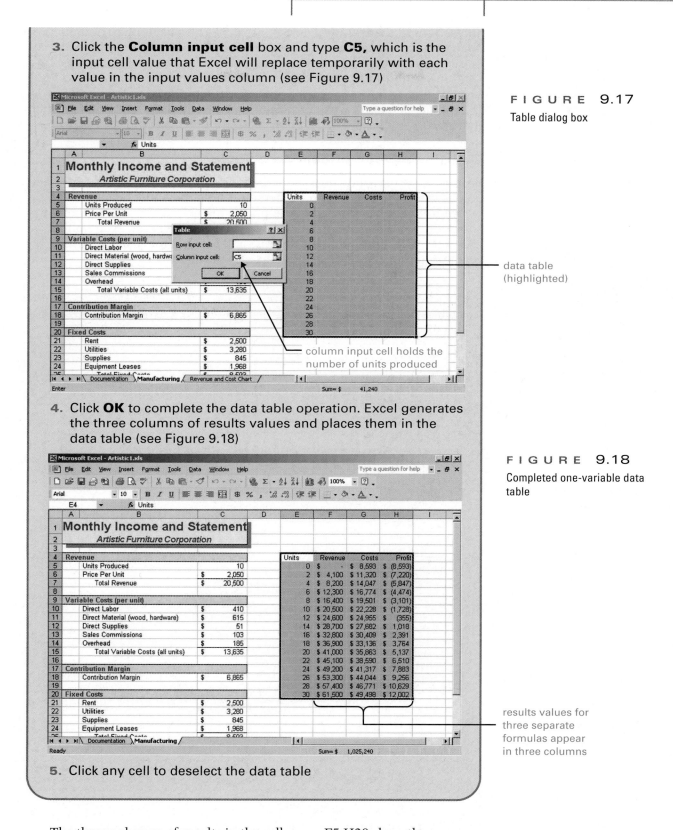

FIGURE 9.17

Table dialog box

data table (highlighted)

column input cell holds the number of units produced

4. Click **OK** to complete the data table operation. Excel generates the three columns of results values and places them in the data table (see Figure 9.18)

FIGURE 9.18

Completed one-variable data table

results values for three separate formulas appear in three columns

5. Click any cell to deselect the data table

The three columns of results in the cell range F5:H20 show the revenue, costs, and profit for units ranging from 0 to 30. By looking at the last column of the data table, you can see clearly that Artistic must manufacture and sell more than 12 units to be profitable. It is likely that 13 units produced is the break-even point. Revenue and costs climb steadily as the number of units produced increases.

Paul would like a line chart of two of the three result variables—revenue and costs—with the number of units produced along the X-axis. Having the chart to review is a clear visual reminder of Artistic's production goals.

Charting a One-Variable Data Table

Producing a chart showing the relationship between volume, revenue, and cost is often the best way to understand how they affect each other and where it makes sense to continue producing goods (or not). A chart that shows cost and revenue lines clearly illustrates the break-even point. The line chart will show a line for revenue and another for cost. The Units column, or input values, forms the X-axis of the chart.

FIGURE 9.19

Selecting a chart type

> ## Charting three sets of results values of a one-variable data table:
>
> 1. Select the cell range **E5:G20,** which encompasses the units produced column, the revenue column, and the costs column
>
> 2. Click the **Chart Wizard** 📊 button on the Standard toolbar
>
> 3. Click the **Standard Types** tab (if necessary), click **XY (Scatter)** in the Chart type list box and click the **Scatter with data points connected by smoothed Lines without markers** chart sub-type (see Figure 9.19)
>
>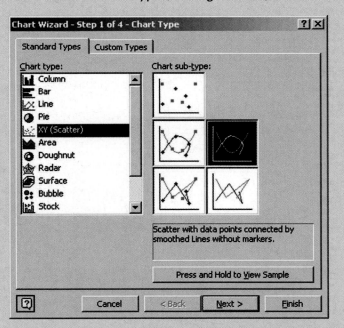
>
> 4. Click the **Next** button, click the **Series** tab, click **Series1** in the Series list box, click in the **Name** text box, and type **Revenue**

5. Click **Series2** in the Series list box, click the **Name** text box, type **Costs,** and click the **Next** button. Excel changes the names in the legend to better document the values each line is charting

6. Click the **Chart title** text box and type **Revenue Versus Cost**

7. Click the **Value (X) axis** text box, type **Units Produced and Sold,** and click the **Next** button to go to the final Chart Wizard step

8. Click the **As new sheet** option button and then click the **Finish** button to produce the chart (see Figure 9.20)

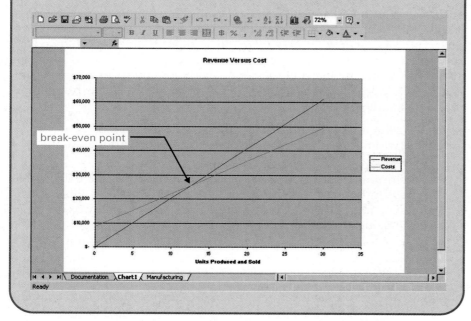

Chart of revenue versus cost

Paul wants you to move the new chart, on the chart sheet called Chart1, so it is after the Manufacturing tab. He wants you to rename the Chart1 tab to *Revenue and Cost Chart.*

Moving the chart and renaming the chart sheet tab:

1. Click the **Chart1** worksheet tab, drag it to the right of the Manufacturing tab, and release the mouse to move the worksheet

tip: *Your chart tab may be called Chart2, Chart3, or some other name depending on the number of charts you have created or attempted to create*

2. Double-click the chart sheet tab to select the tab text, type **Revenue and Cost Chart,** and press **Enter** to complete the sheet tab renaming operation

3. Click the **Manufacturing** tab to make that worksheet active, and click **Ctrl+Home** to move to cell A1. (Because cell A1 is merged with cells B1 and C1, the active cell indicator surrounds the three merged cells)

4. Click **File** on the menu bar and then click **Save** to save your modified workbook and preserve it for future use

PERFORMING WHAT-IF ANALYSIS WITH A TWO-VARIABLE DATA TABLE

The data table you created above displays the effect on the company's profitability of changing a single variable, the number of units produced. You can create a ***two-variable data table*** that computes the effects of two variables on a single formula. Like a one-variable data table, a two-variable data table is rectangular and the results cells contain formulas that compute results values. However, a two-variable data table differs from a one-variable data table in several ways:

- The data table contains input values in the leftmost column (the first variable) and the topmost row (the second variable) of the table.

- The formula that Excel uses to calculate the two-variable data table results must appear in the upper-left corner of the data table at the intersection of the row and column that contains the two sets of input values.

- Although you can include as many formulas as you want in a one-variable data table, you can include only one output formula in a two-variable data table.

Figure 9.21 shows an example of a two-variable data table to compute a monthly payment for different terms (cells C2:G2—variable 1) in months and different annual interest rates (cells B3:B11—variable 2) for a $15,000 loan. The formula into which Excel substitutes each interest rate term pair and that it uses to generate the array of results cells is found in cell B2—the corner of the two-variable data table. The formula in cell B2 is this:

=PMT(A2/12,B1,−15000)

The three blank cells referenced in the formula are empty. Therefore Excel returns the error value you see in Figure 9.21. Excel substitutes each of the column values into cell A2 and substitutes each of the row values into cell B1 to create the result value at the intersection of the pair of row and column values. The table readily shows that a 36-month loan at an 8 percent interest rate requires a monthly payment of $470 (values are rounded to the nearest dollar).

Creating a Two-Variable Data Table

Paul anticipates slowing down production for the summer months as a number of his employees take vacation. By carefully scheduling when the employees take their two-week vacation, he will not have to shut down because there are enough skilled workers to build the entertainment centers. However, he determines that he cannot produce more than 10 to 12 entertainment units in the summer months. As you recall from the analysis earlier in this chapter, Artistic loses money if it produces fewer than 13 units

FIGURE 9.21

Example of a two-variable
data table

formula used to generate results values

row values

results values

column values

	A	B	C	D	E	F	G	H
1			Months					
2		#DIV/0!	12	24	36	48	60	
3	Rate:	6.00%	$ 1,291	$ 665	$ 456	$ 352	$ 290	
4		6.50%	$ 1,294	$ 668	$ 460	$ 356	$ 293	
5		7.00%	$ 1,298	$ 672	$ 463	$ 359	$ 297	
6		7.50%	$ 1,301	$ 675	$ 467	$ 363	$ 301	
7		8.00%	$ 1,305	$ 678	$ 470	$ 366	$ 304	
8		8.50%	$ 1,308	$ 682	$ 474	$ 370	$ 308	
9		9.00%	$ 1,312	$ 685	$ 477	$ 373	$ 311	
10		9.50%	$ 1,315	$ 689	$ 480	$ 377	$ 315	
11		10.00%	$ 1,319	$ 692	$ 484	$ 380	$ 319	
12								

per month at the current level of costs. Paul wants to investigate if there is any combination of units produced per month and sale prices that would yield a profit. In other words, is there a way to produce fewer units and perhaps raise the price per unit and still stay profitable? A two-variable data table helps you answer that question for Paul.

task reference

Creating a Two-Variable Data Table

- Type the formula or a reference to the input cell in the upper-left cell in the data table

- Type the first variable values in the row to the right of the formula

- Type the second variable values in the column below the formula

- Select a cell range that encompasses the formula, row values, and column values

- Click **Data** on the menu bar and then click **Table**

- Type the address of the input cell that corresponds to the row values in the Row input cell text box

- Type the address of the input cell that corresponds to the column values in the Column input cell text box

- Click **OK**

You are ready to begin creating the two-variable data table with the proposed number of units to produce running along a row at the top of the data table and a column of proposed sale prices in the column at the left side of the data table.

Filling in the labels, row values, and column values of the two-variable data table:

1. To save the **Artistic1.xls** workbook under a different name, click **File** on the menu bar, click **Save As,** navigate to the folder in which you want to save the workbook, type **Artistic2** in the File name list box, and click the **Save** button. Excel saves the workbook under its new name

2. Click cell **F22** and type **Units Produced**

3. Click cell **E24,** type **2000,** click cell **E25,** type **2100,** and press **Enter**

4. Select cells **E24:E25,** release the mouse, click the fill handle, drag it down through cell **E34,** and release the mouse. Excel creates a range of values from $2,000 through $3,000

5. Click cell **F23,** type **2,** and press **Enter.** Excel displays $2 because Accounting is the default format

6. Click cell **E20,** click the **Format Painter** button, and click cell **F23** to alter its format

7. Select the cell range **F23:K23,** click **Edit** on the menu bar, point to **Fill,** and click **Series.** Excel displays the Series dialog box (see Figure 9.22)

FIGURE 9.22

Series dialog box

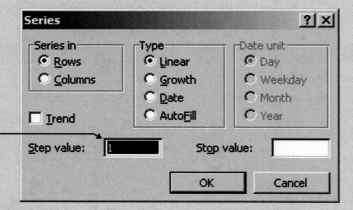

type 2 for the Step value ⎯

8. Type **2** in the Step value text box and then click the **OK** button to create the series of numbers from 2 through 12 (see Figure 9.23)

FIGURE 9.23

Completing a data table's column and row input values

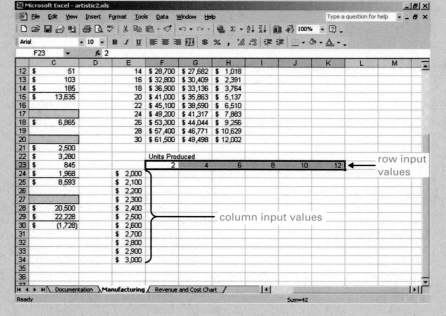

The first row in the developing two-variable data table contains the series of production quantities you want Excel to plug into the revenue, costs, and profit equations to see if varying them, along with the price, generates a profit. The left-most column contains candidate prices for the entertainment center that has been priced at $2,050 up until now. The question that the two-variable data table will answer is this: What profit, if any, is created with the combinations of production quantities and prices. Each results cell will display the profit value for a single quantity-produced/price pair in the data table.

You are ready to create the profit formula and then complete the data table building process. First, you will write in the upper left corner of the data table the formula referencing the profit cell—the model equation for which results will be created. Then, you will execute the Data Table command requesting Excel to fill in a series of results for the quantity/price variable pairs.

Completing the two-variable data table:

1. Click cell **E23** type **=C30** (a reference to the cell that calculates profit), and press **Enter**

   The actual profit for 10 units appears. But, you will use the same procedure presented earlier, to format this entry so it looks like a label

2. Right-click cell **E23,** click **Format Cells** on the shortcut menu to open the Format Cells dialog box

3. Click the **Number** tab, if necessary, click **Custom** in the Category list, click the **Type** text box, press **Home,** press and hold the **Shift** key, and press and release the **End** key, and release the **Shift** key to select the format appearing in the Type list box

4. Type **"Price";"Price"** including the quotation marks and the semicolon separating the identical character strings (see Figure 9.24)

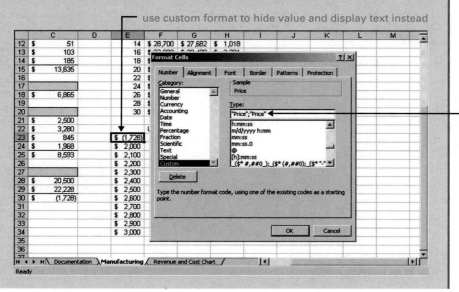

FIGURE 9.24

Formatting a formula to display text

5. Click **OK** to close the Format Cells dialog box and apply the format. Excel displays *Price* in cell E23, even though the cell contains a formula that yields a value

6. Select the cell range **E23:K34,** click **Data** on the menu bar, and click **Table.** The Table dialog box appears

7. Type **C5** in the Row input cell text box, because C5 contains the number of units produced in the original worksheet and corresponds to the changing values in the top row of the data table

8. Press the **Tab** key and type **C6** in the Column input cell text box. C6 holds the original sales price and is used in formulas throughout the worksheet. It corresponds to the column of changing sales price values in the input column of the data table

9. Click **OK** to complete the operation and generate the data table (see Figure 9.25), and click any cell to deselect the cell range

10. Save the workbook by clicking the **Save** button on the Standard toolbar

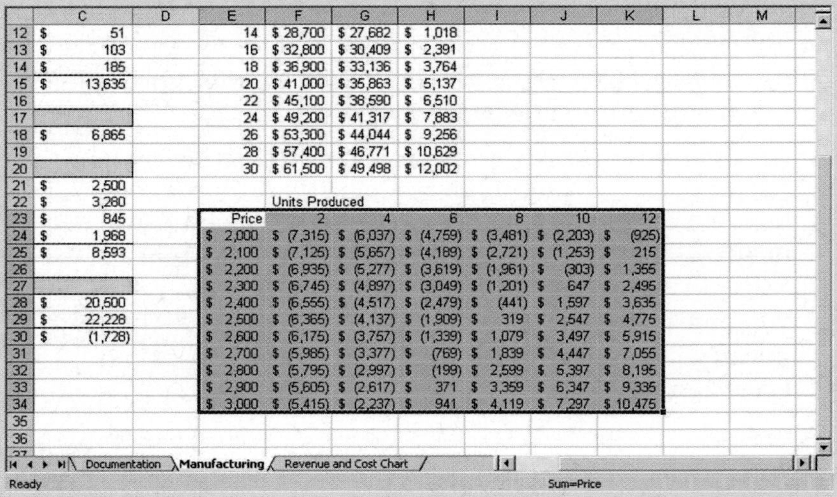

FIGURE 9.25

Completed two-variable data table

	C	D	E	F	G	H
12	$ 51		14	$ 28,700	$ 27,682	$ 1,018
13	$ 103		16	$ 32,800	$ 30,409	$ 2,391
14	$ 185		18	$ 36,900	$ 33,136	$ 3,764
15	$ 13,635		20	$ 41,000	$ 35,863	$ 5,137
16			22	$ 45,100	$ 38,590	$ 6,510
17			24	$ 49,200	$ 41,317	$ 7,883
18	$ 6,865		26	$ 53,300	$ 44,044	$ 9,256
19			28	$ 57,400	$ 46,771	$ 10,629
20			30	$ 61,500	$ 49,498	$ 12,002
21	$ 2,500					
22	$ 3,280		Units Produced			

Data table (rows 23–34):

Price	2	4	6	8	10	12
$ 2,000	$ (7,315)	$ (6,037)	$ (4,759)	$ (3,481)	$ (2,203)	$ (925)
$ 2,100	$ (7,125)	$ (5,657)	$ (4,189)	$ (2,721)	$ (1,253)	$ 215
$ 2,200	$ (6,935)	$ (5,277)	$ (3,619)	$ (1,961)	$ (303)	$ 1,355
$ 2,300	$ (6,745)	$ (4,897)	$ (3,049)	$ (1,201)	$ 647	$ 2,495
$ 2,400	$ (6,555)	$ (4,517)	$ (2,479)	$ (441)	$ 1,597	$ 3,635
$ 2,500	$ (6,365)	$ (4,137)	$ (1,909)	$ 319	$ 2,547	$ 4,775
$ 2,600	$ (6,175)	$ (3,757)	$ (1,339)	$ 1,079	$ 3,497	$ 5,915
$ 2,700	$ (5,985)	$ (3,377)	$ (769)	$ 1,839	$ 4,447	$ 7,055
$ 2,800	$ (5,795)	$ (2,997)	$ (199)	$ 2,599	$ 5,397	$ 8,195
$ 2,900	$ (5,605)	$ (2,617)	$ 371	$ 3,359	$ 6,347	$ 9,335
$ 3,000	$ (5,415)	$ (2,237)	$ 941	$ 4,119	$ 7,297	$ 10,475

Column C values for rows 23–30: 23: $ 845, 24: $ 1,968, 25: $ 8,593, 28: $ 20,500, 29: $ 22,228, 30: $ (1,728)

Sheet tabs: Documentation \ Manufacturing \ Revenue and Cost Chart

Ready   Sum=Price

What are Artistic's options? There are several. The lower right portion of the data table shows several positive values—profits—for combinations of production quantities and prices. For instance, Artistic Furniture Corporation can make a profit making and selling 12 units if it charges $2,100 for each unit. Similarly, it can make a larger profit by producing only 6 units but charging $2,900 per unit. What it does to cover the summer's production is up to Paul and his managers. You have helped them make intelligent choices by producing the two-variable data table showing that there are several acceptable ways to achieve profitability.

EDITING DATA TABLES

One-variable and two-variable data tables contain special formulas that compute and display the results values. These special formulas appearing in a single data table are part of a related group called an ***array formula.***

Deleting Data Table Result Values

If you try to delete any cell that is part of the array formula—cell G30 (see Figure 9.25) for example—Excel displays an alert box with the message *Cannot change part of a table.* If you decide to erase part of a data table and then recreate it, you must select all the results values and then delete the entire array of answers. Once you have deleted the results values, you can select the data table including the input values and formula(s) and then execute the Table command of the Data menu to regenerate the table.

Adding Data Table Input Values

Because the results values are, in fact, formulas, you can alter any of the input values in the input row or input column. After you do so, Excel automatically recalculates the results values to reflect the change in one or more input values. You can add new input values, but you must re-execute the Table command to add the new results values and update the formula array.

Copying Data Table Results

You can copy the table results to another location of the original worksheet. One reason you might want to do this is to preserve a data table's results before you change input values and generate different results values. You can copy all or any portion of the results values to another location using standard copy paste operations. For example, you can select the cell range F24:H30, press Ctrl+C to copy the results to the clipboard, click cell E55, and press Ctrl+V to paste the cells to the new locations. When you copy array formulas out of the data table range, Excel changes the array formulas to constants.

---

making the grade

SESSION 9.1

1. The three-letter abbreviation for the process of examining the relationship between a product's cost, number of units produced, and profit is what?

2. When revenue is equal to total costs and profit is zero, this is called the _____ point.

3. A _____ cost is one that varies directly with the number of units that a company produces, whereas a _____ cost is one that remains constant no matter how many or few goods or services a company sells.

4. A _____ table summarizes key input and output cell values of multiple what-if analyses in a single rectangular cell range.

5. The key input variable that you want Excel to change in a one-variable data table is called the _____ cell, and the _____ cell holds the computed answer that is affected by a change in the variable.

6. A _____-variable data table allows you to perform what-if analysis on more than one formula.

7. The maximum number of variables you can use in a data table is how many?

EXCEL

making **the grade**

8. Make the following modifications to the Artistic Furniture Corporation worksheet, **Artistic2.xls.** First, save the worksheet as **Artistic28.xls** to preserve **Artistic2.xls.** Delete the one-variable analysis located in cell range **E4:H20.** Move the two-variable analysis from its present location—cell range **E22:K34**—to the cell range **E4:K16.** Delete the **Revenue and Cost** Chart sheet. Change the input values by typing **2050** in cell **E6,** typing **2100** in cell **E7,** selecting the cell range **E6:E7,** and dragging the fill handle down through cell **E25.** The new input values range from $2,050 to $3,000 in increments of $50. Next, regenerate new results values by selecting the cell range **E5:K25** and then executing the **Table** command in the **Data** menu. Designate cell **C5** as the Row input cell and cell **C6** as the Column input cell. Click **Page Setup** in the File menu and change the page print orientation to **Landscape.** In the Page Setup dialog box, click the **Fit to** option button on the Page tab so that the output is scaled to fit on one page. Click **OK** to close the Page Setup dialog box. Group both worksheets and then place your name in the worksheet header. Ungroup the worksheets, click **Name Box list arrow** and click the **CreateDate** name to go to that cell on the Documentation page. Type today's date. Click **Name Box list arrow** and click the **CreateName** name to go to that cell on the Documentation page. Type your name. Print both workbook pages, or Save As, according to your instructor's direction.

SESSION 9.2 CREATING AND USING SCENARIOS

In this section, you will learn how use the Excel scenario manager, create scenarios, edit scenarios, delete and hide scenarios, and view scenario results.

DOING MORE COMPLEX WHAT-IF ANALYSIS WITH SCENARIO MANAGER

Data tables are fine for simple situations involving only one or two variables, but most managers' decisions involve many more variables. The combination of values assigned to one or more variable cells in a what-if analysis is called a *scenario.* A scenario consists of selected *variables,* which are cells in which Excel substitutes different values. A scenario identifies the cells that contain values you want to change as *changing cells.* *Scenario management* is the process of examining individual variables or changing cells and assigning a range of values to them. Excel's scenario manager allows you to create scenarios, alter existing scenarios, display individual scenarios, and produce a summary report, called a **scenario report.** By storing values in a scenario, instead of manually changing them in the individual cells, you can accomplish the following:

- Define several scenarios, each with a different group of cell variable values, and then switch between scenarios to view their effects on dependent cells one scenario at a time

- Change cells' values on a worksheet and later recall any of the groups of values you stored in a scenario

- Summarize in a single concise report all of the scenarios including the input or changing cells and any result cells that you designate

Paul carefully studied both your one-variable data table and the two-variable data table that clearly show the break-even point based on varying the number of units produced and the sale price of each unit. However, he wants to examine the effect of changing more of the cells in the Artistic worksheet. For example, Paul knows that there are other variables that Artistic Furniture Corporation can modify to change its profit picture. He has identified four distinct groups of variable values that he would like you to study—four scenarios. Figure 9.26 depicts the four scenarios.

Paul believes that the values of seven variables in the Artistic worksheet will have the largest effect on the company's profit. The variables include variable costs, revenue, fixed costs, units produced (production quantities per month), sales price per unit, labor per unit, material cost per unit, overhead, utilities, and supplies. Utilities and supplies are both fixed costs, but Paul has altered them in the past by watching carefully how they use energy and recycling their supplies when possible. The four scenarios are groups of values that Paul wants to change to see their effect, and they are called Current, Conserve, Efficient, and High Cost.

The Current scenario represents the current conditions in which Artistic produces 10 units per month, sells each unit for $2,050, and maintains the standard variable and fixed costs. It is always a good idea to include typical or average values as one of the scenarios. Under the Conserve

Scenario Name	Cell	Cell Meaning	Cell Value
Current	C5	Units Produced	10
	C6	Price per Unit	$ 2,050
	C10	Labor per Unit	$ 410
	C11	Material per Unit	$ 615
	C14	Overhead per Unit	$ 185
	C22	Utilities	$ 3,280
	C23	Supplies	$ 845
Conserve	C5	Units Produced	25
	C6	Price per Unit	$ 1,950
	C10	Labor per Unit	$ 390
	C11	Material per Unit	$ 554
	C14	Overhead per Unit	$ 170
	C22	Utilities	$ 2,900
	C23	Supplies	$ 650
Efficient	C5	Units Produced	20
	C6	Price per Unit	$ 2,100
	C10	Labor per Unit	$ 425
	C11	Material per Unit	$ 615
	C14	Overhead per Unit	$ 200
	C22	Utilities	$ 3,400
	C23	Supplies	$ 900
High Cost	C5	Units Produced	28
	C6	Price per Unit	$ 2,400
	C10	Labor per Unit	$ 450
	C11	Material per Unit	$ 600
	C14	Overhead per Unit	$ 220
	C22	Utilities	$ 3,600
	C23	Supplies	$ 900

FIGURE   9.26

Four scenarios

scenario, Artistic could produce 25 units, reduce its selling price slightly to $1,950, and reduce the variable costs of labor, material, and overhead while reducing the fixed utilities and supplies costs by carefully conserving energy and recycling some supplies. The Efficient scenario is one in which Artistic produces 20 units but sells each unit for $2,100—slightly more than usual. Labor costs per unit rise because Paul anticipates hiring more skilled carpenters whose labor rate per hour is higher than usual. In this scenario, other costs such as overhead, utilities, and supplies are higher because carpenters work more hours to maintain peak efficiency. The High Cost scenario tweaks the variables by raising production of units to a near-record 28 units per month. Paul raises the wholesale price in this scenario to $2,400, incurs higher labor per unit, but lowers (slightly) the material because he purchases it in higher quantities for the increased production volume. Overhead, utilities, and supplies are all higher due to extended working hours and consumption of more materials.

Paul wants you to work with the changes shown in Figure 9.26 to do a what-if analysis to see the result of each scenario. In particular, Paul wants a summary report showing each of the four groups of input values and the three output results—total revenue, total costs, and profit. You quickly realize that a two-variable data table is out of the question because so many changing cells are involved. Another approach might be to enter each of the seven values into their appropriate cost and units of production cells and then print the worksheet. That would involve making seven changes and printing four worksheets. However, the best solution for evaluating these various proposals is to use scenarios with Excel's built-in Scenario Manager and produce a summary report that outlines each of the input or changing cells and displays output cells of your choice.

Opening the Artistic Furniture Corporation Workbook

Paul has prepared a worksheet for you to use that matches the one you created in Session 9.1 but omits the data tables and does not have a chart sheet. You will use the worksheet as you develop scenarios in this session. Begin by opening the workbook and entering a few preliminary labels.

> #### Opening the Artistic Furniture Corporation scenario workbook:
>
> 1. If you took a break since you completed the last session, ensure that Excel is running
>
> 2. Open the workbook **ex09ArtisticScenarios.xls** and immediately save it under the new name **Artistic3.xls** to preserve the original file
>
> 3. Click the **Name Box list arrow** on the left end of the Formula bar and click the name **CreateDate**
>
> 4. Type today's date and press **Enter**
>
> 5. Click the **Name Box list arrow** on the left end of the Formula bar and click the name **CreateBy**
>
> 6. Type your name and press **Enter**
>
> 7. Click the **Manufacturing** worksheet tab to make that sheet active

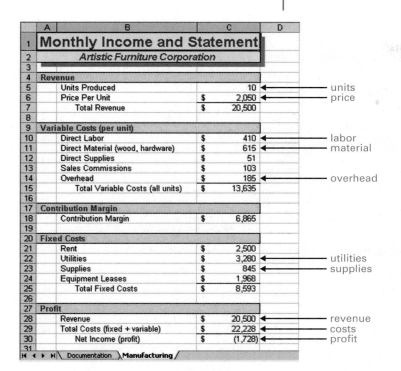

FIGURE 9.27

Input and results cells to receive names

The worksheet is almost identical to the one you created in Session 9.1. Notice that cell C5 contains the current production assumption of 10 units per month, and cell C6 contains the selling price of each entertainment unit, $2,050. The remaining variable and fixed costs are the baseline values found in the Current scenario.

Before you create your first scenario, you will find it very helpful if you name each of the input cells in the scenario as well as the result cells. The reason to name these cells is that names appear in the scenario output when you produce a report, and associating names with input cells and result cells provides built-in documentation. Naming cells is not required, but it makes scenario reports and other associated dialog boxes more intelligible. Figure 9.27 shows the manufacturing worksheet with pointers to the cells you will name and the suggested names you will assign in the exercise that follows.

Create names for seven of the input cells and the three output cells in the next exercise. Be sure to use Figure 9.27 as a guideline while you execute the steps.

Defining names for selected input and result cells:

1. Click cell **C5,** click the **Name Box,** type **Units,** and press **Enter** (see Figure 9.28)

2. Repeat step 1, naming the following cells with the listed names. Remember to press Enter after typing each name:

   C6: **Price**

   C10: **Labor**

   C11: **Material**

FIGURE 9.28

Naming an input cell

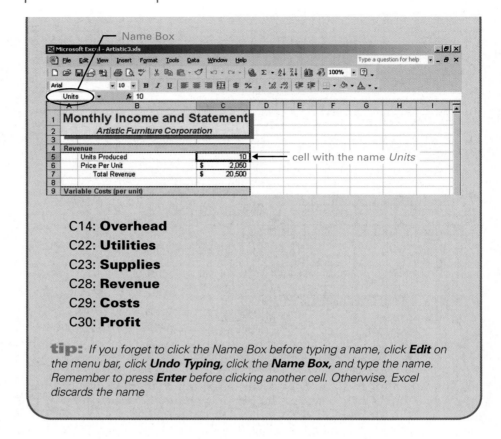

C14: **Overhead**

C22: **Utilities**

C23: **Supplies**

C28: **Revenue**

C29: **Costs**

C30: **Profit**

tip: *If you forget to click the Name Box before typing a name, click **Edit** on the menu bar, click **Undo Typing**, click the **Name Box**, and type the name. Remember to press **Enter** before clicking another cell. Otherwise, Excel discards the name*

Although it is never necessary to use names in an Excel worksheet, it is almost always helpful. Names are easier to remember and to understand when you encounter them in cell formulas or reports. You can create several scenarios now that you have named selected cells.

Creating Scenarios

You create one or more scenarios by using Excel's Scenario Manager. You can specify up to 32 cell values in each scenario, and the number of scenarios you can create is limited only by the amount of memory your computer has.

---

task reference

Creating a Scenario

- Click **Tools** and click **Scenarios** to open the Scenario Manager

- Click the **Add** button and type a scenario name

- Specify the changing (input) cells in the scenario

- Type commentary in the Comment text box and then click the **OK** button

- Type the values for each changing cell, scrolling the list if necessary, and then click **OK**

- Click **Close** to close the Scenario Manager

When you view your first scenario, Excel replaces all the changing cells with the values you specify in the scenario. If you want to preserve the original values in those cells, you should create a scenario that holds the current values in the worksheet. That way, you can quickly restore the worksheet to its original form using the scenario. That will be the first scenario you create—one you will call *Current*.

Creating a default scenario called Current and defining the changing cells:

1. Click **Tools** on the menu bar and then click **Scenarios**. The Scenario Manager dialog box appears (see Figure 9.29)

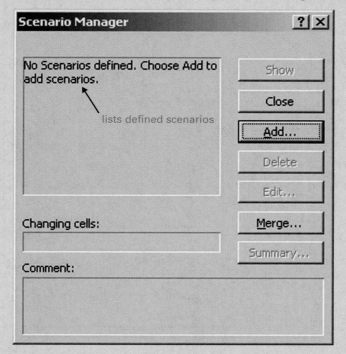

F I G U R E   9.29
Scenario Manager dialog box

2. Click the **Add** button. Excel opens the Add Scenario dialog box

3. Type **Current** in the Scenario name text box and press the **Tab** key to move to the Changing cells box

4. Click the **Collapse dialog box** button to minimize the dialog box

5. Scroll to the top of the worksheet and then click cell **C5** (Units Produced)

6. Press and hold the **Ctrl** key, click cell **C6** (Price Per Unit), click cell **C10** (Direct Labor), click cell **C11** (Direct Material), click cell **C14** (Overhead), click cell **C22** (Utilities), click cell **C23** (Supplies), release the Ctrl key, and press **Enter** to finalize your Changing cells selection

7. Press the **Tab** key to jump to the Comment text box and type **Profit for a typical production level.** This provides documentation for the set of values you are about to set for the selected cells (see Figure 9.30)

FIGURE 9.30

Specifying a scenario's changing cells

scenario's name ───────▶

changing cells for ───────▶
the *Current* scenario

comment about ───────▶
the scenario

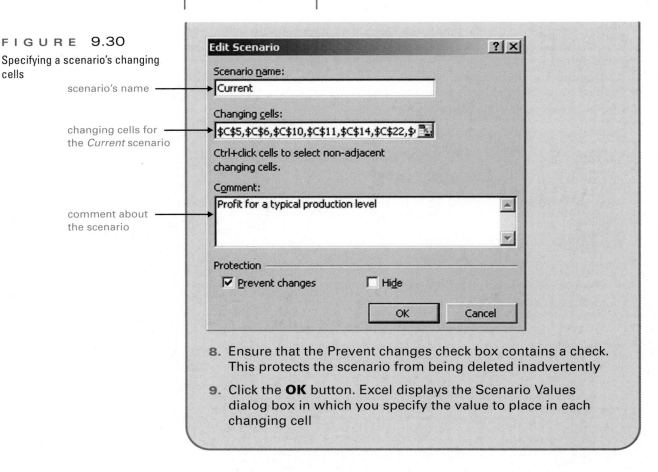

8. Ensure that the Prevent changes check box contains a check. This protects the scenario from being deleted inadvertently

9. Click the **OK** button. Excel displays the Scenario Values dialog box in which you specify the value to place in each changing cell

Once you have told Excel's Scenario Manager which cells it can change, you can specify the exact values for each changing cell for one or more scenarios. You define the values for the Current scenario next.

Specifying values for all changing cells in a scenario:

1. Click and drag the scroll box next to the changing cells values to view all seven of them (see Figure 9.31)

FIGURE 9.31

Scenario Values dialog box

values assigned to each ───────
cell in this scenario

names appear to the left of ───────
each changing-cell text box

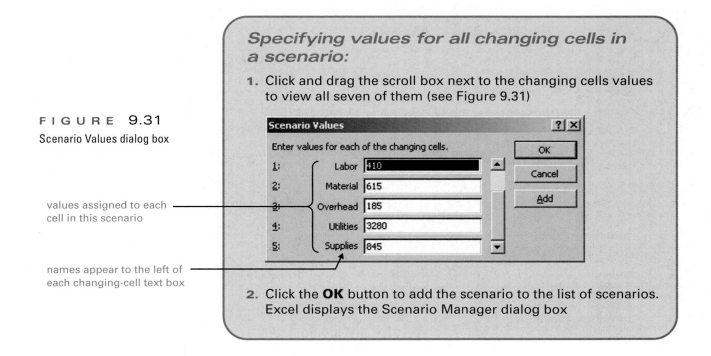

2. Click the **OK** button to add the scenario to the list of scenarios. Excel displays the Scenario Manager dialog box

Having defined one of four scenarios, you can proceed to define the other three. The difficult part is done, because you do not need to specify the changing cells again. Next, you will create three scenarios for the same set of changing cells by typing a complete new set of changing *values* for each scenario.

Adding three other scenarios:

1. Click the **Add** button in the Scenario Manager dialog box, type **Conserve** in the Scenario name text box, and press the **Tab** key twice to select the Comment text box. Conveniently, Excel selects the entire comment

2. With the entire comment selected, type **Produce more units and simultaneously reduce variable and fixed costs,** and click **OK.** Excel displays the Scenario Values text box. You will enter new values for this scenario

3. Type **25** in the Units box and press **Tab**

tip: *If you accidentally press the Enter key after entering a value, Excel closes the Scenario Values dialog box. Simply click the* **Edit** *button in the Scenario Manager dialog box and then click the* **OK** *button in the Edit Scenario dialog box to continue entering values in the Scenario Values dialog box*

4. Type the following values in the indicated text boxes and press the **Tab** key after you type each value:

   Price: **1950**

   Labor: **390**

   Material: **554**

   Overhead: **170**

   Utilities: **2900**

   Supplies: **650**

5. Click **OK** in the Scenario Values dialog box to complete the scenario. Excel displays the Scenario Manager, which now contains two scenarios—Current and Conserve

6. Click the **Add** button in the Scenario Manager dialog box, type **Efficient** in the Scenario name text box, press the **Tab** key twice to move to the Comment text box, and type **Produce 20 units, sell each unit at a higher price, and increase costs,** and click **OK**

7. Type the following values in the indicated text boxes, pressing the **Tab** key after you finish typing each value:

   Units: **20**

   Price: **2100**

   Labor: **425**

   Material: **615**

   Overhead: **200**

   Utilities: **3400**

   Supplies: **900**

EXCEL

8. Click **OK** to complete this scenario

9. Click the **Add** button in the Scenario Manager dialog box, type **High Cost** in the Scenario name text box, press **Tab** twice to move to the Comment text box, type **Produce 28 units, sell each unit at a very high price, and increase costs,** and click **OK**

10. Type the following values in the indicated text boxes, pressing the Tab key after you finish typing each value:

Units: **28**

Price: **2400**

Labor: **450**

Material: **600**

Overhead: **220**

Utilities: **3600**

Supplies: **900**

11. Click **OK** to complete this scenario. Excel displays Scenario Manager containing four scenarios (see Figure 9.32)

FIGURE 9.32

Scenario Manager containing four scenarios

four named scenarios

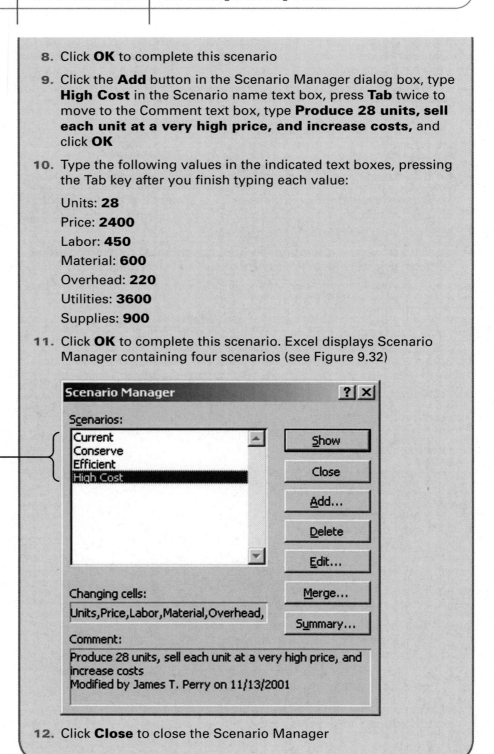

12. Click **Close** to close the Scenario Manager

With four scenarios defined and the Scenario Manager dialog box displayed, you have several choices. You can select a scenario by name and then click the Show button to request that Excel plug in the values you specified earlier into the changing cells. You can also delete a scenario, add a scenario, edit an existing scenario, merge scenarios together, or produce a summary report. In addition, you could click the close button to save all the scenarios you have created. Excel saves scenarios with the worksheet in which they have been created. Each worksheet in a workbook can have its own scenarios, all managed by the Scenario Manager. Each time you load a workbook, all of its scenarios are available to you.

Paul wants to see the consequences of applying these different scenario what-if values. He asks you to show him each one in turn.

Showing Scenarios

After you create one or more scenarios, you can see their effect by opening the Scenario Manager, selecting a scenario, and requesting Excel to apply that scenario's values to their respective cells.

---

task reference

Viewing a Scenario

- Click **Tools** and click **Scenarios** to open the Scenario Manager

- Select a scenario from the Scenarios list

- Click the **Show** button

Next, you will open the scenario manager and view each scenario. Pay particular attention to cell C30, containing profit, after you apply each scenario. First, you will display the worksheet full screen to be able to see as much of it as possible before you apply different scenarios.

Viewing a scenario:

1. Click **View** on the menu bar and then click **Full Screen.** Excel opens the worksheet in full screen view and removes any previously visible toolbars

2. Scroll the worksheet so that you can see cells C5 through C30 on the screen at once. If it is not possible on your screen to see that range of cells, then scroll the worksheet up just enough to display cell C30 at the bottom of the screen

3. Click **Tools** on the menu bar and then click **Scenarios** to display the Scenario Manager dialog box

4. Move the dialog box to the right, if necessary, so it does not obscure column C

5. Click the **Conserve** in the Scenarios list box and then click the **Show** button to apply the scenario's values. Excel inserts the values into the changing cells and recalculates the worksheet (see Figure 9.33). Notice that the Net Income (cell C30) contains $9,170

Excel places the value 25 into cell C5, the number of units produced. In addition, the other six changing-cell values appear in cells C6, C10, C11, C14, C22, and C23. Paul, who is looking at the worksheet on your computer, is pleased to see that the Conserve scenario produces a profit.

FIGURE 9.33

Applying the Conserve scenario

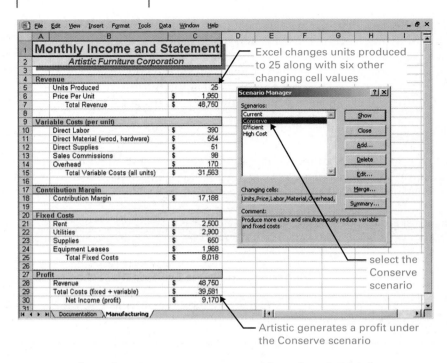

Excel changes units produced to 25 along with six other changing cell values

select the Conserve scenario

Artistic generates a profit under the Conserve scenario

How does this scenario compare to the others? Which one creates the most profit? Apply the other scenarios to answer these questions.

Viewing Artistic's other scenarios:

1. With the Scenario Manager open, double-click the **Efficient** scenario in the Scenarios list box. Excel applies the seven changing-cell values to the worksheet and recalculates it. Profit is $5,312 under the Efficient scenario

2. Double-click the **High Cost** scenario in the Scenarios list box. Excel applies the seven changing-cell values of the High Cost scenario to the worksheet and recalculates it. Profit is $17,884 under the High Cost scenario—the highest value so far

3. Double-click the **Current** scenario in the Scenarios list box to restore the worksheet to its original values

4. Click the **Close** button to close the Scenario Manager dialog box

5. Click **View** on the menu bar, and then click **Full Screen** to restore the screen to its normal display

In the best scenario, High Cost, the company produces at near capacity, charges 20 percent more for its product, and incurs a slight increase in variable and fixed costs. Which course to follow depends on several factors, and Paul will have to mull over the consequences. Meanwhile, Paul wants you to make changes to the High Cost scenario by increasing the unit sale price to $2,250, increasing the utilities to $3,800, and increasing the supplies variable cost to $1,100. Then he wants you to rerun the scenario so that he can review it.

Editing a Scenario

To make changes to one or more scenarios, you click the Scenario Manager's Edit button. The Scenario Manager displays the Edit Scenario dialog box, which is identical to the Add Scenario dialog box. You can change the name of the scenario, remove existing changing cells, or specify a different set of changing cells. When you click OK, the Scenario Values dialog box appears in which you can alter the values of any or all of the changing cells. You may want to reduce the number of scenarios later when you fine-tune your analyses.

---

task reference

Editing a Scenario

- Click **Tools** and click **Scenarios** to open the Scenario Manager

- Select a scenario from the Scenarios list

- Click the **Edit** button

- Make any changes in the Edit Scenario dialog box and click **OK**

- Make any changes in the Scenario Values dialog box and click **OK**

When anyone edits an existing scenario, Excel automatically adds text to the end of the commentary in the Comment box. You will find this information useful when you want to keep track of who is making changes to scenarios. This is particularly useful when you want to route the scenarios to users and allow them to make changes. When you receive the modified scenarios, you can merge the changes together into a unified what-if model.

You are ready to make changes to the High Cost scenario to change the values Paul outlined previously.

Editing Artistic's High Cost scenario:

1. Open the Scenario Manager, click **Tools** on the menu bar and then click **Scenarios**

2. Click **High Cost** in the Scenarios list box and click the **Edit** button. Notice that Excel adds a "Modified by . . ." message below the current comment in the Comment box (see Figure 9.34)

3. Click **OK,** because you do not need to modify the Scenario name, Changing cells, or Comment. The Scenario Values dialog box appears

4. Press the **Tab** key to select the value in the Price box, and then type **2250**

5. Press the **Tab** key *four times* to select the Utilities box, and then type **3800**

6. Press the **Tab** key to select the Supplies box, type **1100,** and click **OK.** Excel redisplays the Scenario Manager

---

EXCEL

FIGURE   9.34

Excel's comment in the Comment list box

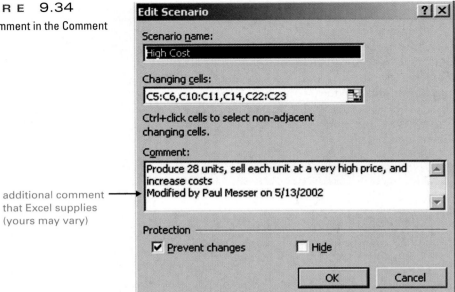

additional comment
that Excel supplies
(yours may vary)

With the changes in place, you can view the newly edited scenario, High Cost, to review its effects.

Viewing an edited scenario:

1. With the Scenario Manager open, double-click the **High Cost** scenario to apply that scenario's values to the designated changing cells

2. Click the **Close** button to close the Scenario Manager, and then scroll the worksheet so that you can see cell C30, Net Income (profit) near the bottom of the screen (see Figure 9.35). Notice that profit has dropped to $13,494, which is probably a more realistic projection

3. Click the **Save** 🖫 button on the Standard toolbar to save the newly created and modified scenarios

Deleting a Scenario

After much thought, Paul has decided that the Current scenario, which you created to preserve the original values of the worksheet, is no longer needed because it shows a negative profit. Paul wants to avoid that situation and knows his company has to produce more than the break-even number (13) of entertainment centers in order to survive. He asks you to delete the scenario called *Current*.

task reference

Deleting a Scenario

- Click **Tools** and click **Scenarios** to open the Scenario Manager

- Select a scenario from the Scenarios list

- Click the **Delete** button

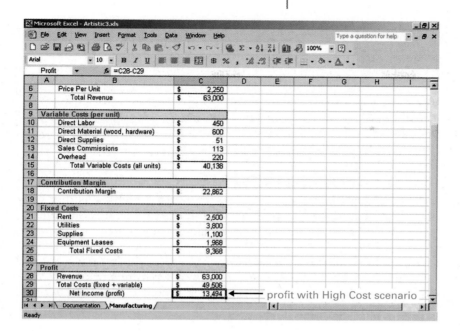

FIGURE 9.35
New results from edited High
Cost scenario

Delete the Current scenario from the list of defined scenarios. Be aware that you cannot revive a scenario once you have deleted it.

Deleting a scenario:

1. Open the Scenario Manager, click **Tools** and then click **Scenarios**

2. Click **Current,** if necessary, in the Scenarios list

3. Click the **Delete** button. Excel deletes the Current scenario, removes its name from the list of scenarios, and redisplays the Scenario Manager dialog box (see Figure 9.36)

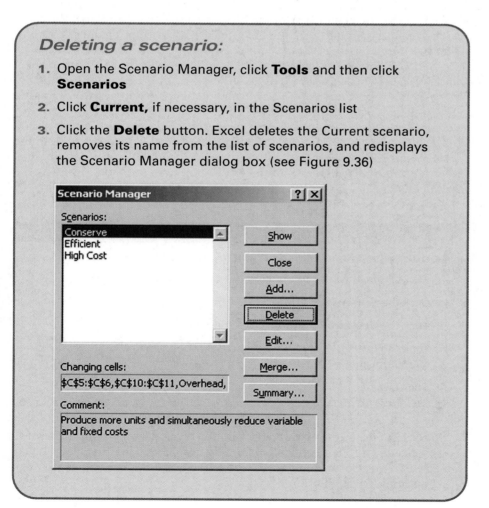

FIGURE 9.36
The Scenario Manager after deleting the Current scenario

tip: *If you do delete the wrong scenario, close the Scenario Manager, close the workbook without saving it, and then reopen the **Artistic3.xls** workbook. That restores the workbook and all the scenarios that existed prior to the deletion operation*

Paul is satisfied with the three scenarios, although he is frustrated because it is difficult to view their results side-by-side. He wishes there were a way to summarize the three scenarios to help him make decisions about production. You can do what Paul wants by producing a scenario report.

CREATING SCENARIO REPORTS

While using scenarios has many benefits, the main drawback is that you cannot view the results of all the scenarios at once. That is, it is difficult to view the results of three or four scenarios side-by-side. Fortunately, Excel provides a way for you to view a condensation or summary allowing you to compare different scenarios. A *scenario summary* outlines each scenario by displaying changing cells and result cells in a separate worksheet. You can produce two types of summary reports: a scenario summary report and a scenario PivotTable report.

Producing a Scenario Summary Report

A scenario summary report helps managers make decisions about which course of action to take. For Artistic Furniture Corporation's manager, a summary report is a handy summary of the values that can affect the company's profitability and the results of tweaking those input values. You produce the report using the Scenario Manager. The Scenario Manager automatically includes all changing cells in the report, but you must select the result cells you want to include. Otherwise, the Scenario Manager includes in the report any cells whose value depends on any of the changing cells. You may want a different selection of result cells. As usual, you can select result cells to include in the report by clicking them or by typing their cell references or names separated by commas. You can also hold the Ctrl key and then click each cell you want to include in the result cells. Excel automatically places commas between each cell you select in the Result cells list.

---

task reference

Producing a Scenario Summary Report

- Click **Tools** and click **Scenarios** to open the Scenario Manager
- Click the **Summary** button
- Click the **Scenario Summary** option button
- Type the cell addresses in the *Result cells* box of all result cells you want to display in the report
- Click **OK**

Paul wants a summary report for the three scenarios that lists the changing cells and the result cells C28, C29, and C30. The three result cells, named Revenue, Costs, and Profit, respectively, are the key values that will help Paul make a production decision.

Creating a Scenario Summary report:

1. With the Scenario Manager dialog box still open, click the **Summary** button. The Scenario Summary dialog box opens. You can produce either a scenario summary or a scenario PivotTable report

2. If necessary, click the **Scenario Summary** option button

3. Type **C28,C29,C30** in the Result cells box (see Figure 9.37). (You do not need to type spaces between the cell references)

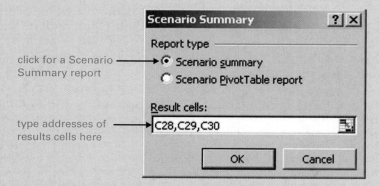

click for a Scenario Summary report

type addresses of results cells here

FIGURE 9.37
Selecting result cells for the Scenario Summary report

4. Click **OK.** Excel's Scenario Manager creates a Scenario Summary report on a separate worksheet called Scenario Summary (see Figure 9.38). Notice the outlining symbols above and to the left of the summary report, allowing you to show and hide details

outlining symbols allow you to hide or reveal details

FIGURE 9.38
Scenario Summary worksheet

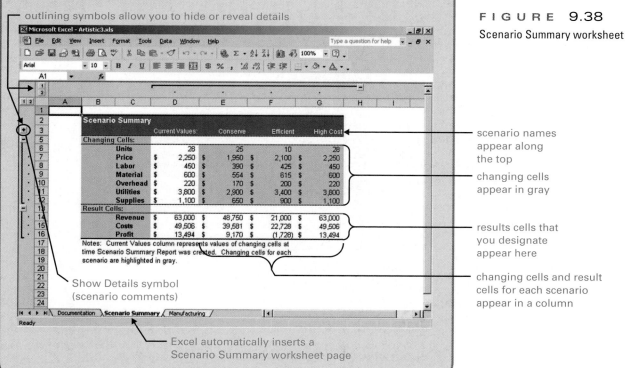

scenario names appear along the top

changing cells appear in gray

results cells that you designate appear here

changing cells and result cells for each scenario appear in a column

Show Details symbol (scenario comments)

Excel automatically inserts a Scenario Summary worksheet page

The Scenario Summary report is chock full of information. The first column contains the names (or cell addresses) of the changing and result cells. The names of the scenarios appear in the order in which you created them. The summary report's second column (labeled "Current Values") lists the contents of the changing cells and result cells currently in the worksheet. The third through fifth columns show both changing cells and result cells for the Conserve, Efficient, and High Cost scenarios. The Changing cells—the cells you designated in the Add Scenario dialog box—are shaded so that you can tell quickly which scenarios control which changing cells. The *show details* symbol to the left of row 3 indicates that Excel has hidden something there. Clicking that symbol reveals the contents of the Comment box that you filled in when creating the scenario. You can hide the Changing Cells rows, the Result Cells rows, or both by clicking the Show Detail symbols in the left portion of the worksheet.

Paul would like to see the comments you typed for each scenario. You will do that next.

Showing scenario comments:

1. With the Scenario Summary worksheet displayed, click the **Show Details** outline symbol next to row 3. Excel displays the previously hidden scenario comments (see Figure 9.39)

FIGURE 9.39

Showing scenario comments

click this Hide (Show) Details symbol to hide (show) scenario comments

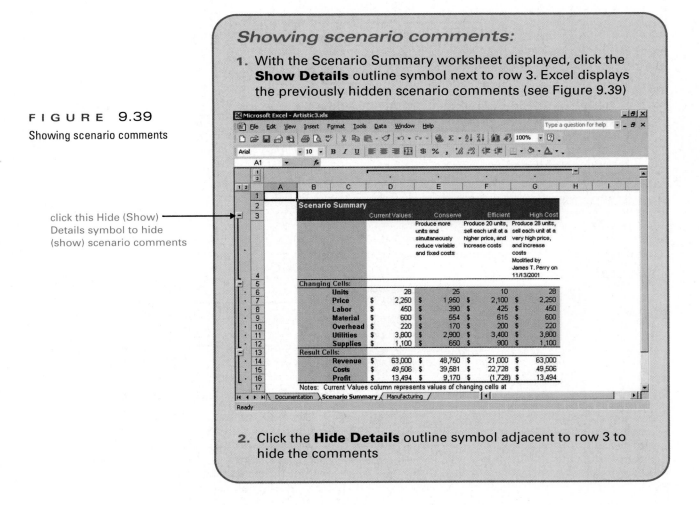

2. Click the **Hide Details** outline symbol adjacent to row 3 to hide the comments

Producing a PivotTable Report

The other report you can create with the Scenario Manager is the Scenario PivotTable. The Scenario PivotTable option inserts a new worksheet into your workbook. Unlike a Scenario Summary report, a PivotTable report is a what-if tool in its own right. You can use the mouse to drag and drop cells and cell ranges onto the pivot table and manipulate it just like any other PivotTable. You can mix and match distinct scenarios to review their effects on result cells.

While pivot tables are tremendously powerful, you will find them most useful for what-if analyses in which you have designated different sets of changing cells—perhaps created by different groups of people. If all of your scenarios contain the same set of changing cells as your Artistic Furniture Corporation worksheet does, then a scenario summary report is as useful as a PivotTable report. Besides, PivotTable reports take longer to create and use more memory than do scenario summaries. When you display a PivotTable report, the Query And Pivot toolbar appears.

---

task reference

Producing a PivotTable Report

- Click **Tools** and click **Scenarios** to open the Scenario Manager

- Click the **Summary** button

- Click the **Scenario PivotTable** option button

- Type the cell addresses in the Result cells of all result cells you want to display in the report

- Click **OK**

Paul wants you to create a simple PivotTable report so that he can review it and decide if it is useful to him.

Creating a Scenario PivotTable report:

1. Click the **Manufacturing** worksheet tab to make that worksheet active

   tip: Because each worksheet holds the scenarios you created for it, you cannot create a scenario summary report or a PivotTable report from the Scenario Summary worksheet

2. Click **Tools** on the menu bar, click **Scenarios,** and click the **Summary** button. The Scenario Manager displays the Scenario Summary dialog box

3. Click the **Scenario PivotTable report** option button, ensure that the Result cells box contains the cell addresses C28, C29, and C30, and then click **OK** to create the PivotTable report (see Figure 9.40)

   tip: Your display may not show the PivotTable Field List or the PivotTable toolbar. Display the PivotTable toolbar: Click **Tools,** point to **Toolbars,** and click **PivotTable.** Click the **Show Field** List button (see Figure 9.40) on the PivotTable toolbar to display the PivotTable Field List

4. Click the **Documentation** worksheet tab to make that worksheet active

FIGURE 9.40

Creating a PivotTable report

scenario names

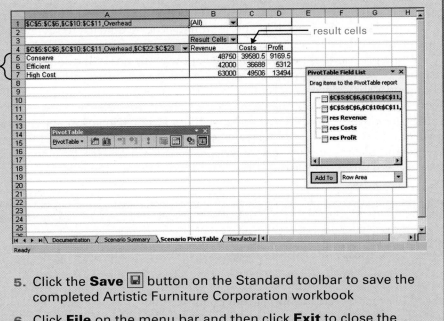

5. Click the **Save** 🖫 button on the Standard toolbar to save the completed Artistic Furniture Corporation workbook

6. Click **File** on the menu bar and then click **Exit** to close the worksheet and exit Excel

The report cells contain row fields displaying changing cells, whose names appear in the rows. The result cells appear, initially, across the top of the table. A scenario pivot table behaves like any other pivot table: you can drag the shaded boxes from one area to another to rearrange the pivot table.

After careful examination of the PivotTable report, Paul decides it is not as useful for him as the Scenario Summary report. He will use the PivotTable report in the future if he decides to create scenarios that contain different sets of changing cells.

Paul is very pleased with you for creating the data tables, scenarios, and scenario reports. By using these feature-rich what-if analysis tools, Paul will be able to fine-tune the Artistic Furniture Corporation production and optimize the company's profit.

SESSION 9.2   *making the grade*

1. A _____ consists of selected variables, which are cells in which you substitute different values.

2. The cells whose values change in a scenario are called _____ cells.

3. Begin creating a scenario by clicking _____ on the Tools menu.

4. Every scenario you create must have a scenario _____.

5. A collection of scenarios is organized by the scenario _____.

6. Scenarios are associated with an individual _____ and are only accessible when it is active.

7. You can create either a scenario _____ report or a scenario _____ to summarize all of a worksheet's scenarios.

8. Make the following modifications to the Artistic Furniture Corporation worksheet, **Artistic3.xls.** First, open the worksheet and immediately save it as **Artistic38.xls** to preserve Artistic3.xls. Delete the Scenario Summary and Scenario PivotTable worksheets (**Edit, Delete Sheet, Delete**) so that only the Documentation and Manufacturing sheets remain. Add a new scenario called **Middle Road** whose changing cells are **C5, C10,** and **C11.** Type the comment **Simpler model including production, direct labor, and direct material.** Click **OK** to proceed to the Scenario Values dialog box. Type **18, 415,** and **620** in the Units, Labor, and Material boxes, respectively. Click **OK** to add the Middle Road scenario to the list. Click the **Efficient** scenario and then click the **Show** button. Then click the **Middle Road** scenario and click the **Show** button. Click the **Summary** button, click the **Scenario Summary** option button, and click **OK** to create a new Scenario Summary worksheet. What do you notice about the scenario summary that is different from the previous scenario summary you created? Enter your name in the worksheet header of all three worksheets—group them first to make it easier. Change the Scenario Summary worksheet to print in landscape orientation. Print Preview each page and adjust the margins so each one fits on one page. Click the **Save** button to save the workbook. Execute **Print** or **Save As,** according to your instructor's direction.

SESSION 9.3 SUMMARY

Cost-Volume-Profit (CVP) analysis examines the relationship between a product's expenses, the number of units produced, revenue, and profit. Two feature-rich Excel tools help you perform what-if analysis by automating substitution of different values in key cells to help you perform CVP analysis. The two tools are data tables and scenarios. With Excel's one- and two-variable data table feature, you can determine the break-even point of a business—the number of units or mix of products and services a company produces in order for profit to be zero. A one-variable data table summarizes key input and output cell values in a what-if analysis by substituting a series of values for an input cell from a choice of several input values. Output of a one-variable data table is one or more rows or columns containing result cells (profits, for example) that display an output value for each input value substituted into the worksheet. Using a one-variable data table, you can view the effects of changing an input value on multiple output formulas. A two-variable data table computes the effects of two variables on a single formula. Excel substitutes values into selected cells of a worksheet to produce a result value for each pair of input values. For example, with a two-variable data table, you can study the effects of altering both the interest rate and the number of months in the period on a loan's monthly payment amount. Similarly, you could perform what-if analysis on the effect of changing the production volume of a product and the selling price of a product on the company's profitability.

Complex what-if analyses on more than two variables require more power than either one- or two-variable data tables provide. Using Excel's Scenario Manager, you can substitute up to 32 input values into the same number of selected input cells and analyze the results on key output cells. A group of values and changing cells is called a scenario, and you can define as many scenarios for a single worksheet as you would like. Once you have created one or more scenarios, you can click the Show button to plug the values of the scenario into the worksheet. Excel recalculates its values and displays the results of the scenario. Using the Scenario Manager, you can edit scenarios, delete scenarios, or create scenario reports. The Scenario Manager provides two types of reports: a Scenario Summary report or a Scenario PivotTable report. A scenario summary creates a separate worksheet with an overview of the changing cell values and result values for each scenario. Scenarios display in columns and changing cells appear across rows. PivotTable reports summarize scenarios on a separate worksheet also. Unlike scenario summaries, PivotTable reports are what-if tools. You can drag and drop cells and cell ranges into a pivot table and change it as you would any other pivot table. PivotTable reports are most useful when you create scenarios with different sets of changing cells.

MOUS OBJECTIVES SUMMARY

- Create Excel scenarios (MOUS Ex2002e-8-3)
- Manage Excel scenarios with the Scenario Manager (MOUS Ex2002e-8-3)
- View, add, edit, and delete scenarios (MOUS Ex2002e-8-3)
- Create a scenario report (MOUS Ex2002e-8-3)

task reference roundup

Task	Page #	Preferred Method
Creating a One-Variable Data Table	EX 9.18	• Decide if you want values for the input cell to appear in a row or down a column
		• If you arrange a data table in columns, then insert the input values in the first column beginning below the first row of the table and place a reference (a formula) to the result cell in the cell above and to the right of the column of input values
		• If you arrange a data table in rows, then insert the input values in the first row beginning in the second column of the data table and place a reference (a formula) to the result cell in the cell below the input row and to its left
		• Select the table, click **Data**, and then click **Table**
		• Enter the cell reference of the input cell in the Row input cell box if input values are in a row or enter the cell reference of the input cell in the Column input cell box if the input values are in a column in the data table
		• Click **OK**
Creating a Two-Variable Data Table	EX 9.25	• Type the formula or a reference to the input cell in the upper-left cell in the data table
		• Type the first variable values in the row to the right of the formula
		• Type the second variable values in the column below the formula
		• Select a cell range that encompasses the formula, row values, and column values
		• Click **Data** on the menu bar and then click **Table**
		• Type the address of the input cell that corresponds to the row values in the Row input cell text box
		• Type the address of the input cell that corresponds to the column values in the Column input cell text box
		• Click **OK**
Creating a Scenario	EX 9.34	• Click **Tools** and click **Scenarios** to open the Scenario Manager
		• Click the **Add** button and type a scenario name
		• Specify the changing (input) cells in the scenario
		• Type commentary in the Comment text box and then click the **OK** button
		• Type the values for each changing cell, scrolling the list if necessary, and then click **OK**
		• Click **Close** to close the Scenario Manager
Viewing a Scenario	EX 9.39	• Click **Tools** and click **Scenarios** to open the Scenario Manager
		• Select a scenario from the Scenarios list
		• Click the **Show** button
Editing a Scenario	EX 9.41	• Click **Tools** and click **Scenarios** to open the Scenario Manager
		• Select a scenario from the Scenarios list

EXCEL

task reference roundup

Task	Page #	Preferred Method
		• Click the **Edit** button
		• Make any changes in the Edit Scenario dialog box and click **OK**
		• Make any changes in the Scenario Values dialog box and click **OK**
Deleting a Scenario	EX 9.42	• Click **Tools** and click **Scenarios** to open the Scenario Manager
		• Select a scenario from the Scenarios list
		• Click the **Delete** button
Producing a Scenario Summary Report	EX 9.44	• Click **Tools** and click **Scenarios** to open the Scenario Manager
		• Click the **Summary** button
		• Click the **Scenario Summary** option button
		• Type the cell addresses in the *Result cells* box of all result cells you want to display in the report
		• Click **OK**
Producing a PivotTable Report	EX 9.47	• Click **Tools** and click **Scenarios** to open the Scenario Manager
		• Click the **Summary** button
		• Click the **Scenario PivotTable** option button
		• Type the cell addresses in the Result cells box of all result cells you want to display in the report
		• Click **OK**

CROSSWORD PUZZLE

Across

4. A(n) _____ formula in a data table is part of an interrelated group of formulas.
7. The name for a combination of values assigned to one or more variable cells in a what-if analysis.
10. The input _____(s) are the set of possible values substituted into the input cell.
12. The result _____(s) are the computed answer(s) for a one-variable data table.

Down

1. A scenario _____ outlines each scenario by displaying changing cells and result cells in a separate worksheet.
2. The _____ cells defined in a scenario contain values you want Excel to change.
3. A cell in which Excel substitutes different values.
5. A _____ cell holds the output value that is affected by a change in the input cell.
6. The point in which profit is zero is called the _____ point.
8. The _____ cell is the key input variable to change in a one-variable data table analysis.
9. Money or items of value a company receives during a given period.
11. A _____ cost is one that remains constant regardless of how many goods or services you make or sell.
12. The relationship between a product's expenses, units produced, revenue, and profit.
13. A data _____ summarizes the key input and output cell values of multiple what-if analyses in a single cell range.

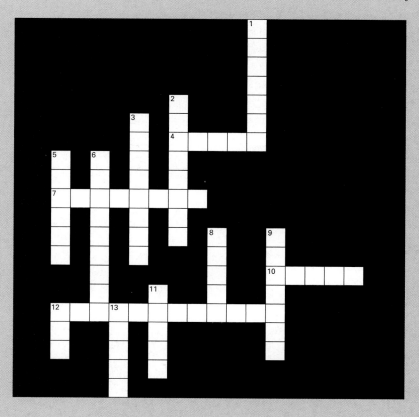

FILL-IN

1. Typically, there are two major categories of costs in building: _____ costs and _____ costs.

2. The point where profits are zero is called the _____ point.

3. A _____ variable data table can evaluate multiple result cells and produce result values.

4. In a two-variable data table, you always place the reference to the result cell in the _____ corner of the table—at the intersection of the row input values and the _____ input values.

5. The Excel _____ Manager allows you to create what-if analyses for more than two variables.

6. Unlike the Scenario summary, the _____ report is, itself, a what-if tool that allows you to drag input cells into it.

REVIEW QUESTIONS

1. Describe, briefly, the difference between fixed costs and variable costs in a manufacturing environment where the company is building products for sale.

2. Describe why a one- or two-variable data table is a good what-if tool compared to a worksheet without the ability to create data tables or similar analyses.

3. From what you have read in this chapter, what would you do if you wanted to see the effect of changing, say, four variables in a what-if analysis? Explain how you might automate the what-if analysis.

4. Explain what happens if you try to delete one of the result values in a two-variable data table.

CREATE THE QUESTION

For each of the following answers, create an appropriate, short question.

ANSWER	QUESTION
1. variable cost	_____
2. the upper-left corner of the data table	_____
3. array formula	_____
4. Scenario Manager	_____
5. result cell	_____
6. PivotTable report	_____

practice

1. Considering Several Scenarios for Outdoor Adventures

Outdoor Adventures manufactures a line of outdoor camping and hiking equipment. Bill Hoskins, the president of Outdoor Adventures, has prepared a preliminary budget and he wants you to create three scenarios for him. He would like to see the effect of changing the labor, materials, and production revenues on the operating income—revenues minus expenses. He would like you to prepare a Scenario Summary report for him.

1. Open **ex09Outdoor.xls** and save it as **OutdoorAdventures.xls**

2. Click the **May** tab to make that sheet active

3. Click cell **B6,** type **=SUM(B3:B5),** click cell **B18,** click the **AutoSum** button on the Standard toolbar, and press **Enter** to sum expenses

4. Click cell **B20** and type **=B6-B18,** press **Enter** to compute Operating Income (or net income). Name selected cells to help identify them in scenario summaries later

5. Select the cell range **A3:B5,** click **Insert** on the menu bar, point to **Name,** click **Create,** and ensure that the **Left column check box** is checked, click **OK,** and click any cell to deselect the range

   Next, create three scenarios

6. Click **Tools** on the menu bar, click **Scenarios,** and click the **Add** button

7. Type **Current budget** in the Scenario name box, press the **Tab** key, type **B3:B5** in the Changing Cells box, press **Tab,** type **Current budget figures for the baseline,** click **OK** in the Add Scenario dialog box, and click **Add** in the Scenario Values dialog box to accept the current values and add another scenario

8. Type **Increase labor** in the Scenario name box, press **Tab** twice, type **Increase labor only,** click the **OK** button, type **72000** in the Labor box, and then click **Add** in the Scenario Values dialog box to add another scenario

9. Type **Increase materials** in the Scenario name box, press **Tab** twice, type **Increase materials only,** click the **OK** button, double-click the **Materials** box, type **2456,** and then click **Add** in the Scenario Values dialog box to add another scenario

10. Type **Increase production** in the Scenario name box, press **Tab** twice, type **Increase production only,** click the **OK** button, double-click the **Production** box, type **7800,** and then click **OK**

11. Click the **Summary** button on the Scenario Manager dialog box, ensure that the **Scenario summary** option button is selected, and click **OK**

12. When the Scenario Summary worksheet appears, click **File** on the menu bar, click **Page Setup,** click the **Page** tab (if necessary), click the **Landscape** option button in the Orientation panel, and click **OK**

13. Click the **Save** button on the Standard toolbar to save your workbook

14. Identify your workbook by placing your name in all three pages' headers, and then either print all three worksheets or execute Save As, according to your instructor's direction

2. Using Two Variables to Determine Optimal Numbers

Parson City Community Recreation Center (PCCRC) is getting ready to open its doors. After years of fundraising and two years of construction, the Center will soon be ready for use by the public. The only income the PCCRC will have to cover all expenses is membership dues that will be collected on a monthly basis. Since the Center has state-of-the-art teaching, and theater and sports facilities, the board expects membership to be high. The board must now decide what the center will charge for monthly dues. Since the PCCRC is a nonprofit organization, it is crucial that the Center be as close as possible to break-even each year. In determining what the membership dues will be, the Center has to work around one restriction placed on it by the city—due to the size of the center, there may be no more than 4,500 members.

Open **PCCRC.xls** and save it as **PCCRC2.xls.** This is the budget determined by the board. A one-variable data table has already been completed with different possible numbers of members with dues set at $25. As you can see, these possible scenarios will not allow the PCCRC to even cover its expenses. In order to decide what to charge for monthly dues, it needs your help in creating a two-variable data table. It wants you to work with monthly dues in the range of $25 to $35, in increments of $2, and number of members from 4,000 to 4,500, in increments of 100.

1. In cell **J18,** enter $**25** as the lowest possible charge for dues. Enter $**27** in **K18,** $**29** in **L18** and so on, up to $**35**
2. In cells **I19** through **I24,** copy the membership numbers from the one-variable data table
3. Since this is a two-variable data table, in cell **I18,** enter **=D23** for Income. Since a currency value appears, format the cell to instead read **Members**

4. In cell **L17,** type **Dues** and align it to the right of the cell. Apply Bold and Italic to *Members* and *Dues* and change the typeface to a green color
5. Select the range **I18:O24,** select **Data** in the menu bar, and then click **Table**
6. In the table dialog box, type **D17** in the Row Input box to reference membership dues
7. For the Column Input box, type **D16** to reference the number of members. Click **OK**
8. After the table is filled, analyze the data. Look for the cell with positive income closest to $0. How many members paying what amount of dues yield this result? Highlight the cell and its corresponding member and dues figures.
9. Include your name in the worksheet header, and print or save as according to your instructor's direction

1. Reviewing Best and Worst Case Scenarios for Abel-Massey Corporation

Abel-Massey's president, Bert Abel, has produced a pro forma income statement in which he is projecting expenses and income for his business. The worksheet, called **ex09AbelMassey.xls,** is preformatted and contains revenue and expenses for 2002 and projections for 2003 and 2004. Bert wants you to create three scenarios and then create a Scenario Summary report that outlines the results of the scenario analysis. To make the analysis easier to understand, Bert has named all the changing cells and the three result cells so that they are self-documenting in the summary report. The changing cells are specially formatted with a gray background so that both the worksheet reader and anyone who creates scenarios can easily identify them. Most of the changing cells represent a percentage of product sales. For example, cell B7 contains 30 percent. That is a what-if estimate of the contract revenues as a percentage of product sales in this model.

FIGURE 9.41

Abel-Massey scenarios and their values

Changing Cell	Range Name	Base	Worst	Best
C6	SalesYear1	$1000	$1000	$1200
D6	SalesYear2	$1200	$1200	$1400
E6	SalesYear3	$1400	$1400	$1600
B7	ContractRevenue	30%	25%	35%
B11	ProductCost	50%	55%	45%
B12	SubcontCost	18%	21%	15%
B16	Equipment	9%	10%	8%
B17	Payroll	25%	28%	22%
B18	Rent	25%	28%	22%
B19	Supplies	2%	2%	2%

Your job is to create three scenarios called Base, Worst, and Best. Start by opening **ex09AbelMassey.xls** and save it as **AbelMassey.xls** to preserve the original workbook. Use the values shown in Figure 9.41 and the corresponding scenario values for the three scenarios. When you have completed the three scenarios, produce a Scenario Summary report—an additional worksheet. Select cells **C22, D22,** and **E22** as the Result cells in the Scenario Summary dialog box when you produce the summary report. Click the Scenario Summary worksheet and then select landscape orientation for the page in the Page Setup dialog box. The other pages print suitably in portrait orientation.

Either print the three Abel-Massey worksheets comprising the workbook or execute File, Save As, depending on your instructor's direction. Here are the three scenarios' values and the cells and names to which they correspond (see Figure 9.41).

2. Examining Car Financing Options with a Two-Variable Data Table

Nancy Webber graduates from college in three months, and she has received three terrific job offers. Having a job in hand and the promise of a good salary, Nancy wants to purchase a new car. She figures she will need a $10,000 loan to buy the car she wants. She's not sure what interest rate she will be able to lock in, but Nancy knows she cannot afford a payment of more than $315 per month. In order to find the best combination of loan duration (years) and interest rate, Nancy wants to build a two-variable data table with interest rates from 6 percent to 10 percent as column values in the table and years—from 1 to 5—along the top of the table.

Begin by opening **ex09Loan.xls** and save it as **Loan2.xls.** The loan worksheet contains the loan amount in cell B1, an interest rate in cell B2, the loan length in years in cell B3, and the monthly payment (a PMT function) in cell B5. Create a two-variable data table whose upper-left corner, containing a reference to cell B5, is cell D2. In cells E2 through I2, type the values **1** through **5** representing the duration in years of the loan. In cells D3 and D4, type **6.00%** and **6.25%,** respectively. Select cells **D3** and **D4,** and then drag the fill handle down through cell D19. In cell D2, type **=ABS(B5),** which is the absolute value of the cell B5 containing the monthly payment. Create a two-variable data table for the cell range D2:I19. Format the values in the resulting data table to display currency symbols and two decimal places. Format cell D2 to display the text **"Interest"** instead of the formula result. In cell E1, type **Years** to label the top row. Conditionally format the cell range **E3:I19** so that any value less than or equal to $315 is red in color. For added interest, select the entire table, open the Drawing toolbar, and select a drop shadow. Identify your worksheet by placing your name in the header. Select the landscape orientation. Either print the worksheet or execute Save As, according to your instructor's direction.

on the web

1. Using Scenarios to Forecast Stock Prices

Travis Lewis inherited his grandfather's investments years ago. In the will, his grandfather indicated that Travis could not sell any of the investments until he reached 26 years of age. Travis' 26th birthday was a few months ago, and he has decided to analyze his holdings and sell some of the stocks. In deciding when to sell these stocks, there are several things Travis needs to take into consideration. He has decided that he wants to at least breakeven when he sells each stock. Since he already paid inheritance tax when he received the investments, he doesn't need to figure that into his calculations. Since the stocks were inherited, the cost basis used for tax purposes will be the price of each stock at his grandfather's death. He will have to pay capital gains tax on the profit of each stock, which his advisor estimates will be 20 percent. He will also have to pay a flat $250 commission to his broker for each stock sold.

Travis has decided to sell the following stocks: Nokia, Siebel Systems, Wells Fargo, Disney, and Baxter International. Open **TravisStock.xls** and save as **TravisStock2.xls.** This workbook records the information Travis needs to determine which stocks to sell now that at least break even. You will have to use the Web to determine the cost basis for each stock and its current price. Go to www.finance.yahoo.com—this is the Web site you will use to determine stock prices. Under Research & Education, select Historical Quotes to find the cost basis and current price of each stock. Once these are determined, enter the gain or loss per share. For total gain or loss, create a formula to multiply the number of shares held by the amount of gain or loss per share. The capital gains tax amount formula will multiply this total by 20 percent (cells H3:H7). Some of the cells may have negative numbers due to a "loss" if the stock is sold. When this occurs, simply reference negative numbers as stocks that should not be sold. Fill the profit column with a formula that will subtract tax and commission for total gain per stock. Which stocks should Travis currently sell? Include your name in the worksheet header. Execute Print or Save As, according to your instructor's direction.

Travis is debating waiting to see how the market changes over the next few years. He asked his advisor to come up with four possible scenarios for the stock market five years from now. Open **TravisScenarios.xls**—it contains the four possible scenarios forecasted by his advisor. Travis needs you to use the Scenario Manager to see what the possible status of his stock holdings will be in five years. Go back to the worksheet **TravisStock2.xls.** Using the four possible forecasts, add a scenario for each possible outcome, using current price and capital gains tax as the changing cells. Create a Scenario Summary report for Travis, using profit as the result cells. Include your name in the header and print the report. In which of the scenarios will Travis receive a profit after selling his stock?

2. Analyzing College Expenses

Karen Roman will be an incoming freshman at the University of California, Santa Barbara, next fall. She has been busy preparing for her new school and the big move across country. She is expecting to receive an academic scholarship for $7,750 and her parents have agreed to give Karen an additional $8,000 a year to go toward expenses. Karen will need to use student loans to cover any additional needs at UCSB.

Using her Web browser, Karen went to www.ucsb.edu to locate more information on what her expenses will be once she starts school. She has asked you to help and look at the Web site with her. Once on the home page, select **Current Students** and then click **Financial Aid.** Click **Cost of Attendance** to display an outline of expenses. Karen's father gave her an expense statement worksheet, called ex09UCExpenses.xls, to use to help her easily understand her sources of funds and her expenses. Open **ex09UCExpenses.xls,** save the workbook as **UCexpenses.xls,** and fill in the current undergraduate expenses for Karen. Remember to note expenses for being an out-of-state student. In cells D5 and D21, create formulas to compute the total sources and expenses. In cell **D24,** enter **=D5** and in cell **D25,** enter **=D21.** Create a formula in cell **D26** for Amount Needed to subtract D25 from D24. Format this row boldface.

Karen is eligible for a few more scholarships and is applying for them. She has asked you to create a one-variable data table to reflect the different possible amounts of scholarships she may receive. Her different possibilities are the current amount of $7,750, $8,500, $11,800, $14,500, and $15, 200. In the cell range **G3:I3,** enter the following headings: **Scholarships, Total Sources,** and **Amount Needed.** Under scholarships, enter the five possibilities for Karen. In cells **G4:I4,** enter references to the appropriate cells in the expense statement.

Select the range of the title, click on **Data** and then click **Table.** Enter **D3** as the column input cell. Format the table so that each cell has a dollar sign and no decimals. Format the Amount Needed cells to be positive numbers in red. Title the worksheet **Loan Amounts.** Type your name in the worksheet header. Execute Print or Save As, according to your instructor's direction.

1. Determining Whether a Project will Produce Income Using Tables

G. Mercer is a retailer with stores throughout the northeast. Sales have been strong for the past few years and the company is thinking about expanding its operations to include locations in large western cities. Before investing in actual store locations, G. Mercer needed to figure out a way to determine the level of demand for its products in areas outside the northeast. Due to the great increase in use of the Internet for shopping, G. Mercer decided on an online store as the best option. An online store will allow the company to record where customers are located throughout the country, help gain name recognition in new areas, and increase sales. While there are many benefits to launching a Web site, G. Mercer wants to be sure that the new project will at least bring in enough total income over the first six months to cover costs for the project.

A local designer has agreed to design the Web site for $30,000. G. Mercer will spread this cost over six months, for $5,000 each month. The online store will use currently unused office space to house a technology department that will run and update the Web site and also a customer service team to assist online customers. Estimated salaries for the technology department total $12,000 a month. New equipment and computers will total $7,000 a month and customer service salaries will be $26,000.

G. Mercer will use its current warehouses and distributors to handle the online orders. However, each order will cost an additional $2.00 in labor and $1.00 in packaging. The customer will pay for all shipping costs. In order to determine whether this venture will be profitable in the first six months, the following estimates have been made for number of orders. For January: 245 orders; February: 298 orders; March: 362 orders; April: 403 orders; May: 476 orders; and June: 495 orders. The company wants to use conservative estimates and believes orders will average $156 in sales during this preliminary period.

Stephanie Peters is director of the finance department and needs you to summarize these figures for a presentation. Open **GMercer.xls** and save as **GMercer2.xls.** This is the spreadsheet Stephanie designed to analyze sales, costs, and income. She has already calculated the results for January, and she wants you to complete the information for February through June. To supply these figures, you will need to create a one-variable data table. For the column headings, use **Orders, Revenue, Costs,** and **Income.** For these column cells, enter references to the appropriate cells in the current worksheet created by Stephanie. (Be sure to use the cell for Total Costs.) Title the column before Orders as **Month** and fill in **January** through **June.** Be sure not to include this column when creating the table. In the Units column, enter the estimates given to you. When the Table dialog box opens, specify the input cell as **D8** and that the table is in column format.

Chart this data table to illustrate when G. Mercer will break even. To create the chart, use the data table you created and the figures for Orders, Revenues and Costs. Use the XY Scatter Chart without markers on the lines. Title the chart **G. Mercer Break-Even** and type **Orders** in the X-axis box. Select for the chart to appear on a new sheet and title the sheet **BE Chart.** Should G. Mercer take on the Web site project? In which month will the company begin to cover its costs? Include your name in the worksheet header. Execute either Print or Save As, according to your instructor's direction.

2. Examining Options to Decrease Fixed Costs

WebVideo is one of the best online stores for movies and videos. Its products range from new releases to hard-to-find and rare videos. The site is easy to navigate and offers competitive prices coupled with quick delivery—all of which contributed greatly to WebVideo's popularity. Since the company has no retail locations, all videos are housed in a single warehouse and distribution center. In order to meet customers' requests and maintain its reputation for service, WebVideo has always maintained large inventories of each movie, resulting in hundreds of thousands of videos. While this has enabled WebVideo to quickly locate and deliver videos, it is a very costly way to operate. All of the videos had to be bought by WebVideo and are an enormous investment. WebVideo receives income from each sale, but since its initial and replenishment costs are so high, the company has not been able to show a profit.

Open **WebVideo.xls** and save as **WebVideo2.xls.** This workbook contains the company's income statement for the past two months. Begin by entering Contribution Margin in cell **B19.** For cells D19 and H19, create a formula to subtract variable costs from revenues. WebVideo clearly has enough revenue to cover variable expenses, so management has decided that fixed costs must be decreased. It has been determined that the best way to achieve this is to sell off some inventory and move to a smaller facility. First, WebVideo needs you to determine how its estimated 10 percent increase in videos sold will affect operating income. Create a one-variable data table to examine how increases in sales will affect current variable and fixed costs and operating margin. In the cell range **K5:N5,** enter the headings **Videos Sold, Var. Costs, Fixed Costs,** and **Op. Income** and bold the text in these cells. In cell **K6,** enter **=H5,** for **L6** enter **=H17,** for **M6** enter **=H26** and for cell **N6** enter **=H28.** Select the table range, click **Data,** and then click **Table.** In the column input cell, enter **H5** and click **OK.** At what number of videos sold will they receive positive income? Bold this number and make its color red. Include your name and print the worksheet.

Next, WebVideo needs you to examine what its income would be if it moved to another facility. The company needs to determine whether it will receive positive income sooner by choosing this option. Another facility will give the firm the following decreased costs: Lease $5,350; Overhead $1,860; Salaries $96,000; and Maintenance $700. Since WebVideo will carry a smaller inventory, some videos ordered by customers online will have to be sent to WebVideo from an outside supplier. This is going to cause an increase in shipping costs to $2.55. This $1.40 increase will be partially passed on to the customer through an increase in video prices to $15.99. WebVideo expects this increase in price to cause some of its customers to choose their competitors to order videos. But WebVideo also believes that its superior customer service will retain a large number of its clients and expects 8,400 videos to sell in April. Open a new worksheet and create an income statement similar to the statement in WebVideo.xls. Title your worksheet **WebVideoOption2.xls** and use all of the forecasted costs and revenues for WebVideo moving to a new facility. Will this option bring positive income for WebVideo in the month of April? Include your name in the worksheet header. Execute Print or Save As, according to your instructor's direction.

1. Using Scenario Manager to Forecast Income

Jeff Livingston owns Leaf Furniture, a large store that sells imported furniture from around the world. Jeff has been busy preparing for the summer and has attended several trade shows where teak furniture was the new trend. He has decided to carry an initial line of teak patio furniture—specifically, sets of a table and four chairs. Jeff contacted many teak furniture makers around the world to inquire about their prices and to see samples of their teak pieces. Based on quality of craftsmanship, Jeff has narrowed it down to four manufacturers located in Zaire, Brazil, the U.S., and Thailand. Initially, Jeff just compared each seller's price for the furniture set. But he then realized that each seller had different shipping charges based on its location. Also, each seller outside of the country adds a surcharge to cover tariff costs. Since each seller's location causes the shipping and tariff charges to vary greatly, Jeff needs to be sure to include these numbers and not look at just the cost per set. After looking at the differences in these additional charges, Jeff has asked you to help him determine from which manufacturer he should purchase the furniture.

Open **Teak.xls** and save as **Teak2.xls.** Jeff expects to charge $1,200 per furniture set based on his competitors' prices. His first order will be for 30 sets of furniture and he will order more though the summer based on sales. Jeff has already started the worksheet by entering revenue information and expects to make $36,000 in sales from the first 30 sets. Jeff has also entered each seller's charge per set (product cost), shipping charge, and surcharge. Complete the Income Statement by entering **Income** in cell A14. Enter the appropriate formula in this row's cells to compute income received after costs are subtracted from revenues. Bold this row. Based on this information, which seller should Jeff use? Include your name and print the Income Statement.

Jeff has looked over these figures and agrees with your recommendation. He wants to consider different options for the sales price and number of units sold. His current scenario would be to charge $1,200 per set, to sell 30 sets, and for his costs to remain the same. The worst case would be if he sold fifteen sets, sold them for $1,200 each, and his product cost increased by $30 per set. The best case would be if he sold 30 sets, was able to increase the price to $1,500 each, and his product costs dropped by $20 each. Use the Scenario Manager to enter the Best Case, Current Case, and Worst Case scenarios. For changing cells, be sure to include the cell ranges for Price per Set, Number of Sets Sold, and Product Cost. Specify the values for these changing cells based on the three scenarios Jeff gave you. Next, create a Scenario Summary report, using the cells that represent Income as the result cells. Include your name in the header, and print the scenario summary.

running project

Pampered Paws

Pampered Paws owner, Grace Jackson, knows a lot of her revenue is from dog food sales. While cat food sales volumes are significant, dogs are larger than cats and eat a significant amount more. Therefore, having the right mix of dog food brands and types for sale can greatly improve Pampered Paws' profitability. Grace knows that the number of bags of the different brands of dog food it offers is one way she can perform an extensive what-if analysis. Grace has put together a preliminary worksheet, called **ex09Paws.xls,** containing her per unit wholesale cost (what she pays) for various brands of dog food, and her typical retail price (the price she charges customers). She has created additional columns indicating typical sales in units of each brand per month. She wants you to complete the worksheet by writing formulas for the Total Cost, Total Sales, and Profit columns.

The Total Cost formula for each dog food is its wholesale cost times the units sold. The Total Sales formula for each dog food is its retail price (column C) times the units sold. The profit for each dog food is the Total Sales minus Total Cost. Format cell range E4:G8 with the Accounting format, display two decimal places, and display the currency symbol.

Write SUM functions in cells E10 through F10 for the Total Cost, Total Sales, and Profit columns. Assign the names TotalCost to cell E10, TotalSales to cell F10, and TotalProfit to cell G10. Next, use the Scenario Manager to create three scenarios with changing cells D4 through D8. The result cells included in the scenario are the totals in the cell range E10:G10. Figure 9.42 lists the details of the three scenarios you are to create. Create a Scenario Summary report, and move the Scenario Summary worksheet to the right of the Dog Food Analysis worksheet. Place your name in the worksheet header of all three worksheets and print all three worksheets. Save the workbook as **Paws92.xls.**

FIGURE 9.42
Pampered Paws' scenarios

Changing Cells	Scenarios Typical	One	Two
D4	100	100	300
D5	266	200	100
D6	221	100	150
D7	314	300	200
D8	222	240	100

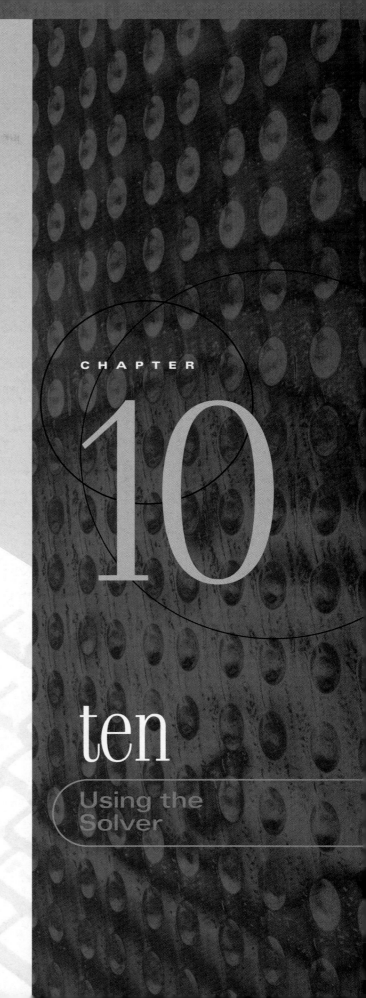

did you

know?

some *Chinese typewriters have 5,700 characters. The keyboard on some models is almost three feet wide, and the fastest someone can type on these machines is 11 words per minute.*

the *colloquial term "mackintosh" for a raincoat comes from Charles Mackintosh, the Scottish chemist who invented and patented the first practical waterproof cloth in 1823.*

the *Chinese invented eyeglasses, and Marco Polo reported seeing many pairs worn by the Chinese as early as 1275.*

there *are more telephones than people in Washington, D.C.*

the *thighbone, the strongest bone in the body, is hollow. Ounce for ounce, it has a greater pressure tolerance and bearing strength than a cast steel rod of equivalent size.*

that *a company other than Microsoft created the Solver add-in for Microsoft Excel? Read this chapter to find out the name of that company.*

Chapter Objectives

- Learn how to use Excel's goal-seeking tools to find a value from an answer formula

- Concisely formulate the goal-seeking objective

- Experiment with attaining a desired goal using trial and error

- Implement goal-seeking by using a graph

- Create goal-seeking reports

- Install the Excel Solver tool

- Use Excel's Solver to unravel more complex problems

- Identify the formula to be optimized

- Specify constraints on the problem that the Solver must satisfy

- Learn how to create Solver Answer, Limit, and Sensitivity reports

CHAPTER

10

ten

Using the
Solver

chapter case
ExerCycle

John Laskowski is an exercise enthusiast whose favorite form of exercise is to ride his bicycle on long weekend trips. John was the manager of a Chicago-area bicycle shop called Bikes4U. More than a few of John's bicycle customers commented how much they missed riding their bicycles during the often bitterly cold winter months. Although many of those customers suggested that the bicycle shop also sell stationary bicycles, Bikes4U owners wanted to maintain their focus on outdoor bikes of all types. John felt there was a big potential market in stationary bikes, so last year he left Bikes4U to open his own store and sell stationary exercise bicycles. He drew up a business plan, found several small retail locations in small shopping centers near his home, and then settled on one model of exercise bicycle that he felt would be

a best seller. In his business plan, John outlined the retail and wholesale prices of a particular exercise bike that he wanted to sell exclusively.

John needs financing to purchase a quantity of the exercise bicycles and wants your help to calculate how many bicycles he can purchase. The bank has looked over John's business plan and agreed to loan him $58,000. If his business proves to be successful over the coming months, the bank has promised him additional financing. John wants you to help him determine how many exercise bicycles he can purchase. Later, John will sell an additional exercise bicycle model and would like your help to determine the best product mix to maximize his profit. Figure 10.1 shows the completed Exercise Bicycle Data worksheet of the ExerCycle workbook.

FIGURE 10.1

Completed Exercise Bicycle Data worksheet

	A	B	C	D	E	F	G	H	I	J	
1	**Single unit information**										
2	Model	**Upright 961**	**Recumbent 268**								
3	Item retail price	$2,400	$2,555								
4	Item wholesale cost	$1,800	$1,855								
5	Item profit	$600	$700								
6											
7	Assembly time (hrs)	4.5	5.5								
8											
9	**Total production information**					Totals		Resources			
10	Number of units	14	17			31		Available	Slack		
11	Cost	$25,200	$31,535			$56,735		$58,000	$1,265		
12	Profit	$8,400	$11,900			$20,300					
13	Assembly time (hrs)	63.0	93.5			156.5		160.0	3.5		
14											
15			$20,300								
16			$2								
17			TRUE								
18			TRUE								
19			TRUE								
20			TRUE								
21			$100								
22											
23											
24											
25											

Documentation / Solver Answer Report / **Exercise Bicycle Products** /

Ready

Chapter 10 covers two sophisticated tools that work backward from a desired solution to determine the values needed to optimize the result. The first of these two tools is the Goal Seek command. The second tool is called the Solver. First, you will learn how to use the Goal Seek command to determine how many products you can purchase from a distributor given an upper limit on the loan you received from a bank. The **Goal Seek** command works backward in a worksheet to compute an unknown value that produces the final optimized result you desire. For example, suppose you want to know what score you must get on the final exam to have an overall course grade of 90 percent. With Goal Seek, you point to the cell containing the formula that computes the final percentage, indicate the *desired* final percentage you want (seek), and indicate the cell's value that Excel can manipulate to achieve the desired result. The alternative to using the goal seek technique is trial and error, which can be a long and error-prone process. Using goal-seeking methods automates the process.

Excel's Solver is a more powerful and capable tool than goal seeking. The Solver can minimize or maximize the value in the result cell by manipulating the values in more than one cell to achieve a desired end result. The Solver can answer the question "How can I allocate my limited resources (time, money, labor, or supplies) among several alternative options to achieve the best result?" Unlike the Goal Seek command, the Solver allows you to specify one or several constraints. For example, suppose you want to sell two products that have different profit margins. You can use the Solver to figure out what **product mix**, or quantities of each product to sell, will generate the greatest profit. Unlike the Goal Seek command, you do not know the amount of the profit—only that you want to create the largest profit possible. Constraints to the values that the Solver manipulates include specification that the quantity of products you sell must be whole numbers—you cannot sell a fraction of a bicycle, for instance. Another constraint the Solver must consider is the maximum amount of cash you have to purchase the products you sell. In decision analysis, the types of problems that the Solver works with are called **linear programming problems,** which involve one or more unknowns and an equal number of equations. Linear programming problems gave rise to the development of spreadsheet solvers, even though you will not need to think of these problems in terms of linear programming. You simply want the best, or optimal, solution to a multiple-variable (quantities of several products) problem from a collection of possible solutions.

SESSION 10.1 USING GOAL SEEK

In this section, you will learn how to use the Goal Seek command to solve a problem by working backward from a desired outcome. You will begin by opening a workbook, formatting and protecting a documentation worksheet, and then entering preliminary values for a product that John wants to sell. Once you have set up the values and formulas in the data portion of the workbook, you will try solving the problem by hand by substituting values into independent cells that affect the final result. Then, you will use Goal Seek to find the values that create the desired result. You will use a graphical method of goal seeking by selecting a chart element and stretching it to the outcome you want. Excel invokes the Goal Seek command to help you.

FIGURE 10.2

Design of the goal seek worksheet

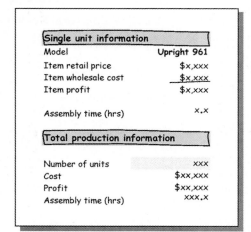

DESIGNING A GOAL-SEEKING WORKBOOK

John wants to design the goal seeking worksheet so that it has two sections. The upper section includes the exercise bicycle's name, its selling or retail price, John's cost to purchase a single exercise bike, and the profit per bike. The exercise bicycles are shipped unassembled, so John will have to assemble each bike before selling it. He wants to include the time needed to assemble each bicycle in the worksheet, even though the assembly time does not play a direct role in his calculations just yet. The lower section of the worksheet describes aggregate information about all the exercise bikes that John hopes to sell, including the total number of units for sale, their cumulative profit, their total cost, and the total time to assemble all bicycles. John has developed a rough sketch of the layout of the worksheet (see Figure 10.2).

John also wants the workbook to contain a documentation worksheet that precedes the data worksheet. It will contain the simple ExerCycle logo, the designer's name, a design date, and modification dates.

FORMATTING AND PROTECTING THE DOCUMENTATION WORKSHEET

John wants you to start by modifying the documentation worksheet, the first worksheet in the ExerCycle workbook. You will format the background color of the worksheet, change its tab name to Documentation, modify the tab's color, insert data validation into two cells to display messages, eliminate the row and column headers on the documentation worksheet, and protect the worksheet so that users can change only three cells on the documentation worksheet.

Renaming and Coloring a Worksheet Tab

First, you will rename a worksheet tab and then apply a color to it.

Opening the ExerCycle workbook and modifying the worksheet tab:

1. Start Excel as usual

2. Open the workbook **ex10ExerCycle.xls** and immediately save it as **ExerCycle2.xls** to preserve the original workbook in case you ever want to revert to it. A documentation worksheet appears

3. Right-click the **Sheet1** worksheet tab, click **Tab Color** in the shortcut menu, click the **Light Turquoise** color square (fifth row from the top, fifth column), and click **OK** to close the Format Tab Color dialog box

4. Double-click the **Sheet1** worksheet tab to select its name, type **Documentation,** and press **Enter** to rename the worksheet tab

Unlocking Selected Cells

Now that you have given the worksheet tab a meaningful name and colored it the same color as the worksheet itself, you can work with three cells that the user enters data into. You will unlock them, provide data validation, and then protect the entire worksheet. John wants any worksheet user to be able to enter his or her name in the designer cell, enter the current date, and type a modification date in cells C12, C14, and C16. A message telling the user what he or she can type into each cell is a helpful addition to the Documentation worksheet.

Unlocking data input cells:

1. Click cell **C12**

2. Press and hold the **Ctrl** key, click cells **C14** and **C16** in turn to select them, and then release the **Ctrl** key

3. Click **Format** on the menu bar, click **Cells,** click the **Protection** tab of the Format Cells dialog box, click the **Locked** check box to clear its checkmark, and click **OK** to complete the three-cell unlocking operation

Adding Simple Data Validation to Selected Cells

Next, you will supply minor data validation for the three input cells (C12, C14, and C16) on the Documentation worksheet to remind the user about what information he or she can type in the cells.

Providing data validation for the three data input cells:

1. Click cell **C12,** click **Data** on the menu bar, click **Validation,** and click the **Input Message** tab

2. Click the **Input message** text box, type the message **Type your first and last names,** and then click **OK** to close the Data Validation dialog box

3. Click cell **C14,** click **Data** on the menu bar and click **Validation**

4. Click the **Input message** text box, type the message **Type today's date (mm/dd/yy),** and then click **OK** to close the Data Validation dialog box

5. Click cell **C16,** click **Data** on the menu bar, and click **Validation**

6. Click the **Input message** text box, type the message **Press F2 and then type the latest modification date. Use a comma to separate the latest date from previous ones.** (include the terminating period), and then click **OK** to close the Data Validation dialog box (see Figure 10.3)

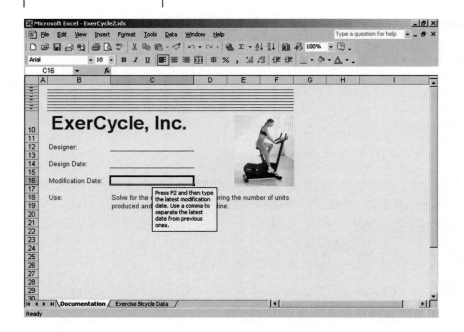

Eliminating Row and Column Headers

Spreadsheet row and column headers are not useful for this Documentation worksheet, so John wants you to eliminate them. When the user opens the ExerCycle workbook, John wants the Documentation worksheet to display cleanly without the additional clutter of the row and column headers.

Hiding a worksheet's row and column headers:

1. Click **Tools** on the menu bar, and then click **Options** (at the bottom of the menu)

2. Click the **View** tab, if necessary, and then click the **Row & column headers** check box, found in the Window options panel, to clear its checkmark (see Figure 10.4)

3. Click **OK** to complete the operation and close the Options dialog box. Excel eliminates the row and column headers from the Documentation worksheet (see Figure 10.5). Other worksheets are unaffected

Applying Worksheet Protection

The last modification to the Documentation worksheet is to engage protection so that the user cannot inadvertently alter any Documentation worksheet cells (except C12, C14, and C16). In applying protection, you will choose an option that allows the user to make active only cells that are unlocked.

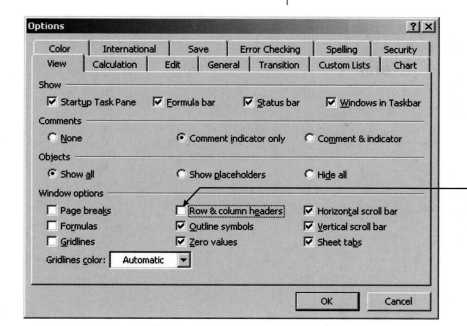

F I G U R E 10.4

Removing a worksheet's row and column headers

clear the *Row & column headers* checkbox

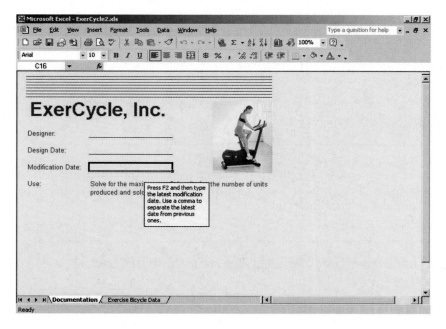

F I G U R E 10.5

Worksheet without row and column headers

Enforcing protection on the Documentation worksheet:

1. Click cell **B12** containing the label *Designer:* (observe cell address in the Name Box. It will display B12 when you click the correct cell)

2. Click **Tools** on the menu bar and point to **Protection**

3. Click **Protect Sheet.** The Protect Sheet dialog box opens

4. Click the **Select locked cells** check box, located at the top of the list of labeled check boxes, to clear its checkmark. Clearing the check box prevents users from selecting any locked cell in the worksheet (see Figure 10.6)

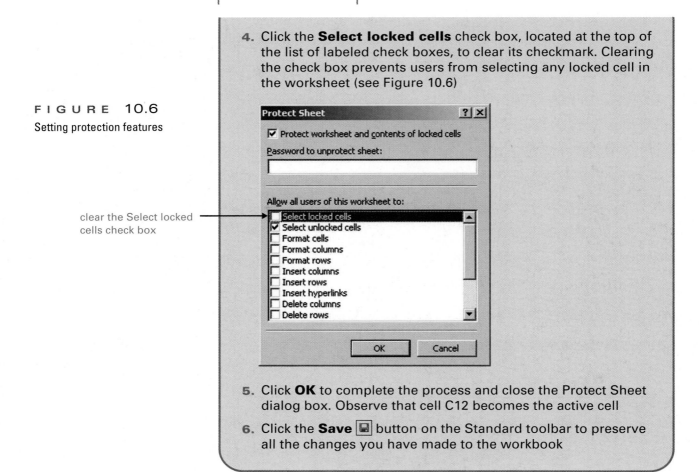

5. Click **OK** to complete the process and close the Protect Sheet dialog box. Observe that cell C12 becomes the active cell

6. Click the **Save** 🖫 button on the Standard toolbar to preserve all the changes you have made to the workbook

See the effect of exempting any locked cell on the Documentation worksheet from becoming active by following the steps below. The steps attempt to make several ineligible cells active.

Experimenting with the newly applied protection:

1. Press and release the **Tab** key four times, slowly. Notice that cells C14, C16, C12, and C14, in turn, become active. That means that you can use the Tab key to move from one unlocked cell to another, skipping locked cells

2. Using the mouse, try to click any cell in the Documentation worksheet *except* cell C12, C14, or C16. Nothing happens. The active cell remains cell C14 (assuming you executed step 1 above)

You show the newly formatted worksheet to John and illustrate how Excel enforces cell protection. John is pleased and suggests you now move to the goal-seeking worksheet to add the necessary values, labels, and formulas.

CREATING A GOAL SEEK WORKSHEET

Using the Goal Seek command, you can compute an unknown value that yields the result you want. In the case of ExerCycle, John wants to know how many exercise bicycles he can purchase with the $58,000 loan he obtained from the bank.

Entering Values and Writing Formulas

You begin building the goal seek worksheet by entering data, labels, and formulas for the upright exercise bicycle called the Upright 961.

Entering labels and values in the Exercise Bicycle Data worksheet:

1. Click the **Exercise Bicycle Data** worksheet tab to make that worksheet active

2. Click cell **B1,** click the **Bold** [B] button on the Formatting toolbar, click the **Align Right** button on the Formatting toolbar [≡], and type **Upright 961**

3. Click cell **B2** and type **2400,** which is the suggested retail price of the upright exercise bicycle

4. Click cell **B3** and type **1800,** which is John's wholesale cost

5. Click cell **B6** and type **4.5,** which is the number of hours John estimates it will take to assemble the exercise bicycle and prepare it for sale

6. Click cell **B8** and type **3,** and then press **Enter** (see Figure 10.7). Cell B8 contains John's initial estimate of the number of bicycles he will buy, assemble, and sell. Later, that value will change as John uses the Goal Seek command to determine how many bicycles he can purchase with his loan

	A	B	C	D	E	F	G	H	I	J
1	Model	Upright 961								
2	Item retail price	2400								
3	Item wholesale cost	1800								
4	Item profit									
5										
6	Assembly time (hrs)	4.5								
7										
8	Number of units	3								
9	Cost									
10	Profit									
11	Assembly time (hrs)									
12										

FIGURE 10.7

Worksheet with price, cost, and labor hours entered

The values you entered in four cells represent known constants in the worksheet that will represent John's simple business of buying, assembling, and selling a single product. Next, you write the formulas that depend on these numeric constants. The formulas include the profit on the sale of a single exercise bicycle—its item profit, total cost, total profit, and total assembly time based on the number of units John can sell. The latter formulas occupy the lower portion of the worksheet containing information about aggregate sales. John wants you to write formulas for Item profit, Number of units, Profit, Cost, and Assembly time (hrs). In addition, you will assign a name to the very important cell B8, which contains the number of units to sell. Near the end of this section, you will use the Goal Seek command to determine the value of that cell if you purchase as many bicycles as your loan allows you to buy.

Entering formulas and naming a cell:

1. Click cell **B4,** type **=B2-B3,** and press **Enter**

2. Click cell **B8,** click in the **Name Box** to the left of the Formula bar, type **UprightUnits** (no spaces), and press **Enter**

3. Click cell **B9,** type **=B3*UprightUnits,** and press **Enter.** The value 5400 appears. It is the John's total cost for the exercise bicycles

4. In cell **B10,** type **=B4*UprightUnits,** and press **Enter.** The value 1800 appears. It is the profit John will realize if he sells all the bicycles

5. In cell **B11,** type **=B6*UprightUnits,** and press **Enter.** The value 13.5 appears. That is the total number of hours needed to assemble all the bicycles (see Figure 10.8)

FIGURE 10.8

Goal seek worksheet with formulas

	A	B	C	D	E	F	G	H	I	J
1	Model	Upright 961								
2	Item retail price	2400								
3	Item wholesale cost	1800								
4	Item profit	600								
5										
6	Assembly time (hrs)	4.5								
7										
8	Number of units	3								
9	Cost	5400								
10	Profit	1800								
11	Assembly time (hrs)	13.5								
12										
13										
14										

Setting a Default Format and Formatting Individual Cells

With the basic goal seek worksheet set up, you can establish the default numeric format and then apply other formatting to dress up the worksheet. First, set the format for all numeric cells in the worksheet to currency with zero decimal places. Recall that you can select all cells in a worksheet by clicking the Select All button at the intersection of the row and column headers or by pressing Ctrl+A.

Setting a default numeric format:

1. Press **Ctrl+A** to select all the worksheet's cells

2. Click **Format** on the menu bar, click **Cells,** click the **Number** tab, click **Currency** in the Category list, type **0** in the Decimal places box, click the **Symbol** list box, click **$,** and click **OK** to close the Format Cells dialog box

3. Click cell **B3** to deselect the range

Next, you will format cell B3 with an underline and then change the format on numeric cells that are not currency values.

Underlining a cell and modifying the format of other numeric cells:

1. With cell B3 selected, click **Format** on the menu bar, click **Cells,** click the **Font** tab, click the **Underline** list box, click **Single Accounting** in the list, and click **OK**

2. Click cell **B6,** press and hold **Ctrl,** click cell **B11,** and release the **Ctrl** key

3. Click the **Comma Style** [,] button on the Formatting toolbar, and then click the **Decrease Decimal** button on the Formatting toolbar. Excel formats cells B6 and B11 by removing the currency symbols and displaying one decimal place in both cells

4. Click cell **B8,** click **Edit** on the menu bar, point to **Clear,** and click **Formats** to restore the cell to the General numeric format (see Figure 10.9)

	A	B	C	D	E	F	G	H	I	J
1	Model	Upright 961								
2	Item retail price	$2,400								
3	Item wholesale cost	$1,800								
4	Item profit	$600								
5										
6	Assembly time (hrs)	4.5								
7										
8	Number of units	3								
9	Cost	$5,400								
10	Profit	$1,800								
11	Assembly time (hrs)	13.5								
12										

FIGURE 10.9

Worksheet with numeric entries formatted

All the numeric entries are formatted in attractive ways, and values that represent currencies are obvious. John is pleased with the way the worksheet is shaping up.

Inserting Rows and Adding Section Banners

John would like you to provide visual headings about the two sections that display "Single unit information" and "Total production information" so that the sections are clearly distinguished. He wants the first heading above the label *Model* in row 1, and he wants the second heading marking the total production information just above the label *Number of units* found in cell A8. Both headings will have a fill color that matches the fill color (light turquoise) in the Documentation worksheet. You will be adding rows to accommodate the two new headings. John also wants you to highlight cell B8, which contains the number of units, with a light yellow fill color.

Inserting rows and adding section banners:

1. Click cell **A1,** click **Insert** on the menu bar, and then click **Rows.** Excel inserts a new row 1

---

*another***way**

. . . to Insert
a Row

Right-click the row
header

Click **Insert** on the
shortcut menu

2. In the empty cell A1, type **Single unit information** and press **Enter**

3. Click cell **A9,** click **Insert** on the menu bar, and then click **Rows.** Excel inserts a new row 9

4. In the empty cell A9, type **Total production information** and press **Enter**

Applying Fill Colors to Selected Cells

With the two section headings in place, you can apply fill colors to them and to cell B10 containing the number of units to sell.

Applying fill colors to selected cells:

1. Click and drag cell range **A1:B1** and click the **Fill Color button list arrow** on the Formatting toolbar to display a palette of color selections

tip: *If you click the **Fill Color** button instead of its list arrow, then click the **Undo** button on the Standard toolbar and repeat step 1*

2. Click the **Light Turquoise** color square in the fifth column of the bottom row in the Fill Color palette.

tip: *If you hover the mouse over any color square, its name appears in a ScreenTip. That ensures you are about to click the correct color square*

3. With cells A1 and B1 still selected, click the **Bold** button on the Formatting toolbar, click the **Borders** button list arrow, and then click the **Outside Borders** button to place an outline around the cell pair

4. With cells A1 and B1 still selected, click the **Format Painter** button on the Standard toolbar in preparation to paste this format on the other section heading

5. Click and drag the cell range **A9:B9.** Excel pastes all the formatting from cells A1:B1 onto the cell range A9:B9

6. Click cell **B10,** click the **Fill Color** button list arrow on the Formatting toolbar, and click the **Light Yellow** color square in the third column of the bottom row in the Fill Color palette (see Figure 10.10)

With the formatting complete and formulas in place, you are ready to use the Goal Seek command.

USING THE GOAL SEEK COMMAND

Recall that the purpose of the worksheet you are developing is to determine how many upright exercise bicycles John can purchase with his

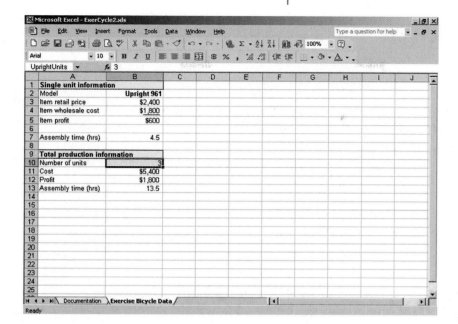

FIGURE 10.10
After applying fill colors

$58,000 loan. That is the ***goal seek objective***—the end result you want to achieve. Now that you have completed the goal seek worksheet's labels, formulas, and formatting, you can focus on the main goal: maximizing John's profit on the sale of exercise bicycles. John stops by your desk and you show him the work you have done so far on the workbook. You ask John why assembly time for each bicycle and total assembly time are part of the worksheet. He tells you that in order to figure out the maximum profit the store can generate, you must consider two constraints in his business model. (A ***constraint*** is limitation on the values that a cell can have.) As you remember, John has a loan for $58,000. That limits how many bicycles he can purchase from the manufacturer. There is another restriction that John has not mentioned yet. Because John is ExerCycle's only employee, his time is split between running the store, selling bicycles, and assembling bicycles. John figures that he has only 160 hours for assembling bicycles each month, and he wants to sell all he can in order to stay in business. He explains that if he had an unlimited supply of money and time, his profit would be enormous. However, you have to help him figure out his profit given the time and money restrictions.

You can use the trial-and-error method to see how many units John can purchase with his loan. Sometimes the solution is relatively easy to find that way. Other times, it is very difficult.

Generating Solutions by Trial and Error

One method to calculate profit John can realize from selling bicycles is to enter different numbers in cell B10, which is the quantity he purchases and sells, and then observe the values for total cost, total profit, and total assembly time. Doing this is typical what-if analysis. In other words, you can ask what-if questions by typing the value 25, then 35, and then 40 in turn into cell B10 and examining the resulting values of those substitutions. That is the traditional approach you have used so far in this textbook. Try that next.

Using what-if techniques to examine cost, profit, and assembly time values:

1. Click cell **B10,** type **25,** and press **Enter.** Cell B11 displays the profit, $15,000. Notice that the cost is $45,000, and assembly time for 25 units is 112.5 hours. Those values are both less than their constraints of $58,000 and 160 hours, respectively

2. Click cell **B10,** type **40,** and press **Enter.** Although profit has risen to $24,000, the purchase cost for 40 units is $72,000 (cell B11), exceeding the bank loan constraint of $58,000. The assembly time, 180 hours, also exceeds the available 160 hours. Figure 10.11 shows the first two analyses side by side

FIGURE   10.11

Comparing two what-if results

purchase 25 units

	A	B
1	Single unit information	
2	Model	Upright 961
3	Item retail price	$2,400
4	Item wholesale cost	$1,800
5	Item profit	$600
6		
7	Assembly time (hrs)	4.5
8		
9	Total production information	
10	Number of units	25
11	Cost	$45,000
12	Profit	$15,000
13	Assembly time (hrs)	112.5

$45,000 is less than the $58,000 loan amount

purchase 40 units

	A	B
1	Single unit information	
2	Model	Upright 961
3	Item retail price	$2,400
4	Item wholesale cost	$1,800
5	Item profit	$600
6		
7	Assembly time (hrs)	4.5
8		
9	Total production information	
10	Number of units	40
11	Cost	$72,000
12	Profit	$24,000
13	Assembly time (hrs)	180.0

$72,000 exceeds the $58,000 loan amount

3. Click cell **B10,** type **35,** and press **Enter.** Profit is $21,000. While assembly time for 35 units, 157.5 hours, is within the constraint limit, the total wholesale cost of $63,000 is still larger than the bank loan

The previous what-if analyses reveal that the number of units John can sell to maximize his profits under the constraints of time and money is between 25 units and 35 units. You could continue using this trial-and-error method, but using this method—even for this relatively simple problem—would waste a lot of time. Excel provides a better approach.

Generating a Solution with the Goal Seek Command

By using the Excel Goal Seek command, you can short-circuit the process of trying different values until you find a solution. Goal seeking starts with the end result that you want and then backtracks from the formula to a precedent value that satisfies the desired result. A **precedent value** is the value on which a formula, or result, is directly (or indirectly) based. In this case, the end result you are seeking is a total wholesale cost (cell B11) that is less than or equal to the loan amount of $58,000. The precedent value, quantity to purchase and then sell, is stored in cell B10. Excel can repeatedly change the value of the precedent value until the end result is less than or equal to the goal value you specify. Of course, total assembly time is also a constraint. However, the previous what-if analyses show that the real constraint is total wholesale cost, cell B11. The difference between what-if analysis and goal seek analysis is the way John asks the question(s). John could ask "*What* would it cost *if* I purchased 25 bicycles?"

Using goal seek analysis, the question John would pose is "If I can spend $58,000 on bicycles, how many can I purchase?" That is exactly the type of problem that the Goal Seek command solves. That is, "the result is this, so what is the independent value that I plug in to get that result?"

You can use goal seek to answer the question of how many bicycles can be purchased for $58,000. Another goal seeking question is "How many bicycles can be assembled under the time constraint of 160 hours?" Goal seek cannot answer both questions at the same time. It works to find only one precedent value at a time. You have to choose either purchase cost or assembling hours as the result and then use goal seeking to determine the maximum precedent value that satisfies either constraint.

---

task reference

Using Goal Seek

- Click **Tools** and then click **Goal Seek**

- Click the **Set cell** box and type the cell address of the result cell

- Click the **To value** box and type the result value you want

- Click the **By changing** cell box and type the address of the changing cell

- Click **OK** to solve the problem, and then click **OK** to close the Goal Seek Status dialog box

---

To use the Goal Seek command, you first identify the changing cell and the result cell. The changing cell is the precedent cell whose value Excel changes to reach the result you want. The result cell, which always contains a formula, is the cell holding your goal. In this case, the goal is cell B11 containing the formula to calculate the total purchase price. Your goal is to set this value as close to $58,000 without going over that value, which will maximize John's profit. Because goal seeking solves for one precedent value only, you have to manually ensure that other constraints are met. In other words, when you solve for the purchase quantity, Excel will ensure that the total wholesale cost does not exceed $58,000. However, you must inspect cell B13 to make sure Excel's solution does not force the assembly time above 160.

Using Goal Seek to find how many bicycles John can purchase:

1. Click **Tools** on the menu bar and then click **Goal Seek.** The Goal Seek dialog box opens

2. Drag the Goal Seek dialog box to the right so that you can see cells B10 and B11

3. Type **B11** in the *Set cell* box, and then press **Tab** to move to the *To value* box

4. In the *To value* box, type **58000** and press **Tab.** $58,000 is John's loan amount and, thus, his spending limit

5. In the *By changing cell* box, type **B10.** Cell B10 is the precedent cell that Excel can change in its attempt to reach the $58,000 cost goal. Your Goal Seek dialog box should resemble Figure 10.12

FIGURE 10.12

Completed Goal Seek dialog box

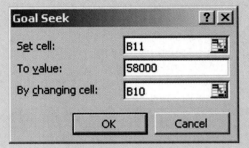

6. Click **OK** to launch the Goal Seek process. The Goal Seek Status dialog box opens and indicates that it found a solution

7. Drag the Goal Seek Status dialog box to the right so that you can see cells B10 and B11. Notice that cell B10 contains the answer, 32.22222222 bicycles (see Figure 10.13)

FIGURE 10.13

Goal Seek has found an answer

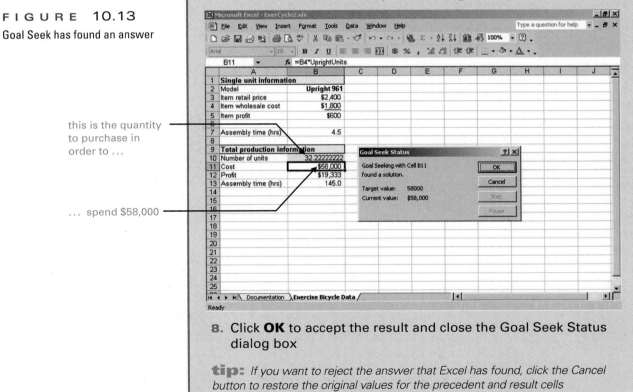

this is the quantity to purchase in order to ...

... spend $58,000

8. Click **OK** to accept the result and close the Goal Seek Status dialog box

tip: *If you want to reject the answer that Excel has found, click the Cancel button to restore the original values for the precedent and result cells*

Of course, you cannot purchase or sell a fraction of a bicycle, so you discard any fraction in the answer and settle on 32 bicycles. The value for the assembly time, 145.0 hours, is less than the available time, so that constraint is met simultaneously. If you are curious about the quantity of bicycles John could assemble in 160 hours, regardless of their cost, you can run another Goal Seek command to see the answer.

Using Goal Seek to find how many bicycles John can assemble in 160 hours:

1. Click **Tools** on the menu bar and then click **Goal Seek.** The Goal Seek dialog box opens

2. Type **B13** in the *Set cell* box, and then press **Tab** to move to the *To value* box

3. In the *To value* box, type **160** and press **Tab.** 160 is the maximum hours John has available to assemble bicycles

4. In the *By changing cell* box, type **B10.** Cell B10 is the precedent cell that Excel can change in its attempt to reach the 160-hour goal

5. Click **OK** to launch the Goal Seek process. The Goal Seek Status dialog box opens and indicates that it found a solution. Notice that cell B10 contains the answer, 35.55555556 bicycles (see Figure 10.14)

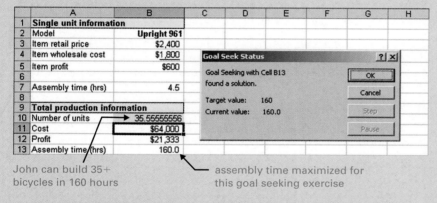

John can build 35+ bicycles in 160 hours

assembly time maximized for this goal seeking exercise

FIGURE 10.14
Goal Seek maximizes assembly hours

6. Click **OK** to accept the result and close the Goal Seek Status dialog box

Though goal seeking has demonstrated that John could assemble 35 bicycles in the allotted 160 hours, the purchase cost of 35 bicycles, $64,000, exceeds the loan amount. It is clear to you that the real constraint John will have to observe is total cash available to purchase bicycles from the manufacturer, not the labor hours available.

Graphic Goal Seeking

Excel also allows you to do goal seeking graphically. For example, you can create a simple column chart of total profit and total cost. Once you have constructed the two-column chart, you may wonder how many bicycles John would have to purchase and subsequently sell in order to have a total profit of $50,000. You can perform that goal seeking procedure by selecting the graph's profit data marker and then drag the column up to the $50,000 mark on the Y-axis. Dragging the profit data marker identifies to Excel your result value and launches the Goal Seek command. See this for yourself by creating a graph and then dragging the profit column.

Creating a simple column chart of cost and profit:

1. Select cell range **A11:B12,** click the **Chart Wizard** [chart icon] button on the Standard toolbar, click **Next,** click **Next** again, click the **Legend** tab, click the **Show legend** check box to clear it, and click **Finish.** Excel creates an embedded column chart

2. Move the chart to the right, if necessary, so that you can see both the chart and worksheet columns A and B

With the embedded chart built, you can perform goal seeking by manipulating either of the chart's columns.

Performing goal seeking by resizing a chart data marker:

1. Click the **Profit** data marker, which is the short blue bar with the label "Profit" below it, and then click the **Profit** data marker again to select just that column. Selection handles surround the Profit data marker (the second blue column in the chart)

2. Move the mouse to the large selection handle in the top middle of the data marker. The mouse changes to a double-headed arrow pointing up and down

3. Click and drag the selection handle up toward the $50,000 horizontal rule until the ScreenTip indicates that the value is approximately $50,000 (see Figure 10.15), and then release the mouse. This takes patience and a steady hand. Excel opens the Goal Seek dialog box

FIGURE   10.15

Dragging a chart's data marker to perform goal seeking

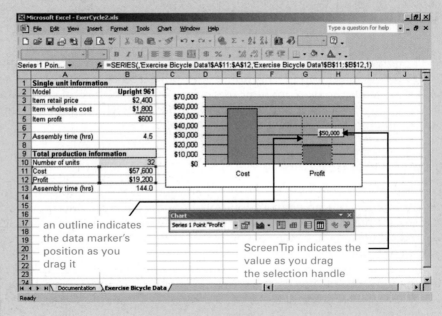

4. With the insertion point in the *By changing cell* box, type **B10**

5. If you were unable to drag the data marker to exactly $50,000, then press **Shift+Tab** to move back to the *To value* box and type **50000.** Your Goal Seek dialog box should look like the one in Figure 10.16

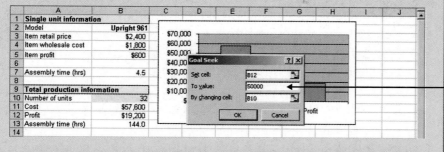

FIGURE 10.16

Goal Seek dialog box after dragging a chart data marker

To value box is set when you drag a data marker

6. Click **OK** to accept your values and cell addresses. Excel finds a solution

7. Click **OK** to accept the solution and close the Goal Seek Status dialog box (see Figure 10.17)

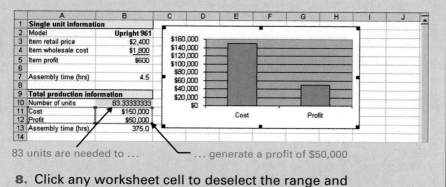

83 units are needed to . . .

. . . generate a profit of $50,000

FIGURE 10.17

Graphic goal seeking results

8. Click any worksheet cell to deselect the range and corresponding data marker in the chart

The Goal Seek command invoked through a chart indicates that John must sell more than 83 exercise bicycles to yield a profit of $50,000.

Deleting the chart and restoring the number of units to its original value:

1. Click the **Chart Area** (the white area near the outermost rectangle surrounding the chart) to select the embedded chart, and then press the **Delete** key. Excel removes the chart

2. Click cell **B10,** type **32,** and press **Enter**

John is pleased with your results and can see that he can purchase enough bicycles with his first round of financing to start his business with sufficient stock. You are ready to save, print, and close the ExerCycle workbook.

Printing, saving, and closing the ExerCycle workbook:

1. Type your first and last names in the Exercise Bicycle Data worksheet header (any section: left, center, or right)

2. Click the **Documentation** worksheet tab, click **C12** next to the Designer label, type your first and last names, press **Tab,** type today's date, and press **Enter**

3. Click **File,** click **Print,** click the **Entire workbook** option button in the Print what section, and click **OK.** Excel prints both worksheets in your workbook

4. Click **File** on the menu bar and then click **Exit**

5. Click the **Yes** button when Excel asks you if you want to save the changes you made to **ExerCycle2.xls.** Excel saves your workbook and exits

---

SESSION 10.1

making the grade

1. Goal seeking works backward from the _____ to determine an answer.

2. A goal seek _____ is another name for the result you want to achieve.

3. In goal seeking, a _____ limits the values that a cell can have.

4. The _____ value is the value on which a formula, or result, is directly (or indirectly) based.

5. Make the following modifications to the ExerCycle worksheet. Open **ExerCycle2.xls** and save it as **ExerCycle210.xls.** Change cell B4, the item wholesale cost, to $1950. Type **3** in cell **B10,** the initial number of units to purchase and sell. In cell **B7,** type **6.5** to change the per unit assembly time. Using the Goal Seek command, determine the number of units John can purchase if he were to get a loan for $74,000. Print the result. Using the Goal Seek command, determine the number of units John must sell in order to realize a profit of $94,500. Print the result.

SESSION 10.2 SOLVING COMPLEX PROBLEMS

In this section, you will learn how to install the Solver tool and how to use the Solver to determine a solution to a more complex problem involving multiple products and multiple constraints. You will use the Solver to decide the best combination of exercise bicycle products to sell in order to maximize profits. You will learn about the three Solver reports: Answer, Limit, and Sensitivity.

INTRODUCING THE PROBLEM

Recently, John received a letter from Biking Industries, the manufacturer from whom John purchases the Upright 961 exercise bicycle. In the letter, Biking Industries' vice president of marketing informed John that one of the recumbent exercise bicycles they manufacture is on sale for the next three months. John can purchase the recumbent bicycle, called the Recumbent 268, at the wholesale price of $1,855. Its suggested retail price is $2,555. John wants to offer more than one exercise bicycle for sale to give customers more choice and so that his sales success does not depend on one exercise bicycle alone. He tells you that the bank is not willing to increase the loan amount from its original $58,000. Thus, John will have to determine how many of each type of exercise bicycle he can purchase for $58,000. You ask John about assembly time for the recumbent model. He asks you to call the manufacturer and find out an estimate of the time it takes to assemble the Recumbent 268.

You find out from Biking Industries that the estimated assembly time for the Recumbent 268, assuming an experienced person is performing the work, is 5.5 hours. That is an hour more than the assembly time for the Upright 961, but the recumbent model is slightly more complex than the upright version.

The data you have learned here, though relatively simple, illustrates the type of problem that you encounter frequently in business. John wants to maximize total profit selling the two bicycles, yet he is restricted by both time and money. Time and money are the problem's constraints—time to assemble the bicycles and the total amount he can spend to acquire the disassembled exercise bicycles. You can't help but wonder exactly how many of each type of exercise bicycle John should sell in order to maximize his profits.

INTRODUCING THE SOLVER

The Goal Seek command is suitable for problems that involve an exact result value that depends on one precedent value. For more complex problems, the Solver is your best choice. You can use the Solver for *equation-solving* in which you use goal seeking or back solving like the Goal Seek command and *constrained optimization* in which you specify a set of constraints and an outcome or result that you want optimized (minimized or maximized). Unlike the Goal Seek command, the Solver can change the value of several cells at once, not just one, to reach the desired final result.

What applications use the Solver? Most often, the Solver is the tool of choice when you need to solve a resource allocation problem. A *resource allocation problem* is one in which productive resources (people, raw materials, time, and so on) can be used in a variety of places or in different products, and in which those resources must be distributed in the best way possible. "Best" usually implies minimizing costs, maximizing profits, or reducing risk to a very low level. For example, a Solver could solve for the best allocation of a fixed number of labor hours between multiple products manufactured by a company. Similarly, the Solver could determine how many of each of several products to sell to maximize profit, which is a *product mix* problem. Determining the best way to ship a variety of packages across different available routes to destination warehouses is another example of a problem that the Solver can disentangle.

Solver problems involve precedent cells, also known as decision variables, and an objective function. Excel's Solver can change decision variables to cause changes in the **object function,** which is the cell containing a function whose value you want to optimize and whose value is affected by a change in the decision variables.

The Solver is an Excel add-in, which means that it might not be available in the Tools menu. An **add-in** is a specialized feature of Excel that not everyone uses on a regular basis. Therefore, it is not necessarily included automatically as one of the available programs on the Tools menu. To see whether or not you have Solver installed, look in the Tools menu. If Solver is not in the menu, you can install it easily by following installation steps provided in this chapter.

Microsoft did not develop the Microsoft Excel Solver. Instead, Frontline Systems, headquartered in Incline Village, Nevada, first produced it for Microsoft after winning a competition among third-party solver developers in 1990. Frontline Systems has continued to work with Microsoft to supply the enhanced Solver add-in that is available for Excel XP.

INSTALLING THE SOLVER

In order to work with the steps in this session, you need the Excel Solver. First, determine if the Solver is installed on the computer you are using.

Determining if the Solver Add-in is installed on your computer:

1. Start Excel as usual. Excel opens and displays a new workbook and empty worksheet

2. Click **Tools** on the menu bar

3. Scan the Tools command list for "Solver . . ." If present, Solver is about two-thirds of the way down the list of commands— just after the Formula Auditing command

4. Press the **Esc** key to close the Tools menu

If the Solver command is not in the Tools menu, the Solver Add-in was not installed when Excel was installed. Check with your instructor to ensure that it is okay to install the Solver. If so, execute the following steps to install the Solver. If the Solver is installed in Excel, skip the next steps labeled "Installing the Solver on your computer."

Installing the Solver on your computer:

1. Click **Tools** on the menu bar and then click **Add-Ins.** The Add-Ins dialog box opens

2. Click the **Solver Add-in** check box to place a checkmark in it (see Figure 10.18)

3. Click **OK** to add the Solver to the Tools menu and close the Add-Ins dialog box

4. Click **Tools** on the menu bar and locate Solver in the list of commands

5. Press **Esc** to close the Tools menu

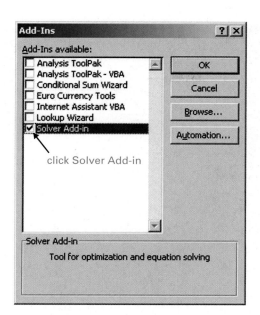

FIGURE 10.18
Adding the Solver to the Tools menu

FORMULATING THE PROBLEM CONCISELY

With the Solver available in the Tools menu, you can turn your attention to examining the problem and reviewing a worksheet partially set up to solve the problem. John has created a revised worksheet with formatting already established so that you can focus on solving the asset allocation problem at hand. Begin by opening the product mix workbook and saving it under a new name.

Opening the product mix worksheet, examining it, and saving it under a new name:

1. Open the workbook **ex10ExerCycleMix.xls** and immediately save it as **ExerCycleMix2.xls** to preserve the original workbook. The Documentation worksheet appears displaying a picture of the Recumbent 268 exercise bicycle (see Figure 10.19)

2. Click cell **C12,** if necessary, to make it active. Cell C12 is the cell to the right of the label *Designer*

tip: *Remember that the cell address of the active cell appears in the Name Box to the left of the Formula bar*

3. Type your first and last names in cell C12 and then press **Tab** to move to the next unlocked cell in the worksheet, cell C14

4. Type today's date and then press **Tab** to move to cell C16

5. Press **F2,** type a comma and a space, type today's date, and then press **Enter.** Cell C12 becomes active

6. Click the **Exercise Bicycle Products** worksheet tab to make that worksheet active. The retail prices, costs, and item profits for the two exercise bicycles are filled in already (see Figure 10.20)

FIGURE 10.19

Documentation worksheet of the product mix workbook

Photo courtesy of Precor, Inc.

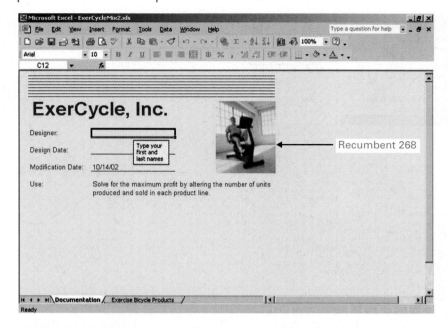

FIGURE 10.20

Exercise Bicycle Products worksheet

product unit cost and price information

aggregate production information about multiple units of both products

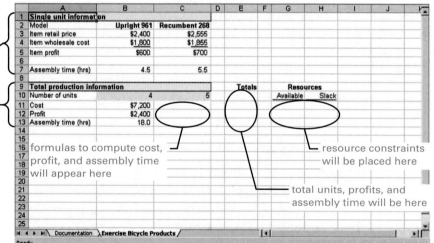

The Exercise Bicycle Products worksheet is similar in structure to the Exercise Bicycle Data worksheet of the goal-seeking workbook you completed in the last session. The main difference is that there are two product columns, columns B and C. Similar to the previous goal-seeking worksheet, the Exercise Bicycle Products worksheet contains data about a single unit in the upper half of the worksheet and aggregate information in the lower half of the worksheet—beginning in row 9.

John has asked you to complete the formulas and values for three areas highlighted in Figure 10.20. First, you are to write formulas for the total cost, total profit, and total assembly time for the Recumbent 268—cells C11 through C13. Then, you can fill in row totals in the cell range E10:E13 that will display the total units purchased and sold, the total cost, total profit, and total assembly time. Finally, you can fill in the resource restrictions in cells G11 and G13 as well as the accompanying formulas for slack in cells H11 and H13. **Slack** is the quantity of a resource that has not been used or allocated. A synonym for slack is "unused," but *slack* is the term you will most often see in applications like this one.

You are ready to write the missing equations and values to complete the worksheet prior to applying the Solver.

Writing formulas for the recumbent exercise bicycle:

1. Click cell **C10** and observe the Name Box. Notice that part of a cell name appears there. The name, RecumbentUnits, refers to cell C10 so that any reports you create will include that name. Using a name can help you quickly identify the quantity cells so important to this analysis

2. Click cell **C11**, type **=C4*RecumbentUnits,** and press **Enter.** The formula calculates the total cost of recumbent exercise bicycles, $9,275 in this case, by multiplying the cost per unit by the number of units purchased

3. In cell C12, type **=C5*RecumbentUnits** and press **Enter.** Excel calculates the total profit and displays $3,500

4. In cell C13, type **=C7*RecumbentUnits** and press **Enter.** Excel calculates the total assembly time for five recumbent exercise bicycles, which is 27.5 hours (see Figure 10.21)

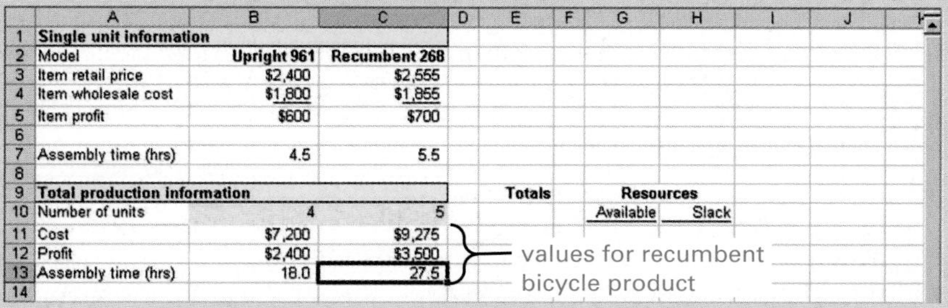

	A	B	C	D	E	F	G	H	I	J	
1	Single unit information										
2	Model	Upright 961	Recumbent 268								
3	Item retail price	$2,400	$2,555								
4	Item wholesale cost	$1,800	$1,855								
5	Item profit	$600	$700								
6											
7	Assembly time (hrs)	4.5	5.5								
8											
9	Total production information					Totals		Resources			
10	Number of units	4	5					Available	Slack		
11	Cost	$7,200	$9,275								
12	Profit	$2,400	$3,500								
13	Assembly time (hrs)	18.0	27.5								
14											

values for recumbent bicycle product

FIGURE 10.21
Recumbent exercise bicycle aggregate values displayed

You show John the recumbent bicycle formulas and calculated results that are based on the assumption that John will purchase, assemble, and then sell five recumbent bicycles. An important series of formulas are the totals you will place into the cell range E10:E13. The values total the number of units purchased and sold, cost, profit, and assembly time. Two of those totals, total number of units and total assembly time, are especially important. They will help you determine the best product mix based on the allocation of limited resources. You enter the totals next.

Writing formulas to sum values for all products:

1. Select the cell range **E10:E13**

2. Click the **AutoSum** button on the Standard toolbar. Excel places SUM functions in cells E10 through E13 that sum the partial rows to the left of each SUM function. (Notice that cell E12 is formatted to display results in boldface)

3. Click cell **E10** and then examine the Formula bar. Notice the summed cell range, B10:D10, includes the extra cell D10 (see Figure 10.22)

FIGURE 10.22

Product summation formulas completed

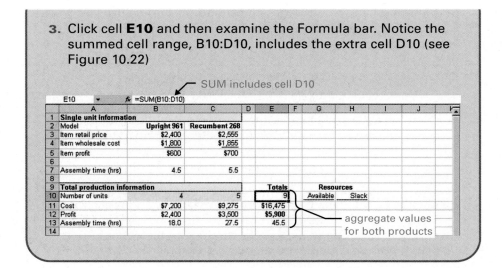

Normally the extra cell in a sum formula would be a problem. In this case, it is a feature. If John ever asks you to insert a column to accommodate another product, you would click the column D header and then insert a column. For example, if you insert one new product column, creating a new column D, Excel pushes the narrow column D to the right and it becomes column E. Excel automatically adjusts the range of cells in all SUM functions by one column. The SUM function in cell F10 is adjusted to =SUM(B10:E10), which automatically includes any newly inserted product columns. The only caveat is that you should keep the narrow column (D in this case) empty.

The only formulas and values needed to complete the Exercise Bicycle Products worksheet prior to using the Solver are the constraints. Part of formulating the problem correctly is knowing all the problem's constraints and stating them precisely in a worksheet. Recall that the constraints, or limitations, are the number of assembly hours available and the cash (loan amount) available to purchase the bicycles. You will enter the total cash available into cell G11 and the total assembly hours into cell G13. In cells H11 and H13, you will enter a simple formula that shows the slack available. Prior to executing the Solver, slack resources will be equal to the total available resources. Once the Solver has completed its work, the slack resources will be the available resources minus the used resources. Execute the following steps to complete the Resources section of the worksheet.

Entering the available resources values (constraints):

1. Click cell **G11,** which is in the same row as total cost, type **58000,** and press **Enter.** That amount is the total available to purchase bicycles

2. Click cell **G13,** type **160,** and press **Enter.** John has available a total of 160 hours of assembly time

Next, enter formulas that indicate how much of the resources remain after they are allocated to building the bicycles. Initially the slack values are equal to the available resources because the resources are uncon-sumed. When you employ the Solver, the values for slack resources should decline. In an ideal situation, you have exactly the resources needed for an optimal outcome, and the values for *all* slack resources are zero. That is, all resources would be completely consumed with no inventory or idle time remaining. In reality, this rarely occurs for all resources.

Next, write the formulas to compute slack values, which are the total available resources minus the consumed resources—represented by totals in column E for total cost and total assembly time.

Entering formulas for slack resources:

1. Click cell **H11,** type **=G11-E11,** and press **Enter.** The value $41,525 appears and indicates that building 4 upright and 5 recumbent exercise bicycles leaves $41,525 available for purchasing more bicycles

2. Click cell **H13,** type **=G13-E13,** and press **Enter.** The slack hours available for building additional bicycles, 114.5, appears (see Figure 10.23)

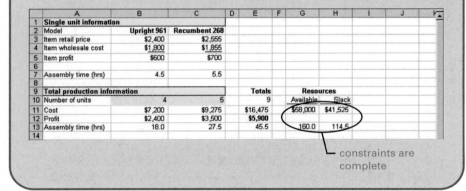

constraints are complete

FIGURE 10.23

Worksheet with constraints complete

SOLVING MORE DIFFICULT PROBLEMS USING TRIAL AND ERROR

You have helped John create a worksheet in which you will be able to find the combination of upright and recumbent bicycles to sell that will maxi-mize John's profit and stay within the cost and assembly time limitations. As with goal seek problems, you can solve more complex problems with multiple constraints using trial and error. What are the precedent values, or variables, that you can alter in your attempt to maximize profit? The two main precedent values are the number of units of each type of exercise bicycle that are stored in cells B10 and C10. Those cells contain the what-if values you can manipulate in an attempt to achieve maximum profit (cell E12) while not violating any of the resource constraints.

In the next steps, you will enter different values for the *Number of units* and then note the total profit and the slack values. Carefully examine each of the slack values to ensure that none of them becomes negative. Negative resources indicate a solution is not feasible. That is, you cannot use re-sources you do not have. Finally, you will graph the results to see if you can detect a pattern.

EXCEL

Entering various quantities and searching for an optimal solution:

1. Select the cell range cell **B10:C10,** the two precedent cells upon which both profit and slack formulas depend. You will continue to search for a feasible solution by entering values and pressing Enter repeatedly

2. Type **10,** press **Enter,** type **12,** and press **Enter.** In this scenario, you propose that John sells 10 upright bicycles and 12 recumbent bicycles. Total profit is $14,400 and there are positive slack values for resources

3. Type **18,** press **Enter,** type **20,** and press **Enter.** Total profit is $24,800, which is better than the previous scenario. However, both the cost and assembly slack values are negative, which means the procedure requires more resources than you have available (see Figure 10.24)

FIGURE 10.24

Infeasible solution

negative cost indicates a cost overrun

	A	B	C	D	E	F	G	H	I	J	
4	Item wholesale cost	$1,800	$1,855								
5	Item profit	$600	$700								
6											
7	Assembly time (hrs)	4.5	5.5								
8											
9	Total production information						Totals		Resources		
10	Number of units	18	20				38		Available	Slack	
11	Cost	$32,400	$37,100				$69,500		$58,000	($11,500)	
12	Profit	$10,800	$14,000				$24,800				
13	Assembly time (hrs)	81.0	110.0				191.0		160.0	(31.0)	
14											

negative assembly hours indicates more time used than is available

4. Type **20,** press **Enter,** type **12,** and press **Enter.** The total profit is $20,400 and the assembly slack time is positive—some assembly time is still available—but the slack value for cost (cell H11) is negative $260. This is an infeasible solution because it would require additional cash

5. Type **4,** press **Enter,** type **5,** and press **Enter** to return the purchase quantities back to their original values

6. Click any cell to deselect the two-cell cell range

You have tried three pairs of numbers and found two solutions that would work, but did you find the best solution? Looking at the answer, you can't help but wonder if the proposed solution of 10 upright and 12 recumbent units is the best solution. The Excel Solver can answer that question for you. It is designed to help you solve constrained optimization problems like this.

USING THE SOLVER

Excel's Solver attempts to find the best solution for the optimization problem. You identify to the Solver the object function (or target cell), the precedent cells (or changing cells), and all constraints that apply to the problem. Solver then goes to work to find the maximum or minimum value for the object function by changing the precedent cells' values. The solution must satisfy all specified constraints, such as a limit on resources. In this case, the constraints are the upper limit on funds available to purchase unassembled exercise bicycles and the total number of hours available to assemble them.

First, make sure you understand how to identify all the important cells that the Solver will either examine or alter. The object function is total profit whose result appears in cell E12. It is a simple expression that sums the profits of the two bicycles.

The precedent cells, which the Solver can change in its search for an optimal solution, are cells B10 and C10. Those are the same cells you modified in your manual search for a solution to the product mix that optimized profit.

The only two constraints for this problem are values, not formulas, found in cells G11 and G13. Cell G11 contains the maximum total cost of all products, $58,000, that John can purchase, and cell G13 holds the maximum hours available for product assembly—160 hours.

With all of the important components identified, you can set up Excel's solver and then have it determine a solution.

---

task reference

Using the Solver

- Click **Tools** and then click **Solver**

- In the *Set Target Cell* box, type the address of the cell containing the objective function

- Click one of the **Equal To** option buttons and, if necessary, type a value in the *Value of* box

- In the *By Changing Cells* box, type the cell addresses of all cells that Excel can change

- Click the **Add** button to add constraints to the Subject to the Constraints box

- Click the **Solve** button to create a solution

- Click the **OK** button

John urges you to begin the process of solving for maximum profit by using the Solver.

Opening the Solver Parameters dialog box to enter parameters:

1. Click **Tools** on the menu bar and then click **Solver.** The Solver Parameters dialog box opens

2. Click the **Set Target Cell** box and type **E12.** Cell E12 contains the object function, total profit

3. If necessary, click the **Max** option button to indicate to the Solver that you want to maximize the value in cell E12

---

4. Click the **Solver Parameters dialog box title bar** and drag the dialog box so that it is below row 13 of your worksheet and you can see all of the occupied cells in rows 9 through 13

5. Click the **By Changing Cells** box and click and drag the cell range **B10:C10** to select the two changing cells (see Figure 10.25)

FIGURE 10.25

Partially complete Solver Parameters dialog box

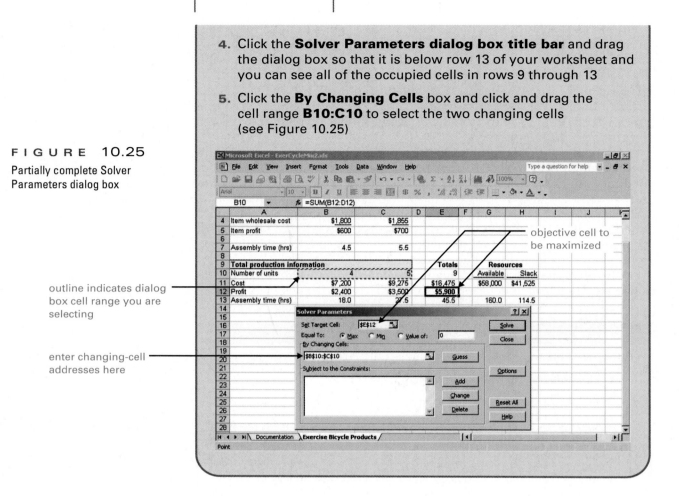

outline indicates dialog box cell range you are selecting

enter changing-cell addresses here

Now you are ready to have Solver look for a solution. John wants the right mix of products to maximize profit.

Solving for maximum profit:

1. Click the **Solve** button on the Solver Parameters dialog box. Solver quickly solves the problem. After a short time, Solver opens the Solver Results dialog box with a message "Set Cell values do not converge" (see Figure 10.26). Notice the enormous number of units in cell E10—over 465 million bicycles!

2. Click the **Cancel** button in the Solver Results dialog box to discard the proposed solution and restore the worksheet cells to their original values

The Solver issued the error message shown above because it has no constraints. The Solver calculated the obvious answer to maximizing profits: Build a few billion bicycles!

The Solver attempts to solve the problem by repeatedly substituting values for the changing cells and examining the target cell value. After a large number of substitutions, the Solver recognizes that it is not getting

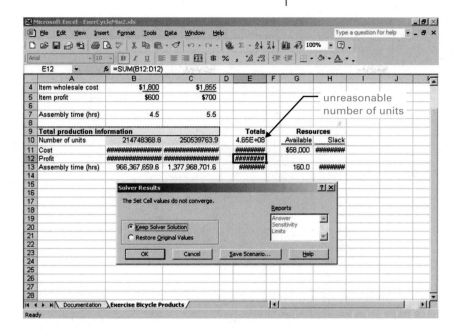

FIGURE 10.26
Solver warning that it cannot generate a solution

any closer to a solution. It halts and issues the error message you see above. To reach a feasible solution, you have to specify constraints.

Adding Constraints

With the target cell and changing cells identified, you next identify the problem's constraints. One constraint is that the total amount available to purchase exercise bicycles—the wholesale purchase amount—is $58,000. That value you placed in cell G11. Cell E11 contains a formula that calculates the total cost of all bicycles to be purchased. You express the constraint that the purchase price must be less than $58,000 by writing an expression, called an *inequality*, this way:

    E11 <= G11

The second and final constraint is that the total assembly time (cell E13) must be less than 160 hours (cell G13). Just as above, you write the second constraint as an inequality too. The inequality is:

    E13 <= G13

You express all Solver constraints by clicking the Add button in Solver Parameters dialog box and then writing the constraint expression. You can add as many constraints as you need.

Entering Solver constraints:

1. Click **Tools** on the menu bar and then click **Solver.** The Solver Parameters dialog box opens and displays the same Set Target Cell, E12, as you set in steps above

2. Click the **Add** button in the *Subject to the Constraints* panel. The Add Constraint dialog box opens

3. Type **E11,** the total value of all bicycles purchased, in the Cell Reference box

4. Click the **Constraint** list box in the center of the Add Constraint dialog box, and then click **<=** in the list

5. Click the **Constraint** box and type **G11** to establish the upper limit of $58,000 (see Figure 10.27)

FIGURE 10.27
Adding a spending constraint

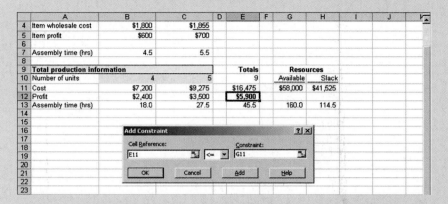

	A	B	C	D	E	F	G	H	I	J	K
4	Item wholesale cost	$1,800	$1,855								
5	Item profit	$600	$700								
6											
7	Assembly time (hrs)	4.5	5.5								
8											
9	Total production information				Totals		Resources				
10	Number of units	4	5		9		Available	Slack			
11	Cost	$7,200	$9,275		$16,475		$58,000	$41,525			
12	Profit	$2,400	$3,500		$5,900						
13	Assembly time (hrs)	18.0	27.5		45.5		160.0	114.5			

Add Constraint
Cell Reference: E11   <=   Constraint: G11
OK   Cancel   Add   Help

tip: *Although you could type 58000 in the Constraint cell, it is better to type a cell reference or a cell name. That way, you can change a constraint by typing a new value in a cell. Next, you will add the second and last constraint that limits the total assembly time to a value less than or equal to 160 hours*

6. Click the **Add** button in the Add Constraint dialog box. The Solver stores the first constraint and then clears the list and text boxes in preparation for you to enter another constraint

7. In the Cell Reference box, type **E13.** Cell E13 contains the total assembly used, so far, to build the bicycles

8. If necessary, click the **Constraint** list box in the center of the Add Constraint dialog box, and then click the **<=** relational operator in the list

9. Click the **Constraint** box and type **G13** to establish the upper limit of 160 hours

10. Click **OK** to close the Add Constraint dialog box and return to the Solver Parameters dialog box (see Figure 10.28)

FIGURE 10.28
Solver Parameters dialog box with newly added constraints

target cell, whose value is to be maximized

Solver Parameters
Set Target Cell: $E$12
Equal To: ● Max ○ Min ○ Value of: 0
By Changing Cells:
changing cells — $B$10:$C$10   Guess
Subject to the Constraints:
two constraints — $E$11 <= $G$11
$E$13 <= $G$13
Add   Change   Delete
Solve   Close   Options   Reset All   Help

The constraints that you just specified appear in the *Subject to the Constraints* text box. Notice that Excel uses absolute cell references. Had you named the cells that are involved in the constraints, their names would appear instead of their cell references.

If your constraints do not match Figure 10.28, you can delete the incorrect one(s) and then click the Add button to enter the correct restraints. Instead of typing a cell reference in the Add Constraints dialog box, you can simply point to the cell by clicking it. The Solver will automatically fill in the absolute cell reference or the cell name when you click a worksheet cell. Move the Add Constraint dialog box, if needed, to reveal the cell you want to click, or click the Collapse Dialog box button to reduce it to a title bar, and then click the cell whose address you want in the Cell Reference or Constraint text box.

With the target cell, changing cells, and constraints specified, the Solver is ready to attempt to solve the problem. Keep in mind what it is you want: the product mix that yields the maximum profit given the limited supply of money and assembly time.

Generating a solution using the Solver:

1. Click the **Solve** button on the Solver Parameters dialog box. The Solver reports that it has found a solution and that all constraints and optimality conditions are satisfied (see Figure 10.29)

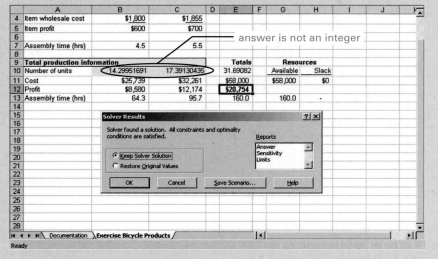

2. If the Solver Results dialog box obscures part of the active worksheet, drag the dialog box out of the way. Leave it open so that you can use it in the steps that follow

FIGURE 10.29

Solver produces a solution

Insisting on Positive Integer Answers

Notice that cells H11 and H13 indicate that all of the resources are completely used. There are exactly zero dollars left (cell H11) and the assembly process has consumed precisely 160 hours (cell H13). The maximized profit, displayed in cell E12, is $20,754. What product mix of upright and recumbent bicycles yields that profit? Cells B10 and C10 contain the answer. They indicate that John must assemble and sell 14.29951691 Upright 961 bicycles and 17.39130435 Recumbent 268 bicycles to maximize profit. However, there's a problem with the answers. You cannot assemble a fraction of an exercise bicycle.

Occasionally, the Solver will make changing cells negative and arrive at an answer. Negative values for production quantities are rarely an acceptable way to solve an optimization problem. You add constraints that prevent the Solver from generating solutions that are either negative or contain fractional values.

> ### Constraining changing cell values to positive numbers:
>
> 1. Click the **Restore Original Values** option, and then click **OK** to close the Solver Results dialog box and restore the original worksheet values
>
> 2. Click **Tools** on the menu bar, click **Solver,** and then click the **Add** button in the *Subject to the Constraints* panel. The Add Constraint dialog box opens
>
> 3. With the insertion point in the Cell Reference box, click and drag the worksheet cell range **B10:C10.** Excel enters $B$10:$C$10 in the Cell Reference box
>
> 4. Click the **Constraint** list box in the middle of the dialog box, and then click the **>=** choice in the list
>
> 5. Click the **Constraint** box and type **0.** This constraint indicates that you will only accept values for the changing cells that are greater than zero (see Figure 10.30)

FIGURE 10.30

Limiting changing cells to positive values

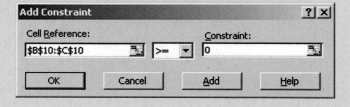

Finally, you limit the changing cell values to integer numbers, because John can only assemble whole bicycles.

> ### Constraining changing cell values to integers:
>
> 1. Click the **Add** button to add the previously created constraints and clear the Add Constraint boxes for the next entry
>
> 2. With insertion point in the Cell Reference box, type **B10:C10**
>
> 3. Click the **Constraint** list box in the middle of the dialog box, and then click the **int** choice in the list. (*Int* is an abbreviation for integer and forces the Solver to return solutions that are whole numbers)
>
> 4. Click **OK** to save this constraint and close the Add Constraint dialog box. The Solver Parameters dialog box reappears (see Figure 10.31)

changing cells must be integer values

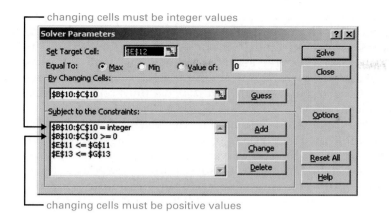

Solver Parameters dialog box
with additional constraints

changing cells must be positive values

Your constraints should match those shown in Figure 10.31. If an individual constraint does not match, delete it and then insert the correct constraint expression.

---

task reference

Deleting a Solver Constraint

- Click **Tools** and then click **Solver**
- Click the constraint you want to delete
- Click the **Delete** button

If you were to create a scatter chart with two lines showing the cost and assembly hours constraint, it would look like Figure 10.32. The Y-axis is the number of recumbent bicycles that John can purchase and assemble, and the X-axis is the number of upright exercise bicycles that John can purchase and assemble. The blue line represents the assembly hours constraint, and the red line represents the cost constraint. Observe where the red line—the cost constraint—intersects the Y-axis. That chart point

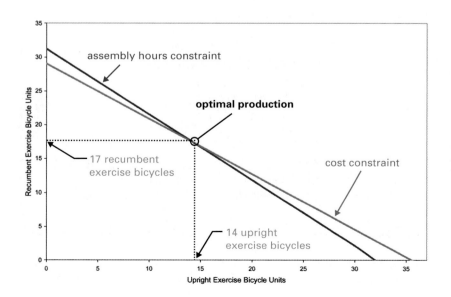

F I G U R E   10.32

Chart showing optimal product mix with constraints

EXCEL

indicates that John could build 29 recumbent exercise bicycles and zero upright exercise bicycles—based on the cost constraint alone. Look at the point where the assembly hours constraint line intersects the X-axis. The data point indicates that under the assembly hours constraint, John has time to assemble approximately 32 upright exercise bicycles and zero recumbent bicycles. Other points on either of the cost lines represent mixtures of both bicycles.

The smallest chart area that is bounded by the assembly line, the cost line, the X-axis, and the Y-axis represents product mix data points that are feasible. The point in which the two curves cross represents the optimal product mix. The dashed line from the crossover point to the X-axis shows the optimal number of upright units subject to both constraints, while the horizontal dashed line from the optimal production point to the Y-axis shows the optimal number of recumbent units subject to both constraints.

While graphic solutions are a convenient way to visualize a solution, the Solver does a faster job of determining the optimal product mix under the constraints you have set forth.

FIGURE 10.33

Solver finds a suitable product mix

Solving the product mix problem with corrected restraints in place:

1. Click the **Solve** button in the Solver Parameters dialog box. The Solver returns an answer with positive integer values for the changing cells B10 and C10 (see Figure 10.33). The Solver determines that John should build and sell 14 upright bicycles and 17 recumbent bicycles

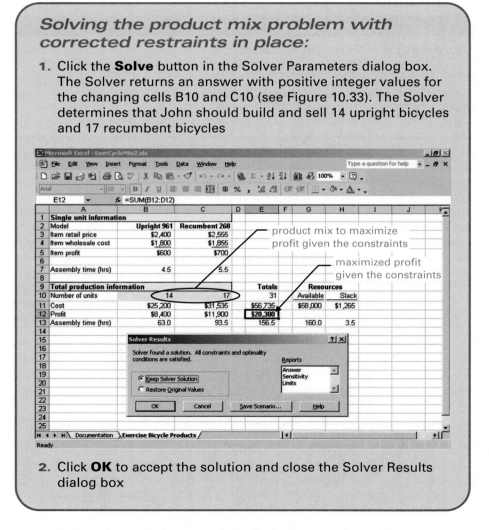

2. Click **OK** to accept the solution and close the Solver Results dialog box

You show the worksheet to John, who happens to be walking past your desk as you complete the preceding exercise. He's very happy and notices that his $58,000 covers his wholesale cost to purchase the exercise bicycles with $1,265 to spare. The total assembly time is 156.5 hours, which is just under the maximum allowed of 160 hours.

John is concerned about saving the Solver parameters in case he wants to rerun the Solver or even try out different constraints. He asks you to investigate how to do this.

SAVING SOLVER PARAMETERS

When you save a workbook after using the Solver, Excel saves all the values you specify in the Solver Parameters dialog box along with the workbook. Therefore, you do not need to reenter the Solver parameters if you want to work with the Solver later. Each worksheet can store one set of Solver Parameter values. Conversely, a worksheet cannot store more than one set of Solver parameters. In order to save more than one set of Solver parameters within a worksheet, you must use the Solver's Save Model option.

Although John does not anticipate that the constraints or any other Solver parameters will change, he asks you to save the current Solver Parameters values so that either you or he can investigate other constraints and find alternative product mix solutions.

---

task reference

Saving Solver Parameters

- Click **Tools** and then click **Solver**

- Click **Options** and then click **Save Model**

- Select an empty cell range into which Excel can store the Solver's parameters, and then click **OK**

- Click **Cancel** in the Solver Options dialog box, and then click **Close**

Saving Solver parameters and naming the saved parameters:

1. Click **Tools** on the menu bar and then click **Solver.** The Solver Parameters dialog box opens and displays the parameters you established earlier

2. Click the **Options** button. The Solver Options dialog box opens (see Figure 10.34)

3. Click the **Save Model** button. The Save Model dialog box opens and prompts you for a cell range in which to store the Solver parameters in the worksheet

4. Click cell **C15,** because that cell is empty as are the cells below it, and then click **OK.** Excel stores parameter values in the cell range C15:C21. Then the Solver Options dialog box reappears

5. Click **Cancel** to close the Solver Options dialog box, and then click the **Close** button to close the Solver Parameters dialog box. Solver parameters are saved (see Figure 10.35)

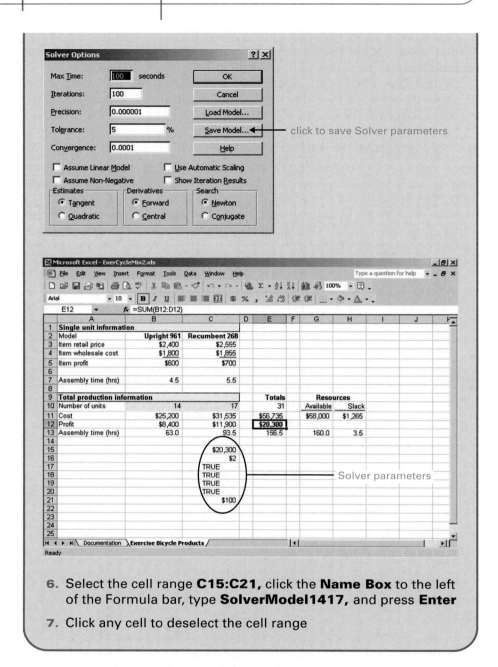

6. Select the cell range **C15:C21,** click the **Name Box** to the left of the Formula bar, type **SolverModel1417,** and press **Enter**

7. Click any cell to deselect the cell range

CREATING REPORTS WITH THE SOLVER

In addition to printing out the worksheet, John wants you to produce an answer report—one of three reports available with the Solver.

The Solver allows you to create three types of reports that you can analyze to better understand the results that the Solver has created. The three reports are the answer report, sensitivity report, and limits report. An *answer report*, the most popular and useful of the three reports, lists the target cell, the changing cells with their original and final values, constraints, and data about the constraints. The most useful part of an answer report lists the constraints and indicates which constraints are binding and the amount of slack in the constraints that are not binding. A *sensitivity report* tells how sensitive the current solution is to changes in the adjustable cells. A *limit report* displays the range of values that the changing cells can assume based on the constraints you have defined. Both the sensitivity report and the limit report allow the user to specify the reliability of the results. However, both reports are available only when the problem does not contain integer constraints. Because both the assembly hours and the total cost constraints are integer constraints, you cannot use the latter two reports. Therefore, you will request the Solver to produce an answer report and you will then examine its contents.

Producing an answer report:

1. Restore the changing cells to their original values: Click cell **B10,** type **4,** click cell **C10,** type **5,** and press **Enter**

2. Click **Tools** on the menu bar, click **Solver,** and then click the **Solve** button. The Excel Solver creates the same solution as before: Purchase, assemble, and sell 14 upright and 17 recumbent exercise bicycles

3. Click **Answer** in the Reports list box and ensure that the **Keep Solver Solution** option is selected (see Figure 10.36)

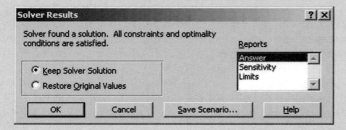

FIGURE 10.36

Preparing to create an answer report

4. Click **OK.** Excel produces an answer report

Excel places the answer report on its own worksheet and names it Answer Report 1. Each time you create another answer report, Excel increases the report number by one (Answer Report 2 would be the name of the next worksheet). Execute the steps that follow to examine the answer report.

Examining an answer report:

1. Click the **Answer Report 1** worksheet tab to view the answer report that the Solver created (see Figure 10.37)

The report contains four parts. The first section contains the report title, workbook and worksheet names, and the date and time when the report was created (rows 1 through 3 of Figure 10.37). The second section describes the characteristics of the target cell. The description includes the optimization (max, min, or value), the cell location, the cell name, its original value, and its final value. In the third section are all of the changing cells, labeled Adjustable Cells in the answer report. They indicate the cells'

FIGURE 10.37

Viewing an answer report

section 1 contains report documentation

section 3 describes the changing cells

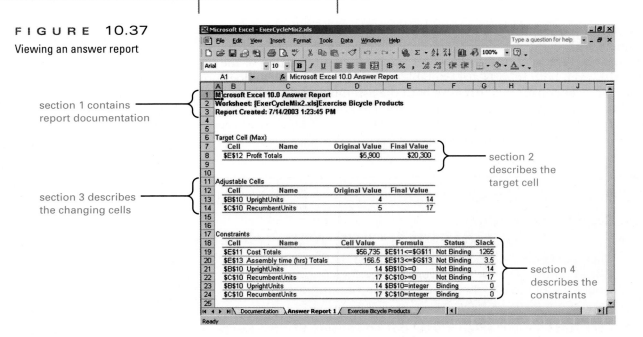

section 2 describes the target cell

section 4 describes the constraints

address, names, original values, and final values. The fourth section lists all of the constraints. The columns in the constraint list display each constraint's cell address, name, final value, constraint expression, status (Binding or Not Binding), and slack value.

The constraint list reveals which of the constraints were limiting factors, indicated by the status of **Binding,** and cells with final values less than the constraint values, indicated by **Not Binding.** The only binding constraints were those requiring that the changing cells be integer values. Although the final values of both the Cost Totals and the Assembly Time constraints were close to their limit values, neither reached their respective limit values. For example, the Cost Totals row indicates that the total cost of $56,735 is less than the limit value of $58,000 by the slack listed, 1265. Notice that the slack assembly time of 3.5 hours, though not binding, is less than the time needed to assemble one more recumbent or upright exercise bicycle. Even though there is enough slack time to make one more bicycle, the slack of the other constraint, available money, is not enough to purchase another bicycle.

You are ready to print the final report for John, including the answer report. First, rename the Answer Report 1 worksheet tab, then add a worksheet header to that page, print the three worksheets, and save the workbook.

Printing and saving the ExerCycleMix2 workbook:

1. Double-click the **Answer Report 1** worksheet tab, type **Solver Answer Report,** and press **Enter.** That assigns a more meaningful name to the worksheet tab and readily identifies the report the worksheet contains

2. Press and hold the **Ctrl** key, click the **Exercise Bicycle Products** worksheet tab, release the **Ctrl** key, click **View** on the menu bar, click **Header and Footer,** click the **Custom Header** button, type your first and last names in the Left section, click **OK,** and click **OK** again

3. Click the **Documentation** worksheet tab and then click the **Save** button on the Standard toolbar to save the workbook and preserve all of the changes you made in this session

4. Click **File** on the menu bar, click **Print,** click the **Entire workbook** option button in the *Print what* panel, and click **OK** to print the workbook's worksheets

5. Click **File** on the menu bar, and then click **Exit** to exit Excel

You show John the printed worksheets. He is glad to know exactly how many of each of the two products he can produce to maximize his profits given his labor and money constraints. John could not have done this work without your help.

making the grade

1. You can use the Solver for constrained _____ in which you specify a set of constraints and an outcome that you want minimized or maximized.

2. The Solver changes decision variables, or changing cells, to cause changes in the object _____, which is the cell containing a function whose value you want to optimize.

3. The Solver goes to work to find the maximum or minimum value for the target cell or object function by changing the value of the _____ cell(s).

4. A(n) _____ is a limitation on the value that a cell can have.

5. Make the following modifications to the ExerCycle Company workbook. Open the **ExerCycleMix2.xls** workbook and save it as **ExerCycleMix3.xls** to preserve the one you finished for Session 10.2. Delete the worksheet named **Solver Answer Report** (Edit, Delete Sheet). Lower the wholesale cost of the Upright 961 to $1,755 (cell B4) and use the Solver to maximize profits using all of the same changing cells, target cell, and constraints as before. How many units of each type should you sell now? Print the worksheet. Increase the labor constraint value in cell G13 to 170. Run the Solver again, and print the worksheet with the newest solution. Finally, click **Tools,** click **Solver,** and then delete the assembly time constraint from the Subject to the Constraints box ($E$13 <= $G$13), rerun the Solver, and print the results.

SESSION 10.3 SUMMARY

The Goal Seek command works backward from a single-valued solution to produce a final, optimized result. The Goal Seek finds a solution by repeatedly changing one cell's value until the specified result cell contains the desired result value, called the goal seek objective. A constraint, or limitation, is a cell that limits the values that a cell can have. By modifying a cell's value within its allowed limits, Goal Seek can produce an optimal result. Goal Seek is useful to determine the maximum profit for a product given a constraint on the number of hours required to sell or manufacture each product. Similarly, Goal Seek can determine a least cost solution to a wide variety of cost minimization problems in wide ranges of disciplines from agriculture to zoology. Without tools such as the Goal Seek command, only the unattractive alternative of exhaustive trial-and-error is available. Using trial and error, you can repeatedly substitute values into independent cells and then examine their effect on the objective cell. This is an error-prone and laborious technique at best.

For more complex optimization problems, Excel provides the Solver. You can use the Solver for equation solving in which you use goal seeking or back solving and for constrained optimization in which you specify a set of constraints and an outcome that you want to optimize. Unlike the Goal Seek command, the Solver provides a solution, where possible, that involves multiple resources that affect the outcome. The Solver can determine the best way to use consumable resources such as energy and raw materials to create one or more products. A slack resource is the quantity of a resource required to produce an optimal result that is unused or unallocated. You can add constraints to limit solutions to values within a range, to positive values, to negative values, and to integer values. Integer value Solver constraints limit a result to integral values and eliminate answers containing fractions.

task reference roundup

Task	Page #	Preferred Method
Using Goal Seek	EX 10.15	• Click **Tools** and then click **Goal Seek**
		• Click the **Set cell** box and type the cell address of the result cell
		• Click the **To value** box and type the result value you want
		• Click the **By changing** cell box and type the address of the changing cell
		• Click **OK** to solve the problem, and then click **OK** to close the Goal Seek Status dialog box
Using the Solver	EX 10.29	• Click **Tools** and then click **Solver**
		• In the *Set Target Cell* box, type the address of the cell containing the objective function
		• Click one of the **Equal To** option buttons and, if necessary, type a value in the *Value of* box
		• In the *By Changing Cells* box, type the cell addresses of all cells that Excel can change
		• Click the **Add** button to add constraints to the Subject to the Constraints box
		• Click the **Solve** button to create a solution
		• Click the **OK** button
Deleting a Solver Constraint	EX 10.35	• Click **Tools** and then click **Solver**
		• Click the constraint you want to delete
		• Click the **Delete** button
Saving Solver Parameters	EX 10.37	• Click **Tools** and then click **Solver**
		• Click **Options** and then click **Save Model**
		• Select an empty cell range and then click **OK**
		• Click **Cancel** and then click **Close**

EXCEL

CROSSWORD PUZZLE

Across

1. The quantity of a resource that is not used or allocated is called what?
3. A(n) _____ function is the cell containing a function whose value you want to optimize.
6. A(n) _____ Solver report shows how sensitive the current solution is to changes in the changing cells.
7. A limitation on the values that a cell or resource can have.
9. A(n) _____ -in feature or command is one that not everyone uses on a regular basis.
10. The _____ value of a formula is the value on which a formula is directly or indirectly based.
12. When a constraint is the limiting factor, it is a _____ constraint.
14. A(n) _____ programming problem involves one or more unknowns and an equal number of equations.

Down

2. A(n) _____ Solver report lists the target cell, the changing cell(s), constraints, and data about the constraints.
3. Constrained _____ is a technique using a set of constraints and an outcome to be minimized or maximized.
4. A product _____ is the quantity of each product to sell in order to generate the greatest profit.
5. A(n) _____ Solver report displays the range of values that the changing cells can assume based on their constraints.
8. A goal seek _____ is the end result that you want to achieve using goal seek techniques.
11. A(n) _____ solving method used by the Goal Seek command, also known as back solving.
13. The _____ Seek command works backward to compute an unknown value that will produce the result you want.

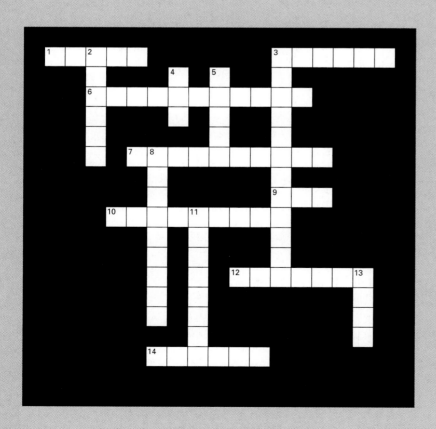

LEVEL TWO

FILL-IN

1. The _____ _____ command works backwards to compute an unknown value that produces a result you want.

2. You specify a _____ when you indicate a limitation on the values that a cell can have.

3. A _____ value is a cell value upon which a formula is directly or indirectly dependent.

4. Excel's _____ is the best choice, instead of the Goal Seek command, when you do not know the desired end result—only that you want to minimize or maximize a value.

5. A specialized feature of Excel that is not automatically included when you install Excel is called a(n) _____.

6. You can create a(n) _____ report that displays which constraints are binding and which are not.

REVIEW QUESTIONS

1. Explain briefly when you would use goal seek techniques versus the Solver.

2. Discuss whether you would use the Goal Seek command or the Solver command to determine what grade you need on the final exam to achieve an overall course average of 90 percent.

3. Discuss why the target cell must always be a formula, not a constant value, when you use the Solver.

4. Discuss what happens if you use the Solver but specify no constraints.

CREATE THE QUESTION

For each of the following answers, create an appropriate, short question.

ANSWER	QUESTION
1. This type of constraint is binding	_____
2. The goal seek objective	_____
3. A limitation on the values that a cell can have	_____
4. A precedent value	_____
5. The quantity of resources that are not used or allocated	_____
6. A sensitivity report	_____

practice

1. Maximizing Ocean Pacific Spas' Profit

Ocean Pacific Spas manufacturers and sells two spa models: the Infinity and the Classic. Ocean Pacific Spas receives spa bodies from another manufacturer and then adds a pump and tubing to circulate the water. The Infinity Spa takes, on average, 15.5 hours of labor to fit a pump and tubing and 14.5 feet of tubing. The Classic model requires 10.5 hours of labor and uses 20 feet of tubing. Based on selling patterns, George Millovich (Ocean Pacific Spas' owner) has determined that the Infinity spa generates a profit of $400 per unit, and the Classic spa generates $345 profit. While George would like a large labor capacity and sufficient tubing and motors to build any number of spas, his resources are limited. For the next production period, George has 2,650 labor hours, 3,450 feet of tubing, and 231 pumps available. Help George figure out how many Infinity spas and Classic spas to build in order to maximize his profit.

1. Open **ex10OceanSpas.xls,** save it as **OceanSpas2.xls,** and type your name to the right of the Modified By label on the Documentation worksheet, press **Tab,** and type today's date near the Modification Date label, press **Enter,** and then click the **Spa Data** tab to display that worksheet

2. Click **D5,** type **=C2*C3+D2*D3,** and press **Enter.** The expression sums the profit for both types of spas

3. Click and drag cell range **C8:D10,** type **15.5,** press **Enter,** type **14.5,** press **Enter,** type **1,** press **Enter,** type **10.5,** press **Enter,** type **20.0,** press **Enter,** type **1,** and press **Enter.** That completes the material and labor constraints for each spa type. Next, enter the system-wide constraints—overall materials and labor available for all products

4. Click cell **C14,** type **=C8*C2+D8*D2,** click cell **C15,** type **=C9*C2+D9*D2,** click cell **C16,** and type **=C10*C2+D10*D2.** These equations multiply the resources per spa type and the number of units of each type produced to display the total resources used

to manufacture all units. At first, these display zero because no units are being produced (cells C2 and D2)

5. Click cell **D14,** type **2650,** click cell **D15,** type **3450,** click cell **D16,** type **231,** and press **Enter.** These values are the total number of labor hours, total length of pipe, and total number of pumps available for producing all spas. Now you are ready to solve for the maximum profit and determine how many Infinity units and Classic units to produce

6. Click **Tools** on the menu bar, click **Solver,** click the **Set Target Cell** box, and type **D5**

7. Click the **Max** option button, click the **By Changing Cells** box, and type **C2:D2**

8. Click the **Add** button, and move the Add Constraint dialog box to the right so that you can see all the entries in column D through row 16. Then click the **Cell Reference** box, click and drag the cell range **C14:C16,** click the **relationships** list box, click **<=,** click the **Constraint** box, click and drag the cell range **D14:D16,** and click the **Add button**

9. Click the **Cell Reference** box, click and drag the cell range **C2:D2,** click the **relationships** list box, click **>=** (greater than or equal to), click the **Constraint** box, type **0,** and click the **Add** button

10. Click the **Cell Reference** box, click and drag the cell range **C2:D2,** click the **relationships** list box, click **int,** and click **OK**

11. Click the **Solve** button, then click the **Answer** in the Reports box, and click **OK**

12. Format the values representing dollar amounts with the currency symbols and zero decimal places. How many units of the Infinity and the Classic spa should Ocean Pacific Spas manufacture to maximize its profits given the constraints you entered?

13. Place your name in the Header of all three worksheets, save your workbook, and either Print all worksheets or execute Save As, according to your instructor's direction

2. Finding a Monthly Payment that Fits the Budget

Jessica Engstrom wants to purchase a newer model automobile to replace her decrepit 1984 car. The bank where Jessica has a checking account, Washington Mutual, is advertising an annual interest rate of 7.75 percent for three-year loans on used cars. By selling her old car and using some cash she has accumulated, Jessica has $3,000 available as a down payment. Under her current budget, Jessica figures that the maximum monthly loan payment she can afford is $300. She wants to find out the maximum car price she can afford and keep the monthly payment no higher than $300. She cannot alter the interest rate, and the three-year term is part of the loan package that cannot be changed either. Use the Excel Goal Seek command to figure out the highest purchase price Jessica can afford.

Jessica has started a worksheet, but you must help her fill in the remaining details. Do the following to complete the worksheet and find Jessica's answer.

1. Open **ex10LoanGoal.xls,** save it as **LoanGoal2.xls,** and type your name near the Modified By label on the Documentation worksheet, press **Tab,** type today's date near the Modification Date label, and click the **Sheet1** tab to open that worksheet

2. Rename Sheet1 to **Loan Analysis,** change the Loan Analysis sheet tab color to Green, and delete the Sheet2 worksheet

3. Type the following values in the corresponding cells: In cell B3, type **19000**; in cell B4, type **3000**; in cell E3, type **7.75%**; in cell, E4 type **3**

4. Click cell **B5** and type the formula to calculate the loan amount **=B3-B4**

5. Click cell **B7** and enter the monthly payment formula **=–PMT(E3/12,E4*12,B5)** Be sure to place the minus sign following the equal sign so the calculated answer is positive

6. Format cells B3, B4, B5, and B7 to display currency symbols and two decimal places

7. Now goal seek the highest purchase price for $300 per month: Click cell **B7,** then click **Tools,** and click **Goal Seek**

8. Ensure that the Set cell text box contains B7, press **Tab,** type **300,** press **Tab,** type **B3,** and click the **OK** button to perform the goal seek

9. Click **OK** to close the Goal Seek Status dialog box

10. Type your name in the worksheet header of the Loan Analysis worksheet, and print or Save As according to the direction of your instructor

challenge

1. University Employees Credit Union Investments

The State University Employee Credit Union (SUECU) is projecting how it will allocate funds for investments next fiscal year. The credit union makes four types of loans to its members-only organization. Besides loans, SUECU also invests members' money in risk-free investments. The projected loan and risk-free investment annual rates of return are as follows:

Loan or Investment Type	Annual Rate or Return
Automobile loans	10%
Furniture loans	10%
Other secured loans	9%
Signature loans	12%
Risk-free investments	5%

This year, the credit union will have $2,000,000 available to invest in loans and risk-free investments. State laws and the credit union association laws restrict the allocation of funds to loans and investments in the following ways:

- Signature loans cannot exceed 10 percent of the funds invested in all loans (automobile, furniture, other, and signature)

- Risk-free investments cannot exceed 30 percent of the total funds available for investment ($2,000,000)

Use the Solver add-in to determine how much money should be allocated to each of the five types of investments to maximize the total annual return. Request that the Solver create an Answer Report worksheet.

Begin by opening **ex10CreditUnion.xls** and save the workbook as **CreditUnion2.xls.** Format all numeric currency entries to zero decimal places and the Accounting format. Ensure that the Solver cannot use negative values for any of the investments. Format all interest rates using the percentage format with zero decimal places. Start the initial allocations of each of the five investments at $100,000, and optimize the amount of interest. Type your name next to the Modified By label on the Documentation sheet, and enter today's date next to the Modification Date label on the Documentation sheet. Place your name in the worksheet header of the Data and Answer Report worksheets. Either Print all worksheets or execute Save As, according to the direction of your instructor.

2. Maximizing Profit for Green Creek Bevels

Green Creek Bevels manufactures linear glass bevels for the art glass industry using a fully automated series of beveling machines. Unlike custom bevel artisans, Green Creek does not produce bevels with curves. Starting with a rectangular piece of glass, a series of four processes are required to produce a finished bevel. The first process is grinding using a steel wheel and steel grit. Following this, a machine smoothes the bevel using a Newcastle stone. Then a cork wheel coated with pumice buffs each bevel. Finally, a felt wheel coated with jeweler's rouge restores the glistening surface to a bevel. Green Creek produces two grades of bevels: Premium and Standard. Premium bevels require more care and time on the machines to produce than standard bevels. The profit for a premium bevel is $10, whereas the profit for a standard bevel is $7.

Tobias Carling wants to use Excel's Solver to compute the number of each bevel type he should produce to maximize his profit. Begin by opening the worksheet, called **ex10GreenCreek.xls,** and save it as **GreenCreek2.xls.** It contains columns for the Premium and Standard bevel information. Under *Steps to Complete,* in cell A5, are the time units needed to grind, smooth, buff, and polish a bevel per hour, along with the maximum time units available for each machine in cells G6 through G9. Write formulas for total profit (premium profit per unit times premium units produced plus standard profit per unit times standard units), and total time units for grinding, smoothing, buffing, and polishing the bevels. Total polish time, for example, is the formula =C9*C2+D9*D2.

Name cell C2 PremiumUnits; name cell D2 StandardUnits; name cell E3 TotalProfit. Format cells appropriately to display currency values (or not). Write formulas for slack time in H6:H9. Use the Solver to maximize profit, cell E3, with changing cells C2:D2 and constraints that total time in E6:E9 must be less than the constraints in

the cell range G6:G9. Produce an Answer report. How many units of Premium and Standard bevels should Tobias produce each hour? Write your name and date in the underlined cells on the Documentation worksheet and in the worksheet headers for the Answer Report Worksheet and the Production Data worksheet. Print the workbook, or execute Save As, according to the direction of your instructor.

on the web

1. Finding the Highest Profit on DVD Sales

Allison Gonzales, the sales manager for DVDs and More, wants to maximize her profit on the sale of portable DVD players. She has created a worksheet with some formatting in place called **ex10DVD.xls.** She would like you to use the Web to locate the retail price of two other portable DVD players and add their data in rows 4 and 5 (items 3 and 4 in the list). Use www.Hotbot.com or a similar Web search engine to find prices for portable DVD players. For the wholesale price of each unit (cells D4 and D5), write a formula that computes 55 percent of the retail price for both units you find. Fill the cells in rows 4 and 5 with appropriate formulas.

The only constraint is that Allison has $200,000 to purchase new DVD players. So, the total wholesale cost of the four types of DVD units must be less than $200,000. Place formulas in cells G6 through I6 that sum the number of units, cost, and profit. You want to maximize total profit, which is in cell I6. Cell H8 contains the slack value (any cash left over after you purchase the proposed units of each product). Name cell H6 **TotalCost,** cell I6 **TotalProfit,** and cell C8 **PurchaseCash.** Solve for maximum profit under the cost constraint, limiting the number of units to positive integers. Produce an answer report. Place your name in all worksheet headers and in the Documentation sheet and include today's date. Print or Save As according to your instructor's direction.

e-business

1. Computing Profit for a Hosted Web Site Store

Otis Toadvine wants to bring his brick-and-mortar coffee bean store online. Investigating online Web hosting packages, he locates Dynamic Store Front (www.dynamicstorefront.com/). Using the Excel goal seek tool, determine what total dollar volume of credit card sales Otis needs in order to realize a monthly profit of $30,000.

Otis has created a rudimentary workbook called **ex10WebHosting.xls.** Save the file as **WebHosting2.xls** to preserve the original file. Next, use your Web browser to display the Dynamic Store Front Web page, click the **Pricing** link, and print the page so that you have the pricing information at hand. Then, fill in cell **C11** with the one-time application fee, cell **C14** with

the monthly hosting fee (minimum), and cell **C17** with the monthly statement fee. Cell C16 contains a formula 1.89 percent times the total sales value from credit card sales plus $0.25 times the number of credit card swipes (see the Web page). Write a formula in cell C21 for profit: total sales minus total variable costs minus the application fee. (Otis has decided to expense the one-time application fee the first month.) Using Goal Seek, determine the value that credit card sales (cell C5) must be in order to achieve a profit of $30,000. Enter your name and today's date in the appropriate cells on the Documentation worksheet, and place your name in the Hosting Cost Calculation worksheet header. Either Print or Save As, according to the direction of your instructor.

around the world

1. Shipping Solutions

Shipping Solutions has manufacturing plants in Philadelphia and Los Angeles. It manufactures doors and ships them to its four warehouses. Its warehouses are located in Philadelphia, Buenos Aires, London, and Tokyo. Each warehouse has a limited amount of storage space for the doors—one of the constraints. The two manufacturing plants each have a maximum capacity to produce doors. The manufacturing facilities can produce more doors than the warehouses can store. The problem is to find the cheapest way to ship doors from both the Philadelphia and Los Angeles facilities to each of the four warehouses and supply them with the number of doors each warehouse requires.

Two tables appear in the worksheet that Winnie Holyoke, the resident Excel expert, created. The topmost table lists the shipping costs in cost unit from each manufacturing facility to each warehouse. The second table—the one whose solution you are going to find—lists the numbers of units shipped from each manufactur-

ing facility to each warehouse. Those numbers start out at zero. Your job is to minimize the total cost of shipping units to each of the warehouses.

Open the worksheet **ex10Shipping.xls.** Cell C16 contains the SUMPRODUCT function, which you may not have used yet. Briefly, it multiplies two cell ranges, one cell at a time, and sums the products. In this case, SUMPRODUCT multiplies the shipping cost per unit and a corresponding number of shipping units for each of eight cell pairs and forms the sum of the products. Cell C16, the total shipping cost, is the value to minimize. All constraints are colored light green so that they are easy to spot. There are two sets: maximum production capacity by manufacturing plant (cells H10:H11) and the warehouse storage limits found in cells C13:F13. The changing cell range, which Solver can manipulate, is C10:F11. Solve for the minimal cost that satisfies all constraints. Produce an answer report, and print all the workbook's worksheets. Identify the worksheets by placing your name in the worksheets' header.

running project

Pampered Paws

In Chapter 9, Grace created several different scenarios in order to investigate the best mix of pet foods to sell. While the scenario analysis allowed her to evaluate her profit under the scenarios in which she varied the amount of each product she sold, she was not able to determine the best product mix. She would like to take the Chapter 9 scenario analysis to the next step and determine how many bags of each of the five pet foods she needs to sell to maximize her profit. Grace has changed the retail selling price of all five products since you examined them in Chapter 9, and those price changes affect the total profit. Open **ex10Paws.xls** and then click the Dog Food Analysis worksheet tab. The dog food products are in alphabetical order, and their new retail prices appear in column C. Grace wants to use the Solver to optimize total profit by having the Solver change the values in

cell range D4:D8. Write formulas for total cost, total sales, and profit and place them in cell ranges E4:E8, F4:F8, and G4:G8, respectively. Place SUM functions in cells D9 through G9 to sum the units sold, total cost, total sales, and profit columns. A Solver constraint is that total cash to purchase pet food at wholesale (column E's sum) must be less than or equal to $4,000 (cell B15). The second and last condition is that there is storage space for only 400 bags (cell B16) of pet food. Write formulas for slack for both constraints in cells D15 and D16. Using the Solver, solve for the optimal number of units sold for each pet food, and create an answer report. Fill in your name and today's date in the Documentation worksheet, place your name in each worksheet's header, and print all three worksheets.

did you know?

Nolan Bushnell, who invented Pong, is credited as the father of video games.

about three percent of the metal in a typical personal computer is precious, and a third of that is gold.

Bell Labs originally conceived of the idea of the cellular phone in 1947.

Nieman Marcus was the first mail order catalog to offer a home computer for sale—a Honeywell H316 in 1969 for $10,600.

the first digital computer in the world, the ENIAC, had 18,000 vacuum tubes.

the Hayes company created the first modem, which set the AT command set standard for modem communications.

prior to founding Apple Computer, Steve Jobs and Steve Wozniak wrote a game for Atari called Breakout.

CHAPTER

11

eleven

Importing
Data

Chapter Objectives

- Import text files into Excel with the Text Import Wizard (MOUS Ex2002e-1-1)

- Move a worksheet from one workbook to another one

- Copy data from a Web page and paste it into an Excel worksheet (MOUS Ex2002e-1-1)

- Convert cell formulas to values with the Paste Special command

- Import database information into Excel using the Query Wizard

- Use Microsoft Query to create a query to filter, sort, and retrieve database records

- Write a database query that joins two related database tables and returns values from each table

- Edit and save database queries

- Write an aggregate query to summarize imported data

chapter case

Mission Bay Boat Works

Mission Bay Boat Works builds some of the world's fastest racing shells and a wide range of recreational shells. Headquartered in Vancouver, British Columbia, Mission Bay Boat Works (MBBW) has a small inside sales office in Seattle, Washington, to serve its U.S. customers. Building boats with patented hull designs, MBBW racing shells are available in sizes ranging from singles to eight-person models. MBBW shells are noted for their durability as well as their lightweight and sleek design. Mission Bay's recreational shells, though slightly heavier than their racing shell counterparts, are carefully crafted for durability, low maintenance, and low water resistance.

Bob Plimpton, who is the manager of inside sales for Mission Bay Boat Works, wants to consol-idate information about his inside salespersons into an Excel workbook. Unfortunately, the information sources he needs are located in disparate locations and are in text and database formats. He wants you to help him bring together the information into an Excel workbook so that he can print, modify, and study it. Employee inside sales information is in text format, and customer information is in an Access database. After you translate the information into Excel format, Bob wants to place some of it on the company Web server so that inside salespersons can access it using a Web browser. Figure 11.1 shows the documentation worksheet of the completed Mission Bay Boat Works workbook.

FIGURE 11.1
Completed Mission Bay Boat
Works workbook

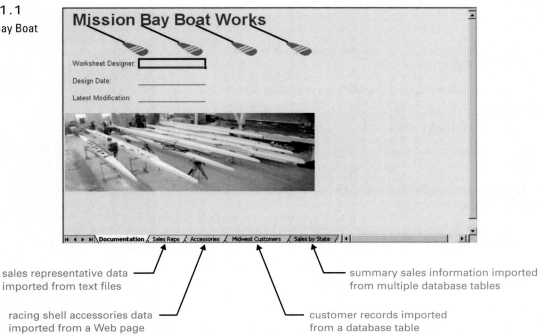

sales representative data imported from text files

racing shell accessories data imported from a Web page

customer records imported from a database table

summary sales information imported from multiple database tables

Chapter 11 covers importing data from sources other than Excel workbooks and producing worksheets and charts that you store on the World Wide Web. External data sources from which you will import data into Excel include comma-delimited text files produced by programs such as Notepad, Web-based data files found on the Internet, and information stored in Microsoft Access databases including tables and information produced by executing Access queries. You will import into an Excel worksheet text data whose fixed length data are stored in columns. Excel can import data whose individual values are separated from one another by commas or another of several possible field separators. Using copy-paste techniques, you can copy data displayed in your Web browser and paste the data into an Excel worksheet. This is particularly handy because a large percentage of the data available on the Web are in text format, not worksheet format.

Excel can import and dissect data stored in Microsoft Access databases as well as in a variety of other database formats. Excel uses structure information about the database's tables to separate distinct fields into Excel columns, and you can choose to use the table column names as column headers in an Excel worksheet. An Excel *query* combines related information from one or more database tables, based on your search and sort criteria, and returns a table as a result. A *database table* is arranged in rows and columns and holds data.

Importing data into Excel using an Access query allows you to be selective about which rows you import and the order in which those rows occur in the worksheet.

SESSION 11.1 IMPORTING TEXT DATA AND WEB DATA

In this section, you will learn how to import data from a text file, using an Excel Wizard to guide you in converting the data into Excel format. Because the Web is such a rich source of information, you will learn how to copy data from a Web page and paste the data into an Excel worksheet. Knowing the forms of text data available for importing and exporting into Excel will aid you in working with the Excel import Wizard. You will learn about text file formats including delimited text and fixed-width text and how to import data from each format. In addition, you will learn about modifying data with formulas and then converting the formulas to values.

IMPORTING TEXT FILES INTO EXCEL

Bob knows that pulling together all of the data he needs will be a big task. Data that he wants you to locate and import into an Excel workbook includes information about the sales representatives he manages, and products he sells.

Mission Bay Boat Works Data Sources

The data you need to complete the workbook are in several locations. The sales representative information is stored in two text files that Bob's predecessor compiled. Some of the parts and accessories that MBBW sells are on Web pages; however, Bob wants them in his Excel workbook so that he can refer to the items easily. The third location for critical business information—customer sales data—is in a Microsoft Access database. The

EX 11.3

EXCEL

company captures sales information including each customer's name, address, and the sale amount. In the same Access database are records of people who have not yet made a purchase but who have indicated interest in receiving a catalog or further information. People on this list represent possible future sales, and Bob wants the marketing staff to contact people in the database to see if MBBW can assist them in purchasing products. Figure 11.2 shows the three data sources you will help Bob pull together into one workbook. Once you consolidate the information from disparate locations and formats into several worksheets of one workbook, Bob can analyze the data and produce various Excel reports.

Understanding Text Files and Data Separation Choices

Text data consists only of characters (letters, digits, and special characters) that you can type on a keyboard—devoid of any special formatting (boldface, italic, etc.). Text data is the most common data format because just about every program that exists today can store your data in text format regardless of the product's native format. Excel, for example, allows you to store worksheet data in text format in addition to the default Excel worksheet format. Similarly, Word provides a "plain text" output format for Word documents. Of course, the Web is the most popular medium for dispersing and displaying information. The Web contains pages in a format that combines text and special text-like tags called HTML. Electronic

FIGURE   11.2

Mission Bay Boat Works data sources

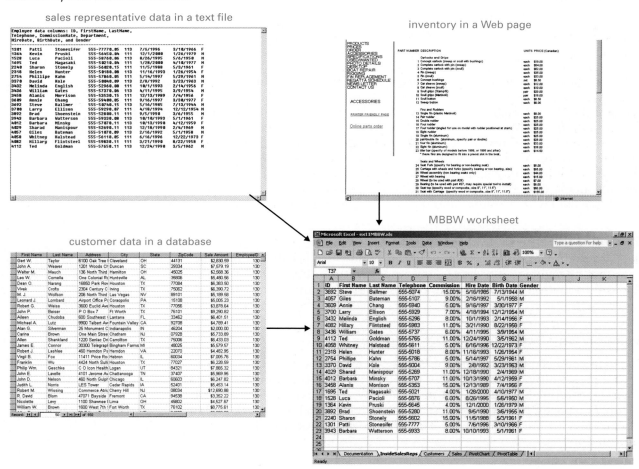

mail, by far the most popular form of business communication, sends messages and attachments in text format, though most e-mail programs display messages in a stylized, nontext format when you read them.

As text data has no internal markers to indicate where data begin and end, text files and programs that read text files rely on delimiters to separate data fields from one another. A *delimiter* is a character or group of characters that separates two pieces of data. Delimiters are used in almost every computer application. For example, the Web uses a slash (/) to separate directories and filenames. This tells the Web server which part of a path's character string represents a directory or series of directories in a hierarchy, and which part represents a filename. Common delimiters you will encounter include blanks, commas, semicolons, quotation marks, brackets, and braces—any character(s) that does not normally occur in the data it is delimiting.

Text files do not require delimiters for Excel or another product to correctly interpret where data fields occur. An alternative to delimited data is to arrange data into specific locations or starting positions. Such an arrangement is know as *fixed width* data. An individual unit of data, either fixed length or separated from others by a delimiter, is called a data *field.*

Fixed length data fields have their roots in 1960s data processing in which nearly all data were stored in specific columns of the input file. In a typical payroll file from the early days of computing, an employee's name might begin in the first position and extend for 15 characters followed by his or her hourly rate beginning in, say, column 16. Other fields such as the number of hours worked, the department number, and so on also appear in the same location in an input record. Programs read data from particular locations in a record and store each of the data groups, called fields, in different locations within the program for processing. Figure 11.3 shows an example of fixed length data in which distinct information about several salespersons begins in the same column for each data field. Figure 11.4 shows comma-separated data fields in a Notepad window. Values

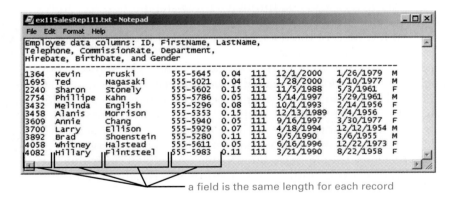

F I G U R E   11.3

Text file with fixed length fields

a field is the same length for each record

F I G U R E   11.4

Text file with comma-separated fields

a comma separates one field from another

EXCEL

separated from one another by commas are called ***comma-separated values,*** abbreviated ***CSV.***

Excel can import either fixed length data fields or delimited data fields. With either type of file, Excel knows where each field begins and ends and assigns each field to its own column when you open either type of file in preparation to import data. Excel places each record in a data file in successive rows of a worksheet. If you choose to import text data beginning in cell B2, then Excel will place the first record into cell row 2, the second record into row 3, and so on. Similarly, the first field of each record goes into column B of its row. The second field of each record goes into column C, and so on.

Bob wants you to import into Excel the sales representative information found in the two text files called **ex11SalesRep111.txt** and **ex11SalesRep113.csv.** There are two text files because the sales employees once worked in two different divisions, each with a different manager. The manager of division 111 kept the sales representative information in a fixed length text file, whereas the manager of division 113 kept information about his sales representatives in a comma-separated text file. Because the two divisions' sales representatives now work in one division, you will import the files into Excel and then merge the two sets of records into one Excel worksheet. You begin by importing the employee records in the fixed length text file.

WORKING WITH A FIXED LENGTH DATA FILE

This file contains information about the inside sales representatives located in the Seattle office who call customers and potential customers around the United States. Bob is not sure about the data's structure, but the office manager who gave him the file assures Bob that it is a text file containing no special characters.

The file extension .txt indicates that the file is a text file. Whenever Excel opens a file whose extension is .txt, it automatically launches the ***Text Import Wizard*** to lead you through a three-step process to covert the text format data into Excel format. In step 1, the Text Import Wizard displays the first few lines of the file and asks you to determine if the data is delimited or fixed length and which row is the first row you want Excel to import. Step 2 asks you to indicate where each data field in the incoming data begins. You can add a line, called a ***column break,*** to indicate the beginning of a field, or you can move or remove column breaks as needed to properly identify where columns begin. In step 3, you can optionally designate a column data format for each field, and you can indicate which text fields to omit from the Excel worksheet. When you have completed the third step, Excel quickly imports the text file and moves individual fields into worksheet columns until all text records are converted and moved into worksheet rows.

Opening the Text Import Wizard

Bob tells you there are two ways to launch the Text Import Wizard. You can open an existing workbook and then execute Import External Data found in the Data menu, or you can open a text file directly. You will use the latter method to open the employee text file. Once Excel imports the employee information into the worksheet, you will then move it to the main Mission Bay Boat Works workbook.

Begin your work on the employee workbook by opening the employee text file. When you execute the Open command on the File menu, Excel

---

task reference

Importing Fixed Length Data Using the Text Import Wizard

- Click **File** and then click **Open**

- In the Files of type list box of the Open dialog box, select **Text Files**

- Using the *Look in* list box, navigate to the folder containing the text file, click the filename in the list of files, and click the **Open** button

- Click the **Fixed Width** option button in the Original data type panel

- Click the **Start import at row** spin box to select the first row to import, and click the **Next** button

- In Step 2, click to the left of each field to add a break line, double-click a break line to remove it, or drag a break line to its correct position at the beginning of a column as needed. Then click the **Next** button to proceed

- In Step 3, for each column, click a **Column data format** option button to select a column format or click the **Do not import column** option button to skip the column, and then click the **Finish** button

---

displays only files whose secondary name is .xls. In order to display files with other extensions—such as .txt, .prn, or .csv—you will have to click the Files of type list box and then select Text Files. Then, names of text files, if any, will appear in the Open dialog box.

Opening the fixed length sales representatives text file:

1. Start Excel

2. Click the **Open** 🖼 button on the Standard toolbar, click the **Files of type** list arrow, click the **Text Files (*.prn; *.txt; *.csv)** entry, navigate to the disk and folder containing the sales representatives text file **ex11SalesRep111.txt,** click **ex11SalesRep111.txt,** and click the **Open** button. The Text Import Wizard—Step 1 of 3 dialog box opens (see Figure 11.5)

3. Click the **Fixed width** option button, if necessary, to indicate that the text file contains fixed width data

---

Specifying the Starting Row

Notice in Figure 11.5 that the text file contains commentary in the first four lines indicating the names of the columns and their ordering. A dashed line follows the three rows of field description information and separates the comments from the data. Comment lines in the beginning of a text file describing the text file's contents and column format are common in many text files. Figure 11.6 shows a text file available from the U.S. Census Bureau showing population estimates for U.S. regions and states from 1990 to 1999. (Go to the Web address www.census.gov/population/estimates/state/st-99-1.txt to view these and related files.) Notice that the

FIGURE 11.5

Text Import Wizard Step 1 of 3
dialog box

select one of two formats
based on the text data

the first few rows of the
text file appear in the
Preview of file panel

comment lines
precede the
employee data

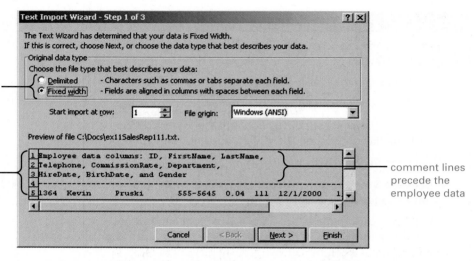

FIGURE 11.6

Fixed length text from the U.S.
Census Bureau

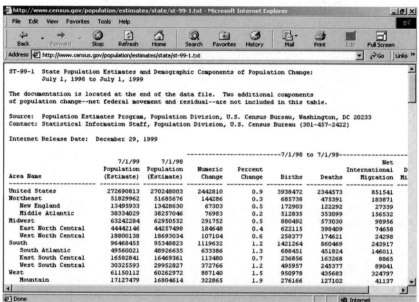

first lines of the text file are comments about the values in the fixed length fields beneath the comment lines. Were you to import this data into an Excel worksheet, you would want to skip the comments and begin importing at row 14—the row below the dashed line.

Because you do not want to import the first four rows of the **ex11SalesRep111.txt** file into the Excel worksheet, you will tell the Text Import Wizard to skip them.

Specifying the first row to import:

1. Click the **Start import at row** spin box up arrow repeatedly until the value 5 appears in the box. This causes Excel to import rows beginning with row 5. After a brief pause, Excel scrolls the display to show row 5 at the top of the Preview of file list box (see Figure 11.7)

2. Click the **Next** button to go to the second Text Import Wizard step

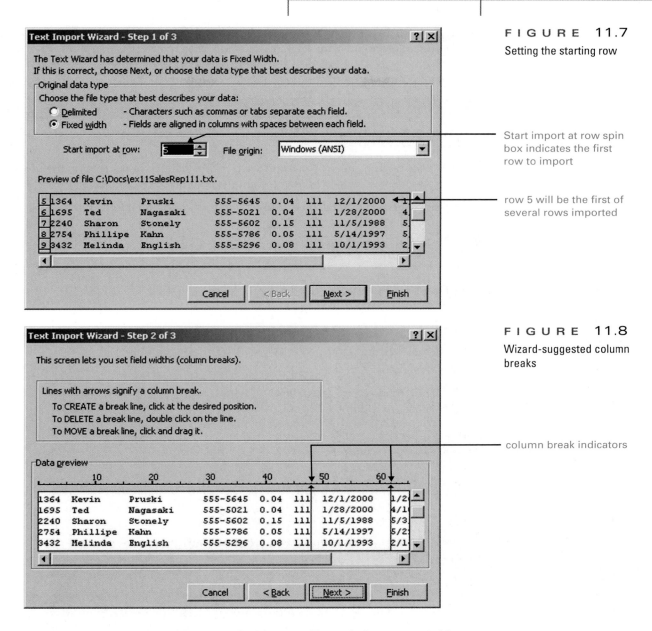

FIGURE 11.7

Setting the starting row

Start import at row spin box indicates the first row to import

row 5 will be the first of several rows imported

FIGURE 11.8

Wizard-suggested column breaks

column break indicators

The Text Import Wizard examines the text file and places vertical lines, called *column breaks,* in the data where it believes new columns begin. Sometimes the Wizard is correct and places all breaks where they belong, but occasionally the Wizard doesn't place enough column breaks or places them in the wrong locations. In any case, you should always check each column break to ensure that it is in the correct location. If necessary, you can drag a line break to move it, delete unneeded line breaks, or add new ones. Remember to drag the horizontal scroll box to view the entire breadth of the text, if needed.

Altering Column Breaks and Adding New Ones

The Wizard does its best to place the column breaks where columns begin. It uses the vertical lines to mark the positions of its proposed column breaks. You observe the line breaks that the Text Import Wizard suggests and see that there are several missing column breaks. In addition, one line break is out of place (see Figure 11.8).

There are no column breaks marking the beginning of the first name, last name, telephone number, commission rate, or department number. The column break for the hire date column is two positions to the left of the actual column beginning.

---

task **reference**

Adding, Moving, and Deleting Column Breaks Using the Text Import Wizard

- Add a column break by clicking the position just above the ruler in the Data preview panel where you want the column break to appear

- Move a column break by clicking it and then dragging it to its new position

- Delete a column break by double-clicking it

Add new column breaks and move the one misplaced column break so that Excel correctly interprets the data.

Modifying Text Import Wizard column breaks:

1. Click the space immediately to the left of the first name *Kevin* to create a column break at the beginning of the first name column. Be sure the line does not cross any data

   tip: *Don't worry if you place a column break in the wrong location. You can move it easily by clicking and dragging the line to its proper location*

2. Click the space immediately to the left of the last name *Pruski* to create a column break at the beginning of the last name column

3. Click the space immediately to the left of the telephone number beginning in position 29 (see the ruler above the data in the Data preview panel) to create a column break

4. Click the space immediately to the left of the commission rate (0.04 in the first record) to create a column break at position 39

5. Click the space immediately to the left of the department number, 111, to create a column break at position 45

6. Click and drag the column break line that is in position 48 (between the department number and the hire date) to position 50—immediately to the left of the hire date column (see Figure 11.9)

7. Click and drag the **Data preview horizontal scroll box** to check the rightmost text fields. The column breaks are fine for the rightmost fields

Specifying Data Formats and Skipping Selected Columns

The third and final step of the Text Import Wizard lets you specify the data type of each column you are importing. You are limited to General, Text,

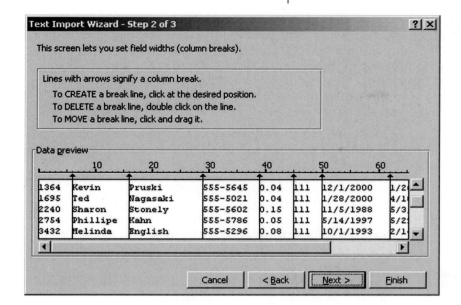

FIGURE 11.9
Adjusted column breaks

Date, and Do Not Import columns. The General option treats text as text and numbers as numbers, the default for all imported columns. The Text option treats all entries in a column as text, even if some entries appear to be numbers. The Date option treats entries as dates. The Do Not Import column option provides a convenient way to skip a data column.

In the third and final Wizard step, you will set the data format for two columns and tell the Wizard to skip the department number column.

Setting the data format for selected columns:

1. Click the **Next** button to go to the third and last Text Import Wizard step. The Text Import Wizard—Step 3 of 3 dialog box appears (see Figure 11.10)

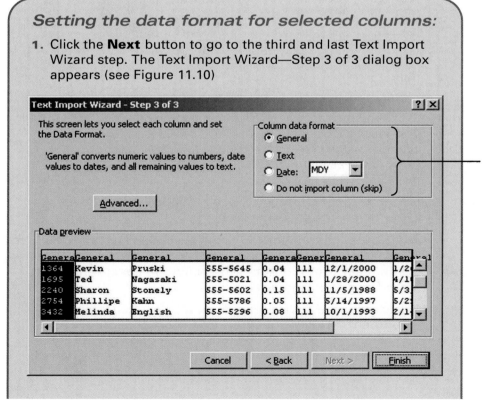

FIGURE 11.10
Text Import Wizard Step 3 of 3 dialog box

data format choices

2. Click anywhere within the sixth column from the left, containing the values 111, and then click the **Do not import column (skip)** option button located in the Column data format panel. You can omit this column from the import operation because the department number is unnecessary in the newly merged sales group

3. Click anywhere within the seventh column containing dates, and then click the **Date** option button to ensure that Excel interprets the dates correctly

4. Click the eighth column containing employees' birth dates, and then click the **Date** option button to ensure that Excel interprets the dates correctly. Notice that the column headers above the three columns whose format option you changed are now Skip, MDY, and MDY, respectively (see Figure 11.11)

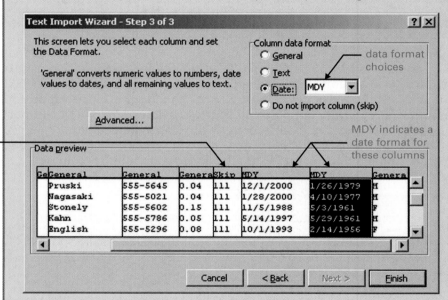

Excel will skip this column while importing others

5. Click **Finish** to complete the three-step process and import the data into an Excel worksheet. Excel creates a new workbook with one worksheet whose tab and workbook name are the same name as the text file you imported—**ex11SalesRep111.txt**

6. Double-click the worksheet tab, type **Sales Reps,** and press **Enter** to rename the worksheet tab

7. Insert a new row 1 at the top of the worksheet and enter the following text in cells **A1** through **H1,** respectively: **ID, First Name, Last Name, Phone, Commission Rate, Hire Date, Birth Date,** and **Gender**

8. Select cell range **A1:H1,** click **Format,** click **Cells,** click the **Alignment** tab, click the **Wrap text** check box (found in the Text control panel), click the **Font** tab, click **Bold** in the Font style list, and click the **OK** button to format the column labels

9. Drag the mouse through the column headings for columns **A** through **H** and then double-click the right dividing line between any two selected column headings to optimize the width of the selected columns

10. Select column **E** (click its column heading), and then drag the dividing line between columns E and F until the word *Commission* in cell E1 appears on one line

11. Click cell **A1** to deselect the cell range (see Figure 11.12)

title bar indicates a text file name

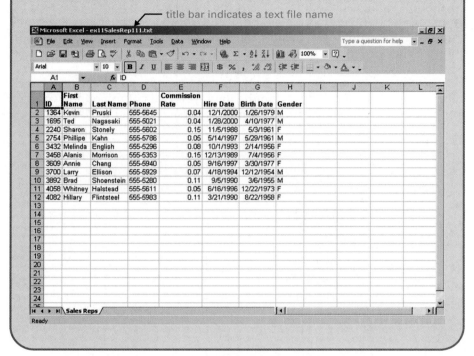

FIGURE 11.12

Imported and formatted employee information

Saving Imported Data as an Excel Workbook

Look carefully at the Excel title bar. Notice that the name *ex11SalesRep111.txt* appears in the title bar. This indicates Excel still believes the file you are viewing is a text file—even though it is in an Excel workbook. Save the imported data as an Excel workbook.

Saving the imported employee text file as an Excel workbook:

1. Click **File** on the menu bar and click **Save As**

2. Click the **Save as type** list box, and then click **Microsoft Excel Workbook (*.xls)** in the list

3. Type **SalesReps2** in the File name list box and click the **Save** button to save the workbook under its new name

4. Click **File** on the menu bar and then click **Close** to close the workbook

Bob is pleased when you show him your work. With one of the two sales representative text files imported, you are ready to import the second one.

WORKING WITH A COMMA-SEPARATED VALUES TEXT FILE

The data file **ex11SalesRep113.csv** contains sales representative information from the old Division 113 of Mission Bay Boat Works. You know that the division's manager kept the sales representative information in a comma-separated, or CSV, format. Excel is particularly adept at importing CSV files because each field is delimited with a comma. That is, a comma occurs following each field except for the last field in a record. There is no ambiguity about where one field ends and another one begins. Naturally, using CSV formatted files means that numeric field values cannot contain commas, because the comma is a field separator. A value such as 10,761.34 is written without a comma in the CSV file: 10761.34.

You are ready to import the CSV file **ex11SalesRep113.csv** into Excel. When you are finished importing the data, you will combine the two sales representative worksheets into the main worksheet, **ex11MBBW.xls.**

Importing comma-separated values into Excel:

1. With Excel open, click the **Open** ![open button] button on the Standard toolbar, click the **Files of type** list arrow, and click **Text Files (*.prn; *.txt; *.csv)** from the list of file types

2. Using the *Look in* list box, navigate to the folder containing the file **ex11SalesRep113.csv,** click **ex11SalesRep113.csv,** and click the **Open** button. Excel imports the CSV file without your help and displays it in a new workbook (see Figure 11.13)

FIGURE 11.13

Importing comma-separated values

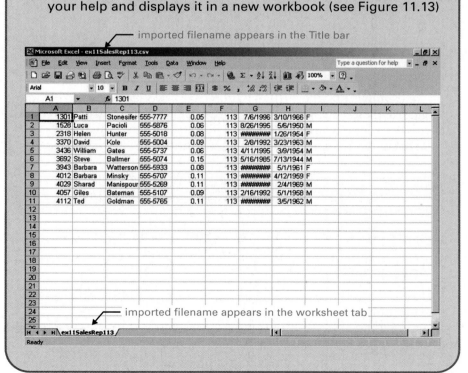

You can eliminate the column containing the old department number, column F. After eliminating that column, the worksheet will be ready to copy into the main workbook.

Eliminating an unwanted column in the imported file:

1. Right-click column F's column heading. Excel selects column F and displays a shortcut menu

2. Click **Delete** in the shortcut menu to delete the column, and click cell **A1** to deselect column F

MOVING, COPYING, AND PASTING DATA BETWEEN WORKBOOKS

Bob wants the imported employee data from both files placed into the workbook **ex11MBBW.xls.** In this section, you will open **ex11MBBW.xls** and **SalesReps2.xls,** and then move the Sales Reps worksheet to the **ex11MBBW.xls** workbook. Next, you will copy the data from **ex11SalesRep113.csv** and paste the data into the Sales Reps worksheet—just below the existing sales rep information. Finally, you will close the **ex11SalesRep113.csv** workbook and tidy up the consolidated Sales Reps worksheet by sorting the data and saving the workbook under a new name.

Opening Other Workbooks

In order to consolidate the two imported text files into the main Mission Bay Boat Works worksheet, open all three workbooks to facilitate moving and copying data between them.

Opening two other workbooks:

1. With the **ex11SalesRep113.csv** workbook open, click the **Open** button on the Standard toolbar

2. Click the **Files of type** list arrow, and click **Microsoft Excel Files** from the list of file types

3. Using the *Look in* list box, navigate to the folder containing the file **SalesReps2.xls,** click **SalesReps2.xls,** and click the **Open** button

4. Click the **Open** button on the Standard toolbar, navigate to the folder containing the file **ex11MBBW.xls,** click **ex11MBBW.xls,** and click the **Open** button

Three workbooks are open in Excel: **SalesReps2.xls, ex11MBBW.xls,** and **ex11SalesRep113.csv.** Notice that the three filenames appear in taskbar buttons.

Moving a Worksheet to another Workbook

Now you can move the **SalesReps2.xls** worksheet over to the **ex11MBBW.xls** workbook.

> ## *Moving the Sales Reps worksheet to the ex11MBBW.xls workbook:*
>
> 1. Click **Window** on the menu bar, and then click **SalesReps2.xls** in the list of active workbooks to make it active
>
> 2. Click **Edit** on the menu bar and click **Move or Copy Sheet.** The Move or Copy dialog box opens
>
> 3. Click the **To book** list box arrow and click **ex11MBBW.xls** in the list of open workbooks
>
> 4. In the *Before sheet* list box, click **(move to end).** Figure 11.14 shows the completed Move or Copy dialog box

FIGURE 11.14

Preparing to move a worksheet

workbook to which the worksheet is moved

move the worksheet to the end of the workbook

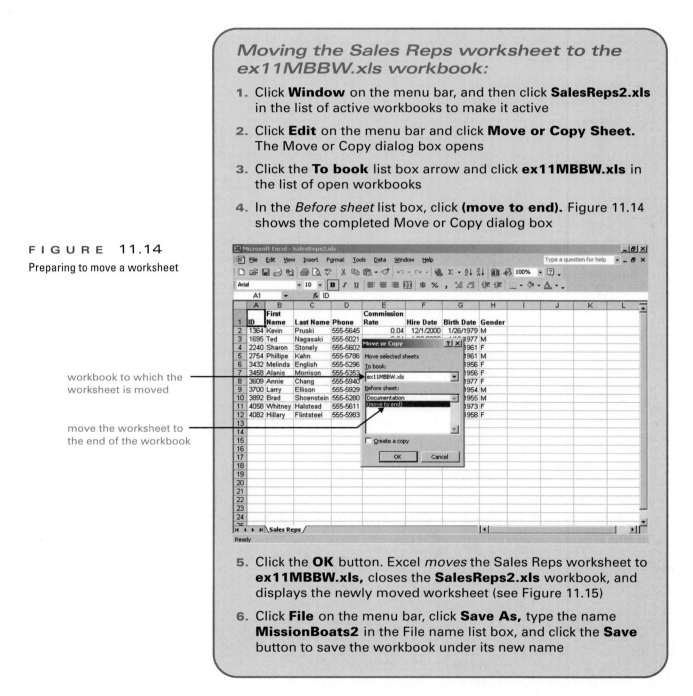

> 5. Click the **OK** button. Excel *moves* the Sales Reps worksheet to **ex11MBBW.xls,** closes the **SalesReps2.xls** workbook, and displays the newly moved worksheet (see Figure 11.15)
>
> 6. Click **File** on the menu bar, click **Save As,** type the name **MissionBoats2** in the File name list box, and click the **Save** button to save the workbook under its new name

Copying and Pasting Data to Another Worksheet

Next, you will copy and paste a worksheet from the **ex11SalesRep113.csv** workbook into the Sales Reps worksheet.

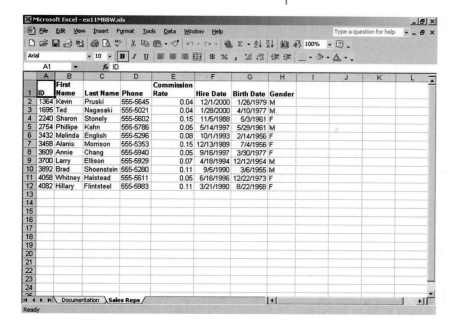

FIGURE 11.15
Moved Sales Rep worksheet

Copying and pasting worksheet data:

1. Click **Window** on the menu bar and then click **ex11SalesRep113.csv** to make that workbook and accompanying worksheet active

2. Click and drag the cell range **A1:H11,** and click the **Copy** button on the Standard toolbar. Excel places the selected cell range onto the Clipboard

3. Click **File** and then click **Close.** When Excel displays a dialog box asking if you want to save the changes you made to ex11SalesRep113.csv, click **No.** The worksheet **MissionBoats2.xls** becomes active

4. Click cell **A13** and then click the **Paste** button on the Standard toolbar to paste in the remaining sales representative data. Excel pastes the data into rows 13 through 23

5. Click Cell **A1** to deselect the range, and click the Save button on the Standard toolbar to preserve your latest changes (see Figure 11.16)

FORMATTING AND SORTING THE IMPORTED DATA

Bob wants the sales rep rows to be sorted by employees' names—by last name and then first name—so that he can easily locate any particular employee. He also wants you to format the commission rate column so that the rates display a percentage with two decimal places and to center the values in the Gender column. You agree that will make the list easier to use, and you also decide to color the column label backgrounds and color-code the worksheet tab.

F I G U R E   11.16

Completed Sales Rep worksheet

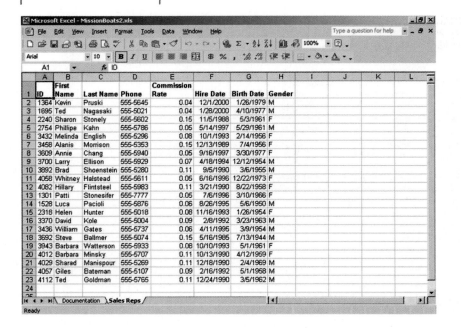

Sorting and formatting the Sales Rep worksheet:

1. Click **Data** on the menu bar, click **Sort,** click the **Sort by** list box arrow, and click **Last Name**

2. Click the **Then by** list box arrow and then click **First Name**

3. Ensure that the **Ascending** option button is selected for both sort fields, and then click **OK** to sort the rows

4. Select cell range **E2:E23,** click the **Percent Style** % button on the Formatting toolbar, and click the **Increase Decimal** button on the Formatting toolbar *twice* so that the commission rates display two decimal places

5. Select cell range **H2:H23** and click the **Center** ≡ alignment button on the Formatting toolbar. Excel centers the Gender column values

tip: *Recall that you can select a filled cell range by clicking the first cell in the range, holding down the **Shift** key, tapping the **End** key, pressing an arrow key, and then releasing the **Shift** key. Excel will select the cell range in the direction of the arrow you pressed until it encounters an empty cell*

6. Select cell range **A1:H1,** click the **Fill Color** list arrow on the Formatting toolbar, click the **Light Yellow** color square (fifth row from the top, third column) from the drop-down color palette, and click cell **A1** to deselect the cell range

7. Right-click the **Sales Reps** worksheet tab, click **Tab Color** in the shortcut menu, click the **Light Yellow** color square, and click **OK** (see Figure 11.17)

8. Click the **Save** button on the Standard toolbar to save the workbook and all changes you have made so far

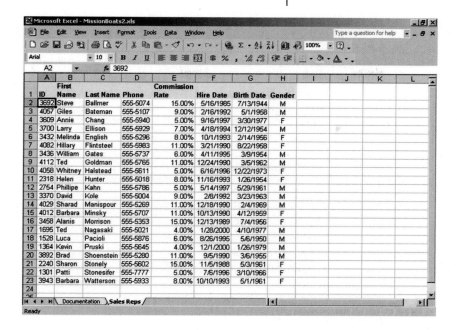

FIGURE 11.17
Sorted and formatted Sales Reps
worksheet

Now you have the two text files containing sales representative information imported into a single worksheet called Sales Reps. It is a simple matter for Bob to review or alter the inside sales reps by consulting his master workbook.

COPYING AND PASTING DATA FROM A WEB PAGE

The Internet is a treasure trove of information. You can find information that you want to download and manipulate in Excel , such as statistics on the U.S. Census Bureau Web site, information about stocks and bonds on Web sites such as E*Trade or Microsoft's Money Central. While a few large data-rich sites offer information in spreadsheet format or rich text format (RTF), Web pages and the data they contain are in HTML format. (**Rich Text Format** is a standard for specifying formatting documents in which the document contains text and special commands holding formatting information.) A particular part of a page displaying values is plain text. Because Excel is particularly adept at reading HTML-format files, you can copy Web information and paste it directly into an Excel worksheet with relative ease.

Bob asks you to browse the Web and locate racing shell parts of various types and then download the Web page into his **MissionBoats2.xls** master worksheet. He suggests you look at the Web site of his main competitor, Hudson Boat Works. He explains that they have an extensive range of rowing parts from backstays to tillers. Because Hudson Boat Works is a Canadian company, the company's prices are specified in Canadian dollars. Therefore, Bob wants you to convert prices into U.S. Dollars using the conversion rate that he will provide.

Download the parts names and prices into Excel using a Web browser. If you do not have a connection to the Internet, or do not want to use the Internet for this next exercise, you can use your browser to open a file containing a Web page similar to the Hudson Boat Works Web page.

Opening a Web Page

Bob wants the parts worksheet to follow the Sales Reps worksheet in the **MissionBoats2.xls** workbook, so keep the **MissionBoats2.xls** workbook open. First, you will launch a Web browser and then type the Uniform Resource Locator (URL) for the Hudson Boat Works accessories page. (A *Uniform Resource Locator,* or *URL,* is the global address of a document or other resource on the Web.)

FIGURE 11.18

Hudson Boat Works accessories Web page

Opening the Hudson Boat Works parts Web page:

1. If you are connected to the Internet, open a Web browser such as Internet Explorer, type the URL **www.hudsonboatworks.com/mainsite/partslist.htm** in the Address list box (Internet Explorer) or the Location list box (Netscape Navigator), press **Enter,** and then *skip* step 2. Your Web browser opens the Hudson Boat Works accessories Web page (see Figure 11.18)

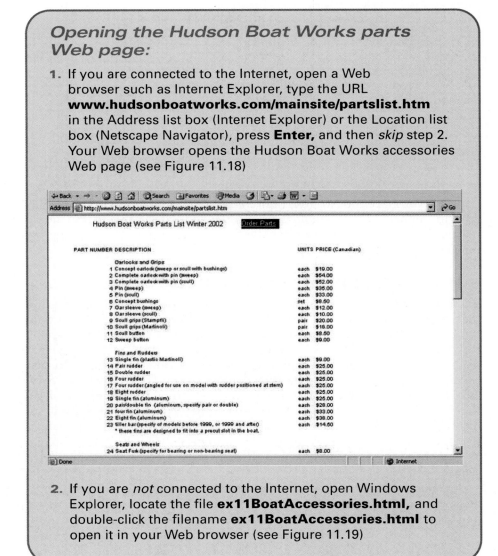

2. If you are *not* connected to the Internet, open Windows Explorer, locate the file **ex11BoatAccessories.html,** and double-click the filename **ex11BoatAccessories.html** to open it in your Web browser (see Figure 11.19)

Copying Portions of a Web Page into an Excel Worksheet

Whenever you display a Web page in a browser, you can download the Web page to the hard disk on your computer, download a picture from within a Web page to your computer, or select text within a page to save on your computer. Besides saving the selected Web page or portion thereof to a

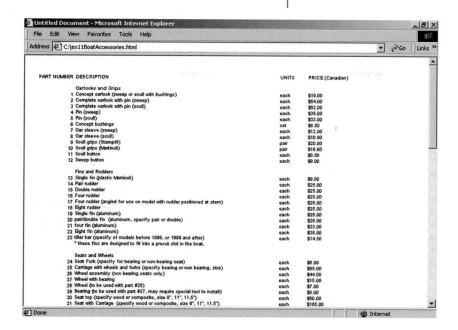

disk on your computer, you can also copy and paste text into an Excel worksheet. Whether you display the accessories page from the Web or from the file, copying the data to an Excel worksheet is the same procedure. Start by adding a new worksheet to the MissionBoat2 workbook.

Creating a new worksheet to hold the Web page data:

1. Click the **Microsoft Excel** button on the taskbar to make the **MissionBoats2.xls** workbook active. Excel displays the Sales Reps worksheet

2. Click **Insert** on the menu bar and then click **Worksheet.** Excel adds a worksheet called Sheet1 to your workbook

tip: *The worksheet you add may not be named Sheet1 if you have added other worksheets to your workbook*

3. Click and drag the newly added worksheet to the position following the Sales Reps worksheet

4. Double-click the **Sheet1** worksheet tab, type **Accessories,** and press **Enter** to rename the worksheet

5. Right-click the **Accessories** worksheet tab, click **Tab Color,** click the **Light Green** color square (fifth row from the top, fourth column from the left), and click **OK**

Now you have an empty worksheet onto which you can paste part of the contents of the Web page you opened in your browser.

Copying Web page data onto the Clipboard:

1. If you opened a Web page on the Internet, click the **Parts List** button on the taskbar to make your browser and the Web page active and jump to step 3

2. If you opened a Web page from the file **ex11BoatAccessories.html,** click the **Untitled Document** button on the taskbar to make your browser and the Web page active

3. Click the **Maximize** button on the browser's title bar to enlarge the window, if necessary

4. Move the mouse just to the left of the word *PART* in the text **PART NUMBER DESCRIPTION** at the top of the Web page. The mouse pointer changes to an I-beam

5. Click and drag the mouse to the right until you select the **UNITS** and **PRICE (Canadian)** labels as well as the prices beneath the PRICE label (see Figure 11.20)

FIGURE 11.20

Web page text selected

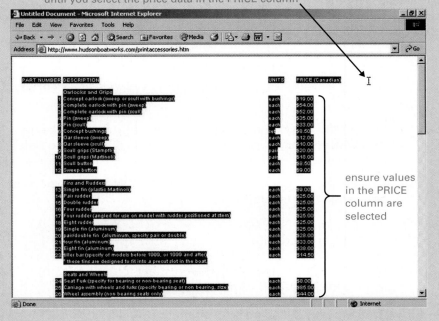

6. Release the mouse

tip: *This takes a little practice. If you have trouble selecting all of the prices, repeat steps 4 through 6.*

7. Press **Ctrl**+**C** to copy the selected text to the Clipboard

Once the Web page text is on the Clipboard, you can copy it to an Excel worksheet easily.

Pasting Web page data from the Clipboard to the worksheet:

1. Click the **Microsoft Excel** button on the taskbar to make the worksheet active, and then click cell **A1,** if necessary, to make A1 active

2. Click the **Paste** 📋 button on the Standard toolbar. Excel pastes the data from the Clipboard to the worksheet

3. Click the **Paste Options** smart tag and click **Match Destination Formatting** to format the data with the Excel default font, typeface, and font size

4. Click cell **A1** to deselect the cell range (see Figure 11.21)

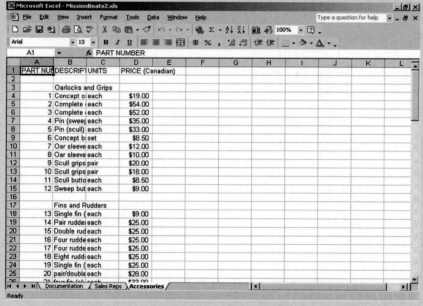

5. Right-click either the **Hudson Boat Works Inc** taskbar button or the **Untitled Document** taskbar button, and then click **Close** from the shortcut menu to close the browser

---

FIGURE 11.21

Pasted Web page data

Converting Prices to U.S. Dollars

The last series of steps to complete the accessory parts worksheet page is to convert the prices from Canadian dollars to U.S. dollars. Bob tells you to use the conversion rate of 1 Canadian dollar equals 0.65 U.S. dollars. You will write formulas to convert prices, then you will convert the formulas to values, and, finally, you will delete the Canadian prices column.

Deleting unneeded rows and writing currency conversion formulas:

1. Reduce the number of items in the accessories page: Click row 29's **row heading** button, press and hold the **Shift** key, tap the **PgDn** key *four times,* and release the **Shift** key. Excel selects several rows, including several below the last accessory row

2. Click **Edit** on the menu bar and then click **Delete** to delete the excess accessories rows. Only parts belonging to the group Oarlocks and Grips and the group Fins and Rudders remain on the Accessories worksheet

3. Click cell **E4** and type =**D4*0.65,** and then press **Enter**

4. Click cell **E4** and drag its fill handle through the cell range **E5:E28** to copy it to that target cell range

5. Select the cell range **E16:E17,** which displays 0.00, and press the **Delete** key to clear their values

6. Select cell range **E4:E28** and then click the **Copy** 📋 button on the Standard toolbar

7. Click **Edit** on the menu bar and click **Paste Special.** The Paste dialog box opens

8. Click the **Values** option in the Paste panel (see Figure 11.22), and click **OK** to paste values back into the worksheet column

FIGURE 11.22

Pasting values into a column of formulas

select Values to convert formulas to values ⟶

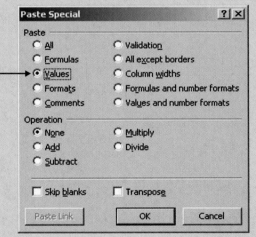

9. Right-click column D's column heading and then click **Delete** to delete column D

10. Click and drag the column headings **A** through **D** to select those four columns, click **Format** on the menu bar, point to **Column,** and click **AutoFit Selection**

11. Click cell **D1,** type **PRICE,** and press **Enter** to label the column

You have copied a Web page to an Excel worksheet and converted the Web page into Excel format. To check that the prices are values and not text entries, you could drag the mouse through any cell range, say D4:D8, and check the sum in the status bar at the bottom of the screen. Now is a good opportunity to save your workbook.

> **Saving your workbook:**
>
> 1. Click the **Documentation** worksheet tab to make that worksheet active
>
> 2. Click the **Save** 🖫 button on the Standard toolbar
>
> 3. Click **File** on the menu bar and then click **Exit** to exit Excel

Bob is quite happy. So far, you have consolidated the sales representatives' information from two different text files and placed the results in a workbook, and you have copied and pasted a parts list from the Web. Additionally, you converted prices from Canadian dollars to U.S. dollars and pasted values instead of formulas. Converting formulas to values removes the dependency on the Canadian values and allows you to delete that unwanted column.

making the grade   SESSION 11.1

1. _____ data consists only of characters that you can type on a keyboard and does not contain any special formatting.

2. Groups or fields of data often are separated from one another with a _____ character that does not otherwise occur in the data.

3. When the Excel Text Import Wizard imports text data, it indicates the beginning of each new column of data with what?

4. Text files in which values are separated from one another with commas have the special name _____ _____ values. People often use the abbreviation _____ to refer to these types of files.

5. Modify the employee worksheet you saved as **MissionBoats2.xls** in the following ways. First, open **MissionBoats2.xls** and immediately save it as **MissionBoats111.xls.** Then make the Accessories worksheet active and delete column A containing sequential part numbers. Add a new worksheet and rename the worksheet to **Shell Prices.** Move the worksheet to the end of the workbook—following the Accessories worksheet. Change the tab's color to **red.** Click cell **A1,** click **Data** on the menu bar, point to **Import External Data,** and click **Import Data.** Using the Look in list box, navigate to the folder containing the text file **ex11Vespoli.txt.** Then click **ex11Vespoli.txt** and click **Open.** Make sure the **Delimited** option is selected. Click **Next** to go to Step 2, ensure that the **Tab** checkbox in the Delimiters panel is checked, click the **Finish** button, and then click the **OK** button to import the data beginning in cell A1. Format the values using the Accounting format with a currency symbol and zero decimal places. Optimize the widths of the six Shell Prices columns. Type your name in all worksheet headers, and print the Documentation and Shell Prices worksheets. Save the workbook and close Excel.

SESSION 11.2 USING QUERIES TO IMPORT DATABASE DATA

In this section, you will learn how to import data from a Microsoft Access database using both the Query Wizard and Microsoft Query. You will select columns from a database table to import, specify which rows to import using criteria, and sort information prior to importing it into Excel—all with the Query Wizard. Using the more powerful Microsoft Query, you will import information from multiple related database tables that compute a summation of grouped records, and you will save queries for later use.

RETRIEVING DATA FROM DATABASES

It is common for companies to store their important data such as customer names and addresses, invoices, product catalogs, and employee information in corporate databases. A *database* is a collection of information organized so that a computer program can select requested information from it quickly—a sophisticated electronic filing system. Special programs called *database management systems,* or *DBMSs,* take in user requests and comb through a database to deliver requested information, update information, or delete information. Data may be stored and managed by a program such as Microsoft Access. Larger databases can contain tens of thousands or millions of individual pieces of related information. These much larger databases are managed by faster and more robust server database management systems such as IBM's DB2, Oracle, or Microsoft SQL Server, and run on large computers managed by a full-time staff of computer professionals.

Excel is incapable of storing millions of database records because of worksheet row limits and computer memory limitations. However, Excel can tap into the power of database systems through a query. Excel passes a query you specify in Excel to database software that translates the query, retrieves the data, and passes the data back to the Excel program. Special software installed with Excel, called a *database driver,* translates Excel information requests into database commands. Database drivers allow you to retrieve data from Access databases, Web pages, text files, Paradox databases, dBASE databases, and a host of other files and database systems.

You can retrieve data from databases by first creating a query and then submitting the query to the database system. In this chapter, you will use two different methods to create a database query: Excel's Query Wizard and Microsoft Query. The Query Wizard, like other Excel Wizards, displays a series of dialog boxes that lead you through the process of locating a database and forming a query based on the table you select from the database. By clicking option buttons and making choices in Query Wizard list boxes, you help the Query Wizard establish communication with the database and define the information you want to import from a database system into Excel.

Microsoft Query is a more powerful tool for importing database information into Excel. It allows you to specify more complex database queries, perform calculations within a query that the Query Wizard cannot perform, join together related tables, and retrieve information from several tables at once. You will import data from a database using the Query Wizard. Then you will create a more complex query to import data from several database tables using Microsoft Query.

USING THE EXCEL QUERY WIZARD

Bob tells you that Mission Bay Boat Works sales information is kept in a Microsoft Access database. Bob wants to analyze sales information in

Excel, and there are two tables in the Access database that will help do that. He asks you to import the data into Excel where you can then perform various calculations and print out Excel worksheets of sales information. One of the tables, called tblCustomers, contains customer name and address data—both customers who have purchased items and those who have made inquiries without making purchases. Another table, called tblSalesTransactions, contains data about sales made in the last six months. Arranged in table columns called fields, the table's fields contain the salesperson's identification number (who made the sale), the customer's identification number (who bought the items), the sale date, and the total sale amount.

Bob wants to mail out a marketing brochure especially designed for customers living in Illinois, Indiana, or Michigan, who have purchased racing shells or merely made an inquiry about the price and availability of boats. The information is in the Access database called **ex11MBBW.mdb.** Bob wants you to import the customer names and addresses of the customers from each of the three states into Excel. You will use the Excel Query Wizard to write a query, connect to the database, and retrieve the desired customer data. Bob tells you that each customer's information is stored in its own *record*, which is a collection of related information about one object (a person in this case) that is stored in a database table.

There are two general steps to get data out of a database and into an Excel worksheet. The first step is to specify a data source, which is the name and location of the database. The second step is to define a query that is responsible for searching the database and returning information to Excel. In the next section, you will learn how to specify a data source. The remainder of this session shows you how to build a query and then use it to import database data into Excel.

Creating a Data Source Definition

Before importing data, open Excel, open your Mission Bay Boat Works workbook, and insert a new worksheet into it.

Opening the Excel workbook and adding a new worksheet:

1. Open the workbook **MissionBoats2.xls** that you saved in the previous session, and then immediately save it under the new name **MissionBoats3.xls** (click **File,** click **Save As,** type the name **MissionBoats3.xls,** and click the **Save** button) to preserve the original workbook

2. Click **Insert** on the menu bar, click **Worksheet,** drag the newly added worksheet tab to the right of the Accessories worksheet, double-click the newly added worksheet tab, type **Midwest Customers,** and press **Enter**

3. Right-click the **Midwest Customers** worksheet tab, click **Tab Color,** click the **Tan** color square (fifth row from the top, second from the left) in the Format Tab Color dialog box, and click **OK**

The first step to import database data into Excel is to choose a data source—the database from which you will import data. Once you have chosen a data source, you can refer to the named data source for other queries you will build in this session.

Creating a connection to a data source:

1. With the Midwest Customers worksheet active, click **Data** on the menu bar, point to **Import External Data,** and click **New Database Query.** The Choose Data Source dialog box opens (see Figure 11.23)

Choose Data Source

Databases | Queries | OLAP Cubes

<New Data Source>
dBase Files - Word*
dBASE Files*
Excel Files*
FoxPro Files - Word*
MS Access Database*
Presidents
Visual FoxPro Database*
Visual FoxPro Tables*

OK
Cancel
Browse...
Options...
Delete

☑ Use the Query Wizard to create/edit queries

very important: make sure that this check box contains a checkmark. If it does not, then click it to place a checkmark in it.

2. Ensure that the **Use the Query Wizard to create/edit queries** check box contains a checkmark, and then double-click the **<New Data Source>** selection. The Create New Data Source dialog box appears containing four boxes that you must fill out in order, 1 through 4

3. Type **MBBW** in text box number 1 to name your data source, and then click in list box number 2 and select **Microsoft Access Driver (*.mdb)** (see Figure 11.24)

Create New Data Source

What name do you want to give your data source?
1. MBBW

Select a driver for the type of database you want to access:
2. Microsoft Access Driver (*.mdb)

Click Connect and enter any information requested by the driver:
3. Connect...

Select a default table for your data source (optional):
4.

☐ Save my user ID and password in the data source definition

OK   Cancel

4. Click the **Connect** button that appears next to the number *3.* This displays a new dialog box in which you select a specific database by name (see Figure 11.25)

5. Click the **Select** button in the Database panel. The Select Database dialog box opens

6. Use the Directories list box to navigate to the folder in which the file **ex11MBBW.mdb** appears, click **ex11MBBW.mdb** in the Database Name list box (see Figure 11.26), and click the **OK** button. The ODBC Microsoft Access Setup dialog box reappears

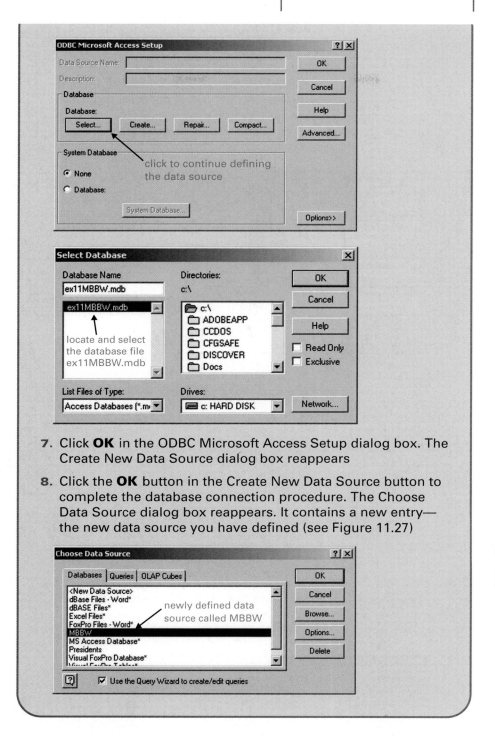

FIGURE 11.25
ODBC Microsoft Access Setup
dialog box

FIGURE 11.26
Select Database dialog box

7. Click **OK** in the ODBC Microsoft Access Setup dialog box. The Create New Data Source dialog box reappears

8. Click the **OK** button in the Create New Data Source button to complete the database connection procedure. The Choose Data Source dialog box reappears. It contains a new entry— the new data source you have defined (see Figure 11.27)

FIGURE 11.27
Choose Data Source dialog box
with the new data source

Choosing and Arranging Columns

After creating the data source, which you named MBBW in this case, you can launch the actual Query Wizard. Then you will be able to specify which table(s) and which column(s) of the database table you want the query to import into your Excel worksheet. Bob tells you that the customer information is stored in a database table named tblCustomers. He wants you to import all the data columns, except CustomerID, for customers who live in Illinois, Indiana, or Michigan.

Choosing the table and table columns to import:

1. In the Choose Data Source dialog box, click **MBBW** in the list of data sources to select it and then click the **OK** button. The Query Wizard executes and then displays the Query Wizard—Choose Columns dialog box displaying a list of tables and queries stored in the database (see Figure 11.28)

FIGURE 11.28

Query Wizard—Choose Columns dialog box

click the expand button (+) to display the table's columns

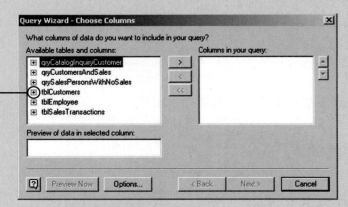

tip: *In large databases, the list of tables and queries may be very long. You can sort the table names and query names into alphabetical order by clicking the **Options** button and then checking the **List Tables and Columns in alphabetical order** check box in the Table Options dialog box that appears*

2. Click the **plus symbol** (+) in front of tblCustomers in the *Available tables and columns* list box. The table's list of columns appears below the table name

3. Click the **FirstName** column name, and then click the > button to place the column name in the *Columns in your query* list. Notice that a column name is moved from one list to another, disappears from the available column list, and the Query Wizard highlights the next name in the list

4. Click the > button repeatedly to move the **LastName, Address, City, State, ZipCode,** and **PhoneNumber** columns, in turn, to the *Columns in your query* list box (see Figure 11.29)

FIGURE 11.29

After selecting columns

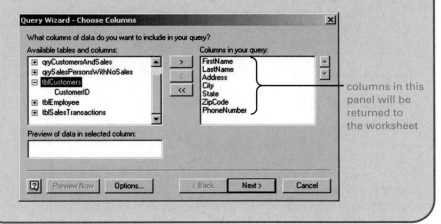

columns in this panel will be returned to the worksheet

tip: *If you aren't sure what information is in a particular column, highlight the column name and then click the **Preview Now** button to display a sample of the actual data in the Preview of data in selected column box*

Filtering Data

You have specified the columns from the tblCustomers table that you want to import into Excel. Next, you must specify record ***selection criteria***, also called a ***filter***, which limits the records retrieved from a table. In this case, the process of limiting records, called filtering data, means you will restrict the retrieved customer records to three states: Illinois, Indiana, or Michigan. In the Query Wizard's next step, you will limit how many and which rows you will retrieve in the completed query.

> ### Limiting retrieved records to those matching selection criteria:
>
> 1. Click the **Next** button. The Query Wizard—Filter Data dialog box opens
>
> 2. Click **State** in the *Column to filter* list. The first list box, located in the *Only include rows where* group, lightens
>
> 3. Click the leftmost list box in the first row of the *Only include rows where* group and click **equals** from the list of relational operations
>
> 4. Type **IL,** (the abbreviation for Illinois) in the rightmost list box in the first row of the *Only include rows where* group
>
> 5. Click the **Or** option button below the first condition in the *Only include rows where* group
>
> 6. Click the leftmost list box in the second row and select **equals**
>
> 7. Click the **list box arrow** in the rightmost list box in the second row. Then scroll down the list box to locate and then click the entry **IN** (the abbreviation for Indiana)
>
> 8. Click the **Or** option button below the second condition in the *Only include rows where* group
>
> 9. Click the leftmost list box in the third row and select **equals**
>
> 10. Click the **list box arrow** in the rightmost list box in the third row. Then scroll down the list box to locate and then click the entry **MI** (see Figure 11.30)

The filtering criteria tells the Query Wizard to only retrieve records in which the customer's State column has the value IL, IN, or MI. The query will exclude all other rows.

Sorting the Resulting Set

The Query Wizard's next to the last step is simple and quick. You can select up to three columns to sort the retrieved data, and you can sort each column either in ascending or descending order. Although you can sort the

2

FIGURE 11.30

Query Wizard—Filter Data
dialog box completed

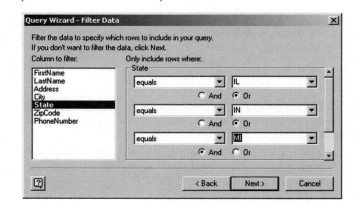

data after they are retrieved into Excel, it usually saves time to let the query do the work. The sort columns you specify must be among the columns returned by the query. For example, you cannot ask the Query Wizard to sort the CustomerID data, because that is not one of the columns that the query will return.

Sorting the data in the query:

1. Click the **Next** button to display the Query Wizard—Sort Order dialog box

2. Click the **Sort by** list box and then click **State** in the list that appears. The Query Wizard automatically selects the Ascending sort option for the column

3. Click the topmost **Then by** list box and then click **City** from the list of sort fields (see Figure 11.31)

FIGURE 11.31

Query Wizard—Sort Order
dialog box

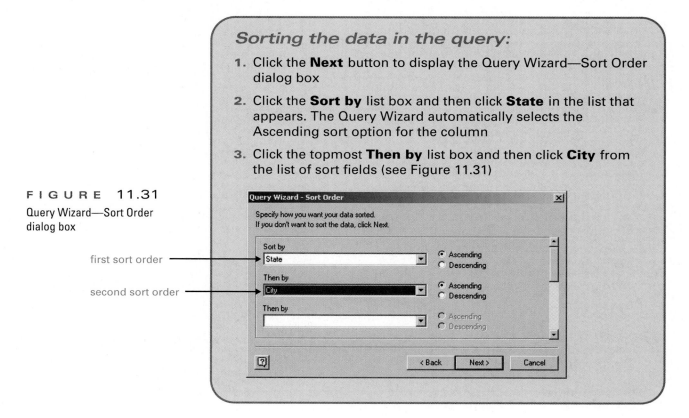

Returning Data to Microsoft Excel and Saving a Query for Later Use

Now the query is complete and there is only one more step remaining. You can instruct the Query Wizard to retrieve the data from the database table and return the data to Excel. Additionally, you can save the query so that you can rerun it later. Why would you ever want to rerun a query? The answer is that the database data will probably change over time as more customers are added to the table and others place orders. If you rerun the query you saved now in two weeks, you are likely to retrieve a slightly different set of customer records. In other words, it is always a good idea to save your query so that you have the option of rerunning it again in the future. Otherwise, you may be stuck running through the Query Wizard steps again.

Bob wants to run this particular query four times in the next month—once each week—to analyze the customer data. Therefore, he wants you to save the query under the name MidwestCustomers. After you save the query, you will return the data to the Excel worksheet.

Saving the customer query:

1. Click the **Next** button to display the Query Wizard—Finish dialog box

2. Click the **Save Query** button, type **MidwestCustomers** in the File name list box, and click **Save.** The Query Wizard saves the query in a special folder called Queries and then redisplays the Finish dialog box. The External Data toolbar probably appears also (see Figure 11.32)

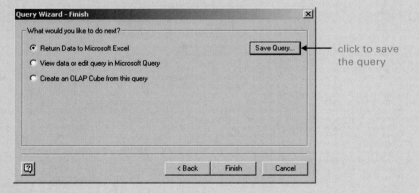

tip: *If a dialog box appears indicating that the query already exists, that is probably because someone else using this computer already created a query definition. Click the Yes button to replace the existing query definition with yours*

3. If the External Data toolbar appears, click the Close button on its title bar to remove the toolbar

FIGURE 11.32
Query Wizard—Finish dialog box

Now you can retrieve the customer information with the query you created and return it to the Excel worksheet.

Returning query results to a worksheet:

1. Ensure that the **Return Data to Microsoft Excel** option button is selected in the Query Wizard—Finish dialog box. Then click the **Finish** button. The Import Data dialog box appears asking where you want to place the data (see Figure 11.33)

EXCEL

F I G U R E   11.33

Import Data dialog box

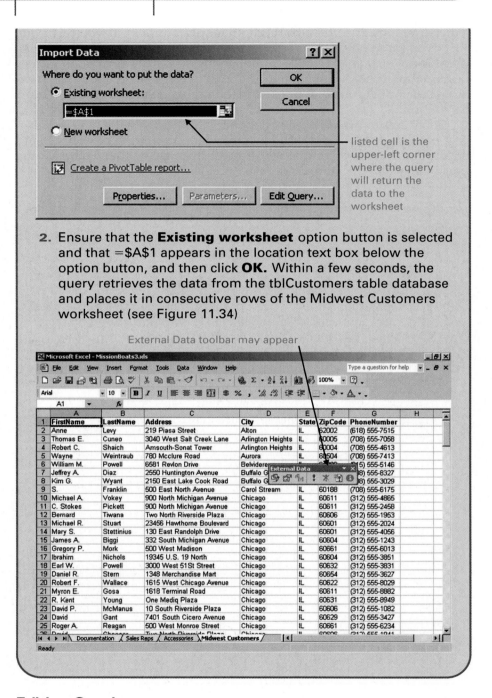

listed cell is the upper-left corner where the query will return the data to the worksheet

2. Ensure that the **Existing worksheet** option button is selected and that =$A$1 appears in the location text box below the option button, and then click **OK.** Within a few seconds, the query retrieves the data from the tblCustomers table database and places it in consecutive rows of the Midwest Customers worksheet (see Figure 11.34)

F I G U R E   11.34

Data returned by the query

Editing Queries

If you work with Excel's Query Wizard quite a bit, you may create a large collection of saved queries. You can rerun any of your saved queries. Suppose you have created a query and discover that you forgot an important column from the database table you imported. That's not a problem since you can simply edit the query and then rerun it.

Bob wants you to remove the PhoneNumber column from the query and thus the column's imported data. Although you could simply delete the PhoneNumber column from the worksheet, the query would continue to import the PhoneNumber column whenever the query is run. For long-term results, edit the database query.

task reference

Editing a Query

- Make sure that one of the cells containing imported database data is active

- Click **Data,** point to **Import External Data,** and click **Edit Query**

- Step through each of the Query Wizard's steps, make any necessary changes at each step, and then press **Next** to go to the next step

- On the Query Wizard's final step, click the **Save Query** button to save your changes and then click the **Finish** button to refresh the imported data

Editing the MidwestCustomers query to delete an unwanted column:

1. Click cell **A1** to ensure that the active cell is one of the imported data elements

2. Click **Data** on the menu bar, point to **Import External Data,** and click **Edit Query.** The Query Wizard—Choose Columns dialog box opens

3. Click **PhoneNumber** in the *Columns in your query* list box (see Figure 11.35), and then click the < button to move the column name back to the tblCustomers table

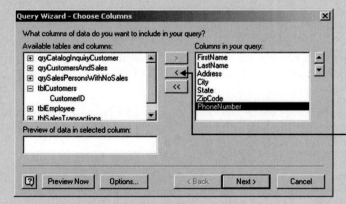

FIGURE 11.35

Preparing to remove a column from a query definition

click to move the highlighted column from the right panel to the left—to delete it from a query

4. Click **Next** to go to the Filter Data step, click **Next** again to go to the Sort Order step, and click **Next** once again to go to the Finish step

5. Click the **Save Query** button to save the modified query. The Save As dialog box opens

6. Click the **Save** button, and then click the **Yes** button when you are asked if you want to replace the query that already exists. The Query Wizard—Finish dialog box reappears

7. Click the **Finish** button to requery the database and import the new data into your Excel worksheet. Notice that the PhoneNumber column does not appear in the refreshed data

Refreshing Data

Databases are continuously changing as database personnel add new customers and delete customers. That's why it is important to refresh data whenever you are working with an Excel worksheet of imported database data. Excel displays a static picture of the data taken sometime in the past. To ensure that your Excel data are current, you have to refresh the data. You can set up a query so that it automatically refreshes the spreadsheet data each time a user opens the workbook. Bob thinks that's a good idea and asks you to do that next.

---

task reference

Automatically Refreshing Data Each Time a Workbook Is Opened

- Ensure that the active worksheet cell is one of the imported data values

- Click **Data,** click **Import External Data,** click **Data Range Properties**

- Click the **Refresh data on file open** check box to place a checkmark in it

- Click **OK**

Forcing a query to automatically refresh data:

1. If necessary, click cell **A1** to ensure that the active cell is one of the imported data elements

2. Click **Data** on the menu bar, point to **Import External Data,** and click **Data Range Properties.** The External Data Range Properties dialog box opens

3. Click the **Refresh data on file open** check box in the Refresh control section to place a checkmark in it (see Figure 11.36)

FIGURE 11.36

Ensuring a query refreshes the data

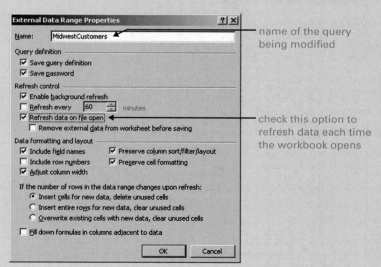

name of the query being modified

check this option to refresh data each time the workbook opens

tip: The next time you open this workbook, Excel will display a Query Refresh dialog box indicating that the workbook contains queries to external data that refresh automatically. Click the **Enable automatic refresh** button to refresh the data

tip: In the Query Refresh dialog box is a check box that allows Excel to refresh the query without bothering you with the dialog box. Check the **Enable automatic query refresh** check box to prevent the warning from occurring for all workbooks you open.

4. Click OK

Each time someone opens the **MissionBoats3.xls** workbook, the query you created with Microsoft Query will import the latest database table data into the Midwest Customers worksheet.

What about creating more complicated queries involving more criteria or more than one database table? You have to use software that is more powerful than the Query Wizard.

USING MICROSOFT QUERY

Bob wants to analyze sales amounts for the last six months. In particular, he would like to see the total sales for the states of Illinois, Indiana, and Michigan to determine any pattern in customer demand by state. Some of the information Bob wants is in the tblCustomer table—the state in which each customer resides. Another part of the information, total sales for each customer transaction, is in another table in the same database called tblSalesTransactions. It contains information about each sale including the sale amount, the salesperson's identification number, and the customer's number. To extract total sales by state, you will have to form a query that extracts information from two separate, but related, tables. Pulling information from two tables requires the database system to perform a join operation on the two tables. A *join* operation matches records in two tables based on a common field, such as a customer number or an inventory number. Joining two tables together in Query Wizard is difficult at best. The more powerful query tool you need is called Microsoft Query.

When to Use Microsoft Query

Microsoft Query is a powerful database query tool that is included with Excel. It allows you to take full advantage of all the capabilities of your database system—including joining two or more tables together. The price you pay for this power is a slightly more complex and less intuitive query-building interface than the Query Wizard. Microsoft Query is a more powerful tool than the Query Wizard because Microsoft Query allows you to:

- add more criteria to restrict which rows are returned to your worksheet
- perform calculations on groups of information—calculations such as summing values, averaging values, or counting unique values
- write SQL (pronounced "sequel") statements. **SQL** is an abbreviation for *structured query language* and is a standard language for requesting information from a database
- join multiple database tables together

Whenever you need to do any of the preceding, then Microsoft Query is a better choice than using the Query Wizard.

Starting Microsoft Query

Because you have to create a multi-table join, extract values from two different tables, and sum those values by state, you quickly decide that Microsoft Query is the tool to use. You ask Bob how to execute Microsoft Query instead of using the Query Wizard. He tells you to clear the checkmark from the *Use the Query Wizard to create/edit queries* check box in the Choose Data Source dialog box (examine Figure 11.27 again). Once you clear the check box, Microsoft Query dialog boxes appear as you define a new query. You are ready to create the new query to extract summary data by state that Bob wants. First, create a new worksheet and name its tab Sales by State.

> ### Creating a new worksheet to hold the sales summary by state:
>
> 1. Click **Insert** on the menu bar, click **Worksheet,** click and drag the newly added worksheet to a new position following the Midwest Customers worksheet
>
> 2. Double-click the new worksheet tab, type **Sales by State,** and press **Enter**
>
> 3. Right-click the **Sales by State** worksheet tab, click **Tab Color,** click the **Rose** color square (fifth row from the top, leftmost column), and click **OK**

Choosing Database Tables and Joining Them

With the new worksheet available to hold the imported summary sales information, you begin to build the query.

> ### Joining two tables together with Microsoft Query:
>
> 1. Click **Data** on the menu bar, point to **Import External Data,** and click **New Database Query.** The Choose Data Source dialog box appears
>
> 2. Click **MBBW,** which is the name of the data source you created in previous steps
>
> 3. Click the **Use the Query Wizard to create/edit queries** check box to clear its checkmark (see Figure 11.37)
>
> 4. Click **OK.** The Add Tables dialog box appears
>
> 5. Double-click the **tblCustomers** table name in the Table list box
>
> 6. Double-click the **tblSalesTransactions** table name. Microsoft Query displays a small panel in its query pane listing the

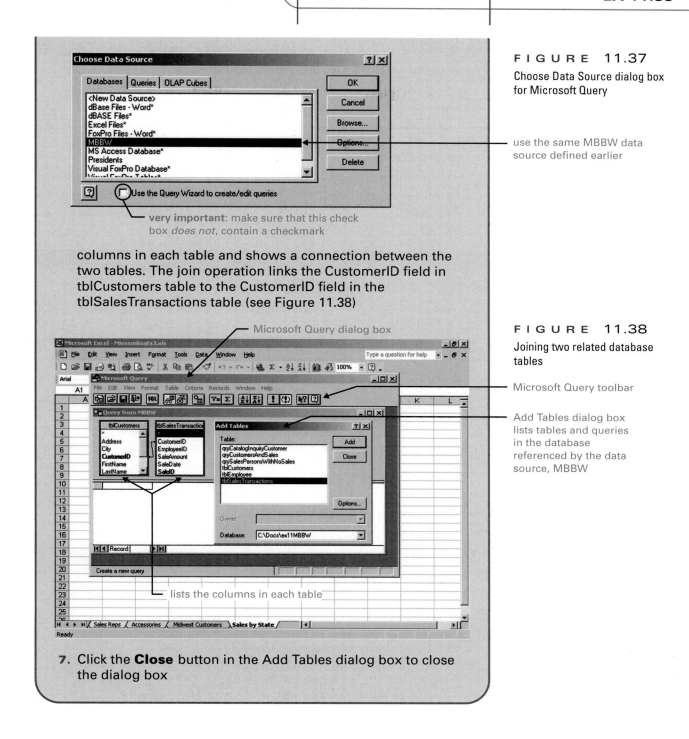

FIGURE 11.37
Choose Data Source dialog box for Microsoft Query

use the same MBBW data source defined earlier

very important: make sure that this check box *does not*, contain a checkmark

columns in each table and shows a connection between the two tables. The join operation links the CustomerID field in tblCustomers table to the CustomerID field in the tblSalesTransactions table (see Figure 11.38)

FIGURE 11.38
Joining two related database tables

Microsoft Query dialog box

Microsoft Query toolbar

Add Tables dialog box lists tables and queries in the database referenced by the data source, MBBW

lists the columns in each table

7. Click the **Close** button in the Add Tables dialog box to close the dialog box

Microsoft Query automatically creates joins between two tables when it determines that one table has a column name that is identical to a special column in another table called a primary key. A ***primary key*** is a table column whose values are unique for each record in a table. If the two tables had different common, or join, column names, you would have to join the two tables together. You would drag and drop a primary key column from one table to its counterpart, called a ***foreign key,*** in the other table. Microsoft then draws a line between the two column names indicating it has joined the two tables on their primary key and foreign key pairs.

Manually Joining Two Tables in a Query

- Drag and drop the primary key from one table to the corresponding foreign key in the second table

Selecting Table Columns

Now that you have selected the correct tables containing the State and Sales Amount columns and joined the tables together, you are ready to select the columns you want to retrieve from the database tables and return to your Excel worksheet.

Adding a Column to a Query

- Double-click a column name to add it to the lower half of the query window

or

- Drag and drop the column name to the lower half of the query window

Because Bob wants you to display the total sales by each state, your query must return two columns: the State column from the tblCustomers table and the SaleAmount column from the tblSalesTransactions table. (Although the SaleAmount column is not a statewide sum, later in this chapter you will modify the results to sum the sales by state.)

anotherway

. . . to Add a Table Column to a Query

Double-click the column name in the table's list of column names

Adding the State and SaleAmount columns to the query:

1. Scroll the column names in the tblCustomer field roster until you see the State column name

2. Drag and drop the **State** column name to the lower panel of the query. State names appear in the first column of the lower panel

3. Drag and drop the **SaleAmount** column name, in the tblSalesTransactions field roster, to the first row, second column in the lower panel of the query. Values for sale amounts appear in the second column (see Figure 11.39)

Removing a Column from a Query

- Move the mouse pointer over the column name in the lower panel of the query

- When the pointer changes to a down arrow, click to select the column

- Press the **Delete** key

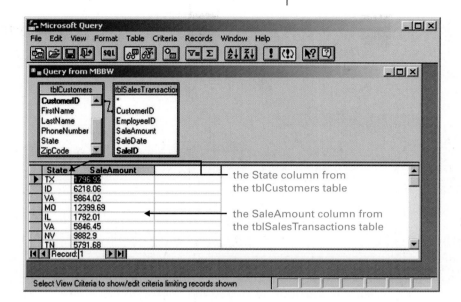

Query with two column names
from two tables

Limiting Which Rows the Query Returns

You restrict which rows a query returns by adding criteria to the query. You used criteria before with the Query Wizard. The effects are the same when you apply criteria using Microsoft Query. Simply specify examples of the values for a particular column that you want to appear in the result, and Microsoft Query will return only records satisfying the criteria for those column(s).

task reference

Adding Criteria to a Query Using Microsoft Query

- Click **Criteria** on the Microsoft Query menu bar and then click **Add Criteria**

- Fill in the list and text boxes in the Add Criteria dialog box

- Click the **Add** button to add the criteria to the query

- Continue adding additional criteria, if needed

- Click the **Close** button when the criteria are complete

Limiting values returned by the query to the states of Illinois, Indiana, or Michigan means you must add the criteria to limit rows to those states.

Adding criteria to a query:

1. Click **Criteria** on the Microsoft Query menu bar, and then click **Add Criteria.** The Add Criteria dialog box appears

2. Click the **Field** list box arrow, scroll the list until you see tblCustomers.State, and then click the entry **tblCustomers.State**

3. Double-click the **Value** field text box to select its value, type **IL,** and click the **Add** button to add the criteria to the query

4. Click the **Or** option button at the top of the Add Criteria dialog box (see Figure 11.40)

FIGURE 11.40

Adding criteria to a query

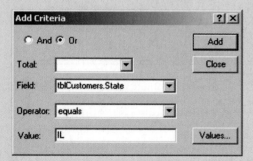

5. Double-click the **Value** field text box to select its value, type **IN,** and click the **Add** button to add the criteria to the query

6. Double-click the **Value** field text box to select its value, type **MI,** and click the **Add** button to add the criteria to the query

7. Click the **Close** button to close the Add Criteria dialog box

8. Click the **Maximize** button on the Query from the MBBW dialog box title bar

9. Move the mouse to the bottom edge of the Query from the MBBW dialog box. When the mouse pointer turns to a double-headed arrow, click and drag the bottom edge down to enlarge the dialog box. Notice that the query preview list contains, in the first few rows, only State column values of IL, IN, or MI. This indicates that the results are restricted by the criteria (see Figure 11.41)

FIGURE 11.41

Previewing filtered results

preview shows only IL, IN, or MI in the State column

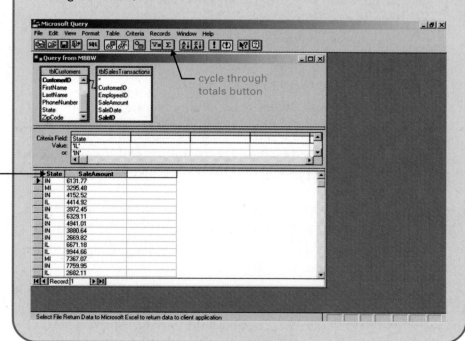

Adding Totals

Bob comments that the preview of the query results apparently display individual sales. He adds that there are over one hundred rows in the result, so far. Bob wants a summary of sales in the three states, not the details. He asks you to figure out a way to have the query display total sales in each of the three states.

You discover that Microsoft Query can provide five types of calculations on query data. They are average, count, maximum, minimum, and sum. The calculations are called **aggregate** calculations because they cumulate information about groups of data. The sum calculation, when used with the SaleAmount column in the query, will group all the sales results by State value and then sum the groups—just what you need here. For example, you sum a column by selecting the column and then clicking the Cycle Through Totals button in the Microsoft Query toolbar (see Figure 11.41).

task reference

Summing a Value Column in a Query

- Click any result in the column you want to sum
- Click the **Cycle Through Totals** button

Summing the SaleAmount column by State:

1. Click the first value in the SaleAmount column in the lower panel of the query

2. Click the **Cycle Through Totals** button (see Figure 11.41). The SaleAmount column header changes to *Sum of SaleAmount,* and the preview list of results shrinks to just three entries—one for each state that Bob wants to review (see Figure 11.42)

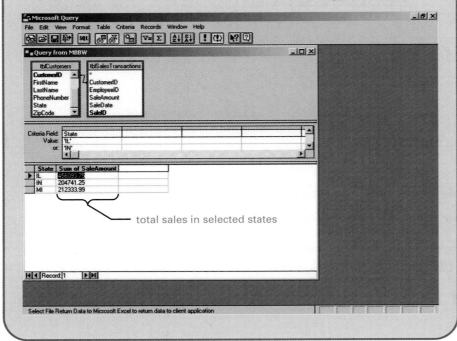

FIGURE 11.42

Preview of query results after summing

tip: *If some other aggregate title appears such as Avg of SaleAmount or Min of SaleAmount, then repeatedly click the* **Cycle Through Totals** *button until Sum of SaleAmount appears in the columns header of the second column in the lower query panel*

Editing a Query's Column Name

Whenever you return results from a query that calculates sums, averages, minimums, maximums, or counts, Query creates a column name prefix indicating the type of calculation that appears in the column. Notice, for example, that the states' total values appear in a column named Sum of SaleAmount.

You can change the name in the query or you can change it in Excel. The problem with changing a returned column's name in Excel is that Query changes it back to the original name when you rerun the query. It is best to change a column's name in the query. That way, the name sticks. Bob wants the sum of sales column to be named Total Sales. He asks you to make the change.

FIGURE 11.43

Changing a query column's name

column's new name

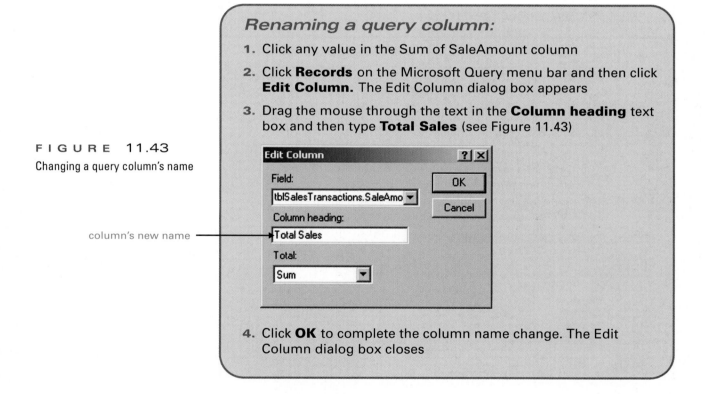

Renaming a query column:

1. Click any value in the Sum of SaleAmount column

2. Click **Records** on the Microsoft Query menu bar and then click **Edit Column.** The Edit Column dialog box appears

3. Drag the mouse through the text in the **Column heading** text box and then type **Total Sales** (see Figure 11.43)

4. Click **OK** to complete the column name change. The Edit Column dialog box closes

Saving a Microsoft Query

Before returning the results to your Excel worksheet, save the query in case Bob wants to rerun it next month. That way, he will simply select the query and return the new results to a worksheet rather than creating a query from scratch.

Returning Results to Excel

You have defined the query completely and are ready to transfer the query results from database tables.

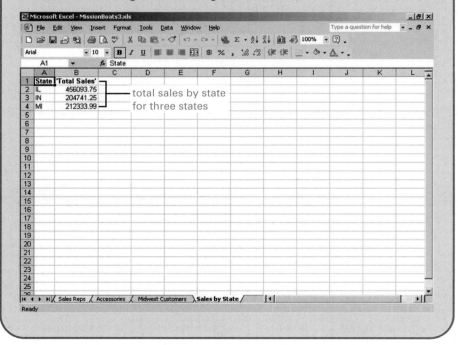

FIGURE 11.44

Returned results

Refreshing Query Data

Bob is concerned that the customer data in the database are ever changing, but that his Excel summary worksheet is a static picture of the database. He asks you how he can be sure the data are accurate. You remind him that he can simply refresh the data.

Manually refreshing query data:

1. Right-click anywhere in the returned data set

2. Click **Refresh Data.** Excel sends the query you created to the database and the updated results appear in your worksheet. Of course, none of the database table data are altered, so the Excel cells remain unchanged

---

Save your workbook, because you have completed your work on the Mission Bay Boat Works workbook and you want to preserve all your changes.

Saving your Mission Bay Boat Works workbook and exiting Excel:

1. Right-click the **tab scrolling** buttons located left of the worksheet tabs and then click **Documentation** in the shortcut menu. The Documentation worksheet becomes active

2. Click the **Save** 🔲 button on the Standard toolbar to save the workbook

3. Click **File** on the menu bar and then click **Exit.** Excel closes

---

Bob is pleased with your work. He can review the data in his Excel workbook, manipulating the numbers any way he wants, and refresh the data periodically when necessary.

SESSION 11.2

making the grade

1. A _____ is a collection of related information about one object that is stored in a database table.

2. By using _____ _____, also called filtering, you limit the records retrieved from a table to those matching certain characteristics.

3. When Excel reruns a database query, it retrieves the most recent information from a database table. You can right-click anywhere in the imported data and then click the _____ Data command to obtain the latest information.

4. To use a query to import information from two related tables, you must first link two tables based on a column found in both tables. You (or Microsoft Query) perform a(n) _____ operation to link the tables.

5. Modify the **MissionBoats3.xls** workbook in the following ways. First, open **MissionBoats3.xls.** If the Query Refresh dialog box appears, click the **Enable automatic refresh** button to proceed to open the workbook. Immediately save the workbook as **MissionBoats112.xls.** Then add a new worksheet, move the worksheet so that it follows the Sales by State worksheet, rename the worksheet tab to **Sales by Employees,** and color the worksheet tab light yellow. Create a new database query (**Data, Import External Data, New Database Query**) by using Microsoft Query (clear the **Use the Query Wizard to create/edit queries** check box), not the Query Wizard. Select **MBBW** from the Data Source dialog box, use the tblEmployee and tblSalesTransactions tables in the Add Table dialog box, and insert the columns **EmployeeFirstName** and **EmployeeLastName** into the query. Then insert the **SaleAmount** column *twice* into the query. Click any value in the first **SaleAmount** column, and then click the **Cycle Through Totals** button *three times* to display the Count of SaleAmount. Click any value in the second **SaleAmount** column and then click the **Cycle Through Totals** button once to display Sum of SaleAmount. Click the **Sort Descending** button on the Query toolbar to sort the rightmost Sum of SaleAmount column from largest to smallest. Rename the two Sum of SaleAmount columns, left to right, to **Sales Count** and **Total Sales.** Return the data to the Excel worksheet. Place your name in the Sales by Employees worksheet header and print the worksheet. Save the workbook and exit Excel.

SESSION 11.3 SUMMARY

Excel can import data in a variety of formats including delimited text. Text data have no internal structure to indicate where data for one column end and another column begins. Excel relies on a delimiter character or characters to distinguish one column from another when importing text data into a worksheet. Possible delimiters include commas, semicolons, spaces, or tabs. Text data columns that occur in specific locations for each record are called fixed length data fields, and Excel can import this text file format also. The Text Import Wizard automatically opens whenever you open a file whose name ends with .prn, .txt, or .csv. The Text Import Wizard guides you through the three-step import process.

You can double-click a comma-separated values data file in Windows Explorer to open the file directly into Excel. The Text Import Wizard does not appear, because Excel knows how to import CSV files quickly.

You can use copy and paste techniques to copy information from a Web page directly into an Excel worksheet. Columnar data in a Web page appears in Excel columns after you paste the data into a worksheet. Using Copy and Paste Special commands available in the Edit menu, you can copy formulas to the Clipboard and then paste back values in their place. This is particularly handy when you want to reduce formula recalculation time in a workbook.

Databases are the most popular choice for corporate data storage. Both large and small organizations use databases to hold customer, invoice, and employee information. Excel can import data from a wide variety of popular database systems including Microsoft Access, Oracle, Microsoft SQL Server, FoxPro, and IBM's DB2. You can use either Excel's built-in Query Wizard or Microsoft's separate Query program to import data from database systems. The Excel Query Wizard is slightly easier to use, but it is not quite as powerful as Microsoft Query. Using either product is a two-step process: You define and connect to a database data source and then you build a query that Excel sends to the database to retrieve information and return it to an Excel worksheet.

MOUS OBJECTIVES SUMMARY

- Import text files into Excel with the Text Import Wizard (MOUS Ex2002e-1-1)
- Copy data from a Web page and paste it into an Excel worksheet (MOUS Ex2002e-1-1)

task reference roundup

Task	Page #	Preferred Method
Importing Fixed Length Data Using the Text Import Wizard	EX 11.7	• Click **File** and then click **Open**
		• In the Files of type list box of the Open dialog box, select **Text Files**
		• Using the *Look in* list box, navigate to the folder containing the text file, click the filename in the list of files, and click the **Open** button
		• Click the **Fixed Width** option button in the Original data type panel
		• Click the **Start import at row** spin box to select the first row to import, and click the **Next** button
		• In Step 2, click to the left of each field to add a break line, double-click a break line to remove it, or drag a break line to its correct position at the beginning of a column as needed. Then click the **Next** button to proceed
		• In Step 3, for each column, click a **Column data format** option button to select a column format, or click the **Do not import column** option button to skip the column, and click the **Finish** button
Adding, Moving, and Deleting Column Breaks Using the Text Import Wizard	EX 11.10	• Add a column break by clicking the position just above the ruler in the Data preview panel where you want the column break to appear
		• Move a column break by clicking it and then dragging it to its new position
		• Delete a column break by double-clicking it

task reference roundup

Task	Page #	Preferred Method
Editing a Query	EX 11.35	• Make sue that one of the cells containing imported database data is active
		• Click **Data**, point to **Import External Data,** and click **Edit Query**
		• Step through each of the Query Wizard's steps, make any necessary changes at each step and then press **Next** to go to the next step
		• On the Query Wizard's final step, click the **Save Query** button to save your changes and then click the **Finish** button to refresh the imported data
Automatically Refreshing Data Each Time a Workbook is Opened	EX 11.36	• Ensure that the active worksheet cell is one of the imported data values
		• Click **Data,** click **Import External Data,** click **Data Range Properties**
		• Click the **Refresh data on file open** check box to place a checkmark in it
		• Click **OK**
Manually Joining Two Tables in a query	EX 11.40	• Drag and drop the primary key from one table to the corresponding foreign key in the second table
Adding a Column to a Query	EX 11.40	• Double-click a column name to add it to the lower half of the query window
		or
		• Drag and drop the column name to the lower half of the query window
Removing a Column from a Query	EX 11.40	• Move the mouse pointer over the column name in the lower panel of the query
		• When the pointer changes to a down arrow, click to select the column
		• Press the **Delete** key
Adding Criteria to a Query Using Microsoft Query	EX 11.41	• Click **Criteria** on the Microsoft Query menu bar and then click **Add Criteria**
		• Fill in the list and text boxes in the Add Criteria dialog box
		• Click the **Add** button to add the criteria to the query
		• Continue adding additional criteria, if needed
		• Click the **Close** button when the criteria are complete
Summing a Value Column in a Query	EX 11.43	• Click any result in the column you want to sum
		• Click the **Cycle Through Totals** button

EXCEL

CROSSWORD PUZZLE

Across

5. A Uniform _____ Locator is a Web address.
6. An individual unit of data in a text file.
7. Information organized so that a computer program can select information quickly.
9. A _____ key is a unique identifier for each record in the table.
10. A line that appears in a text import step to indicate the beginning of a field is a column _____.
12. A database _____ is software that translates Excel requests into database commands.
14. The abbreviation for text data whose values are separated by commas.
16. Called _____ width data, fields occur at particular locations in the input file.

Down

1. An operation that links two related tables together.
2. Another name for selection criteria.
3. Specifying selection _____ limits the records retrieved from a database.
4. A character or group of characters that separates two pieces of text data.
8. Pronounced "sequel," this is the abbreviation for a standard database command language.
11. The "R" in RTF stands for _____ Text Format.
13. A collection of related information about one object stored in a database table.
15. What type of data consists only of characters that you can type on a keyboard?

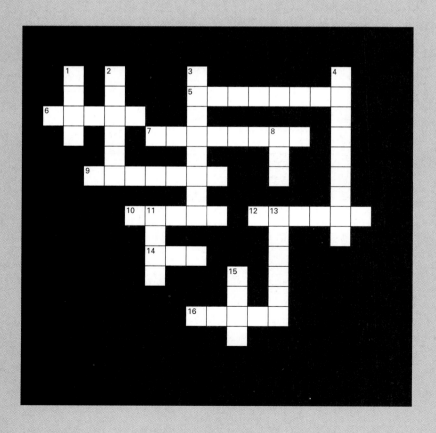

FILL-IN

1. The _____ _____ Wizard appears when you open a text file in Excel.

2. Text data appearing in the same columns throughout the data are called _____ length data.

3. Data in which fields are separated by commas are called _____ separated _____, or CSVs.

4. Double-click a column break in the Text Import Wizard to _____ the column break.

5. Before you can use Microsoft Query to retrieve information from a database, you must first define a _____ source.

6. The standard language for sending commands to databases is called SQL, which stands for _____ Query _____.

REVIEW QUESTIONS

1. Explain why you have to use an import Wizard to import a text file into Excel.

2. Explain why you might ask a database query to sort data, using Microsoft Query, before returning the data to the Excel worksheet. After all, you could perform a sort in Excel after the data is returned. (Hint: Think of a large amount of data.)

3. Explain why you might want to save a query. Once you have returned data into an Excel worksheet, is that it?

4. What does the term "aggregate data" mean when considering a database query?

CREATE THE QUESTION

For each of the following answers, create an appropriate, short question.

ANSWER	QUESTION
1. Comma-separated values	_____
2. Column break	_____
3. General, Text, Date, and Do Not Import column	_____
4. Edit, Paste Special, Values	_____
5. Filter	_____
6. The Refresh command	_____

practice

1. Importing Faculty Teaching Assignments from a Database

Lincoln College, located in Lincoln, Nebraska, teaches a full range of business courses including undergraduate and graduate accounting, general business, and economics courses. Each semester, Dean Nancy Rivetti produces a list of faculty and the courses that they teach. Recently, the registrar placed all information about faculty, students, schedules, and course catalogs into an Access database. Nancy just received a database containing faculty teaching assignments, class scheduling table, and the School of Business course catalog table in an Access database. Nancy is not comfortable using an Access database and wants you to import this coming semester's teaching assignments into an Excel worksheet so she that can print and post it around the campus.

1. Open **ex11LincolnCollege.xls** and save the workbook as **LincolnCollege2.xls**
2. Click the **Teaching Assignments** worksheet tab
3. Click **Data,** point to **Import External Data,** click **New Database Query,** ensure **<New Data Source>** is highlighted in the Choose Data Source dialog box, and then click **OK.** The Create New Data Source dialog box opens
4. Type **Teaching Assignments** in the first textbox; click the second text box and then click **Microsoft Access Driver (*.mdb);** click the **Connect** button to open the ODBC Microsoft Access Setup dialog box
5. Click the **Select** button, navigate to the **ex11LincolnCollege.mdb** database in the Select Database dialog box, click **ex11LincolnCollege.mdb,** click **OK,** and click **OK** again to close the ODBC Microsoft Access Setup dialog box
6. Click **OK** to close the Create New Data Source dialog box
7. Clear the **Use the Query Wizard to create/edit queries** check box, if necessary, to use Microsoft Query; click **OK**

8. In the Add Tables dialog box, double-click **tblFacultyNames,** double-click **tblFacultyCourseAssignments,** double-click **tblCourseNames,** and click the **Close** button
9. Drag the **FacultyID** field name from the tblFacultyNames field roster and drop it on the **ProfessorID** field name in tblFacultyCourseAssignments field roster to join the two tables
10. To add fields to the lower portion of the query, double-click the following fields in the order listed: **FirstName, LastName, Name, Number,** and **Title**
11. Click any entry in the **LastName** column in the lower portion of the query, and then click the **Sort Ascending** button on the Microsoft Query toolbar
12. Click **File** on the Microsoft Query menu bar, and then click **Return Data to Microsoft Excel**
13. Click **OK** to approve the choices presented in the Import Data dialog box
14. Place your name in both worksheet headers, type your name in the Designed by location on the Documentation worksheet, and type today's date in the Design date cell. Save the workbook and then print both worksheets

2. Importing U.S. Population Data from a Text File

Alicia Spencer, an editor with the Lafayette Journal and Courier newspaper, is writing an article about population shifts in the United States during the period 1996 through 1999. She would like to display population information in an Excel worksheet and develop percentages to show net inflow or outflow of population. Alicia tells you that a summer intern looked up information on the U.S. Census Bureau Web site and downloaded the information into a text file. The intern has gone back to college, and Alicia does not know how to move the data into an Excel worksheet. She asks you to help her.

1. Open a new Excel workbook, click the **Open** button on the Standard toolbar, click the **Files of type list box arrow,** and click the entry **Text Files (*.prn; *.txt; *.csv)**

2. With the Look in list box, navigate to the folder containing the file **ex11StatePopulation.txt,** click **ex11StatePopulation.txt,** and click the **Open** button

3. Double-click the **Start import at row** spin control box, type **6** to start the import at row 6, and click the **Next** button

4. Ensure that only the **Tab** check box is checked and then click the **Finish** button

5. Click cell **F1,** type **% Change,** and press **Enter**

6. Bold the column labels in the cell range **A1:F1**

7. Click cell **F2,** type the formula **=(E2-B2)/B2,** and press **Enter**

8. Click cell **F2,** drag its fill handle down through cell **F52,** and release the mouse

9. With the cell range F2:F52 selected, click the **Percent Style** button on the Formatting toolbar, and click the Formatting toolbar **Increase Decimal** button *twice*

10. Click any cell in column **F** and then click the **Sort Descending** button on the Standard toolbar

11. Select cell range **B2:E52,** click the **Comma Style** button, and click the **Decrease Decimal** button *twice*. (Both buttons are on the Formatting toolbar)

12. Drag the mouse through column headings **A** through **F,** click **Format,** point to **Column,** click **AutoFit Selection,** and click cell **A1** to deselect the cell range

13. Double-click the **ex11StatePopulation** worksheet tab, type **State Population,** and press **Enter**

14. Place your name in the worksheet header

15. Click **File,** click **Page Setup,** click the **Page** tab, and click the **Fit to** option button in the Scaling section, click the **Print** button, and click **OK**

16. Click **File,** click **Save As,** click the **Save as type** list box arrow, scroll to the top of the list and click **Microsoft Excel Workbook (*.xls),** drag through the text in the **File name** list box, type **StatePopulation2,** and click the **Save** button

1. Using Importing and Pivot Tables to Consolidate Purchasing and Sales Data

Off the Wall is an eclectic home furnishings store in Hollywood, CA. The store has clients ranging from young to old and classic to modern, all looking for unique pieces for their home. Joe Bradley, the storeowner, recently started carrying a new line of sofas, Maripa, featuring bright colors and patterns. Joe wants to determine how well the line is selling and which of his salespeople are successfully moving the line. Joe currently maintains ordering information on the Maripa line in a text file and employee sales information in an Excel workbook. He assigned each of his top six salespeople a model of the Maripa line so that it would be easier to track employee sales. He wants a single Excel worksheet that details Maripa sales information.

Open **ex11OTWSales.xls,** which is Joe's record of the number of Maripa sofas sold in June, sorted by employee ID number. Using Excel, open the file **ex11MaripaOrders.txt** to invoke the Text Import Wizard. The file **ex11MaripaOrders.txt** is Joe's record of Maripa sofas ordered, including both purchase price and sales price. Joe wants you to create an Excel worksheet, titled **June Maripa Sales,** using information from these two data sources. He wants the column headings to be **Item Number, Number ordered, Purchase Price, Sales Price, Number Sold,** and **Employee Name.** Begin by opening a new Excel workbook. Then use the Text Import Wizard to import the **ex11MaripaOrder.txt** data. Data are in fixed width columns. Import the labels in row 3 along with the data. Be sure to adjust columns, if needed, in Step 2 of the Text Import Wizard. Adjust columns in the Excel worksheet, if needed, to display all data adequately. Sort the information in ascending order by the values in the Item Number column. From the **ex11OTWSales.xls** workbook, copy the number sold and employee name columns and paste them in the appropriate cells in the Maripa Sales worksheet. (Hint: Sort the **ex11OTWSales.xls** columns into Item Number order, and then copy cells by matching Item Number values in the two worksheets.) Joe asks you to insert a column to the right of Purchase Price with the heading **Total Cost** and another column to the right of Sales Price with the heading **Total Sales.** Use formulas to fill these columns with the total cost and sales for each item number.

Next, create a pivot table for Joe, sorted by item number, which includes the number of items purchased and sold as well as the total cost and total sales. Allow Joe to either view all of the data, or just by one item number at a time. Improve the appearance of the worksheet and then create a Documentation sheet as the first sheet of the workbook. Include the title **June Maripa Sales** in cell A2. Type **Created by:** followed by your name in cells A5 and B6. Type **Date:** in cell A7 followed by the current date in cell B7. Type **Re:** in cell A9, and type **Ordering and Sales Figures** in cell B9. Insert column headers in all worksheets. Save the workbook as **JuneMaripaSales.xls** and print all worksheets.

Joe's assistant has just given him the updated sales figures for July. He wants you to change the current workbook of June sales to include July sales. Make the Maripa Sales worksheet active and fill the Number Sold column with the following figures, from the first row to the last, in order: **7, 3, 7, 3, 6,** and **11.** Refresh your pivot table to reflect the new sales and change the Documentation sheet title to **July Maripa Sales.** Save your workbook and print the Maripa Sales worksheet again.

on the web

1. Importing and Using Queries to Summarize Presidential Data

Mrs. Borstel is a third-grade teacher at East Ridge Elementary School in Virginia. The class is learning about the U.S. government. Next week, Mrs. Borstel will begin lessons on the American presidents and wants to make the lessons both fun and interesting for the students. She asked her aide to gather a variety of information on all of the U.S. presidents that will be stored in an Excel worksheet. To make it more interesting, she also asked her aide to gather more specific information on presidents who were born in Virginia. Her hope is that the students will be more curious about learning about the presidents if they know that some were born in their home state.

Mrs. Borstel's aide placed the data in an Access database. It contains one table, called Presidents. The table contains these columns: PresidentID, LastName, FirstName, Party, Term, BirthState, InaugurationAge, and Height. PresidentID is a number indicating order in which the Presidents were elected. The Height field is each President's height in inches. The remaining fields are self-explanatory. The second table, called VirginiaPresidents, is supposed to contain data for those presidents born in Virginia. Mrs. Borstel wants you to organize this information in an Excel workbook.

Begin by opening Excel and saving a new workbook as **Presidents.xls.** Use the Query Wizard to import data from the Presidents table in the **ex11Presidents.mdb** database. Specify in the Query Wizard that you do not want to import the Height column. Import all other rows from the Presidents table. Once all the President rows are imported, sort the Excel data in ascending order by the LastName field and then by the FirstName field for matching LastName field values. Name a worksheet **All Presidents.** Insert a new worksheet into the workbook and name it **Virginia Details.** Use the Query Wizard again to retrieve information from the **VirginiaPresidents** table. Import all fields and then sort the table by the President field.

As you can see, three columns of information are missing from the VirginiaPresidents table: the Vice President's name, the President's birth date, and the President's date of death. Go to a reference Web site, such as www.ipl.com (Internet Public Library), or use a search engine, such as www.dogpile.com or www.hotbot.com, to find the needed information on these presidents. Insert the missing information into the VirginiaPresidents worksheet.

Create a new first worksheet titled **Documentation** in the workbook. In **row 3,** enter **Presidents of the United States of America.** Below this title, enter **Created for: Mrs. Borstel, Created by:** followed with your name, **Date:** followed by the date, and **Details: Presidents from Virginia.** Make the appearance of the workbook uniform and attractive using colors and formatting. Remember that this will be given to the students and needs to get their attention. Save your work and print the workbook.

2. Importing Data and Creating Pivot Charts to Compare Racing Records

Jackson Raceway is a racetrack in Kentucky built by Samuel B. Jackson. Sam was a fan of car races as a child and eventually built his own oval 2.5-mile racetrack, modeled after the Daytona International Speedway. Lately, Samuel has hosted several fundraisers at the track for local charities. He allows groups to hold parties at the track and all proceeds from guests that race during the event go to the charity. This goodwill has brought attention to the charities as well as to Jackson Raceway.

A friend of Samuel is chair of a charity that raises money for the families of children with cancer. He approached Samuel about hosting a fundraising event for the organization and Samuel quickly agreed. Samuel decided to use his recent fame to make this event special. In hopes of drawing a large attendance to the event, Samuel has asked several of the regular racers at the track to compete that evening in a mock Daytona 500 race. Many businesses have agreed to advertise in a special program for the evening that will include each driver's information and their lap record at the track for the years 2000 and 2001.

Begin work for Samuel by opening Excel and then importing **ex11Racers.txt** using the Text Import Wizard. The text file contains the information on each driver that will be included in the event program: name of the driver, car number, make of car, record laps for 2000, and record laps for 2001. A semicolon separates one data item from another. Import data beginning in row 3, which is the row containing labels identifying the data columns in subsequent rows. Save your workbook as **Racers2.xls.** Samuel has persuaded some professional racers to support the charity by coming to the event. In order to print the driver's information in time for the race, Samuel has asked for your help.

Go to www.nascar.com and click the **Drivers** hyperlink on the left-hand side. Use this page to gather information on four racers and the number of laps each completed at the Daytona 500 in the years 2000 and 2001 to complete the worksheet.

In order to clearly compare past records for the program, Samuel wants you to prepare a pivot table and pivot chart comparing each driver's record for 2000 and 2001. Place the racers' names in the column section and the sum of 2000 and 2001 figures in the data section. Insert the pivot chart, in a line chart format, on a new worksheet titled **Racer Chart** and move this worksheet to the end of the workbook. Specify the Y axis scale values as follows: Min 100, Max 200, Major Unit 10, and Category X Axis Crosses at 100. Add a documentation worksheet to the beginning of the workbook with the title **Jackson Raceway Charity Program Information.** Include your name and date, place your name in all worksheet headers, save your work, and print the workbook.

e-business

1. Retrieving and Using Queries Regarding Web Auction Clients

Kellson's auction house in Maine has held public auctions of fine antiques and collectibles for over 40 years. Damion Kellson, president of the company, wanted to expand Kellson's client base, but their location in Maine made it difficult to attract clients from the west and central states. Instead of opening another auction house in the west, Damion thought it would be best to expand the firm's operations with a Web site. The site was designed to include detailed information and photographs of all items being auctioned and the capability for clients to place bids for items through the Web site. After one year, the Web division of the company has been very successful. Kellson's has been able to establish a solid client base in several new areas.

In two months, Kellson's will be holding the largest fine art auction in its history. All east coast clients will be receiving mailers previewing the auction. In order to ensure that Kellson's Web clients know about the auction, Damion will send e-mails to all clients who have previously purchased art through Kellson's Web site. In addition, he will send an attachment with scanned pictures of all the art to clients whose most recent art purchase was over $50,000. Damion's assistant, Ruth, has started retrieving the information for the mailing by summarizing July's Web sales, based on Damion's criteria. Unfortunately, Ruth incorrectly included information on too many clients and saved her records in both a text document and Access. Damion needs you to import the correct information into Excel so that he can easily view all necessary information for the auction announcement. Open **ex11KWeb.xls,** the Excel workbook into which Damion wants you to import the data, and save it as **KWeb2.xls.** Ruth has already formatted the Documentation sheet and labeled the worksheets for you. Select the **WebEMail** worksheet and import all of Kellson's Web clients' information from **ex11KWebMail.txt.** Be sure to use the correct delimited format and do not import any state or profession information. This will give Damion the e-mail addresses he needs to send the auction announcements to everyone. Select the Priority worksheet, which will include data on clients who are to receive the additional attachment. For this worksheet, use the Query Wizard to retrieve information from the **KWebSales** table within the **ex11Kellson.mdb** database. Be sure to save your query. Do not include the columns ID, Age, or Purchases data, and filter your query to only include clients whose last purchase was *Art* that cost at least $50,000. (Only use numbers or letters when defining your query.) Copy and paste the e-mail addresses of these clients into column **D** and give it the column heading **E-mail Addresses.** Improve the format and appearance of both worksheets and enter your name and date into the Documentation worksheet. Save your workbook and print all worksheets.

around the world

1. Using a Pivot Table to Summarize Imported Software Sales Figures

ModelWare is a software company based in Cambridge, England, specializing in designing software for the construction industry. Its programs range from those that design machinery to graphics programs that simulate new neighborhoods. Due to the European Union and introduction of the Euro, expanding business across European nations has become easier than ever before. ModelWare's president, Richard Hearn, believes that the future of the company's success rests upon how well the firm capitalizes on the new opportunities in Europe.

Recently, management established sales operations in France, Germany, Ireland, Sweden, and Italy. Instead of sending only current English ModelWare employees to these markets, management also hired native representatives from each of the countries. The goal of this was to determine whether English or native representatives were able to more quickly build rapport with clients, establish client relationships, and sell software programs.

It has been four months since ModelWare began its new sales divisions in France, Germany, Ireland, and Sweden and Richard wants to analyze the representatives' sales. The sales manager, Connie Triffit, was supposed to give him sales information for the last four months, organized by country. For Richard's purposes, no representatives were named; instead English and Native are used to represent the sum for each type of representatives' sales. Open **ex11EuropeanSales.txt** using Excel. Be sure to scroll through the data while using the Text Import Wizard to ensure that the proper delimiter(s) is selected. Improve the appearance of the worksheet and ensure that there are no blank rows between data. Name the worksheet **EuropeanSales.** Richard has asked you to now create a pivot table and pivot chart reflecting each country's data. Using the data in the European Sales worksheet you just created, create a pivot table that allows Richard to either look at all of the data at once or by individual country, sorted by representative type. Select rep type for the column area and sums of the monthly figures for the data section.

Create the pivot chart in a line format on a new worksheet labeled **CountrySales.** Be sure that each representative type has its own line showing sales for each month. Create a Documentation sheet to be the first page of the workbook. Include the title, **ModelWare European Sales, Requested by: Richard Hearn, Created by:** followed by your name, and **Presented on:** followed by today's date. Place your name in the header of each worksheet. Save your workbook as **ModelWareSales.xls** and print all worksheets.

running project

Pampered Paws

Grace Jackson learned that the American Pet Products Manufacturers Association (APPMA®), Inc. has published an Access database containing a small survey detailing shopping outlets where owners of small pets shop for pet products. The survey compares six stores and shows the percentage of people who claim to shop in each type of store. The store types listed in the survey instrument APPMA sent out are feed store, pet store, pet super store, discount store, and grocery store. In addition, the survey asked whether or not the customer actually purchased an item and which type of item it was. (The survey lists 14 types of pet products.) Grace wants you to import the database table, called OutletsShopped, from the database file, called **ex11Paws.mdb,** and place the data in the second worksheet, called Outlets Shopped Analysis. Begin by opening the Pampered Paws workbook, which is called **ex11Paws.xls.** Then, make the second worksheet active and import the data from the database to the worksheet. Be sure to import the Product field as the *first* column. Format the values as percentages, identify the worksheet with your name in the header, save the workbook as **Paws112.xls,** and print both worksheets.

Chapter Objectives

- Record a macro instruction (MOUS Ex2002e-5-2)

- Examine and use the Visual Basic Editor

- Run macro instructions using a dialog box and a command button (MOUS Ex2002e-5-2)

- Save a macro in your Personal Macro Workbook

- Create and modify Visual Basic code in the Visual Basic Editor (MOUS Ex2002e-5-2)

- Use Visual Basic objects, methods, properties, and variables (MOUS Ex2002e-5-2)

- Create a macro that automatically executes when you open a workbook (MOUS Ex2002e-5-2)

- Create custom functions

- Protect a worksheet to preserve its integrity (MOUS Ex2002e-9-1)

CHAPTER

12

twelve

Automating Applications with Visual Basic

chapter case
King's Stained Glass Studio

Mike King is the owner and creative designer of King's Stained Glass Studio, a small stained glass store and design studio, stocking art glass, glass bevels, and art glass-working supplies. Mike's only full-time employee, his wife Charlotte, works in the store selling glass and supplies. When time permits, she also helps Mike construct art glass windows. Mike spends almost all of his time designing and building stained glass panels commissioned by churches, businesses, and individuals. Mike and Charlotte's 1,200-square-foot store provides enough room for both Mike's studio and the retail store. Over 70 percent of the revenue is derived from store sales of glass and supplies.

Mike wants to make it easier for shoppers to locate the glass and supplies he sells and to list their prices. He envisions using his computer and Excel to provide a list of items and their prices that will make it simple for customers to quickly find what they want. Although he cannot afford to hire another full-time person to help Charlotte run the store, he has enough money to hire a part-time student to implement his in-store glass and supplies locator program. He has asked you to use the information already entered into an Excel workbook to create a simple interface that anyone can use to look up glass and supplies prices—whether he or she is familiar with Excel or not. Figure 12.1 shows the first page of a menu-based Excel workbook that allows customers to choose from three types of art glass or examine the supplies on hand in Mike's store.

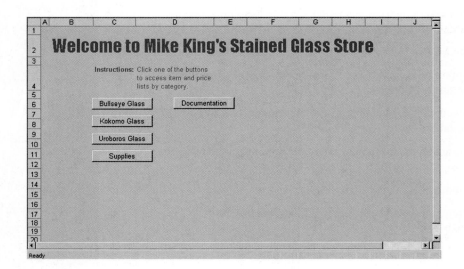

F I G U R E 12.1
King's Stained Glass Studio
main menu

Chapter 12 covers creating Visual Basic macro instructions and functions to automate Excel. Office XP products employ a powerful programming language called Visual Basic for Applications (VBA) that allows you to write macro instructions to automate procedures and create procedures and functions. Fortunately, you do not have to be a programmer to create a macro. You can create a VBA macro by turning on the macro recorder, executing Excel commands and using the mouse as you would to manually accomplish a task, and then save the recorded instructions to a named macro instruction. Once you have saved a sequence of instructions that Excel writes for you in VBA code, you can play back the macro instruction anytime you want to reproduce the sequence of instructions. When you store macro instructions in Excel's Personal Macro Workbook, Excel makes them available to all workbooks you open.

Excel provides the Visual Basic editor in which you can write instructions that go beyond what macros provide. For example, you can write a sub procedure of VBA instructions to repeat a series of instructions such as examining a group of selected cells to determine which contain negative values—a procedure you could record with the macro instruction recorder. When you use a particular formula frequently in a workbook, you can turn it into a custom function that returns a value when you write an expression using the custom function. Saving a procedure or macro instruction as auto_open causes it to execute automatically when you first open the workbook to which it is attached.

SESSION 12.1 CREATING MACROS

In this section, you will learn how to record and save macro instructions using the Macro Recorder. Then you will view a macro instruction using the Visual Basic editor and learn alternative ways to run a macro. You will learn how to run macros with the Macro dialog box and by assigning a macro to a command button. Finally, you will store a macro instruction so that the workbook containing it will execute the macro whenever the workbook opens.

WHAT IS A MACRO?

Mike knows that many of his customers do not have finely honed computer skills. If his idea of placing products and prices in an Excel workbook is to be successful, he cannot rely on customers knowing how to use Excel. For example, he knows he cannot assume a customer will know how to move from one worksheet of stained glass prices to another worksheet containing art glass tools. Therefore, he will have to automate the *Art Glass Catalog* (or AGC), as Mike calls the proposed workbook, so that it is as simple to operate as a television set. To do so, Mike reasons, will require the use of macro instructions to move from one worksheet to another when the customer clicks a clearly marked button on a worksheet. In addition, Mike would like to automate some parts of his customer information system using macro instructions and custom Excel functions.

A *macro instruction,* or *macro,* is a *VBA procedure,* which is a group of VBA statements that collectively performs a particular task or returns a result. You can create two types of VBA procedures: functions and subroutines. A *VBA function* is a procedure that returns a result, similar to the way Excel's built-in functions such as SUM and PMT return values. A *VBA subroutine* is a procedure that performs a particular task. A macro is a

VBA procedure, because a macro does not return a value. It does accomplish a task by executing the steps that the macro contains, though. Figure 12.2 shows a VBA macro procedure called *PrintFormulas* that prints a worksheet's formulas.

Using the Visual Basic editor, you can write your own Excel custom functions. Functions begin with the word *Function* and end with *End Function.* Between them are the lines of Visual Basic statements that define the function. Functions usually have **arguments,** which are symbolic names for values, expressions, and cell references that are passed to the function for its use in calculating an answer. Figure 12.3 shows the Bonus function that computes the bonus a salesperson earns based on the sale price of the item he or she sold. The salesperson earns a bonus if the sale is over $5,000. The bonus amount is 12 percent of the difference between the sale amount and $5,000.

WHY BOTHER CREATING A MACRO?

Macros allow you to create your own commands. Doing so can save you a lot of time and effort—especially for tasks you perform repeatedly in a workbook or a few times in many workbooks. Some of the examples of time-consuming and somewhat tedious tasks that you can automate and simplify by using macros are:

- Place your name in a worksheet header
- Apply an AutoFormat to a range of worksheet cells
- Print a worksheet, print its formulas, and then redisplay the workbook in nonformula view
- Trace the precedent cells for each of a group of worksheet cells using one command
- Assign a group of instructions that accomplish a particular task to a command button

FIGURE 12.2

A macro to print a worksheet's formulas

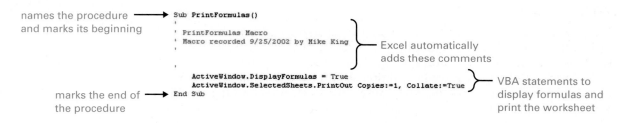

FIGURE 12.3

A function to calculate sales bonus

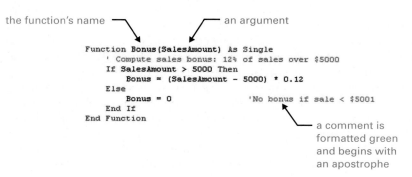

DECIDING WHICH MACROS YOU NEED

You meet with Mike on Tuesday to discuss which macros you should write to automate the workbook so that customers can view the glass and supplies available at Mike's store. Mike's workbook currently contains five worksheets: Documentation, Welcome, Bullseye, Kokomo, Uroboros, and Supplies (see Figure 12.4). The Documentation worksheet contains brief comments about the workbook including the date when it was created. On the Welcome worksheet, Mike wants several buttons that open different product pages of the workbook when customers click them. In addition, Mike wants the Welcome worksheet to appear when anyone opens the workbook, because it is the main page from which customers go to product pages. The Bullseye, Kokomo, and Uroboros worksheets contain stained glass products from three like-named glass manufacturers. On the Supplies worksheet is a list of all the supplies Mike carries including copper foil, glass cutters of all descriptions, lead, solder, and so forth.

You discover that you can create a complete Excel application with Excel macro instructions written in Visual Basic that will encapsulate instructions that you can assign to buttons you place on the worksheet surface. This user interface, forming the communication between the Excel workbook and customers using it, makes it easy for anyone to use the Excel application without knowing anything about Excel.

F I G U R E   12.4

Worksheets comprising King's product catalog workbook

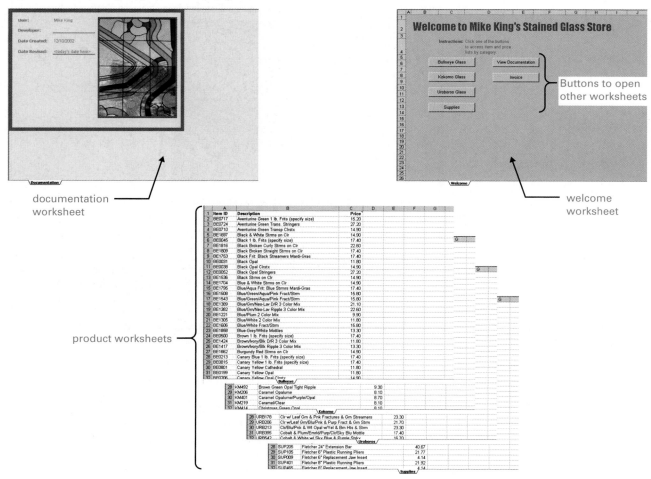

Designing and creating the interface does not appear to be a daunting task. Discussions with Mike make it clear that he wants a simple interface in which a customer clicks a product button and then a product page corresponding to the label on the button becomes active. Of course, you will need to design another series of buttons that appear on each product page to redisplay the Welcome worksheet containing all the product buttons.

You begin work by opening the Art Glass Catalog (AGC) workbook. Then you will begin work creating the macros needed to automate the catalog.

FIGURE 12.5

Documentation worksheet

Opening the Art Glass Catalog workbook and saving it under a new name:

1. Start Excel

2. Open the workbook **ex12ArtGlass.xls** and immediately save it as **Catalog2.xls** to preserve the original workbook in case you want to revert to that version. Excel displays the first worksheet, Documentation (see Figure 12.5)

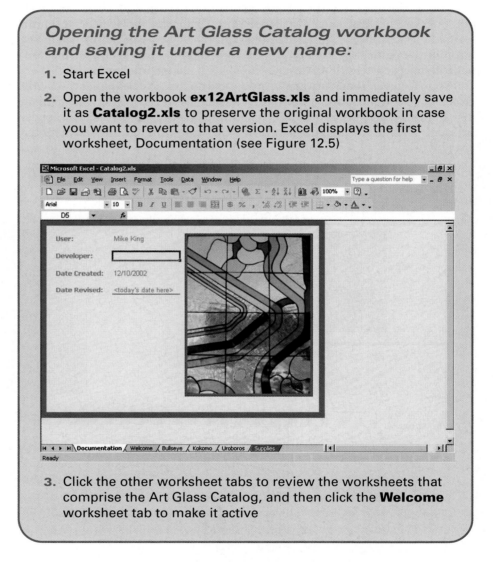

3. Click the other worksheet tabs to review the worksheets that comprise the Art Glass Catalog, and then click the **Welcome** worksheet tab to make it active

The Welcome worksheet will hold all of the buttons that customers will click to display the product worksheets. For example, a customer will examine the prices of Bullseye glass by clicking a button labeled Bullseye. Similarly, buttons on the Welcome worksheet will contain labels corresponding to the other glass manufacturers, a supply worksheet, and the Documentation worksheet. You are now ready to create your first macro instruction.

RECORDING A MACRO

Excel provides an efficient tool for creating macros called the Excel Macro Recorder. As its name implies, the Macro Recorder records your actions. Recording a macro involves three steps. First, you start the Macro Recorder, and then you perform the actions you want Excel to record including clicking menus and commands and typing information into cells. Finally, you stop the recorder. Excel saves the recorded actions, including any mistakes you may make, in a macro instruction. Subsequently, you can replay the macro instruction any time you want to reproduce the results. Naturally, a macro's playback facility is particularly useful for long and often-used procedures, because a macro repeats the series of instructions exactly the same way you do manually in a fraction of the time.

Macros are saved in a special Excel object called a **Module.** A module can contain many macros, and a workbook can hold an unlimited number of modules.

Macro Storage Choices

You can instruct Excel to save your macros in one of three locations: the current workbook, the Personal Macro Workbook, or a new workbook. Excel's **Personal Macro Workbook** is a workbook that Excel always loads, and subsequently hides, whenever you launch Excel. Macros stored in the Personal Macro Workbook are available for any workbook. The option to store a macro in a new workbook is less commonly used. The most common storage option is the current workbook, which is the default choice. If you store macros in the current workbook, you can execute them whenever the workbook is open. This is the option you will use in this chapter.

Choosing between Absolute and Relative Cell References

When the macro recorder is active, it records all commands you execute as well as the addresses of any cells you click. For example, if you click cell B4 while recording a macro, the recorder stores the instruction

> Range("B4").Select

When the macro recorder stores the actual cell reference in recorded code, it is storing an absolute cell reference. An alternative way to record cell references in a macro instruction is to store cells' relative cell references. A relative cell reference refers to a clicked cell's location relative to the previously active cell. If cell B8 is active and you click cell B4 while recording a macro using relative cell reference, Excel stores the instruction

> ActiveCell.Offset(−4,1).Range("A1").Select

"ActiveCell.Offset" is a relative reference, or offset, from the previously active cell, B8. That is, the notation "(−4,1)" indicates that cell B4 is −4 rows (up) and 1 column to the right of the previously active cell.

When you replay a macro recorded using absolute cell references, the macro affects the same cells every time it is played. When you record a macro using relative cell references, the cells affected are all relative to the cell that was active prior to executing the macro instruction. In other words, using relative cell references in macro instructions results in more versatile macros because they are not tied to particular worksheet cells.

Because the macros you record in this chapter do not need to take advantage of relative cell references, you will record all macros using absolute cell references. Next, you will learn how to assure that the macro recorder uses absolute references.

Recording a Macro

Your first macro simply selects and displays the Bullseye worksheet and then selects cell A1 on that worksheet. Although it is a simple procedure and hardly seems worthy of a macro, keep in mind that you are automating a process for people who may not know anything about worksheets or the programs that display them.

---

task reference

Recording a Macro Instruction

- Click **Tools,** point to **Macro,** click **Record New Macro**
- Type a macro name in the Macro name text box
- Type a description in the Description text box
- Click **OK**
- Execute the tasks you want to record
- Click the **Stop Recording** button

Set up to begin recording the BullseyeWorksheet macro:

1. Click **Tools** on the menu bar, point to **Macro,** and then click **Record New Macro.** The Record Macro dialog box appears
2. Type **BullseyeWorksheet** in the Macro name text box, replacing the suggested name. (The suggested name is usually Macro1, Macro2, and so forth.)

tip: *Make sure you spell all macro names* without *spaces. The macro name above,* BullseyeWorksheet, *is one word*

3. Drag the mouse through the text in the **Description** text box to select it, and then type **Make the Bullseye worksheet active** (see Figure 12.6)

FIGURE 12.6

Record Macro dialog box

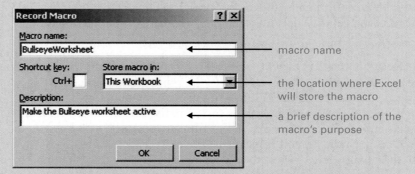

— macro name

— the location where Excel will store the macro

— a brief description of the macro's purpose

4. Click **OK** to begin the actual macro recording process. The floating Stop Recording toolbar appears.

tip: *Be careful what you do from now until you stop the Macro Recorder because it records every action you take. The Macro Recorder does not record mouse movements, so you can move the mouse to the menu bar or around the screen. Be sure not to click any commands unless you want your actions recorded—the recorder does not miss anything*

With the Macro Recorder active, you will record the commands that make the Bullseye worksheet active and make cell A1 active. Like a faithful scribe, the Macro Recorder will write down every action you perform.

another**word**

. . . on Naming Macros

Keep macro names short (25 characters or fewer, for example) and ensure that they describe the task they perform. It is okay to use multiple words for the macro name, but separate each word with an underscore or place words one after another with each word capitalized. For example, PrintWorksheetFormulas or Print_Formulas are good, descriptive macro names. In any case, do not use spaces anywhere in a macro name

---

Recording the BullseyeWorksheet macro:

1. Ensure that the **Relative Reference** button on the Stop Recording toolbar is not pressed in. If it is, then click the Relative Reference button to pop it out (see Figure 12.7)

Stop Recording button ———— Relative Reference button

2. Click the **Bullseye** worksheet tab to make that worksheet active, and then click cell **A1**

3. Click the **Stop Recording** button (see Figure 12.7). The Macro Recorder stops recording the macro instruction and places the BullseyeWorksheet macro in a module along with other macros that you may record in this session

4. Preserve your work by saving the workbook, including the macro instructions Excel holds in modules, by clicking the **Save** 🖫 button on the Standard toolbar

FIGURE 12.7

The Stop Recording toolbar

RUNNING A MACRO

There are a variety of ways to play back a macro. You can run a macro by

- assigning it to a keyboard shortcut
- assigning it to a graphic object on a worksheet
- assigning it to a toolbar button
- assigning it to a menu
- selecting it from a list of macros in the Macro dialog box

Some methods are more convenient than others, and you can decide which method works best for you. Users who are not accustomed to Excel will prefer either a toolbar button or a graphic object, like a button, to launch a macro.

Using the Macro Dialog Box

Test the macro instruction by using the last method—running it from the Macro dialog box—to ensure that it works properly. After determining the macro works properly, you can consider a simpler method to execute macros.

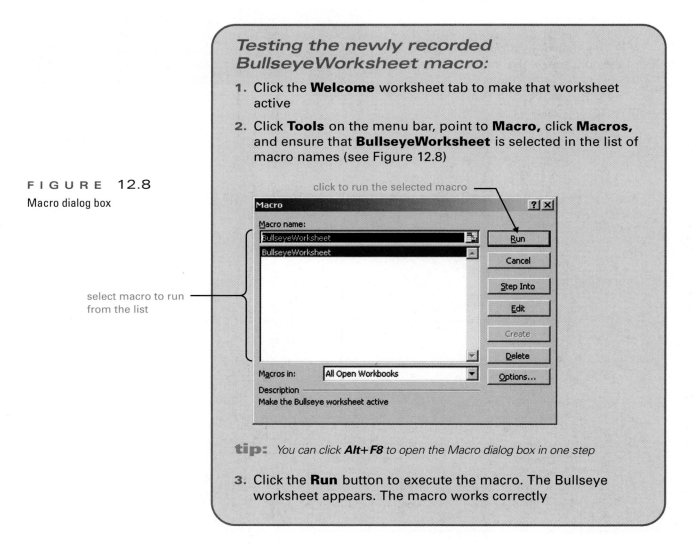

Testing the newly recorded BullseyeWorksheet macro:

1. Click the **Welcome** worksheet tab to make that worksheet active

2. Click **Tools** on the menu bar, point to **Macro,** click **Macros,** and ensure that **BullseyeWorksheet** is selected in the list of macro names (see Figure 12.8)

FIGURE 12.8

Macro dialog box

select macro to run from the list

click to run the selected macro

tip: *You can click **Alt+F8** to open the Macro dialog box in one step*

3. Click the **Run** button to execute the macro. The Bullseye worksheet appears. The macro works correctly

Assigning a Macro to a Button

Perhaps the most convenient way to replay a macro instruction is by clicking a button or other graphic object assigned to it. The most common graphic object to assign to a macro is a button, but you can choose any graphic object created with the Forms or Drawing toolbar.

Mike reminds you that most of his customers are probably not Excel experts. Therefore, Mike wants you to create a clearly labeled button to open the Bullseye worksheet when customers click the button. You proceed to create a button and assign the BullseyeWorksheet macro to it.

task reference

Assigning a Macro to a Button

- Click **View,** point to **Toolbars,** click **Forms**
- Click the **Button** tool in the Forms toolbar
- Click a worksheet cell to place a button on the worksheet
- Select the macro to assign to the button from the Macro name list
- Click **OK**
- Drag the mouse across the button's caption and type a descriptive name
- Click any cell to deselect the button

Creating a button and assigning the BullseyeWorksheet to it:

1. Click the **Welcome** worksheet tab to make that worksheet active

2. Click **View** on the menu bar, point to **Toolbars,** and click **Forms** to open the Forms toolbar (see Figure 12.9)

Button tool —

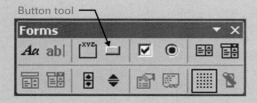

tip: *The exact shape of your toolbar may be different from the figure. Normally, the Forms toolbar floats on the screen. You can reshape any toolbar by dragging one of its edges, and you can dock it by dragging it to one of the four edges of the screen*

3. If necessary, drag the Forms toolbar out of the way so that you can see cell C6

4. Click the **Button** tool in the Forms toolbar, and then click worksheet cell **C6.** (It is not important to be exactly in cell C6— just close to it.) Excel places a default-named button on the worksheet and opens the Assign Macro dialog box

5. Click **BullseyeWorksheet** in the *Macro name* list (see Figure 12.10) and then click **OK.** Excel closes the Assign Macro dialog box

6. With the newly added button still selected, drag the mouse through the button's caption to select its characters. (The button's default caption is similar to *Button 12.* The exact default name assigned depends on how many objects you have created so far.)

F I G U R E   12.9
Forms toolbar

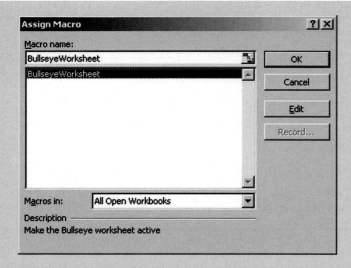

7. Type **Bullseye Glass** (place a space between the two words)

8. If you cannot see the button's entire caption, move the mouse to the center selection handle on the right edge. When the mouse pointer changes to a double-headed arrow, click the selection handle and drag it to the right. Release the mouse when you think the button is wide enough.

9. Repeat step 8, as needed, to fine tune the button's width until the button is sufficiently wide

10. Click any worksheet cell to deselect the button (see Figure 12.11)

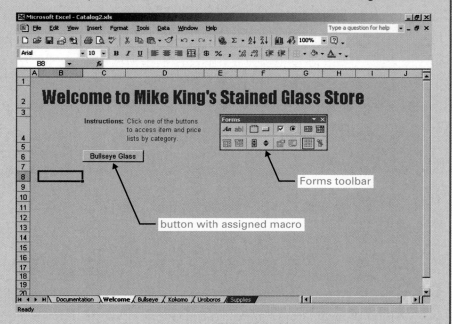

11. Close the Forms toolbar by clicking the **Close** button in its title bar

Assigning a Macro to a Graphic

You can assign a macro to any graphic object in a way that is similar to the method you follow for a button. The difference is that the Assign Macro dialog box does not appear automatically after you draw the object. For example, you can place a Horizontal Scroll object, found in the AutoShapes section of the Drawing toolbar, on the worksheet. Then right-click the object and proceed as you did in steps 5 through 10 above to assign a macro to the graphic. Figure 12.12 shows another worksheet containing a graphic that is assigned to a macro instruction. The shortcut menu contains the Assign Macro command you click to assign a macro to the selected graphic.

Making a Button Visible on Printouts

Buttons are designed for on-screen use, and they are convenient for worksheet users. By default, buttons *do not* display on a printed worksheet because users cannot interact with printed buttons. However, you may want to display worksheet buttons on printouts so that others can evaluate your work. If so, then you must execute an extra step to make a button visible on printouts.

Mike wants you to make the Bullseye Glass button visible on any printouts you produce as a reminder that the Welcome worksheet contains buttons.

---

task reference

Making Buttons Visible on a Printout

- Right-click the button you want to display on a printout
- Click **Format Control** on the shortcut menu
- Click the **Properties** tab
- Click the **Print object** check box, and then click **OK**

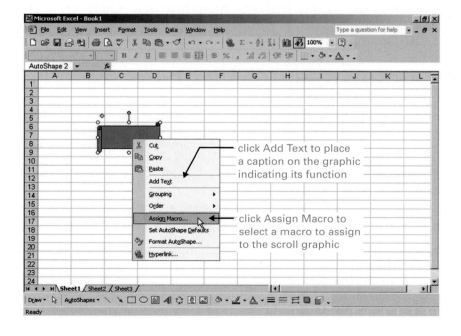

F I G U R E   12.12

Assigning a macro to a graphic

click Add Text to place a caption on the graphic indicating its function

click Assign Macro to select a macro to assign to the scroll graphic

EXCEL

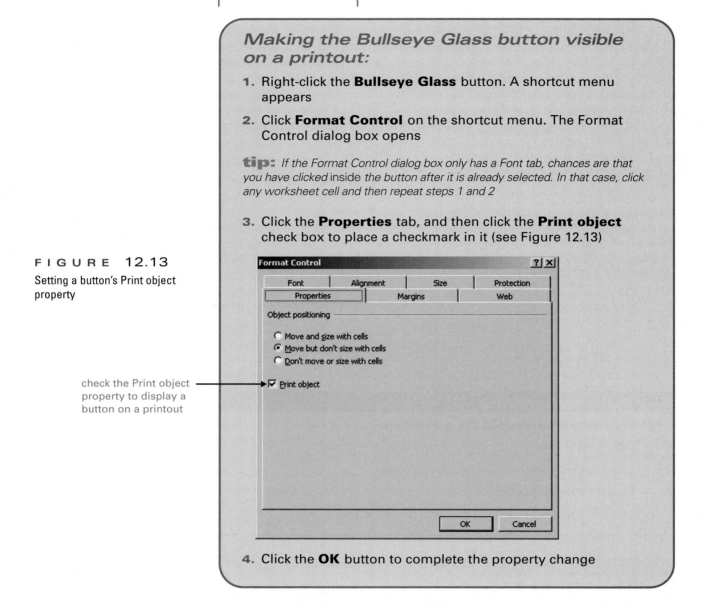

FIGURE 12.13

Setting a button's Print object property

Making the Bullseye Glass button visible on a printout:

1. Right-click the **Bullseye Glass** button. A shortcut menu appears

2. Click **Format Control** on the shortcut menu. The Format Control dialog box opens

tip: *If the Format Control dialog box only has a Font tab, chances are that you have clicked inside the button after it is already selected. In that case, click any worksheet cell and then repeat steps 1 and 2*

3. Click the **Properties** tab, and then click the **Print object** check box to place a checkmark in it (see Figure 12.13)

check the Print object property to display a button on a printout

4. Click the **OK** button to complete the property change

RECORDING MACROS FOR THE OTHER PRODUCT WORKSHEETS

Mike points out that you will need to create three more buttons and three more macros to display the Kokomo, Uroboros, and Supplies worksheets. Because few customers will be interested in viewing the Documentation worksheet, he tells you there is no need to create a button to make it active. After all, you or he can simply click the Documentation worksheet tab to display the worksheet if necessary.

Recording the Kokomo, Uroboros, and Supplies Macros

Creating macros to go to the three other glass and supplies worksheets is a snap. You've done the process recently. Here, you will record three new macros and assign buttons to them, although there are alternative approaches available for seasoned macro writers. These alternatives include copying and pasting code and making small changes to the clones, but doing so incurs some risk of mistake. It's best to stick to tried-and-true methods.

You prepare to record the macro to make the Kokomo worksheet active. Then, you record similar macros to display the other worksheets.

Recording the KokomoWorksheet, UroborosWorksheet, and SuppliesWorksheet macros:

1. If necessary, click the **Welcome** worksheet tab to make it active

2. Click **Tools** on the menu bar, point to **Macro,** and click **Record New Macro**

3. Type **KokomoWorksheet** in the Macro name text box, replacing the suggested name. Remember: No spaces in macro names

4. Drag the mouse through the text in the Description text box to select it, type **Make the Kokomo worksheet active,** and click **OK** to begin the actual macro recording process

5. Click the **Kokomo** worksheet tab, click cell **A1,** and then click the **Stop Recording** button

6. Click the **Welcome** worksheet tab to make the worksheet active

7. Repeat steps 2 through 6 to create the UroborosWorksheet macro, substituting **UroborosWorksheet** in step 3, **Make the Uroboros worksheet active** in step 4, and **Uroboros** in step 5

8. Repeat steps 2 through 6 to create the SuppliesWorksheet macro, substituting **SuppliesWorksheet** in step 3, **Make the Supplies worksheet active** in step 4, and **Supplies** in step 5

9. Click the **Save** 🖫 button on the Standard toolbar to save all the work you have done so far

---

Attaching Buttons to the Kokomo, Uroboros, and Supplies Macros

Next, you place buttons on the Welcome worksheet and attach them to the macros you created above.

Creating and assigning buttons to the Kokomo, Uroboros, and Supplies worksheets:

1. Click the **Welcome** worksheet tab, if necessary, to make that worksheet active

2. Click **View** on the menu bar, point to **Toolbars,** click **Forms** to open the Forms toolbar, and drag it to the right so that you can see column C

Assigning the KokomoWorksheet
macro to a button

3. Click the **Button** tool in the Forms toolbar, click the cell below the last button, drag the mouse pointer down and to the right so that the button outline is approximately the same size as the button above it, and release the mouse. The Assign Macro dialog box opens

4. Click **KokomoWorksheet** in the Macro name list (see Figure 12.14), and then click **OK**

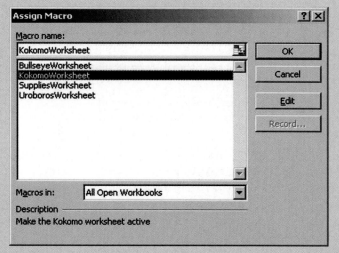

5. Drag the mouse through the button's caption and type **Kokomo Glass** (two words)

6. If necessary, resize the button so that you can see the entire caption

7. Click any worksheet cell to deselect the button

8. Repeat steps 3 through 7, substituting **UroborosWorksheet** in step 4 and **Uroboros Glass** in step 5

9. Repeat steps 3 through 7, substituting **SuppliesWorksheet** in step 4 and **Supplies** in step 5

10. Close the Forms toolbar by clicking the **Close** button in its title bar. The four buttons are in place on the Welcome worksheet (see Figure 12.15)

tip: *If your worksheet buttons are not all uniform in size, don't worry. They still work fine when you click them*

You may want to alter a button's properties. One of the only tricky parts of doing that is selecting the button without clicking it and causing it to activate.

task reference

Selecting a Button Control without Activating it

- Press and hold the **Ctrl** key
- Click the button on the worksheet
- Release the **Ctrl** key

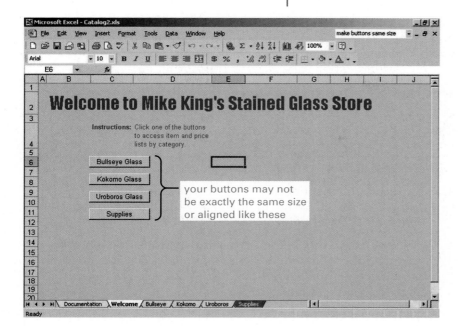

FIGURE 12.15
Welcome worksheet with four buttons

Mike notes that you have not provided an obvious or easy way for a customer to return to the Welcome worksheet after opening one of the other worksheets. He would like you to place a button on each of the glass and supplies worksheets which, when pushed, will make the Welcome worksheet active.

Recording a Return Macro and Assigning It to Multiple Buttons

You realize that the macro instruction to return to the Welcome worksheet will be the same for all four worksheets, so you can save time by creating one macro that is activated by four different buttons—one on each glass or supplies worksheet.

In preparation to record the macro, you first make the Bullseye glass worksheet active. Then you can record the macro and create four buttons to access the macro.

Creating a Return to Menu macro:

1. Click the **Bullseye Glass** button to make the Bullseye worksheet active

2. Click **Tools** on the menu bar, point to **Macro,** and click **Record New Macro**

3. Type **ReturnToMenu** in the Macro name text box, replacing the suggested name

4. Press **Tab** three times to move to the Description text box, type **Make the Welcome worksheet active,** and click **OK** to begin the actual macro recording process

5. Click the **Welcome** worksheet tab and then click the **Stop Recording** button

---

Next, you will create a button to activate the new macro and place it on the Bullseye worksheet. Then you can copy the button to the glass and supplies worksheets using a simple copy-and-paste technique.

Assigning the ReturnToMenu macro to a button and copying it to other worksheets:

1. Click the **Bullseye Glass** button to make the Bullseye worksheet active

2. Click **View** on the menu bar, point to **Toolbars,** click **Forms** to open the Forms toolbar, and drag it to the right, if necessary, so that you can see cell D1

3. Click the **Button** tool in the Forms toolbar, move the plus-shaped mouse to the upper-left corner of cell **D1,** and click the mouse. Excel places a button on the worksheet and opens the Assign Macro dialog box.

4. Click **ReturnToMenu** in the list of macro names, and then click **OK**

5. Drag the mouse through the button's caption and type **Menu**

6. Move the mouse to the border around the button. When the mouse pointer becomes a four-headed arrow, click the button's border to select the button. The border changes from a series of slash marks (////) to dots, indicating that you have selected the button object and not the button's caption

7. Press **Ctrl+C** to copy the button to the Clipboard, and click cell **A1** to deselect the button

tip: *If you accidentally deselect the button, you can select it by pressing* **Ctrl,** *clicking the button, and releasing the* **Ctrl** *key. If you simply click the button without first holding down the Ctrl key, then you activate the attached macro*

8. Click the **Documentation** worksheet tab, click cell **C10** (below the entry *Date Revised*), press **Ctrl+V** to paste the button on the Documentation worksheet, and click the underlined cell to the right of the label *Developer* to deselect the button

9. Click the **Kokomo** worksheet tab, click cell **D1,** press **Ctrl+V** to paste the button near cell D1 on the Kokomo worksheet, and click cell **A1** to deselect the button

10. Click the **Uroboros** worksheet tab, click cell **D1,** press **Ctrl+V** to paste the button near cell D1 on the Uroboros worksheet, and click cell **A1** to deselect the button

11. Click the **Supplies** worksheet tab, click cell **D1,** press **Ctrl+V** to paste the button near cell D1 on the Supplies worksheet, and click cell **A1** to deselect the button

12. Click the Forms toolbar **Close** button (see Figure 12.16)

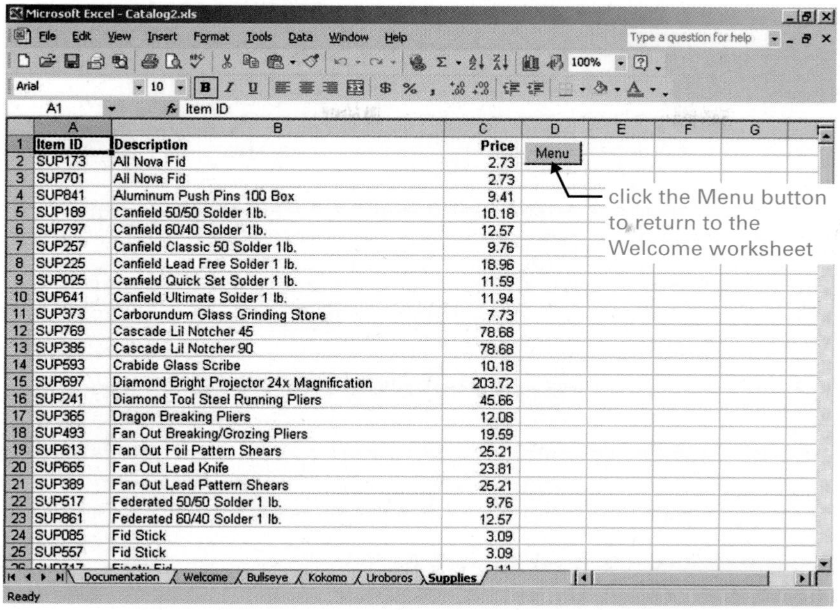

FIGURE   12.16
Supplies worksheet with the
Menu button in place

CREATING AND RUNNING MACROS STORED IN THE PERSONAL MACRO WORKBOOK

Excel placed all the macros you have recorded so far in a module that belongs to the current (active) workbook. A macro recorded in a workbook is available only when the workbook containing it is open. That is, if you were to open another workbook, leaving the King's Stained Glass Studio workbook open (but not active), all the King's Glass macros would be available for execution in the new workbook as well. However, you have to remember to first load any workbooks containing macros you want to use.

Creating and Saving a Macro in the Personal Macro Workbook

A superior solution that makes macros you choose available at all times is to store macros in the Personal Macro Workbook. Excel automatically creates the Personal Macro Workbook the first time you choose that option for macro storage. Excel stores the workbook, called Personal.xls, in the XLStart folder, which is created when you install Microsoft Office. (Depending on your operating system, you can locate the XLStart folder by using the Search Find command on your Window's Start menu.) Excel automatically opens and hides the Personal.xls workbook each time you open Excel, thereby making all macros stored in it available to all Excel workbooks you open.

Mike wants you to create a macro instruction that types King's Stained Glass Studio into the header of a worksheet and places the page number in the worksheet footer. He wants the macro instruction available for any workbook he may load. Therefore, you will create it in the Personal Macro Workbook.

Creating a macro and storing it in the Personal Macro Workbook:

1. With the Supplies worksheet still active, click **Tools** on the menu bar, point to **Macro,** and click **Record New Macro**

2. Type **KingHeaderFooter** in the Macro name text box, replacing the suggested name

3. Click the **Store macro in** list box to display a list of locations where you can store macros: Personal Macro Workbook, New Workbook, and This Workbook

4. Click the **Personal Macro Workbook** choice, press the **Tab** key to select the Description text box, type **Enter King's header and footer into a worksheet** to replace the existing description text (see Figure 12.17), and click **OK.** Excel starts the macro recorder

FIGURE   12.17

Creating a Personal Macro Workbook macro

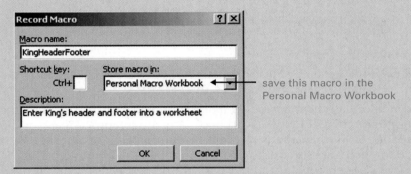

save this macro in the Personal Macro Workbook

5. Click **View** on the menu bar, click **Header and Footer,** click the **Custom Header** button, click in the **Right section** panel, type **King's Stained Glass Studio,** and click **OK**

6. Click the **Custom Footer** button, click in the **Center section** panel, click the **Page number** button in the Footer toolbar, and click **OK.** The Page Setup dialog box reveals your choices (see Figure 12.18)

FIGURE   12.18

The Page Setup dialog box

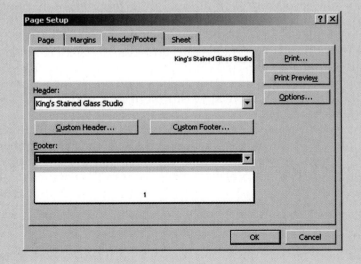

7. Click **OK** in the Page Setup dialog box to complete the procedure

8. Click the **Stop Recording** button. Excel stops recording the macro and closes the Stop Recording toolbar

Unhiding the Personal Macro Workbook

In case you want to examine or delete macros stored in the Personal Macro Workbook, you must first unhide the workbook. Then you can examine the macro instructions it contains. Although you will not unhide or hide the **Personal.xls** workbook, you should know how to do it.

---

task reference

Unhiding a workbook

- Click **Window** on the menu bar
- Click **Unhide**
- Click a workbook in the Unhide workbook list and then click **OK**

Similarly, you can hide any active workbook by reversing the previous procedure.

---

task reference

Hiding a workbook

- Make active any worksheet of the workbook you want to hide
- Click **Window** on the menu bar
- Click **Hide**

SETTING THE MACRO SECURITY LEVEL

Viruses that can cause damage to your computer system can exist in the form of macro instructions attached to Excel workbooks. If you download workbooks from the Internet, you want to beware of the potential viruses hidden in macro instructions. To guard against viruses or unwanted macro instructions in Excel worksheets, you can use any number of antivirus software packages. In addition, Excel provides a measure of security through settings you establish. Three security levels are available in Excel: Low, Medium, and High. You should set your macro security level to Medium, at least. When Excel macro security is Medium, Excel will display a warning dialog box whenever you open a workbook containing macros.

Mike wants you to determine the macro security level he has, and he wants you to set it to Medium, if necessary. Then you will save, close, and re-open the **Catalog2.xls** workbook to review the warning dialog box that Excel displays.

task reference

Setting the Macro Security Level

- Click **Tools** on the menu bar, click **Options,** and click the **Security** tab

- Click the **Macro Security** button

- Click the security level option button of your choice

- Click **OK** to close the Security dialog box and then click **OK** to close the Options dialog box

Setting the Excel macro security level to Medium:

1. Click **Tools** on the menu bar, click **Options,** and then click the **Security** tab

2. Click the **Macro Security** button near the bottom of the Security panel. Excel opens the Security dialog box

3. Click the **Medium** option button, if necessary (see Figure 12.19), to set the security level to Medium

FIGURE 12.19

Setting the macro security level to Medium

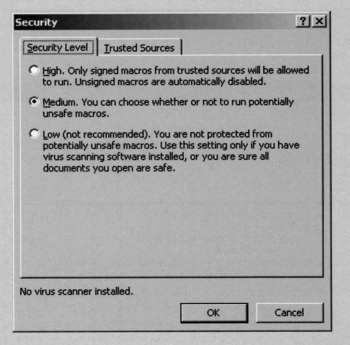

4. Click **OK** to close the Security dialog box and then click **OK** to close the Options dialog box

OPENING A WORKBOOK CONTAINING MACROS

You have made a lot of changes to the **Catalog2.xls** workbook since you last saved it, so you should save it now to preserve all the work you have done so far.

Saving your workbook and closing Excel:

1. Click the **Save** 🖫 button on the Standard toolbar

2. Click **File** on the menu bar, and then click **Exit** to close the workbook and exit Excel. Excel displays a dialog box with the message "Do you want to save the changes you made to 'PERSONAL.XLS'?" (see Figure 12.20)

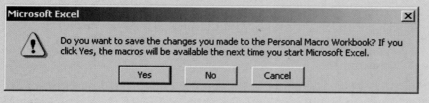

3. Click **Yes** to save the newly created macro and save the altered Personal Macro Workbook, **Personal.xls**

FIGURE 12.20
Saving the Personal Macro
Workbook

Now you can reopen the **Catalog2.xls** workbook and observe the macro security warning that Excel displays.

Opening the Catalog2.xls workbook:

1. Start Excel

2. Click **File** on the menu bar and then click **Open.** Excel displays the Open dialog box and the **Catalog2.xls** workbook appears in the list of available workbooks

3. Click the **Catalog2.xls** workbook in the list of workbooks and then click **Open.** Excel displays a warning indicating that the workbook contains macros (see Figure 12.21)

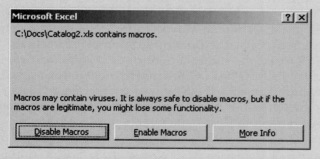

FIGURE 12.21
Excel macro warning

4. Click the **Enable Macros** button to open the workbook and allow its attached macros. Excel loads the workbook and displays the Supplies worksheet

tip: *If you click the Disable Macros button, Excel will open the workbook but disallow use of any of the macros it contains. The macros remain stored in the workbook's module(s)*

Mike is pleased with the macro instructions. He tries out each of the buttons on the menu bar and is delighted with them. The Menu button on each worksheet makes the Welcome worksheet active. You close the workbook, save the workbook under a new name, exit Excel, and take a break.

> ## Saving the workbook under a new name and exiting Excel:
>
> 1. Click the **Menu** button on the Supplies worksheet and then click cell **A1**
>
> 2. Click **File** on the menu bar and then click **Save As**
>
> 3. Type **Catalog3** in the File name text box and then click the **Save** button
>
> 4. Click **File** on the menu bar and then click **Exit** to close the workbook and exit Excel

SESSION 12.1   *making the grade*

1. A _____ is a VBA procedure that performs a particular task or returns a result.

2. A VBA _____ is a procedure that returns a result similar to Excel's built-in functions.

3. Excel's _____ _____ Workbook is a workbook that automatically loads whenever you load any Excel workbook.

4. Excel saves macros in a special object called a _____, which is stored with the workbook.

5. You can assign a macro to a _____ to facilitate running the macro by those unaccustomed to using Excel commands.

6. Open Excel and then open **Catalog2.xls.** Save the workbook as **Catalog22.xls** to preserve the changes you made to **Catalog2.xls** for use in the next section. Modify **Catalog22.xls** by following these instructions. Click the **Documentation** worksheet tab. Press **Alt+F8** to use the shortcut to open the Macro dialog box. Click the entry **PERSONAL.XLS!KingHeaderFooter** in the list of macro names, and click the **Run** button. The macro places a header and footer on the Documentation worksheet. Click the **Welcome** worksheet tab. Save the modified workbook and exit Excel.

SESSION 12.2 WRITING SUBROUTINES AND CUSTOM FUNCTIONS

In this section, you will learn about the Visual Basic Editor, how to edit macros in the Visual Basic Editor, how to create and name a macro that automatically executes when you open a workbook, how to write code to gather data from a user with an input box, how to display special message boxes to a user signaling errors and posting information, and how to write iteration structures that repeat a sequence of instructions.

EXAMINING THE VISUAL BASIC EDITOR

Having recorded several macros, you may wonder where Excel stores the macro instructions and exactly what they look like. As you recall, Excel writes Office XP macros in VBA, or Visual Basic for Applications. When you recorded your first macro, Excel created an object called a module in the active workbook. Recall that a module is where Excel stores VBA code. As you created the BullseyeWorksheet macro, for example, Excel recorded your keystrokes and commands and placed the VBA code in the BullseyeWorksheet and saved it in a module. Modules do not appear in the workbook along with worksheets. To view a module and the VBA procedures it contains, you have to open the Visual Basic Editor (VBE). The Visual Basic Editor is a program that contains multiple windows and allows you to view objects, VBA Code, and objects' properties in a convenient development environment. The editor is identical in all Office XP products and also has a strong resemblance to the Visual Basic 6 programming language editor interface.

The Visual Basic Editor provides an easy way for you to print, view, or modify any macros you have recorded. You will use the Visual Basic Editor several times in this session.

Viewing a Macro with the Visual Basic Editor

task reference

Opening the Visual Basic Editor

- Click **Tools,** point to **Macro,** and click **Visual Basic Editor**

or

- Press **Alt+F11**

or

- Click **Tools,** point to **Macro,** and click **Macros**
- Select the name of the macro you want to edit
- Click the **Edit** button

Mike notices that there is no automated way for a customer to view the Documentation worksheet. You have created buttons to open the glass and supplies worksheets, so Mike would like a button on the Welcome worksheet that opens the Documentation worksheet. You realize that the code to open the Documentation worksheet will be similar to the code to open any of the other worksheets. The only difference is that the target worksheet's name is different. You decide to use the Visual Basic Editor to copy an existing macro, rename it, and then assign it to a button on the Welcome worksheet. Using this technique is slightly faster than recording a new macro to do the job. Before creating the new macro, you want to become familiar with the Visual Basic Editor. First, you open the workbook Catalog3.xls.

Opening the Catalog3 workbook:

1. Start Excel
2. Open the workbook **Catalog3.xls**
3. Click the **Enable Macros** button when the Microsoft Excel dialog box appears

Now you can open the Visual Basic Editor and investigate its several windows.

FIGURE 12.22
The Visual Basic Editor window

Project Explorer window

objects stored in this workbook: woorksheets and modules

Project Explorer window

Properties window

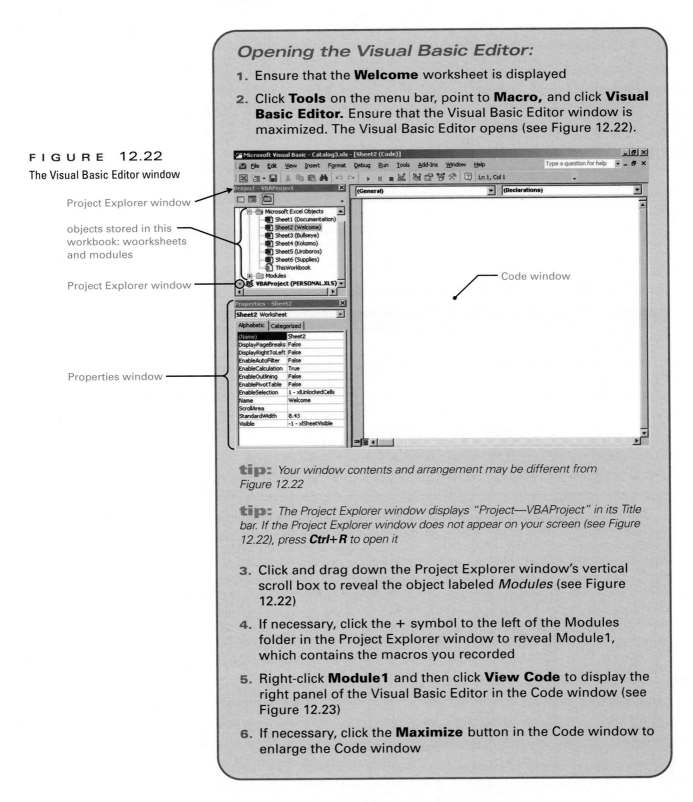

Opening the Visual Basic Editor:

1. Ensure that the **Welcome** worksheet is displayed

2. Click **Tools** on the menu bar, point to **Macro,** and click **Visual Basic Editor.** Ensure that the Visual Basic Editor window is maximized. The Visual Basic Editor opens (see Figure 12.22).

Code window

tip: *Your window contents and arrangement may be different from Figure 12.22*

tip: *The Project Explorer window displays "Project—VBAProject" in its Title bar. If the Project Explorer window does not appear on your screen (see Figure 12.22), press **Ctrl+R** to open it*

3. Click and drag down the Project Explorer window's vertical scroll box to reveal the object labeled *Modules* (see Figure 12.22)

4. If necessary, click the + symbol to the left of the Modules folder in the Project Explorer window to reveal Module1, which contains the macros you recorded

5. Right-click **Module1** and then click **View Code** to display the right panel of the Visual Basic Editor in the Code window (see Figure 12.23)

6. If necessary, click the **Maximize** button in the Code window to enlarge the Code window

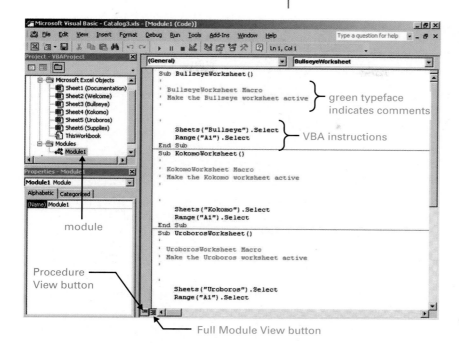

FIGURE 12.23

Visual Basic Editor with
Module 1 code visible

Editing a Macro with the Visual Basic Editor

Office XP's Visual Basic Editor displays several windows that allow you to review and alter various parts of your Excel project. A ***project*** contains forms, modules, and the Excel workbook objects. You can see two of these elements, a workbook with its worksheets and a module, in the Project Explorer window. ***Workbook objects*** are a workbook's worksheets and chart sheets. A special object called ThisWorkbook provides a convenient way to refer to all of the workbook's objects with one name (see Figure 12.23). A project may contain one or more forms. A ***form*** is a dialog box that appears in response to a user-defined command key click or other event. A form can contain command buttons, text boxes, list boxes, and a large number of other controls. Modules, as described previously, contain your VBA code, and there can be many modules in a project. Click an object in the Project Explorer window to activate it in the Properties window. Clicking one of the workbook's sheet names in the Project Explorer window activates its properties in the Properties window. In the Properties window, for example, you can change a worksheet's name. Double-clicking a module or form in the Project Explorer reveals its properties in the Properties window and reveals module code in the Code window.

You are ready to insert another VBA procedure to make the Documentation worksheet active. Because the code will be similar to the ReturnToMenu code, you will insert a new procedure, copy code from the ReturnToMenu code, and edit the code slightly so that it opens the Documentation worksheet.

Creating a sub procedure and copying code from another sub procedure:

1. Drag the Code window scroll button down until you can see the ReturnToMenu code in the Code window, and then click anywhere *inside* the ReturnToMenu sub procedure code

2. Click the **Procedure View** button located in the lower-left corner of the Code window. Only the ReturnToMenu code is visible in the Code window

3. Press **Ctrl+A** to select all of the ReturnToMenu code, and then press **Ctrl+C** to copy the code to the Clipboard

4. Click the **Full Module View** button in the lower-left corner of the Code window, and then click anywhere *below* the "End Sub" statement of the ReturnToMenu macro to deselect the code and position the insertion point

5. Click **Ctrl+V** to paste the code into the Code window. The Code window displays both the original ReturnToMenu code and the newly inserted copy

6. Drag the mouse through the code line **ReturnToMenu()** in the copy of the sub procedure

7. Type **DocWorksheet()** to rename the sub procedure

8. Double-click **ReturnToMenu** in the comment line of the DocWorksheet sub procedure and type **DocWorksheet**

9. Double-click **Welcome** in the second comment line of the DocWorksheet sub procedure and type **Documentation**

10. Double-click the word **Welcome** in the DocWorksheet sub procedure code line *Sheets("Welcome").Select* and then type **Documentation** (see Figure 12.24)

FIGURE 12.24

Modifying a copied sub procedure

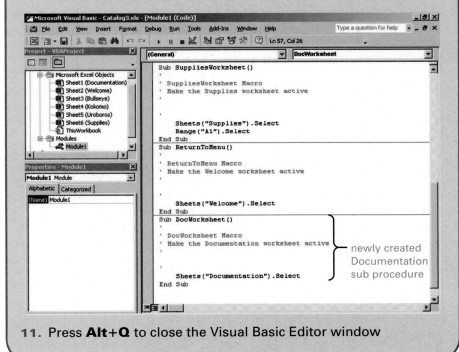

11. Press **Alt+Q** to close the Visual Basic Editor window

Now you have code that you can execute to make the Documentation worksheet active. To finish this work, you will create a new button and attach the newly minted code to it.

Creating a Documentation button and attaching code to it:

1. Press and hold the **Ctrl** key, click the **Bullseye Glass** button on the Welcome worksheet, release the **Ctrl** key, press **Ctrl+C** to copy the button to the Clipboard, and press **Ctrl+V** to paste the button onto the worksheet

2. Drag the copied button to the right of the original Bullseye Glass button until the bottom edge of the two buttons are aligned

3. Drag the mouse through the copied button's caption and then type **Documentation**

4. Move the mouse to the border of the Documentation button. When it changes to a four-headed arrow, right-click the button, click **Assign Macro** in the shortcut menu, click **DocWorksheet** in the list of macro names, and click **OK**

5. Click cell **A1** to deselect the Documentation button

Deleting a Macro

If you make a mistake while recording a macro and don't want to bother editing the recorded macro to correct it, you can delete a macro and start over. Although you do not need to delete any macros you have recorded in this session, you should know how to do so. If you record several macros, you will have occasion to delete unwanted macros eventually.

task reference

Deleting a Macro

- Click **Tools,** point to **Macro,** and click **Macros**

- Click the name of the macro in the Macro name list that you want to delete

- Click the **Delete** button

- Click **Yes** to confirm the deletion

WRITING SUBROUTINES

With the exception of the DocWorksheet procedure, you have created VBA sub procedures using the macro recorder. Using the macro recorder to create sub procedures has the advantage of precisely reproducing your keystrokes and commands. However, there are a number of situations where the macro recorder falls short. You cannot use the macro recorder to create a sub procedure that repetitively executes a series of instructions. Such a structure, called *repetition* or *looping* by programmers, repeats a series of steps until a special condition is recognized to halt the repetition. Excel applications developers use looping frequently. Another feature that the macro recorder is incapable of recording is branching. **Branching,** or **selection,** is a program structure that evaluates a condition and then takes one of two actions based on the outcome of condition evaluation. Selection is vital to writing robust VBA sub procedures. It allows you to evaluate whether the user's response is appropriate or not. Similar in design to the IF function, selection allows you to write an unlimited number of VBA statements for each of the two possible outcomes of a test—true or false. By writing your own sub procedures, or subroutines, you can take advantage of the full power of VBA and break the limits imposed by using the macro recorder alone.

Writing a Subroutine that Executes Whenever the Workbook Opens

Mike would like to have the Welcome worksheet active whenever the Catalog workbook opens regardless of which worksheet was active when the workbook was closed. In addition, he would like to remove the worksheet tabs so that customers have to use the buttons you created to move from one worksheet to another. Mike points out that making the worksheet tabs unavailable allows Mike to add other worksheets to the workbook in which Mike can record information that he does not want customers to view easily. Examples of information he wants to hide in the workbook include data about upcoming stained glass classes and customer catalog requests.

To run a VBA sub procedure automatically whenever you open the Catalog3.xls workbook, you create an event procedure. An **event procedure** is one that executes whenever a particular event occurs. For example, a click event occurs when a user clicks a button, a worksheet becomes active, or the user presses the Enter key when completing an Excel formula. There are a large number of events to which Excel can react. The workbook open event, which occurs whenever a workbook opens, is the event for which you will write a sub procedure. You write the workbook open sub procedure next.

Writing a workbook open event procedure:

1. Press **Alt+F11** to open the Visual Basic Editor

2. In the Project Explorer window, double-click the **ThisWorkbook** entry in VBAProject(Catalog3.xls) Microsoft Excel Objects. An empty Code window opens, and a blinking cursor appears in the Code window

   tip: *If necessary, click the + outline control to open the* ThisWorkbook *heading if it is not visible*

3. Click the leftmost list box at the top of the Code window and then click **Workbook.** The rightmost list box at the top of the Code window displays *Open,* and two code lines automatically appear in the Code window

4. Between the two code lines, type the following code. Press **Tab** at the beginning of the first line—before typing it—to indent the comment line four spaces. (Excel automatically indents subsequent lines by the same amount.) Press **Enter** after typing each line (see Figure 12.25). Type *no* spaces in the second and fourth lines below

'Activate Welcome worksheet

Sheets("Welcome").Select

'Remove worksheet tabs

ActiveWindow.DisplayWorkbookTabs = False

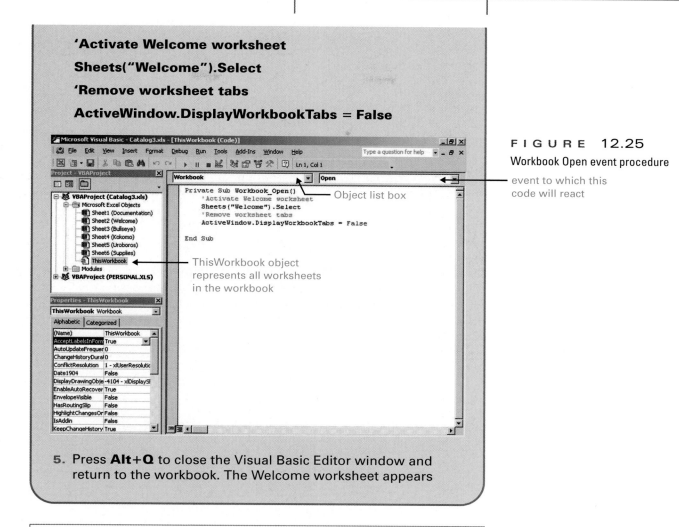

FIGURE 12.25
Workbook Open event procedure

event to which this
code will react

Object list box

ThisWorkbook object
represents all worksheets
in the workbook

5. Press **Alt+Q** to close the Visual Basic Editor window and
   return to the workbook. The Welcome worksheet appears

*another*word

. . . on Adding Code to the Workbook Open Event Procedure

If you want to include additional code in the Workbook Open event procedure but are not sure how to write the code, record the steps and copy them
to the Workbook Open procedure. Turn on the Macro Recorder and then
manually carry out the actions. After you have stopped the Macro Recorder,
simply open the newly recorded macro and copy the recorded code to the
Workbook Open procedure. Then delete the macro you just recorded since
it is no longer needed.

You decide to test the new code. It will be easy to spot any mistakes in
short code segments like this.

Testing the Workbook Open event procedure:

1. Press the **Supplies** worksheet tab to activate that worksheet prior to saving it. Doing this will help you determine whether the Workbook Open event procedure is working properly

2. Click the **Save** button on the Standard toolbar to save the changed workbook

3. Click **File** on the menu bar and then click **Close** to close the **Catalog3.xls** workbook

4. Click the **Open** button on the Standard toolbar, locate and click the **Catalog3.xls** workbook in the Open dialog box, and click the **Open** button to open the workbook

5. Click the **Enable Macros** button to open the workbook and test the Workbook Open event procedure. Excel opens the workbook, makes the Welcome worksheet active, and removes all worksheet tabs (see Figure 12.26)

FIGURE 12.26

Testing the Workbook Open event procedure

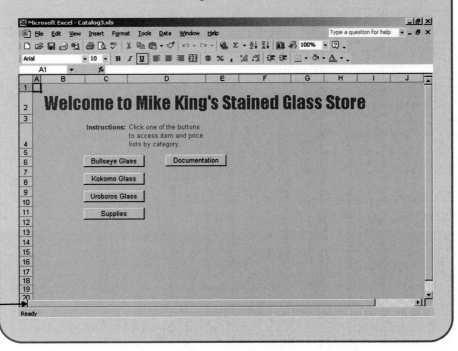

worksheet tabs and tab scrolling buttons are absent

Getting Data with the InputBox Function

Mike wants to add a little security to the Catalog workbook by requiring a workbook user to enter a password before the workbook opens. The password that Mike has selected is the word *Excel*. Later, you can change the password if you want.

The logical location for the password code is in the Workbook Open event code—the VBA code that Excel executes first when you attempt to open a workbook. Inserting password protection in VBA code requires just a few new elements including the InputBox function and the If-Then-Else selection structure.

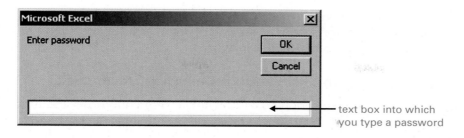

text box into which
you type a password

FIGURE 12.27
Example InputBox display

The InputBox function displays a dialog box with a text box, into which a user can type a string of characters and two buttons: OK and Cancel. The InputBox function has the following form:

```
InputBox (prompt, title)
```

Prompt is the message displayed within the dialog box, and it explains what the user is to input. *Title* is the title that appears in the dialog box's title bar. Figure 12.27 shows the InputBox display that Mike wants you to create.

You modify the Workbook_Open code with code to implement the password requirement. The process you will follow is to write some code, test the code, and then add more code to the Workbook_Open event procedure. By using this code test cycle, you ensure that any coding mistakes will be easy to spot.

Writing an InputBox function:

1. Press **Alt+F11** to open the Visual Basic Editor

2. In the Project Explorer window, double-click the **ThisWorkbook** entry in VBAProject(Catalog3.xls)\Microsoft Excel Objects. The Workbook_Open event procedure appears in the Code window

3. Click the empty line above End Sub, ensuring that the blinking insertion point is indented four characters, and then press **Enter** to open up another blank line

4. Type **strAnswer = InputBox("Enter password")** and then press **Enter** (see Figure 12.28). In the next steps, you will test your new code line

```
Private Sub Workbook_Open()
    'Activate Welcome worksheet
    Sheets("Welcome").Select
    'Remove worksheet tabs
    ActiveWindow.DisplayWorkbookTabs = False

    strAnswer = InputBox("Enter password")

End Sub
```

FIGURE 12.28
Completed InputBox function code

5. Press **Alt+Q** to close the Visual Basic Editor, press the **Save** button on the Standard toolbar, click **File** on the menu bar, and click **Close.** Excel closes the workbook

6. Click the **Open** button on the Standard toolbar, click **Catalog3.xls** in the Open dialog box, click **Open,** and click **Enable Macros.** Excel displays an input box with the prompt Enter password

7. Type your last name in the text box and then click the **OK** button. The dialog box disappears

The InputBox function works correctly. The next step is to add VBA code to process the information a user enters in the InputBox text box, ensuring that it is the prescribed password.

Controlling Program Flow with a Selection Structure

VBA provides several selection structures for testing conditions and executing alternative sets of instructions based on the outcome of the test. The most frequently used selection structure is If-Then. The form of the If-Then structure you will use, with its optional Else clause, is as follows:

```
If <condition to test> Then
    <true statement code lines>
Else
    <false statement code lines>
End if
```

Where <condition to test> is an expression that results in true or false (Name = "Fred", or C15 < 12). Expressions usually involve using comparison operators (<, <=, >, >=, =, <>) to compare the left side of the expression with the right side. The <true statement code lines> are one or more VBA statements that are executed if the condition is true. The <false statement code lines> contain the code lines that are executed if the condition is false. Only one set of code statements can be executed.

You will enhance the password enforcement code by adding an If-Then-Else selection structure to test whether the user has entered the correct password.

Writing an If-Then-Else selection structure:

1. Press **Alt+F11** to open the Visual Basic Editor

2. In the Project Explorer window, double-click **ThisWorkbook**

3. Click the empty line above End Sub, ensuring that the blinking insertion point is indented four characters

4. Type the following lines, pressing **Enter** at the end of each line. Press **Tab,** when needed, to indent the lines to match the code shown here and in Figure 12.29

   If UCase(strAnswer) <> "EXCEL" Then

   　　MsgBox "Incorrect password", vbOKOnly, "Error"

   Else

   　　Exit Sub

   End if

   tip: *Make sure you have spelled EXCEL correctly in the above code. When you complete this code, you will find it almost impossible to open the workbook if you forget the password or misspell it in the code*

5. Press **Alt+Q** to close the Visual Basic Editor, press the **Save** button on the Standard toolbar, click **File** on the menu bar, and click **Close.** Excel closes the workbook

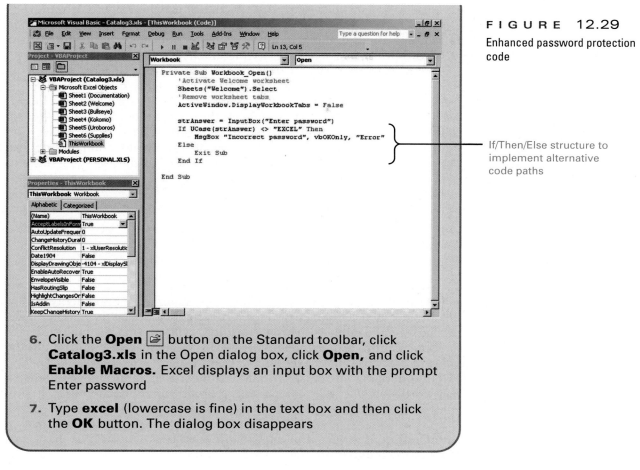

FIGURE 12.29
Enhanced password protection code

If/Then/Else structure to implement alternative code paths

6. Click the **Open** button on the Standard toolbar, click **Catalog3.xls** in the Open dialog box, click **Open,** and click **Enable Macros.** Excel displays an input box with the prompt Enter password

7. Type **excel** (lowercase is fine) in the text box and then click the **OK** button. The dialog box disappears

The condition part of the If statement is

```
UCase(strAnswer) <> "EXCEL"
```

UCase is a function that converts the string strAnswer, holding the user's input password. Once the input is converted, temporarily, to uppercase, Excel compares it to the uppercase string EXCEL. The relational operator <> means "not equal to." So the condition determines whether the upper-case version of the input password is not equal to EXCEL. If that is true, then the MsgBox statement executes. The MsgBox statement displays a di-alog box and allows the user to click the OK button. (vbOKOnly places only the OK button on the dialog box.) If the condition is false, then the statement Exit Sub executes. It exits the sub procedure without further processing—the statement executed for a correct password.

Writing an Iteration Structure

The password checking code you have written does not actively prevent a user from opening the workbook, because the code accepts any password. The code displays an error message when it detects an incorrect password and then exits the sub procedure, allowing the workbook to open. Detecting a correct password has the same result: Excel executes the Exit Sub statement, which transfers control to the End Sub statement directly and thereby exits the sub procedure. Mike has decided that the result of entering an incorrect password should be that the workbook is closed. Mike may give the authority to open the workbook to other employees.

Because typing mistakes can occur, Mike wants the password procedure to allow the user up to three attempts to enter a correct password. On the third failed attempt, the workbook will close. Your task in finishing up the password protection scheme is to implement two new features.

First, you will create an *iteration* structure—one or more statements that execute a series of VBA instructions repeatedly *until* a condition is true or *while* a condition is true. (Iteration structures are also called loops.) Second, you will code a VBA statement that closes the workbook following the third incorrect attempt to enter a password.

Excel provides several ways to repeatedly execute a section of code. The one you will use is the For-Next structure, which has the following form:

```
For <counter> = <start value> To <end value>
    Statement₁
    Statement₂
    . . .
    Statementₙ
Next <counter>
```

The <counter> is the initial value of a counter that keeps track of how many times the statements within the loop, Statement₁, Statement₂, and so on, are executed. The <start value> is the first value that the counter takes on, and <end value> is the highest value, or limit, that the counter takes on. Statements between the For and Next statements are executed until the value of the <counter> exceeds the <end value> or code within the loop exits the looping structure. To allow someone three attempts to enter a password, you will code a loop using the following For statement:

```
For intCount = 1 To 3
```

where intCount is the name you will give to the counter variable that keeps track of the number of times a loop executes.

> ## Writing an iteration structure:
>
> 1. Press **Alt+F11** to open the Visual Basic Editor
>
> 2. In the Project Explorer window, double-click the **ThisWorkbook** entry
>
> 3. In the Code window, click immediately to the left of the first letter in the code line strAnswer = InputBox("Enter password"), and then press **Enter** to open a new line
>
> 4. Press the **up arrow** key to move to the line above the InputBox code line and type **For intCount = 1 To 3**
>
> 5. Press the **down arrow** key, press the **Home** key to move the insertion point in front of the first letter of the InputBox line, and then press **Tab** to indent the line
>
> 6. Repeat step 5 for the next five lines to indent each of them to the next tab stop
>
> 7. With the insertion point at the beginning of *End If,* press the **down arrow,** ensure that the insertion point is lined up with the letter *F* in the For statement seven lines above it, and type **Next intCount**

8. Press **Enter**

9. Type **'Exhausted loop means allowable attempts exceeded** and then press **Enter.** Notice that Excel colors comments green

tip: *Be sure to type an apostrophe as the first character in the preceding line so that Excel interprets the line as commentary, not code. Your Workbook_Open event procedure should match Figure 12.30*

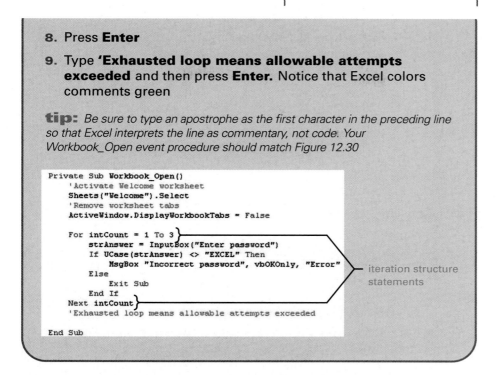

```
Private Sub Workbook_Open()
    'Activate Welcome worksheet
    Sheets("Welcome").Select
    'Remove worksheet tabs
    ActiveWindow.DisplayWorkbookTabs = False

    For intCount = 1 To 3
        strAnswer = InputBox("Enter password")
        If UCase(strAnswer) <> "EXCEL" Then
            MsgBox "Incorrect password", vbOKOnly, "Error"
        Else
            Exit Sub
        End If
    Next intCount
    'Exhausted loop means allowable attempts exceeded

End Sub
```

iteration structure statements

FIGURE   12.30
Workbook Open event procedure with iteration structure

The preceding code executes the InputBox code line and the If-Then-Else code lines up to three times, if necessary. On the third unsuccessful attempt, the MsgBox code executes and displays the error message to the user and then jumps to the line of code following the Next statement terminating the loop.

Closing a Workbook with VBA Code

The line following the "Exhausted loop" comment is where you will place a code line to close the workbook. That works because the only possible way to reach the line following the Next statement is looping three times and filling in the incorrect password each of the three times. Otherwise, if the user enters the correct password—even on the third attempt, then control transfers outside the Workbook Open event procedure entirely. The statement to close the current workbook is *ThisWorkbook.Close. ThisWorkbook* is the symbolic name for the entire workbook, an object, and *Close* is a method that operates on the object ThisWorkbook. A ***method*** is an action that takes place on behalf of the object to which it is attached.

You make the final modification to the Workbook_Open event procedure by adding the statement to close the workbook when the user fails after three times to enter a correct password.

Modifying the Workbook Open event procedure with the Close method:

1. With the Visual Basic Editor displayed and the Workbook_Open event procedure displayed in the Code window, ensure that the insertion point is below the "Exhausted loop" comment line

Completed Workbook Open
event procedure

2. Type **ThisWorkbook.Close** (see Figure 12.31)

```
Private Sub Workbook_Open()
    'Activate Welcome worksheet
    Sheets("Welcome").Select
    'Remove worksheet tabs
    ActiveWindow.DisplayWorkbookTabs = False

    For intCount = 1 To 3
        strAnswer = InputBox("Enter password")
        If UCase(strAnswer) <> "EXCEL" Then
            MsgBox "Incorrect password", vbOKOnly, "Error"
        Else
            Exit Sub
        End If
    Next intCount
    'Exhausted loop means allowable attempts exceeded
    ThisWorkbook.Close
End Sub
```

closes the current
workbook, but leaves ——→
Excel running

tip: *As you type statements such as the preceding one, you will notice that
Excel displays pop-up help showing allowed choices to add to the code. Simply
ignore the help and continue typing*

3. Press **Alt+Q** to close the Visual Basic Editor

4. Press the **Save** 🖫 button on the Standard toolbar to save
   your changes

5. Click **File** on the menu bar and then click **Close.** Excel closes
   the **Catalog3.xls** workbook, but Excel remains open

Now you can test your work. First, you will pretend to forget the password and observe what Excel does to protect the workbook. In the second
test, you will enter the correct password (Excel) the first time and observe
the workbook open. Mike walks by just before you test the new code, so
you beckon him over to observe your tests.

*Testing password protection by entering
incorrect passwords three times:*

1. Click the **Open** 🖼 button on the menu bar, click **Catalog3.xls**
   in the Open dialog box, click the **Open** button, and click the
   Enable Macros button. The Microsoft Excel password dialog
   box appears

2. Type **mcgraw** in the text box and press **Enter.** (Pressing the
   Enter key is the same as clicking the OK button in this case.)
   The Error dialog box appears

3. Press **Enter** to dismiss the Error dialog box. The Enter
   Password dialog box reappears

4. Repeat steps 2 and 3 two more times, typing **macros** and
   then **testing** in step 2 for the second and third attempts,
   respectively. After you enter the third incorrect password
   and press Enter, Excel closes the workbook

Wonderful! Entering an incorrect password three times in a row works correctly—the workbook closes. Now, try entering the correct password, Excel, to ensure that it opens the workbook.

Testing password protection by entering the correct password:

1. Click the **Open** 🖻 button on the menu bar, click **Catalog3.xls** in the Open dialog box, click the **Open** button, and click the **Enable Macros** button. The Microsoft Excel password dialog box appears

   tip: *To prove that the password is case insensitive, you will use odd capitalization but correct spelling of the password to open the workbook in the next step*

2. Type **excEL** (three lowercase letters followed by two uppercase letters) in the text box and press **Enter.** The workbook opens and displays the Welcome worksheet. Notice that the worksheet tabs and tab scroll buttons are absent

3. Click **File** on the menu bar and then click **Close.** Excel closes the **Catalog3.xls** workbook, but Excel remains open

---

Mike is pleased. He's so happy with your progress, he offers to buy you lunch.

WRITING CUSTOM FUNCTIONS

Although Microsoft Excel has a large number of built-in functions, chances are that Excel does not have a few functions you work with regularly. If this is the case, you can create your own custom functions from VBA code. Any function you create is called a ***user-defined function,*** or ***UDF.*** Like sub procedures, you place user-defined functions in modules.

Mike wants you to insert a customer invoice worksheet as the last worksheet in the Catalog workbook. Mike has created the basic invoice worksheet in a workbook called ex12ArtGlassInvoice. He will use the invoice worksheet to create and print invoices for his large accounts. Excel does not supply two functions in its built-in functions that Mike needs to complete his invoice worksheet. One of the missing functions computes a discount percentage for qualifying customer orders based on the number of units ordered for each item. A second function that Mike wants determines whether the customer's order is tax exempt or not. If not, then it calculates the tax owed based on the tax rate in his home state, Nebraska, and charges the customer accordingly.

Differentiating between Functions and Sub Procedures

A function and a sub procedure are similar because they both contain a sequence of VBA code lines. They both appear in a module attached to a workbook. Their purposes are different, however. A sub procedure contains VBA statements that affect a worksheet or workbook. A custom function cannot delete a worksheet column, format worksheet cells, insert a worksheet, or perform an action that alters a workbook. Unlike a sub procedure, a custom function can only return a value to a worksheet formula by assigning the function name the result of the function's calculations—just like Excel's built-in functions. Functions are available only in the workbook where they are created.

Custom functions contain VBA statements that start with *function* instead of *sub.* The end of a function is marked with *end function,* instead of *end sub.* At least one statement in a function must assign the function name to a value or expression that is the result of the function prior to the end of the function. The general form of a custom function is the following:

```
Private Function <function name> (argument₁,…,argumentₙ)
As <function data type>
    <one or more VBA statements>
    <function name> = <expression>
    . . .
End Function
```

Opening the Invoice Workbook

Before writing any custom functions, you will open the invoice worksheet that Mike has created and then write functions to perform the invoicing operation. You ask Mike for a copy of the invoice workbook. He tells you it is called **ex12ArtGlassInvoice.xls.** He also mentions that another person wrote a VBA sub procedure to clear the invoice entries that do not contain formulas. The workbook has protection turned on so that anyone entering data can press the Tab key to move from one cell to another. There are some cells that require formulas that you are to write. You open the ex12ArtGlassInvoice worksheet next.

Opening the Invoice workbook:

1. Click the **Open** 🖝 button on the Standard toolbar, navigate to the folder containing **ex12ArtGlassInvoice.xls,** click **ex12ArtGlassInvoice.xls,** and click **Open**

2. Click the **Enable macros** button in the dialog box that appears warning you that the workbook contains macros

3. Click **File** on the menu bar, click **Save As,** type **Invoice2** in the File name text box, and click the **Save** button. Excel saves the workbook under its new name (see Figure 12.32)

4. Press the **Tab** key a dozen times. Notice which cells Excel activates. Excel moves to the next unlocked cell on the Invoice page, making it convenient for anyone to fill out the invoice row by row

---

Creating Custom Functions

Mike points out that the custom function you will write computes a discount based on the quantity ordered for each item. The custom function, to be called Discount, will occupy the cell range F13:F18. Cell G20 will hold the custom formula that computes tax, if any, on the sale. The custom function will be called Tax.

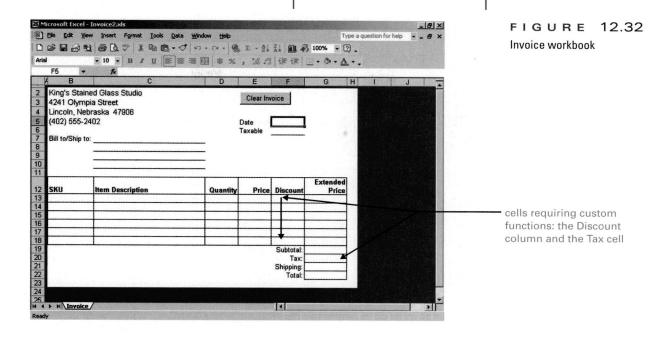

FIGURE 12.32

Invoice workbook

cells requiring custom functions: the Discount column and the Tax cell

Mike explains how he calculates a discount, if any, for each invoice line—he did this in the past by hand. Discounts are based on the quantity of each item a customer purchases. If a customer purchases three items, for example, there are three entries on the invoice, one for each item, in cells B13 through G15. If the item quantity is less than 50, there is no discount for the item. The purchase price of any item in which the quantity is between 50 and 99 receives a 5 percent discount. The discount for a quantity greater than 99 of any one item is 10 percent.

Rather than write a formula to implement this three-tier discount scheme, Mike wants you to write a custom function called Discount. Like nearly all functions, the Discount function will have two arguments. The function uses the values in cells passed as arguments to calculate an answer that the function returns to the cell containing the function. The answer returned by a function can be any of several data types allowed by VBA. You indicate the function answer's data type with a type that follows the As phrase at the right end of the function's prototype statement (see Figure 12.33). The ***prototype statement*** is the first line of the function definition.

The ***data type*** of a variable reveals the type of information that is stored in the memory space. VBA has several data types. These are listed in Figure 12.34.

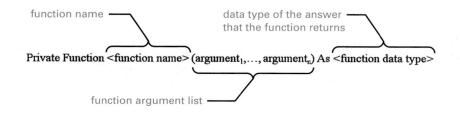

function name

data type of the answer that the function returns

Private Function <function name> (argument$_1$,..., argument$_n$) As <function data type>

function argument list

FIGURE 12.33

General form of a function prototype

EXCEL

FIGURE 12.34

Popular VBA data types

Data Type	Use For
Currency	Numbers containing decimal amounts such as dollars and cents
Date	An eight-character date (mm/dd/yy)
Integer	Whole number in the range of -32768 to $+32767$
Long	Large whole numbers
Single	Single-precision numbers with decimal amounts (six digits of precision)
String	Alphanumeric data including digits, letters, and special characters
Variant	Default data type if not declared; allows conversion from one data type to another

Writing a custom function to calculate a discount percentage:

1. Press **Alt+F11** to open the Visual Basic Editor, click **Insert** on the menu bar, and then click **Module** to create a new module. The Visual Basic Editor creates Module1 and places it below the existing InvoiceModules module.

2. In the code window, type the following VBA code (press **Enter** at the end of each line except the last line, End If). Press the **Tab** key before typing the second line (a comment) to indent it, and press the Tab key, as needed, to match the indentation of the code below

```
Private Function Discount(Quantity) As Single
    'Calculate the discount percentage
    If Quantity >= 100 Then
        Discount = 0.1
    ElseIf Quantity >= 50 Then
        Discount = 0.05
    Else
        Discount = 0
    End If
```

tip: When you complete the Private Function line, Excel automatically adds End Function to the last line in the function (see Figure 12.35)

Next, you can implement the second function called Tax. The Tax function will compute sales tax for any sale that is taxable. If a sale is not taxable, the computed tax will be zero. If a sale is taxable, then cell F6 will contain Y (for yes). If it is not, then cell F6 will contain N (for no). The taxable status can be either uppercase or lowercase, because the Tax function will recognize either one.

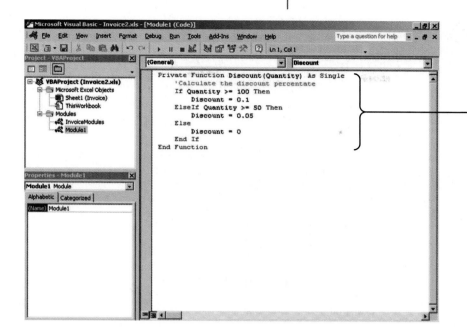

Completed Discount custom function

Discount custom function

Writing a custom function to compute sales tax:

1. Move the blinking cursor in the Code window to the end of the End Function line and press **Enter** to move to the beginning of a new line

2. Type the following VBA code (press **Enter** at the end of each line except the last line, End If):

Private Function Tax(Subtotal, Taxable) As Currency
    'Calculate Tax
    If UCase(Taxable) = "N" Or UCase(Taxable) = "NO" Then
        Tax = 0
    Else
        Tax = Subtotal * 0.075
    End If

    Figure 12.36 shows the completed Tax custom function

3. Press **Alt+Q** to close the Visual Basic Editor and display the Invoice worksheet

With the two functions completed, you can write custom functions in your workbook that call upon the custom functions to deliver an answer.

Using Custom Functions

Once you have defined one or more functions, you can activate a worksheet cell and write an expression containing the function and any arguments, such as cell references, that you pass to the function. Suppose that

EXCEL

FIGURE 12.36
Completed Tax custom function

Tax custom function ——

you entered information about a purchased item in the first row, row 13, of the invoice list of line items. You enter the SKU, or stock keeping unit (inventory number) of the item in cell B13, the item description in cell C13, the quantity (sheets of glass) in cell D13, and the price per unit in cell E13. In the cell range F13:F18 are expressions that reference the Discount function you defined to compute the percentage discount. (All the cells in the invoice are formatted to display percentages, currency, or integers as needed.) In cell F13, for example, you would write the expression

```
=Discount(D13)
```

The argument, cell D13, references the cell containing the quantity of that item ordered. When Excel computes the discount using your Discount function, the reference to cell D13 is passed to the function and, in effect, is substituted for every occurrence of the word Quantity in the function definition. The function returns the result, zero in this case, to the cell containing the expression.

You will type in cell F13 the Discount expression shown above and then copy that expression down through the cell range F14:F18. Because the worksheet is formatted to suppress displaying zero values, nothing will display in the Discount column at first. Later, when you enter values larger than 49 in the Quantity column to test the worksheet, you will see values appear in the Discount and Extended Price columns. In order to make changes to the Invoice worksheet, you first disengage protection so that you can alter the contents of cells.

Temporarily removing worksheet protection:

1. Click **Tools** on the menu bar and point to **Protection**

2. Click **Unprotect Sheet.** Excel removes protection from the Invoice worksheet

With protection removed, you are free to write the Discount expression in a locked cell. Once all new formulas are in place, you will reestablish worksheet protection.

Using a custom function in a worksheet cell:

1. Click cell **F13** and type **=Discount(D13)** (see Figure 12.37)

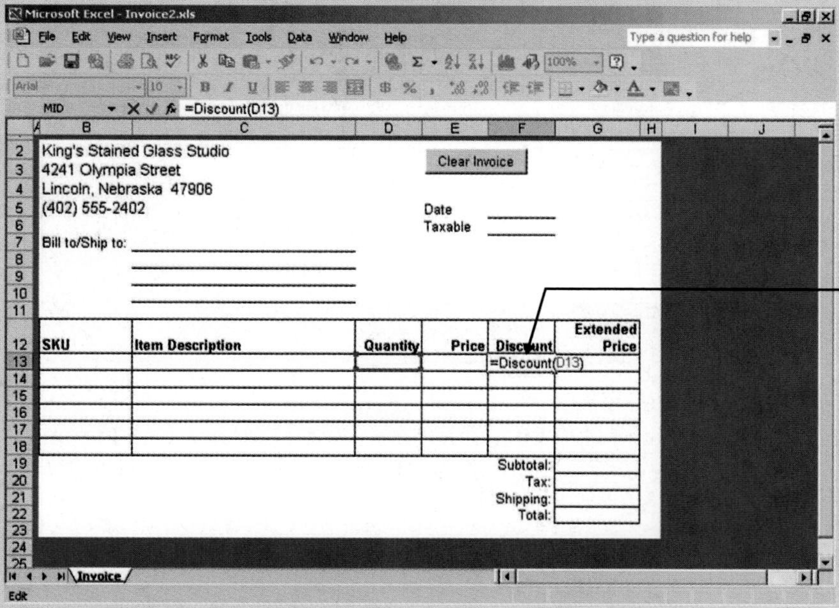

discount function with argument

FIGURE 12.37
Entering the Discount function in cell F13

2. Press **Enter** to complete the expression

3. Click cell **F13**, click and drag the fill handle through the cell range **F14:F18**, and then release the mouse. The Discount expression appears in cell range F13:F18, though no value appears in the cells because the argument of each function refers to an empty cell

The final function you will write is the one to calculate tax, if any. The Tax function will appear in cell G20. The Tax function contains two arguments. The first argument refers to cell G19, which contains the subtotal. The second argument refers to cell F6, which indicates whether the transaction is taxable or not. When an invoice is completed, cell F6 will contain Yes or No, which indicates the taxable status. In other words, if cell F6 contains either "n" or "no," then the taxable amount returned by the Tax function is zero. Otherwise, tax is computed at 7.5 percent of the subtotal.

Writing the worksheet expression containing the Tax function:

1. Click cell **G20** and type **=Tax(G19,F6)** (see Figure 12.38)

EXCEL

F I G U R E   12.38

Entering the Tax function in cell G20

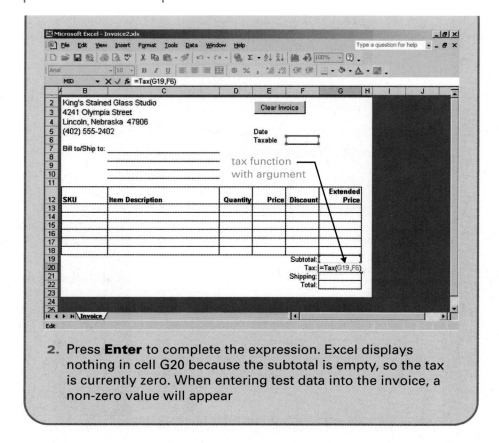

2. Press **Enter** to complete the expression. Excel displays nothing in cell G20 because the subtotal is empty, so the tax is currently zero. When entering test data into the invoice, a non-zero value will appear

Cells in the fill-in fields—Date, Taxable, Bill to-Ship to, the invoice lines, and Shipping—are unlocked so that you can enter data into them. All other cells are locked to protect the formulas and labels they hold. With all formulas in place, you can protect your worksheet before entering data to test your two custom functions.

Restoring worksheet protection:

1. Click **Tools** on the menu bar and point to **Protection**

2. Click **Protect Sheet.** Excel displays the Protect Sheet dialog box

3. Click **OK** to finalize protection and accept the dialog box protection values displayed

4. Click the **Save** button on the Standard toolbar to save all the changes you have made so far

Testing Custom Functions

A simple way to test the worksheet is to type a few test values into a blank invoice.

Entering test data to test the Discount and Tax custom functions:

1. Click cell **F5,** type today's date, and press **Tab** to move to the next unlocked cell

2. In cell **F6,** type **yes,** and press **Tab** to move to the next unlocked cell—the first Bill to-Ship to entry

3. Fill out the shipping address of the customer by typing the following three lines, pressing **Tab** after finishing each line to move to the next line

   Tobias Carling

   12843 Glider Port Road

   La Jolla, CA 92111

   Next, you will enter the number, description, quantity, and price of several products that were purchased by this customer

3. Press **Tab** to move to the first row just below the SKU label and enter the following lines for three items purchased. When you are finished, your invoice should match the one in Figure 12.39

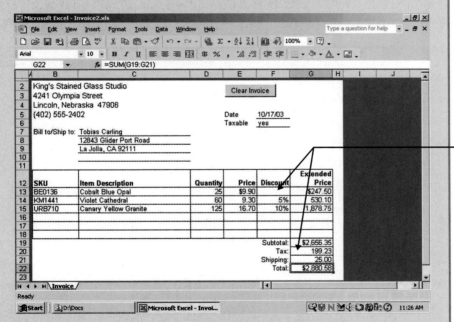

FIGURE 12.39
Completed test invoice

compare your discount and tax numbers to these results

4. Type **BE0136,** press **Tab,** type **Cobalt Blue Opal,** press **Tab,** type **25,** press **Tab,** type **9.9,** and press **Tab** to complete the first line and move to the beginning of the second one

5. In cell **B14,** type **KM1441,** press **Tab,** type **Violet Cathedral,** press **Tab,** type **60,** press **Tab,** type **9.3,** and press **Tab** to complete the second line and move to the beginning of the third one

6. In cell **B15,** type **URB710,** press **Tab,** type **Canary Yellow Granite,** press **Tab,** type **125,** press **Tab,** and type **16.7** to complete the third invoice item line

7. Click cell **G21,** the Shipping cell, type **25,** and press **Enter.** Figure 12.39 shows the completed invoice. Compare your results to the figure

tip: *If the figure and your calculations do not match, recheck the values you entered and make changes where needed*

tip: *If you think your custom functions are incorrect, press **Alt+F11** and then compare your two functions to Figures 12.35 and 12.36. Make any necessary changes, press **Alt+Q** to move back to the worksheet, and press function key **F9** to recalculate the worksheet*

8. Print your worksheet by clicking the **Print** button on the Standard toolbar

9. Clear the data you just entered by pressing the **Clear Invoice** button found near cell E2

Printing VBA Code

Printing your VBA code is an excellent way to document your work and preserve a hard copy of it that you can pass around for others to examine.

task reference

Printing VBA code

- Click **Alt+F11** to open the Visual Basic Editor
- Double-click the module in the Project Explorer window containing the VBA code you want to print
- Click **File** on the menu bar
- Click the **Code** check box in the Print What panel
- Click the **Current Project** option button in the Range panel to select all of the code in a project, or click the **Current Module** option button in the Range panel to select only the current module
- Click **OK**

Now that your work is complete, Mike wants you to print the VBA function code you created for the Invoice2 worksheet.

Printing the Discount and Tax function code:

1. Press **Alt+F11** to open the Visual Basic Editor

2. Double-click the **Module1** module in the Project Explorer window to reveal the Discount and Tax functions in the Code window

3. Click **File** on the menu bar and then click **Print.** The *Print— VBAProject* dialog box appears

4. Ensure that the **Current Module** option in the Range panel is selected, and ensure that the **Code** check box contains a checkmark (see Figure 12.40)

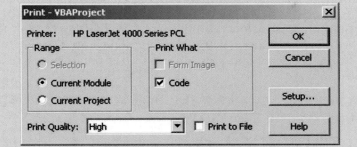

FIGURE 12.40

Preparing to print a code module

5. Click **OK.** Excel prints the code contained in the module

6. Press **Alt+Q** to close Visual Basic Editor and return to the worksheet

You are done with your work on the Invoice workbook, so save it and close Excel.

Saving the Invoice2 workbook and exiting Excel:

1. Click the **Save** button on the Standard toolbar to save the workbook

2. Click **File** on the menu bar and then click **Exit.** Excel closes

---

You show Mike your work. He is especially pleased with the two custom functions you created for the Invoice workbook. That will make invoicing selected customers easier for Mike.

---

making the grade   SESSION 12.2

1. A _____ is where Excel stores VBA code.

2. A _____ contains forms, modules, and the Excel workbook objects.

3. You can use a _____ or repetition structure to repeat a series of VBA instructions.

4. The instruction that makes a decision to do one action or another is called a _____ structure.

5. You can pass a cell reference to a custom function through one of its _____.

6. Make the following modifications to the Invoice2 workbook. Open the **Invoice2.xls** workbook (click **Enable Macros** to allow macros) and save it as **Invoice3.xls.** Press **Alt+F11** to open the Visual Basic Editor. Insert a new custom function called ShippingCost below the Tax custom function in Module1. Type the following code to define the function (press **Enter** at the end of each line and press **Tab** to indent the lines as indicated below):

Private Function ShippingCost(QtyTotal As Integer) As Single
    If QtyTotal < 10 Then
        ShippingCost = 5
    ElseIf QtyTotal < 50 Then
        ShippingCost = 12
    ElseIf QtyTotal < 150 Then
        ShippingCost = 45
    Else
        ShippingCost = 70
    End If
End Function

Press **Alt+Q** to close the Visual Basic Editor window, click cell **G21**, and type **=ShippingCost(SUM(D13:D15)).** Click cell **D13** and type **10,** click cell **D14** and type **50,** and click cell **D15** and type **20,** and then press **Enter.** Examine the shipping cost in cell G21. It should display the value 45. Place your name in the worksheet header, print the worksheet, print the VBA code for the three custom functions, save the workbook, and then close Excel.

SESSION 12.3 SUMMARY

Visual Basic for Applications, or VBA, is a powerful programming language that allows you to automate Excel procedures and create custom functions. Using the macro recorder, you can record your commands and keystrokes and capture them in a macro that you can replay whenever you need to. Alternatively, you can use the Visual Basic Editor to write macro instructions and custom functions by hand. Sub procedures that you create using the macro recorder are more limited than those that you code by hand. Recorded macros cannot perform If tests, and they cannot create code that loops. When you require selection (If) or iteration (loop) structures, you can manually write VBA code to implement sub procedures.

Sub procedures affect Excel objects in some way such as deleting columns, making a cell active, selecting a worksheet, and so on. Using the form menu, you can attach sub procedures to command buttons. By clicking a command button, the associated sub procedure executes. A specially named sub procedure, called Workbook_Open, automatically executes whenever the workbook containing it opens. The Workbook_Open sub procedure is a handy location for initialization procedures or welcome messages that must occur. Sub procedures in any open workbook are available to all open workbooks. Sub procedures that you want to be available to all workbooks should be saved in the Personal Macro Workbook. The Personal Macro Workbook is a hidden workbook stored in Excel's XLStart folder. Whenever Excel is started, Excel also opens the Personal Macro Workbook and then hides it—making any sub procedures it holds available to all open workbooks.

Unlike sub procedures, custom functions cannot affect Excel objects. Instead, they return a value, or answer, to the cell containing the function. Functions return a value in VBA code by assigning the function name to the value or expression that computes a value. Custom functions can return one of several different data types. A function's answer data type is declared in the prototype statement following the optional argument list. Data types include string, integer, date, currency, single, and double.

MOUS OBJECTIVES SUMMARY

- Record a macro instruction (MOUS Ex2002e-5-2)
- Run macro instructions using a dialog box and a command button (MOUS Ex2002e-5-2)
- Create and modify Visual Basic code in the Visual Basic editor (MOUS Ex2002e-5-2)
- Use Visual basic objects, methods, properties, and variables (MOUS Ex2002e-5-2)
- Create a macro that automatically executes when you open a workbook (MOUS Ex2002e-5-2)
- Protect a worksheet to preserve its integrity (MOUS Ex2002e-9-1)

task reference roundup

Task	Page #	Preferred Method
Recording a Macro Instruction	EX 12.8	• Click **Tools,** point to **Macro,** click **Record New Macro**
		• Type a macro name in the Macro name text box
		• Type a description in the Description text box
		• Click **OK**
		• Execute the tasks you want to record
		• Click the **Stop Recording** button
Assigning a Macro to a Button	EX 12.11	• Click **View,** point to **Toolbars,** click **Forms**
		• Click the **Button** tool in the Forms toolbar
		• Click a worksheet cell to place a button on the worksheet

EXCEL

task reference roundup

Task	Page #	Preferred Method
		• Select the macro to assign to the button from the Macro name list
		• Click **OK**
		• Drag the mouse across the button's caption and type a descriptive name
		• Click any cell to deselect the button
Making Buttons Visible on a Printout	EX 12.13	• Right-click the button you want to display on a printout
		• Click **Format Control** on the shortcut menu
		• Click the **Properties** tab
		• Click the **Print object** check box, and click **OK**
Selecting a Button Control without Activating It	EX 12.16	• Press and hold the **Ctrl** key
		• Click the button on the worksheet
		• Release the **Ctrl** key
Unhiding a Workbook	EX 12.21	• Click **Window** on the menu bar
		• Click **Unhide**
		• Click a workbook in the Unhide workbook list and then click **OK**
Hiding a Workbook	EX 12.21	• Make active any worksheet of the workbook you want to hide
		• Click **Window** on the menu bar
		• Click **Hide**
Setting the Macro Security Level	EX 12.22	• Click **Tools** on the menu bar, click **Options,** and click the **Security** tab
		• Click the **Macro Security** button
		• Click the security level option button of your choice
		• Click **OK** to close the Security dialog box, and click **OK** to close the Options dialog box
Opening the Visual Basic Editor	EX 12.25	• Click **Tools,** point to **Macro,** and click **Visual Basic Editor**
		or
		• Press **Alt+F11**
		or
		• Click **Tools,** point to **Macro,** and click **Macros**
		• Select the name of the macro you want to edit
		• Click the **Edit** button

task reference roundup

Task	Page #	Preferred Method
Deleting a Macro	EX 12.29	• Click **Tools**, point to **Macro**, and click **Macros**
		• Click the name of the macro in the Macro name list that you want to delete
		• Click the **Delete** button
		• Click **Yes** to confirm the deletion
Printing VBA code	EX 12.48	• Click **Alt+F11** to open the Visual Basic Editor
		• Double-click the module in the Project Explorer containing the VBA code you want to print
		• Click **File** on the menu bar
		• Click the **Code** check box in the Print What panel
		• Click the **Current Project** option button in the Range panel to select all of the code in a project, or click the **Current Module** option button in the Range panel to select only the current module
		• Click **OK**

CROSSWORD PUZZLE

Across

2. A programming structure that repeats a series of steps until a special condition is recognized to halt the repetition.
8. Unlike a function, this VBA code can affect Excel objects.
9. A data _____ is the type of information that is stored in a variable.
10. A procedure that returns a result or answer.
11. An Excel object where macros are stored.
13. A dialog box that appears in response to a user-defined command key click or other event.

Down

1. A programming structure that evaluates a condition and then takes one of two actions based on the condition.
3. Contains forms, modules, and the Excel workbook objects.
4. The worksheets and chart sheets stored are collectively known as _____ objects.
5. A _____ statement is the first line of a function or sub procedure definition.
6. A symbolic name for a value, expression, or cell reference that is passed to a function for its use in calculating an answer.
7. Store any macros in the _____ macro workbook to make them available to all Excel workbooks.
11. A group of VBA statements that collectively performs a particular task or returns a result.
12. When you create your own Excel function, it is called a _____-defined function.

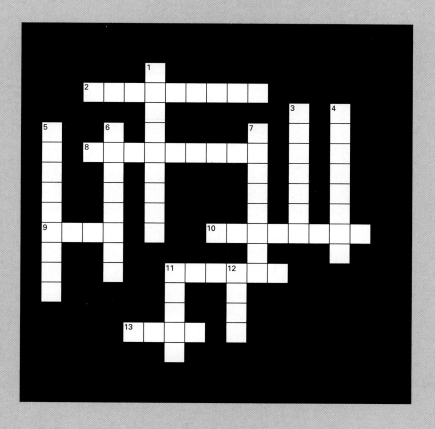

FILL-IN

1. Excel stores in a _____ all macros and user-defined functions.

2. Store a macro in Excel's _____ _____ workbook to make it available to any workbook you open.

3. A variable's _____ _____ restricts the type of information it holds.

4. You pass a cell reference to a sub procedure or a function through a(n) _____.

5. A _____ is an action that takes place on behalf of the object to which it is attached.

6. The _____ statement is the first line of a function or sub procedure definition.

REVIEW QUESTIONS

1. Buttons you add to an Excel worksheet to launch sub procedures normally do not appear on printouts. Why not?

2. You can create a macro by using the Macro Recorder or by creating it yourself in the Visual Basic Editor. Using the Macro Recorder is usually a simpler way to create a macro. Why would you use the Visual Basic Editor to create a sub procedure?

3. What is the main difference between a sub procedure and a user-defined (custom) function?

4. Why does Excel display a warning dialog box when you open a workbook containing macros?

CREATE THE QUESTION

For each of the following answers, create an appropriate, short question.

ANSWER	QUESTION
1. The Macro Recorder	_____
2. Save it in the Personal Macro Workbook	_____
3. A function can, but a sub procedure cannot	_____
4. The Visual Basic Editor	_____
5. The Project Explorer	_____
6. A selection structure	_____

practice

1. The Voice of the Midwest, Radio Station WWWA

WWWA is a radio station in the Midwest that plays classical music. The station reaches an estimated audience of 1.5 million listeners. WWWA is supported by advertising revenues and must continually seek new advertisers to support the station. Seven full-time sales and marketing people are responsible for obtaining new advertisers and generating the required revenue to keep the station afloat. The station pays each salesperson a base salary ($2,000 per month), a commission on their month's sale amounts, and a bonus when applicable. Each salesperson's commission rate may be different and is based on a combination of seniority and past sales. The company awards a bonus to salespersons who sell more than $10,000 in new advertising each month. The bonus is 10 percent of the sales revenue over $10,000.

Margaret Perkins, the sales manager, wants you to help her create a worksheet to compute salespersons' commissions and bonuses. She wants you to write VBA functions to implement both the commission and bonus calculations. Margaret has created a fundamental workbook called **exSalesQuota.xls.**

1. Open **exSalesQuota.xls** and save it as **SalesQuota2.xls.** Type your name in the underlined cell to the right of the User label. Press the **Tab** key and type the current date adjacent to the Date Revised label

2. Click the **January Sales** worksheet tab, click cell **B8,** click the **Sort Ascending** button on the Standard toolbar, select cell range **C8:G8,** press and hold the **Ctrl** key, select cell range **C15:G15,** release the **Ctrl** key, and click the **Currency Style** button on the Formatting toolbar

3. Select cell range **C9:G14,** click the **Comma Style** button on the Formatting toolbar, select cell range **D8:D14,** click the **Percent Style** button on the Formatting toolbar, and click **Increase Decimal** button (also on the Formatting toolbar) *twice*

4. Press **Alt+F11** to open the Visual Basic Editor. Maximize the code window, if necessary. Click **Insert** on the menu bar,

and click **Module** to insert a code module to the workbook

5. Click in the code window and type the following code (indent as shown). Note that Excel automatically inserts the two End Function statements, so you do not have to type those statements:

```
Function Commission(TotalSales, CommRate As
Currency) As Currency
'Compute commission on total sales
Commission = TotalSales * CommRate
End Function
Function Bonus(TotalSales, BonusRate, BonusFloor
As Currency) As Currency
'Compute bonus based on a percent of 'sales over
minimum sales
If TotalSales < BonusFloor Then
    Bonus = 0
Else
    Bonus = (TotalSales − BonusFloor) * BonusRate
End If
End Function
```

6. Press **Alt+Q** to close the Visual Basic Editor and return to the worksheet

7. Set your macro security to Medium: Click **Tools,** click **Options,** click the **Security** tab, click the **Macro Security** button, click the **Medium** option button, click **OK,** and click **OK** again

8. Click cell **E8,** type **=Commission(C8,D8),** and press **Enter**

9. Click cell **F8,** type **=Bonus(C8,B$3,B$4),** and press **Enter**

10. Click cell **G8,** type **=B$2+E8+F8,** and press **Enter**

11. Select cell range **E8:G8,** press **Ctrl+C,** select cell range **E9:E14,** press **Ctrl+V,** click the **Paste Options** smart tag, and click the **Match Destination Formatting** option in the Paste Options list

12. Click cell **B15,** press **Ctrl+B,** click the **Align Right** button on the Formatting toolbar, type **Totals,** and press **Enter**

13. Select cell range **C8:C15,** click the **AutoSum** button on the Standard toolbar, select cell range **E8:G15,** click the

AutoSum button on the Standard toolbar, and click any cell to deselect the cell range

14. Place your name in the January Sales worksheet header, print both the Documentation and January Sales worksheets, and print the January Sales worksheet formulas. (Click **Tools,** click **Options,** click the **View** tab, and click the **Formulas** check box, and click **OK.**) Remember to reverse the Formulas setting once you have printed the worksheet formulas

15. Press **Alt+F11** to open the Visual Basic Editor, and with the two functions displayed in the code window click **File,** click **Print,** click **OK,** and press **Alt+Q** to close the VB editor

16. Save your workbook and exit Excel

2. Creating a Macro to Trace Precedents of a Cell Range

Dr. Phil Hinman sometimes has difficulty tracking down errors in formulas he writes for various Excel workbooks he uses. For example, he believes there is a mistake in the formulas he has written for the grade book he maintains for his Philosophy 101 class, but he is having trouble locating it. He knows he can use the Formula Auditing command to locate cells that a formula references. He would like to generalize formula auditing so that he can select several cells and locate their precedent cells in one operation—something that Excel's Formula Auditing command cannot do. He has asked you to help him create a macro instruction he can call from any Excel workbook to audit one or more cell formulas. You will create a macro instruction and store it in your Personal Macro Workbook.

1. Open **ex12GradeBook.xls** and briefly review the Documentation page, and then click the **Phil 101** worksheet tab to move to that worksheet. Save the workbook as **GradeBook2.xls**

2. Click cell **B16,** which contains a formula computing the lowest score for Exam 1

3. Click **Tools** on the menu bar, point to **Macro,** and then click **Record New Macro**

4. Type **PointOutPrecedents** in the *Macro name* text box, press **Tab,** hold down the **Shift** key and type **P** in the Shortcut key text box, and release the **Shift** key

5. Click the **Store macro in** text box, select **Personal Macro Workbook,** press **Tab,**

type **Trace precedents of a selection of cells** in the Description text box, and click **OK**

6. Click **Tools** on the menu bar, point to **Formula Auditing,** click **Trace Precedents,** and click the **Stop Recording** button on the Stop Recording toolbar.

7. Click **Tools,** point to **Formula Auditing,** and click **Remove All Arrows**

8. Press **Alt+F11,** click the Microsoft Visual Basic window **Maximize** button, drag down the **Project—VBAProject** scroll box in the Project Explorer window until you see the VBAProject (PERSONAL.XLS) object

9. Click the + symbol to the left of VBAProject (PERSONAL.XLS) to reveal Modules, click the + symbol to the left of Modules (if necessary) to reveal its modules, and double-click the **Module1** object under Modules in the Project Explorer window to display the macro code in the Code window. (If you do not see the PointOutPrecedents macro, then double-click the next module in the list, Module2. Repeat step 9 as needed until you see PointOutPrecedents in the Code window)

10. Replace the Selection.ShowPrecedents code statement with the following code, and type your own name in place of <your name here> in the comment (match the indenting, too):

  Modified by <your name here>
    For Each FormulaCell in Selection
      FormulaCell.ShowPrecedents
    Next

11. Click **File** on the menu bar, click **Print,** and click **OK** to print your code

12. Press **Alt+Q** to save the revised macro and close the VB editor

13. Select cell range **B16:D18** and then press **Ctrl+Shift+P** (hold down **Ctrl** and **Shift,** tap and release **P,** and release **Ctrl** and **Shift**). Excel shows the precedent cells

14. Add your name to the worksheet header and print the Phil 101 worksheet

15. Save the workbook, exit Excel, and click **Yes** when asked if you want to save changes to the Personal Macro Workbook

www.mhhe.com/i-series

challenge

1. Ticket Sale Proceeds at Latron Theater

Latron Theater is a local playhouse whose proceeds provide scholarships for performing arts students. In addition to raising money through ticket sales, the theater has a fundraising campaign in which donors become playhouse members based on their donation amount. The top three levels of membership are platinum, gold, and silver. As a token of appreciation for the support of members in these levels, the theater provides them with discounted tickets for each performance.

The newest production, *The Wrong Door,* is opening in two months and tickets will go on sale to the public this Saturday. Playhouse members have the ability to purchase tickets two weeks before the general public. Madison Lawson is the director of membership at the theater and responsible for member ticket sales. Madison uses a workbook, called Ticket Sales, to record information on member ticket purchases. It is organized by membership level and contains each member's last name, the evening for which they bought tickets, and the quantity of tickets purchased. Madison has asked you to insert macros and formulas into the workbook to help her record and monitor ticket sales.

Begin by opening **ex12TicketSales.xls,** unprotect the worksheet, and save the workbook as **TicketSales2.xls.** Madison has already created a documentation sheet and typed *Main Page* into its tab. In cell A9, she wants you to insert in bold type, **Modified By,** followed by your name, and in cell A11, **Modified On:,** followed by the current date. Create macros that will quickly take Madison from the main page to cell A1 of each of the membership level worksheets. Name the macros **View_Platinum, View_Gold,** and **View_Silver.** In the assigned buttons, type **Platinum, Gold,** and **Silver,** and make the text bold. Place the buttons side by side starting in A15. Test your macros to make sure they run as Madison requested. She is appreciative of how the macros will make the workbook more efficient and asks you to add an additional macro. She would like a button placed in cells F1:G1 of each membership level worksheet that will take her back to cell A1 of the Main Page. Name the macro **Return_Main** and type **Return to Main Page** in the buttons. Hide the gridlines in the Main Page.

Madison wants to additionally be able to determine total tickets sold and their proceeds by membership level and the total proceeds from the members. In row 33 of each membership level worksheet, enter **"Total <level> Tickets Sold:",** and type Platinum, Gold, and Silver where appropriate. In row 35 of these worksheets, enter **"Total <level> Ticket Proceeds:"** and enter **"Total Membership Ticket Proceeds:"** in row 37. In cell **E33,** enter a formula that will calculate the sum of the total number of tickets sold based per each membership level. In cell **E35,** create a formula that results in the total proceeds for that level, based on ticket price and number of tickets sold. Finally, in cell **E37,** enter a formula that will calculate the total sum of membership ticket proceeds. Save your work, and print both the Main Page and your code procedures in Visual Basic Editor.

2. Automating an Employee Information Form

Bass Pro Fishing Outfitters, a large sporting goods store in Columbia, Missouri, conducts an annual review of each employee's performance and updates employee data using an Excel workbook. Corky Westfield, the human resources department manager, has developed a simple Excel workbook that meets his needs, but he'd like to automate it with buttons to open each of the workbook's worksheets. Corky wants you to create buttons and any VBA code needed to automate the workbook. In particular, he wants a button on the Cover Sheet that prints all three worksheets and buttons (and associated VBA code) on each of the two employee data worksheets that make the Cover Sheet active. He also asks you to remove the row and column headers and worksheet tabs from all three worksheets after you have tested the new macro instructions to open the worksheets.

Open **ex12EmployeeForm.xls** and save it as **EmployeeForm2.xls.** Begin by recording a macro instruction named **PrintWorksheets** that prints all workbook worksheets. Create a button and attach the button to the PrintWorksheets macro. Label the button **Print Workbook** and place it over cell **C10.**

Record a macro to make the worksheet Employee Data 1 active and select the merged cells **C5:E5.** Name the macro **ED1Active.** Attach it to the Cover Sheet button labeled **Employee Data 1.** Record another macro (or copy and rename it in the VB editor) that makes the Employee Data 2 worksheet active and selects the merged cells **C5:E5** on that worksheet. Name the macro **ED2Active.** Attach it to the Cover Sheet button labeled **Employee Data 2.** Record a macro that makes the Cover Sheet worksheet active and selects cell **A1.** Name the macro **CoverActive.** Place

a button on the Employee Data 1 worksheet and another button on the Employee Data 2 worksheet. Attach the CoverActive macro to both buttons. Shift-click each worksheet tab to group the worksheets, then click **Tools,** click **Options,** and click the **View** tab. Clear the **Row & column headers** check box and clear the **Sheet tabs** check box. Close the Options dialog box. Click the appropriate buttons to move to the Employee Data 1 worksheet. Fill out the white worksheet cells with data, move to the Employee Data 2 worksheet (go to the Cover Sheet and then to the Employee Data 2 worksheet), fill out white worksheet cells with data, and return to the Cover Sheet. Place your name in the header of all three worksheets, and click the **Print Workbook** button to print the three worksheets. Press **Alt+F11** to display the Visual Basic Editor and then print the Visual Basic code. Save your workbook.

1. Following Stocks on the Internet

Brian Lucas has been handling his own investments for the past 12 years. After getting his graduate degree in finance, he started his career with an investment research firm. He has moved into another area of business since then, but still uses his investment skills learned years ago. Brian tends to be a conservative investor and mainly invests in value stocks. He carefully collects and analyzes data on companies' stock prices and fundamentals before determining if any are appropriate investments for him.

Brian hasn't had much time recently to research new investments. He has asked you to collect data from the Internet in order to help him. Open **ex12StockWatch.xls** and save as **StockWatch2.xls.** This is the workbook format Brian uses to record and update company information. Insert your name and today's date in the appropriate cells in the documentation worksheet. The other worksheets in the workbook are labeled Stock 1, 2, and 3. Brian wants you to pick three companies that you feel will be successful

for the long term. Go to a Web site such as www.msn.com to find the companies' ticker symbols and the information Brian has requested for each company. Enter the data you find into the corresponding cell in row D. The workbook already contains a macro that prompts Brian to enter which stock worksheet he would like to view. He wants you to add a message box that will tell him if he has entered an incorrect stock worksheet. Edit the Stock_Data macro to include the If-Then-Else control structure. Above the **Sheets(Sheetname).Select** line, enter **If Sheetname="Stock 1" or Sheetname="Stock 2" or Sheetname="Stock 3" Then.** Under the line that selects cell D1, enter **ElseIf Sheetname <>"" Then.** In the next line, enter the message box function to display **"Please Select Stock 1, Stock 2, or Stock 3"** and title the box **Incorrect Stock Worksheet.** Be sure to end the If function and test your macro. Save your work, and print both the workbook and the macro.

e-business

1. Viewing Audit Assignments at Dawson's Corporation

Dawson's Corporation is a specialty coffee company founded by Peter Dawson in 1974 in Oakland, California. Dawson's popularity grew quickly and Peter decided to both start a Web site and to begin franchising the company throughout the United States. Within 10 years, Dawson's had grown to 119 locations with two corporate offices. A unique aspect of the company's Web site guarantees delivery of all orders within 24 hours. This is possible because the Web site routes each online order to the closest franchise location. That location then packages and delivers orders to each customer daily. It was crucial to Peter that each franchise truly represented Dawson's quality, so he designed the Quality Assurance department to monitor each franchisee's location. Each of the corporate offices has such a department, with six analysts to supervise the quality and daily operations of the franchises.

The analysts are each assigned a new group of locations, called branches, each quarter to supervise. Peter requires that each branch be audited four times a year by a different analyst in order to give thorough audits. This requires the analysts to visit each of their assigned locations unannounced in order to see how the franchisees truly manage and run their locations and order fulfillment process. The new director of Quality Assurance, Julie Whitfield, feels that there needs to be stronger communication and support between the Oakland and Boston offices. Her first project was to prepare a new way to assign analysts their branches in an easy-to-understand accessible document. Since most of her communication with the analysts is through e-mail, she wants to make the audit assignments available on the company's network. Open **AuditAssignments.xls,** which is Julie's workbook of audit assignments for next quarter. The worksheets are sorted alphabetically by analyst and include the branch number, franchisee name, state of the branch, and the office in which the analyst works.

Julie has given you the project of creating a Documentation sheet and macro buttons to help the analysts find their audit assignments for the quarter. Start by saving the workbook as **AuditAssignments2.xls** and insert a Documentation sheet. In the Documentation sheet, enter the title **Dawson's Corporation,** and the sub-title **Audit Assignments for Third Quarter.** Beneath these, enter **Created for: Julie Whitfield, Created by:** followed with your name, and **Date:** followed with today's date. Next, you will create macros to take analysts to the audit assignments for their office.

Use the Macro Recorder to record the steps taken to move from the Documentation sheet to cell A1 of the Boston Assignments worksheet. Name the macro **Boston_Assignments,** and add the description **Displays the Boston office audit assignments worksheet.** Record the same steps for the Oakland Assignments, name the macro **Oakland_Assignments,** and add the description **Displays the Oakland office audit assignments.** Insert a button in cells D16:F17 for the Boston_Assignments macro. Type **View Boston Assignments** into the button. Insert another button into cells D20:F21 for Oakland_Assignments macro. Type the caption **View Oakland Assignments** for this button. Test your macros to ensure that they function correctly.

Julie wants to use this workbook as her master copy for creating new workbooks. She needs you to create another macro, titled **New_Audit_Workbook,** which will open a new workbook with the same documentation information as her master workbook. Create a macro that copies the documentation sheet titles, Created for:, Created by:, and Date:, then opens a new workbook, pastes the Documentation sheet information into the first worksheet, and types Documentation in the worksheet tab. Save your work and print both the master Documentation sheet and the New_Audit_Workbook sub procedure in Visual Basic Editor.

around the world

1. Bottling Options at Serechini Vineyards

Serechini Vineyards has been producing and selling red wine from southern Italy for six generations. Serechini's bottle supplier is closing its business and the owner has offered to sell the manufacturing plant to the vineyard. The plant will close in four months, and the owner needs an answer from Serechini by the end of the month. Pietro Serechini, the vineyard owner, has asked his accountant to determine whether this is a good investment for the vineyard. Pietro's main concern isn't the capital needed to buy or run the plant, but rather the cost profit per bottle.

Pietro's accountant prepared a spreadsheet including the revenues and costs per bottle of wine. While buying the plant and making its own bottles would increase the company's profit per bottle, Pietro wants to look at other options. He asked his accountant to research the three largest bottle manufacturers in the world and determine how much it would cost to outsource bottles from them. Pietro is concerned that performing his own maintenance and repairs at the plant will cause a greater increase in overhead costs than what he will save in materials and shipping costs. The sale price and selling and administrative costs are to be the same for each plant since the selling price is constant and all sales and administrative duties are performed at Serechini's headquarters.

Open **ex12SerechiniVineyards.xls,** which is the workbook Pietro's accountant has prepared detailing the revenue, costs, and profit per bottle for either producing its own bottles or outsourcing its manufacturing. The workbook compares the figures for self-production in Italy or using manufacturers in Korea, Mexico, and Germany. Several of Serechini's managers want to buy the manufacturing plant because they are convinced that the savings from producing the bottles near the vineyard will outweigh any lower labor costs abroad. Pietro wants to use the workbook to clearly show them that the best alternative for the vineyard is to outsource from another bottle.

Insert your name and today's date in the Documentation sheet and save the workbook as **SerechiniVineyards2.xls.** Since Pietro and other managers will use the workbook, he wants you to place macros in the Documentation sheet that will open any of the worksheets. He wants the macro to display an input box that prompts users for the name of the worksheet they want to view. It needs to ensure that one of the four worksheets in the workbook is correctly chosen. Record a macro named **View_Macro** that takes you from the Documentation sheet to the Italy sheet tab and selects cell A1. For the description, type **Displays chosen bottling alternative.** Through the Visual Basic Editor, edit the View_Macro procedure so that the macro contains an input box that prompts the user to **"Type Italy, Korea, Mexico, or Germany."** Title the input box **"Country of Alternative"** and use the variable **"Sheetname."** Place a button in cells D16:F18 of the Documentation sheet to run this macro and type **"View Bottling Alternative"** into the button.

Pietro also wants you to add a macro that will return users to the Documentation sheet from any of the alternative worksheets. In the Italy worksheet, create a macro that will return the user to cell A1 of the Documentation sheet. Name the macro **Return_Documentation** and for the description, type **"Returns user to Documentation Sheet."** Insert a button in cells E20:F22 for this macro and type **"Return to Documentation Sheet"** in the button. Copy and paste this button into each of the other alternative worksheets.

After reviewing the workbook, Pietro feels that to be effective, the percentage of profit per bottle should be added. In each of the alternatives worksheets, type **Profit per Bottle (%)** in cell A15. Through Visual Basic editor, use the Insert Module command and the Insert Procedure command to create a function to determine this figure. Name the function **Profit** and use the parameters **Bottle_Price** and **Bottle_Cost.** (Hint: Profit = (Bottle Price-Bottle Cost)/Bottle Price). The syntax for the function should be as follows:

```
Function Function_Name (Parameters As Single) As Single
    Function_Name=Expression
End Function
```

If you are having trouble, make sure that each argument and the entire function is declared **As Single.** Place this function in cell **H15** of each alternative worksheet and format the cell to display a percentage with two decimal points.

Remove all gridlines and column and row headers, save your work, and print the workbook and the Procedure code in Visual Basic Editor.

running project

Pampered Paws

Grace Jackson, Pampered Paws' owner, keeps a worksheet containing information about unpaid (outstanding) invoices. Located on the second worksheet, called Unpaid Invoices, a list contains the customer name, address, date the invoice was mailed, and the invoice amount. Grace wants you to write a custom function called PastDue that will return one of three values, depending on how long ago the invoice was mailed. If the invoice date, in column G, is less than 30 days ago, the PastDue function returns 0 (zero) to the worksheet. If the invoice date is between 30 and 59 days ago, the function returns 30. If the invoice date is more than 59 days ago, then the PastDue function returns 60. PastDue has the form =PastDue(invoice date, today's date). (Remember to type both arguments in the custom function prototype with "As Date" to properly identify the incoming argument data types. The entire function returns an integer, so type "As Integer" following the argument list in the prototype.)

After you define the PastDue custom function, type today's date in cell G1. Then write the PastDue expression in the cell range I3:I53. The first argu-ment references the invoice date for the current customer, whereas the second argument refer-ences cell G1 containing today's date. Copy the ex-pression from cell I3 to the remaining cells (I4:I53).

Record a macro to switch from the Unpaid Invoices worksheet to the Documentation work-sheet, create a command button and place it on the Unpaid Invoices worksheet, and assign the Documentation worksheet activation macro to it. Similarly, create a macro to make the Unpaid Invoices worksheet active, place a command but-ton on the Documentation worksheet, and assign the macro you recorded to the button. (Unprotect the worksheet, place the button on it, and then pro-tect the worksheet.) Set the properties of the two command buttons so that they will print along with the worksheet. Fill out the empty lines on the Documentation worksheet, print the two com-pleted worksheets, and print the PastDue custom function code.

Excel file finder

Location in Chapter	Data File to Use	Student Saves Data File as . . .
CHAPTER 1		
Opening a workbook	ex01Scrip.xls	
Saving a workbook	ex01Scrip.xls	ex01Scrip.xls
Saving a workbook/new name	ex01Scrip.xls	Scrip2.xls
Clearing several cells' contents	Scrip2.xls	Scrip3.xls
Closing a workbook	Scrip3.xls	Scrip3.xls
Formulas	ex01Income.xls	Income2.xls
Protected cells	ex01Timecard.xls	
Label	ex01Johnsons.xls	
Entering values	ex01Computer.xls	Computer2.xls
Cell references	ex01GNP.xls	GNP2.xls
CHAPTER 2		
Saving a worksheet		Recycle.xls
Saving modified workbook	Recycle.xls	Recycle.xls
Setting print margins	Recycle.xls	Recycle.xls
Insert comments in cell	Recycle.xls	Recycle.xls
Autoformat	Recycle.xls	Recycle2.xls
Insert	ex02Wages.xls	Wages2.xls
Creating an invoice	ex02Randys.xls	Randys2.xls
Comment indicator	ex02Payroll.xls	Payroll2.xls
Sorting		Brokerage2.xls
Comparing records	ex02E-Merchant.xls	E-Merchant2.xls
CHAPTER 3		
Start Excel	ex03Fruit.xls	ExoticFruit.xls
Indenting text	ExoticFruit.xls	ExoticFruit.xls
Save workbook/new name	ExoticFruit.xls	ExoticFruit2.xls
Formatting	ExoticFruit2.xls	ExoticFruitModified.xls
Increasing row height	ExoticFruit2.xls	

Location in Chapter	Data File to Use	Student Saves Data File as . . .
Remove drawing toolbar	ExoticFruit2.xls	ExoticFruit2.xls
Save workbook	ExoticFruit2.xls	ExoticFruit2.xls
Header	ExoticFruit2.xls	ExoticFruit3.xls
Cell formatting	ex03Bookstore.xls	Bookstore2.xls
Create business card		BusinessCard.xls
Formatting	ex03Schedule.xls	
Formatting	ex03Payment.xls	
Comparing data	ex03Headphones.xls	headphones2.xls
Formatting Borders	ex03Rowing.xls ex03Paws.xls	Paws33.xls
CHAPTER 4		
Opening a worksheet	ex04BigWave.xls	BigWave2.xls
Saving, previewing, and printing	BigWave2.xls	BigWave2.xls
Modifying a chart	BigWave2.xls	BigWaveModified.xls
Selecting nonadjacent data ranges	BigWave2.xls	BigWave3.xls
Saving and printing	BigWave3.xls	BigWave3.xls
Creating Web pages	BigWave3.xls	[web page name]
Saving workbook	BigWave3.xls	BigWave4.xls
Stacked bar chart	ex04BigWave.xls	BigWave5.xls
3-D chart	ex04Olympics.xls	Olympics2.xls
Selection handle	ex04Rainfall.xls	Rainfall2.xls
Headers	ex04California.xls	California2.xls
Pie chart	ex04RentalCar.xls	RentalCar2.xls
Column graph	ex04Crop.xls	
Pie chart	ex04ExportCoffee.xls	ExportCoffee2.xls
Formatting	ex04HourlyLabor.xls	
Labeling	ex04Unemployment.xls	Unemployment2.xls
Chart comparison	ex04Paws.xls	
CHAPTER 5		
Opening a worksheet	Ex05Employee.xls	Employee1.xls
Freezing label rows/columns	Employee1.xls	
Adding a new record—data form	Employee1.xls	
Making the grade	Employee1.xls	EmployeeS3.xls

Location in Chapter	Data File to Use	Student Saves Data File as . . .
Filtering a list	EmployeeS3.xls	Employee2.xls
Making the grade	Employee2.xls	Employee52.xls
Selecting another pivot table data summary function	Employee52.xls	Employee3.xls
Printing/saving	Employee3.xls	Employee3.xls
Making the grade	Employee3.xls	Employee3Modified.xls
Filtering	Ex05Fairmont.xls	Fairmont2.xls
Sorting/filtering	Ex05Grades.xls	Grades2.xls
Subtotals/pivot tables	Ex05Doctors.xls	Doctors2.xls
Analyzing differences in salaries	Ex05Salaries.xls	Salaries2.xls
E-Business	Ex05Service.xls	Service2.xls
Analyzing global marketing opportunities	Ex05Tennis.xls	Tennis2.xls
CHAPTER 6		
Opening/saving	Ex06Loan.xls	Loan1.xls
Saving	Loan1.xls	Loan1.xls
Making the grade	Loan1.xls	Loan11.xls
Opening	Loan1.xls	Loan2.xls
Autofill	Loan2.xls	Loan2.xls
Making the grade	Loan2.xls	Loan22.xls
Saving	Loan2.xls	Loan3.xls
Making the grade	Loan3.xls	Loan33.xls
Data validation	Ex06Savings.xls	Savings2.xls
Total payment	Ex06CarLoan.xls	CarLoan2.xls
Amortization schedules	Ex06Desserts.xls	Desserts2.xls
Future values	Ex06Conservative.xls	Conservative2.xls
Lookup tables	Ex06Stocks.xls	Stocks2.xls
Amortization schedule	Ex06Paws.xls	(unspecified different name)
CHAPTER 7		
Opening/saving	Ex07Avicon.xls	Avicon2.xls
Inserting a graphic	Avicon2.xl (Ex07Bevel.jpg)	Avicon2.xls
Mailing a workbook as an e-mail attachment	Avicon2.xls	
Pasting a graphic	Ex07Letter.doc (Ex07Bevel.jpg)	Letter2.doc

Location in Chapter	Data File to Use	Student Saves Data File as . . .
Embedding an object	Letter2.eod (Avicon2.xls)	
Altering a bar chart	Letter2.doc	
Linking worksheet cells to a Word document	Avicon2.xls (Letter2.doc)	Avicon2.xls
Altering data	Avicon2.xls	
Altering data	Avicon2.xls	Letter2Link.doc
Making the grade	Letter2Link.doc	Letter22Link.doc
Creating a new document	Letter2Link.doc	Letter3Merge.doc
Container document	Letter3Merge.doc	
Source file/merge fields	Letter3Merge.doc (Ex07Customers.xls)	
Creating/printing merged documents	Ex07Customers.xls	Ex07Customers.xls
Saving/deleting	Letter3Merge.doc	Letter3Merge.doc
Making the grade	Letter3Merge.doc	Letter33Merge.doc
Data/merge fields	Ex07SatLetter.doc (Ex07SatScores.xls) (Ex07SatAddresses.xls)	SatLetter2.doc
Creating a fax	Ex07Amalgamated.xls	Amalgamated2.doc
Fax—multiple recipients	Ex07CattleNews.doc (Ex07CattleClients.xls)	
Mailer	Ex07Realtor.doc Ex07Realtor.xls	
Brochure	Ex07CoffeeBrochure.doc (Ex07CoffeeLogo.jpg)	
Managing a firm's clients	Ex07Tax.doc (Ex07TaxList.xls) (ex07TaxClients.xls)	Tax2.doc
Billing clients	Ex07FloraInvoice.xls (exFloraPrices.xls)	Invoice2.xls
Reporting new accounts	Ex07NewAccounts.xls (Ex07NewAccountsMemo.doc)	NewAccounts2.xls NewAccountsMemo2.doc
Running project	Ex07PawsCustomers.xls (Ex07PawsLetters.doc) (Ex07PawsItems.xls)	Ex07PawsLetters.doc
CHAPTER 8		
Copying worksheets	Ex08Beco.xls (ex08VanBuren.xls)	Beco2.xls

Location in Chapter	Data File to Use	Student Saves Data File as . . .
Copying a worksheet into the master worksheet	Ex08WestLafayette.xls (Beco2.xls)	Ex08WestLafayette.xls
Adding a new worksheet	Beco2.xls	
Making the grade	Beco2.xls	Beco21.xls
Opening a workbook	Ex08Danielli.xls	Danielli3.xls
Opening a workbook and entering a link formula	Beco3.xls (Danielli3.xls)	
Modifying values	Danielli3.xls	Danielli3.xls
Redirecting link references to a renamed supporting workbook	Beco3.xls (Danielli3.xls)	Beco3.xls Acquisition2002.xls
Saving/exiting	Beco3.xls	Beco3.xls
Making the grade	Beco3.xls (Acquisition2002.xls)	Beco4.xls Danielli4.xls
Summarizing sales data	Ex08ReedReps.xls	ReedReps2.xls
Consolidated income statement	Ex08DelzuraHawthorne.xls (Ex08DelzuraPortland.xls) (Ex08DelzuraMain.xls)	DelzuraMain2.xls
Summarizing billing/bonuses	Ex08Kelleher.xls	Kelleher2.xls
Consolidating information	Ex08Robot.xls (Ex08RobotPets.xls)	Robot2.xls
Analyzing law schools	Ex08LawSchools.xls	LawSchools2.xls
Summarizing multiple worksheets	Ex08AIFlorida.xls (Ex08AiGeorgia.xls) (Ex08AILouisiana.xls)	AIFlorida2.xls (AIGeorgia2.xls) (AILouisiana2.xls)
Sales consolidation	Ex08Wilton.xls	Wilton2.xls
Running project	Ex08Paws.xls	Paws8.xls
CHAPTER 9		
Entering revenue values and formulas, and applying a default numeric format	ex09Artistic.xls	Artistic1.xls
Opening the scenario workbook	ex09Artistic Scenarios.xls	Artistic3.xls
Making the grade	Artistic3.xls	Artistic38.xls
Practice Project #1	ex09Outdoor.xls	OutdoorAdventures.xls
Practice Project #2	ex09PCCRC.xls	PCCRC2.xls
Challenge Project #1	ex09AbelMassey.xls	AbelMassey.xls
Challenge Project #2	ex09Loan.xls	Loan2.xls
On the Web Project #1	ex09TravisStock.xls	TravisStock2.xls

Location in Chapter	Data File to Use	Student Saves Data File as . . .
On the Web Project #1	ex09TravisScenarios.xls	
On the Web Project #2	ex09UCExpenses.xls	UCexpenses.xls
E-Business Project #1	ex09GMercer.xls	GMercer2.xls
E-Business Project #2	ex09WebVideo.xls	WebVideo2.xls
Around the World Project #1	ex09Teak.xls	Teak2.xls
Running project	ex09Paws.xls	Paws92.xls
CHAPTER 10		
Renaming and coloring a worksheet tab	ex10ExerCycle.xls	ExerCycle2.xls
Making the grade	ExerCycle2.xls	ExerCycle210.xls
Formulating the problem concisely	ex10ExerCycleMix.xls	ExerCycleMix2.xls
Making the grade	ExerCycleMix2.xls	ExerCycleMix3.xls
Practice Project #1	ex10OceanSpas.xls	OceanSpas2.xls
Practice Project #2	ex10LoanGoal.xls	LoanGoal2.xls
Challenge Project #1	ex10CreditUnion.xls	CreditUnion2.xls
Challenge Project #2	ex10GreenCreek.xls	GreenCreek2.xls
On the Web Project #1	ex10DVD.xls	
E-Business Project #1	ex10WebHosting.xls	WebHosting2.xls
Around the World Project #1	ex10Shipping.xls	
Running project	ex10Paws.xls	
CHAPTER 11		
Understanding text files and data separation choices	ex11SalesRep111.txt	
Understanding text files and data separation choices	ex11SalesRep113.csv	
Setting the data format for selected columns	ex11SalesRep111.txt	ex11SalesRep111.txt
Working with a comma-separated values text file	ex11SalesRep113.csv	ex11MBBW.xls
Moving, copying, and pasting data between workbooks	ex11MBBW.xls and SalesReps2.xls	
Opening two other workbooks	ex11SalesREp113.csv, SalesReps2.xls, and ex11MBBW.xls	MissionBoats2.xls
Opening a Web page	MissionBoats2.xls and ex11BoatAccessories.html	
Creating a new worksheet to hold the Web page data	MissionBoats2.xls	

Location in Chapter	Data File to Use	Student Saves Data File as . . .
Making the grade	MissionBoats2.xls and ex11Vespoli.txt	MissionBoats111.xls
Creating a data source definition	MissionBoats2.xls	MissionBoats3.xls
Creating a connection to a data source	ex11MBBW.mdb	
Making the grade	MissionBoats3.xls	MissionBoats112.xls
Practice Project #1	ex11LincolnCollege.xls	LincolnCollege2.xls
Practice Project #1	ex11LincolnCollege.mdb	
Practice Project #2	ex11State Population.txt	
Challenge Project #1	ex11OTWSales.xls and ex11Maripaorders.txt	JuneMaripaSales.xls
On the Web Project #1	Presidents.xls and ex11Presidents.mdb	
On the Web Project #2	ex11Racers.txt	Racers2.xls
E-Business Project #1	ex11KWeb.xls	KWeb2.xls
E-Business Project #1	ex11KwebMail.txt and ex11Kellson.mdb	
Around the World Project #1	ex11EuropeanSales.txt	ModelWareSales.xls
Running project	ex11Paws.mdb and ex11Paws.xls	Paws112.xls
CHAPTER 12		
Creating macros	ex12ArtGlass.xls	Catalog2.xls
Making the grade	Catalog2.xls	Catalog22.xls
Opening the invoice workbook	Ex12ArtGlassInvoice.xls	Invoice2.xls
Making the grade	Invoice2.xls	Invoice3.xls
Practice Project #1	ex12SalesQuota.xls	SalesQuota2.xls
Practice Project #2	ex12GradeBook.xls	GradeBook2.xls
Challenge Project #1	ex12TicketSales.xls	TicketSales2.xls
Challenge Project #2	ex12EmployeeForm.xls	EmployeeForm2.xls
On the Web Project #1	ex12StockWatch.xls	StockWatch2.xls
E-Business Project #1	ex12AuditAssignments.xls	AuditAssignments2.xls
Around the World Project #1	ex12SerenchiniVineyards.xls	SerenchiniVineyards2.xls
Running project	ex12Paws.xls	

REFERENCE

MOUS Certification Guide

MOUS Objective	Task	Session Location	End-of-Chapter Location
Note: MOUS objectives do not apply to Chapter 1.			
CHAPTER 2 EX2002-1-1	**Planning and Creating a Worksheet** Move text, values, and formulas	2.1	EX 2.48
EX2002-3-1	Format cells	2.2	EX 2.48
EX2002-3-2	Insert and delete rows and columns, adjust column width	2.2	EX 2.48
EX2002-3-7	Set a print area	2.2	EX 2.48
EX2002-5-1	Create formulas containing cell references and mathematical operators	2.1	EX 2.48
EX2002-5-1	Differentiate between absolute, mixed and relative cell reference	2.1	EX 2.48
EX2002-7-3	Create cell comments	2.2	EX 2.48
CHAPTER 3 EX2002-1-2	**Formatting a Worksheet** Clear all formatting from selected cells	3.1	EX 3.48
EX2002-3-1	Applying currency and accounting formats to numbers	3.1	EX 3.48
EX2002-3-1	Modify the typeface and point size of text and numbers	3.1	EX 3.48
EX2002-3-1	Apply boldface, italics, and underlines to cells	3.1	EX 3.48
EX2002-3-1	Left-, center-, and right align text	3.1	EX 3.48
EX2002-3-1	Clear all formatting from selected cells	3.2	EX 3.48
EX2002-3-2	Hide and reveal rows and columns	3.2	EX 3.48
EX2002-3-7	Modify the worksheet's print characteristics	3.2	EX 3.48
CHAPTER 4 EX2002-4-1	**Creating Charts** Delete embedded charts and chart sheets	4.2	EX 4.48
EX2002-6-1	Create an embedded chart and chart sheet	4.1	EX 4.48
EX2002-6-1	Modify an existing chart by revising date, altering chart text and labeling data	4.1	EX 4.48
EX2002-6-1	Use color and patterns to embellish a chart	4.2	EX 4.48
EX2002-6-1	Alter a chart type and create a three-dimensional chart	4.2	EX 4.48
EX2002-6-1	Create a pie chart with a title, exploding slice, labels and floating text	4.2	EX 4.48
EX2002-6-1	Add texture to chart	4.2	EX 4.48
EX2002-6-2	Add a new data series to a chart	4.1	EX 4.48

MOUS Objective	Task	Session Location	End-of-Chapter Location
CHAPTER 5 EX2002-3-2	**Exploring Excel's List Features** Freeze rows and columns	5.1	EX 5.61
EX2002-3-2	Create and apply conditional formatting	5.2	EX 5.62
EX2002-4-1	Use worksheet labels and names in formulas	5.1	EX 5.62
EX2002-7-1	Create subtotals	5.2	EX 5.61
EX2002-7-2	Create filters with AutoFilter	5.2	EX 5.62
EX2002-7-3	Group and outline structured data	5.1	EX 5.61
EX2002-8-1	Create a pivot table and pivot chart	5.3	EX 5.62
CHAPTER 6 EX2002-4-1	**Common Functions** Define and use names in functions in place of cell reference	6.1	EX 6.53
EX2002-4-1	Add, delete, move, and rename worksheets	6.3	EX 6.53
EX2002-4-2	Learn about index functions and write the index function VLOOKUP	6.1	EX 6.53
EX2002-4-2	Add, delete, move, and rename worksheets	6.3	EX 6.53
EX2002-5-2	Write financial functions including PV, PMT, PPMT, and IPMT	6.2	EX 6.53
EX2002-5-2	Write and apply the NOW date function	6.3	EX 6.53
EX2002-7-4	Provide data validation for selected worksheet cells	6.1	EX 6.53
EX2002-9-1	Apply worksheet protection	6.3	EX 6.53
CHAPTER 7 EX2002-1-2	**Integrating Excel and Office Objects** Embed an Excel object within a Word document	7.2	EX 7.43
CHAPTER 8 EX2002-4-3	**Developing Multiple Worksheet and Workbook** Consolidate and summarize data using three-dimensional formulas	8.1	EX 8.43
CHAPTER 9 EX2002e-8-3	**Using Data Tables and Scenarios** Create Excel Scenarios	9.	EX 9.50
EX2002e-8-3	Manage Excel scenarios with the Scenario Manager	9.	EX 9.50
EX2002e-8-3	View, add, edit, and delete scenarios	9.	EX 9.50
EX2002e-8-3	Create a scenario report	9.	EX 9.50
CHAPTER 11 EX2002e-1-1	**Importing Data** Import text files into Excel with the Text Import Wizard	11.	EX 11.48
EX2002e-1-1	Copy data from a Web page and paste it into an Excel worksheet	11.	EX 11.48
CHAPTER 12 EX2002e-5-2	**Automating Applications with Visual Basic** Record a macro instruction	12.	EX 12.51
EX2002e-5-2	Run macro instructions using a dialog box and a command button	12.	EX 12.51
EX2002e-5-2	Create and modify Visual Basic code in the Visual Basic Editor	12.	EX 12.51
EX2002e-5-2	Use Visual Basic objects, methods, properties, and variables	12.	EX 12.51
EX2002e-5-2	Create a macro that automatically executes when you open a workbook	12.	EX 12.51
EX2002e-9-1	Protect a worksheet to preserve its integrity	12.	EX 12.51

reference roundup

Task	Page #	Preferred Method
Worrkbook, open	EX 1.11	• Click **File**, click **Open,** click workbook's name, click the **Open** 🖝 button
Formula, entering	EX 1.17	• Select cell, type =, type formula, press **Enter**
Sum function, entering	EX 1.20	• Select cell, type =**SUM(**, type cell range, type), and press **Enter**
Editing cell	EX 1.22	• Select cell, click formula bar, make changes, press **Enter**
Workbook, saving	EX 1.24	• Click **File,** click **Save As,** type file name, click **Save** 💾 button
Help, obtaining	EX 1.25	• Click the **Microsoft Excel Help** command from the **Help** menu (or click the Microsoft Excel **Help** 🔲 button on the Standard toolbar)
		• Click the **Answer Wizard** tab
		• In the *What would you like to do* text box, type an English-language question (replacing the words displayed and highlighted in blue) on the topic with which you need help and click the **Search** button
Contents, clearing	EX 1.27	• Click cell, press **Delete** keyboard key
Header/Footer, creating	EX 1.31	• Click **View,** click **Header and Footer,** click **Custom Header** or **Custom Footer,** select section, type header/footer text, click the **OK** button, and click the **OK** button
Printing worksheet	EX 1.33	• Click **File,** click **Print,** click the **OK** button
Worksheet formulas, printing	EX 1.36	• Click **Tools,** click **Options,** Click the **View** tab, click **Formulas** check box, click **OK,** click **File,** click **Print,** click the **OK** button
Workbook, closing	EX 1.37	• Click **File,** click **Close,** click **Yes** to save (if necessary)
Writing formulas	EX 2.9	• Select a cell, type **5,** type the formula, press **Enter**
Modifying an AutoSum cell range by pointing	EX 2.11	• Press an arrow key repeatedly to select leftmost or topmost cell in range, press and hold **Shift,** select cell range with arrow keys, release **Shift,** press **Enter**
Writing a function using the Paste Function button	EX 2.17	• Select a cell, click **Paste Function**, click a function category, click a function name, click **OK,** complete the formula palette dialog box, click **OK**
Copying and pasting a cell or range of cells	EX 2.21	• Select source cell(s), click **Edit,** click **Copy,** select target cell(s), click **Edit,** click **Paste**
Copying cell contents using a cell's fill handle	EX 2.23	• Select source cell(s), drag the fill handle to the source cell(s) range, release the mouse button
Changing relative references to absolute or mixed references	EX 2.27	• Double-click the cell, move insertion point to the cell reference, press **F4** repeatedly as needed, press **Enter**
Moving cells' contents	EX 2.29	• Select the cell(s), move the mouse pointer to an edge of the selected range, click the edge of the selected cell or cell range, drag the outline to the destination location, release the mouse

task reference roundup

Task	Page #	Preferred Method
Spell-checking a worksheet	EX 2.31	• Click cell **A1**, click the **Spelling** [✓] button, correct any mistakes, click **OK**
Inserting rows	EX 2.34	• Click a cell, click **Insert**, click **Rows**
Inserting columns	EX 2.34	• Click a cell, click **Insert**, click **Columns**
Applying AutoFormat to cells	EX 2.36	• Select a cell range, click **Format**, click **AutoFormat**, select a format style, click **OK**
Modifying a column's width	EX 2.39	• Select the column heading(s), click **Format**, point to **Column**, click **Width**, type column width, and click **OK**
Inserting a comment	EX 2.45	• Click a cell, click **Insert**, click **Comment**, type a comment, and click another cell
Formatting numbers	EX 3.7	• Select cell(s)
		• Click **Format**, click **Cells**, click **Number**
		• Click format category and select options
		• Click **OK**
Copying a cell format to a cell or cell range	EX 3.10	• Select the cell whose format you want to copy
		• Click the **Format Painter** [✓] button
		• Click (click/drag) the target cell(s)
Wrapping long text within a cell	EX 3.17	• Select the cell or cell range to which you will apply a format
		• Click **Format**, click **Cells**, and click the **Alignment** tab
		• Click the **Wrap text** check box
		• Click **OK**
Applying fonts and font characteristics	EX 3.18	• Select the cell or cell range that you want to format
		• Click **Format**, click **Cells**, and click the **Font** tab
		• Select a typeface from the Font list box
		• Select a font style and a font size
		• Click **OK**
Clearing formats from a cell, cell selection, rows, or columns	EX 3.21	• Select the cell, cell range, rows, or columns
		• Click **Edit**, point to **Clear**, and click **Formats**
Modifying a row's height	EX 3.23	• Click the row heading
		• Click **Format**, point to **Row**, and click **Height**
		• Type the row height in the Row height text box
		• Click **OK**

task reference roundup

Task	Page #	Preferred Method
		• Click the **Selection: Chart** option
		• Optionally type a page title and click **OK**
		• Click **Save**
Freezing rows and columns	EX 5.6	• Select cell at upper-left corner
		• Click **Window;** click **Freeze Panes**
Adding a record to a list using a data form	EX 5.8	• Click list cell, click **Data,** click **Form**
		• Click **New,** type values in fields, press **Enter,** and click **Close**
Deleting a record from a list with a data form	EX 5.12	• Click list cell, click **Data,** click **Form**
		• Click **Criteria** button, Click **Find Next** as needed, click **Delete,** and click **OK**
Sorting a list on one column	EX 5.15	• Click cell in list
		• Click the **Sort Ascending** or **Sort Descending** button
Sorting a list on more than one field	EX 5.17	• Click list cell, click **Data,** click **Sort**
		• Specify Sort by and Ascending/Descending options
		• Repeat for up to two Then by fields
		• Click **OK**
Creating a custom sort order	EX 5.19	• Click **Tools,** click **Options,** click **Custom Lists** tab
		• Click **NEW LIST,** type each new member of the list in order
		• Click the **Add** button and click **OK**
Filtering a list with AutoFilter	EX 5.24	• Click list cell, click **Data**
		• Click **list arrow** on filtering column, click filter value from list
Clearing All AutoFilter filtering criteria	EX 5.26	• Click **Data,** point to **Filter**
		• Click **Show All** to remove all existing filters
Subtotaling a list's entries	EX 5.29	• Sort list by grouping column
		• Click a cell inside the list
		• Click **Data,** click **Subtotals**
		• Choose group column, choose aggregate function
		• Click **OK**

task reference roundup

Task	Page #	Preferred Method
Displaying row or column headings on each page	EX 5.34	• Click **File**, click **Page Setup**, click the **Sheet** tab
		• Click **Collapse** dialog button on the **Specify Rows to repeat at top** or the **Specify Columns to repeat at left**
		• Specify row(s) or column(s)
		• Click **OK**
Applying a conditional format to cells	EX 5.37	• Click cell range to conditionally format
		• Click **Format**, Click **Conditional Formatting**, specify criteria
		• Click **Format** button on the Conditional Formatting dialog box and specify formatting options
		• Click **OK**
		• Click **OK**
Creating a pivot table with the PivotTable Wizard	EX 5.43	• Click **Data**, click the **PivotTable and PivotChart Report**
		• Specify the data's location (worksheet, external list, etc)
		• Select the **PivotTable** option and click the **Layout** button
		• Design pivot table layout by selecting row, column, data, and page fields
		• Designate location for pivot table as separate page or object on worksheet
		• Click the **Finish** button
Selecting pivot table fields	EX 5.46	• Click and drag selected field(s) to summarize to Data Items area
		• Click and drag field buttons to Column, Row, and Page fields
Formatting pivot table fields	EX 5.48	• Select any cell in the pivot table data item area
		• Open the PivotTable toolbar, click **Field Settings,** and click the **Number** button
		• Select a format from the Category list and make associated format choices
		• Click **OK** to close the Format Cells dialog box and then click **OK** to close the Pivot Table Field dialog box
Naming a cell or cell range	EX 6.14	• Select the cell or cell range you want to name
		• Click the **Name box** in the formula bar
		• Type the name and press **Enter**
Deleting a name	EX 6.17	• Click **Insert**, point to **Name**, and then click the **Define** button

task reference roundup

Task	Page #	Preferred Method
		• Click the name in the *Names in workbook* list that you want to delete
		• Click the **Delete** button and then click the **OK** button
Using the VLOOKUP function	EX 6.22	• Create a lookup table and sort the table in ascending order by the leftmost column
		• Place in columns to the right of the search columns values you want to return as answers
		• Write a VLOOKUP function referencing a cell containing the lookup value, the lookup table, and the column containing the answer
Deleting a worksheet from a workbook	EX 6.39	• Right-click the worksheet tab of the worksheet you want to delete
		• Click **Delete** on the shortcut menu
Adding a worksheet to a workbook	EX 6.40	• Click the worksheet tab before which you want to add a worksheet
		• Click **Insert** on the menu bar and then click **Worksheet**
Moving a worksheet to a new position within a workbook	EX 6.41	• Click the worksheet tab of the worksheet you want to move
		• Drag the worksheet to its new position indicated by the down-pointing arrow and release the mouse
Renaming a worksheet	EX 6.42	• Double-click the worksheet tab of the worksheet you want to rename
		• Type the new worksheet name and press **Enter**
Locking cells	EX 6.46	• Select the cells you want to be unprotected (unlocked)
		• Click **Format,** click **Cells,** and then click the **Protection** tab
		• Click **Locked** check box to clear its checkmark and click **OK**
Enabling worksheet protection	EX 6.48	• Click **Tools,** point to **Protection,** and click **Protect Sheet**
		• Optionally enter (and remember) a password twice and click **OK**
Mailing a workbook as an e-mail attachment	EX 7.11	• Open the Excel workbook you want to send as an e-mail attachment
		• Click **File** on the menu bar, point to **Send To,** and then click **Mail Recipient (as Attachment)**
		• Enter the recipient's e-mail address in the To text box
		• Click the **Send** button
Embedding an object	EX 7.14	• Start the source program, open the source document, select the object you want to copy, and click the **Copy** button on the Standard toolbar
		• Start the container (destination) program, open the container document that will contain the embedded object, and place the insertion point at the destination point in the container document

task reference roundup

Task	Page #	Preferred Method
		• Click **Edit**, click **Paste Special**, click the **Paste** option button, click an option in the As list box, and click **OK**
Linking an object	EX 7.19	• Start the source program, open the source document, select the object you want to link, and click the **Copy** button on the Standard toolbar
		• Start the container (destination) program, open the container document that will contain the linked object, and place the insertion point at the destination point in the container document
		• Click **Edit**, click **Paste Special**, click the **Paste link** option button, click an option in the As list box, and click **OK**
Deleting a mail merge field	EX 7.35	• Click the mail merge field you want to delete
		• Press the **Delete** key
Copying worksheets from other workbooks	EX 8.6	• Open the master workbook—the workbook into which you want to copy worksheets from other workbooks
		• Open all other workbooks containing worksheets you want to copy to the master workbook
		• In any of the open Excel workbooks, click **Window**, click **Arrange**, click the **Tiled** option button, and click **OK**
		• Press and hold the **Ctrl** key, and then click and drag to the master workbook the tab of the worksheet you want to copy
		• Release the mouse when the down-pointing arrow is in the correct tab location in the master workbook, and then release the **Ctrl** key
Grouping contiguous worksheets	EX 8.11	• Click the worksheet tab of the first worksheet in the group
		• Use the tab scrolling buttons if necessary to bring the last worksheet tab of the proposed group into view
		• Hold down the **Shift** key and click the last worksheet tab in the group
Grouping noncontiguous worksheets	EX 8.11	• Click the worksheet tab of the first worksheet you want in the group
		• Press and hold the **Ctrl** key and then click each worksheet you want to include in the group
		• When you are done, release the **Ctrl** key
Ungrouping worksheets	EX 8.12	• Click the worksheet tab of any worksheet not in the worksheet group
		• If all worksheets in the workbook are grouped, right-click any worksheet tab and click **Ungroup Sheets** from the shortcut menu
Writing a formula containing a 3-D reference	EX 8.25	• After clicking the cell where you want the formula to appear, type =, type a function name, and type the left parenthesis. If no function is needed, type =
		• Click the sheet tab of the worksheet containing the cell or cell range you want to reference
		• If a worksheet range is needed, press and hold the **Shift** key and click the last worksheet tab in the range

task *reference roundup*

Task	Page #	Preferred Method
		• Click the cell or cell range you want to reference
		• Complete the formula (type a concluding right parenthesis for a function, for instance) and then press **Enter**
Printing multiple worksheets	EX 8.29	• Group the worksheets you want to print by pressing **Ctrl** and then clicking the worksheet tabs or pressing **Shift** and clicking the first and last worksheets in a contiguous group
		• Click **File**, click **Print**, ensure the **Active sheet(s)** option button is selected, and click **OK**
Building link references by pointing	EX 8.32	• Open the supporting workbook
		• Make active the workbook to contain the link reference and the cell to contain the link reference
		• Type the formula up to the point in which you reference the cell or cell range in another workbook
		• Click the taskbar button corresponding to the supporting workbook to make it active
		• Click the worksheet tab containing the cell or cell range to reference
		• Click the cell or drag the cell range of the cell(s) you want to reference and press **Enter**
Opening a supporting workbook from a dependent workbook	EX 8.37	• Open the dependent workbook containing the link reference
		• Click **Edit** and then click **Links**
		• Click the name of the supporting workbook you want to open from the Links list
		• Click the **Open Source** button
Creating a one-variable data table	EX 9.18	• Decide if you want values for the input cell to appear in a row or down a column
		• If you arrange a data table in columns, then insert the input values in the first column beginning below the first row of the table and place a reference (a formula) to the result cell in the cell above and to the right of the column of input values
		• If you arrange a data table in rows, then insert the input values in the first row beginning in the second column of the data table and place a reference (a formula) to the result cell in the cell below the input row and to its left
		• Select the table, click **Data**, and then click **Table**
		• Enter the cell reference of the input cell in the Row input cell box if input values are in a row or enter the cell reference of the input cell in the Column input cell box if the input values are in a column in the data table
		• Click **OK**

task reference roundup

Task	Page #	Preferred Method
Creating a two-variable data table	EX 9.25	• Type the formula or a reference to the input cell in the upper left cell in the data table
		• Type the first variable values in the row to the right of the formula
		• Type the second variable values in the column below the formula
		• Select a cell range that encompasses the formula, row values, and column values
		• Click **Data** on the menu bar and then click **Table**
		• Type the address of the input cell that corresponds to the row values in the Row input cell text box
		• Type the address of the input cell that corresponds to the column values in the Column input cell text box
		• Click **OK**
Creating a Scenario	EX 9.34	• Click **Tools** and click **Scenarios** to open the Scenario Manager
		• Click the **Add** button and type a scenario name
		• Specify the changing (input) cells in the scenario
		• Type commentary in the Comment text box and then click the **OK** button
		• Type the values for each changing cell, scrolling the list if necessary, and then click **OK**
		• Click **Close** to close the Scenario Manager
Viewing a Scenario	EX 9.39	• Click **Tools** and click **Scenarios** to open the Scenario Manager
		• Select a scenario from the Scenarios list
		• Click the **Show** button
Editing a Scenario	EX 9.41	• Click **Tools** and click **Scenarios** to open the Scenario Manager
		• Select a scenario from the Scenarios list
		• Click the **Edit** button
		• Make any changes in the Edit Scenario dialog box and click **OK**
		• Make any changes in the Scenario Values dialog box and click **OK**
Deleting a Scenario	EX 9.42	• Click **Tools** and click **Scenarios** to open the Scenario Manager
		• Select a scenario from the Scenarios list
		• Click the **Delete** button
Producing a Scenario Summary Report	EX 9.44	• Click **Tools** and click **Scenarios** to open the Scenario Manager
		• Click the **Summary** button
		• Click the **Scenario summary** option button
		• Type the cell addresses in the Result cells box of all result cells you want to display in the report

task reference roundup

Task	Page #	Preferred Method
		• Click **OK**
Producing a PivotTable Report	EX 9.47	• Click **Tools** and click **Scenarios** to open the Scenario Manager
		• Click the **Summary** button
		• Click the **Scenario PivotTable** option button
		• Type the cell addresses in the Result cells box of all result cells you want to display in the report
		• Click **OK**
Using Goal Seek	EX 10.15	• Click **Tools** and then click **Goal Seek**
		• Click the **Set cell** box and type the cell address of the result cell
		• Click the **To value** box and type the result value you want
		• Click the **By changing** cell box and type the address of the changing cell
		• Click **OK** to solve the problem, and then click **OK** to close the Goal Seek Status dialog box
Using the Solver	EX 10.29	• Click **Tools** and then click **Solver**
		• In the *Set Target Cell* box type the address of the cell containing the objective function
		• Click one of the **Equal To** option buttons and, if necessary, type a value in the *Value of* box
		• In the *By Changing Cells* box type the cell addresses of all cells that Excel can change
		• Click the **Add** button to add constraints to the Subject to the Constraints box
		• Click the **Solve** button to create a solution
		• Click the **OK** button
Deleting a Solver constraint	EX 10.35	• Click **Tools** and then click **Solver**
		• Click the constraint you want to delete
		• Click the **Delete** button
Saving Solver parameters	EX 10.37	• Click **Tools** and then click **Solver**
		• Click **Options,** and then click **Save Model**
		• Select an empty cell range, and then click **OK**
		• Click **Cancel,** and then click **Close**
Importing fixed length data using the Text Import Wizard	EX 11.7	• Click **File** and then click **Open**
		• In the Files of type list box of the Open dialog box, select **Text Files**

task reference roundup

Task	Page #	Preferred Method
		• Using the *Look in* list box, navigate to the folder containing the text file, click the file name in the list of files, and click the **Open** button
		• Click the **Fixed Width** option button in the Original data type panel
		• Click the **Start import at row** spin box to select the first row to import, and click the **Next** button
		• In Step 2, click to the left of each field to add a break line, double-click a break line to remove it, or drag a break line to its correct position at the beginning of a column as needed. Then, click the **Next** button to proceed
		• In Step 3, for each column, click a **Column data format** option button to select a column format, or click the **Do not import column** option button to skip the column, and click the **Finish** button
Adding, moving, and deleting column breaks using the Text Import Wizard	EX 11.10	• Add a column break by clicking the position just above the ruler in the Data preview panel where you want the column break to appear
		• Move a column break by clicking it and then dragging it to its new position
		• Delete a column break by double-clicking it
Editing a query	EX 11.25	• Make sure that one of the cells containing imported database data is active
		• Click **Data,** point to **Import External Data,** and click **Edit Query**
		• Step through each of the Query Wizard's steps, make any necessary changes at each step and then press **Next** to go to the next step
		• On the Query Wizard's final step, click the **Save Query** button to save your changes and then click the **Finish** button to refresh the imported data
Automatically refreshing data each time a workbook is opened	EX 11.36	• Ensure that the active worksheet cell is one of the imported data values
		• Click **Data,** click **Import External Data,** click **Data Range Properties**
		• Click the **Refresh data on file open** check box to place a checkmark in it
		• Click **OK**
Manually joining two tables in a query	EX 11.40	• Drag and drop the primary key from one table to the corresponding foreign key in the second table
Adding a column to a query	EX 11.40	• Double-click a column name to add it to the lower half of the query window
		or
		• Drag and drop the column name to the lower half of the query window
Removing a column from a query	EX 11.40	• Move the mouse pointer over the column name in the lower panel of the query

task reference roundup

Task	Page #	Preferred Method
		• When the pointer changes to a down arrow, click to select the column
		• Press the **Delete** key
Adding criteria to a query using Microsoft Query	EX 11.41	• Click **Criteria** on the Microsoft Query menu bar and then click **Add Criteria**
		• Fill in the list and text boxes in the Add Criteria dialog box
		• Click the **Add** button to add the criteria to the query
		• Continue adding additional criteria, if needed
		• Click the **Close** button when the criteria are complete
Summing a value column in a query	EX 11.43	• Click any result in the column you want to sum
		• Click the **Cycle Through Totals** button
Recording a Macro instruction	EX 12.8	• Click **Tools**, point to **Macro**, click **Record New Macro**
		• Type a macro name in the Macro name text box
		• Type a description in the Description text box
		• Click **OK**
		• Execute the tasks you want to record
		• Click the **Stop Recording** button
Assigning a Macro to a button	EX 12.11	• Click **View**, point to **Toolbars**, click **Forms**
		• Click the **Button** tool in the Forms toolbar
		• Click a worksheet cell to place a button on the worksheet
		• Select the macro to assign to the button from the Macro name list
		• Click **OK**
		• Drag the mouse across the button's caption and type a descriptive name
		• Click any cell to deselect the button
Making buttons visible on a printout	EX 12.13	• Right-click the button you want to display on a printout
		• Click **Format Control** on the shortcut menu
		• Click the **Properties** tab
		• Click the **Print object** check box, and click **OK**
Selecting a button control without activating It	EX 12.16	• Press and hold the **Ctrl** key
		• Click the button on the worksheet
		• Release the **Ctrl** key

task reference roundup

Task	Page #	Preferred Method
Unhiding a workbook	EX 12.21	• Click **Window** on the menu bar
		• Click **Unhide**
		• Click a workbook in the Unhide workbook list and then click **OK**
Hiding a workbook	EX 12.21	• Make active any worksheet of the workbook you want to hide
		• Click **Window** on the menu bar
		• Click **Hide**
Setting the Macro security level	EX 12.22	• Click **Tools** on the menu bar, click **Options,** and click the **Security** tab
		• Click the **Macro Security** button
		• Click the security level option button of your choice
		• Click **OK** to close the Security dialog box, and click **OK** to close the Options dialog box
Opening the Visual Basic Editor	EX 12.25	• Click **Tools,** point to **Macro,** and click **Visual Basic Editor**
		or
		• Press **Alt+F11**
		or
		• Click **Tools,** point to **Macro,** and click **Macros**
		• Select the name of the macro you want to edit
		• Click the **Edit** button
Deleting a Macro	EX 12.29	• Click **Tools,** point to **Macro,** and click **Macros**
		• Click the name of the macro in the Macro name list that you want to delete
		• Click the **Delete** button
		• Click **Yes** to confirm the deletion
Printing VBA code	EX 12.48	• Click **Alt+F11** to open the Visual Basic Editor
		• Double-click the module in the Project Explorer containing the VBA code you want to print
		• Click **File** on the menu bar
		• Click the **Code** check box in the Print What panel
		• Click the **Current Project** option button in the Range panel to select all of the code in a project, or click the **Current Module** option button in the Range panel to select only the current module
		• Click **OK**

reference 4

Making the Grade Answers

making the grade

CHAPTER 1

SESSION 1.1

1. Spreadsheet
2. What-if
3. Workbook, worksheets
4. Standard, formatting
5. Active

SESSION 1.2

1. Function
2. **a.** Formula
   b. Value
   c. Text
   d. Text
   e. Text
   f. Text
   g. Value
3. =Sum(B4:C6)
4. Save, Save As
5. Clear Contents
6. What-if
7. Header
8. Solutions file is **ex01scrip-solution.xls**

CHAPTER 2

SESSION 2.1

1. AutoSum automatically creates a sum formula with selected cells adjacent to it in its argument list. An AutoSum on the right end of a row contains the sum of the row, whereas an AutoSum below a column includes all the contiguous cells above it in the argument list. Sometimes AutoSum guesses the range incorrectly. In that case, you have to adjust the cell range.

2. Because an equal sign (=) does not precede the formula, Excel creates a text entry that is "D5+F5."
3. Fill handle
4. Order of precedence consists of rules that govern the order in which Excel evaluates mathematical operators in an expression. Excel first evaluates D5*D6 and then adds that product to D4 to produce the result. In other words, multiplication occurs first in the expression =D4+D5*D6 because multiplication has precedence over addition, the first operator in the formula.
5. You can produce the average of a range by dividing its sum by the number of elements in the range. The equivalent of the formula =AVERAGE(A1:B25) is =SUM(A1:B25)/50

SESSION 2.2

1. Test a worksheet by entering zero to observe the computed values. Use a calculator to compare one or two worksheet formula results with the calculator's answers.
2. Undo, Edit
3. c
4. b
5. See the file **Recycle2.xls**

CHAPTER 3

SESSION 3.1

1. Formatting does not change the *contents* of a cell. It changes the *appearance* of a cell's displayed results.
2. The General format is the default Excel cell format.
3. right; left
4. currency; decimal places
5. Solution file is **ex03ExoticFruitMTG31.xls**

SESSION 3.2

1. Select a row by clicking its row heading. Then click Format, Row, Height, type in the height, and click OK.
2. Border (not Borders)
3. toolbar; Menu
4. selection handles
5. Solution file is **ex03ExoticFruitMTG32.xls**

CHAPTER 4

SESSION 4.1

1. data series
2. category
3. embedded; chart sheet
4. chart wizard
5. Solution file is **ex04BigWaveMTG41.xls**

SESSION 4.2

1. Ctrl
2. embedded; chart sheet
3. pie
4. elevate
5. Solution file is **ex04BigWaveMTG42.xls**

making the grade

CHAPTER 5
SESSION 5.1

1. field
2. row
3. Freeze Panes
4. data form
5. solution file is **ex05EmployeeMTG51.xls**

SESSION 5.2

1. Data, AutoFilter (and then filter the Location column with the address "Olin Hall").
2. Execute Data, Sort, select City in the Sort by list box, and select Bank Name in the Then by list box. The City (or whatever the column is labeled containing the city name) is the primary sort key, and Bank Name is the secondary sort key breaking ties in the City column.
3. Create an AutoFilter (Data, Filter, AutoFilter) and then create a custom filter (click Custom in the Salary list box) that reads "is less than or equal to" in the first Salary Custom AutoFilter text box and type "40000" in the second Salary Custom AutoFilter text box.
4. First, sort the customer list into order by customer name. Next, execute Data, Subtotals and specify "Customer" as the *At each change* in field on which subtotals are calculated. Click Sum in the *Use function* list box to produce a sum for each customer's sales. Check the Sales check box in the *Add subtotal to* list box to total the sales column.
5. Solution file is **ex05EmployeeMTG52.xls**

SESSION 5.3

1. row, column, or page
2. data
3. SUM is the default function
4. Each time the pivot table refreshes data or changes, it "forgets" formatting applied through the Format menu. Formatting pivot table data cells within the pivot table wizard through the PivotTable Field dialog box applies formats that are not "forgotten" each time the pivot table is refreshed.
5. solution file is **ex05EmployeeMTG53.xls**

CHAPTER 6
SESSION 6.1

1. arguments
2. assumption(s) or input(s)
3. validation
4. alert
5. solution file is **ex06LoanMTG61.xls**

SESSION 6.2

1. amortization
2. PMT
3. interest
4. PV; present
5. Solution file is **ex06LoanMTG62.xls**

SESSION 6.3

1. NOW

2. locked
3. password
4. Tab
5. Solution file is **ex06LoanMTG63.xls**

CHAPTER 7
SESSION 7.1

1. link
2. clipboard
3. Paste
4. object, linking, embedding
5. solution file is the Word document, **ex07LetterMTG71.doc**

SESSION 7.2

1. mail merge
2. merge
3. source; container
4. labels
5. solution file is **ex07LetterMTG72.doc**

CHAPTER 8
SESSION 8.1

1. Arrange
2. Shift
3. Before the current, active worksheet
4. drilling
5. solution file is **ex08BecoMTG81.xls**

SESSION 8.2

1. link, link, external
2. path
3. brackets, or square brackets
4. apostrophes

making *the grade*

5. solution file is
ex08BecoMTG82.zip.
(Notice that it is a zip file
because the solution
involves two workbooks,
and one contains link
references to the other)

CHAPTER 9
SESSION 9.1

1. CVP

2. break-even

3. variable; fixed

4. data

5. input; result

6. one

7. two

8. Solution file is
ex09ArtisticMTG91.xls.

SESSION 9.2

1. scenario

2. changing

3. scenarios

4. name

5. manager

6. worksheet

7. PivotTable; summary

8. The difference is that not all
the variables in the Middle
Road scenario can be
changed and display in
white instead of gray. The
solution file is
ex09ArtisticMTG92.xls.

CHAPTER 10
SESSION 10.1

1. solution or result

2. objective

3. constraint

4. precedent

5. Solution file is
ex10ExerCycleMTG101.xls.

SESSION 10.2

1. optimization

2. function

3. changing (or precedent)

4. constraint

5. Solution file is
ex10ExerCycleMTG102.xls.

CHAPTER 11
SESSION 11.1

1. text

2. delimiter

3. column break

4. comma-separated; CSV

5. Solution file is
ex11MissionBoatsMTG111.xls.

SESSION 11.2

1. record

2. selection criteria

3. Refresh

4. join

5. Solution file is
ex11MissionBoatsMTG112.xls.

CHAPTER 12
SESSION 12.1

1. macro

2. function

3. Personal Macro

4. module

5. button

6. Solution file is
ex12CatalogMTG121.xls.

SESSION 12.2

1. module

2. project

3. looping

4. branching or selection

5. arguments

6. Solution file is
ex12InvoiceMTG122.xls.

glossary

Absolute cell reference: A cell reference in which a dollar sign ($) precedes both the column and row portions of the cell reference.

Activating (toolbar): Making a toolbar appear on the desktop.

Active cell: The cell in which you are currently working.

Active sheets: Sheets that are selected.

Add-in: A specialized feature of Excel that not everyone uses on a regular basis.

Aggregate: Calculations that cumulate information about groups of data.

Alignment: The position of the data relative to the sides of a cell.

Amortization: The process of distributing periodic payments over the life of a loan.

Amortization schedule: Lists the monthly payment, the amount of the payment applied toward reducing the principal (loan amount), and the amount of the payment that pays the interest due each month.

Answer report: The most popular Solver report, which lists the target cell, the changing cells with their original and final values, constraints, and data about the constraints.

Argument: A symbolic name for a value, expression, or cell reference that is passed to the function for its use in calculating an answer.

Argument list, function: The data that a function requires to compute an answer in which commas separate individual list entries.

Argument list: *See* Arguments.

Argument list: The collection of cells, cell ranges, and values listed in the comma-separated list between a function's parentheses.

Arguments: A list of zero or more items enclosed in parentheses and following the function name.

Arguments, function: They specify the value that the function uses to compute an answer, and comprise the argument list that can be values, cell references, expressions, a function, or an arbitrarily complex combination of the preceding that results in a value.

Array formula: Special formula in a data table that is part of an interrelated group of formulas.

Ascending order: Arranges text values alphabetically from A to Z, arranges numbers from smallest to largest, and arranges dates from earliest to most recent.

Assumption cells: Cells upon which other formulas depend and whose values can be changed to observe their effect on a worksheet's entries.

Attached text: Chart objects such as X-axis title, Y-axis, title and tick marks.

AutoComplete: Excel offers to fill in the remainder of the cell with information that matches your partial entry from another cell in the same column.

Axis: Line that contains a measurement by which you compare plotted values.

Binding: A resource constraint that is a limiting factor.

Bottom margin: The area at the bottom of the page between the bottom-most portion of the print area and the bottom edge of the page.

Branching: A programming structure that evaluates a condition and then takes one of two actions based on the outcome of condition evaluation.

Break-even: Profit is zero.

Categories: Organizes values in a data series.

Category names: Correspond to worksheet text you use to label data.

Cell: The Excel worksheet element located at the intersection of a row and a column and identified by a cell reference.

Cell border: A format that applies lines of various types to one or more edges of cells (left, right, top, bottom) of the selected cell(s).

Cell contents: The text, formulas, or numbers you type into a cell.

Cell range: One or more cells that form a rectangular group.

Cell reference: A cell's identification consisting of its column letter(s) followed by its row number.

Changing cells: The cells defined in a scenario that contain values you want Excel to change.

Chart area: The area in which all chart elements reside.

Chart sheet: Chart on a separate sheet.

Chart title: Labels the entire chart.

Charts: Sometimes called graphs, they are a graphical representation of data.

Client: The program that receives the information copied from another program.

Column break: A line that appears in a text import step to indicate the beginning of a field.

Comma-separated values: Values separated from one another by commas.

Comments: Worksheet cell notes that are particularly helpful to indicate special instructions about the contents or formatting of individual cells.

Compound document: A document containing linked and embedded data drawn from several sources.

Conditional test: An equation that compares two values, functions, formulas labels, or logical values.

Consolidate: Summarizing data from multiple worksheets.

Consolidation worksheet: *See* Summary worksheet.

Constrained optimization: A technique whereby you specify a set of constraints and an outcome or result that you want minimized or maximized.

Constraint: A limitation on the values that a cell can have.

Container or container program: *See* Client.

Contribution margin (CM): The amount remaining from revenue after deducting all variable costs.

Cost-Volume-Profit (CVP) analysis: Examines the relationship between a product's expenses (cost), the number of units of the product produced (volume), revenue, and profit.

CSV: *See* Comma-separated values.

Custom sorting series: An ordered list you create to instruct Excel in what order to sort rows containing the list items.

Data fields (pivot table): Numeric data that appears in the pivot table's central position and is summarized.

Data form: A dialog box displaying one row of a list in text boxes in which you can add, locate, modify, or delete records.

Data label: The value or name assigned to an individual data point.

Data marker: A graphic representation of the value of a data point in a chart.

Data points: The values that comprise a data series.

Data series: The set of values that you want to chart.

Data table: Summarized key input and output cell values of multiple what-if analyses in a single, rectangular cell range.

Data type: The type of information that is stored in a variable.

Date constant: A date such as 12/12/2003.

Database: A collection of information organized so that a computer program can select requested information from it quickly.

Database driver: Special software that translates Excel information requests into database commands.

Database management system: A program that takes in user requests and combs through a database to deliver requested information, update information, or delete information.

Database table: A two-dimensional arrangement of rows and columns and holds data.

DBMS: *See* database management system.

Delimiter: A character or group of characters that separates two pieces of data.

Dependent workbook: A workbook containing a link to a supporting worksheet.

Descending order: Arranges text values alphabetically from Z to A, arranges numbers from largest to smallest, and arranges dates from most recent to earliest.

Disintermediation: Eliminating the often expensive intermediary in a transaction.

Dock (toolbar): Toolbar adheres to one of the four edges of the window.

Drilling down: Entering data in the same cell of several workbooks simultaneously.

Drop shadow: The shadow that is cast by an object.

Dynamic link: *See* link.

Editing: Modifying the contents of a cell.

Embedded chart: Chart on a worksheet near the data you are charting.

Embedding: Placing a copy of an object from one program within another program's file.

Equation-solving: Goal seeking or back solving method such as the method used by the Goal Seek command.

Error value: A special Excel constant that indicates something is wrong with the formula or one of its components.

Event procedure: A procedure that executes whenever a particular event occurs.

Exact match criteria: Criteria in which a row's field exactly matches a particular filter value.

External reference: *See* link.

Field: An individual unit of data, either fixed length or separated from others by a delimiter. Each column of a list of related information describing some characteristic of the object, person, or place.

Filter: Selection criteria applied to a merge operation to restrict the source data records chosen to those that satisfy the criteria.

Filtering: A list displaying only records that match particular criteria and hiding the rows that do not.

Fixed cost: A cost that remains constant no matter how many or how few goods or services you manufacture and sell.

Fixed pitch (font): Every character is the same width.

Fixed-width: Data arranged into specific locations or starting positions.

Floating (toolbar): Toolbar that can appear anywhere on the work surface.

Font: The combination of typeface and qualities including character size, character pitch, and spacing.

Footer: Text that appears automatically at the bottom of each printed page in the footer margin.

Foreign key: A table column that identifies records in a different table.

Form: A dialog box that appears in response to a user-defined command key click or other event.

Format: Cosmetic changes to a worksheet that make the text and numbers appear different.

Formatting: The process of altering the appearance of data in one or more worksheet cells.

Formula: An expression that begins with an equal sign and consists of cell references, arithmetic operators, values, and Excel built-in functions (see Chapter 6) that result in calculated value.

Formula bar: Appears below the menu bar and displays the active cell's contents.

Function: A built-in or prerecorded formula that provides a shortcut for complex calculations.

General (format): Formatting that aligns numbers on the right side of a cell, aligns text on the left side, indicates negative numbers with a minus sign on the left side of a number, and displays as many digits in a number as a cell's width allows.

Goal seek: A worksheet command that works backward to compute an unknown value that produces the final, optimized result you desire.

Goal seek objective: The end result you want to achieve using goal seek techniques.

Gridlines: Extensions of tick marks that help identify the value of the data markers.

Grouping: Joining two objects into one object.

Header: Text that appears automatically at the top of each printed page in the header margin.

Headings row: The list row containing the column headings appearing at the top of the list.

Hide (data): Reduce a row's height to zero.

Input cell: The key input variable that you want Excel to change in a one- or two-variable data table analysis.

Input values: The set of possible input values substituted into the input cell.

Iteration: *See* repetition.

Join: An operation that matches records in two tables based on a field that each one has in common, such as a customer number or an inventory number.

Label text: Chart text such as tick mark label, category axis labels, and data series names.

Landscape: Print orientation in which the width is greater than the length.

Left margin: Defines the size of the white space between a page's left edge and the leftmost edge of the print area.

Legend: Indicates which data marker represents each series when you chart multiple series.

Limit report: A Solver report that displays the range of values that the changing cells can assume, based on the constraints you have defined.

Linear programming problem: Such problems involve one or more unknowns and an equal number of equations.

Link or linking: To paste a copy of an object into a document in such a way that it retains its connection with the original object. Updates to the original object appear automatically in the documents in which they are pasted.

Link: Formulas that reference cells in other worksheets.

List definition table: A table with column names and their definitions.

List: A collection of data arranged in columns and rows in which each column displays one particular type of data.

Lookup function: Uses a search value to search a table—a range of cells—for a match or close match and then return a value from the table as a result.

Lookup table: The table that a lookup function searches.

Lookup value: The value being used to search a lookup table.

Looping: *See* repetition.

Macro: *See* macro instruction.

Macro instruction: A group of VBA statements that collectively performs a particular task or returns a result.

Main document: The document containing merge fields from which merged documents are created.

Mathematical operator: A symbol that represents an arithmetic operation.

Menu bar: Contains Excel menus.

Merge field: A special tag placed in a document into which an actual field value from a source data file is substituted.

Method: An action that takes place on behalf of the object to which it is attached.

Mixed cell reference: A cell reference in which either the column or the row is never adjusted if the formula containing it is copied to another location.

Model row: Contains distinct formulas that you can copy to other rows and not have to modify any copied cell formulas afterward.

Module: An Excel object where macros are saved.

Mouse pointer: Indicates the current position of the mouse.

Name box: Appears on the left of the formula bar and displays either the active cell's address or its assigned name.

Object function: The cell containing a function whose value you want to optimize and whose value is affected by a change in the decision variables.

Object linking and embedding: A technology developed by Microsoft that enables you to create objects with one application and then link or embed them in a second application.

Paste: Placing information into one document that is copied from another document.

Path: The disk drive and folders that lead to a referenced workbook.

Personal Macro Workbook: A workbook that Excel always loads, and subsequently hides, whenever you launch Excel.

Pitch: The number of characters per horizontal inch.

Pivot table: An interactive table enabling you to quickly group and summarize large amounts of data.

Plot area: Rectangular area bounded by the X-axis on the left and the Y-axis on the bottom.

Point: The height of characters in a typeface; equal to $1/72$ of an inch.

Pointing: Using the mouse to select a cell range while writing a formula.

Portrait: Print orientation in which the length is greater than the width.

Positional arguments: Arguments whose position in the argument list is important and inflexible.

Precedence order: Determines the order in which to calculate each part of the formula—which mathematical operators to evaluate first, which to evaluate second, and so on.

Precedent cell: A cell upon which a formula depends.

Precedent value: The value on which a formula, or result, is directly or indirectly based.

Primary key: A table column whose values are unique for each record in a table.

Primary sort field: The first sort field of multiple sort fields required to reorder a list.

Principal: Amount of money borrowed.

Product mix: The quantity of each product to sell in order to generate the greatest profit.

Project: Contains forms, modules, and the Excel workbook objects.

Properties dialog box: Contains several text boxes that you can fill in with helpful information including the fields Title, Subject, Author, Manager, Company, Category, Keywords, and Comments.

Proportional (font): Each character's pitch varies by character.

Protect (worksheet): Excel disallows modifications to cells or new values in cells.

Prototype statement: The first line of the function definition.

Prototype: A proposed worksheet model.

Query: Combines related information from one or more database tables, based on your search and sort criteria, and returns a table as a result.

Range errors: Values that are either too large or too small (negative or too close to zero, for example) that do not make sense in the context of the application.

Range Finder: A feature that color-codes an outline surrounding each cell referenced by a formula.

Range name: A name that you assign to a cell or cell range that can replace a cell address or cell range in expressions or functions.

Rate: Percentage interest rate.

Record: A collection of related information about one object stored in a database table.

Record: Each row of a list containing the fields that collectively describe a single object, person, or place.

Reference: A link to an object identifying the filename and its location.

Refresh (pivot table): Make Excel recalculate the values in the pivot table based on the data list's current values.

Relational operator: Compares two parts of a formula.

Relational operator: Compares two values and the result in either true or false.

Relative cell reference: Cell references in formulas that change when Excel copies them to another location.

Repetition: A programming structure that repeats a series of steps until a special condition is recognized to halt the repetition.

Resource allocation problem: An optimization problem in which productive resources (people, raw materials, time, and so on) can be used in a variety of places or in different products, and in which those resources must be distributed in the best way possible.

Result cell: Holds the result that is affected by a change in the input cell.

Result values: The computed answer for each input value in a one-variable data table.

Revenue: Money or items of value a company receives during a given period.

Rich Text Format: A standard for specifying formatting documents in which the document contains text and special commands holding formatting information.

Right margin: Defines the white space between the print area's rightmost position and the right edge of a printed page.

Scenario: The combination of values assigned to one or more variable cells in a what-if analysis.

Scenario management: The process of examining individual variables or changing cells and assigning a range of values to them.

Scenario summary: Outlines each scenario by displaying changing cells and result cells in a separate worksheet.

Search criteria: Values that the data form should match in specified data form fields.

Secondary sort field: The field used to break ties on a group of matching primary sort field values.

Selection: *See* branching.

Selection criteria: Specifying values to limit the records retrieved from a table.

Selection handles: Small, white squares that appear around an object that is selected.

Sensitivity report: A Solver report that shows how sensitive the current solution is to changes in the adjustable cells.

Series in: Option that establishes the way the data series is represented—either by rows or by columns.

Server: The program from which you copy information pasted into another program.

Sheet tab scroll buttons: The buttons you click to scroll through an Excel workbook's sheet tabs.

Sheet tab: Contains the sheet's name.

Sizing handles: *See* Selection handles.

Slack: The quantity of a resource that has not been used or allocated.

Sort field: The field or fields you use to sort a list.

Sort key: *See* Sort field.

Source cell(s): The copied cell(s).

Source program: *See* Server.

Spreadsheet: A popular program used to analyze numeric information and help make meaningful business decisions based on the analysis.

SQL: An abbreviation for structured query language, it is a standard language for requesting information from a database.

Stacked bar chart: A subtype of the bar chart, combines the data markers in a data series together to form one bar, placing each marker at the end of the preceding one in the same data series.

Standard toolbar: Contains buttons that execute popular menu bar commands such as Print, Cut, and Insert Table.

Status bar: Bar appearing at the bottom of the display that shows general information about the worksheet and selected keyboard keys.

Summary worksheet: Contains a digest or synopsis of the information contained in the individual worksheets.

Supporting workbook: A workbook containing a worksheet to which a link formula refers.

Supporting worksheets: Worksheets that are referenced by other worksheets.

Syntax: Rules governing the way you write Excel functions.

Target cell(s): The cell or cells to which the contents are copied.

Task Pane: A dialog window that provides a convenient way to use commands, gather information, and modify Excel documents.

Term: Time period over which you make periodic payments.

Text (entry): Any combination of characters that you can type on the keyboard including symbols.

Text box: A rectangular-shaped drawing object that contains text.

Text data: Data that consists only of characters (letters, digits, and special characters) that you can type on a keyboard—devoid of any special formatting.

Text Import Wizard: A three-step process to help convert text-format data into Excel format.

Three-dimensional formulas: Formulas that reference other worksheets in the current workbook.

Tick marks: are small lines, similar to marks on a ruler, which are uniformly spaced along each axis and identify the position of category names or values.

Tie (sort): Exists when one or more records have the same value for a field.

Time value of money: $100 today is more valuable than $100 is next year.

Top margin: The area between the top of page and top-most edge of the print area.

Two-dimensional formulas: Formulas that reference cells on a single worksheet.

Two-variable data table: Computes the effects of two variables on a single formula.

UDF: *See* user-defined function.

Unattached text: Chart objects such as comments or text boxes.

Uniform Resource Locator: The global address of a document or other resource on the Web.

Unlocked: An attribute of a cell that leaves it unprotected.

URL: *See* Uniform Resource Locator.

User-defined function: A function you create.

Value (entry): Numbers that represent a quantity, date, or time.

Variables: Cells in which Excel substitutes different values.

VBA function: A procedure that returns a result just as do Excel's built-in functions such as SUM and PMT.

VBA procedure: *See* macro instruction.

VBA subroutine: A VBA procedure that performs a particular task.

What-if analysis: Making changes to spreadsheets and reviewing their affect on other values.

Wild card character: A special character that stands for zero or more characters.

Workbook objects: A workbook's worksheets and chart sheets.

Workbook window: The document window open in Excel.

Workbook: A collection of one or more individual worksheets.

Worksheet: They resemble pages in a spiral-bound workbook like the ones you purchase and use to take class notes.

Wrap text: Formatting that continues long text on multiple lines within a cell.

X-axis title: Which briefly describes the X-axis categories.

X-axis: Contains markers denoting category values.

Y-axis title: Identifies the values being plotted on the Y-axis.

Y-axis: Contains the value of data being plotted.

Glossary for Common Microsoft Office XP Features

Access 2002: Relational database tool that can be used to collect, organize, and retrieve large amounts of data. With a database you can manipulate the data into useful information using tables, forms, queries, and reports.

Answer Wizard: Located in the Microsoft Help dialog box, it provides another means of requesting help through your application.

Application: A program that is designed to help you accomplish a particular task, such as creating a slide show presentation or creating a budget.

Ask a Question: A text box located in the top right corner of your window, it is perhaps the most convenient method for getting help.

Clipboard: A temporary storage location for up to 24 items of selected text that has been cut or copied.

Clippit: The paper clip office assistant.

Excel 2002: An electronic spreadsheet tool that can be used to input, organize, calculate, analyze, and display business data.

F1: The robot office assistant.

Formatting toolbar: A collection of buttons that allows you to change the appearance of text, such as bold, italicize, or underline.

FrontPage 2002: A powerful Web publishing tool that provides everything needed to create, edit, and manage a personal or corporate Web site, without having to learn HTML.

Integrated application suite: A collection of application programs bundled together and designed to allow the user to effortlessly share information from one application to the next.

Links: The Cat office assistant.

Menu bar: Displays a list of key menu options available to you for that particular program.

Office Assistant: Character that will appear ready to help you with your question.

Office XP: The newest version of the popular Microsoft integrated application suite series that has helped personal computer users around the world to be productive and creative.

Outlook 2002: A desktop information management tool that allows you to send and receive e-mail, maintain a personal calendar of appointments, schedule meetings with co-workers, create to-do lists, and store address information about business/personal contacts.

Paste Options button: Button that appears when you paste into your document. It will prompt the user when clicked with additional features such as allowing you to paste with or without the original text formatting.

PowerPoint 2002: A popular presentation tool that allows users to create overhead transparencies and powerful multimedia slide shows.

Professional edition: Office XP version that includes Access, in addition to the Standard version of Word, Excel, PowerPoint, and Outlook.

Professional Special edition: Office XP version that includes Access, FrontPage, and Publisher, in addition to the Standard version of Word, Excel, PowerPoint, and Outlook.

Publisher 2002: A desktop publishing tool that provides individual users the capability to create professional-looking flyers, brochures, and newsletters.

Rocky: The dog office assistant.

Smart tag button: Buttons that appear as needed to provide options for completing a task quickly.

Standard edition: Office XP version that consists of Word, Excel, PowerPoint, and Outlook.

Standard toolbar: A collection of buttons that contains the popular icons such as Cut, Copy, and Paste.

Task pane: This window allows you to access important tasks from a single, convenient location, while still working on your document.

Title bar: Located at the top of each screen, it displays the application's icon, the title of the document you are working on, and the name of the application program you are using.

Toolbar: A collection of commonly used shortcut buttons.

Word 2002: A general-purpose word-processing tool that allows users to create primarily text-based documents, such as letters, résumés, research papers, and even Web pages.

index